NASCLA CONTRACTORS GUIDE TO BUSINESS, LAW AND PROJECT MANAGEMENT

Utah 3rd Edition

Supplemental forms and links are available at NASCLAforms.org
using access code UT129354.

**National Association of State
Contractors Licensing Agencies
(NASCLA)**
23309 N. 17th Drive
Building 1, Unit 110
Phoenix, Arizona 85027
(623) 587-9354
(623) 587-9625 fax
Visit our web site:
www.nascla.org

NASCLA Contractors Guide to Business, Law and Project Management

Utah 3rd Edition

Revised March 2016

Copyright © 2008, 2012, and 2016 by

National Association of State Contractors Licensing Agencies (NASCLA)
23309 North 17th Drive, Building 1, Unit 110
Phoenix, Arizona 85027

ISBN-10 1-934234-82-6

ISBN-13 978-1-934234-82-2

INTRODUCTION

The construction industry is one of the strongest industries in America. To keep the construction industry thriving and to be a successful construction contractor, you must be knowledgeable in both your trade and managing a business.

Thorough business planning and good management skills are the keys to success in today's market. A solid business plan lays the foundation for your financial, marketing, and management strategies and helps you maximize your potential. Competition can be fierce in the construction industry. In developing a business plan, you analyze your market and competition and understand where you can gain an edge.

Good management skills entail applying knowledge from all aspects of the business to create a successful operation. Effective managers know how to win customers, satisfy employees, meet all legal obligations, and increase the bottom line. If this is where you want to take your business, this book can help you get there.

About This Book

This book is organized into three sections. Part 1 focuses on planning and starting your business. This section will help you formulate a business plan, choose a business structure, understand licensing and insurance requirements and gain basic management and marketing skills.

Part 2 covers fundamentals you will need to know in order to operate a successful construction business. This section covers estimating, contract management, scheduling, project management, safety and environmental responsibilities, and building good relationships with employees, subcontractors, and customers.

Part 3 provides valuable information to assist you in running the administrative functions of your business. Financial management, tax basics, and lien laws are covered. Effective management of these areas of business is vital and failure to give them proper attention can cause serious problems.

Part 1: Getting Your Business Off the Ground

✓ Chapter 1 covers tips for writing a business plan and discusses key characteristics of entrepreneurship. A sample business plan is provided in Appendix A and at **NASCLAforms.org** using access code **UT129354**.
✓ Chapter 2 describes each type of business entity and summarizes their advantages and disadvantages.
✓ Chapter 3 reviews the licensing process and the requirements for getting a license.
✓ Chapter 4 discusses insurance and bonding options to protect your business against unmitigated risk.
✓ Chapter 5 is your business toolbox with tips on time management, delegation, business ethics, and technology. It also provides information on resources available to assist small businesses.
✓ Chapter 6 helps you execute your marketing plan through promotional materials, public relations and effective selling skills.

Part 2: Fundamentals for the Field

✓ Chapter 7 shows you how to formulate estimates and evaluate bid opportunities.

✓ Chapter 8 takes you through the key elements of contracts and what is needed to make them enforceable.

✓ Chapter 9 covers scheduling techniques and the fundamental skills needed to effectively manage construction projects.

✓ Chapter 10 explains the importance of understanding customer expectations and handling change orders effectively. The basics of successful negotiation are also addressed.

✓ Chapter 11 is your resource for employment law, hiring and retaining of good employees, and discipline and termination of employees if unfortunate employment circumstances arise.

✓ Chapter 12 gives you the fundamentals for understanding OSHA laws and setting up a safety program for your company. Environmental considerations and possible permitting situations are covered in the event you are creating or working with environmental hazards.

✓ Chapter 13 covers the basics of finding and hiring good subcontractors and establishing good working relationships with them.

Part 3: Office Administration

✓ Chapter 14 takes you through the accounting cycle, the preparation and analysis of financial statements and payroll procedures.

✓ Chapter 15 gives you federal and state tax basics and helps you understand the forms you need to file.

✓ Chapter 16 covers lien law regulations and the process for filing a lien.

Supplemental forms and links are available at **NASCLAforms.org** using access code **UT129354**.

Whether you are studying for the contractors' licensing exam or need an ongoing reference manual for managing your business, the *NASCLA Contractors Guide to Business, Law and Project Management* will serve as a valuable resource. We hope you find this reference useful in your daily operations and that the concepts discussed give you the tools for running a successful business.

TABLE OF CONTENTS

PART I
Getting Your Business Off the Ground

PART II
Fundamentals for the Field

CHAPTER 12: JOBSITE SAFETY AND ENVIRONMENTAL FACTORS

CHAPTER 13: WORKING WITH SUBCONTRACTORS

PART III
Office Administration

CHAPTER 14: FINANCIAL MANAGEMENT

CHAPTER 16: UTAH PRECONSTRUCTION AND CONSTRUCTION LIEN LAW

APPENDIX A: GLOSSARY

APPENDIX B: BUSINESS PLAN TEMPLATE

APPENDIX C: USEFUL LINKS

APPENDIX D: NEW BUSINESS CHECKLIST

APPENDIX E: UTAH CONSTRUCTION TRADES LICENSING ACT

APPENDIX F: UTAH CONSTRUCTION TRADES LICENSING ACT RULE

APPENDIX G: GENERAL RULE OF THE DIVISION OF OCCUPATIONAL AND PROFESSIONAL LICENSING

APPENDIX H: UTAH WORKERS' COMPENSATION LAW

APPENDIX I: UTAH OCCUPATIONAL DISEASE ACT

APPENDIX J: UTAH INJURED WORKER REEMPLOYMENT ACT

APPENDIX K: UTAH PRECONSTRUCTION AND CONSTRUCTION LIEN LAW

APPENDIX L: RESIDENCE LIEN RESTRICTION AND LIEN RECOVERY FUND ACT

APPENDIX M: RESIDENCE LIEN RESTRICTION AND LIEN RECOVERY FUND RULE

APPENDIX N: DIVISION OF OCCUPATIONAL AND PROFESSIONAL LICENSING ACT

APPENDIX O: STATE CONSTRUCTION CODE ADMINISTRATION AND ADOPTION OF APPROVED STATE CONSTRUCTION CODE RULE

APPENDIX P: STATE CONSTRUCTION AND FIRE CODES ACT

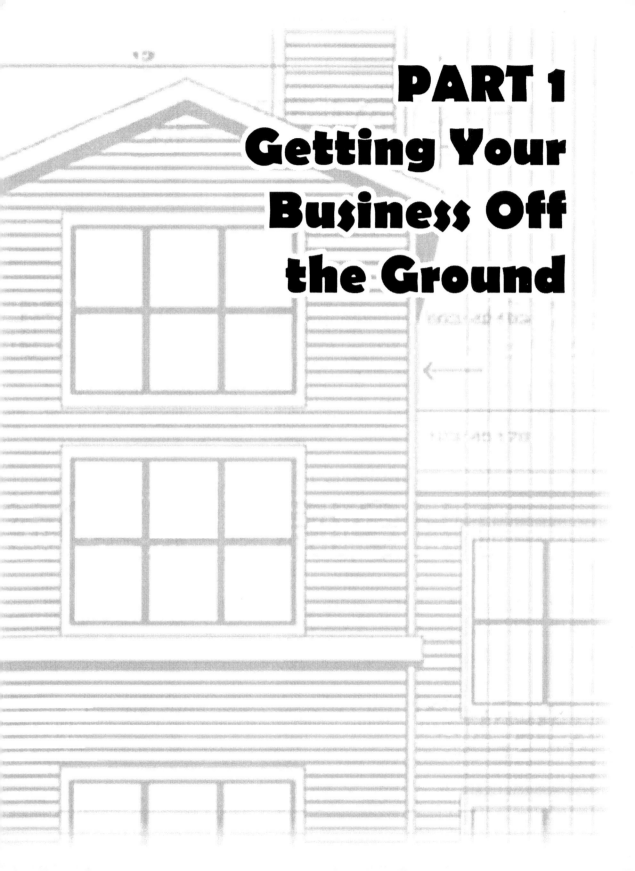

PART 1
Getting Your
Business Off
the Ground

Chapter 1
THE PLAN

Chapter Survey...

⇨ *Being an Entrepreneur*

⇨ *The Benefits of a Business Plan*

⇨ *Elements of a Business Plan*

⇨ *Business Plan Pitfalls*

Just as you need trade tools to successfully complete contracting jobs, you need organization tools to successfully manage your business. As a business owner you go from being an expert in your trade to requiring expertise in project management, marketing, employee management, financial management, contract management and much more.

Success Factors: It takes an organized, consistent approach to achieve success in today's market. Businesses fail every day. The top reasons businesses fail are

✓ poor sales,

✓ competitive weakness,

✓ high operating expenses,

✓ difficulty collecting on invoices,

✓ inventory problems,

✓ too many fixed assets,

✓ poor location, and

✓ fraud.

To Sum It Up...

Poor planning and inadequate management are overriding factors in business failure.

From this point forward, we will build your business management expertise so you can identify and understand these obstacles, thereby, increasing your chances of building and operating a successful business.

Being an Entrepreneur

Understanding Entrepreneurship: As a business owner, you may be referred to as an entrepreneur. There are many definitions of "entrepreneur." For our purposes, an entrepreneur is a person engaged in strategic activities that involve the initiation and development of a new business, created to build long-term value and steady cash flow streams.

Risk Taking: Entrepreneurs are often regarded as risk takers. There is risk associated with any venture, but entrepreneurs understand the importance of taking calculated risks. A calculated risk is a risk that is well-thought through where all outcomes are considered. This chapter will introduce the business planning process and help you understand the risks and opportunities associated with business ownership and how to manage them.

Something to Consider...

Entrepreneurship has its rewards as well as its drawbacks. Before embarking on any business venture, an entrepreneur must weigh all of these factors carefully.

Rewards and Challenges: Rewards of owning your own business include

✓ being your own boss;

✓ having flexibility of time;

✓ having more freedom and independence;

✓ making your own decisions; and

✓ receiving personal satisfaction from completing a job.

Entrepreneurship also has many frustrations and challenges, including

✓ long working hours;

✓ managing cash flow and payroll;

✓ high potential for overwhelming responsibility;

✓ finding and keeping qualified employees;

✓ paying taxes; and

✓ knowing and following government regulations.

Entrepreneurs need to decide if the rewards of entrepreneurship outweigh the challenges.

The Benefits of a Business Plan

Preparing a business plan that outlines strategies and goals for your business is useful for a newly-formed or early-stage business. It can also be a helpful tool for a company that is making major strategic changes (i.e., providing additional product or service offerings). A business plan should be a living document that changes as your business and the market change.

Think of the business plan as a blueprint for your business. Just as you would not perform your trade without a blueprint or plan from the customer, you should not operate your company without a business plan.

Key Functions: A business plan serves three key functions:

✓ **Planning Tool:** Your business plan is a road map for the growth of the business. Putting together the plan helps you think through all possible scenarios for growth in the market.

✓ **Loan or Investor Document:** If you are planning to seek loan financing or approach an investor, you will need a business plan. Investors or loan officers will review this document to evaluate the qualifications of your management team, your projected growth, and your competitive advantage.

✓ **Benchmarking Tool:** Your business plan should also serve as a base against which to measure and monitor the company's performance. If your company exceeds or falls short of your projections, you can investigate the reasons for the difference.

A business plan will allow you to think through all aspects of your business, thus providing you with a competitive edge.

Elements of a Business Plan

The following are the typical elements found in a business plan:

✓ **Cover Page:** Contact information and a confidentiality statement are stated on the cover page.

✓ **Executive Summary:** Placed after the cover page at the beginning of the business plan, the executive summary includes highlights of the plan and gains the interest of the reader. It is usually written last.

✓ **Company Summary:** The company vision and mission, legal structure, management personnel, business location, and facilities are outlined in the company summary section.

✓ **Products and Services:** Your specific products and services, primary subcontractors and suppliers, the use of technology on your business, and expansion opportunities are all covered in the products and services section.

✓ **Market Analysis:** Your target market, market trends, and major competitors are defined under market analysis.

✓ **Marketing Strategy:** The uniqueness of your product or service as well as your pricing, advertising, and promotional strategies are outlined in the marketing strategy.

✓ **Financial Plan:** If you already have financial statements, you should include a balance sheet, an income statement, and a cash flow statement as part of your business plan. New and existing businesses can put together financial projections as additional documentation.

A business plan template that can be customized for your company is located in Appendix B. The template provides specific guidance for completing each section.

Samples: The websites listed below offer sample business plans:

✓ www.allbusiness.com

✓ www.bplans.com

✓ www.inc.com

✓ www.sba.gov/starting_business

✓ www.americanexpress.com/us/small-business/
  openforum

✓ www.bizmove.com/small-business/
  business-plan.htm

Business planning software packages that provide a step-by-step guide to creating a business plan are also available for purchase.

- -
Your business plan is the blueprint for your business.
- -

Business Plan Pitfalls

 As you start creating your business plan, there are guidelines you should follow to make sure you are giving investors an accurate and honest picture of your business.

✓ Make sure your assumptions are realistic.

✓ Keep the language simple. Don't use technical terminology or jargon.

✓ Cover the risks as well as the opportunities.

✓ Analyze your competition thoroughly.

By applying these simple guidelines, your business plan will have a solid foundation.

Final Inspection...

Being an Entrepreneur: Entrepreneurs should be willing to take calculated risks and weigh all factors when making business decisions.

The Benefits of a Business Plan: A business plan is sometimes required by bank loan officers or by investors. It can also be used as a planning and benchmarking tool.

Elements of a Business Plan: A business plan typically contains a cover page, an executive summary, a company summary, a listing of products and/or services, a market analysis, an explanation of the marketing strategy, and a financial plan.

Business Plan Pitfalls: It is important to portray an accurate picture of your business when formulating your business plan.

Supplemental Forms

Supplemental forms and links are available at **NASCLAforms.org** using access code **UT129354**.

Business Plan Template	This template gives an outline for the business plan, including questions that help create detailed assumptions for each section of the plan.
Profit and Loss Pro Forma	This spreadsheet automatically calculates totals when you enter profit and loss numbers. You can adjust the numbers to determine your revenue and expense break-even point.

Chapter 2
CHOOSING YOUR BUSINESS STRUCTURE

Chapter Survey...

⇨ Sole Proprietorships

⇨ Partnerships

⇨ C Corporations

⇨ S Corporations

⇨ Limited Liability Company (LLC)

⇨ Summary of Business Legal Structures

⇨ Joint Ventures

⇨ Naming Your Business

⇨ Reserving Your Name in Utah

⇨ Contacting the Utah Division of Corporations and Commercial Code

When starting a business, one of the first things you need to decide is the legal structure your business will take. Each form of business has its advantages and disadvantages. The right choice depends on the nature of your business, plus various tax and liability issues. To ensure you are making the appropriate choice, it is best to consult with an attorney and an accountant.

Sole Proprietorships

Getting Started: Many businesses begin as sole proprietorships because it is the simplest ownership form to set up. In a sole proprietorship, you are the sole owner of the company. If the sole proprietorship does business under a name different than your own, typically, a fictitious name certificate needs to be filed at a local or state government office.

If you are doing significant business, a sole proprietorship may be a risky legal business structure, because it exposes you to unlimited liability for the business' debt.

Key Characteristics of Sole Proprietorships:

✓ **Existence:** You own the assets of the company. If you decide to sell your sole proprietorship business, in actuality you are selling the assets of the business. You would have to close out your business license and the new buyer would have to obtain all appropriate licenses and accounts in his or her name. A sole proprietorship is terminated upon the owner's death.

✓ **Financial Management:** Business and personal expenses must be separated and careful records must be kept, because the IRS may question the handling of these funds and you may be asked to provide documentation.

✓ **Liability:** You bear personal liability for all actions undertaken in the name of the business.

✓ **Taxes:** Your net income from the business is reported as ordinary income. Sole proprietors do not pay corporate income taxes.

Advantages of a Sole Proprietorship:

✓ Minimal legal restrictions

✓ Simple ownership form

✓ Low startup costs

✓ Sole ownership of profits

✓ Freedom in decision-making process

Disadvantages of a Sole Proprietorship:

✓ Unlimited personal liability

✓ Less available capital

✓ Possible difficulty obtaining long-term financing

✓ Dissolution of the business in the event of the owner's death

Sole proprietorships are easy to form but are risky because the owner has unlimited personal liability.

Partnerships

Partnering Up: A partnership is a relationship between two or more persons who join to carry on a trade or business. Each person contributes money, property, labor, or skill, and each partner expects to share in the profits and losses of the business. A partnership may be considered when neither partner can operate the business alone. Each partner should bring specific advantages to the business. There are two types of partnerships—general and limited. The differences are outlined in the following key characteristics.

Key Characteristics of Partnerships:

✓ **Existence:** A general partnership can be formed through an oral agreement, but it is recommended that a written partnership agreement be made. General partners own the assets of the company, just as an individual owns assets in a sole proprietorship. A limited partnership consists of one or more general partners and one or more limited partners. Limited partners have limited liability in the company. A partnership exists as long as the partners agree it will and as long as all of the general partners remain in the partnership. If a general partner leaves the partnership or dies, the partnership dissolves and the assets of the partnership must be sold or distributed to first pay the creditors and then the partners.

✓ **Financial Management:** The partnership should keep separate bank accounts and financial records for the business so that partners know whether there are profits and losses and the distribution of these amounts. The use of an outside accountant for record-keeping is recommended to prevent suspicion or doubt among partners.

✓ **Liability:** All owners in a general partnership have personal and unlimited liability for all actions undertaken in the name of the business, including all debts. Each partner is responsible for the acts of other partners when they act in the name of the business. Limited partners have no personal liability for the business of the partnership. Limited partners are liable only for the previously agreed-upon contribution to or investment in the business.

✓ **Taxes:** Business, income, and sales taxes are the responsibility of every partner. For federal income taxes, partners must file returns on IRS Form 1065.

Advantages of a General Partnership:

✓ Ease of formation

✓ Direct profit rewards

✓ Larger management base than that of a sole proprietorship

Disadvantages of a General Partnership:

✓ Unlimited personal liability of general partners

✓ Multiple decision makers

✓ Limited life of the business

✓ Changes of partners or partnership agreement may be difficult

✓ Partnership dissolves in the event of the death of a general partner

Use Caution: Partnerships should be entered into carefully. Potential partners should discuss their expectations of the business before deciding to go into business together.

Questions to ask include these:

✓ Do the partners want to grow and operate a company long-term?

✓ Do the partners want to grow a short-term company to sell?

✓ How will profits be distributed: 100 percent to partners, or a part to the business, the rest to partners? What are the profit distribution percentages?

✓ Do the partners agree on the nature of the business, including the types of jobs the business will accept?

Also, be sure to define each partner's individual responsibilities as well as the group responsibilities.

✓ Who can sign debt instruments, such as notes, bonds, and leases for the partnership?

✓ Who determines the amount and frequency of compensation, salaries, draws, or profit-sharing for the partners?

✓ Who will handle record-keeping?

✓ If required, who oversees recruitment of additional partners or dissolution of the partnership?

✓ Who can make amendments to the partnership agreement?

Utah Limited Partnership Registration: To register a Utah limited partnership, you must file the Certificate for a Limited Partnership with the Utah Division of Corporations and Commercial Code.

Foreign Limited Partnership Registration: To register a foreign (not formed in Utah) limited partnership, you must file the Application for Foreign Limited Partnership with the Utah Division of Corporations and Commercial Code.

Utah Limited Liability Partnership Registration: To register a Utah limited liability partnership, you must file the Application for Limited Liability Partnership with the Utah Division of Corporations and Commercial Code.

Foreign Limited Liability Partnership Registration: To register a foreign limited liability partnership, you must file the Application for Foreign Limited Liability Partnership with the Utah Division of Corporations and Commercial Code.

Carefully examine business expectations and responsibilities before entering into a partnership.

C Corporations

Your Corporate Identity: If you decide to do business under a corporate identity, you will have to comply with the formal requirements of state law to create the corporation. A business assumes a corporate identity in Utah when it files as a corporation with the Utah Division of Corporations and Commercial Code.

Key Characteristics of Corporations:

✓ **Existence:** Incorporation gives your business a legal existence. That is, the business can own assets and conduct business in its own name. A corporation lasts as long as the stockholders determine it should. A corporation continues to exist even if one or more of the shareholders die.

✓ **Financial Management:** The corporation needs separate bank accounts and separate business records. The corporation, not the shareholders, owns the money that the shareholders pay to buy the corporation's stock, all the assets, and the money earned by the corporation.

✓ **Liability:** The owners of the corporation, known as stockholders, are not personally liable for the losses of the business. Generally speaking, the corporate entity is responsible for business debts.

✓ **Taxes:** The corporation must file income tax returns and pay taxes on the profits. Dividends paid to shareholders by the corporation are also taxed to each shareholder individually. That is why there is said to be a "double tax" on corporations.

Other requirements for a corporation include

✓ a board of directors and corporate officers;

✓ stockholders as owners of the company;

✓ periodic board meetings, maintenance of board minutes, and approval of corporate resolutions; and

✓ a board empowered to authorize certain actions such as borrowing money, entering into contracts, and allocating corporate resources beyond routine business transactions.

Advantages of a C Corporation:

✓ Separate legal entity

✓ Limited liability for stockholders

✓ Unlimited life of the business

✓ Availability of capital resources

✓ Transfer of ownership through sale of stock

Disadvantages of a C Corporation:

✓ Complex and expensive organization

✓ Limitations on corporate activities and decisions by the corporate charter

✓ Extensive regulation and record-keeping requirements

✓ Double taxation (one on corporate profits and again on dividends)

Utah Corporation Registration: To register a Utah corporation, you must file Articles of Incorporation with the Utah Division of Corporations and Commercial Code.

Foreign Corporation Registration: To register a foreign (not formed in Utah) corporation, you must file the Application for Authority to Conduct Affairs for a Foreign Corporation with the Utah Division of Corporations and Commercial Code. An original certificate of existence or good standing from the state of incorporation, not more than 90 days old, must accompany the application.

Corporations are more complex to form and operate but reduce personal liability of the owners.

S Corporations

If your business is an eligible domestic corporation, you can avoid double federal taxation (corporate and shareholder taxes on the same earnings as in a C corporation) by electing to be treated as an S corporation under the rules of Subchapter S of the Internal Revenue Code. In this way, the S corporation passes its items of income, loss, deduction, and credits through to its shareholders to be included on their separate returns.

Requirements for an S Corporation:

✓ Domestic corporation with one class of stock

✓ No more than 75 shareholders who are citizens or legal residents of the U.S.

✓ All shareholders must consent to S corporation status

✓ Use of a permitted tax year

✓ Filing of IRS Form 2553

S corporations have special tax considerations. Consult with the appropriate financial and legal professionals to find out if this option is right for you.

Limited Liability Company (LLC)

A Hybrid Structure: This legal arrangement shares characteristics of both sole proprietorships and corporate identities. LLCs must consist of at least one member. The ownership in your LLC is invested in memberships rather than shares of stock.

Limited liability companies offer some protection from liability for actions taken by your company or by other members of your company. It does not protect from liability for personal actions. In this way, it resembles a sole proprietorship rather than a corporation.

Like an S corporation, federal income taxes are paid only on income distributed to members as ordinary income. A limited liability company can be expensive to organize and requires more administrative work. This form of organization is useful to professionals and general partnerships.

Advantages of a Limited Liability Company:

✓ Limited disclosure of owners

✓ Limited documentation

✓ No advance IRS filings

✓ No public disclosure of finances

✓ Limited liability for managers and members

✓ Ability to delegate management to a non-member

Tax Implications: LLCs are not taxed at an entity level. Depending on the number of business owners, the LLC is taxed differently.

✓ An LLC with one owner is taxed as a sole proprietorship.

✓ An LLC with more than one owner may elect to be taxed as a partnership or as a corporate entity.

Utah Limited Liability Company Registration: To register a Utah limited liability company, you must file Articles of Organization with the Utah Division of Corporations and Commercial Code.

Foreign Limited Liability Company Registration: To register a foreign (not formed in Utah) corporation, you must file the Application for Authority to Transact Business for a Foreign Limited Liability Company with the Utah Division of Corporations and Commercial Code. An original certificate of existence or good standing from the state of organization, not more than 90 days old, must accompany the application. The filing fee is $70.

Summary of Business Legal Structures

	Ownership	Liability	Formation Documents	Taxation	Management
Sole Proprietorship	One Owner	Unlimited personal liability	Doing Business As (DBA) Filing	Entity not taxed; profits and losses claimed on personal taxes	Owner
General Partnership	Unlimited number of general partners	Unlimited personal liability	General Partnership Agreement	Entity not taxed; profits and losses claimed on personal taxes of general partners	General partners
Limited Partnership	Unlimited number of general and limited partners	Unlimited personal liability of the general partners; limited partners generally have no personal liability	Limited Partnership Certificate Limited Partnership Agreement	Entity not taxed; profits and losses claimed on personal taxes of general and limited partners	General partners
Limited Liability Company (LLC)	Unlimited number of members	Generally no personal liability of the members for obligations of the business	Articles of Organization Operating Agreement	Entity not taxed (unless chosen to be taxed); profits and losses are passed through to the members	Manager or members designated in Operating Agreement
C Corporation	Unlimited number of shareholders	Generally no personal liability of the shareholders	Articles of Incorporation Bylaws Organizational Board Resolutions Stock Certificates Stock Ledger	Corporation taxed on its earnings at the corporate level and the shareholders may have a further tax on any dividends distributed ("double taxation")	Board of Directors
S Corporation	Up to 75 shareholders allowed	Generally no personal liability of the shareholders	Articles of Incorporation Bylaws Organizational Board Resolutions Stock Certificates Stock Ledger IRS and State S Corporation Election	Entity generally not taxed, as profits and losses are passed through to the shareholders ("pass-through" taxation)	Board of Directors

Joint Ventures

Complement Your Strengths: A joint venture is a special business arrangement that exists when two or more companies join to undertake a specific project.

The management of a joint venture is often assigned to one individual or company. This arrangement brings together companies with complementary resources and strengths. When forming this type of venture, it is important to consult an attorney to ensure that all aspects of risk are covered.

Naming Your Business

Choose Wisely: Selecting a name is an important part of forming your business. The name you choose affects your customers' impression of your company. The individuality of the name affects future trademarks and service marks. It is important to select a name that is distinctive.

Do your homework before you decide on a name for your company. A search can be conducted using the following sources:

✓ U.S. Patent and Trademark Office 1-800-786-9199 or at www.uspto.gov

✓ Secretary of State Office in the state where you intend to do business

✓ Internet search engines such as www.yahoo.com or www.google.com

In addition to registering a legal business name, business owners often register a trade name, also called a fictitious name or DBA (doing business as) name. Registering a trade name assists an owner in providing documentation to a bank, creditors, and others to support the use of the business name. It also helps in establishing priority if a competing trade name is used after a name has been registered. Trade names are filed on the local or state level.

A business may choose to file for a trademark. A trademark can be a word, name, symbol, sound, or color used to represent and distinguish a company's products or services. A trademark is not the same as a trade name. Although, a business can trademark a trade name. Trademarks can be filed on the state and federal level. State information is available through the Utah Division of Corporations and Commercial Code. Federal information is available through the U.S. Patent and Trademark Office.

Reserving Your Name in Utah

You can reserve a limited partnership, corporate, or limited liability company name through the Utah Division of Corporations and Commercial Code.

A corporate name availability database is located at the Utah Division of Corporations and Commercial Code website where you can find existing and available business names. If you file a name that is too similar to another registered business name, your application will be rejected and you will need to re-file with another unique name.

The Utah Division of Corporations and Commercial Code website also has an online name reservation form. Reserved names expire after 5:00 p.m. on the 120th day.

Contacting the Utah Division of Corporations and Commercial Code

For questions about registering your business in Utah or obtaining forms, contact the Utah Division of Corporations and Commercial Code:

Utah Division of Corporations and Commercial Code
160 East 300 South
2nd Floor
Salt Lake City, Utah 84111

Telephone: (801) 530-4849
Toll-free: (877) 526-3994
Fax: (801) 530-6438

Email: corpucc@utah.gov

Website: www.corporations.utah.gov

The Utah Division of Corporations and Commercial Code website also offers other valuable information, such as business forms, online business filing, and filing guide sheets. Domestic and foreign corporations, limited liability companies, and limited partnerships must file with the Division of Corporations and Commercial Code before commencing business in Utah.

Final Inspection...

Sole Proprietorships: This business structure offers easy formation and operation. However, unlimited personal liability is a concern because the business and owner are considered the same legal entity.

Partnerships: Partnerships can bring together two or more people with strengths and resources in different areas but also allow for unlimited personal liability of general partners. To reduce conflicts among partners, responsibilities and business goals must be clearly outlined at the beginning of the business arrangement.

C Corporations: C corporations offer liability protection to the owners and easy ownership transfer through stock sales. This business structure is more complex to operate and shareholders may be "double-taxed" on their earnings.

S Corporations: S corporations are similar to C corporations but offer special tax considerations. S corporation status can be filed with the IRS, if companies meet the specified criteria.

Limited Liability Company (LLC): LLCs have characteristics of both sole proprietorships and corporations.

Summary of Business Legal Structures: Each type of business entity has unique ownership, liability, taxation, and management characteristics.

Required formation documents differ for each business structure.

Joint Ventures: Joint ventures are generally formed on a project basis in order to integrate positive attributes and resources of two or more companies.

Naming Your Business: An appropriate business name is important and defines how your customers perceive you.

Reserving Your Name in Utah: A limited partnership, corporate, or limited liability company name can be reserved through the Utah Division of Corporations and Commercial Code. All names must be distinguishable from other registered business names.

Contacting the Utah Division of Corporations and Commercial Code: The Utah Division of Corporations and Commercial Code can be contacted about registering your business in Utah, obtaining various business forms, and filing guidelines for businesses.

Supplemental Forms

Supplemental forms and links are available at **NASCLAforms.org** using access code **UT129354**.

Summary of Business Legal Structures	Table showing the primary features of each type of business entity (featured earlier in the chapter).
IRS Form 2553	IRS form to elect S corporation status

Chapter 3
BECOMING A LICENSED CONTRACTOR

Chapter Survey...

⇨ *Purpose of Licensing*

⇨ *Division of Occupational and Professional Licensing*

⇨ *When is a Contractor's License Needed?*

⇨ *Licensing Process*

⇨ *License Renewals*

⇨ *Reciprocity (Endorsement)*

⇨ *Disciplinary Action*

Purpose of Licensing

A major purpose of contractor licensing is to protect the health, safety, and welfare of the public. Licensing also defines the work that a contractor is allowed to do under a particular license.

Licensing establishes entrance requirements, standards of practice, and disciplinary authority to protect the public from unqualified, incompetent, and unethical contractors.

✓ **Entrance Requirements:** Licensing ensures that those practicing a trade or occupation have met a minimum set of qualifications, such as experience, training, and required examination.

✓ **Standards of Practice:** Contractors are required to adhere to standards of practice established by law. The standards ensure an appropriate level of quality workmanship is given to the public. Continuing education may be required for certain trades.

✓ **Disciplinary Authority:** Statutes and regulations define illegal and prohibited activities. The law provides licensing authorities with a mechanism to conduct investigations and to administer discipline to problem contractors. Violations can result in penalties, including fines and loss of license.

Division of Occupational and Professional Licensing

The Division of Occupational and Professional Licensing oversees contractor licensing in the state of Utah.

State statutes create the Construction Services Commission within the Division to administer and enforce contractor licensing law. The Construction Services Commission is comprised of nine members. Commission members are appointed by the Executive Director of the Division with the approval of the Governor and serve a four-year term. Commission members include:

✓ one licensed general engineering contractor;

✓ one licensed general building contractor;

✓ two licensed residential and small commercial contractors;

✓ one chair person each from the Plumbers Licensing Board, the Alarm System Security and Licensing Board, and the Electricians Licensing Board; and

✓ two members from the general public.

The Commission is responsible for

✓ issuing licenses;

✓ determining examination requirements and required passing scores;

✓ determining standards for supervision of students and persons in training to become qualified for licensure;

✓ determining standards of conduct for licensees; and

✓ setting fees for the division.

For further information, contact

Utah Division of Occupational and Professional Licensing
160 East 300 South
Salt Lake City, Utah 84111

*Mailing address: P.O. Box 146741
Salt Lake City, Utah 84114-6741*

*Phone: (801) 530-6628
Toll-free in Utah: (866) 275-3675*

Email: doplweb@utah.gov

Website: www.dopl.utah.gov

When is a Contractor's License Needed?

Under state statute 58-55-102(12)(a), a contractor is defined as "any person who for compensation other than wages as an employee undertakes any work in the construction, plumbing or electrical trade for which licensure is required." This includes:

- ✓ any person who builds a structure on his/her own property with the intention to sell or for public use;

- ✓ any person that presents him- or herself as a contractor through advertising or any other means;

- ✓ any person engaged as a maintenance person, other than an employee, who regularly engages in activities set forth under the definition of "construction trade";

- ✓ any person engaged in any construction trade for which licensure is required under the Utah Construction Trades Licensing Act; or

- ✓ a construction manager who performs management and counseling services on a construction project for a fee.

Contractors as defined by the Utah Construction Trades Licensing Act are required to be licensed. The definition of contractor does not include alarm companies or alarm company agents but these parties are also required to be licensed.

Construction trade is defined by state statute 58-55-102(10) as

- ✓ construction, alteration, remodeling, repairing, wrecking or demolition, addition to, or improvement of any building, highway, road, railroad, dam, bridge, structure, excavation or other project, development or improvement to other than personal property, and constructing, remodeling, or repairing a manufactured home or mobile home as defined in Section 15A-1-302; or

- ✓ installation or repair of a residential or commercial natural gas appliance or combustion system.

Exemptions: Several exemptions to the licensing law exist. These are detailed in state statute §58-55-305.

License Classifications: The Division issues licenses in the following classifications:

- ✓ general engineering contractor;
- ✓ general building contractor;
- ✓ residential and small commercial contractor;
- ✓ elevator contractor;
- ✓ specialty contractor;
- ✓ master plumber;
- ✓ residential master plumber;
- ✓ journeyman plumber;
- ✓ apprentice plumber;
- ✓ residential journeyman plumber;
- ✓ master electrician;
- ✓ residential master electrician;
- ✓ journeyman electrician;
- ✓ residential journeyman electrician;
- ✓ apprentice electrician;
- ✓ construction trades instructor:
  - general engineering classification;
  - general building classification;
  - electrical classification;
  - plumbing classification; and
  - mechanical classification;
- ✓ alarm company;
- ✓ alarm company agent; and
- ✓ elevator mechanic.

Detailed descriptions for each classification are listed in R156-55a-301 of the Utah Construction Trades Licensing Act Rules.

You may apply for a license in one or more classification or specialty contractor sub-classification. You must meet all qualifications and a separate application and fee must be submitted for each classification or sub-classification for which you are applying.

Licensing Process

To become licensed as a contractor in Utah, you are required to

1. confirm all experience requirements are met;

2. pass required examinations through PSI (to contact PSI, call 1-800-733-9267 or go online at www.psiexams.com);

3. complete a written application as required by the Utah Division of Occupational and Professional Licensing and include the Qualifying Questionnaire (if there is a history of unprofessional or unlawful conduct);

4. provide proof of registration with:

   ✓ Utah Department of Commerce;

   ✓ Utah Division of Corporations and Commercial Code;

   ✓ Unemployment Insurance Division in the Utah Department of Workforce Services; and

   ✓ Utah State Tax Commission and the Internal Revenue Service.

5. produce satisfactory evidence of:

   ✓ two years full-time paid employment experience in the construction industry, which experience, unless more specifically described in this section, may be related to any contracting classification; and

   ✓ knowledge of the principles of the conduct of business as a contractor, reasonably necessary for the protection of the public health, safety, and welfare;

6. complete a 20-hour course established by rule by the commission with the concurrence of the director, which course may include:

   ✓ construction business practices;

   ✓ bookkeeping fundamentals;

   ✓ mechanics lien fundamentals; and

   ✓ other aspects of business and construction principles considered important by the commission with the concurrence of the director;

7. demonstrate financial responsibility through appropriate financial documentation, obtaining a license bond, or obtaining a guaranty agreement;

8. obtain a certificate of general liability insurance with a minimum coverage of $100,000 per incident and $300,000 in total coverage;

9. provide a certificate of workers' compensation coverage or proof that the company does not have or intend to hire employees;

10. provide an unemployment insurance registration number, a signed agreement with a Professional Employer Organization, or proof that the company does not have or intend to hire employees;

11. provide a Utah State tax ID number, a signed agreement with a Professional Employer Organization, or proof that the company does not have or intend to hire employees;

12. file application with the Utah Division of Occupational and Professional Licensing and pay appropriate licensing fees;

13. register with the Residence Lien Recovery Fund (if required) and pay assessment; and

14. obtain approval for licensure before performing work requiring a contractor's license.

The following graph shows a summary of the licensing process.

Summary of Licensing Process

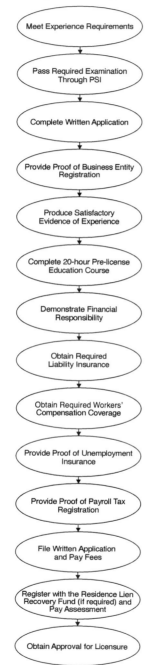

Meet Experience Requirements

Pass Required Examination Through PSI

Complete Written Application

Provide Proof of Business Entity Registration

Produce Satisfactory Evidence of Experience

Complete 20-hour Pre-license Education Course

Demonstrate Financial Responsibility

Obtain Required Liability Insurance

Obtain Required Workers' Compensation Coverage

Provide Proof of Unemployment Insurance

Provide Proof of Payroll Tax Registration

File Written Application and Pay Fees

Register with the Residence Lien Recovery Fund (if required) and Pay Assessment

Obtain Approval for Licensure

License Number Use: The contractor's license number must be used on all permit applications, contracts, agreements, or bids whenever a license is required.

For more information, see statute 58-55-301 License required—License classifications in Appendix E.

License Renewals

Licenses renew once every two years. Contractor licenses expire on November 30 in the odd numbered years. The Utah Division of Occupational and Professional Licensing (DOPL) sends out a notice of license renewal approximately two months before the expiration date of the license. It is important to maintain a current address with the DOPL so proper notification reaches you in a prompt manner. Even if you do not receive the notice of license renewal, it is your responsibility to renew your license and pay appropriate fees in a timely manner. For expiration dates, see www.dopl.utah.gov/renewal_dates.html.

Reciprocity (Endorsement)

The Utah Division of Occupational and Professional Licensing has reciprocity, referred to as endorsement, agreements with the following states:

- ✓ Arizona
- ✓ California
- ✓ Louisiana
- ✓ Nevada
- ✓ South Carolina

Licenses from the reciprocal state must be active. Only specific licenses are granted reciprocity. The Utah Division of Occupational and Professional Licensing website has an easy-to-read license comparison located at www.dopl.utah.gov/licensing/contractor_reciprocate_charts.html.

Disciplinary Action

The Division is responsible for investigating unlawful and unprofessional conduct of licensed and unlicensed contractors.

Unlawful Conduct: A detailed list of actions that constitute unlawful conduct is contained in §58-55-501. A summary is listed as follows.

- ✓ Performing work regulated by the Utah Construction Trades Licensing Act without proper licensure
- ✓ Performing work beyond the scope of the license held

✓ Hiring or employing an unlicensed contractor other than an employee for wages who is not required to be licensed under this chapter

✓ Applying for or obtaining a building permit either for oneself or another when not licensed or excepted from licensure as a contractor

✓ Issuing a building permit to an unlicensed contractor

✓ Applying for or obtaining a building permit for an unlicensed contractor

✓ Failing to obtain required building permits

✓ Submitting a bid as an unlicensed contractor for any work for which a license is required

✓ Providing false or misleading information on an application to obtain or renew a contractor's license

✓ Allowing one's license to be improperly used by another

✓ Doing business under a name other than the name appearing on the license

✓ If licensed as a specialty contractor in the electrical trade or plumbing trade, journeyman plumber, residential journeyman plumber, journeyman electrician, master electrician, or residential electrician, failing to directly supervise an apprentice under one's supervision or exceeding the number of apprentices one is allowed to have under his supervision

✓ If licensed as a contractor or representing oneself to be a contractor, receiving any funds in payment for a specific project from an owner or any other person, which funds are to pay for work performed or materials and services furnished for that specific project, and after receiving the funds to exercise unauthorized control over the funds by failing to pay the full amounts due and payable to persons who performed work or furnished materials or services within a reasonable period of time

✓ Employing as an alarm company an unlicensed individual as an alarm company agent

✓ If licensed as an alarm company or alarm company agent, filing fingerprint cards for an applicant which are not those of the applicant or are in any other way false or fraudulent and intended to mislead the division in its consideration of the application for licensure

✓ Willfully or deliberately disregarding or violating building or construction laws, safety and labor laws, any provision of the health laws, workers' compensation insurance laws, laws governing withholdings for employee state and federal income taxes, unemployment taxes, FICA, or other required withholdings, or reporting, notification, and filing laws

✓ Aiding or abetting any person in evading the licensing law or rules

✓ Engaging in the residential construction trade when not currently registered as a qualified beneficiary under Title 38, Chapter 11, Residence Lien Restriction and Lien Recovery Fund Act

✓ Failing, as an original contractor, to include in a written contract the notification required in Section 38-11-108

✓ Wrongfully filing a mechanics' lien

✓ If licensed as a contractor, not completing a three-hour core education class and an additional three hours of professional education approved by the division and the Construction Services Commission within each two-year renewal cycle

✓ Performing work outside the scope of a temporary alarm company license

✓ Ownership in an unincorporated entity and engaging in construction trade work or an unincorporated entity providing labor while maintaining unlawful status in the United States

✓ Failing to provide workers' compensation coverage or pay unemployment compensation coverage for employees engaging in the construction trade

✓ Failing to properly display the contractor's license number or carry a copy of the contractor's license while performing sign installation or non-electrical outdoor advertising signage work

Unprofessional Conduct: A detailed list of actions that constitute unprofessional conduct is contained in §58-55-502. A summary is listed below.

✓ Failing to establish, maintain, or demonstrate financial responsibility while licensed as a contractor

✓ Disregarding or violating building or construction laws, safety and labor laws, any provision of the health laws, workers' compensation insurance laws, laws governing withholdings for employee state and federal income taxes, unemployment taxes, FICA, or other required withholdings, or any reporting, notification, and filing laws

✓ Willful, fraudulent, or deceitful act by a licensee, caused by a licensee, or at a licensee's direction which causes material injury to another

✓ Contract violations that pose a threat or potential threat to the public health, safety, and welfare including:

• Willful, deliberate, or grossly negligent departure from or disregard for plans or specifications, or abandonment or failure to complete a project without the consent of the owner or his duly authorized representative or the consent of any other person entitled to have the particular project completed in accordance with the plans, specifications, and contract terms

• Failure to deposit funds to the benefit of an employee as required under any written contractual obligation

• Failure to maintain health insurance coverage as extended by any written contractual obligation or representation by the licensee, unless the employee is given written notice of cancellation or reduction of benefits at least 45 days before the effective date

• Failure to reimburse the Residence Lien Recovery Fund

• Failure to provide the information required by Section 38-11-108 (Residence Lien Recovery Fund)

• Willfully or deliberately misrepresenting or omitting a material fact in connection with an application to claim recovery from the Residence Lien Recovery Fund

✓ Failing as an alarm company to notify the division of the cessation of performance of its qualifying agent, or failing to replace its qualifying agent

✓ Failing as an alarm company agent to carry or display a copy of the licensee's license

✓ Failing to comply with operating standards established by rule in accordance with Section 58-55-308 (installation, repair, or replacement of gas appliance or combustion system)

✓ Ownership in an unincorporated entity and engaging in construction trade work or an unincorporated entity providing labor while maintaining unlawful status in the United States

✓ Failing to provide workers' compensation coverage or pay unemployment compensation coverage for employees engaging in the construction trade

✓ Failing to inform customers of county, city, or town policy regarding the installation of an alarm system

Penalties: Contractors who perform an unlawful or unprofessional act are subject to monetary fines, criminal penalties, and loss of license. Unlicensed contractors performing work requiring licensure may be found guilty of a Class A misdemeanor plus monetary penalties. Criminal and administrative penalties for unlawful actions are outlined in detail in §58-55-503.

Final Inspection...

Purpose of Licensing: A major purpose of licensing is to protect the health, safety, and welfare of the public.

Division of Occupational and Professional Licensing: The Division of Occupational and Professional Licensing regulates contracting activities through examination, licensure, and disciplinary action.

When is a Contractor's License Needed?: The Department of Occupational and Professional Licensing requires licensure for "any person who for compensation other than wages as an employee undertakes any work in the construction, plumbing or electrical trade for which licensure is required."

Licensing Process: You must complete the licensing process in order to obtain a contractor's license.

License Renewals: Contractor licenses must be renewed every two years and expire on November 30 in the odd numbered years.

Reciprocity (Endorsement): Contractors from several different states can obtain reciprocity from the Division of Occupational and Professional Licensing.

Disciplinary Action: Contractors who perform unlawful and/or unprofessional conduct may be subject to criminal and administrative penalties.

Chapter 4
MANAGING RISK

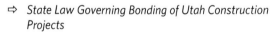
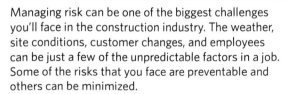

Managing risk can be one of the biggest challenges you'll face in the construction industry. The weather, site conditions, customer changes, and employees can be just a few of the unpredictable factors in a job. Some of the risks that you face are preventable and others can be minimized.

Risk assessment is one of the most important steps in the risk management process. You must determine the probability of loss occurring and the consequences if the loss occurs. Your approach to a risk with the potential for a large loss and a low probability of occurring is handled differently from a risk with a potential for minimum loss but a high likelihood of occurring.

Potential risk must be examined on both a project and overall business basis. Future chapters will focus on the skills you need to assess, manage, and ultimately protect yourself against risks for certain situations, such as environmental and safety risks.

Risk Management Benefits

Unmanaged risk can harm your business, resulting in financial loss, lower profit margins, and unnecessary liabilities. Risk management involves assessing all areas of your business from operations to administrative functions. Good risk management provides several benefits that can affect your reputation and bottom line:

✓ Lower business and liability insurance premiums

✓ Reduce chances of being sued

✓ Improve chances of prevailing in a lawsuit

Risk is managed in several ways. There may be provisions added to a contract to reduce your risk (discussed in Chapter 8), or safety programs or operating procedures can be put in place.

Other risks can be minimized through insurance coverage and bonding, which will be discussed in this chapter.

Insurance

While some risks can be minimized, others are uncontrollable. Insurance is a way to supplement your risk management program to protect your business against unforeseen events, such as accidents and theft. Without it, you could lose your business in a lawsuit as a result of one bad accident. The less coverage your business has, the more risk you assume. As you increase coverage, you reduce your risk.

Insurance Defined: Insurance is a protective measure in which coverage is obtained for a specific risk (or set of risks) through a contract. In this contract or policy, one party indemnifies another against specified loss in return for premiums paid. Indemnity is a way to transfer risk and exemption from loss incurred by any course of action. Sometimes an insurance payout is called an indemnity.

An insurance policy outlines the specifics of the contract between your business and the insurance company. At a minimum, the policy lists the policy term, coverage, premiums, and deductibles.

Finding the Right Insurance Company and Agent: Large companies often employ full-time risk managers. Most small business owners do not have this benefit, and this makes finding the right insurance company and agent important to the risk management process. There are two types of agents: those who work with only one insurance company and independent agents who can shop around for policies with competing companies. Regardless of which type of agent you choose, it is important to find a professional you can trust. Your agent will provide you with a wealth of knowledge on insurance and risk management topics and help you assess your insurance needs.

Required Coverage: The law may require you to carry a certain level of coverage, such as workers' compensation, unemployment, and vehicle insurance.

Many construction contracts require a contractor to maintain certain types of insurance and coverage levels. The following chart gives an example of how insurance coverage requirements might be outlined in a contract.

Type of Insurance	Minimum Insurance Coverage (Combined Single Limit Per Occurrence / Aggregate)
Commercial General Liability including Premises - Operations Products / Completed Operations Contractual Insurance Property Damage Independent Contractors Bodily Injury	$3,000,000 / $3,000,000
Automobile Liability Owned, Non-owned, or Rented	$3,000,000 / $3,000,000
Workers' Compensation and Occupational Diseases	As Required by Applicable Laws
Employer's Liability	$3,000,000

It is important to conduct a site survey to assess any special conditions that may cause added risk to a project. You should also consider the nature of each project to be sure you have adequate coverage for the work you are performing. You may want to talk this over with your insurance agent and add supplemental coverage when necessary.

In this chapter, we will focus on policies that apply to the construction industry, but you should consult with your insurance carrier for a plan that is right for you and provides your business with the best protection.

Property Insurance

Property insurance typically covers your business and personal property when damage, theft, or loss occurs. You can buy property insurance to cover specific risks such as fire or theft or you can purchase a broad-based policy to cover a variety of risks (including fire, theft, vandalism, and "acts of God" such as lightning strikes). In considering property insurance, evaluate your physical location and the region in which you do business to determine which risks are likely to occur, such as hurricanes or floods.

Types of Property You May Want to Cover:

✓ Buildings and other structures (owned or leased)

✓ Furniture, equipment, and supplies

✓ Inventory

✓ Machinery

✓ Computers

✓ Intellectual property (i.e., books and documents)

✓ Automobiles, trucks, and construction equipment

✓ Intangible property (i.e., good will, trademarks, etc.)

✓ Leased equipment

All-Risk Builders' Risk Insurance

All-risk builders' risk insurance is a form of property insurance that covers property owners and builders for buildings under construction. This type of insurance typically covers machinery, equipment, materials, supplies, and fixtures that are part of the structure or will become part of the structure. Additional coverage can be added for items, such as temporary structures and scaffolding, used during construction. In general, major construction defects such as poor workmanship and faulty design are not covered. Your tools also may not be covered under this type of policy. You should talk to your insurance agent about getting separate coverage for these items.

All-risk coverage provides for direct loss by those perils that are not specifically excluded by the policy. It generally provides coverage for almost all risks, including theft, vandalism, accidental losses, and damage or destruction. Construction must be in progress for coverage to exist.

The American Institute of Architects (AIA) and the Associated General Contractors of America (AGC) publish contract documents useful for owners and contractors (for AIA documents, check the AIA website at www.aia.org/contractdocs/index.htm; for AGC documents, see the organization's website at www.agc.org). These standard documents require the purchase of all-risk coverage. An owner has the option of giving the responsibility of purchasing all-risk coverage to the general contractor. If this is the case, the owner is required to notify the general contractor in writing. General contractors may prefer to purchase the insurance because they have a deeper understanding of the project and the potential risk. The cost of the insurance is then passed on to the owner.

The standard AIA and AGC documents require replacement cost coverage for losses that occur. Replacement cost coverage replaces damaged property without any allowances or deductions, such as depreciation.

If you use documents other than the AIA and AGC standard forms, carefully examine the insurance obligations for both you and the owner and discuss any concerns with your insurance agent.

A subrogation clause is generally included in the builders' risk insurance policy. Subrogation typically occurs when the insurance company pays the insured for damage or loss and then sues the negligent third party to pay for the loss. This can lead to a situation where the contractor is sued by the owner's insurance company for a loss that occurred.

To avoid this situation between the owner, contractor, and subcontractors, the contract may contain a clause waiving the parties' right to sue one another.

Named Peril Builders' Risk Insurance

Named peril builders' risk insurance policies have narrower coverage than all-risk insurance and specify what perils are covered. Typical named peril policies are written for fire and lightning but can also include events such as wind damage, explosion, water damage, terrorism, or earthquake.

Inland Marine/Equipment Theft Insurance

Inland marine insurance is a type of property insurance that you can purchase for your tools and equipment. It provides coverage for goods in transit and projects under construction. The cost of the insurance may be more than the cost of putting preventive measures in place to deter theft. It is important to secure your equipment by using the proper locks, creating limited access through fencing and locked storage areas, and removing keys from the ignition of all vehicles. Equipment theft increases the cost of insurance premiums, and if it happens often, you might find it difficult to obtain coverage.

Equipment Floater Policy

An equipment floater policy is a type of inland marine insurance. Coverage for equipment is available on an all-risk or specified-peril basis. The coverage provided is for direct physical loss to the equipment and is designed to cover mobile equipment while it is stored on premises, in transit, or at temporary locations or jobsites. An endorsement can be added for rented or leased equipment. Normal wear and tear is generally not covered by the equipment floater policy.

Transportation Floater and Motor Truck Cargo Insurance

Both transportation floater and motor truck cargo insurance are types of inland marine insurance. A transportation floater policy protects the transporter against damage that occurs to freight during transport. Motor truck cargo insurance protects the transporter in the event of damaged or lost freight. This protection also applies to contractors who transport equipment or materials to and from the jobsite.

Liability Insurance

Liability insurance is designed to protect against third-party claims that arise from alleged negligence resulting in bodily injury or property damage. Payment is not typically made to the insured but rather to someone suffering loss who is not a party to the insurance contract.

Commercial General Liability (CGL)

Commercial general liability (CGL) insurance offers basic liability coverage. CGL covers four types of injuries, including

- ✓ bodily injury that results in actual physical damage or loss for individuals who are not employees;
- ✓ damage or loss to property not belonging to the business;
- ✓ personal injury, including slander or damage to reputation; and
- ✓ advertising injury, including charges of negligence that result from promotion of goods or services.

Most businesses in the construction industry will need to supplement their CGL policy with other types of insurance, such as a vehicle insurance policy.

Umbrella Liability Insurance

An umbrella liability insurance policy can supplement your CGL policy. The umbrella policy provides additional coverage in the areas that are not covered in the CGL policy. This type of insurance takes effect once a certain deductible or self-insured retention level is met. Umbrella insurance coverage can be customized to meet the needs of your business.

Director's and Officer's Liability Insurance (D and O)

Director's and officer's liability insurance protects directors and officers from liability due to actions connected with their corporate positions. These actions include such things as misstatement of financial reports, misuse of company funds, and failure to honor an employment contract. This insurance does not cover intentional or illegal acts.

Other Types of Liability Insurance

Other types of liability insurance may be purchased in order to cover exclusions that exist in your CGL policy. Examples of additional liability coverage include:

- ✓ **Contractual liability insurance** provides contractors with protection for damages that result from their negligence while under written contract.
- ✓ **Completed operations liability insurance** provides coverage for loss arising out of completed projects.
- ✓ **Contractor's protective public and property damage liability insurance** protects contractors who supervise and subsequently are held liable for actions of subcontractors from claims for personal injury and property damage.
- ✓ **Professional liability insurance** (sometimes called errors and omissions insurance) protects contractors from negligence resulting from errors or omissions of designers and architects.
- ✓ **Construction wrap-up liability insurance** bundles liability and workers' compensation insurance for general contractors and subcontractors on large construction projects. This type of insurance helps eliminate gaps in coverage. To qualify for this type of insurance, certain contract cost requirements must be met. These requirements vary by state.

Business Owner's Policies (BOPs)

Business owner's policies (BOPs) bundle property and liability coverage together. This type of coverage can eliminate gaps or overlaps between separate property and liability policies. Small and mid-sized companies usually qualify for this type of policy. A business selects the amount of liability coverage it needs based on its assets. Additional coverage can be purchased depending on the particular risks of the company.

Automobile Insurance

If you have a company vehicle or a fleet of vehicles, auto insurance provides coverage for liability and physical damage associated with vehicles owned by your company. All states require vehicle owners to carry some level of liability insurance covering bodily injury and property damage incurred in a vehicle accident. Physical damage coverage pays for the damage to the insured vehicle. Different types of automobile insurance are available. Various options include coverage for only vehicles owned; vehicles owned, leased or hired; and for all automobiles, including those not owned, leased, or hired.

Burglary and Theft Insurance

Burglary and theft insurance covers loss or damage by burglary, theft, larceny, robbery, forgery, fraud, and vandalism. However, this type of insurance generally does not cover employee acts.

A fidelity bond or employee theft insurance is used to cover criminal acts of burglary and theft by employees.

Key Man Life Insurance

This type of coverage is beneficial if your company depends on specific individuals for continuing success of your business. For example, if your legal structure is a partnership, the success or ongoing existence of the company would not continue if one of the partners died or became incapacitated. Key man insurance is available as life insurance, disability insurance, or both.

Coverage Gaps and Overlaps

It is important to understand the coverage that each of your policies provides. You must be aware of gaps and overlaps that may exist between policies. Differences in coverage can cause difficulties in claim settlement, particularly when a claim falls in the gray area between coverages. For example, if a claim involves both an automobile and property, there may be a conflict between which policy covers the damage. To minimize these conflicts, you may want one insurer for all policies. If you have overlapping coverage, make sure that each policy has fairly equal reimbursement levels. This will ensure that you receive equal coverage if more than one policy covers a claim.

Carefully evaluate your risk management program and supplement it with the appropriate insurance coverage.

Employment-Related Insurance

Workers' Compensation Insurance

Workers' compensation insurance provides coverage for employees who are injured on the job. The insurance is purchased by the employer; no part of it should be paid for by employees or deducted from their pay.

Utah Coverage Requirements: The Utah workers' compensation program provides wage replacement and medical care program for employees due to injury, illness, and death resulting from a compensable work-related claim.

Workers' Compensation benefits pay for

✓ hospital bills, medical bills, and prescriptions for work-related injuries and illnesses;

✓ wage replacement for time lost from work due to work-related injuries and illnesses;

✓ burial and dependent benefits in the case of death;

✓ mileage for all authorized medical care;

✓ permanent partial impairment; and

✓ permanent total disability.

In return for providing workers' compensation benefits, the employer is free from lawsuits from the injured employee.

Under Utah law, all employers are required to carry workers' compensation insurance with the exception of sole proprietorships and partnerships as outlined below. The following information and additional publications are available on the Labor Commission website at www.laborcommission.utah. gov. The website has easy-to-read information for employers and employees including a publication titled Employer's Guide to Workers' Compensation.

Labor Commission of Utah
Division of Industrial Accidents
P.O. Box 146610
160 East 300 South, 3rd Floor
Salt Lake City, Utah 84111

Phone: (801) 530-6800

Email: iaccd@utah.gov

Website: www.laborcommission.utah.gov

Sole Proprietorships and Partnerships: A sole proprietor or partner, with no employees other than the sole proprietor or partners, is not required to obtain workers' compensation coverage. If you are a subcontractor, you or the general contractor are required to obtain workers' compensation coverage.

Corporations and LLCs: Corporate officers and directors are considered employees and required to have workers' compensation coverage, however, an exemption from coverage may be obtained.

Contractor Coverage: General contractors who sublet any part of contract work to a subcontractor, including sole proprietors, partners, and corporate officers, may be liable for workers' compensation coverage if the subcontractor has not obtained workers' compensation insurance coverage. In order to protect your business, it is recommended that you verify insurance coverage of all subcontractors before beginning work. If the subcontractor is a sole proprietor, partner, or corporate officer, an exemption is available through the Workers' Compensation Fund of Utah. Exemptions are not valid until an application is made and approved through the Workers' Compensation Fund of Utah.

Obtaining Coverage: Every employer subject to the workers' compensation law must obtain workers' compensation insurance or qualify as a self-insurer to ensure payment of benefits to injured workers. To obtain workers' compensation insurance, employers can contact an insurance agency representing a company licensed to write workers' compensation insurance in Utah. The Workers' Compensation Fund of Utah also provides workers' compensation coverage and will not turn away any employer. Employers are required to pay for 100 percent of the workers' compensation premium. Programs that may reduce the cost of this insurance are introduced in Chapter 12, Jobsite Safety and Environmental Factors. The Utah Labor Commission OSHA Consultation Services provides free safety consultations for companies. Contact (801) 530-6901 or 1-800-530-6855 for further information.

Self-Insurance: To qualify as a self-insurer, employers must file an application with the Labor Commission of Utah. Employers must have a minimum net worth of ten million dollars to qualify for self-insurance.

Penalties: Failure to carry workers' compensation can result in hefty penalties. Uninsured employers are subject to fines of $1,000 or three times the amount of the premium the employer would have paid during the period of non-compliance by the Labor Commission. In addition, an employer failing to provide coverage as required by law may be sued in a court of law by the injured employee.

Required Posting: Employers must post a typewritten or printed notice of compliance with the workers' compensation law in a prominent location in the workplace. Notices are available free of charge from the Labor Commission. The posting should include the insurance company's name and phone number and steps to reporting an industrial claim.

Reporting an Injury: Upon knowledge of an injury, an employer must complete an Employer's First Report of Injury or Illness (Form 122) and file it with the Labor Commission within seven days. A copy of the report must be submitted to the employer's workers' compensation carrier and given to the injured employee. Injured employees have up to 180 days to report an injury or work-related illness. Form 122 must be completed and properly filed for all injuries or illnesses requiring treatment by a physician regardless of the severity.

Chapter 11, Employee Management, covers workers' compensation insurance in more detail.

Follow the Law...

Workers' compensation insurance coverage may be required by law for your business. It is 100 percent employer-paid and premiums cannot be deducted from the employee's pay.

Employer's liability insurance can be purchased to supplement your workers' compensation insurance in the event you are sued for negligence as a result of an employee injury or death.

Unemployment Insurance

Unemployment insurance (UI) programs provide unemployment benefits to eligible workers who become unemployed through no fault of their own and meet certain other eligibility requirements. This program is jointly financed through federal and state employer payroll taxes (federal/state UI tax).

Generally, employers must pay both state and federal unemployment taxes if

✓ they pay wages to employees totaling $1,500 or more in any quarter of a calendar year; or

✓ they had at least one employee during any day of a week during 20 weeks in a calendar year, regardless of whether or not the weeks were consecutive.

Utah State Unemployment Program: Employers are subject to unemployment taxes as defined in the Utah Employment Security Act if

✓ wages of $1 or more were paid during a calendar quarter;

✓ the business was acquired from an employer who was subject to the Act; or

✓ the business is subject to the Federal Unemployment Tax Act (FUTA).

Additional rules exist for those who employ domestic or agricultural workers and for non-profit companies.

Registering a Business: All new and acquired business in Utah must register with the Department of Workforce Services. Registration for an unemployment tax account is available in the following ways:

✓ online at jobs.utah.gov/ui/employer/ employerhome.aspx

✓ fax by completing Status Report, Form 1 and sending it to (801) 526-9377

✓ telephone by calling (801) 526-9400 or 1-800-222-2857 (toll free in Utah)

✓ mail by completing Status Report, Form 1 and sending it to

Utah Department of Workforce Services
Employer Accounts
140 East 300 South
P.O. Box 45288
Salt Lake City, Utah 84145-0288

Tax Base: The taxable wage base is the amount that Utah employers are required by law to pay on unemployment insurance tax. For the most current taxable wage base information, visit the website at http://jobs.utah.gov.

Rate Calculations: Utah unemployment tax rates may change periodically. Each employer's overall tax rate is recalculated each year. For the most up-to-date, tax rates and rate calculation formulas, visit the Department of Workforce Services website at jobs.utah.gov/ui/employer/Public/Questions/ TaxRates.aspx.

Paying Unemployment Tax: Employers subject to the Utah Employment Security Act are required to file wage reports and pay tax quarterly. Wages are reported on the Employer's Quarterly Wage List, Form 3H. Even if no wages were paid during the quarter, employers must still send wage reports. Wages that must be reported include

✓ hourly wages, salaries and commissions;

✓ meals, lodging and other payments in kind;

✓ tips and gratuities;

✓ remuneration for services of an employee with equipment;

✓ vacation and sick pay;

✓ separation and dismissal pay;

✓ bonuses and gifts;

✓ payments in stock; and

✓ contributions to deferred compensation plans, including 401(k) plans.

The employer's tax contributions must be reported using the Employer's Quarterly Wage List, Form 3.

The reporting due dates are as follows:

Quarter Ending:	Reports mailed to Employers the Last week of:	Wage Report and Contributions Due:
March 31	March	April 30
June 30	June	July 31
September 30	September	October 31
December 31	December	January 31

Recordkeeping: Employers must keep the following records for at least four calendar years:

✓ Name and social security number of each employee

✓ Date each employee was hired

✓ Place of employment

✓ Date and reason each employee was separated from employment

✓ Beginning and ending date of each pay period and the date wages were paid

✓ Total amount of wages paid in each pay period, showing separately wages and other payments such as tips and bonuses

✓ Special payments such as bonuses, commissions, gifts, severance pay or accrued leave pay, etc

✓ Cash value of living quarters, meals, or anything else paid to an employee as compensation for work done

Fraud: Unemployment insurance fraud is considered a crime and, if convicted, is punishable by fines, penalties, and/or criminal prosecution. Fraud by employers includes

✓ misclassification of workers;

✓ incorrectly reporting wages;

✓ providing false information to prevent an otherwise eligible claimant from obtaining benefits; and

✓ failure to pay unemployment insurance taxes, report necessary information, or prohibit inspection from the Department.

SUTA dumping is a transfer of employees between businesses for the purpose of obtaining a lower unemployment compensation tax rate. SUTA dumping is prohibited and subject to criminal and/or civil penalties according to state law.

Further Information: For more information on the Utah unemployment program, contact:

Utah Department of Workforce Services
140 East 300 South
Salt Lake City, Utah 84145

Phone: (888) 848-0688

Website: www.jobs.utah.gov

Chapter 11, Employee Management, covers unemployment insurance in more detail.

Social Security

The Social Security Administration (SSA) is a federal agency responsible for paying retirement, disability, and survivors benefits to workers and their families. The SSA is also responsible for administering the Supplemental Security Income program. The SSA issues Social Security numbers, which are required for employees to legally work in the United States. Chapter 15, Tax Basics, explains how to submit Social Security tax for employees.

Insurance Coverage for Subcontractors

When hiring subcontractors, you should verify their insurance coverage to ensure it is adequate enough to cover any liability arising from their work.

There are a few simple questions you can ask to assess proper coverage.

✓ **Does the subcontractor carry the appropriate insurance?** Determine what type of insurance is needed. For example, you may require the subcontractor to carry commercial general liability (CGL) insurance.

✓ **Is the coverage adequate for the type of work being performed?** You can be held responsible for damages not covered by the subcontractor's insurance. Make sure their coverage limits are large enough to cover your project.

✓ **Is the insurance coverage current?** You can check with the insurance company listed on the insurance certificate to verify that the subcontractor's insurance coverage is current and that it will cover your project.

If insurance coverage is required, it is prudent to write the requirements into the contract. Chapter 8, Contract Management, talks about indemnification clauses as a contract provision to limit risk. This provision can also be included in your contract with the subcontractor. Indemnification absolves your company or holds your company free from liability from any losses or damages incurred by the subcontractor.

What is a Bond?

A surety bond is a risk transfer mechanism between a surety bonding company, the contractor, and the project owner. The agreement binds the contractor to comply with the terms and conditions of a contract. If the contractor can not perform the contract, the surety bonding company assumes the contractor's responsibilities and ensures that the project is completed.

Statutory and Common-Law Bonds: The federal government uses surety bonds on construction projects as a way to pre-qualify prospective construction firms. A surety bond is often required by law for public projects. It is referred to as a statutory bond. The owner of a private construction project may also opt to require a bond as an added guarantee that a project will be completed on-time, on budget, and within specified requirements. These private construction bonds are sometimes referred to as common-law bonds.

Surety Bonding Companies: When selecting a surety bonding company, check with the U.S. Department of the Treasury or a similar state agency (i.e., Department of Insurance) to ensure that the company is licensed for bonding. The surety company is the primary risk-taker in a bonding agreement, so it is important that it complies with all applicable laws and regulations.

Bond Language

Bonds generally contain four basic requirements:

✓ **Total dollar amount required for the bond**
 The bond amount is generally set as a percentage of the estimated cost. This number can vary and can be up to 100 percent of the estimated cost of construction. Maintenance bonds often use a figure of 10 percent of construction cost as the required amount.

✓ **Length of the bond**
 Bond lengths are typically required for a fixed rate of time following a project milestone, after which the bond is released. For construction performance bonds, this is usually after completion and final approval of the project.

✓ **Requirements for notice of defect or lack of maintenance**
 A period for completion of corrections is generally outlined after a notice of defect. The bond also establishes a time period for response from the bonding company, if the contractor fails to meet the obligations of the contract.

✓ **Bond enforcement**
 If the contractor does not successfully complete all required work or violates any requirement of the bond, enforcement measures are outlined to ensure project completion and proper maintenance.

Types of Bonds

A **bid bond** guarantees that the contractor, if awarded the job, will do work at the submitted bid price, enter into a contract with the owner, and furnish the required performance and payment bonds. Bid bonds serve as a deterrent against frivolous or unqualified bidders. If the contractor defaults on the bid agreement, the bid bond can be used to make up the pricing difference with the next lowest bidder.

A **performance bond** guarantees that the contractor will complete a contract within its time frame and conditions.

A **payment bond** guarantees subcontractors and suppliers that they will be paid for work if they perform properly under the contract.

A **maintenance bond** guarantees that for a stated period, typically for one year, no defective workmanship or material will appear in the completed project.

A **completion bond** provides assurance to the financial backers of a construction project that it will be completed on time.

A **fidelity bond** covers business owners for losses due to dishonest acts by their employees.

A **lien bond** guarantees that liens cannot be placed against the owner's property by contractors for payment of services. This type of bond allows someone to "bond around" a labor or materialmen's lien.

Just as the owner may require the general contractor to obtain a performance bond, a payment bond, or both, the general contractor may require the same of the subcontractor. The **subcontractor's bond** protects the general contractor in the event that the subcontractor does not fully perform the contract and/ or pay for labor and materials.

A **bank letter of credit** is not a bond but is a cash guarantee to the owner. It is not a guarantee of performance but can be converted to a payment to the owner by a bank or lending institution. The letter of credit typically does not cover 100 percent of the contract but customarily 5 percent to 10 percent of the contract.

· ·

Various types of bonds are issued as a protective measure in the event that contractual obligations are not met.

· ·

Qualifying for a Bond

Before issuing a bond, a surety company will examine your business thoroughly to make sure it is established, profitable, and well-managed. Some of the items the surety company will evaluate to make this determination include

✓ good references;

✓ ability to meet current and future obligations;

✓ experience matching contract requirements;

✓ necessary equipment to complete the work;

✓ financial stability;

✓ good credit; and

✓ established bank relationship and line of credit.

A surety's underwriting process consists of an extensive prequalification process in order to guarantee to the project owner that the contractor will fulfill the terms of the contract.

Bonds are priced on the basis of a percentage of the contract amount. Market conditions and prevailing industry practices set the percentage. Bond premiums vary among surety companies, but typically range from a half percent to two percent of the contract amount.

Bond Claims

Filing Process: Construction law and contractual relationships govern the bond claims process. The filing process is outlined in the bond language for common-law bonds. Government statutes outline the filing process for statutory bonds.

Project Changes: Unless specifically outlined in the bond agreement, the surety company will not cover changes to the original contract. In most cases, a request for additional coverage must be made and the bonding company must be notified of the contract changes.

Payment in the Event of Default: In the event of contractor default, the surety has several options. The surety may

✓ provide additional financing for the contractor to finish the project;

✓ arrange for a new contractor or hire subcontractors to complete the work; or

✓ pay out the amount of the bond.

Laws Governing Bonding of Federal Construction Projects

Miller Act: As a result of the high failure rate for completion of public construction projects, the Heard Act was enacted in 1894, allowing the use of surety bonds for federally funded projects. In 1935, the Miller Act replaced the Heard Act. The Miller Act is the current law requiring performance and payment bonds on all federal construction projects valued at greater than $100,000.

The surety amounts are defined as follows:

✓ A performance bond is required in an amount that the contracting officer regards as adequate. The bond is normally 100 percent of the contracted price.

✓ A separate payment bond is required for the protection of the suppliers of labor and materials. The sum of the payment bond varies, based on the size of the contract. These amounts include:

• Fifty percent of the contract amount for projects less than $1 million

• Forty percent of the contract amount for projects between $1 million and $5 million

• $2.5 million payment bond for contracts in excess of $5 million

Little Miller Acts: Most states and local governments also have similar surety laws on public works projects that are referred to as "Little Miller Acts."

Construction Industry Payment Protection Act of 1999: The Construction Industry Payment Protection Act of 1999 makes several amendments to the Miller Act of 1935. Its purpose is to improve payment bond protections for persons who furnish labor or material for use on federal construction projects. This law was passed because the bonding amounts specified in the Miller Act may not provide subcontractors with adequate protection.

The Construction Industry Payment Protection Act of 1999 outlines three specific requirements:

✓ The general contractor of a project generally must obtain a payment bond in an amount that is equal to the total value of the federal contract, unless a lesser amount is specified by the contracting officer. The payment bond cannot be less than the performance bond.

✓ Subcontractors are permitted to notify contractors of intent to sue by any means which provides written, third-party verification of delivery.

✓ Waivers of Miller Act payment bond protections are void before the work begins. Any waiver of a subcontractor's right to sue on a payment bond must be in writing, signed, and executed after the subcontractor has first furnished labor or materials for use in the project.

State Law Governing Bonding of Utah Construction Projects

Bonding requirements for public and private construction projects in Utah are contained in Title 14 of the Utah Code.

Public Construction Projects: If a public entity issues a commercial contract exceeding $50,000 it must obtain a payment bond from the general contractor. If it does not, the public entity must make prompt payment to the construction project's subcontractors and suppliers, upon demand. Subcontractors and suppliers have a direct right of action against the public entity.

Subcontractors and suppliers may make a payment claim if payment not received within 90 days after the last day of providing labor and/or materials. Subcontractors and suppliers have one year to make a claim. To protect payment claim rights, subcontractors and suppliers must file a preliminary notice. Preliminary notice filing is discussed in more detail in Chapter 16, Utah Mechanics' Lien Law.

Private Construction Projects: Before awarding a commercial contract exceeding $50,000, a general contractor is required to furnish the owner with a payment bond. The payment bond must be in the amount of the original contract price and it becomes binding upon award of the contract. The purpose of the payment bond is to protect subcontractors and suppliers who provide labor, services, equipment, and materials. If an owner fails to obtain a bond from the general contractor, the owner becomes liable to each person who provides labor, services, equipment, and materials.

Subcontractors and suppliers may make a claim against the bond if payment in full is not received within 90 days after the last day of providing labor and/or materials. Subcontractors and suppliers have one year to make a claim against the bond. To protect bond claim rights, subcontractors and suppliers must file a preliminary notice. Preliminary notice filing is discussed in more detail in Chapter 16, Utah Mechanics' Lien Law.

Final Inspection...

Risk Management Benefits: Managing risk is challenging but is important to your reputation and bottom line.

Insurance: Insurance should supplement your risk management program. It provides protection against unforeseen events and is sometimes required by law. Several different types of insurance coverage are available to fit the needs of your business.

Property Insurance: Property insurance typically covers your business and personal property when damage, theft, or loss occurs. All-risk builders' risk, named peril builders' risk, inland marine/equipment theft, equipment floater, transportation floater, and motor truck cargo policies are types of property insurance that may benefit your business.

Liability Insurance: Liability insurance is designed to protect against third-party claims that arise from alleged negligence resulting in bodily injury or property damage. Several types of liability insurance policies are available, such as commercial general, umbrella, and director's and officer's liability insurance.

Business Owner's Policies (BOPs): Property and liability coverage are bundled under business owner's policies.

Automobile Insurance: Liability and physical damage associated with vehicles owned or leased by your company are covered under automobile insurance. Several types of coverage are available.

Burglary and Theft Insurance: Loss or damage by burglary, theft, larceny, robbery, forgery, fraud, and vandalism is covered under burglary and theft insurance.

Key Man Life Insurance: This type of insurance is available as life insurance or disability insurance, or both, to protect the continuing success of the business.

Coverage Gaps and Overlaps: It is important to evaluate all of your insurance coverage. Using one insurer may minimize gaps and overlaps in coverage.

Employment-Related Insurance: Workers' compensation, unemployment, and social security are employment-related insurance regulated by state and/ or federal government.

Insurance Coverage for Subcontractors: When hiring subcontractors, ensure that they carry proper insurance coverage. These requirements should be outlined in the construction contract.

What is a Bond? Bonds provide protection in the event that contractual obligations are not met.

Bond Language: At a minimum, bonds should contain the total dollar amount, length of the bond, requirements for notice of defect or lack of maintenance, and bond enforcement.

Types of Bonds: Several types of bonds are available depending on the desired coverage.

Qualifying for a Bond: Before issuing a bond, the surety company will review your business to ensure it is established, profitable, and well-managed.

Bond Claims: The bond claim filing process is outlined in the bond language for common-law bonds and in the government statutes for statutory bonds.

Laws Governing Bonding of Federal Construction Projects: The Miller Act and Construction Industry Payment Protection Act of 1999 outline bonding requirements for federal construction projects.

State Law Governing Bonding of Utah Construction Projects: Utah law specifies payment bond requirements for Utah public and private construction projects.

Chapter 5
YOUR BUSINESS TOOLBOX

Just as you need a toolbox filled with tools to accomplish jobs in your trade, you need a toolbox of resources and skills to help you run your business. This chapter will introduce a few of these tools and will lay a foundation for tools covered in subsequent chapters.

Time Management

Time Is Money: This familiar phrase holds special meaning for business owners. Your ability to manage time effectively can make the difference between completing a job successfully and failing to meet customer expectations. Time is one of your most important tools. Use it wisely.

Setting Goals: Effective goal setting is a key cornerstone to time management success. Once goals are set, they should be documented. This gives you a visual reminder and ensures proper communication to the whole work team. A methodical approach should be used to move forward towards achieving your goals. Your management team and employees should understand your goals and can help put together the plan tactics.

Four Time Management Tips: These habits will help you organize and manage your time.

✓ Prioritize tasks daily
✓ Delegate effectively when possible
✓ Use checklists and calendars (find a time management system that works for you)
✓ Do not procrastinate

Advantage of Technology: Learning about new technology and using it in your operations can save you time. Research ways to automate your operations without taking away from the quality of your products and services. Putting a new technology or process in place can give you more time to focus on strategic activities.

Competitive Edge: Although multitasking is an important skill, effective time management requires that you focus on the necessary task at hand to move forward towards achievement of the set goals. It gives you a competitive edge and helps you anticipate problems before they occur. Planning your time puts you in control, gives you the ability to be proactive and helps reduce anxieties caused by "putting out fires". Your professionalism will be appreciated by your customers, subcontractors, and suppliers.

Time is money.
Use it wisely.

Delegation

You Can't Do It All: When you become a business owner, you go from a tradesperson to a manager of many jobs and a business administrator. Delegation is a key tool that will ensure that you get all tasks accomplished. You simply cannot do it all and be efficient.

Preparing to Delegate: Learning to delegate is often difficult because you are giving up control of certain tasks. You may feel that a task won't be done correctly or that it takes longer to explain a task than just doing it yourself.

Delegation is a way of developing your employees and building a solid team. Giving your employees increased responsibility builds their self-confidence, provides motivation, and makes them more productive and loyal. Delegation gives you the chance to concentrate strategically on running your business.

How to Delegate: Here are simple steps on how to delegate:

1. Identify a person for the task.

2. Explain the task clearly and make sure you are understood. You may want to ask the person to repeat their understanding of the task back to you.

3. Follow up with the person throughout the process.

4. Give positive feedback and provide guidance on how the task can be improved, if necessary.

Effective delegation increases your efficiency.

Business Ethics

Your Reputation: Good business ethics are a must if you want to safeguard your reputation in the industry. Practicing good business ethics, when dealing with customers, employees, subcontractors, and suppliers, is not only the right thing to do, it is the best way to avoid litigation.

Defining Ethics: You may ask, "What are ethics?" In general, the term as it applies to business means behaving in a trustworthy, fair, honest, and respectful manner toward everyone with whom you interact. Your core values serve as your moral compass and guide this standard.

Studies Say...

Top management has the strongest influence on employees' ethical behavior. If top managers demonstrate unethical behavior, employees are likely to do the same.

Establishing a code of conduct is the first step to ensuring that good ethics are practiced throughout your company. A code of conduct is a documented way that an organization should operate.

This document can include

✓ guidelines for employees, management, subcontractors, and suppliers;

✓ standards for doing business; and

✓ a statement of commitment to the community.

You may want to provide your customers with your code of conduct. It will reinforce your commitment to good ethics and demonstrate professionalism.

Make the right ethical choices to protect your reputation and avoid litigation.

Technology

Technology as an Essential Tool: Technology is an essential tool for communicating and keeping your business competitive. Purchasing technology is becoming increasingly cost-effective. There are many technological tools specifically designed for the construction industry. These tools increase efficiency and aid in various tasks, such as

✓ estimating and bidding,

✓ accounting,

✓ job costing,

✓ scheduling, and

✓ construction management.

If you have not jumped into the technology age, here are a few basics to start with:

Computer: For a business owner, a computer has many uses which will help in streamlining administrative functions. This is the basic tool you will need to operate programs for applications such as writing, accounting, scheduling, estimating, and e-mail. Some builders opt to have laptop computers to perform these functions on the jobsite.

Phone: Cell phone technology has advanced in the area of two-way radio communications (sometimes referred to as a push-to-talk feature), use of e-mail, photography, and calendar management. Regardless of the features you choose for your business cell phone, it is important that you are always accessible to your customers and employees.

Fax Machine: Although e-mail has become a prevalent means for communication, it is still important for businesses to have a fax machine so that copies of important documents can be transmitted quickly and efficiently.

Printer: A printer allows you to produce hard copies of the files you have on your computer. A printer will come in handy when creating customer correspondence and contracts. Portable printers small enough to bring to the jobsite are also available.

Scanner: Documents and small objects can be copied or scanned in a form that can be stored on a computer and then these files can be manipulated and printed for use.

Multifunction Hardware: You can purchase a single machine that works as a photocopier, fax, printer, and scanner. This type of hardware can be convenient and cost-effective if your business uses such functions frequently. However, bear in mind that if the unit breaks, you may lose several or all of the functions until it is repaired or replaced.

Digital Camera: A digital camera is a great way to store your photos on the computer. It is important for you to document your work every step of the way, and digital pictures are a cost effective way to organize that information. Your pictures can be stored on a disk with the project files and e-mailed as necessary.

Internet: The Internet is a powerful tool. It can be used for research, communication, or marketing your company.

Word Processing Software: Word processing can save you a lot of time because the information you need is stored in the computer. Handwritten documents need to be rewritten each time, while documents entered in the computer can be modified and reused. Many word processing programs have templates of commonly used documents for business, and these can be used, modified, and reused at any time.

Spreadsheet Program: This type of software gives you the flexibility to create financial worksheets on the computer. You can set up the worksheet to automatically calculate figures, reducing mathematical errors.

A Warning about Software: Although software is designed to streamline your processes, you must still understand the basics. For example, if you purchase accounting software but do not understand the fundamentals of accounting, the software is useless to you. In future chapters, we will cover basic skills that will help you utilize software packages.

Once you become comfortable with technology, you may want to purchase other advanced tools and software.

. . . .
*Using technology can increase your
efficiency and keep you competitive.*
. . . .

Small Business Assistance and Loans

Various federal, state and local resources can help you with small business services or education you might need. Many of these services may be free or available at a minimal cost to business owners. Below are some of the resources available to you.

State of Utah Official State Website

The Utah state website provides comprehensive resources for small business owners and prospective entrepreneurs. Information on the site includes small business financing, business requirements, human resource assistance, business forms, business registration and links to key state agencies.

Additional information is available on the website at www.business.utah.gov.

Local Community Colleges & Universities

Business education opportunities are available through local community colleges and universities. Seminars, workshops, and courses are offered on business skills and small business management.

Small Business Administration (SBA)

The Small Business Administration's mission is to counsel, assist, and protect the interests of small business. The SBA provides training and online help for small businesses.

The SBA website at www.sba.gov has several online resources to Federal, state, and local information for business owners. Resources include:

✓ Starting a Business

✓ Registrations, Licenses, and Permits

✓ Finance and Taxes

✓ Expanding Your Business

✓ Legal Compliance

✓ Industry Specifics

✓ State and Local Resources

A partnership program through the SBA links business owners from across the nation to create a social network and provide access to experts.

The SBA Headquarters is located in Washington, D.C., but you can check the website at www.sba.gov or call 1-800-U-ASK-SBA to find an office near you.

> *Utah District Office*
> *125 South State Street, Room 2227*
> *Salt Lake City, Utah 84138*
>
> *Phone: (801) 524-3209*
>
> *Website: www.sba.gov/ut*

Service Corps of Retired Executives (SCORE)

SCORE is a national volunteer organization of retired executives who can provide counseling and training to you if you are an entrepreneur and/or business owner. There are several SCORE offices located throughout the state. You can find the SCORE office nearest to you on the website.

> *SCORE Association*
> *409 3rd Street, SW*
> *6th Floor*
> *Washington, D.C. 20024*
> *1-800-634-0245*
>
> *Website: www.score.org*

Business.USA.gov Website

The Business.gov website provides several online resources to Federal, state, and local information for business owners. Resources include:

✓ Starting a Business

✓ Registrations, Licenses, and Permits

✓ Finance and Taxes

✓ Expanding Your Business

✓ Legal Compliance

✓ Industry Specifics

✓ State and Local Resources

A partnership program through Business.gov links business owners from across the nation to create a social network and provide access to experts.

Appendix C contains additional references and website links on topics covered in this book.

Small Business Certifications

Federal and state governments often have opportunities for businesses to bid on contracts. These contracts are highly sought after for a number of reasons. To level the playing field, the government has established certifications for small, minority-owned, and women-owned businesses. If your company fits the criteria, you can obtain one or more certifications, which can provide additional opportunities for you to bid on government contracts.

The U.S. Small Business Administration has several different certification and assistance programs for small businesses. These programs include the following:

✓ Historically Underutilized Business Zone (HUBZone) Certification

✓ 8(a) Business Development Program

✓ Small Business Certification

✓ Women-Owned Small Business Federal Contract Program

✓ Veteran and Service-Disabled Veteran Owned Business Assistance Program

✓ Native American Owned Business Certification

✓ Alaskan Owned Business Assistance Program

✓ Native Hawaiian Owned Business Assistance Program

Information on these certifications is found on the SBA website at www.sba.gov/contracting/resources-small-businesses or by calling 1-800-U ASK SBA. In addition to certification information, the SBA website contains helpful links about government contracting and business development.

Certifications are also available at the state and local level. The Utah Department of Transportation (UDOT) offers a Unified Certification Program for the Disadvantaged Business Enterprise (DBE) certification. Information is available on the UDOT website at www.udot.utah.gov.

Final Inspection...

Time Management: Effective time management gives you a competitive edge and helps you anticipate problems before they occur.

Delegation: Effective delegation increases your efficiency and helps develop your employees.

Business Ethics: The right ethical choices help protect your reputation and avoid litigation.

Technology: Technology is an essential tool for communicating and keeping your business competitive.

Small Business Assistance and Loans: Several organizations are available to help small businesses with a variety of functions.

Small Business Certifications: Certifications for small, minority, and women-owned businesses are available through the government. If your company qualifies, certifications can provide additional opportunities for you to bid on government contracts.

Chapter 6
MARKETING AND SALES

Chapter Survey...

⇨ *Executing Your Marketing Plan*

⇨ *Logos, Stationery, and Business Cards*

⇨ *Promotional Materials*

⇨ *Public Relations*

⇨ *Effective Selling Skills*

⇨ *Organizing the Sales Process*

⇨ *Your Sales Presentation*

Start Off on the Right Foot: First impressions can tell your potential customers a lot about your business. Customers may judge your professionalism or reputation on this initial contact. Marketing, in some cases, may be the first impression of your business, and you want to make sure customers feel comfortable with you and your company from this point on.

The purpose of marketing is to bring in new customers and retain current customers. A good marketing program helps ensure a steady flow of leads and customers and, more important, a steady flow of incoming cash.

- -

First impressions are lasting ones.
Make your company's first impression a
positive one.

- -

Executing Your Marketing Plan

Maximize Your Marketing Potential: When developing your market analysis and marketing strategy (featured in the business plan template in Appendix B), you should answer questions such as these:

✓ What is the vision for my business?

✓ Who are my customers?

✓ What is the best way to reach these customers?

✓ What is my competitive advantage?

✓ What is the best way to promote my products and services (e.g. advertising, public relations, online marketing, direct sales, etc.)?

✓ What will my marketing efforts cost?

✓ How much revenue do I expect to gain as a result of marketing efforts?

✓ Who will manage the marketing program? Will I need to hire outside help to execute the program?

✓ What growth opportunities exist in my industry?

✓ What challenges for growth exist in my industry?

Now it is time to put these thoughts into action. Developing a promotion plan will help you bring these ideas to life.

Logos, Stationery, and Business Cards

Create Your Identity: A simple start to developing your promotion plan is to create a logo. Not only will your name distinguish you in the market but a logo will set you apart from your competitors. Logos become part of your company identity and convey a professional look, which is important for that first impression.

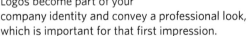

A good logo design should be

✓ simple and easy to remember;

✓ attractive in color and black and white;

✓ limited to one or two colors;

✓ representative of your company identity; and

✓ scalable up or down and attractive in any size.

Once your logo is created, you should include it on your business cards and stationery.

Promotional Materials

You may also apply your logo to several different promotional items. These items include

- ✓ brochures,
- ✓ direct mailings,
- ✓ jobsite signs,
- ✓ truck signs,
- ✓ yellow pages, and
- ✓ websites.

Using promotional materials will give you name recognition. When potential customers have an upcoming job, they may be more likely to approach your company to put in a bid because your name is out in the market.

Business promotion through social media has become a prevalent means of marketing. You can create a business account on social media websites, such as Facebook, Twitter, and LinkedIn, to advertise your services, post updates on your business, and gain name recognition. Participation in social media can be an inexpensive way to market and increase traffic to your business website. In addition to creating a business page on social media sites for promotion, these sites have areas where you can buy advertising space.

A good marketing program is an investment that can help you gain customers and strengthen your reputation.

Public Relations

Benefits of Networking: Public relations are an inexpensive but effective marketing tool. It is important to build name recognition;

good public relations constantly keeps your business in the eye of the public—your potential customers. The downside to public relations is its labor-intensive nature, but the time invested will give you great rewards. You may use this approach to not only get potential customers but as a way to get referrals to good subcontractors, suppliers, or employees.

In the Public Eye: Here are some ideas to get you started.

- ✓ ***Join local trade associations***
  This is a good opportunity to meet new people in your industry. You can also volunteer to speak at meetings and conferences to showcase your knowledge and expertise.

- ✓ ***Participate in a local non-profit initiative (for example, be a volunteer Habitat for Humanity worker)***
  High-profile projects will put you in a positive light in the public eye and may get some press coverage.

- ✓ ***Volunteer for local leadership opportunities***
  Leadership positions in organizations such as schools or the local Chamber of Commerce may give you time with other influential people in the community who can make good referrals about you and your business.

- ✓ ***Sponsor community events***
  When you sponsor community events, your business name is often featured in event brochures, signage, and media promotions such as newspapers and radio advertisements.

- ✓ ***Send press releases to the local media***
  This public relations technique offers exposure to a broad audience and gives you credibility because it is communicated through a third-party. Press releases can report your involvement in the local community, new construction trends, or any ideas that might be interesting to the public and will promote your company.

- ✓ ***Hold an open house***
  You can hold an open house at your office or at a job where you can showcase your work. An open house gives you a chance to reinforce current business relationships and make new ones.

Effective Selling Skills

Don't Underestimate Your Selling Skills: Selling is often perceived as a salesperson pitching a product or service and the customer saying yes or no. Many people don't feel comfortable with the process of selling, because it makes them feel pushy and overbearing. Selling should be the simple process of matching your company's skills and expertise with what the customer needs.

Listen Up: Active listening is the golden rule to effective selling. Without listening, you cannot clearly understand what your customer needs. You may ask yourself, "What exactly is active listening?" Here are a few simple rules:

✓ Maintain good eye contact.

✓ Be attentive.

✓ Keep an open mind.

✓ Don't interrupt.

✓ Ask clarifying questions.

✓ Put yourself in the "shoes" of the other person.

✓ Pay attention to body language (i.e., facial expressions).

Using these simple guidelines, you will gain a more thorough understanding of your potential customers and be able to target your response to their needs.

A Word of Caution...

Be careful not to make unrealistic or inaccurate statements just to make a sale. You will hurt your business in the long run and potentially leave yourself open to a lawsuit. All advertising and marketing claims must be truthful and not deceptive. Individual state contractor licensing boards may have specific guidelines regarding licensed contractor advertising such as including a licensing number and specific verbiage required by law.

Organizing the Sales Process

Put It in Writing: Selling is a process. Generally speaking, higher-value sales have a longer selling process than a lower-value sale. To manage this selling process and provide the best service possible, you must be organized. Tracking potential customers is made simple by developing a sales tracking sheet for each contact you make. Your tracking sheet should contain the contact information for the potential customer, the type of work the customer wants, a

summary of communication, the source of referral for that customer, and any other information you feel is necessary.

The next step is to prioritize your sales leads. Prioritizing leads is a way to manage your time in the sales process and can give you key insights into the effectiveness of your marketing program. You want to concentrate most of your time on the strong leads.

Tracking and prioritizing leads makes the sales process most effective.

Your Sales Presentation

Present Your Best Side: Once you have determined your strongest sales leads, you should schedule time to make a sales presentation. This is your opportunity to show customers how your company can meet their needs; in the sales presentation you try to gain a commitment to perform the work.

Presentation materials are important visuals and give the customer something concrete to take away and read after the meeting. These materials can include

✓ a company information sheet,

✓ brochures,

✓ business cards,

✓ past customer testimonials,

✓ warranty information, and

✓ photographs of past projects.

To avoid awkward stumbling in the presentation, have materials prepared ahead of time. This demonstrates your professionalism and ensures that you have thought through the presentation.

Overcoming "No": Handling objections is one of the more difficult parts of the sales process. This is the time to use your active listening skills and overcome the objection.

✓ Repeat the objection to ensure that you completely understand the potential customer's reservation.

✓ No question is a stupid question. The person with the objection may just not understand the process.

✓ Give an example of a customer with the same question and how you effectively fulfilled his/her needs.

Communication Is Key: Closing the sale is a very important part of the process. Try to gain a commitment from the potential customer, whether it is hiring your company to do the work or even just scheduling a follow-up appointment.

Follow up on all sales presentations. This may be as simple as making a phone call or sending a card or small gift. Consistent follow-up ensures that you are at the top of your potential customer's mind and gives you an advantage over competitors.

Clearly understanding your potential customer's needs is imperative.

Final Inspection...

Executing Your Marketing Plan: Once you develop your marketing plan, the next step is implementing it.

Logos, Stationery, and Business Cards: These simple marketing tools can help establish your company's identity.

Promotional Materials: You can extend your marketing program by using various promotional materials.

Public Relations: This is an inexpensive but effective way to market your company.

Effective Selling Skills: Effective selling involves carefully listening to your potential customer's needs.

Organizing the Sales Process: Tracking potential sales leads can help you organize the process of selling.

Your Sales Presentation: Preparation and follow-up are important when presenting to potential customers.

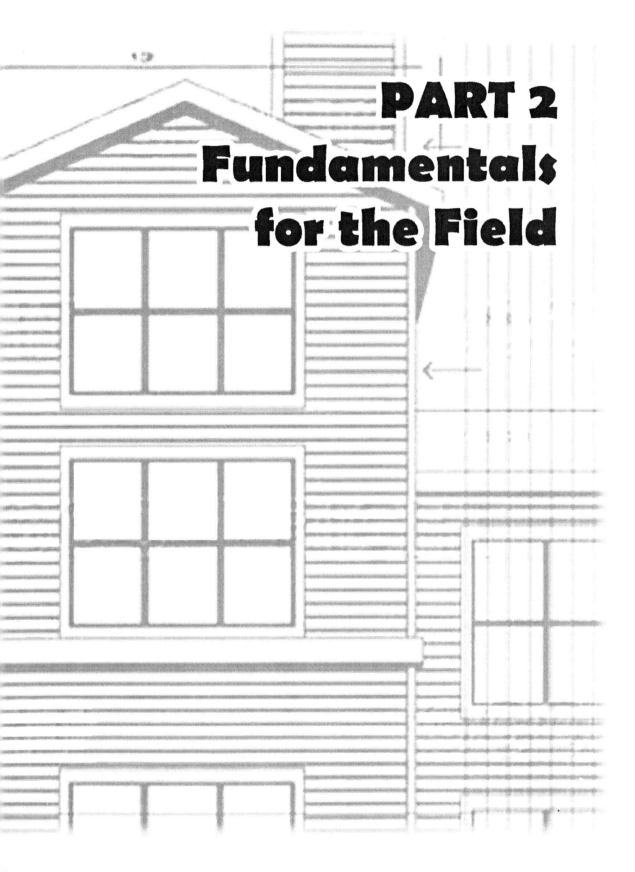

PART 2
Fundamentals for the Field

Chapter 7
BIDDING AND ESTIMATING

Chapter Survey...

⇨ Bid Documents

⇨ Ethics in Bidding

⇨ Estimate Planning

⇨ Estimating Framework

⇨ Determining Estimated Costs

⇨ Other Methods of Estimating

⇨ Estimating Pitfalls

⇨ Using an Estimator

⇨ Submitting Your Bid

⇨ Job Cost Recording System

⇨ Technology Tools for Estimating

Accurate estimating is important to the profitability of a construction company. If a job is estimated correctly, the contractor has a good chance at getting the job and making money. If the job is poorly estimated, the contractor may lose the bid or win the bid and lose money on the project.

The estimator must ask these questions when assessing whether to bid on a project.

✓ **Company Resources and Type of Work:** Does our company have the resources to perform this work? Is this project consistent with the type of work we do?

✓ **Site Considerations:** Are there any special site considerations that we need to consider? Do the site conditions create any additional costs for our company?

✓ **Location and Cost Effectiveness:** How can we do the work efficiently and in the most cost effective manner? Does the location present special considerations and added cost through travel time and limited accessibility?

✓ **Risk Assessment:** What are the risks and how will we manage them?

✓ **Profitability of Project:** What is our profit margin on this work?

If you know you cannot complete the job on time or there is a chance you could lose money on the project, we recommend that you *do not bid the job*. The jobs you choose should contribute to your long-term goals and the reputation you want your company to have in the market.

Bid Documents

In a competitive bid situation, a bid package is often put together that includes

✓ **an invitation to bid** that gives a brief overview of the project, deadlines, and general requirements;

✓ **bid instructions** that contain specifics of how the bid should be completed and submitted;

✓ **bid forms,** including but not limited to items such as a bid sheet, bid schedule, bidder's questionnaire on experience, financial responsibility and capability, and a copy of the contract; and

✓ **supplements**, including items important to the overall bid process such as a property survey and soil analysis.

It is important to follow all the instructions in the bid package carefully and submit all documents according to the required specifications. The bidder can be found unresponsive if information is incorrectly submitted or omitted altogether.

Pre-bid meetings may also be scheduled, especially for larger projects. In a pre-bid meeting, the project specifications and any changes to the bid package are discussed.

If changes are made to a bid package before it is due, an **addendum** is issued. The addendum becomes part of the bid documents and, ultimately, part of the contract when awarded. It is important to carefully review all addenda to evaluate the impact on your bid.

Changes in plans and specifications may affect your bid pricing or even your decision to bid at all.

Carefully evaluate whether bidding on a project is the right decision for your company.

Ethics in Bidding

Good ethical conduct is necessary to maintain the integrity of the bidding process. The situations listed below are not only a poor way to do business, but some state statutes forbid these practices on public projects.

✓ **Bid Shopping**
   Bid shopping occurs when the general contractor approaches subcontractors other than those who have submitted bids to seek a lower offer than what was quoted in original bids. In this situation, the general contractor reveals the original bids submitted and tries to reduce the price.

✓ **Bid Peddling**
   Bid peddling occurs when the subcontractor approaches the general contractor after the project was awarded with the intent of lowering the original price submitted on bid day.

✓ **Bid Rigging**
   Bid rigging is a form of collusion where contractors coordinate their bids to fix the award outcome of a project.

Estimate Planning

Once you have determined that you want to submit a bid, you must prepare your estimate. An estimate is the sum of the costs to complete the project, plus your added overhead and profit margin. Before you start putting numbers down on paper, you should understand all the factors that impact the cost of the job. A good estimate will fall within 1 percent to 2 percent of actual construction costs.

Project Documents

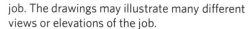

A complete set of project documents is required to prepare an accurate cost estimate. These documents include the following:

✓ **Construction or architectural drawings** that show a schematic diagram of the job. The drawings may illustrate many different views or elevations of the job.

✓ **Specifications** are details that determine the type of materials or methods to be used in construction. If there is a conflict between the specifications and applicable codes, you must follow the stricter of the two. The codes are the minimum requirements by law. You must always meet or exceed the applicable codes.

✓ **The contract** is the agreement between you and your customer to complete the specified work. The conditions outlining the obligations of each party, such as the owner and contractor, are included in the contract. If your bid is accepted, the construction drawings and specifications become part of the contract package. Contracts are covered in more detail in Chapter 8.

✓ **Bonds** may be required as part of the bid submittal (discussed in Chapter 4). Bonds commonly required are bid and performance bonds.

You should carefully review these documents to understand the project and the expectations of the customer.

Site Visit

There may be specifics about the site that influence the cost estimate. These details cannot always be determined from the construction documents. It is important that you go to the actual site and look at any factors that may impact the project. Soil type, grading, vehicle access, and availability to electricity and water are some of the variables that could affect the cost of the project. You want to anticipate as many of these problems as you can before beginning work.

During this time, you should consider the environmental aspects of the project. If you need to obtain environmental permits, this process will affect your estimated costs. Your project may also require special equipment and processes that should be factored into your estimate. Chapter 12, Safety and Environmental Considerations, discusses environmental impacts in more depth.

Estimating Framework

Estimating should be a systematic process. Approaching the estimate in an organized way will help you avoid errors or omissions. Taking the extra time to construct a framework for the estimate will increase your accuracy.

Your estimating framework essentially lists the process for completing the job. This can be accomplished by

✓ defining the phases of the project; and

✓ listing each task and materials needed within each phase.

Once your framework is established, you can enter the time and cost for each task. If you are awarded the job, you can easily convert your estimating framework into your job schedule.

Define the Phases

The first thing you need to consider when you build your estimate is the phases of the project that you are working on. For example, you might list the phases as preconstruction, construction, and post-construction. The order of tasks will drive your scheduling process.

List Each Task and Materials Needed

Once you list the phases of the project, you need to develop a list of tasks and materials for each phase. Be very specific in this step. If you omit an item or add an unnecessary item, your estimate will be inaccurate. The task and material list should also include labor time needed and material amounts. By identifying these items early in the process, you may also determine the need for items such as overtime to meet certain project deadlines and temporary storage. All of these items play a part in the cost estimate.

Estimating Checklist

The Construction Specifications Institute publishes a classification system called MasterFormat. This system includes numbers and job tasks grouped by major construction activities. This is a helpful tool when setting up your estimating framework to ensure that you have accounted for all aspects of materials and labor. After you become familiar with the estimating process, you may develop your own estimating checklist customized for your needs.

Determining Estimated Costs

Quantity Take-off Method

One accurate method of estimating is the quantity take-off method. Using this method, you individually estimate units of materials and labor for each task you listed in your estimating framework.

After estimating materials and labor, the following items are added:

✓ subcontractor fees,

✓ labor burden,

✓ project overhead costs,

✓ project equipment,

✓ contingencies,

✓ allowances,

✓ company overhead, and

✓ profit.

By going through the items individually, you can adjust your estimate to accommodate the unique aspects of the project you may have uncovered when reviewing the construction documents or during your site survey.

 STEP 1 Determine Labor Cost for Each Task

Using your estimating framework, you can begin to enter your labor cost. Information from previous jobs can help you determine accurate job costs. There are also published costs available through books such as the RSMeans cost data series, but this is no substitute for your knowledge of the industry. Your experience with your local labor market and wages should be factored into your estimated costs.

For each labor item on your estimating framework list, use the following formula to determine the labor cost.

Required Labor Hours per Task x Labor Rate = Labor Cost per Task

The required labor hours can vary based on several different factors, such as employee skill level, size of crew, and weather conditions. These factors must be taken into account when determining the required labor hours. Hours spent planning and scheduling must also be figured into the labor cost equation.

Another helpful tool when determining labor cost is your historical cost data. Determining your final labor cost from past projects will help you put together more accurate estimates for future jobs. Developing a cost-tracking system is discussed later in this chapter.

Add Labor Burden

As an employer, you incur costs such as employment taxes and insurance. These obligations add approximately 30 percent to your labor cost. This additional amount is referred to as labor burden.

Labor burden includes items such as

✓ Medicare and social security (discussed in Chapter 15),
✓ federal unemployment insurance (discussed in Chapter 15),
✓ workers' compensation,
✓ liability insurance,
✓ state unemployment insurance, and
✓ company benefits (such as medical insurance, vacations, etc.).

Labor burden must be factored into your total labor cost.

 Determine Materials Cost

Just as you plugged the labor cost into your estimating framework, you can do the same with the materials cost. For each material item listed on your estimating framework, you need to obtain a cost.

Your suppliers can provide you with the materials price per unit or a lump sum. The cost of materials can fluctuate according to the availability of raw materials and demand, so it is important to keep current cost data. In addition to tracking wage, earnings, employment, and benefit statistics, the Bureau of Labor Statistics (www.bls.gov) tracks the prices of major groups of construction materials as part of its Producer Price Index (PPI) program. Periodically reviewing this resource can help you understand potential increases and decreases in materials cost.

You may receive the materials cost as a unit cost. If necessary, use the following formula to determine the total material cost per unit for each of the materials categories on your take-off sheet.

Price per Unit x Number of Units Needed = Total Material Unit Cost

To make sure you receive the best price, obtain at least three bids from suppliers. You should also add a small contingency for waste. Depending on the type of material and the job specifications, your waste contingency will vary.

Determine Project Equipment Costs

Equipment needed to complete the job is figured as a direct cost of the project and added to your estimate.

For example, if you need a crane to set an air handling unit on top of a building as part of a HVAC project, it is considered a direct cost.

Small tools and pickup trucks are considered an indirect cost and not part of project equipment. These indirect costs are figured into project overhead.

Figuring the direct cost of equipment differs depending if you rent or own the equipment.

Owned Equipment: To estimate owned equipment, you must arrive at a unit cost for the equipment. To calculate unit cost, consider the following factors:

✓ actual value of equipment factoring in its age and amount of depreciation from the original purchase price;
✓ maintenance and operating costs;
✓ taxes and fees;
✓ labor to operate equipment, including any training or licensing costs; and
✓ insurance.

Unit cost is calculated by estimating the number of hours you will use the equipment per year and dividing this number by the total yearly cost of the equipment calculated by considering the operational factors.

For example, if you figure the total cost of the equipment for the year is $30,000 and you plan to use the equipment for a total of 1,000 hours, your unit cost to operate the equipment is $30 an hour.

If you estimate using the equipment for 40 hours on a project, your estimated project equipment cost for that project is $1,200.

Rental Equipment: The following items are considered when figuring the cost of rental equipment:

✓ equipment rental rate;
✓ labor cost to pick up and return equipment or delivery fees;
✓ labor cost to operate equipment; and
✓ other costs associated with operating the equipment (e.g., cost of fuel).

Subcontracting: You may decide that neither option is cost effective or feasible and subcontract the work. In this case, this line item would appear under subcontractor fees.

Rent, Lease, or Buy? Construction equipment is vital to the completion of construction projects. Equipment can range from cranes to computers. The decision to rent, lease, or purchase this equipment is a challenging one, and there are many considerations to each option.

Leasing is a long-term rental agreement that provides the benefits of using the equipment without purchasing. Lease payments are made to the owner of the equipment in exchange for the use of the equipment. At the end of the lease term, the owner takes possession of the equipment.

Leasing equipment has many advantages. One of the biggest is the ability to use the equipment with a limited capital expenditure. Other advantages compared to purchasing include

✓ no down payment;

✓ duration of payments over a longer period making them lower;

✓ lease payments (as defined by the IRS) are deductible as operating expenses; and

✓ obsolete equipment is returned to the owner at end of the lease.

Equipment ownership allows you to take advantage of certain tax benefits and usually costs are less than leasing in the long run. Leases are long-term contractual agreements that generally cannot be cancelled. If you no longer need the equipment, you must still make payments for the full term of the lease.

Purchasing equipment is advantageous when the equipment has a long and useful life and will not become obsolete in the short-term. You gain ownership of the equipment after the purchase is made but you should consider how the equipment will hold value over a long-term period. For this reason, salvage value is a benefit to purchasing equipment.

Renting equipment may be an alternative to purchasing or leasing. Although renting equipment is usually the costliest, it is the best option in certain circumstances. These include

✓ short-term, specialized projects;

✓ replacement for equipment being repaired;

✓ equipment with high maintenance costs; and

✓ jobs that require transportation and storage to distant locations.

The decision to rent, purchase, or lease is one that should be analyzed carefully to provide the most cost-effective solution for your company.

 Add Subcontractor Fees

Subcontractors will be a consideration if you need to outsource work that your company does not have the resources to complete. Chapter 13 covers hiring and working with subcontractors. You should get at least three bids from subcontractors, so you have a good measure for comparison. Carefully evaluate your subcontractors to determine that they have the proper qualifications, licensure, and insurance coverage. The subcontractor fees must be added to the estimate that you give your customer.

 Add Allowances

There may be items that are not specified in the project plans, such as finish materials (carpeting, fixtures, lighting, etc.). For these items, you can specify an allowance in your estimate. This is the owner's budget for these items. If the owner's choices exceed or fall short of the allowance amount, the contract should clearly address who is responsible for the difference. Typically, a change order is created stating the amount under or over what is stated in the contract. Change orders are discussed in Chapter 8.

 Add Contingencies

A contingency percentage is sometimes added to an estimate to protect the contractor if an unanticipated problem or condition arises during the course of the project. Contingency markups are generally based on the risk level of the project.

For example, a low risk level project might have a 2 percent contingency markup, but a project that has more unknown factors would have a higher markup.

Add Project Overhead

Project overhead costs are items that are necessary to complete the project but are not directly associated with labor and materials. These costs typically account for 5 percent to 10 percent of the total bid, but these costs should be itemized as much as possible to achieve the most accurate result.

Examples of project overhead costs include

✓ bonds,

✓ temporary storage,

✓ temporary office,

✓ security guard,

✓ utilities,

✓ dumpsters, and

✓ portable toilets.

Project overhead differs from company overhead. Company overhead cannot be directly linked with a project.

STEP 9   Add Company Overhead

Company overhead is the cost of doing business. These expenses are necessary to keeping the operation running. Examples of these expenses are

✓ office rent,

✓ accounting fees,

✓ taxes,

✓ telephone,

✓ legal fees, and

✓ administrative labor.

Calculating an Overhead Percentage

Using historical information from the past year is the best way to predict overhead for the following year. Overhead percentages generally average between 5 percent and 20 percent, so it is best to calculate the overhead rates specific to your company.

Company Overhead: To arrive at a company overhead percentage, you can make the following calculations.

✓ Add up all of your overhead costs from the previous year. These numbers may be found on your income statement as part of your administrative expenses.

✓ Divide your overhead costs by your revenues (found on your income statement) to arrive at your overhead percentage.

Project Overhead: Project overhead is a similar calculation.

✓ Add up all of your project overhead costs from the previous year.

✓ Divide your project overhead costs by your revenues (found on your income statement) to arrive at your overhead percentage.

Adding Overhead to the Bid: You must add these overhead percentages to your estimate to cover your overhead costs.

For example, let's say you calculated the direct costs for your bid at $100,000, your project overhead at 9 percent, and company overhead percentage at 11 percent. Your direct costs are then 80 percent of your total bid price. Since overhead is a percentage of revenue, you should divide the direct costs of your bid by 80 percent (.80).

Here is what the calculation should look like:

$$\$100,000 \div .80 = \$125,000$$

After adding in overhead, the bid price with direct costs and overhead is $125,000.

STEP 10   Add Markup and Determine Profit Margin

Considerations for properly pricing a job include

✓ cost estimate,

✓ customer needs and expectations,

✓ local market and competition, and

✓ expected profit margin.

Determining the right pricing based on these factors is important to maximizing your profit and satisfying your customers.

Cost-based pricing is one of the most common ways to price a bid. Essentially, the cost of the project is determined through the cost estimate and an overhead percentage, plus a markup percentage. The markup percentage is divided into the direct costs of the project, just like the overhead costs in the previous example. If you estimated correctly, you will achieve your internal profit margin goals.

The standard industry markup is 15 percent, but you should consider the market and competition. You must be careful to keep your estimate in line with your competition and understand how much your customers are willing to pay for your work.

In your estimate, markup is applied to the direct costs of the project, such as labor, material, project equipment, project overhead, and subcontractors.

If your markup is too low, you may not cover your costs to complete the project, causing you to break even, or lose money on the job. To get the work, you may decide to bid low by lowering your profit markup and make it up on future projects, but this should not be a common practice. You will eventually go out of business if an insufficient amount of profit is achieved over time.

On the flip side, if your markup is too high, you may bid yourself out of jobs. Typically, the higher the markup, the fewer jobs you receive. The lower the markup, the more jobs you receive. You must estimate and choose your markup carefully to ensure a steady flow of jobs and profits for your company.

Attention to detail is important to preparing an accurate estimate.

Other Methods of Estimating

Quantity take-off is generally the most accurate way to estimate, but there are other estimating methods you can use.

✓ A **conceptual estimate** is generally prepared by the architect using cost models from previous projects. The contractor may arrive at a much different cost because of the project's unique characteristics.

✓ Using the **square-foot method** of estimating, the project cost is a calculation of the square footage of the project multiplied by a unit cost. This is a quick way to arrive at an estimated cost, but this method does not account for project specifics that affect cost. Another variation of this method is putting together an estimate using cubic feet of the project multiplied by a unit cost.

✓ The **unit price method** of estimating bundles all of the cost factors such as labor, materials, equipment, and subcontractors to come up with a unit price for the entire task. For example, let's say you are placing and finishing a 2,000-square-foot concrete slab and you determined that your unit price is $2.00 per square foot for this task. The total unit price is $4,000.

Estimating Pitfalls

Accurate estimating is a vital function for construction businesses and can make the difference between getting the right jobs and making a profit on a job. There are pitfalls that are detrimental to the estimating function that you want to avoid.

Preliminary Estimates

Your customers may be eager to determine what their project will cost and will ask for an estimate on the spot. Quoting a price before you have a chance to make accurate calculations is a risky practice. If you quote a price too high, it is possible that you could lose the bid. If you quote a price too low, the potential customer may be disappointed and feel you were dishonest in your initial contact.

Inaccurate Estimates

Inaccuracies occur when you make errors and omissions in your estimate. To avoid inaccuracies, you should always check your estimates. Errors to look for:

✓ **Mathematical errors:** Always check your work and if possible, have someone else check the mathematical accuracy of the estimate.

✓ **Omissions in labor or materials:** Be as thorough as possible when setting up the framework for your estimate. The use of a standard format, such as MasterFormat, will help you avoid this mistake.

✓ **Non-standard abbreviations:** Non-standard abbreviations may be interpreted as a different measurement or material. Spell out the actual word rather than inventing an abbreviation that is unclear or vague.

✓ **Units of measure:** Define linear, square, and cubic measure accurately. The difference between these measures can make a drastic difference in cost.

The more accurately you prepare your estimates, the better chance you have to make your expected profit.

Accurate estimates help you get the right jobs and make a profit.

Using an Estimator

Estimators develop the cost information business owners or managers need to bid for a contract. Small business owners or managers may perform this function without the use of a professional estimator. Large companies or a large project may need to use an estimator.

Estimators follow the same estimating process: performing the quantity take-off, analyzing subcontractor bids, determining equipment needs and sequence of operations, analyzing physical constraints at the site and contingencies, and determining allowances and overhead costs. The estimator may also have a say in setting the profit for the project and the terms and conditions of the contract. The estimator's job is solely to perform the estimating function and, if used, the estimator is an important member of the project team.

Submitting Your Bid

Once your estimate is complete and you are ready to submit your bid, you must make sure to follow all of the instructions in the bid package. These instructions include submitting all of the required documents and the exact information requested by the bid submission deadline. Even though you may have a template put together for the estimating process, you may need to customize your bid so as to respond to the specifications of the bid. Once your bid is submitted, it is reviewed by the owner. Bid review is generally a 30- to 90-day process. You are notified of the acceptance or rejection of your bid after this review process is complete.

Job Cost Recording System

A job cost recording system provides many benefits to the estimating and project management process.

✓ Current projects are monitored more closely with a cost tracking system. Cost overruns are identified and corrective action is taken sooner.

✓ Information from a job cost recording system helps with future estimates by creating more accurate unit costs.

✓ Many analytical reports can be generated from cost data to review performance by project, activity, year, etc. Using this data can help you make more strategic decisions.

There are many ways to set up a job cost recording system, but to ensure accuracy, it must remain consistent for all projects.

The first step is to develop a cost code system. A cost code system includes the following components.

✓ **Project Number:** A project numbering system could be as simple as starting with the number one (1) and consecutively numbering subsequent projects. A more complex project numbering system might also include a code for the type of project and the year it was started. For example, let's say you are working on a remodel project (R) that started in 2006 (06) and was the first (01) project of the year. Your project number could be R-06-01.

✓ **Activity Classification Code:** You may want to develop your own system or use a classification system such as the CSI MasterFormat. For example, for a finish carpentry job you could use MasterFormat number 06200. If you use the same classifications on your estimate, it will be easier to compare estimated to actual costs.

✓ **Distribution Code:** These are items such as material, labor, equipment, and project overhead. For example, coding might be as simple as one-letter abbreviations:

Material = M
Labor = L
Equipment = E
Project Overhead = P

This code can be placed behind the activity classification code. For example, the labor for finish carpentry could be classified as 06200L and materials as 06200M.

Once your system is set up, you can begin entering the cost data. Materials, equipment, and project overhead costs can be gathered from purchase orders, receipts, and invoices. Labor costs can be taken from timecards. It is important that employees fill out timecards completely and with enough detail so you can accurately record labor costs. A sample time card is located in Chapter 14.

Technology Tools for Estimating

Many computer tools are available to help streamline the estimating process. This technology provides many benefits:

✓ shorter time to prepare the estimate;

✓ improved accuracy; and

✓ professional presentation to the customer.

Estimating software ranges from a basic spreadsheet format to complex databases. However, the programs share some common features:

✓ databases for unit cost items, such as material and labor;

✓ multiple estimate report formats to present to the customer (hard copy and electronic);

✓ tracking method for historical information;

✓ ability to recall and modify past projects; and

✓ job costing capabilities.

As with any software, you must understand the fundamentals. If you do not know how to estimate, the software available will provide limited benefits to the process.

Final Inspection...

Bid Documents: All bid documents should be completed according to the specific requirements of the bid.

Ethics in Bidding: Good ethical practices are important to maintaining the integrity of the bid process.

Estimate Planning: Careful review of construction documents and a site visit are important first steps to creating an accurate estimate.

Estimating Framework: An estimating framework includes the project phases and the labor and materials needed for each phase.

Determining Estimated Costs: The quantity take-off method is one of the more accurate estimating methods. All direct and indirect costs must be added to ensure the estimate is complete.

Other Methods of Estimating: Estimates can be prepared using different methods with varying degrees of accuracy.

Estimating Pitfalls: It is important to be accurate and detailed when estimating a job. You may not make your expected profit if you make mistakes in your estimate.

Using an Estimator: An estimator is used to perform the estimating function on a project. The estimator may also make recommendations on the project profit margin and terms of the contract.

Submitting Your Bid: All instructions in a bid package must be followed or the bid may be rejected. There is typically a 30- to 90-day bid review process.

Job Cost Recording System: Monitoring current projects, creating more accurate future estimates, and providing reports for analysis are benefits of implementing a job cost recording system.

Technology Tools for Estimating: There are several computer tools to help you create your estimate, but it is still important to fully understand the process.

Chapter 8
CONTRACT MANAGEMENT

Chapter Survey...

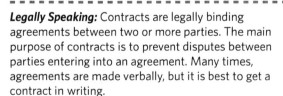

Legally Speaking: Contracts are legally binding agreements between two or more parties. The main purpose of contracts is to prevent disputes between parties entering into an agreement. Many times, agreements are made verbally, but it is best to get a contract in writing.

Contracts serve many purposes including

✓ **defining the obligations of the agreement;**

✓ **outlining payment terms; and**

✓ **limiting the liability of the parties involved.**

Contracts need to be worded carefully to protect your company. It is recommended you consult with an attorney experienced in construction law to ensure you have a legally enforceable contract.

Required Contract Elements

Make it Binding: You may have reached an agreement to do work for a customer, but that does not mean that you have a contract. There are four key elements that must be in effect to make a contract binding.

✓ **Offer and Acceptance**

✓ **Consideration**

✓ **Competent Parties**

✓ **Legal Purpose**

Offer and Acceptance

The Offer is on the Table: An offer specifically outlines the obligations of the contract, including the work to be done and compensation for this work. When you submit an estimate or bid for work, this is considered an offer. All parties must be clear on the essential details and obligations of the contract to have a valid offer. Once an offer is made, you are bound to what you have agreed to do.

An offer generally has a specific amount of time in which an acceptance needs to be made. This time frame is typically 30 days, but it should be stated in the offer. If a deadline for acceptance is not outlined in the offer, it expires in a "reasonable time." Reasonable time is up to court interpretation and is considered on an individual case basis.

Negotiation: Negotiation is the process where the owner and contractor come to an agreement on the price and terms of the contract. Chapter 10 discusses techniques that help guide you through the negotiation process. An offer is usually the outcome of a negotiation, but parties are not bound to the contract terms until an offer is made and acceptance is achieved. It is important to be clear when a communication is for negotiation purposes so it is not misconstrued as an offer.

Acceptance: The next step of the process is acceptance. Acceptance is agreeing to the offer made and generally is done by signing the offer. In some cases, a counteroffer is made. A counteroffer is not considered acceptance. It is only when both parties agree to the contract terms that you obtain acceptance.

Offer Checklist: Your offer should contain certain components because, if accepted, you are contractually bound to it:

- ✓ Date of offer
- ✓ Names and contact information of contracting parties
- ✓ Name and location of project
- ✓ Description of the work to be performed
- ✓ Contract time or start and completion date
- ✓ Payment terms, including progress payment schedule and final payment
- ✓ Conditions for schedule delays
- ✓ List of contract documents, including general conditions, drawings, and specifications
- ✓ Contract sum, including contract type such as lump sum, unit price, or cost plus (discussed later in this chapter)
- ✓ Expiration date of offer

Once accepted, this agreement becomes part of the contract's Standard Form of Agreement.

Consideration

An Exchange: Both parties must give up something of value to have consideration. Most likely this will be money, but it could be anything of value. Payment terms should be clearly outlined in the contract. Typically, the contractor provides services and in exchange, the owner provides monetary compensation.

Competent Parties

Legal Capacity: The parties in agreement should have the legal capacity to enter into a contract. Simply put, the parties must both be of sound mind in order for the contract to be valid. A situation where parties may not have legal capacity might be if you contracted with someone who is heavily under the influence of drugs or alcohol. The courts may rule someone incompetent

if they are mentally disabled. Minors are prohibited from entering into contracts without parental consent.

Legal Purpose

Contracts must be possible to perform, not intended to harm anyone, and cannot require any illegal activity. For example, a contract that requires the contractor to build a house that does not comply with building codes does not have a legal purpose and is invalid.

- -
Consult with an attorney to ensure your contracts are legally enforceable.
- -

Contract Provisions

Make it Clear: Contracts should be clear and concise. It is important that both parties understand the terms of the contract. There are provisions that you need to include in your contracts to ensure that all details are clearly outlined. Provisions are simply clauses that outline the stipulations of the contract.

Key Contract Provisions: Contracts are full of provisions, but a few key ones you will want to include:

- ✓ **Contract Price and Payment Terms**
- ✓ **Obligation of the Parties**
- ✓ **Supplemental Conditions**
- ✓ **Breach of Contract**

Contract Price and Payment Terms

Getting Paid: The contract should specify how the contract price is calculated. Whether you choose to use a lump-sum, unit-price or cost-plus method, include all fees the customer is expected to pay.

Payment terms should be very specific and include

- ✓ who is issuing payment,
- ✓ amount of the payment,
- ✓ form of payment, and
- ✓ when the payment will be issued.

Progress Payments: Progress payments are partial payments made after specified phases of construction are complete. Payments are generally calculated by taking the difference between the completed work and materials delivered and a predetermined schedule of unit costs.

Requirements for the schedule of progress payments should be clearly outlined in the construction contract including

✓ number of payments,

✓ amount of each payment,

✓ stage of progress between payments, and

✓ date or stage when each one is due.

It is important to monitor the progress payment schedule to ensure timeliness. You may be required to submit a partial payment estimate to the project architect or engineer prior to the payment due date. The partial payment estimate outlines the work performed and proof of materials and equipment delivery required for the next stage of construction. The architect or engineer certifies each progress payment by confirming the information in the partial payment estimate.

Progress payments have two functions: one, to protect the owner by holding the contractor responsible for following the planned schedule and two, to allow the contractor to pay for labor and material expenditures as they occur. This method of payment also protects both parties in the event of a contract breach on either side.

Retainage: Retainage is used by the owner to ensure completion of the construction project and provide protection against liens, claims, and defaults. It is calculated as a percentage (generally 10 percent) withheld from each progress payment. The retainage amount may be reduced further after substantial completion of the project (for example, retainage amounts may drop to 5 percent after 75 percent completion of the project). Retainage amounts must be clearly stated in the construction contract. Prime contractors generally hold the same percentage of retainage for their subcontractors.

The architect or engineer certifies when the project is complete and the work meets the conditions of the contract documents.

The retained amounts are generally due to the contractor upon completion and acceptance of the work.

Final Payment: Once the structure can be used for its intended purpose, the architect issues a certificate of substantial completion. A certificate of occupancy,

issued by a building inspector, deems the structure meets all applicable codes and is safe for occupancy.

Final payment is generally due when all punch list items are complete as agreed between the owner and contractor, proper approvals are obtained, and all paperwork is complete.

To receive a final payment, the following documentation should be prepared and delivered to the owner upon completion of the project:

✓ Completion certificates issued by the architect

✓ Inspection certificates

✓ Guaranties and warranties

✓ Affidavits that all subcontractors and project bills have been paid

✓ Equipment operation manuals

✓ Final lien waivers for those who submitted preliminary notices

✓ Final project drawings

✓ Any other documents as required by contract

It is important to organize paperwork throughout the construction process. A delay in putting the final paperwork together can consequently delay the final payment.

Obligations of the Parties

Contract Conditions: The obligations of the parties should be specifically outlined in the contract and include both the contractor's obligations and the owner's obligations. The obligations of the parties are the contract conditions.

Contractor's obligations include but are not limited to

✓ having proper licensure;

✓ securing building permits;

✓ ordering all materials and supplies and arranging for site delivery;

✓ furnishing all labor, including obtaining required subcontractors to complete the job;

✓ completing all work in compliance with all applicable codes and scheduling inspections on a timely basis;

✓ completing all work according to plans and specifications; and

✓ keeping the construction site clean and removing all debris during and upon completion of construction.

Owner's obligations include but are not limited to

✓ ensuring prompt approval of all plans and specifications;

✓ ensuring project meets zoning specifications;

✓ issuing payments according to the specified progress payment schedule;

✓ paying for all required permits, assessments, and charges required by public agencies and utilities;

✓ furnishing all surveys and recording plats and a legal description of the property; and

✓ providing access to the construction site in a timely manner.

Each list of obligations must be customized according to the agreement reached and the individual job being performed. Most contracts require agreement by both parties if obligations are assigned to another party.

Supplemental Conditions

The supplemental conditions modify the general conditions of the contract and are often prepared in a separate document. Supplemental conditions are tailored specifically to each project. They may outline items such as specific insurance requirements, project procedures, and local law requirements.

- -

Be very specific when outlining the obligations of both parties.

- -

Breach of Contract

A breach of contract occurs when one of the parties involved fails to perform in accordance with any of the terms and conditions of the contract.

A breach may occur when a party

✓ **refuses to perform the contract;**

✓ **performs an act prohibited by the contract; or**

✓ **prevents the other party from performing its obligations.**

There are two types of breaches: **material** and **immaterial**.

A **material breach** is a serious violation of the contract. For example, if a contractor refuses to perform or complete a job or if an owner refuses to pay for completed or partial jobs, this is considered a breach of contract. This type of breach may void the contract and will most likely end up in litigation.

The injured party can seek monetary damages for the loss suffered as a result of the breach. Sometimes the damages are written into the contract. These are called **liquidated** or **stated damages**.

Breach of contract can occur if contracts are not completed within the time frame specified in the contract. If a time is not specified in the contract, the project must be completed in a "reasonable time." If the project has an unexcused delay, the owner may be entitled to liquidated damages for the "loss of use." Some contracts specify a per-day rate for liquidated damages. For example, if a contract specifies a $400 per day assessment and the contractor finished 30 days late, $12,000 in liquidated damages is assessed to the contractor. An owner who sues for liquidated damages cannot sue for actual damages.

If you sue for breach of contract, you must do so within the statute of limitations. Statutes of limitations are laws that set a maximum period of time within which a lawsuit or claim may be filed. The deadlines vary depending on the circumstances of the case and the type of claim. If a claim is not filed before the statutory deadline, you may lose the right to file a claim.

An **immaterial** or **partial breach** is a less serious violation and usually does not result in termination of the contract. The injured party may only sue for the value of the damages.

Boilerplate Provisions

Standard Language: The term "boilerplate" refers to standard language or clauses used in a legal contract. Sometimes they are referred to as "miscellaneous" clauses. They generally appear at the end of the contract and their purpose is to protect the business in the event of a lawsuit. Attorney's fees, arbitration, and consent to jurisdiction (meaning where the disputes will be settled) are a few examples of boilerplate provisions. When dealing with contracts, make sure to draft and read the boilerplate provisions carefully. These provisions affect your legal rights just as much as the other parts of the contract.

Provisions to Limit Risk

Allocating Risk: As mentioned at the beginning of the chapter, one of the purposes of a contract is to limit the liabilities of the parties involved. Your contract should address the allocation of risk among parties. Examples of risk allocation provisions are listed below:

✓ **Force majeure** addresses "acts of God" and other external events such as war or labor strikes. This provision is written to either absolve the owner or contractor of costs associated with these occurrences.

✓ **Indemnification** absolves the indemnified party from any payment for losses and damages incurred by a third party. Simply put, it is a way to shift payment or liability for any loss or damage that has occurred. Indemnification clauses must be examined carefully to ensure the proper liability is distributed between the contractor and owner.

✓ **Differing site conditions** provision allocates the responsibility for extra costs due to unexpected site conditions. As discussed in Chapter 7, the site conditions must be investigated and taken into consideration when putting together the bid. The owner is responsible for disclosing all site information during the bid process. If errors or omissions occur, the owner may be responsible for incurring the extra construction cost.

✓ **Warranties or guarantees** define the contractor's responsibility for the repair of defects to the construction project after the completion of work. Warranties are often set forth for a defined time period.

✓ **Delays and extensions of time** provide a contingency in case the completion deadline is not met. Delays at no fault of the contractor, such as changes by the owner or architect and environmental or severe weather delays, are generally not considered breach of contract. These types of delays are considered excusable and are granted time extensions. This contingency needs to be clearly outlined in the contract.

✓ **Schedule acceleration** provides assignment of costs incurred to complete a project ahead of schedule. In general, if the owner requires the contractor to accelerate the schedule, the owner is responsible for all associated costs. If the owner requests the schedule be accelerated due

to project delays caused by the contractor, the contractor is generally liable for additional costs incurred.

✓ **Artistic changes** clause addresses changes made by the architect or design professional during the course of the project for artistic or creative purposes. The drawings and specifications outline the technical aspects of the project, but may not show the artistic objectives of the project. Including an artistic changes clause will put a limit on the number of changes that can occur as a result of artistic decisions.

Standard legal language must be used when specifying risk assignments to make the contract enforceable. Since legal language is often difficult to understand, it is recommended that you consult with legal counsel when drafting and/or interpreting these provisions.

What Are Recitals?

Background Information: Recitals are language at the beginning of the contract that provide background to the contract, such as the parties entering into the contract, the contract contents, and reasons for the parties' entering into the contract. Recitals cannot always be enforced by law, so it is important to provide specific terms throughout the contract.

Types of Construction Contracts

The differences in the types of contracts are primarily

✓ **who takes the risk that the work will be performed for the estimated cost;**

✓ **who pays for cost overruns; and**

✓ **who keeps the cost savings if the project performed is less than the estimate.**

Contracts between the owner and primary contractor may differ from contracts between the primary contractor and the subcontractors.

Lump-Sum Contract

In a lump-sum contract, the contractor agrees to complete the project for a predetermined, specified price. The contractor essentially assumes all of the risk under this contract agreement because the contractor is responsible for additional costs associated with unforeseen circumstances. For example, if extra cost is incurred due to inclement weather, the contractor must absorb these costs. Conversely, the contractor gets to keep any cost savings achieved.

If you use this type of contract, you may be required to formally submit a specific schedule and your quality assurance program so your customer knows you are completing the project to the highest standards. You should avoid this type of contract unless plans and specifications are detailed enough that a final cost can be determined in advance.

Unit-Price Contract

A unit-price contract may be used for jobs where the extent of work cannot be fully determined, or the actual quantities of required items cannot be accurately calculated in advance. A price per unit is calculated for each item and the contractor is paid according to the actual quantities used.

Cost-Plus Contract

Using the cost-plus contract method, the contractor is reimbursed for the actual cost of labor and materials and is paid a markup fee for overhead and profit. The cost-plus contract can be calculated different ways. The owner may pay the actual costs, plus a percentage markup or a fixed fee markup.

Contracting Methods

Single Prime

The single prime method is the traditional form of contracting. The project owner typically hires an architectural firm to design the project. The contractor then performs the work according to the specifications of the project and is responsible for the costs of all materials and labor to obtain project completion.

Design/Build

Using the design/build method of construction, the owner contracts with one company to complete the process from start to finish. The company awarded the design/build contract puts together a team of construction professionals, which may include designers, architects, engineers, and contractors that take a project from design through completed construction. The team works closely to satisfy the owner's needs within a predetermined budget.

Construction Management

Under the construction management method, the project owner contracts with a professional construction manager to coordinate and manage the project. The construction manager generally receives a fee to manage, coordinate, and supervise the construction process from the conceptual development stage through final construction. Work must be performed in a timely manner and on an economical basis.

Turnkey

Turnkey construction is similar to the design/build construction model. In addition to managing the construction and design team, the contractor also obtains financing and land. Under the turnkey model, the construction firm is obligated to complete a project according to pre-specified criteria but with expanded responsibilities and liability. A price is generally fixed at the time the contract is signed.

Fast-Track Construction

Under fast-track construction management, the construction process begins before completion of the contract documents. Fast-track construction involves a phased approach to the project. A contract may be drawn up for each phase. Generally, the cost is not fixed until after construction documents are complete and some construction commitments have already been made.

Multiple Prime Contracts

Large construction projects may involve multiple prime contracts. The owner may contract with two or more prime contractors to complete the same project. This contracting method may integrate elements of the construction management and fast-track construction models. The owner takes on a more active role in managing the different prime contractors. Contractor and owner obligations must be clearly defined in the contract.

Partnering

Partnering starts with setting common objectives and goals for a construction project. All parties involved, such as the owner, design professionals, engineers, and contractors, work together to achieve these objectives and goals. Several meetings are held throughout the bid and construction process to evaluate the decisions made by all parties and adjustments occur when necessary. Partnering increases communication and trust, consequently reducing potential litigation and claims.

Sources of Contracts

Standard forms for contracts are readily available through many sources. There are numerous books available that provide sample contracts and forms. Associations such as the American Institute of Architects (AIA) or the Associated General Contractors (AGC) also have standard forms for contracts.

In situations where the form of the contract is not written by you, it is important to

- ✓ read the contract very carefully;
- ✓ highlight anything that is vaguely worded for further clarification;
- ✓ make necessary additions;
- ✓ review changes with the other party;
- ✓ make sure any requested changes have been added prior to signing; and
- ✓ review the contract again, prior to signing.

Always make sure you keep a signed copy of every contract you sign, in case you need to refer to it in the future.

Making Changes to the Contract

A **change order** is a written agreement between the owner and contractor to change the contract. Change orders add to, delete from, or otherwise alter the work set forth in the construction documents. Change orders are standard in the construction industry as a legal means for making changes to the contract.

Common reasons for generating a change order include

- ✓ change in scope (for example, owner requests a design change or owner exceeds allowance amount);
- ✓ unforeseen conditions when site conditions differ from expected; and
- ✓ errors or omissions in construction plans or specifications.

The AIA and AGC have standardized forms that you can use to execute change orders. Change orders are legally binding and it is important that all of the provisions are clear to both parties. Change orders should include

- ✓ date of change order;
- ✓ description of the change in work;
- ✓ reason for change;
- ✓ change in contract price;
- ✓ change, if any, in contract time; and
- ✓ signatures from both parties.

Chapter 10 also discusses how to handle change orders from a customer relations perspective.

Changes prior to the contract award are called **addenda**. Changes made after the contract is signed and executed are called **modifications**.

Resolving Claims

The claims resolution process provides a way for the owner and contractor to resolve disputes about additional amounts owed as a result of contract changes. As discussed in the previous section, the purpose of written change orders is to avoid disputes. If a change is made to the contract without a change order, claims may arise.

Claims Procedure: The contract may stipulate specific procedures for handling claims. Many times, the contract defers to the architect to initially resolve claims. If claims cannot be resolved by the architect, the contractor and owner may proceed to mediation. If mediation fails, the next step is arbitration. The contract should specify the time allowed to request arbitration. A typical deadline for an arbitration request is 30 days from the time the architect makes a decision on the claim.

Project Schedule: During the claims resolution process, the project cannot be delayed. All schedules and deadlines must be followed. The only exception is disputes involving safety. Work must cease on disputed activities until all safety issues are resolved.

Alternative Dispute Resolution

Alternative dispute resolution (ADR) involves settling legal disputes by avoiding the often costly and time intensive process of a government judicial trial.

The most common forms of ADR are: negotiation, mediation, collaborative law, and arbitration.

Negotiation: Negotiation is a dialogue entered into for the purpose of resolving disputes or producing an agreed upon course or courses of action. Negotiation is inexpensive and generally the first step in ADR. Negotiation allows for an unstructured discussion between both parties and generally does not involve anyone other than the affected parties. If an agreement is not reached, more formal methods of dispute resolution are required.

Mediation: In mediation, the parties themselves set forth the conditions of any agreement with dialogue facilitated by an independent, third party mediator. The mediator is not a judge or arbitrator who sets forth the terms of an agreement, rather a mediator is a trained professional in negotiations and the process of mediation. The goal of mediation is to find areas of agreement between the parties involved by using strategies and techniques designed to allow the parties to work towards a mutual and fair agreement. If a settlement is not reached, the dispute may go through mediation again or sent to arbitration. The option to take legal disputes to mediation is desirable from a cost perspective because it is generally less expensive and allows for a quicker resolution than going to trial.

Collaborative Law: Collaborative law is a facilitative process wherein all parties agree at the onset to work to identify a solution that is beneficial to all parties involved. In collaborative law, the parties use their advocates, most often their lawyers, to facilitate a mutually beneficial result through the process of negotiation. There is no neutral mediator or arbitrator involved and the parties are expected to reach a settlement without using further methods of ADR or litigation.

Arbitration: Arbitration uses a third-party arbitrator or arbitrators to act as a judge or judges to render a decision by which all parties are legally bound. Arbitration is held in a format less formal than a trial. The arbitrator(s), unlike a mediator, is not involved in the negotiation discussion towards a settlement. Arbitrators may be attorneys or retired judges who serve individually or as a panel. They are either chosen by the parties involved in the dispute or appointed by the court according to the terms of the contract. Arbitrators with industry-specific experience (such as construction litigation experience) may be appointed

to certain types of disputes. The decision or arbitral award made by the arbitrator(s) is legally binding unlike in mediation. Many times, contracts call for disputes to be resolved through arbitration over taking matters to a costly trial. Arbitration may be required by law for certain types of disputes. Nearly all states have adopted the federal Uniform Arbitration Act making arbitral awards binding by both state and federal law.

Making Substitutions

When bidding on a project, many contractors bid from their normal manufacturers and suppliers and not the manufacturer that appears on the plans. When bidding, you need to make sure you can pay for the cost of all items and products as specified. Failure to do so could cost you a lot of money.

Substitution Approval Process: The best way to ensure a specific substitution is by the "prior approval" process. A "prior approval" occurs during the bid stage only. If a particular product or item is desired other than the specified item, you must submit a request while the project is being bid. If approved, all bidders will be allowed to use that item or product in their bids. That is why the "prior approval" is done in the bidding stage. It keeps the playing field level for all competitors.

Substitutions After the Bid Process: A substitution may be made after the bid has been accepted. Nevertheless, any substitution must meet certain criteria to even be considered. The specifications should describe the conditions for such substitutions. Usually there are only four reasons that a substitution would be entertained:

✓ the specific item or product is no longer available;

✓ a cost savings;

✓ a time savings; or

✓ combination of cost and time savings.

Discontinued Products: A product no longer available is generally the only event that will not require a change order reducing cost and/or time, unless it was approved under the "prior approval" process. Do not forget to note those reductions in the substitution request. The reason a reduction of cost and/or time is required is due to the fact that it is understood that the bid was based on the specific item or product. To make a change, the result must benefit the owner; otherwise, there is no reason to make the substitution.

Substitution Specifications: If there is a basis for the substitution, the next requirement is that the item or product must be equal to that which was specified. Just as the reference of a 2 x 4 to contractors is not measured as 2" x 4", its nomenclature is referred to as "nominal." Many other products are referred to as "nominal" sizing. HVAC systems are especially that way. Just because one manufacturer references a unit as five-tons, it does not mean that it produces the same capacity as a five-ton unit from another manufacturer under the same conditions.

The specifications must be analyzed carefully before submitting the substitution request. Be sure to cover the cost of the specified item, as a substitution may not be granted, not even in the "prior approval" process.

Contract Documents and Project Manual

The project manual is a central location for bid documents, contract provisions, technical specifications, and addenda. This bound manual is a useful tool easily referenced on the jobsite. It can be reproduced and distributed to contractors, subcontractors, and suppliers. The following is a detailed summary of the documents contained in a typical project manual.

Bid Documents:

✓ Invitation to bid

✓ Bid instructions

✓ Bid forms

✓ Supplements

✓ Addenda

Contract Provisions:

✓ Form of agreement

✓ General conditions or obligation of parties

✓ Supplemental conditions

✓ Change orders

✓ Index of drawings

Supplemental Forms:

✓ Required bonds

✓ Certificate of insurance

Technical specifications are generally organized by a classification system, such as the CSI MasterFormat.

The **construction drawings** are also part of the contract documents. For larger projects, the drawings are divided by design discipline and trades. Drawings may include but are not limited to:

✓ architectural,

✓ structural,

✓ plumbing,

✓ electrical,

✓ mechanical,

✓ landscape, and

✓ civil.

The drawings are kept separate but can be indexed in the project manual.

Are Oral Agreements Legally Binding?

Under most circumstances, oral agreements are just as binding as written agreements with a few exceptions. Exceptions include contracts which have a high risk of fraud such as the sale or purchase of land. Oral agreements present a challenge because it is difficult to prove what terms were agreed upon if a dispute arises. Needless to say, it is a risky way to do business and it is best to get everything in writing.

Sometimes parties enter into agreements that are partially oral and partially written. For example, you may have carefully put together a written contract to do work. The customer then verbally gives you a change order. Now you are in a situation where you have an oral agreement for the change. To protect yourself, it is best to follow up with a written change order. In a legal judgment, written agreements always take precedence over oral agreements.

- -

Oral agreements are not a good way to do business. Get it in writing!

- -

Legal Interpretation

Clarity of language and meaning is one of the most important aspects of interpreting contracts and avoiding disputes. It is strongly recommended that you use an attorney when drafting contracts to ensure that the contract will stand up in a dispute. There are also necessary provisions that should be included in a contract. A contract lawyer can advise you on this matter.

The use of plain language is important when establishing intent in a contract. If a dispute arises, the contract will be interpreted using the plain meaning of the words in the contract. If your contract goes to litigation, the judge may not have a background in the construction industry. This is why it is important to clearly state the terms in the contract using plain language.

Technical terminology in contracts between parties who understand their technical meaning may be used. However, many customers may not understand technical jargon so you may want to use caution putting these terms in a contract. Rather, you should express your intentions in layman terms. Disputes may arise when parties do not understand undefined technical language and contract interpretation may not end up in your favor.

If the provision being disputed is vague, the actions of the parties will be examined first. If the parties conducted themselves consistently with what they thought the provision meant at that time, the provision would likely take that meaning. If the contract cannot be clarified based on this method, the interpretation will go against the party who wrote it.

Subcontracting

Subcontractors contract with the general contractor or other subcontractors to complete a portion of a larger project. The same principles that apply to owner/contractor contracts also apply to subcontracts.

Subcontracts should include similar content as owner/contractor contracts, such as

✓ Date

✓ Names and contact information of contracting parties

✓ Name and location of project

✓ Description of the work to be performed

✓ Subcontract time or start and completion date

✓ Payment terms, including progress payment schedule and final payment

✓ Conditions for schedule delays

✓ Drawings and specifications

✓ Contract sum

✓ Any general and supplemental conditions that apply

✓ Signatures from both parties

Depending on the stipulations in the owner/contractor agreement, the owner may need to approve subcontractors.

It is also important to get subcontracts in writing to avoid disputes. In providing a written contract, both parties have a clear understanding of the agreement. Oral contracts can lead to ambiguity and one party may interpret the agreement differently than the other.

Clarity is very important to an enforceable contract.

Final Inspection...

Required Contract Elements: Required contract elements include offer and acceptance, consideration, competent parties, and legal purpose.

Contract Provisions: Your contract should contain provisions that clearly outline the terms of the contract. A few key provisions you want to include are contract price and payment terms, obligation of the parties, and breach of contract.

Breach of Contract: A breach of contract occurs when one of the parties involved fails to perform in accordance with any of the terms and conditions of the contract.

Boilerplate Provisions: These provisions contain standard language designed to protect you in the event of a lawsuit.

Provisions to Limit Risk: These provisions limit the liability of the contracting parties by addressing allocation of risk.

What Are Recitals? This language appears at the beginning of the contract and is intended to give background information.

Types of Construction Contracts: Different types of contracts address who is responsible for cost savings and overruns for estimated work.

Contracting Methods: Depending on the level of involvement in a construction project, different types of contracting methods are used.

Sources of Contracts: Contracts are available through several different sources, including associations such as the American Institute of Architects (AIA) or the Associated General Contractors (AGC).

Making Changes to the Contract: To change the contract, a change order is written and agreed to by the owner and contractor.

Resolving Claims: The claims resolution process provides a way for the owner and contractor to resolve disputes about additional amounts owed as a result of contract changes.

Alternative Dispute Resolution (ADR): This process involves settling legal disputes by avoiding the process of a government judicial trial. The most common forms of ADR are: negotiation, mediation, collaborative law, and arbitration.

Making Substitutions: Specifications must be analyzed carefully before submitting the substitution request. Substitutions may be granted if products are discontinued or to provide a cost or time savings.

Contract Documents and Project Manual: The project manual is a central location for bid documents, contract provisions, technical specifications, and addenda.

Are Oral Agreements Legally Binding? Oral agreements can be binding, but it makes good business sense to get a contract in writing.

Legal Interpretation: Clarity of language and meaning in contracts is important to avoid disputes and ensure proper legal interpretation in the event of a lawsuit.

Subcontracting: The same principles that apply to owner/contractor contracts also apply to subcontracts. Similar language is used to ensure that each party is clear on terms and conditions of the contract.

Chapter 9
SCHEDULING AND PROJECT MANAGEMENT

Many construction jobs are performed every day without using a formal scheduling method. Knowing how to schedule and organize tasks helps you complete projects on time, which increases customer satisfaction and ultimately your competitive edge.

Using the quantity take-off method, as explained in Chapter 7, you developed the basis for your project schedule. Each task was assigned the number of labor hours for completion to determine labor cost. Scheduling takes the list of tasks and labor hours and assigns an order of completion.

Scheduling Process

Planning is a key element to formulating an accurate schedule and effectively managing the project. Planning allows you to visualize the project and anticipate potential conflicts and challenges. The project start and completion dates are outlined in the contract. It is the job of the scheduler to fit in all necessary tasks within this time frame in the most efficient manner.

Sequence of Tasks: Understanding the correct sequence of tasks is critical to completing your project on time. As you created your estimate (discussed in Chapter 7), you probably listed your tasks in the order of completion. This determination is particularly important when scheduling subcontractors. Be sure to review the tasks outlined in the estimate and make any necessary corrections to the sequence of tasks.

Some tasks may be completed at the same time while other tasks must come before starting the next task. For example, interior and exterior paint may be applied at the same time but drywall must be completed before paint is applied.

Activity Duration: When creating your estimate, you determined the number of labor hours it takes to complete each task on the project. Using this estimate, you need to determine the duration of the task. The duration of each task depends on a few factors:

✓ size of the project;

✓ labor hours estimated; and

✓ length of time dedicated to the task each day. For example, if a task is estimated at four hours but your crew only has two hours per day to work on the task, the activity duration is two working days.

When determining activity duration, it is important to get input from your subcontractors and the experienced members of your crew.

Once the duration is determined for each activity, you can compare the total time against the project completion time outlined in the contract. If the total time exceeds the project completion time, adjustments must be made. Consideration must be given to increasing labor resources, requiring overtime, or extending the project completion date. These options must be weighed carefully due to added costs and possible timeline conflicts with the owner.

Contingency Time: Contingency time is used as a buffer between tasks to protect against unforeseen task delays. To determine contingency time, the task is analyzed to determine the likelihood of a delay occurring. A few general rules apply to determining contingency time.

✓ Tasks subject to weather delays require more contingency time.

✓ Standard work requires less contingency time than custom work.

✓ Tasks performed in areas with limited access require more contingency time.

With contingency time in place, the likelihood of a delayed task impacting the entire schedule is reduced.

Task Time Ranges: After completing the sequence of tasks, activity duration, and contingency time, the earliest and latest start date and earliest and latest end date are calculated. If the task completion falls outside these dates during the construction process, the project manager has an accurate calculation of the amount of time the project is ahead or behind.

Float Time: Float time is the remaining time after a task is complete and before the next task begins.

✓ The amount of time an activity can be delayed without impacting the early start of the next activity is called free float time.

✓ Total float time refers to the amount of leeway allowed in starting or completing an activity without delaying the project completion date.

✓ Activities with "zero float" are considered critical activities.

Scheduling Methods

A schedule is your blueprint to finishing the project on time. There are three main types of scheduling methods used in the construction industry:

✓ **Calendar Scheduling**

✓ **Bar Chart Scheduling**

✓ **Critical Path Method**

The type of schedule you use depends on factors such as project size, complexity, and location.

Calendar Scheduling

Calendar scheduling is a simple method and can be done on a regular desk calendar. The primary advantage to this method is that you can link project tasks to specific dates, such as

✓ dates of other projects,

✓ delivery dates of materials,

✓ payment schedules, and

✓ employee vacations and holidays.

To create a calendar schedule, you need to know the sequence of tasks and activity duration. After these factors are determined, you can plug the activities into the calendar.

The following is a sample calendar schedule. Calendar scheduling works for smaller, less complex projects but is not recommended for large ones.

SAMPLE CALENDAR SCHEDULE

Project Name:		Start Date:			End Date:	

Sunday	Monday	Tuesday	Wednesday	Thursday	Friday	Saturday
1 Off	**2** Excavation—	**3**	**4** Layout Slab Foundation Forms	**5** Under-ground Plumbing	**6** Pour Concrete	**7** Concrete Cure Time
8 Concrete Cure Time	**9**	**10**	**11** Frame Exterior Walls	**12**	**13**	**14** Off
15 Off	**16** Frame Roof— Install Doors & Windows	**17**	**18**	**19** Lay Roofing Materials	**20**	**21**
22 Off	**23** Electrical Rough-In Plumbing Rough-In	**24**	**25** HVAC	**26** Siding—	**27** Off	**28** Off
29 Off	**30** Siding Insulation	**31**	**1** Install Drywall Paint Exterior	**2**	**3** Off	**4**
5 Off	**6** Install Wood/Tile Flooring	**7**	**8**	**9** Install Trim	**10** Off	**11**
12 Off	**13** Paint Interior	**14**	**15** Finish Electrical Finish Plumbing	**16**	**17** Install Carpeting	**18** Site Clean-up

Bar Chart Scheduling

Similar to the calendar scheduling method, the bar chart schedule shows the activity duration and sequence of tasks to be completed. It is an easy-to-read graphical depiction of the schedule in its entirety.

One of the main weaknesses of the bar chart and calendar scheduling methods is that they do not show the interdependencies of activities.

For example, if there is a delay in a task, the bar chart does not show the impact it has on other tasks. The following is a sample bar chart schedule.

SCHEDULE BAR CHART FOR RETAIL STORE CONSTRUCTION

Description of Tasks	March				April				May				June			
	W1	W2	W3	W4	W1	W2	W3	W4	W1	W2	W3	W4	W1	W2	W3	W4
Contract Award	■															
Field Survey		■														
Documents Reviewed		■														
Building Permit			■	■												
Pre-Meeting				■												
Demolition					■											
Door & Windows					■											
Electrical Rough In						■										
Plumbing Rough In					■											
Lighting						■										
HVAC						■										
Fire Protection						■										
Ceiling					■											
Drywall						■										
Plumbing Fixtures							■									
Caulking & Sealants								■								
Flooring								■								
Cash Wrap										■						
Product Racks										■	■					
Electrical Fixtures											■					
Painting												■				
Signage												■				
Construction Cleaning													■			
Project Closeout														■		

Critical Path Method

The critical path method (CPM) of scheduling illustrates the interdependent relationship of tasks. To develop a CPM schedule, you start by determining the sequence of tasks and activity duration as you would with bar chart or calendar scheduling. In addition, you need to outline the following:

✓ Relationship between tasks

✓ Simultaneous events

✓ Critical path

Relationship between Tasks: Most construction tasks are interrelated. For example, you can't start framing until you pour the foundation. A CPM schedule graphically shows which tasks are related and which

ones are not. When you create your CPM schedule, you need to determine how each task impacts another.

Simultaneous Events: If you know which tasks can be performed simultaneously, you can shorten project completion time. When creating the CPM schedule, you must show when simultaneous tasks are possible.

Critical Path: The critical path is the sequence of tasks that determines the duration of the project. If a task on the critical path is delayed by one week, the project is delayed by one week. You must know which subsequent tasks cannot begin until a critical path item is completed.

The following diagram illustrates a simple critical path example.

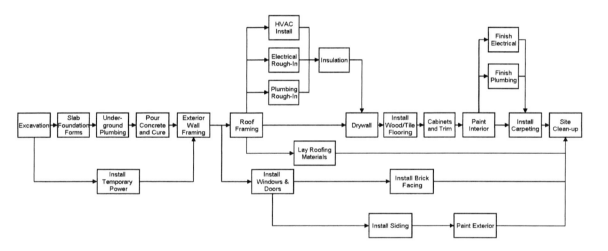

Adding Activity Duration to the CPM Schedule: The CPM schedule can be placed against a timeline. An example of this is illustrated in the bar chart schedule earlier in the chapter. Another alternative is to place the activity duration with each task. You can also put a code with the activity to correlate it to your estimate. If you use your estimating format, you could use the CSI MasterFormat to code the tasks in your schedule. For example, let's say the task of painting the interior has a three-day duration and you use MasterFormat code 09900. Your task might look like this on the CPM chart.

Paint Interior	
09900	3

Many different types of software are available to help you create schedules. You want to choose a program that is right for your needs whether it is simple or more complex. Some programs allow you to adjust the timelines if, for example, you experience a delay in the project. Scheduling software also facilitates the tracking function of a project schedule, which is a key project management tool.

Scheduling and Cash Management

It is important to track incoming cash and expenditures during the construction project to ensure you have enough working capital to complete the job. "Working capital" refers to the amount of cash available after the liabilities or debts are paid. Balancing incoming progress payments and outgoing expenditures is important to manage the project effectively and should be a consideration when preparing your schedule.

If you have more expenditures than incoming cash in any stage of construction, you may not have enough money to proceed to the next stage of construction or pay your debts.

A preliminary cash flow budget, outlining stages of construction with anticipated revenues and expenditures, should be completed during the scheduling phase to anticipate any cash shortages. Cash flow should be tracked through the duration of the project.

What is Project Management?

Effective project management is a challenging task on a construction project. It requires a carefully balanced combination of management skills with an understanding of the design and construction process. Project managers may manage several projects at the same time with projects at different stages of the process. A project manager not only has to manage time through the scheduling process but must also consider many other factors:

✓ Budget constraints

✓ Quality standards

✓ Project plans and specifications

✓ Resource management such as labor, materials, etc.

Project management has applications that are unique in nearly every industry, including construction.

The ability to effectively manage significantly contributes to the success or failure of the project.

Who is the Project Manager?

Construction project managers plan and coordinate construction projects to meet the overall goals of the project and serve as the main contact with the owner. Responsibilities generally include but are not limited to

✓ preparing budgets;

✓ reviewing shop drawings to determine appropriate construction methods;

✓ determining labor requirements and preparing schedules;

✓ monitoring overall progress of the project and preparing job records;

✓ monitoring compliance with building and safety codes;

✓ ensuring proper handling of change orders; and

✓ regularly meeting with owners, trade contractors, architects, and other design professionals on project progress.

Construction project managers work closely with the project superintendent who manages daily site operations.

Construction managers may be owners or salaried employees of a construction management or contracting firm, or they may work under contract or as a salaried employee of the owner, developer, contractor, or management firm overseeing the construction project. They may plan and direct a whole project or just a part of a larger project.

What Qualities Does a Good Manager Need?

A good manager must possess several qualities to effectively lead a team.

✓ Good communication skills

✓ Honesty and integrity

✓ Positive attitude

✓ Effective delegation skills

✓ Team and morale building skills

Project Supervisory Team

While the project manager has a high level understanding of the project, supervisors coordinate and monitor the daily aspects of the project. Depending on the size of the project, the number of supervisory team members may vary.

Superintendent: The superintendent is the onsite supervisor responsible for daily operations. Depending on the size of the project and amount of responsibility the project manager wants to delegate, the superintendent's duties may include

✓ coordinating project activities and serving as a liaison with subcontractors, architects, utilities, and others;

✓ participating in project construction development and planning;

✓ processing utility requests for construction projects;

✓ representing the company regarding onsite construction quality control reviews;

✓ making recommendations and processing change order requests;

✓ reviewing punch lists;

✓ assuring construction specifications are met;

✓ tracking deviations from project schedules and costs; and

✓ maintaining project records and reports.

Communication between the project manager and superintendent is important to keeping the project on-time and within budget and providing a quality product.

Foreman: The foreman assists the superintendent with daily project operations. The superintendent generally oversees all of the daily operations, but the foreman usually supervises specific areas by trade. For example, a carpentry foreman may supervise rough and finish carpentry while the masonry foreman supervises formwork and concrete installation.

The foreman assists the supervisor by

✓ reviewing project plans and blueprints;

✓ providing input on estimated time, material, equipment and supplies needed;

✓ developing schedules and crew assignments;

✓ inspecting work areas;

✓ evaluating employee and subcontractor performance;

✓ completing time sheets, accident reports, and work orders; and

✓ training employees.

Materials Expediter: Timely delivery of materials is important to keeping a project schedule on track.

A materials expediter supervises the materials procurement process to ensure accurate and timely delivery of materials.

Later in the chapter, we will discuss the importance of effective materials management.

Architect and Owner's Representative: The owner will sometimes defer to an appointed representative to oversee a project. In this case, the owner's representative and/or architect will deal with the project manager. The owner's representative and architect usually do not have supervisory authority over the employees and subcontractors but they may communicate with the project manager in order to express any concerns with the project work.

In general, the owner's representative and architect have access to the jobsite and work records and can contribute to quality control on the project. The architect (or sometimes the engineer) must certify each progress payment, so it is in the best interest of the project manager to work closely with the architect and owner's representative.

Project Life Cycle

Each project has a start point, project life cycle, and end point. Through each phase of the project life cycle, you must manage each aspect of the project such as customer relations, materials, budget, and subcontractors. Using the customer relations category as an example, the following illustrates various management aspects in the project life cycle.

Contract Award

After you are successfully offered the job, you should get a contract signed as soon as possible. A few weeks before the job starts, schedule a pre-construction meeting with your customer and any other relevant parties (i.e., architect, subcontractors, etc.).

Pre-Construction Phase

During the pre-construction meeting, you should go over customer expectations. Chapter 10 discusses creating realistic expectations for your customer to avoid disappointment. At this time, you should have a preliminary schedule prepared, so potential scheduling conflicts can be discussed. Be sure to follow up with written meeting notes and distribute to those in attendance as well as those who could not attend.

Construction Phase

As the project progresses, you should carefully monitor the budget, schedule, and project quality. Regularly meet with your customer to discuss the progress of the project and any issues or questions that arise. If you are billing in progress payments, make sure you are invoicing regularly and collecting payments within the defined terms.

Job Completion and Closeout

After the job is complete, you must do a walkthrough and develop a punch list of follow-up items. Discuss any warranties contained in your contract and how the customer can request warranty repairs. Send a customer satisfaction survey to gather feedback for future improvements.

Key Elements for a Successful Project Outcome

Many elements go into a successful project outcome:

✓ Project manager who understands the total project as a big picture

✓ Early preparation and planning

✓ Good management and front-line supervision

✓ Effective responses to problems and changes

✓ Active customer involvement

✓ Good communication skills

Tracking the Progress of the Project

Daily Reports

Many contractors find that keeping a daily log is a useful project tool. You can use a log  to track the progress of a project and as legal back up in case any disputes arise.

The daily log can list:

✓ Project name and location

✓ Date

✓ Weather conditions

✓ Personnel on the job

✓ Description of work

✓ Hours worked on each task

✓ Change orders

✓ Progress of the job

✓ Other relevant information

Personal comments should not be made in the daily report. It should contain only factual information.

There are specific guidelines you should follow to increase the credibility of the daily report, if a legal dispute arises.

✓ The report should be completed daily. If there was no work completed, note that fact and the reason for it.

✓ Writing should be in ink and not altered.

✓ Pages should be in consecutive order and in a bound book.

Photos are a good way to document the progress of a project and can serve as a supplement to the daily log. Photos should be taken of the site prior to starting work and at critical points during the project to document any problem areas. Digital cameras make photo-taking easy with instant results. You also have the flexibility to store photos on your computer and send them through e-mail.

Status Reports

Status reports summarize project highlights, addressing items completed, in progress, and outstanding. This report is a helpful tool to communicate with the customer, managers, subcontractors, and suppliers periodically throughout the project.

To support your status reports, you should have work records easily accessible for review. These work records include

✓ daily reports,

✓ project photographs,

✓ previous status reports,

✓ safety and accident reports,

✓ change orders,

✓ shop drawings,

✓ purchase orders,

✓ receiving documentation, and

✓ relevant written correspondence.

You should solicit feedback on any anticipated problems or concerns and encourage two-way communication throughout the project. Status reports are a good way to initiate this communication.

Tracking the Schedule

A good project manager makes sure that deadlines are met on time. As discussed earlier, the first step is to develop the schedule. Next, you want to make sure you communicate the schedule to anyone who is impacted by it, such as your crew, subcontractors, and suppliers. You need to make sure they understand the deadlines and their assignments. You may want to present the schedule in a graphical format so team members can get a visual snapshot of the timeline.

Budget and Cost Controls

Project management involves working with budget constraints. A good project manager will control costs and make sure that the project comes in on budget.

If the budget is not monitored carefully, a job that was estimated correctly can turn into a loss for the company.

Materials

Just-In-Time (JIT): Just-in-time deliveries will keep your inventory cost low. This process allows you to time deliveries to arrive as you need the materials in the construction process. Using your schedule, you can closely predict when you need materials according to the work being completed and then coordinate timing with your suppliers. Less inventory onsite will also cut down the risk of theft or vandalism.

Purchase Orders: Using a purchase order system can help you organize and document your materials purchases. If you prepare your purchase orders in advance, you can review these with your customers. This process can potentially reduce change orders by allowing customers to make decisions and sign off on them in advance. Your purchase orders can also serve as delivery date documentation so you can organize just-in-time deliveries.

Receiving: You can control material costs through proper receiving. When materials are delivered, someone should check the materials against the purchase order to confirm the correct quantity and items ordered were received. If there are discrepancies, follow up with the supplier as soon as possible to ensure you receive the proper credits or replacements.

To the best of your ability, you want to estimate and order the correct amount of materials. If you have excess materials, check with your supplier for a return policy. Excess materials should be stored correctly to preserve their condition. Some suppliers charge a restocking fee, but it is generally nominal and worth your time to receive a materials credit.

Budget Tracking

The easiest way to track your budget is to use the cost estimate and a job cost system to determine if you have any cost overruns.

Cost overruns occur when you exceed budgeted amounts in your estimate. These overruns can happen in many areas of the project such as exceeding the amount of labor through improper scheduling and excessive materials waste. Chapter 8, Contract Management, summarizes types of contracts that address who is responsible for cost overruns.

It is important to track costs as the project progresses because cost overruns can indicate a possible problem. The sooner these problems are identified, the easier it will be to take corrective action.

Cost overruns may occur because you have a bad estimate. Tracking your budget will help you or your estimator prepare more accurate estimates in the future.

Cost overruns reduce the amount of profit you make on the job. If you are not making a profit or you are losing money on your projects, you will eventually go out of business.

Quality Assurance

Ensuring the customer receives a quality built product is one of the most important aspects of project management. You may find ways to cut corners, but neglecting quality can cost you in the long run. You may also run into ethical considerations when neglecting quality. Concealing defective work and design flaws can leave you open to a lawsuit and ruin your reputation.

Accurate and Detailed Specifications and Plans

Accurate and detailed specifications and plans are important to setting quality standards for the project. These items will help you put together a more accurate estimate and should be part of the contract documents. If details are vague, your decisions on material quality and construction methods may differ from the owner's. This misunderstanding can cause conflict and disappoint your customer. It is best to set expectations and obtain agreement from the customer early in the project.

Detailed Shop Drawings

In addition to specifications and plans, shop drawings are often required to detail specific aspects of a project. Shop drawings outline specific details, materials, dimensions, and installation for specific items. Product data and samples may accompany shop drawings to provide additional information. Shop drawings are produced by the material supplier, contractor, subcontractor, or manufacturer. As part of the quality control process, the architect and contractor must review and approve shop drawings.

Quality Assurance Program

Setting up a quality assurance program is a good way to let your employees and customers know the importance of producing a high quality product. Internal inspections should take place at different stages of the construction process to review the completed work and confirm that it meets your quality standards.

Your company philosophy should stress quality. You want your employees to take pride in their work. As an employer, you can create a positive work atmosphere and provide the tools employees need to be successful. Providing ongoing training for employees so they can expand their knowledge base helps improve the quality of their work. Employees should know the standards they are expected to follow. Documenting work standards and conducting regular performance reviews are good ways to create a mutual understanding of the level of quality you expect.

Customer Satisfaction Surveys

Customer satisfaction surveys are also a good tool to receive feedback about the quality of your work. Customer surveys are good for asking about the professionalism of your employees, quality of work, and overall service. Potential customers may be interested that you have a continuous improvement program. Positive feedback from your current or former customers can serve as a good marketing tool to gain new business.

Value Engineering

Value engineering is a project management approach. The objective is to understand the owner's cost, quality, and time priorities to deliver a product of the highest value. Many owners will provide incentives to contractors to meet these objectives. For example, an owner may provide a bonus for a contractor who can cut costs without sacrificing quality while meeting all deadlines. If value engineering bonuses exist, it is important that they are included in the construction contract.

The Society of American Value Engineering International (SAVE) publishes a methodology for the construction industry. The purpose of this methodology is to reduce costs, improve productivity, and develop innovative ways to solve problems.

Final Inspection...

Scheduling Process: During the project scheduling process, the sequence of tasks, activity duration, contingency time, task time ranges, and float time are determined.

Scheduling Methods: The three main types of scheduling are calendar scheduling, bar chart scheduling, and critical path method (CPM).

Scheduling and Cash Management: Effective cash management helps ensure you have enough working capital to complete your project.

What is Project Management? Project management involves managing several different factors including budgets, quality controls, project plans and specifications, and resource management.

Who is the Project Manager? Construction project managers plan and coordinate construction projects to meet the overall goals of the project and serve as the main contact with the owner. The ability to manage effectively contributes significantly to the success or failure of a project.

Project Supervisory Team: Depending on the size of the project, the supervisory team may consist of a superintendent, foreman, materials expediter, architect, and owner's representative.

Project Life Cycle: Through each phase of the project life cycle, you must manage each aspect of the project such as customer relations, materials, budget, and subcontractors.

Tracking the Progress of the Project: A good project manager makes sure that deadlines are met on time. Daily reports and status reports are tools you can use to track your progress.

Budget and Cost Controls: A good project manager will control costs and make sure the project comes in on budget.

Quality Assurance: Ensuring that the customer receives a quality built product is one of the most important aspects of project management.

Value Engineering: Balancing the owner's cost, quality, and time priorities while delivering the highest value product are objectives of the value engineering approach.

Chapter 10
CUSTOMER RELATIONS

Understanding Expectations: You will find customers have specific expectations of the outcome of your work. If those expectations are not satisfied, your customers will be disappointed, which will reflect poorly on your company. Instead of promising your customers an unrealistic outcome, it is easier to be honest and bring expectations to a realistic level. If customers have a realistic picture of the project, you can avoid disappointing them. The best way to accomplish this is through consistent and effective communication with your customers.

Communication with Customers

It is important for customers to understand the status of their project and have all the information needed to make informed decisions. This communication will not only keep the customer's expectations realistic but also build a trusting relationship with you and your company.

Communication Opportunities: You have several opportunities to communicate with your customers and keep their expectations at a realistic level, including

✓ contract negotiations,
✓ contract acceptance,
✓ weekly meetings,
✓ punch list and final walkthrough, and
✓ post-job follow-up.

Establishing communication at these times will ensure that your customer is aware of your progress and of issues that arise during any step of the process.

Communication Basics: Now that we have established when to communicate with customers, let's go over a few basics on how to communicate.

✓ Understand that your customer may not have the same level of technical knowledge as you. Avoid using technical terminology and clarify when necessary.

✓ Give your customer a chance to ask questions and express any concerns. Use active listening skills, and remember that all questions are important to the customer.

✓ When dealing with difficult customers, always remain professional.

✓ Use e-mail or written communication as a follow-up to verbal conversations to document key items discussed and any changes agreed to.

✓ Don't forget the personal touch. E-mail and fax are great tools, but schedule time to talk to the customer in person.

✓ Return phone calls promptly.

Good communication can build customer trust and help you understand customer expectations.

Handling Customer Change Orders

Proper handling of customer change orders is very important. This is a critical point in the customer-contractor relationship and can result in a positive or negative outcome. If you do not follow through with the change order as the customer expects, it will result in disappointment and mistrust. If you follow through to the customer's specifications, you will reinforce that you are responsive and understand the importance of customer service.

You should always apply a few general rules when change orders arise:

✓ Always obtain a signed change order for significant amounts of change work.

✓ Small changes done with verbal approval should be followed up with a written and signed change order.

✓ Invoice for change order work promptly.

✓ Include any complementary work done without charge on the invoice.

✓ Show labor and quantity details when pricing change orders as you would when creating your initial estimate.

Negotiation Basics

Good negotiation skills can benefit you personally and in all areas of your business. When a successful negotiation occurs, both parties are satisfied with the outcome.

Preparing to Negotiate: Negotiation is a process and it is important to prepare ahead of time to get the most out of the negotiation. Considering these questions will help:

✓ What are you negotiating (i.e., money, time, conditions, etc.)?

✓ What is the ideal outcome?

✓ How much are you willing to compromise?

✓ What is the other person trying to achieve?

A negotiation may not always involve price. Consider what is valuable to your business. For example, if time is a critical factor to completing your current projects, you may want to negotiate on project timelines. It is important not to compromise your reputation in a negotiation. You don't want to lose your best customer or future referrals.

Confident Negotiations: Now that you are prepared, you can come to the negotiation confident in knowing what you want. Aim high in your negotiation and you will get more. If you ask for more than you want, people will tend to meet you in the middle. It is important to be flexible during the negotiation. Even though you have prepared ahead of time, the other party may change the direction of the negotiation to different terms. For example, you may have prepared to negotiate on price, but your counterpart may want to deal on the timeline of the work.

When possible, it is important to get the final outcome of your negotiation in writing. Once it is in writing, both parties can sign off on what they agreed to, which will help avoid any disappointment or confusion.

Final Inspection...

Communication with Customers: Good communication helps you build trust and understand customer expectations.

Handling Customer Change Orders: Change orders should be handled carefully and accurately documented.

Negotiation Basics: Come to a negotiation prepared, and, when possible, make sure you get any agreement in writing.

Chapter 11
EMPLOYEE MANAGEMENT

Finding good, hardworking employees can sometimes mean the difference between success and failure in business. It is easier to delegate to good employees and produce high-quality work from employees who care about their job. Poor employees can cost a company wasted time and ultimately money. The first step to finding good employees is taking the extra time to hire the right people for the job.

Employees should start off with a few fundamental qualities. They should be

✓ qualified for the position;

✓ motivated to do the job and show initiative;

✓ responsible for their work and actions;

✓ dependable to show up on time and keep work commitments; and

✓ open to learning new skills.

These basic qualities will result in an employee who is capable of performing their present job responsibilities and taking on more tasks in the future.

Interviewing and Hiring Employees

Asking Questions: Asking the right interview questions is key to finding the right employee. The wrong interview questions can get you into trouble. You must convey that you are a fair and non-discriminatory employer. If you ask questions implying otherwise, you will open yourself to a lawsuit. Some questions could lead to legal action and are strictly off-limits, especially the following:

✓ How old are you?

✓ Do you have any disabilities?

✓ Are you pregnant?

✓ Are you married?

✓ Do you have children?

✓ What is your religious affiliation?

✓ What is your sexual orientation?

✓ What ethnic background are you?

Now that you know what questions not to ask, here are some areas to cover during the job interview that will be helpful in determining if an employee is the right fit for your company.

Questions should be asked to elicit information about the candidate's

✓ ability to work with other members of a construction team;

✓ ability to handle conflict;

✓ expectations of the job (e.g. salary, benefits, working hours, etc.);

✓ past work history and reasons for leaving previous jobs;

✓ level of skill or expertise;

✓ training and education;

✓ safety record;

✓ ability to solve problems;

✓ knowledge of your company; and

✓ questions about the job.

Appendix C contains links to websites that provide sample job interview questions for the construction industry that you can customize for your business.

- -

Hiring the right people for the job is the first step to finding good employees.

- -

New Hire Reporting

Reporting Requirements: You are required to report all new employees to the ***Utah New Hire Reporting Program*** no later than 20 days after an employee is hired or rehired. There are several reporting methods you can use:

✓ Internet: Use the online data entry form or secure file upload at jobs.utah.gov/ui/employer/ employerhome.aspx

✓ Magnetic Cartridge, Tape, or Diskette: Download the new hire information onto a magnetic cartridge, tape, or diskette and mail it to:

Utah New Hire Registry
P.O. Box 45247
140 East 300 South
Salt Lake City, Utah 84145

✓ Fax: Fax the Utah New Hire Registry Reporting Form 6, W-4's, or a spreadsheet in the approved new hire reporting format to (801) 526-4391

✓ Mail: Mail the Utah New Hire Registry Reporting Form 6, W-4's, or a spreadsheet in the approved new hire reporting format.

✓ Telephone: Employers may register up to three new hires at a time by calling the New Hire Registry at (801) 526-9235 or 1-800-222-2857.

✓ Payroll Service: Some payroll services will report new hires automatically for you.

Employers submitting data electronically or magnetically may do so twice a month, no more than 16 days apart.

Employers must report the employee's name, social security number, and mailing address.

The employer's name, federal employer identification number, and mailing address must be provided to the new hire reporting program. It is optional, but strongly recommended, to report the employee's date of hire or rehire and date of birth.

Failure to comply with the New Hire Law could result in a $25 fine per failure to report each newly-hired employee or up to a $500 fine if conspiracy to avoid reporting is determined.

The purpose of new hire reporting is to aid in child support enforcement. The National Directory of New Hires compiles new hire information from all states to track child support obligations on a national basis. It is also a good tool in preventing fraudulent unemployment and welfare benefit payments.

For further information, contact

Utah New Hire Registry
P.O. Box 45247
140 East 300 South
Salt Lake City, Utah 84145

Phone: (801) 526-9235
Toll-free: 1-800-222-2857
Fax: (801) 526-4391

Website: jobs.utah.gov/ui/employer/employerhome. aspx

Hiring Minors for Construction Work

The State of Utah and the U.S. Department of Labor have strict rules about the hiring of minors. The Utah youth employment laws are found in Utah Code §34-23-1 et.seq. These statutes define working hours and prohibited tasks for minors. State law requires employers to obtain an age certificate (commonly referred to as a work permit) for minors under the age of 18. Although the rules and prohibitions governing the employment of minors are extensive, we will focus on those related to construction activities.

Working Hours for minors under age 16: Minors under 16 may not be employed before 7:00 a.m. and after 7:00 p.m. (nighttime hours are extended to 9:00 p.m. from June 1 through Labor Day), or

✓ more than four hours during a school day,

- ✓ more than eight hours a day in a 24-hour period, and

- ✓ not more than 40 hours a week.

Minors under the age of 16 may not be employed during school hours, unless the minor has an approved excuse as authorized by proper school authorities.

Prohibited Tasks: Federal and state law prohibits minors under the age of 16 from being employed in a dangerous occupation, which involves many of the tasks associated with construction work. Office and sales work are allowed if that work does not take place at the actual site of construction operations. Although 16- and 17-year-old minors are allowed to do construction work, there are several prohibited jobs defined by the U.S. Department of Labor. The tasks include:

- ✓ mixing, handling, or transporting explosive compounds;

- ✓ operating power-driven woodworking machines;

- ✓ driving a motor vehicle or working as an outside helper (exceptions exist for 17-year-olds on an incidental and occasional basis if certain criteria is met);

- ✓ operating an elevator, crane, hoist, or forklift;

- ✓ operating power-driven metal forming, punching, and shearing machines;

- ✓ operating power-driven circular saws, band saws, and guillotine shears;

- ✓ wrecking or demolition work;

- ✓ roofing work; and

- ✓ excavation jobs.

Exceptions are also provided for 16- and 17-year-old minors who are apprentices as defined by law.

Penalties: Employers who violate the Utah Youth Employment Laws are subject to criminal and civil penalties.

Further Information: The Labor Commission of Utah administers the Youth Employment Laws. Additional information is available at www.laborcommission.utah.gov.

Employee Documentation

Once you hire an employee, you should make sure you set up an employee file.

These items should be included in your employee files:

- ✓ **Form I-9**: The United States Customs and Immigration Service requires this form. It shows that the worker has legal immigration status in the United States. (For more information on I-9s, see the following section on the Immigration and Nationality Act.)

- ✓ **IRS Form W-4**: This form is required to determine the appropriate level of federal tax withholding. Employees can change the amount of federal tax withholding at anytime by completing a new W-4 form.

- ✓ **IRS Form W-5**: To receive earned income credit (EIC) in advance, employees can complete a W-5 form. Advance EIC is a special tax benefit for working people who earn low or moderate incomes. If the employee wants to continue to receive advance EIC, he or she must complete a new W-5 form each year.

- ✓ **State Tax Form**: This form is required to determine the appropriate level of state tax withholding, if applicable. Utah employees must use the information on the employee's W-4 form to determine withholding amounts.

- ✓ **Employment Application**: All employees should complete an application before being hired. It should contain basic information such as the employee's name, address, and phone number. The application should also be signed, giving your company authorization to check references on the employment history section.

- ✓ **Policy Signoffs**: If you have written policies or an employee handbook, have your employees sign a receipt that the employee has received and reviewed it.

- ✓ **Emergency Notification Form**: It is important that you know who to contact in the event of an emergency. Make sure to update this information periodically.

The employee file should be maintained throughout employment and other relevant documentation can be added, such as disciplinary action forms or insurance enrollment forms.

Setting up employee files will help keep you organized.

Key Employment Laws

There are several key laws governing equal employment opportunities and prohibiting discrimination in employment. It is important to understand and abide by these laws, not only to protect your company from a lawsuit but also to safeguard your reputation as a good employer.

Fair Labor Standards Act (FLSA)

The Fair Labor Standards Act, which prescribes standards for the basic minimum wage and overtime pay, affects most private and public employment. It applies to employers who have one or more employees. Individual states may also have additional minimum wage requirements.

✓ Effective July 24, 2009, federal minimum wage increased to $7.25 per hour. Many states have individual minimum wage laws. If the state minimum wage rate differs from the federal rate, the employer must pay the higher of the two rates. Minors under 20 years of age may be paid a minimum wage of not less than $4.25 per hour during the first 90 consecutive calendar days of employment. Employers may not displace any employee to hire someone at the youth minimum wage. Utah does not have a minimum wage dollar amount but has adopted the federal minimum wage and coverage provided in the FLSA.

✓ Employers must pay overtime compensation of one-and-one-half-times the regular rate after 40 hours of work in a workweek.

✓ Wages must be paid on the regular payday for the pay period covered.

✓ The act restricts the hours that children under age 16 can work and forbids the employment of children under age 18 in certain jobs deemed too dangerous.

FLSA is administered by the Employment Standards Administration's Wage and Hour Division within the U.S. Department of Labor.

Determining Exemption Status: Some employees are exempt from the overtime pay provisions or both the minimum wage and overtime pay provisions as defined under the Fair Labor Standards Act (FLSA). This rule would apply to the following examples of employees who might be employed in the construction industry:

✓ Executives

✓ Administrative personnel

✓ Professional employees

✓ Outside sales employees

✓ Employees in certain computer-related occupations as defined in the Department of Labor regulations

Workweek Defined under FLSA: A workweek is a period of 168 hours during seven consecutive 24-hour periods. It may begin on any day of the week and at any hour of the day established by the employer. Generally, for purposes of minimum wage and overtime payment, each workweek stands alone; you may not average two or more workweeks. Employee coverage, compliance with wage payment requirements, and the application of most exemptions are determined on a workweek basis.

Work Hours Defined Under FLSA: Work hours ordinarily include all time during which an employee is required to be on the employer's premises, on duty, or at a prescribed work place.

Bona fide meal periods (typically 30 minutes or more) generally need not be compensated as work time. The employee must be completely relieved from duty for the purpose of eating regular meals. The employee is not relieved if he or she is required to perform any duties, whether active or inactive, while eating.

Employment Practices Not Covered: While FLSA does set basic minimum wage and overtime pay standards and regulates the employment of minors, there are a number of employment practices that FLSA does not regulate.

FLSA does not require

✓ vacation, holiday, severance, or sick pay;

✓ meal or rest periods, holidays off, or vacations; or

✓ premium pay for weekend or holiday work.

Also, FLSA does not limit the number of hours in a day or days in a week an employee may be required or scheduled to work, including overtime hours, if the employee is at least 16 years old.

These matters not covered by FLSA are left for agreement between the employer and the employees or their authorized representatives. Individual state labor departments may have specific regulations separate from FLSA regarding these requirements.

> *Utah Labor Commission*
> *160 East 300 South, Suite 300*
> *Salt Lake City, Utah 84111*
>
> *Phone: (801) 530-6800*
> *Toll-free: 1-800-530-5090*
>
> *Website: www.laborcommission.utah.gov*

Recordkeeping under the FLSA

The FLSA requires employers to keep records on wages, hours, and other items as specified in Department of Labor recordkeeping regulations. Most of this information is maintained by employers in ordinary business practice and in compliance with other laws and regulations. The records do not have to be kept in any particular form, and time clocks need not be used.

Required Information: For employees subject to the minimum wage provisions or both the minimum wage and overtime pay provisions, the following records must be kept:

✓ personal information, including employee's name, home address, occupation, sex, and birth date (if under 19 years of age);

✓ hour and day when workweek begins;

✓ total hours worked each workday and each workweek;

✓ total daily or weekly straight-time earnings

✓ regular hourly pay rate for any week when overtime is worked;

✓ total overtime pay for the workweek;

✓ deductions from or additions to wages;

✓ total wages paid each pay period; and

✓ date of payment and pay period covered.

Special information is required for home workers, for employees working under uncommon pay arrangements, for employees to whom lodging or other facilities are furnished, and for employees receiving remedial education.

Chapter 14, Financial Management, covers the basics of payroll accounting and how to process the listed information.

Penalties

Enforcement of FLSA is carried out by investigators stationed across the U.S. They conduct investigations and gather data on wages, hours, and other employment conditions or practices in order to determine compliance with the law. Where violations are found, they may recommend changes in employment practices to bring an employer into compliance.

Retaliation against an employee for filing a complaint or for participating in a legal proceeding under FLSA is against the law.

Willful violations of employment under FLSA may be prosecuted criminally, and the violator fined up to $10,000. A second conviction may result in imprisonment.

Employers who willfully or repeatedly violate the minimum wage or overtime pay requirements are subject to a civil money penalty of up to $1,100 for each violation.

Immigration and Nationality Act

The employment eligibility provisions of the Immigration and Nationality Act require employers to verify the employment eligibility of all individuals hired. Immigration and Naturalization Service forms (I-9) must be kept on file for at least three years after the date of hire or for one year after the date employment ends, whichever is later.

I-9 forms must be completed with required documentation within three days of hire. A sample I-9 form is located at the end of this chapter.

The law does not require businesses to obtain I-9 documentation for independent contractors and their employees.

Unlawful Discrimination: Discrimination based on national origin or citizenship status is prohibited. If an Office of Special Counsel for Unfair Employment-Related Discrimination (OSC) or Equal Employment Opportunity Commission (EEOC) investigation reveals employment discrimination covered by the Immigration and Nationality Act, the employer will be ordered to cease the prohibited practice and may be ordered to take one or more of the following steps:

✓ hire or reinstate, with or without back pay, individuals directly injured by the discrimination;

✓ lift any restrictions on an employee's assignments, work shifts, or movements;

✓ post notices to employees about their rights and about employers' obligations;

✓ educate all personnel involved in hiring and in complying with employer sanctions and anti-discrimination laws; and

✓ remove a false performance review or false warning from an employee's personnel file.

Employers may also be ordered to pay civil monetary penalties of $375 to $3,200 per individual discriminated against for the first offense, $3,200 to $6,500 per individual discriminated against for the second offense, and $4,300 to $16,000 per individual discriminated against for subsequent offenses.

Completing the I-9 Form for New Hires

Form I-9 is available for download on the U.S. Citizenship and Immigration Services website at www.uscis.gov or by calling 1-800-870-3676. The National Customer Service Center at 1-800-375-5283 can answer questions on USCIS forms and information on immigration laws, regulations and procedures.

The following gives step-by-step instructions on how to complete the form properly.

Section One

The employee completes section one of the I-9 form at the start of employment. The employee's name, address, date of birth, and social security number (optional unless the employer participates in the USCIS E-Verify Program), certification of legal status, and expiration date for temporary work authorization are required. Permanent aliens and authorized aliens must fill in either their alien number or authorization number. The employee must sign and date the form. If a preparer or translator is used, the appropriate signature block must be completed.

Section Two

An authorized employee representative completes section two by examining one document from list A or by examining one document from list B and one document from list C (a summary of approved documents is listed in the following section and a complete list is on the back of the I-9 form). The representative must view original documentation and keep copies of the front and back of this documentation on file.

Acceptable Documentation: The purpose of providing documentation is to establish identity and employment eligibility. Listed below are common forms of identification used when completing the I-9 form. A complete list is included on the back of the I-9 form located at the end of this chapter. If employers participate in the USCIS E-Verify Program, only documents from List B on the I-9 form that bear a photograph are acceptable. I-9 forms must be updated when identity and employment eligibility documents are changed or renewed.

Employees can provide one of the following documents that establishes both identity and employment eligibility:

✓ U.S. passport

✓ Certificate of U.S. citizenship

✓ Certificate of naturalization

✓ Unexpired foreign passport with I-551 stamp or attached I-94 form indicating current employment authorization

✓ Permanent resident card or alien registration receipt with photograph

Employees also have the option of providing two documents–one to establish identity and the other to establish employment eligibility.

Documents that establish identity include

✓ state-issued driver's license with photo;

✓ ID card with photo issued by federal, state or local government agencies;

✓ voter's registration card; and

✓ U.S. military card.

Documents that establish employment eligibility include

✓ U.S. Social Security card issued by the Social Security Administration;

✓ original or certified birth certificate;

✓ U.S. citizen ID card (form I-197);

✓ resident ID card; and

✓ Native American tribal document.

Certification

The date to be used in the certification section must correspond with the current employment date. The authorized employee representative must sign and date this section.

Additional Information: U.S. Citizen and Immigration Services publishes a Handbook for Employers which is a helpful resource for completing the I-9 form. This publication is available online at www.uscis.gov/files/nativedocuments/m-274_3apr09.pdf.

Americans with Disabilities Act (ADA)

This law prohibits discrimination against persons with disabilities and applies to employers with 15 or more employees. In general, the employment provisions of the ADA require

- ✓ equal opportunity in selecting, testing, and hiring qualified applicants with disabilities;
- ✓ job accommodation for applicants and workers with disabilities when such accommodations would not impose "undue hardship;" and
- ✓ equal opportunity in promotion and benefits.

Employment Discrimination: ADA prohibits discrimination in all employment practices, including job application procedures, hiring, firing, advancement, compensation, training, and other terms, conditions, and privileges of employment. It applies to recruitment, advertising, tenure, layoff, leave, fringe benefits, and all other employment-related activities.

Qualified Individuals with Disabilities: Employment discrimination is prohibited against "qualified individuals with disabilities" including applicants for employment and employees. An individual is considered to have a "disability" if that individual has a physical or mental impairment that substantially limits one or more major life activities or has a record of such an impairment, or is regarded as having such an impairment.

Conditions Covered: The ADA applies to persons who have impairments that substantially limit major life activities such as seeing, hearing, speaking, walking, breathing, performing manual tasks, learning, caring for oneself, and working.

Examples include an individual with

- ✓ epilepsy,
- ✓ paralysis,
- ✓ HIV infection,
- ✓ AIDS,
- ✓ substantial hearing or visual impairment,
- ✓ mental retardation, or
- ✓ specific learning disability.

An individual with a minor, non-chronic condition of short duration, such as a sprain, broken limb, or the flu, generally would not be covered by the ADA.

Reasonable Accommodations: An employer is required to accommodate a "known" disability of a qualified applicant or employee unless it imposes an "undue hardship" on the operation of the employer's business. A reasonable accommodation is any modification or adjustment to a job or the work environment that will enable a qualified applicant or employee with a disability to participate in the application process or to perform essential job functions. Reasonable accommodations also include adjustments to assure that a qualified individual with a disability has rights and privileges in employment equal to those of employees without disabilities.

Additional Resources: The Equal Employment Opportunity Commission has developed several resources to help employers and people with disabilities understand and comply with the employment provisions of the ADA. Resources include

- ✓ a technical assistance manual that provides "how-to" guidance on the employment provisions of the ADA as well as a resource directory to help individuals find specific information; and
- ✓ a variety of brochures, booklets, and fact sheets.

For more information about the ADA, contact:

U.S. Equal Employment Opportunity Commission
131 M Street, NE
Fourth Floor, Suite 4NWO2F
Washington, D.C. 20507

Phone: (202) 669-4000
TTY: (202) 669-6820

Website: www.eeoc.gov

Other Labor Laws

Many other labor laws protect the rights of employees.

- ✓ The **Davis-Bacon Act** requires payment of prevailing wage rates and fringe benefits on federally-financed or assisted construction.

✓ The **Walsh-Healey Public Contracts Act** requires payment of minimum wage rates and overtime pay on contracts that provide goods to the federal government.

✓ The **Service Contract Act** requires payment of prevailing wage rates and fringe benefits on contracts to provide services to the federal government.

✓ The **Contract Work Hours and Safety Standards Act** sets overtime standards for service and construction contracts on federal projects.

✓ The **Wage Garnishment Law** limits the amount of an individual's income that may be legally garnished and prohibits firing an employee whose pay is garnished for payment of a single debt.

✓ The **Employee Polygraph Protection Act** prohibits most private employers from using any type of lie detector test, either for pre-employment screening of job applicants or for testing current employees during the course of employment.

✓ The **Family and Medical Leave Act** entitles eligible employees of covered employers to take up to 12 weeks of unpaid job-protected leave each year, with the maintenance of group health insurance, for the birth and care of a child, for the placement of a child for adoption or foster care, for the care of a child, spouse, or parent with a serious health condition, or for the employee's serious health condition.

✓ **Title VII of the Civil Rights Act of 1964** prohibits discrimination on the basis of race, color, religion, national origin, and sex. Sexual harassment is considered a form of sex discrimination and is a violation of Title VII. An amendment to Title VII provides protection against sex discrimination on the basis of pregnancy, childbirth, and related medical conditions.

✓ The **Equal Pay Act of 1963** prohibits employers from paying different wages to men and women who perform essentially the same work under similar working conditions.

✓ The **Age Discrimination in Employment Act (ADEA)** prohibits discrimination against individuals who are age 40 or older. It applies to employers with 20 or more employees.

✓ The **Worker Adjustment and Retraining Notification Act (WARN)** offers protection to workers, their families, and communities by requiring employers to provide notice 60 days in advance of covered plant closings and covered mass layoffs.

✓ **Title III of the Consumer Credit Protection Act (CCPA)** protects employees from being discharged by their employers because their wages have been garnished for any one debt and limits the amount of employees' earnings that may be garnished in any one week.

✓ The **Uniformed Services Employment and Reemployment Rights Act (USERRA)** protects service members' reemployment rights when returning from a period of service in the uniformed services, including those called up from the reserves or National Guard, and prohibits employer discrimination based on military service or obligation.

✓ **Numerous labor organizing, collective bargaining and dispute resolution acts** give employees the right to organize, join labor unions, bargain collectively, and strike.

✓ **Right-to-work laws** secure the right of employees to decide for themselves whether or not to join or financially support a union. Utah is a right-to-work state.

Be aware of the labor laws that apply to your business.

Required Postings

Some of the statutes and regulations enforced by agencies within the U.S. Department of Labor require that posters or notices be posted in the workplace. A complete list of postings can be found at www.dol.gov. A summary of postings that may apply to you as listed on U.S. Department of Labor website is as follows:

Poster	Description of Employers Required to Post Notice
Safety and Health Protection on the Job	Employers located in states with OSHA-approved state plans should obtain and post the state's equivalent poster.
Equal Opportunity is the Law	Businesses holding federal contracts or subcontracts or federally assisted construction contracts of $10,000 or more

Poster	Description of Employers Required to Post Notice
Employee Rights for Workers with Disabilities/Special Minimum Wage Poster	All employers having workers employed under special minimum wage certificates must post this notice
National Labor Relations Act (NLRA) Poster (effective January 31, 2012)	All private-sector employers (excluding agricultural, railroad and airline employers) must post this notice.
Your Rights Under the Family and Medical Leave Act	Public agencies (including state, local, and federal employers), public and private elementary and secondary schools, as well as private sector employers who employ 50 or more employees in 20 or more work weeks and who are engaged in commerce or in any industry or activity affecting commerce, including joint employers and successors of covered employers
Fair Labor Standards Act (FLSA): Minimum Wage Poster	All private, federal, state and local government employers subject to the FLSA
Uniformed Services Employment and Reemployment Rights Act	The full text of the notice must be provided by each employer to persons entitled to rights and benefits under USERRA.
Notice to All Employees Working on Federal or Federally Financed Construction Projects	Any contractor/subcontractor engaged in contracts in excess of $2,000 for the actual construction, alteration/repair of a public building or public work or building or work financed in whole or in part from federal funds, federal guarantee, or federal pledge
Notice to Employees Working on Government Contracts	Every contractor or subcontractor engaged in a contract with the United States or the District of Columbia in excess of $2,500 the principal purpose of which is to furnish services in the U.S. through the use of service employees.
Notice: Employee Polygraph Protection Act	Any employer engaged in or affecting commerce or in the production of goods for commerce. Does not apply to federal, state and local governments, or to circumstances covered by the national defense and security exemption.

Notification of Employee Rights Under Federal Labor Laws	Federal contractors and subcontractors are required to post the prescribed employee notice conspicuously in plants and offices where employees covered by the National Labor Relations Act (NLRA) perform contract-related activity, including all places where notices to employees are customarily posted both physically and electronically.

Additional postings may be required for federal contractors.

Employers in Utah are required by the Labor Commission to display the following posters:

✓ *Job Safety and Health Protection*

✓ *Utah OSHA Statistics*

✓ *Workers' Compensation Act Notice*

These posters are downloadable from the Labor Commission website at www.laborcommission.utah.gov.

The Utah Department of Workforce Services requires display of the Unemployment Insurance Notice to Workers. This poster is available by calling (801) 526-9400 or toll-free 1-800-222-2857.

Other state agencies may also require display of specific documents in the workplace. Please contact the appropriate agencies directly to verify any poster display requirements.

Employee Handbook and Policies

Having clear and well-documented policies helps employees understand the rules of the workplace and protects you if a disgruntled employee files a lawsuit or complaint against you.

Enforcing Policies and Procedures: An employee handbook is a document you put together that lists company policies and employee benefits and rights. It is important for employees to sign a receipt that they have read and understood the contents of the handbook. This documentation is helpful in enforcing the policies and procedures of your company.

Changing Your Handbook: An employee handbook is not a static document. You can add items to the handbook but make sure that you distribute these amendments to employees and have them sign off on the changes.

Writing Your Employee Handbook

It may be difficult to determine where to start when writing your employee handbook and policies. Consider the following sections when putting your handbook together:

✓ Company history

✓ Compensation guidelines (i.e., introductory period, full-time status requirements, etc.)

✓ Payroll distribution dates and times

✓ Benefits

✓ Normal working hours

✓ Overtime pay

✓ Vacation time

✓ Sick days

✓ Policy on sexual harassment

✓ Policy on the use of illegal drugs or alcohol

✓ Non-discrimination policy

✓ Rules of conduct (i.e., disciplinary action for insubordination, fighting, etc.)

✓ Safety policies

✓ Equipment and tool policies

✓ Disciplinary action procedures

You may want to have an attorney review your employee handbook. In many states, the employee handbook is considered an employment contract. There may be certain wording and disclaimers that should be contained in your employee handbook to protect you against legal action.

Employee Satisfaction

Benefits of Employee Satisfaction: Keeping your employees happy and motivated can have a tremendous effect on the performance of your work teams. Your company can benefit from satisfied employees in several ways:

✓ Stronger company loyalty and corporate culture

✓ Higher quality work and customer satisfaction

✓ Lower employee turnover

✓ Increased productivity

Maintaining employee satisfaction is not as easy as it sounds. Even though employers may have good intentions, when faced with tight deadlines and day-to-day operations, employee satisfaction sometimes drops to the bottom of the priority list.

Motivating Employees: The following checklist includes simple ways you can motivate your employees and give them a feeling of achievement:

✓ Provide informal and formal training opportunities for employees to learn new skills.

✓ Empower employees to make decisions and give positive and constructive feedback.

✓ Provide clear expectations for your employees.

✓ Conduct performance reviews on a regular basis.

✓ Mentor your employees and tell them about advancement opportunities in your company and the industry.

✓ Recognize and reward employees for good work.

The Value of Job Descriptions

Job descriptions give employees a guideline for the responsibilities of their job. Job descriptions benefit the employee because employees understand your expectation for their performance. It also makes it easier for you to monitor their performance, give reviews, and conduct disciplinary action if necessary.

Job descriptions should contain a few basic elements:

✓ Job title

✓ Job description, including who the position reports to and summary of job purpose

✓ Key responsibilities

✓ Required licenses and/or certifications

✓ Skills and knowledge needed

Sample Job Description: Listed below is a sample job description for a construction superintendent position using the above categories. All job descriptions must be carefully reviewed and modified to fit the individual company's requirements.

Job Title: Construction Superintendent

Description: Under general direction of the company owner, the construction superintendent serves as a member of the construction management team with broad authority over assigned projects, participating in all phases of construction from project planning to completion. Emphasis is on quality control, evaluation of change order requests, and timely completion of construction schedules.

Key Responsibilities: The duties listed below are intended only as illustrations of the various types of work that may be performed by the construction superintendent:

✓ Coordinates activities associated with the company's construction projects.

✓ Serves as liaison with subcontractors, architects, utilities, and others.

✓ Participates in project construction development and planning.

✓ Processes utility requests for construction projects.

✓ Represents the company regarding onsite construction quality control reviews.

✓ Makes recommendations and processes change order requests.

✓ Reviews punch lists.

✓ Assures construction specifications are met.

✓ Notes deviations from project schedules and costs.

✓ Maintains records and prepares reports.

The omission of specific statements of duties does not exclude them from the position if the work is similar, related, or a logical assignment to this class.

Required Licenses or Certifications: Requires a valid driver's license

Skills and Knowledge Needed:

✓ Principles and practices of construction management, building operation and maintenance, quality assurance programs and systems, budget administration, construction specifications, and bidding processes.

✓ Ability to plan, organize, and manage time to track progress and elements of assigned construction projects effectively.

✓ Establish and maintain effective working relationships with coworkers, employees of subcontractors, and outside entities.

✓ Prepare or participate in the development of construction and other budgets and monitor performance against the approved budget.

✓ Communicate effectively, both orally and in writing.

✓ Ability to lift up to 50 pounds.

Providing Benefits

Offering benefit plans can be an effective means of attracting and retaining good employees, keeping up with the competition, and boosting employee morale. Traditional employee plans include

✓ health insurance,

✓ dental insurance,

✓ vision insurance,

✓ long-term disability,

✓ life insurance, and

✓ 401(k) or other retirement plan.

Some employers also opt to offer more creative benefit options, such as tuition reimbursement, gym subsidies, and child care referral services.

However you decide to package your benefits plan, a few key laws are important.

Workers' Compensation Laws provide monetary compensation to employees who are injured or disabled on the job. These laws also provide benefits for dependents of those workers who are killed because of work-related accidents or illnesses. Some laws protect employers by limiting the amount an injured employee can recover from an employer and by eliminating the liability of coworkers in most accidents. Workers' compensation laws and programs are established at the state level for most employment.

Workers' compensation fraud is committed when an individual willfully intends to provide false or inaccurate information to receive workers' compensation benefits. Examples of fraud include

✓ reporting an injury as work-related when it was not;

✓ continuing to work and receive benefits at the same time; and

✓ misrepresenting an injury.

Employers are in the best position to identify workers' compensation fraud. Workers' compensation fraud is illegal. Your workers' compensation administrator should be notified if you suspect fraud.

Workers' compensation insurance is purchased by the employer; no part of it should be paid for by employees or deducted from their pay.

Utah Coverage Requirements: The Utah workers' compensation program provides wage replacement and medical care program for employees due to injury, illness, and death resulting from a compensable work-related claim.

Workers' Compensation benefits pay for

✓ hospital bills, medical bills, and prescriptions for work-related injuries and illnesses;

✓ wage replacement for time lost from work due to work-related injuries and illnesses;

✓ burial and dependent benefits in the case of death;

✓ mileage for all authorized medical care;

✓ permanent partial impairment; and

✓ permanent total disability.

In return for providing workers' compensation benefits, the employer is free from lawsuits from the injured employee.

Under Utah law, all employers are required to carry workers' compensation with the exception of sole proprietorships and partnerships as outlined below. The following information and additional publications are available on the Labor Commission website at www.laborcommission.utah.gov. The website has easy-to-read information for employers and employees including a publication titled Employer's Guide to Workers' Compensation.

> Labor Commission of Utah
> Division of Industrial Accidents
> P.O. Box 146610
> 160 East 300 South, 3rd Floor
> Salt Lake City, Utah 84111
>
> Phone: (801) 530-6800
>
> Email: iaccd@utah.gov
>
> Website: www.laborcommission.utah.gov

Sole Proprietorships and Partnerships: A sole proprietor or partner, with no employees other than the sole proprietor or partners, is not required to obtain workers' compensation coverage. If you are a subcontractor, you or the general contractor are required to obtain workers' compensation coverage.

Corporations and LLCs: Corporate officers and directors are considered employees and required to

have workers' compensation coverage, however, an exemption from coverage may be obtained.

Contractor Coverage: General contractors who sublet any part of contract work to a subcontractor, including sole proprietors, partners, and corporate officers, may be liable for workers' compensation coverage if the subcontractor has not obtained workers' compensation insurance coverage. In order to protect your business, it is recommended that you verify insurance coverage of all subcontractors before beginning work. If the subcontractor is a sole proprietor, partner, or corporate officer, an exemption is available through the Workers' Compensation Fund of Utah. Exemptions are not valid until an application is made and approved through the Workers' Compensation Fund of Utah.

Obtaining Coverage: Every employer subject to the workers' compensation law must obtain workers' compensation insurance or qualify as a self-insurer to ensure payment of benefits to injured workers. To obtain workers' compensation insurance, employers can contact an insurance agency representing a company licensed to write workers' compensation insurance in Utah. The Workers' Compensation Fund of Utah also provides workers' compensation coverage and will not turn away any employer. Employers are required to pay for 100 percent of the workers' compensation premium. Programs that may reduce the cost of this insurance are introduced in Chapter 12, Jobsite Safety and Environmental Factors. The Utah Labor Commission OSHA Consultation Program provides free safety consultations for companies. Contact (801) 530-6901 or 1-800-530-6855 for further information.

Self-Insurance: To qualify as a self-insurer, employers must file an application with the Labor Commission of Utah. Employers must have a minimum net worth of ten million dollars to qualify for self-insurance.

Penalties: Failure to carry workers' compensation can result in hefty penalties. Uninsured employers are subject to fines of $1,000 or three times the amount of the premium the employer would have paid during the period of non-compliance by the Labor Commission. In addition, an employer failing to provide coverage as required by law may be sued in a court of law by the injured employee.

Required Posting: Employers must post a typewritten or printed notice of compliance with the workers' compensation law in a prominent location in the workplace. Notices are available free of charge from the Labor Commission. The posting should include the insurance company's name and phone number and steps to reporting an industrial claim.

Reporting an Injury: Upon knowledge of an injury, an employer must complete an Employer's First Report of Injury or Illness (Form 122) and file it with the Labor Commission within seven days. A copy of the report must be submitted to the employer's workers' compensation carrier and given to the injured employee. Injured employees have up to 180 days to report an injury or work-related illness. Form 122 must be completed and properly filed for all injuries or illnesses requiring treatment by a physician regardless of the severity.

Unemployment Compensation programs provide unemployment benefits to eligible workers who become unemployed through no fault of their own and meet certain other eligibility requirements. This program is jointly financed through federal and state employer payroll taxes through the federal/state unemployment insurance tax.

Generally, employers must pay both state and federal unemployment taxes if

- ✓ they pay wages to employees totaling $1,500 or more in any quarter of a calendar year; or

- ✓ they had at least one employee during any day of a week during 20 weeks in a calendar year, regardless of whether or not the weeks were consecutive.

Utah State Unemployment Program: Employers are subject to unemployment taxes as defined in the Utah Employment Security Act if

- ✓ wages of $1 or more were paid during a calendar quarter;

- ✓ the business was acquired from an employer who was subject to the Act; or

- ✓ the business is subject to the Federal Unemployment Tax Act (FUTA).

Additional rules exist for those who employ domestic or agricultural workers and for non-profit companies.

Registering a Business: All new and acquired business in Utah must register with the Department of Workforce Services. Registration for an unemployment tax account is available in the following ways:

- ✓ online at jobs.utah.gov/ui/employer/ employerhome.aspx

- ✓ fax by completing Status Report, Form 1 and sending it to (801) 526-9377

- ✓ telephone by calling (801) 526-9400 or 1-800-222-2857 (toll free in Utah)

- ✓ mail by completing Status Report, Form 1 and sending it to

  Utah Department of Workforce Services
  Employer Accounts
  140 East 300 South
  P.O. Box 45288
  Salt Lake City, Utah 84145-0288

Tax Base: The taxable wage base is the amount that Utah employers are required by law to pay on unemployment insurance tax. For the most current taxable wage base information, visit the website at http://jobs.utah.gov.

Rate Calculations: Utah unemployment tax rates may change periodically. Each employer's overall tax rate is recalculated each year. For the most up-to-date, tax rates and rate calculation formulas, visit the Department of Workforce Services website at jobs.utah.gov/ui/employer/Public/Questions/ TaxRates.aspx.

Paying Unemployment Tax: Employers subject to the Utah Employment Security Act are required to file wage reports and pay taxes quarterly. Wages are reported on the Employer's Quarterly Wage List, Form 3H. Even if no wages were paid during the quarter, employers must still send wage reports. Wages that must be reported include

- ✓ hourly wages, salaries and commissions;

- ✓ meals, lodging and other payments in kind;

- ✓ tips and gratuities;

- ✓ remuneration for services of an employee with equipment;

- ✓ vacation and sick pay;

- ✓ separation and dismissal pay;

- ✓ bonuses and gifts;

- ✓ payments in stock; and

- ✓ contributions to deferred compensation plans, including 401(k) plans.

The employer's tax contributions must be reported using the Employer's Quarterly Wage List, Form 3.

The reporting due dates are as follows:

Quarter Ending:	Reports mailed to Employers the Last week of:	Wage Report and Contributions Due:
March 31	March	April 30
June 30	June	July 31
September 30	September	October 31
December 31	December	January 31

Recordkeeping: Employers must keep the following records for at least four calendar years:

✓ Name and social security number of each employee

✓ Date each employee was hired

✓ Place of employment

✓ Date and reason each employee was separated from employment

✓ Beginning and ending date of each pay period and the date wages were paid

✓ Total amount of wages paid in each pay period, showing separately wages and other payments such as tips and bonuses

✓ Special payments such as bonuses, commissions, gifts, severance pay or accrued leave pay, etc

✓ Cash value of living quarters, meals, or anything else paid to an employee as compensation for work done

Fraud: Unemployment insurance fraud is considered a crime and, if convicted, is punishable by fines, penalties, and/or criminal prosecution. Fraud by employers includes

✓ misclassification of workers;

✓ incorrectly reporting wages;

✓ providing false information to prevent an otherwise eligible claimant from obtaining benefits; and

✓ failure to pay unemployment insurance taxes, report necessary information, or prohibit inspection by the Department.

SUTA dumping is a transfer of employees between businesses for the purpose of obtaining a lower unemployment compensation tax rate. SUTA dumping is prohibited and subject to criminal and/or civil penalties according to state law.

Further Information: For more information on the Utah unemployment program, contact:

Utah Department of Workforce Services
140 East 300 South
Salt Lake City, Utah 84145

Phone: (888) 848-0688

Website: www.jobs.utah.gov

The **Consolidated Omnibus Budget Act of 1985 (COBRA)** includes provisions for continuing health care coverage. These provisions apply to group health plans of employers with 20 or more employees on 50 percent of the typical working days in the previous calendar year. COBRA gives "qualified beneficiaries" (a covered employee's spouse and dependent children) the right to maintain, at their own expense, coverage under their health plan that would be lost due to a "qualifying event," such as termination of employment, at a cost comparable to what it would be if they were still members of the employer's group.

Health Insurance Portability and Accountability Act of 1996 (HIPAA) provides for improved portability and continuity of health insurance coverage connected with employment. These provisions include rules relating to exclusions of preexisting conditions, special enrollment rights, and prohibition of discrimination against individuals based on health status-related factors. HIPAA also addresses an employee's right to privacy concerning their health information. As an employer, you need to be aware of this act and keep records concerning any employee's medical conditions in a confidential file.

Disciplining Employees

Corrective action may be necessary from time to time for employees who are not following employment policies and procedures properly. Employers need to administer discipline fairly to promote a respectful work environment and to avoid trouble later.

Progressive Discipline: Progressive discipline is a method of corrective action where the consequences of the improper behavior become more significant if it continues. Progressive discipline gives the employee a chance to take corrective action to prevent future disciplinary action. There are certain offenses that may be cause for immediate termination (i.e., theft, endangering the safety of others, etc.) and are not subject to progressive discipline.

The employee manual is a good place to have written disciplinary policies and a comprehensive list of offenses that lead to immediate dismissal.

Terminating Employees

At one time or another, most employers run into circumstances where they need to terminate employees. It is not a fun or rewarding task but sometimes a necessary one. When terminating an employee, you want to make sure that you have followed the proper procedures to minimize your risk of a wrongful termination lawsuit.

Employment relationships are either contractual or at-will; the definition of the relationship influences the procedures for termination.

Contractual Employees

Union employees and some executives have employment contracts. When terminating a contractual employee, it is important to comply with the terms of the contract. If the contract is breached, you may be subject to a lawsuit.

At-Will Employees

"At-will employment" means that either the employer or the employee may terminate employment at any time without notice or cause. It is not exactly that easy, and there are restrictions that you should be aware of as an employer. These restrictions include:

✓ An employer may not terminate an employee for discriminatory reasons (i.e., race, gender, etc.).

✓ An employer cannot terminate an employee for taking time off to serve on a jury.

✓ Reporting health and safety violations and abuses of power cannot lead to termination. There are "whistle-blower laws" that protect employees if this circumstance does occur.

✓ All employers should use good faith and fair dealing throughout employment. This is why documenting poor performance is strongly

recommended. Without documentation, the termination may be perceived as a breach of good faith.

These are general guidelines, and it is recommended you consult with an expert in Human Resources or an attorney regarding specific situations.

- -
Proper documentation is important when disciplining and terminating employees.
- -

Final Inspection...

Interviewing and Hiring Employees: Your interviews should focus on skills, experience, and qualities. There are certain questions you should avoid because they are not legal to ask.

New Hire Reporting: Utah has mandatory new hire reporting requirements.

Hiring Minors for Construction Work: The State of Utah and U.S. Department of Labor have strict rules for the hiring of minors, including limited working hours and prohibited tasks.

Employee Documentation: Employee files should be maintained throughout employment with relevant documents, such as tax forms and disciplinary forms.

Key Employment Laws: There are several employment laws that you must comply with, such as the Fair Labor Standards Act (FLSA), Immigration and Nationality Act, and the Americans with Disabilities Act (ADA).

Fair Labor Standards Act (FLSA): Standards for basic minimum wage and overtime pay are outlined in the Fair Labor Standards Act. The Act applies to most private and public employers who have one or more employees.

Immigration and Nationality Act: Employers are required to verify the employment eligibility of all individuals hired through I-9 forms. These forms must be kept on file for at least three years after the date of hire or for one year after the date employment ends, whichever is later.

Americans with Disabilities Act (ADA): This law prohibits discrimination against persons with disabilities. It applies to employers with 15 or more employees.

Other Labor Laws: Several other labor laws protect the rights of employees. Specific laws exist that set guidelines for federal contractors, wage garnishment, and an employee's right to join a union. Other laws provide protection against the discriminatory actions of employers.

Required Postings: Employers must post certain notices for employees under federal and state law.

Employee Handbook and Policies: An employee handbook is a useful document for communicating your policies and procedures.

Employee Satisfaction: Your company can benefit in several ways from putting employee satisfaction programs in place.

Providing Benefits: There are some mandatory benefits you must provide employees. Other benefits, such as health insurance, may also be offered to attract and retain employees.

Disciplining Employees: Discipline should be administered in a fair manner and documented appropriately.

Terminating Employees: Using proper termination procedures will help minimize your risk of a wrongful termination lawsuit.

 Supplemental Forms

Supplemental forms and links are available at **NASCLAforms.org** using access code **UT129354.**

IRS Form W-4	IRS form to determine federal income tax withholding
IRS Form W-5	IRS form for employees to elect advance earned income credit
Form I-9	Required form to confirm legal immigration status
Fair Labor Standards Act (FLSA)	Copy of the FLSA law from the U.S. Department of Labor
Americans with Disabilities Act (ADA)	ADA guide for small businesses published by the U.S. Department of Justice
Job Description Template	Form featured earlier in the chapter that shows a sample job description
Employer's Tax Guide (Circular E)	Publication used to determine federal income tax withholding for employees

Instructions for Employment Eligibility Verification	USCIS
	Form I-9
Department of Homeland Security	OMB No. 1615-0047
U.S. Citizenship and Immigration Services	Expires 03/31/2016

Read all instructions carefully before completing this form.

Anti-Discrimination Notice. It is illegal to discriminate against any work-authorized individual in hiring, discharge, recruitment or referral for a fee, or in the employment eligibility verification (Form I-9 and E-Verify) process based on that individual's citizenship status, immigration status or national origin. Employers **CANNOT** specify which document(s) they will accept from an employee. The refusal to hire an individual because the documentation presented has a future expiration date may also constitute illegal discrimination. For more information, call the Office of Special Counsel for Immigration-Related Unfair Employment Practices (OSC) at 1-800-255-7688 (employees), 1-800-255-8155 (employers), or 1-800-237-2515 (TDD), or visit **www.justice.gov/crt/about/osc**.

What Is the Purpose of This Form?

Employers must complete Form I-9 to document verification of the identity and employment authorization of each new employee (both citizen and noncitizen) hired after November 6, 1986, to work in the United States. In the Commonwealth of the Northern Mariana Islands (CNMI), employers must complete Form I-9 to document verification of the identity and employment authorization of each new employee (both citizen and noncitizen) hired after November 27, 2011. Employers should have used Form I-9 CNMI between November 28, 2009 and November 27, 2011.

General Instructions

Employers are responsible for completing and retaining Form I-9. For the purpose of completing this form, the term "employer" means all employers, including those recruiters and referrers for a fee who are agricultural associations, agricultural employers, or farm labor contractors.

Form I-9 is made up of three sections. Employers may be fined if the form is not complete. Employers are responsible for retaining completed forms. Do not mail completed forms to U.S. Citizenship and Immigration Services (USCIS) or Immigration and Customs Enforcement (ICE).

Section 1. Employee Information and Attestation

Newly hired employees must complete and sign Section 1 of Form I-9 **no later than the first day of employment.** Section 1 should never be completed before the employee has accepted a job offer.

Provide the following information to complete Section 1:

Name: Provide your full legal last name, first name, and middle initial. Your last name is your family name or surname. If you have two last names or a hyphenated last name, include both names in the last name field. Your first name is your given name. Your middle initial is the first letter of your second given name, or the first letter of your middle name, if any.

Other names used: Provide all other names used, if any (including maiden name). If you have had no other legal names, write "N/A."

Address: Provide the address where you currently live, including Street Number and Name, Apartment Number (if applicable), City, State, and Zip Code. Do not provide a post office box address (P.O. Box). Only border commuters from Canada or Mexico may use an international address in this field.

Date of Birth: Provide your date of birth in the mm/dd/yyyy format. For example, January 23, 1950, should be written as 01/23/1950.

U.S. Social Security Number: Provide your 9-digit Social Security number. Providing your Social Security number is voluntary. However, if your employer participates in E-Verify, you must provide your Social Security number.

E-mail Address and Telephone Number (Optional): You may provide your e-mail address and telephone number. Department of Homeland Security (DHS) may contact you if DHS learns of a potential mismatch between the information provided and the information in DHS or Social Security Administration (SSA) records. You may write "N/A" if you choose not to provide this information.

All employees must attest in Section 1, under penalty of perjury, to their citizenship or immigration status by checking one of the following four boxes provided on the form:

1. **A citizen of the United States**

2. **A noncitizen national of the United States:** Noncitizen nationals of the United States are persons born in American Samoa, certain former citizens of the former Trust Territory of the Pacific Islands, and certain children of noncitizen nationals born abroad.

3. **A lawful permanent resident:** A lawful permanent resident is any person who is not a U.S. citizen and who resides in the United States under legally recognized and lawfully recorded permanent residence as an immigrant. The term "lawful permanent resident" includes conditional residents. If you check this box, write either your Alien Registration Number (A-Number) or USCIS Number in the field next to your selection. At this time, the USCIS Number is the same as the A-Number without the "A" prefix.

4. **An alien authorized to work:** If you are not a citizen or national of the United States or a lawful permanent resident, but are authorized to work in the United States, check this box.

   If you check this box:

   a. Record the date that your employment authorization expires, if any. Aliens whose employment authorization does not expire, such as refugees, asylees, and certain citizens of the Federated States of Micronesia, the Republic of the Marshall Islands, or Palau, may write "N/A" on this line.

   b. Next, enter your Alien Registration Number (A-Number)/USCIS Number. At this time, the USCIS Number is the same as your A-Number without the "A" prefix. If you have not received an A-Number/USCIS Number, record your Admission Number. You can find your Admission Number on Form I-94, "Arrival-Departure Record," or as directed by USCIS or U.S. Customs and Border Protection (CBP).

      (1) If you obtained your admission number from CBP in connection with your arrival in the United States, then also record information about the foreign passport you used to enter the United States (number and country of issuance).

      (2) If you obtained your admission number from USCIS *within the United States*, or you entered the United States without a foreign passport, you must write "N/A" in the Foreign Passport Number and Country of Issuance fields.

Sign your name in the "Signature of Employee" block and record the date you completed and signed Section 1. By signing and dating this form, you attest that the citizenship or immigration status you selected is correct and that you are aware that you may be imprisoned and/or fined for making false statements or using false documentation when completing this form. To fully complete this form, you must present to your employer documentation that establishes your identity and employment authorization. Choose which documents to present from the Lists of Acceptable Documents, found on the last page of this form. You must present this documentation no later than the third day after beginning employment, although you may present the required documentation before this date.

Preparer and/or Translator Certification

The Preparer and/or Translator Certification must be completed if the employee requires assistance to complete Section 1 (e.g., the employee needs the instructions or responses translated, someone other than the employee fills out the information blocks, or someone with disabilities needs additional assistance). The employee must still sign Section 1.

Minors and Certain Employees with Disabilities (Special Placement)

Parents or legal guardians assisting minors (individuals under 18) and certain employees with disabilities should review the guidelines in the *Handbook for Employers: Instructions for Completing Form I-9 (M-274)* on **www.uscis.gov/ I-9Central** before completing Section 1. These individuals have special procedures for establishing identity if they cannot present an identity document for Form I-9. The special procedures include **(1)** the parent or legal guardian filling out Section 1 and writing "minor under age 18" or "special placement," whichever applies, in the employee signature block; and **(2)** the employer writing "minor under age 18" or "special placement" under List B in Section 2.

Section 2. Employer or Authorized Representative Review and Verification

Before completing Section 2, employers must ensure that Section 1 is completed properly and on time. Employers may not ask an individual to complete Section 1 before he or she has accepted a job offer.

Employers or their authorized representative must complete Section 2 by examining evidence of identity and employment authorization within 3 business days of the employee's first day of employment. For example, if an employee begins employment on Monday, the employer must complete Section 2 by Thursday of that week. However, if an employer hires an individual for less than 3 business days, Section 2 must be completed no later than the first day of employment. An employer may complete Form I-9 before the first day of employment if the employer has offered the individual a job and the individual has accepted.

Employers cannot specify which document(s) employees may present from the Lists of Acceptable Documents, found on the last page of Form I-9, to establish identity and employment authorization. Employees must present one selection from List A **OR** a combination of one selection from List B and one selection from List C. List A contains documents that show both identity and employment authorization. Some List A documents are combination documents. The employee must present combination documents together to be considered a List A document. For example, a foreign passport and a Form I-94 containing an endorsement of the alien's nonimmigrant status must be presented together to be considered a List A document. List B contains documents that show identity only, and List C contains documents that show employment authorization only. If an employee presents a List A document, he or she should **not** present a List B and List C document, and vice versa. If an employer participates in E-Verify, the List B document must include a photograph.

In the field below the Section 2 introduction, employers must enter the last name, first name and middle initial, if any, that the employee entered in Section 1. This will help to identify the pages of the form should they get separated.

Employers or their authorized representative must:

1. Physically examine each original document the employee presents to determine if it reasonably appears to be genuine and to relate to the person presenting it. The person who examines the documents must be the same person who signs Section 2. The examiner of the documents and the employee must both be physically present during the examination of the employee's documents.

2. Record the document title shown on the Lists of Acceptable Documents, issuing authority, document number and expiration date (if any) from the original document(s) the employee presents. You may write "N/A" in any unused fields.

    If the employee is a student or exchange visitor who presented a foreign passport with a Form I-94, the employer should also enter in Section 2:

    a. The student's Form I-20 or DS-2019 number (Student and Exchange Visitor Information System-SEVIS Number); **and** the program end date from Form I-20 or DS-2019.

3. Under Certification, enter the employee's first day of employment. Temporary staffing agencies may enter the first day the employee was placed in a job pool. Recruiters and recruiters for a fee do not enter the employee's first day of employment.

4. Provide the name and title of the person completing Section 2 in the Signature of Employer or Authorized Representative field.

5. Sign and date the attestation on the date Section 2 is completed.

6. Record the employer's business name and address.

7. Return the employee's documentation.

Employers may, but are not required to, photocopy the document(s) presented. If photocopies are made, they should be made for **ALL** new hires or reverifications. Photocopies must be retained and presented with Form I-9 in case of an inspection by DHS or other federal government agency. Employers must always complete Section 2 even if they photocopy an employee's document(s). Making photocopies of an employee's document(s) cannot take the place of completing Form I-9. Employers are still responsible for completing and retaining Form I-9.

Unexpired Documents

Generally, only unexpired, original documentation is acceptable. The only exception is that an employee may present a certified copy of a birth certificate. Additionally, in some instances, a document that appears to be expired may be acceptable if the expiration date shown on the face of the document has been extended, such as for individuals with temporary protected status. Refer to the *Handbook for Employers: Instructions for Completing Form I-9 (M-274)* or I-9 Central (www.uscis.gov/I-9Central) for examples.

Receipts

If an employee is unable to present a required document (or documents), the employee can present an acceptable receipt in lieu of a document from the Lists of Acceptable Documents on the last page of this form. Receipts showing that a person has applied for an initial grant of employment authorization, or for renewal of employment authorization, are not acceptable. Employers cannot accept receipts if employment will last less than 3 days. Receipts are acceptable when completing Form I-9 for a new hire or when reverification is required.

Employees must present receipts within 3 business days of their first day of employment, or in the case of reverification, by the date that reverification is required, and must present valid replacement documents within the time frames described below.

There are three types of acceptable receipts:

1. A receipt showing that the employee has applied to replace a document that was lost, stolen or damaged. The employee must present the actual document within 90 days from the date of hire.

2. The arrival portion of Form I-94/I-94A with a temporary I-551 stamp and a photograph of the individual. The employee must present the actual Permanent Resident Card (Form I-551) by the expiration date of the temporary I-551 stamp, or, if there is no expiration date, within 1 year from the date of issue.

3. The departure portion of Form I-94/I-94A with a refugee admission stamp. The employee must present an unexpired Employment Authorization Document (Form I-766) or a combination of a List B document and an unrestricted Social Security card within 90 days.

When the employee provides an acceptable receipt, the employer should:

1. Record the document title in Section 2 under the sections titled List A, List B, or List C, as applicable.

2. Write the word "receipt" and its document number in the "Document Number" field. Record the last day that the receipt is valid in the "Expiration Date" field.

By the end of the receipt validity period, the employer should:

1. Cross out the word "receipt" and any accompanying document number and expiration date.

2. Record the number and other required document information from the actual document presented.

3. Initial and date the change.

See the *Handbook for Employers: Instructions for Completing Form I-9 (M-274)* at **www.uscis.gov/I-9Central** for more information on receipts.

Section 3. Reverification and Rehires

Employers or their authorized representatives should complete Section 3 when reverifying that an employee is authorized to work. When rehiring an employee within 3 years of the date Form I-9 was originally completed, employers have the option to complete a new Form I-9 or complete Section 3. When completing Section 3 in either a reverification or rehire situation, if the employee's name has changed, record the name change in Block A.

For employees who provide an employment authorization expiration date in Section 1, employers must reverify employment authorization on or before the date provided.

Some employees may write "N/A" in the space provided for the expiration date in Section 1 if they are aliens whose employment authorization does not expire (e.g., asylees, refugees, certain citizens of the Federated States of Micronesia, the Republic of the Marshall Islands, or Palau). Reverification does not apply for such employees unless they chose to present evidence of employment authorization in Section 2 that contains an expiration date and requires reverification, such as Form I-766, Employment Authorization Document.

Reverification applies if evidence of employment authorization (List A or List C document) presented in Section 2 expires. However, employers should not reverify:

1. U.S. citizens and noncitizen nationals; or

2. Lawful permanent residents who presented a Permanent Resident Card (Form I-551) for Section 2.

Reverification does not apply to List B documents.

If both Section 1 and Section 2 indicate expiration dates triggering the reverification requirement, the employer should reverify by the earlier date.

For reverification, an employee must present unexpired documentation from either List A or List C showing he or she is still authorized to work. Employers CANNOT require the employee to present a particular document from List A or List C. The employee may choose which document to present.

To complete Section 3, employers should follow these instructions:

1. Complete Block A if an employee's name has changed at the time you complete Section 3.

2. Complete Block B with the date of rehire if you rehire an employee within 3 years of the date this form was originally completed, and the employee is still authorized to be employed on the same basis as previously indicated on this form. Also complete the "Signature of Employer or Authorized Representative" block.

3. Complete Block C if:

    a. The employment authorization or employment authorization document of a current employee is about to expire and requires reverification; or

    b. You rehire an employee within 3 years of the date this form was originally completed and his or her employment authorization or employment authorization document has expired. (Complete Block B for this employee as well.)

    To complete Block C:

    a. Examine either a List A or List C document the employee presents that shows that the employee is currently authorized to work in the United States; and

    b. Record the document title, document number, and expiration date (if any).

4. After completing block A, B or C, complete the "Signature of Employer or Authorized Representative" block, including the date.

    For reverification purposes, employers may either complete Section 3 of a new Form I-9 or Section 3 of the previously completed Form I-9. Any new pages of Form I-9 completed during reverification must be attached to the employee's original Form I-9. If you choose to complete Section 3 of a new Form I-9, you may attach just the page containing Section 3, with the employee's name entered at the top of the page, to the employee's original Form I-9. If there is a more current version of Form I-9 at the time of reverification, you must complete Section 3 of that version of the form.

What Is the Filing Fee?

There is no fee for completing Form I-9. This form is not filed with USCIS or any government agency. Form I-9 must be retained by the employer and made available for inspection by U.S. Government officials as specified in the **"USCIS Privacy Act Statement"** below.

USCIS Forms and Information

For more detailed information about completing Form I-9, employers and employees should refer to the *Handbook for Employers: Instructions for Completing Form I-9 (M-274)*.

You can also obtain information about Form I-9 from the USCIS Web site at www.uscis.gov/I-9Central, by e-mailing USCIS at I-9Central@dhs.gov, or by calling 1-888-464-4218. For TDD (hearing impaired), call 1-877-875-6028.

To obtain USCIS forms or the *Handbook for Employers*, you can download them from the USCIS Web site at www.uscis.gov/forms. You may order USCIS forms by calling our toll-free number at 1-800-870-3676. You may also obtain forms and information by contacting the USCIS National Customer Service Center at 1-800-375-5283. For TDD (hearing impaired), call 1-800-767-1833.

Information about E-Verify, a free and voluntary program that allows participating employers to electronically verify the employment eligibility of their newly hired employees, can be obtained from the USCIS Web site at www.dhs.gov/E-Verify, by e-mailing USCIS at E-Verify@dhs.gov or by calling 1-888-464-4218. For TDD (hearing impaired), call 1-877-875-6028.

Employees with questions about Form I-9 and/or E-Verify can reach the USCIS employee hotline by calling 1-888-897-7781. For TDD (hearing impaired), call 1-877-875-6028.

Photocopying and Retaining Form I-9

A blank Form I-9 may be reproduced, provided all sides are copied. The instructions and Lists of Acceptable Documents must be available to all employees completing this form. Employers must retain each employee's completed Form I-9 for as long as the individual works for the employer. Employers are required to retain the pages of the form on which the employee and employer enter data. If copies of documentation presented by the employee are made, those copies must also be kept with the form. Once the individual's employment ends, the employer must retain this form for either 3 years after the date of hire or 1 year after the date employment ended, whichever is later.

Form I-9 may be signed and retained electronically, in compliance with Department of Homeland Security regulations at 8 CFR 274a.2.

USCIS Privacy Act Statement

AUTHORITIES: The authority for collecting this information is the Immigration Reform and Control Act of 1986, Public Law 99-603 (8 USC 1324a).

PURPOSE: This information is collected by employers to comply with the requirements of the Immigration Reform and Control Act of 1986. This law requires that employers verify the identity and employment authorization of individuals they hire for employment to preclude the unlawful hiring, or recruiting or referring for a fee, of aliens who are not authorized to work in the United States.

DISCLOSURE: Submission of the information required in this form is voluntary. However, failure of the employer to ensure proper completion of this form for each employee may result in the imposition of civil or criminal penalties. In addition, employing individuals knowing that they are unauthorized to work in the United States may subject the employer to civil and/or criminal penalties.

ROUTINE USES: This information will be used by employers as a record of their basis for determining eligibility of an employee to work in the United States. The employer will keep this form and make it available for inspection by authorized officials of the Department of Homeland Security, Department of Labor, and Office of Special Counsel for Immigration-Related Unfair Employment Practices.

Paperwork Reduction Act

An agency may not conduct or sponsor an information collection and a person is not required to respond to a collection of information unless it displays a currently valid OMB control number. The public reporting burden for this collection of information is estimated at 35 minutes per response, including the time for reviewing instructions and completing and retaining the form. Send comments regarding this burden estimate or any other aspect of this collection of information, including suggestions for reducing this burden, to: U.S. Citizenship and Immigration Services, Regulatory Coordination Division, Office of Policy and Strategy, 20 Massachusetts Avenue NW, Washington, DC 20529-2140; OMB No. 1615-0047. **Do not mail your completed Form I-9 to this address.**

Employment Eligibility Verification

Department of Homeland Security
U.S. Citizenship and Immigration Services

USCIS
Form I-9
OMB No. 1615-0047
Expires 03/31/2016

▶START HERE. Read instructions carefully before completing this form. The instructions must be available during completion of this form.

ANTI-DISCRIMINATION NOTICE: It is illegal to discriminate against work-authorized individuals. Employers **CANNOT** specify which document(s) they will accept from an employee. The refusal to hire an individual because the documentation presented has a future expiration date may also constitute illegal discrimination.

Section 1. Employee Information and Attestation *(Employees must complete and sign Section 1 of Form I-9 no later than the **first day of employment**, but not before accepting a job offer.)*

Last Name *(Family Name)*	First Name *(Given Name)*	Middle Initial	Other Names Used *(if any)*

Address *(Street Number and Name)*	Apt. Number	City or Town	State	Zip Code

Date of Birth *(mm/dd/yyyy)*	U.S. Social Security Number	E-mail Address	Telephone Number
	☐☐☐-☐☐-☐☐☐☐		

I am aware that federal law provides for imprisonment and/or fines for false statements or use of false documents in connection with the completion of this form.

I attest, under penalty of perjury, that I am (check one of the following):

☐ A citizen of the United States

☐ A noncitizen national of the United States *(See instructions)*

☐ A lawful permanent resident (Alien Registration Number/USCIS Number): _____

☐ An alien authorized to work until (expiration date, if applicable, mm/dd/yyyy) _____ . Some aliens may write "N/A" in this field.
(See instructions)

For aliens authorized to work, provide your Alien Registration Number/USCIS Number **OR** Form I-94 Admission Number:

1. Alien Registration Number/USCIS Number: _____

OR

2. Form I-94 Admission Number: _____

If you obtained your admission number from CBP in connection with your arrival in the United States, include the following:

Foreign Passport Number: _____

Country of Issuance: _____

Some aliens may write "N/A" on the Foreign Passport Number and Country of Issuance fields. *(See instructions)*

3-D Barcode
Do Not Write in This Space

Signature of Employee:	Date *(mm/dd/yyyy)*:

Preparer and/or Translator Certification *(To be completed and signed if Section 1 is prepared by a person other than the employee.)*

I attest, under penalty of perjury, that I have assisted in the completion of this form and that to the best of my knowledge the information is true and correct.

Signature of Preparer or Translator:	Date *(mm/dd/yyyy)*:

Last Name *(Family Name)*	First Name *(Given Name)*

Address *(Street Number and Name)*	City or Town	State	Zip Code

🛑 *Employer Completes Next Page* 🛑

Section 2. Employer or Authorized Representative Review and Verification

(Employers or their authorized representative must complete and sign Section 2 within 3 business days of the employee's first day of employment. You must physically examine one document from List A OR examine a combination of one document from List B and one document from List C as listed on the "Lists of Acceptable Documents" on the next page of this form. For each document you review, record the following information: document title, issuing authority, document number, and expiration date, if any.)

Employee Last Name, First Name and Middle Initial from Section 1:

List A	OR	List B	AND	List C
Identity and Employment Authorization		**Identity**		**Employment Authorization**

List A	List B	List C
Document Title:	Document Title:	Document Title:
Issuing Authority:	Issuing Authority:	Issuing Authority:
Document Number:	Document Number:	Document Number:
Expiration Date *(if any)(mm/dd/yyyy)*:	Expiration Date *(if any)(mm/dd/yyyy)*:	Expiration Date *(if any)(mm/dd/yyyy)*:
Document Title:		
Issuing Authority:		
Document Number:		
Expiration Date *(if any)(mm/dd/yyyy)*:		
Document Title:		**3-D Barcode**
Issuing Authority:		**Do Not Write in This Space**
Document Number:		
Expiration Date *(if any)(mm/dd/yyyy)*:		

Certification

I attest, under penalty of perjury, that (1) I have examined the document(s) presented by the above-named employee, (2) the above-listed document(s) appear to be genuine and to relate to the employee named, and (3) to the best of my knowledge the employee is authorized to work in the United States.

The employee's first day of employment *(mm/dd/yyyy)*: _____ *(See instructions for exemptions.)*

Signature of Employer or Authorized Representative	Date *(mm/dd/yyyy)*	Title of Employer or Authorized Representative
Last Name *(Family Name)*	First Name *(Given Name)*	Employer's Business or Organization Name

Employer's Business or Organization Address *(Street Number and Name)*	City or Town	State	Zip Code

Section 3. Reverification and Rehires *(To be completed and signed by employer or authorized representative.)*

A. New Name *(if applicable)* Last Name *(Family Name)* First Name *(Given Name)*	Middle Initial	**B.** Date of Rehire *(if applicable) (mm/dd/yyyy)*:

C. If employee's previous grant of employment authorization has expired, provide the information for the document from List A or List C the employee presented that establishes current employment authorization in the space provided below.

Document Title:	Document Number:	Expiration Date *(if any)(mm/dd/yyyy)*:

I attest, under penalty of perjury, that to the best of my knowledge, this employee is authorized to work in the United States, and if the employee presented document(s), the document(s) I have examined appear to be genuine and to relate to the individual.

Signature of Employer or Authorized Representative:	Date *(mm/dd/yyyy)*:	Print Name of Employer or Authorized Representative:

LISTS OF ACCEPTABLE DOCUMENTS
All documents must be UNEXPIRED

Employees may present one selection from List A
or a combination of one selection from List B and one selection from List C.

LIST A		LIST B	LIST C
Documents that Establish Both Identity and Employment Authorization	OR	**Documents that Establish Identity** AND	**Documents that Establish Employment Authorization**
1. U.S. Passport or U.S. Passport Card		1. Driver's license or ID card issued by a State or outlying possession of the United States provided it contains a photograph or information such as name, date of birth, gender, height, eye color, and address	1. A Social Security Account Number card, unless the card includes one of the following restrictions: (1) NOT VALID FOR EMPLOYMENT (2) VALID FOR WORK ONLY WITH INS AUTHORIZATION (3) VALID FOR WORK ONLY WITH DHS AUTHORIZATION
2. Permanent Resident Card or Alien Registration Receipt Card (Form I-551)			
3. Foreign passport that contains a temporary I-551 stamp or temporary I-551 printed notation on a machine-readable immigrant visa		2. ID card issued by federal, state or local government agencies or entities, provided it contains a photograph or information such as name, date of birth, gender, height, eye color, and address	
4. Employment Authorization Document that contains a photograph (Form I-766)		3. School ID card with a photograph	2. Certification of Birth Abroad issued by the Department of State (Form FS-545)
		4. Voter's registration card	3. Certification of Report of Birth issued by the Department of State (Form DS-1350)
5. For a nonimmigrant alien authorized to work for a specific employer because of his or her status: **a.** Foreign passport; and **b.** Form I-94 or Form I-94A that has the following: (1) The same name as the passport; and (2) An endorsement of the alien's nonimmigrant status as long as that period of endorsement has not yet expired and the proposed employment is not in conflict with any restrictions or limitations identified on the form.		5. U.S. Military card or draft record	4. Original or certified copy of birth certificate issued by a State, county, municipal authority, or territory of the United States bearing an official seal
		6. Military dependent's ID card	
		7. U.S. Coast Guard Merchant Mariner Card	
		8. Native American tribal document	5. Native American tribal document
		9. Driver's license issued by a Canadian government authority	6. U.S. Citizen ID Card (Form I-197)
		For persons under age 18 who are unable to present a document listed above:	7. Identification Card for Use of Resident Citizen in the United States (Form I-179)
6. Passport from the Federated States of Micronesia (FSM) or the Republic of the Marshall Islands (RMI) with Form I-94 or Form I-94A indicating nonimmigrant admission under the Compact of Free Association Between the United States and the FSM or RMI		10. School record or report card	8. Employment authorization document issued by the Department of Homeland Security
		11. Clinic, doctor, or hospital record	
		12. Day-care or nursery school record	

Illustrations of many of these documents appear in Part 8 of the Handbook for Employers (M-274).

Refer to Section 2 of the instructions, titled "Employer or Authorized Representative Review and Verification," for more information about acceptable receipts.

Chapter 12
JOBSITE SAFETY AND
ENVIRONMENTAL FACTORS

Chapter Survey...

⇨ *Safety Standards*

⇨ *Safe Hiring and Training*

⇨ *Substance Abuse Policies*

⇨ *Safety Equipment*

⇨ *Emergency Action Plan*

⇨ *OSHA Recordkeeping*

⇨ *OSHA Injury Decision Tree*

⇨ *Material Safety Data Sheets (MSDS)*

⇨ *Underground Utility Safety*

⇨ *Overhead Power Line Safety*

⇨ *Benefits of Providing a Safe and Healthy Workplace*

⇨ *Employee Rights*

⇨ *Penalties*

⇨ *Environmental Considerations*

⇨ *U.S. Environmental Protection Agency*

⇨ *Utah Department of Environmental Quality*

⇨ *Environmental Law*

⇨ *Air Quality*

⇨ *Asbestos*

⇨ *Clean Water Act*

⇨ *Sedimentation and Erosion Control Measures*

⇨ *Hazardous and Non-Hazardous Waste*

⇨ *Hazardous Substances*

⇨ *Lead*

⇨ *Remodeling or Renovating a Home with Lead-Based Paint (Lead PRE)*

⇨ *Sample OSHA Forms 300, 300A, and 301*

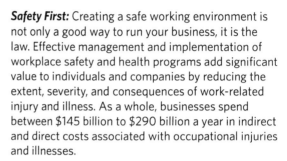

Safety First: Creating a safe working environment is not only a good way to run your business, it is the law. Effective management and implementation of workplace safety and health programs add significant value to individuals and companies by reducing the extent, severity, and consequences of work-related injury and illness. As a whole, businesses spend between $145 billion to $290 billion a year in indirect and direct costs associated with occupational injuries and illnesses.

✓ Workplace injuries and illnesses are reduced by approximately 20 to 40 percent when employers establish safety and health programs.

✓ Workers' compensation premiums, employee retraining costs, and absenteeism are decreased by reducing workplace injuries and illnesses.

✓ Increased workplace safety results in increased productivity and morale and ultimately, profits.

Safety Standards

Understanding OSHA: The Occupational Safety and Health Administration (OSHA) was established by the Occupational Safety and Health Act of 1970 (OSH Act). All employers are subject to federal OSHA requirements and some states have adopted a state plan. State standards are at least as strict as the federal plan. The first step to complying with OSHA is to learn the published standards.

The OSHA standards that apply to the construction industry are

✓ 29 CFR 1926, Safety and Health Regulations for the Construction Industry;

✓ 29 CFR 1910, Occupational Safety and Health Standards; and

✓ 29 CFR 1904, Recording and Reporting Occupational Injuries and Illnesses.

It is the employer's responsibility to understand the OSHA standards and quickly correct any violations.

Putting together a safety program with these standards in mind can help maximize employee safety and prevent violations before they occur.

OSHA Poster: All employers must post the OSHA poster (or state plan equivalent) in a prominent location in the workplace. In construction, employees are generally dispersed to different sites and the OSHA poster must be posted at the location to which employees report each day.

The OSHA poster is downloadable from the OSHA website (www.osha.gov). This website also has useful links to many safety and environmental topics including compliance assistance and laws and regulations. For more information about OSHA, contact

> *Occupational Safety and Health*
> *Administration (OSHA)*
> *Office of Small Business Assistance*
> *Directorate of Cooperative and State Programs*
> *200 Constitution Avenue, NW*
> *Washington, DC 20210*
>
> *Phone: 1-800-321-6742 (OSHA)*
>
> *Website: www.osha.gov*

✓ **OSHA Construction Safety Act:** The Contract Work Hours and Safety Standards Act, commonly known as the Construction Safety Act, sets safety standards for construction contracts on federal projects.

Utah OSHA: Utah has a state-adopted OSHA plan that is "at least as effective" as the federal OSHA program. The Utah Occupational Safety and Health (UOSH) program is administered through the Utah Occupational Safety and Health Administration (UOSHA) of the Labor Commission. The Utah Occupational Safety and Health Act is found in the Utah Code §34A-6-101 through §34A-6-307. The administrative rules are found in the Utah Administrative Code, Title R614.

For further information, contact:

> *Utah OSHA*
> *160 East 300 South, 3rd Floor*
> *P O Box 146650*
> *Salt Lake City UT 84114-6650*
>
> *Phone: (801) 530-6901*
> *Fax: (801) 530-7606*
> *Toll-free in Utah 1-800-530-5090*
>
> *Website: laborcommission.utah.gov/divisions/UOSH*

SHARP Program: The Utah OSHA Consultation program provides employers with services to evaluate workplace safety and health concerns. This program uses a non-penalty approach and is free of charge to the employer. The Safety and Health Achievement Recognition Program (SHARP) provides a free and effective worksite safety program to smaller businesses. Businesses who satisfy specific SHARP requirements are removed from Utah OSH's programmed inspection list for a period of 18 months. To qualify, a business must have fewer than 250 employees at one site (or no more than 500 total employees nationwide). If your company successfully completes the SHARP program, it will receive formal recognition from the Secretary of Labor, UOSH, and the Utah Labor Commission. Many insurance carriers offer discounts to businesses who successfully complete the SHARP program. All requests to participate in the SHARP program are directed to the OSHA Consultation Division at (801) 530-6855.

The Compliance Division of the Utah OSHA has several resources available to employers. Resources include

✓ online training resources and useful links;

✓ special training programs for the construction industry;

✓ seminars and workshops; and

✓ reference materials including posters, sample programs, and recordkeeping resources.

Safe Hiring and Training

Hire Safe: The first step to improving safety in the workplace is to hire employees who have a good safety track record. The majority of accidents are caused by unsafe actions, not unsafe conditions. It is important to do thorough applicant screening and check all employment references. If you find that an applicant had safety accidents with a previous employer, chances for additional accidents while working for you are greater.

Regular Training: Training on safety practices and policies should be conducted regularly. New employees should receive a copy of your safety policies and sign off on them. Brief 10-minute training sessions can be conducted at the jobsite with your crew daily. During these training sessions, you can review policies and receive feedback from your employees on potential hazards that occur on the jobsite.

* *
Conduct regular safety training for your employees.
* *

Substance Abuse Policies

Your Bottom Line: Substance abuse in the workplace can have a profound effect on your business and significantly impact your bottom line. This problem costs American businesses more than $100 billion every year. This loss occurs in

✓ workers' compensation claims,

✓ medical costs,

✓ absenteeism,

✓ lost productivity, and

✓ employee turnover.

For this reason, you should develop a substance free workplace program and make sure that all employees know that substance abuse is not permitted.

Employee Program: Develop your program together with your employees. Talk about the benefits of having a substance free workplace and your concern for them to have a safe and healthy work environment. Eliminating substance abuse increases productivity, reduces accidents, and lowers insurance claim costs. Solicit input from your employees on how to implement the program in the workplace and any other suggestions they have.

Consider this...

Ninety percent of large businesses have drug-free workplace programs in place today, while 5 percent to 10 percent of small- and medium-sized businesses have implemented similar programs. The irony here is that 75 percent of employed Americans work for small- and medium-sized businesses.

Communicate Your Policy: Once you have developed a program, distribute the policy to all employees and have them sign off on it. Your policies should expressly prohibit the illegal use of drugs and/or abuse of alcohol by any employee and spell out the consequences of policy violations. All new employees should receive

your policy as part of their orientation. You should also check with your workers' compensation carrier to see if you can receive a credit for having this policy in place.

* *
Encourage employee participation in developing company safety programs.
* *

Safety Equipment

Prevent Injuries: Using the proper safety equipment can lower the occurrence of injuries on the job. This equipment might include

✓ hard hats,

✓ safety shoes/boots,

✓ protective eyewear,

✓ gloves,

✓ fall protection,

✓ hearing protection,

✓ respirators,

✓ protective coveralls, and

✓ face shields.

Make sure you consult OSHA safety standards to determine what safety equipment is required by law and assess your jobsite to determine additional equipment you want your employees to have.

Emergency Action Plan

Your Plan of Action: OSHA regulations require you have an emergency action plan. If you have more than 10 employees, your plan must be in writing. If you have fewer than 10 employees, you may communicate the plan orally to employees. The emergency action plan must include procedures for

✓ reporting a fire or other emergency;

✓ emergency evacuation;

✓ employees who remain for critical operations before evacuating;

✓ accounting for all employees after evacuation; and

✓ employees performing rescue or medical duties.

The plan should also include the name or job title of the plan administrator. You must review the plan with your employees, designate and train employees to assist in a safe evacuation, and have a distinctive signal that serves as an employee alarm system.

Other OSHA recommendations, although not required, for inclusion in the emergency action plan are

✓ a description of the employee alarm system defining each of the alarm signals and corresponding employee action;

✓ an alternative site for communication in the event of a fire or explosion; and

✓ a secure location, either onsite or offsite, where important information, such as accounting documents, legal files, and employee emergency contact numbers, can be stored.

OSHA Recordkeeping

For the Record: Every employer covered by OSHA who has more than 10 employees, except for employers in certain low-hazard industries in the retail, finance, insurance, real estate, and service sectors, must maintain three types of OSHA-specified records of job-related injuries and illnesses.

These forms are located at the end of the chapter.

✓ OSHA Form 300

✓ OSHA Form 300A

✓ OSHA Form 301

The OSHA Form 300 is an injury/illness log, with a separate line entry for each recordable injury or illness. Such events include work-related deaths, injuries, and illnesses other than minor injuries that require only first aid treatment and that do not involve medical treatment, loss of consciousness, restriction of work, days away from work, or transfer to another job. Construction site operations that last for more than one year must keep a separate OSHA 300 log.

Each year, the employer must conspicuously post in the workplace a Form 300A, which includes a summary of the previous year's work-related injuries and illnesses. The data from Form 300 is used to complete this form. Form 300A must be posted by February 1 and kept in place until at least April 30 following the year covered by the form.

OSHA Form 301 is an individual incident report that provides added detail about each specific recordable injury or illness. An alternative form, such as an insurance or workers' compensation form that provides the same details may be substituted for OSHA Form 301.

Who Needs to Complete the Forms? Employers with 10 or fewer employees are exempt from maintaining these records. However, such employers must keep these records if they receive an annual illness and injury survey form either from the Bureau of Labor Statistics (BLS) or from OSHA. Employers selected for these surveys will be notified before the end of the prior year to begin keeping records during the year covered by the survey.

Timeframe to Retain Records: OSHA records must be kept by the employer for five years following the year to which they pertain.

Exposure Records and Medical Records: Exposure records (including employee exposure to toxic substances and harmful physical agents) must be maintained for 30 years and medical records for the duration of employment plus 30 years. Analysis using exposure or medical records must be kept for 30 years.

Toxic substances and harmful agents include

✓ any material listed in the National Institute for Occupational Safety and Health (NIOSH) Registry of Toxic Effects of Chemical Hazards (RTECHS);

✓ substances which have evidenced an acute or chronic health hazard in testing conducted by or known to the employer; and

✓ substances in a material safety data sheet kept by or known to the employer, indicating that the material may pose a health hazard.

Reporting Fatalities and Hospitalizations: When a work-related fatality or incident that requires hospitalization of three or more employees occurs,

✓ employers must orally report the fatality or incident to the nearest OSHA Area Office within eight hours; and

✓ if a death occurs within 30 days of the incident, employers must report it within eight hours.

Employers do not need to report a death occurring more than 30 days after a work-related incident.

Recordable Illnesses and Injuries: Cases that meet the general recording criteria involve a significant injury or illness diagnosed by a physician or other licensed health care professional, even if it does not result in death, days away from work, restricted work or job transfer, medical treatment beyond first aid, or loss of consciousness.

Medical Treatment Defined: Medical treatment means the management and care of a patient to combat a disease or disorder. It does not include

✓ visits to a physician or other licensed health care professional solely for observation or counseling;

✓ conduct of diagnostic procedures, such as x-rays and blood tests, including the administration of prescription medications used solely for diagnostic purposes (i.e., eye drops to dilate pupils); or

✓ first aid.

First Aid Defined: The following treatments are considered first aid according to 29 CFR 1904:

✓ Using a non-prescription medication at the non-prescription strength

✓ Administering tetanus immunizations (other immunizations, such as the Hepatitis B vaccine or rabies vaccine, are considered medical treatment)

✓ Cleaning, flushing or soaking wounds on the surface of the skin

✓ Using wound coverings such as bandages, Band-Aids™, gauze pads, etc.; or using butterfly bandages or Steri-Strips™; other wound closing devices such as sutures, staples, etc., are considered medical treatment

✓ Using hot or cold therapy

✓ Using any non-rigid means of support, such as elastic bandages, wraps, non-rigid back belts, etc.; devices with rigid stays or other systems designed to immobilize parts of the body are considered medical treatment for recordkeeping purposes

✓ Using temporary immobilization devices while transporting an accident victim (i.e., splints, slings, neck collars, back boards, etc.)

✓ Drilling of a fingernail or toenail to relieve pressure or draining fluid from a blister

✓ Using eye patches

✓ Removing foreign bodies from the eye using only irrigation or a cotton swab

✓ Removing splinters or foreign material from areas other than the eye by irrigation, tweezers, cotton swabs or other simple means

✓ Using finger guards

✓ Using massages; physical therapy or chiropractic treatment are considered medical treatment for recordkeeping purposes

✓ Drinking fluids for relief of heat stress

OSHA Injury Decision Tree

The OSHA injury decision tree shows the steps involved in making the determination for recording work-related injuries or illnesses.

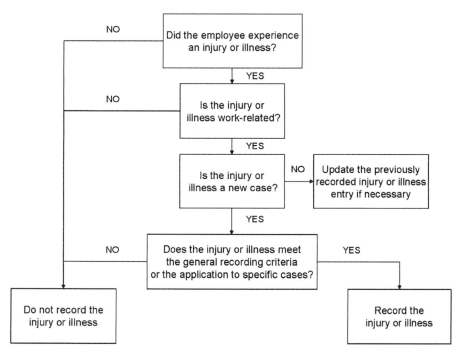

Material Safety Data Sheets (MSDS)

Chemical Safety: Material safety data sheets (MSDS) are a requirement of OSHA's Hazard Communication Standard (HCS). The purpose of the HCS is to ensure chemical safety in the workplace. Requirements of the MSDS program include:

✓ Manufacturers and importers of hazardous materials are required to conduct hazard evaluations of the products they manufacture or import.

✓ If a product is found to be hazardous under the terms of the standard, the manufacturer or importer must so indicate on containers of the material, and the first shipment of the material to a new customer must include a material safety data sheet (MSDS).

✓ Employers must use these MSDSs to train their employees to recognize and avoid the hazards presented by the materials.

Emergency Treatment: Employers must keep MSDSs on hand for all chemicals used in the workplace. The MSDS provides emergency information in case of contact with the chemical either internally or externally. The MSDS also explains the proper precautions to take when using a chemical. In the event of an OSHA inspection, the compliance officer will confirm that all MSDSs are at the worksite.

Inspection Guidelines: OSHA publishes inspection guidelines for enforcement of the Hazard Communication Standard. A summary of items that are reviewed during an inspection is included below:

✓ Is there a written hazard communication plan?

✓ Who is responsible for obtaining and maintaining MSDSs?

✓ Is there an MSDS for every chemical used?

✓ How are the MSDSs maintained (i.e., in notebooks in the work area(s), in a pickup truck at the jobsite, etc.) and do employees have proper access to them?

✓ Who is responsible for conducting training on chemicals and what are the elements of the training program?

The detailed procedure can be downloaded off the OSHA website (www.osha.gov).

Underground Utility Safety

Excavating without identifying underground utilities is a safety issue and can cost you unnecessary fines, repair costs, and utility outages. Although laws on marking underground utilities vary from state to state, contractors should identify underground utilities before digging on

✓ public and private property;

✓ public streets;

✓ alleys;

✓ utility easements; and

✓ all other rights-of-way.

In order to request a locater to come out to your site and locate underground utilities, the Common Ground Alliance (CGA) can be reached by calling 811. Your call is then routed to a local One Call Center. If you prefer to contact your local One Call Center directly, contact information for each state is located on the CGA website at http://call811.com/811-your-state.

Overhead Power Line Safety

OSHA has several programs focused on safety for those who work around overhead power lines. Listed below are a few key points from OSHA to consider when formulating a health and safety program and worksite planning.

Considerations include the following:

✓ perform a thorough site survey prior to beginning construction work;

✓ stay at least 10 feet away from overhead power lines;

✓ assume that all power lines are energized unless confirmed by proper authorities;

✓ call the utility company if overhead lines are present to determine voltage and if the lines can be shut off or insulated during construction work;

✓ use non-conductive ladders when working around overhead power lines;

✓ keep conductive objects at least 10 feet away from overhead power lines unless otherwise trained and qualified to use insulated tools specifically designed for high voltage lines; and

✓ perform thorough research on the location and voltage of overhead power lines when using cranes and heavy equipment to determine a minimum safe distance for operation.

Additional information on overhead power line safety is available on the OSHA website at www.osha.gov.

Benefits of Providing a Safe and Healthy Workplace

Ignoring safety and health regulations in the workplace is detrimental in many ways. Employees are put at risk, company reputation is at stake, and costs are high when accidents happen which effects overall company profits.

The most frequent citations that OSHA issues to the construction industry are for violations pertaining to

✓ scaffolding;

✓ fall protection (scope, application, definitions);

✓ excavations (general requirements and requirements for protective systems);

✓ ladders;

✓ head protection;

✓ hazard communication;

✓ fall protection (training requirements);

✓ construction (general safety and health provisions); and

✓ electrical (wiring methods, design and protection).

Ensuring workers are healthy and safe provides many direct benefits to employers.

✓ lower workers' compensation insurance costs;

✓ reduced medical expenditures;

✓ smaller expenditures for return-to-work programs;

✓ fewer faulty products;

✓ lower costs for job accommodations for injured workers;

✓ less money spent for overtime benefits.

Following safety and health regulations and proper procedures has indirect benefits as well.

✓ increased productivity;

✓ higher quality products;

✓ increased morale;

✓ better labor/management relations;

✓ reduced turnover;

✓ better use of human resources.

The impact of a safety and health program extends beyond the workplace providing employees and their families the security that their incomes are protected, family life is not hindered by injury, and overall reduced stress.

Employee Rights

The OSH Act grants employees several important rights. Among them are the rights to

✓ complain to OSHA about safety and health conditions in their workplace and, to the extent permitted by law, have their identities kept confidential from their employer;

✓ contest the amount of time OSHA allows for correcting violations of standards; and

✓ participate in OSHA workplace inspections.

Retaliation is Prohibited: Private sector employees who exercise their rights under OSHA can be protected against employer reprisal. Employees must notify OSHA within 30 days of the time they learned of the alleged discriminatory action. OSHA will then investigate. If it agrees that discrimination has occurred, OSHA will ask the employer to restore any lost benefits to the affected employee. If necessary, OSHA can initiate legal action against the employer. In such cases, the worker pays no legal fees. The OSHA-approved state plans have similar employee rights provisions, including protections against employer reprisal.

Penalties

OSHA Enforcement: Every establishment covered by the OSH Act is subject to inspection by OSHA

compliance safety and health officers (CSHOs). These individuals are chosen for their knowledge and experience in occupational safety and health. They are thoroughly trained in OSHA standards and in the recognition of occupational safety and health hazards. In states with their own OSHA-approved state plan, state officials conduct inspections, issue citations for violations, and propose penalties in a manner that is at least as strict as the federal program.

The following table illustrates penalty types, descriptions, and amounts assessed to the employer.

Penalty Type and Description	Penalty Amount
Other Than Serious Violation - A violation that has a direct relationship to workplace safety and health, but probably would not cause death or serious physical harm.	Discretionary penalty up to $7,000 for each violation
Serious Violation - A violation where there is substantial probability that death or serious physical harm could result and that the employer knew, or should have known, of the hazard.	Mandatory penalty up to $7,000 for each violation
Willful Violation - A violation that the employer knowingly commits or commits with plain indifference to the law. The employer either knows that what he or she is doing constitutes a violation, or is aware that a hazardous condition existed and made no reasonable effort to eliminate it.	Penalties of up to $70,000 with a minimum penalty of $5,000 for each violation. *If an employer is convicted of a willful violation of a standard that has resulted in the death of an employee, the offense is punishable by a court-imposed fine or by imprisonment for up to six months, or both. A fine of up to $250,000 for an individual, or $500,000 for a corporation, may be imposed for a criminal conviction.*

Repeated Violation - A violation of any standard, regulation, rule, or order where, upon reinspection, a substantially similar violation is found.	Penalties of up to $70,000
Failure to Abate Prior Violation - A violation given when a previous violation has not been corrected.	Civil penalty of up to $7,000 for each day the violation continues beyond the prescribed abatement date
De Minimis Violation – A violation of standards which have no direct or immediate relationship to safety or health.	Violation documented but not cited

Violations may be adjusted depending on the employer's good faith (demonstrated by efforts to comply with the act), history of previous violations, and size of business.

Additional violations for which citations and proposed penalties may be issued upon conviction include the following:

✓ Falsifying records, reports, or applications can bring a fine of $10,000 or up to six months in jail, or both.

✓ Violations of posting requirements can bring a civil penalty of up to $7,000.

✓ Assaulting a compliance officer, or otherwise resisting, opposing, intimidating, or interfering with a compliance officer while they are engaged in the performance of their duties is a criminal offense, subject to a fine of not more than $5,000 and imprisonment for not more than three years.

Citation and penalty procedures may differ somewhat in states with their own occupational safety and health programs.

Inspections: OSHA conducts two general types of inspections: **programmed** and **unprogrammed**.

✓ **Programmed inspections** are performed on establishments with high injury rates.

✓ **Unprogrammed inspections** are used in response to fatalities, catastrophes, and complaints.

Various OSHA publications and documents detail OSHA's policies and procedures for inspections and the penalties for violations.

Environmental Considerations

You need to be aware of the environmental considerations surrounding construction during all phases of the project.

✓ During the **pre-bid phase**, you must learn the regulations that pertain to the project and factor in the cost of compliance into the estimate.

✓ Obtaining the necessary permits occurs during the **pre-construction phase** and environmental responsibilities should be assigned to the construction crew.

✓ Self-audits help ensure compliance during the **construction phase**.

✓ For **post-construction**, you need to ensure that all the close-down procedures were done properly.

Going Green: Integrating eco-friendly practices in your business may help you control costs, tap into a new customer base, and enhance your socially responsible reputation. The demand for energy-efficient building design and construction is increasing. The Energy Star website at www.energystar.gov provides numerous resources on home improvement and commercial and residential construction. The EPA website at www.epa.gov/greenbuilding has information on components of green building, national, state and local funding opportunities, and publications on various environmental topics.

U.S. Environmental Protection Agency

Environmental Regulation: The U.S. Environmental Protection Agency (EPA) leads the nation's environmental science, research, education, and assessment efforts. The EPA works to develop and enforce regulations that implement environmental laws enacted by Congress. The EPA is responsible for researching and setting national standards for a variety of environmental programs and delegates to states the responsibility for issuing permits and for monitoring and enforcing compliance. If national standards are not met, the EPA can issue sanctions and take other steps to assist the states in reaching the desired levels of environmental quality.

Compliance Assistance: The EPA publishes a guide called Managing Your Responsibilities: A Planning Guide for Construction and Development. This publication is available for download at: http://www.epa.gov/compliance/resources/ publications/assistance/sectors/constructmyer.pdf

This guide provides comprehensive information for all types of environmental hazards and compliance requirements. Summarized briefly below are some of the environmental hazards impacting construction projects.

Utah Department of Environmental Quality

The Utah Department of Environmental Quality (DEQ) has several programs and activities available to provide environmental assistance. Permits are required for activities that will have a negative impact on the environment, including the air, land, or water. The website has information about when you are required to obtain an environmental permit and the process for doing so.

Small business assistance is available through the DEQ. These programs help small businesses understand applicable laws and ways to prevent pollution and save money. The small business compliance assistance program includes self-audits and checklists for businesses and free technical assistance and onsite consultation by DEQ employees. The DEQ will meet with businesses in pre-design meetings to determine proper permitting and pollution prevention techniques.

Businesses may also implement an environmental management systems that includes the following steps:

✓ Planning to identify environmental aspects and creating goals to reduce negative impacts;

✓ Implementing a training program and putting operational controls in place;

✓ Monitoring environmental impacts and providing corrective action where needed; and

✓ Reviewing the current program and making continuous improvements.

The DEQ website has additional information on environmental management systems.

The DEQ has three locations each housing different divisions.

Division of Air Quality and Division of Drinking Water
DEQ Building 1
195 North 1950 West
Salt Lake City, Utah 84116

Department of Environmental Quality, Division of Radiation Control, and Division of Environmental Response/ Remediation
DEQ Building 2
195 North 1950 West
Salt Lake City, Utah 84116

Division of Water Quality and Division of Solid and Hazardous Waste
Cannon Health Building
195 North 1950 West
Salt Lake City, Utah 84116

Website: www.deq.utah.gov

Environmental Law

There are several environmental laws that may impact your construction activities.

✓ The Clean Water Act establishes the basic structure for regulating discharges of pollutants into the waters of the United States. This act gives the EPA authority to implement pollution control programs, such as setting wastewater standards for the industry and water quality standards for all contaminants in surface waters. This act is discussed in more depth later in this chapter.

✓ Through the Clean Air Act, the EPA sets limits on how much of a pollutant is allowed in the air anywhere in the United States.

✓ The Endangered Species Act (ESA) protects threatened or endangered species from further harm. You should consider the impact of your construction activities on these species before you start your project.

✓ The National Environmental Policy Act (NEPA) applies to your construction project only if it is considered a "federal action." This act ensures that federal agencies consider environmental impacts in federal planning and decision making and covers construction and post-construction activities.

✓ The National Historic Preservation Act (NHPA) applies to your construction project if your project might have a potential impact on a property that is eligible for or included on the National Register of Historic Places (NRHP).

A thorough environmental assessment of your construction site is recommended for all projects. This assessment allows you to understand the environmental impacts of your project early, causing fewer delays and problems.

Air Quality

Outdoor Air Quality: Air regulations for construction activities are designed to limit the generation of particulate and ozone depleting substances.

Air quality issues that may impact your business are

✓ uncontrolled open burning of debris,

✓ dust generation,

✓ vehicle emissions,

✓ combustion gases from oil-fired equipment, and

✓ releases of chlorofluorocarbons (CFCs).

Indoor Air: Indoor air quality can be just as important as outdoor air quality. For the safety of those on the construction site, you should give special consideration to materials that contain harmful chemicals including

✓ paint/primers,

✓ adhesives,

✓ floor coatings,

✓ carpet, and

✓ plywood/particle board.

Properly installed HVAC units and drain pans are important to avoid biological contaminants that breed in stagnant water. Most air permitting requirements for construction activities are at the state and local level.

Utah Program: The Utah Division of Air Quality Small Business Assistance Program helps small businesses with all aspects of permitting, including approval orders and operating permits.

Approval orders are generally required for most new or modified operations. An approval order is required before starting construction or operation of any emitting equipment and puts limits on these activities.

Operating permits may be required depending on the amount of hazardous air pollutants an operation may potentially emit.

The Utah Division of Air Quality Source Compliance Section conducts inspections and enforces rules and policies to ensure regulatory requirements are met. Businesses are subject to source compliance action notices, compliance advisories, or a notice of violation if violations occur.

Source compliance action notices are issued by the Source Compliance Section for minor compliance issues. These are written warnings and are given to companies where penalties might not be warranted.

Compliance advisories are issued when apparent violations are found during an inspection or review. If a settlement is reached and corrective action is taken in a timely manner, no further administrative action is taken.

A notice of violation is issued if a compliance advisory settlement is not reached or if the action of a business warrants more direct warning. For more information, contact:

Division of Air Quality
195 North 1950 West
Salt Lake City, Utah 84116

Office phone: (801) 536-4400

Hotline: 1-800-458-0145

Website: www.airquality.utah.gov

Be aware of both indoor and outdoor pollution.

Asbestos

Before beginning any demolition or renovation activities on existing buildings, you should evaluate the potential for releasing asbestos. Exposure to asbestos can cause serious health problems and the EPA and OSHA have published rules regulating its production, use, and disposal.

Evaluation Guidelines: When evaluating whether or not asbestos may be present, you want to note possible asbestos-containing material, such as

✓ Insulation, including blown, rolled and wrapped

✓ Resilient floor coverings (tiles)

✓ Asbestos siding shingles

✓ Asbestos-cement products

✓ Asphalt roofing products

✓ Vermiculite insulation

The EPA has a comprehensive list of suspected asbestos-containing materials at: www.epa.gov/region06/6pd/asbestos/asbmatl.pdf.

Inspections: If you are working with asbestos, you should have your site inspected by a certified asbestos inspector prior to construction. You must submit a written Notice of Intent 10 working days prior to starting construction activities. Written notices should be submitted to your delegated state/local pollution control agency and your EPA Regional Office.

Utah Program: The Utah Department of Air Quality has specific notification requirements for asbestos demolition, abatement, and renovation projects.

✓ All demolition projects must be inspected for asbestos and are subject to notification requirements, even if no asbestos is present.

✓ If asbestos removal takes place, it must be done by a Utah state-certified asbestos contractor.

✓ All structures and components on renovation projects must be inspected for asbestos. Asbestos containing materials must be properly removed by a certified asbestos contractor.

Additional information, including notification forms, asbestos inspector and contractor lists, and information on asbestos rules, is available online at www.deq.utah.gov/ProgramsServices/programs/air/asbestos or by calling (801) 536-4424.

Clean Water Act

Water pollution can negatively affect the use of water for drinking, household needs, recreation, fishing, transportation and commerce. The EPA enforces federal clean water and safe drinking water laws, provides support for municipal wastewater treatment plants, and takes part in pollution prevention efforts aimed at protecting watersheds and sources of drinking water.

The Clean Water Act establishes the basic structure for regulating discharges of pollutants into the waters of the United States. This includes

✓ giving the EPA the authority to implement pollution control programs such as setting wastewater standards for industry;

✓ continuing requirements to set water quality standards for all contaminants in surface waters; and

✓ making it unlawful for any person to discharge any pollutant from a point source into navigable waters, unless a National Pollutant Discharge Elimination System (NPDES) permit was obtained under its provisions.

Stormwater Discharges and Construction Site Runoff: Before beginning any construction project, you must consider runoff and stormwater discharges that may originate from your site. These discharges often contain sediment and pollutants such as phosphorous and nitrogen (fertilizer), pesticides, oil and grease, concrete truck washout, construction chemicals, and solid wastes in quantities that could adversely affect water quality.

National Pollutant Discharge Elimination System (NPDES): The EPA has estimated that about 30 percent of known pollution to our nation's waters is attributable to stormwater runoff. In 1987, Congress directed the EPA to develop a regulatory program to address the stormwater problem. The EPA issued regulations in 1990 authorizing the creation of a NPDES permitting system for stormwater discharges from a select group, including construction activities disturbing five or more acres.

In 1999, the EPA expanded this program (called Phase II). This phase brought about two major new permittees:

✓ Construction sites that disturb one acre but less than five acres with possible exceptions allowing a waiver

✓ Small municipal separate storm sewer systems (MS4)

A "larger common plan of development or sale" is subject to stormwater permitting, even if the land is parceled off or sold, and construction occurs on plots that are less than one acre by separate, independent builders.

Assessing Stormwater Discharge: Listed below are questions that you need to consider when determining the need for a stormwater permit for your construction project:

✓ Will your construction project disturb one or more acres of land?

✓ Will your construction project disturb less than one acre of land, but is part of a larger common plan of development or sale that will disturb one or more acres?

✓ Will your construction project disturb less than one acre of land, but is designated by the NPDES (state agency or EPA) permitting authority as a regulated construction activity?

✓ Will stormwater from the construction site flow to a separate municipal storm sewer system or a body of water in the United States such as a lake, river, or wetland?

Municipal Technologies Agency: The EPA's Municipal Technologies Agency provides assistance in the area of municipal wastewater treatment technologies. Available assistance includes

✓ consultation on design, operation, and maintenance of systems;

✓ identification and solution of problems;

✓ contributions in the development of regulations; and

✓ technical information, guidance, assessments, evaluation, and cost estimates for the design, construction, and operation and maintenance of municipal wastewater treatment facilities.

Utah Program: The Utah Division of Water Quality manages surface and underground water quality in Utah. It works to control non-point sources of pollution, including erosion and sedimentation, and manages storm water discharges. Water quality permits issued by the Division of Water Quality include:

✓ Surface Water Discharge Permits

✓ Wastewater Construction Permits

✓ Indirect Charges (to municipal sanitary sewers)

✓ Storm Water Permits

✓ Ground Water Permits

✓ Underground Injection Control Permits

For more information, contact:

Utah Division of Water Quality
195 North 1950 West
P.O. Box 144870
Salt Lake City, Utah 84114

Phone: (801) 538-6146
Fax: (801) 538-6016

Website: www.waterquality.utah.gov/

Sedimentation and Erosion Control Measures

During a short period of time, construction sites can contribute more sediment to streams than can be deposited naturally during several decades. Excess sediment can quickly fill rivers and lakes, requiring dredging, and destroying aquatic habitats.

Measures can be taken to minimize erosion and sedimentation on construction sites:

✓ Sediment control measures include a silt fence or hay bales placed at the down gradient side of the construction site.

✓ Erosion control measures include placing mulch and vegetation as soon as feasible to permanently stabilize the site soil.

✓ A water misting system can control dust generated on the jobsite and loss of soil.

Erosion and sediment control minimizes pollution and contractor costs to rework eroded areas and replace lost soil. Individual states may have required sedimentation and erosion control measures.

Hazardous and Non-Hazardous Solid Waste

In general, construction sites generate more non-hazardous waste than hazardous waste. You should be aware of the regulations surrounding both.

Non-Hazardous Waste: Common non-hazardous waste generated at construction sites includes

✓ scrap wood,

✓ drywall,

✓ bricks,

✓ concrete,

✓ plumbing fixtures and piping,

✓ roof coverings,

✓ metal scraps, and

✓ electrical wiring and components.

Non-hazardous waste is regulated at the state and local level and you should identify any requirements. For more information on state requirements, refer to the Construction Industry Compliance Assistance Center at www.cicacenter.org.

Hazardous Waste: Hazardous waste is regulated at the federal level and your state may have additional requirements.

Examples of hazardous waste are

✓ lead-based paint,

✓ used oil,

✓ hydraulic fluid,

✓ gypsum drywall (due to sulfate), and

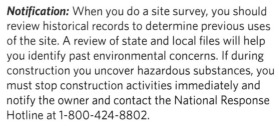

✓ mercury-containing demolition wastes such as batteries and thermostats.

Proper Notification: If you discover hazardous waste on your jobsite, you must notify state and local authorities or the National Response Center Hotline at 1-800-424-8802. Criminal charges may be filed if hazardous wastes are present at the site and proper notification does not take place. If hazardous waste is produced through construction activities, the party that generated the waste is generally responsible for cleaning it up. Hazardous waste must be treated and disposed of at a facility permitted or licensed for that purpose by the state or federal government.

Utah Program: Businesses that generate or store hazardous waste are regulated through the Division of Solid and Hazardous Waste. This branch oversees corrective action, characterization, storage, treatment, and disposal of solid and hazardous waste. The website has several technical assistance links.

For more information, contact:

Division of Solid and Hazardous Waste
195 North 1950 West
P.O. Box 144880
Salt Lake City, Utah 84114

Phone: (801) 536-0200
Fax: (801) 536-0222
Used Oil Hotline: 1-800-458-0145

Website: wasteandradiation.utah.gov

Hazardous Substances

Site Survey: Before beginning any construction or demolition activities at your construction site, you should evaluate the site for any hazardous substances.

Hazardous substances referred to in this section are chemicals that most likely induce serious acute reactions from short-term airborne exposure.

Notification: When you do a site survey, you should review historical records to determine previous uses of the site. A review of state and local files will help you identify past environmental concerns. If during construction you uncover hazardous substances, you must stop construction activities immediately and notify the owner and contact the National Response Hotline at 1-800-424-8802.

Underground Storage Tanks (UST): An underground storage tank system (UST) is defined by the EPA as "a tank and any underground piping connected to the tank that has at least 10 percent of its combined volume underground." The federal UST regulations apply only to underground tanks and piping storing either petroleum or certain hazardous substances. Federal regulations do not apply to the following types of underground storage tanks:

✓ Farm and residential tanks of 1,100 gallons or less capacity holding motor fuel used for noncommercial purposes

✓ Tanks storing heating oil used on the premises where it is stored

✓ Tanks on or above the floor of underground areas, such as basements or tunnels

✓ Septic tanks and systems for collecting storm water and wastewater

✓ Flow-through process tanks

✓ Tanks of 110 gallons or less capacity

✓ Emergency spill and overfill tanks

- -
Conduct a thorough site survey to anticipate any environmental hazards.
- -

Lead

Exposure Hazards: Lead is considered a toxic and hazardous substance and can cause a serious risk of lead poisoning if overexposure occurs. OSHA regulates the amount of lead that workers can be exposed to (no more than 50 micrograms of lead per cubic meter of air averaged over an 8-hour day). Traditionally, most over-exposure occurs in trades such as plumbing, welding, and painting.

Hazard Protection: The most effective way to protect workers is through good work practices and engineering controls. Respirators are not a substitute for these practices, but should be an additional measure of safety. Employers are required to supply respirators at no cost to employees who will potentially be exposed to lead and adopt a respirator program, including a written standard operating procedure, training, and regular equipment inspection.

Engineering controls to reduce worker exposure include

✓ exhaust ventilation, such as power tools with dust collection shrouds or other attachments exhausted through a high-efficiency particulate air (HEPA) vacuum system;

✓ enclosure or encapsulation of lead particles (for example, lead-based paint can be made inaccessible by encapsulating it with a material that bonds to the surface such as epoxy coating);

✓ substituting lead-based products or products that create lead exposure with a comparable product;

✓ replacing lead components with non-lead components;

✓ process or equipment modifications that create less lead exposure from dust; and

✓ isolating the lead exposure area so other areas are not contaminated.

Construction Assistance: OSHA has downloadable software on its website designed to help small business owners understand the Lead in Construction standard. Users should still refer to OSHA standards for specific details as it represents the most up-to-date source.

Utah Program: The Division of Air Quality Lead-Based Paint Program has specific notification requirements for most lead abatement projects and strict disposal requirements. Only companies certified by the Department of Environmental Quality/Division of Air Quality can perform lead abatement projects.

For more information, contact:

> *Division of Air Quality*
> *Lead-Based Paint Program*
> *150 North 1950 West*
> *P.O. Box 144820*
> *Salt Lake City, Utah 84114*
>
> *Phone: (801) 536-4000*
>
> *Website: www.airquality.utah.gov/HAPs/lead/index.htm*

Remodeling or Renovating a Home with Lead-Based Paint (Lead PRE)

If not conducted properly, certain types of renovations can release lead from paint and dust into the air. The Lead Pre-Renovation Education Rule (Lead PRE) is a federal regulation involving those performing renovations for compensation in residential housing that may contain lead paint.

In December 2008 (with amendments in 2010 and 2011), the EPA passed the Lead-Based Paint Renovation, Repair and Painting Program Rule that imposes additional lead-based paint regulations. Under this rule, only certified contractors can perform renovation, repair and painting projects that disturb lead-based paint in homes, child care facilities, and schools built before 1978. The EPA has authorized Alabama, Georgia, Iowa, Kansas, Massachusetts, Mississippi, North Carolina, Oregon, Rhode Island, Utah, Washington, and Wisconsin to administer their own Renovation, Repair and Painting Program. Contractors working in these states must follow the regulations put forth by the state program.

Contractors can become certified renovators by submitting an application and fee to the EPA or state-based program and taking an eight-hour training course from an EPA-accredited training provider. Certified contractors must follow specific work practices to prevent lead contamination. Three simple principles are applied when working with lead which includes:

✓ containing the work area to minimize lead contamination in other work areas;

✓ minimizing dust to prevent harmful airborne particles from being inhaled; and

✓ cleaning up the work area thoroughly.

Required Notification: Under Lead PRE, federal law requires that contractors provide lead information to residents before renovating pre-1978 housing. The EPA publishes a pamphlet titled Protect Your Family from Lead in Your Home which must be distributed to the owner and occupants before starting work. Confirmation of receipt of the lead pamphlet or a certificate of mailing must be kept for 3 years. For work in common areas of multi-family housing, renovation notices must be distributed to all tenants.

For renovations to child-occupied facilities, renovators must distribute the pamphlet titled Renovate Right: Important Lead Hazard Information for Families, Child Care Providers and Schools to owners, administrators, and parents or guardians of children under the age of six that attend these facilities.

Exemptions: This rule applies to nearly all remodeling or renovation work with the exception of the following circumstances:

✓ Housing for the elderly or disabled persons unless children will reside there

✓ Zero-bedroom dwellings

✓ Emergency renovations or repairs

✓ Minor repair and maintenance that disturb two square feet or less of paint per component

✓ Housing or components declared lead-free by a certified inspector or risk assessor

Lead Abatement: Work designed to permanently eliminate lead-based paint hazards is considered lead abatement and is not subject to the guidelines under Lead PRE. This does not include renovation, remodeling, landscaping, or other activities designed to repair, restore, and redesign a given building. The EPA outlines strict regulations for this type of work as discussed in the previous section on lead.

Renovation: Renovations under Lead PRE are modifications of all or part of any existing structure that disturbs a painted surface. This includes

✓ removal/modification of painted surfaces, components or structures;

✓ surface preparation activities (sanding/scraping/ other activities that may create paint dust); and

✓ window replacement.

Penalties: Failure to comply with regulations concerning lead is a serious violation. Non-compliance carries substantial fines of up to $37,500 per day for each violation. Criminal penalties of imprisonment for up to one year also apply to willful or intentional violation of the regulation.

Assistance: You can obtain additional information by going online to the EPA website at www.epa.gov/lead or by contacting The National Lead Information Center (NLIC) at 1-800-424-LEAD.

Final Inspection...

Safety Standards: It is important to know the OSHA standards that pertain to the construction industry.

Safe Hiring and Training: Background checks can help you hire workers with good safety records. Regular training contributes to a safe working environment.

Substance Abuse Policies: Substance abuse compromises safety in the workplace. Clearly written and communicated policies are useful tools in reducing substance abuse.

Safety Equipment: Certain safety equipment may be required according to OSHA regulations, depending on the work being performed.

Emergency Action Plan: Either a written or an orally communicated emergency action plan is required by OSHA, depending on the number of employees you have.

OSHA Recordkeeping: Your company may be required to complete OSHA forms 300, 300A and 301.

OSHA Injury Decision Tree: The OSHA injury decision tree outlines the steps in making the determination for recording work-related injuries and illnesses.

Material Safety Data Sheets (MSDS): A material safety data sheet (MSDS) is required for all chemicals used.

Underground Utility Safety: Although laws on marking underground utilities vary from state to state, contractors should identify underground utilities before excavating.

Overhead Power Line Safety: Overhead power line safety should be considered when formulating a health and safety program and worksite planning. As a general rule, workers should keep a minimum distance of 10 feet from overhead power lines.

Benefits of Providing a Safe and Healthy Workplace: OSHA can assess citations for failing to provide a safe work environment. Ensuring workers are healthy and safe provides many direct and indirect benefits to employers.

Employee Rights: Employees are allowed to report OSHA violations without fear of retaliation.

Penalties: Penalties vary depending on the severity of OSHA violations. OSHA may conduct programmed or unprogrammed inspections.

Environmental Considerations: Environmental factors should be considered throughout all phases of construction. Obtaining proper permits is important for following environmental regulations.

U.S. Environmental Protection Agency (EPA): The EPA works to develop and enforce regulations that implement environmental laws enacted by Congress.

Utah Department of Environmental Quality: The Utah Department of Environmental Quality has several programs and activities that provide environmental and permitting assistance.

Environmental Law: Several laws exist to protect the environment. An assessment of environmental impacts should be done early on in the construction project.

Air Quality: Indoor and outdoor quality should be monitored throughout the construction project.

Asbestos: Before beginning remodeling or demolition of any project, assess whether you may encounter asbestos-releasing materials. Certain permitting and notification requirements may apply.

Clean Water Act: The Clean Water Act establishes the basic structure for regulating discharges of pollutants into the waters of the United States.

Sedimentation and Erosion Control Measures: Erosion and sediment control measures minimize pollution and contractor costs to rework eroded areas and replace lost soil.

Hazardous and Non-Hazardous Waste: Most construction waste is non-hazardous. Both hazardous and non-hazardous waste must be disposed of properly.

Hazardous Substances: Early identification of hazardous substances is important and proper notification is required.

Lead: Contact with lead can cause lead poisoning and you and your employees must follow specific regulations when working with it.

Remodeling or Renovating a Home with Lead-Based Paint: The Lead Pre-Renovation Education Rule (Lead PRE) is a federal regulation involving those performing renovations for compensation in residential housing that may contain lead paint.

Supplemental Forms

Supplemental forms and links are available at **NASCLAforms.org** using access code **UT129354**.

OSHA Forms for Recording Work-Related Injuries and Illnesses	OSHA forms 300, 300A and 301 with instructions
OSHA Compliance Assistance Employment Law Guide	OSHA guide summarizing employer responsibilities under the OSH Act
Managing Your Environmental Responsibilities: A Planning Guide for Construction and Development	EPA guide customized for the construction industry that outlines specific environmental responsibilities
Protect Your Family From Lead in Your Home	Mandatory brochure to distribute to the owner if you are doing renovations on pre-1978 housing

OSHA's Form 300 (Rev. 01/2004)

Log of Work-Related Injuries and Illnesses

You must record information about every work-related death and about every work-related injury or illness that involves loss of consciousness, restricted work activity or job transfer, days away from work, or medical treatment beyond first aid. You must also record significant work-related injuries and illnesses that are diagnosed by a physician or licensed health care professional. You must also record work-related injuries and illnesses that meet any of the specific recording criteria listed in 29 CFR Part 1904.8 through 1904.12. Feel free to use two lines for a single case if you need to. You must complete an Injury and Illness Incident Report (OSHA Form 301) or equivalent form for each injury or illness recorded on this form. If you're not sure whether a case is recordable, call your local OSHA office for help.

Attention: This form contains information relating to employee health and must be used in a manner that protects the confidentiality of employees to the extent possible while the information is being used for occupational safety and health purposes.

Year 20 ___

U.S. Department of Labor
Occupational Safety and Health Administration

Form approved OMB no. 1218-0176

Establishment name: _____

City: _____ State: _____

Identify the person

(A) Case no.	(B) Employee's name	(C) Job title (e.g., Welder)	(D) Date of injury or onset of illness

Describe the case

(E) Where the event occurred (e.g., Loading dock north end)	(F) Describe injury or illness, parts of body affected, and object/substance that directly injured or made person ill (e.g., Second degree burns on right forearm from acetylene torch)

Classify the case

CHECK ONLY ONE box for each case based on the most serious outcome for that case:

Death (G)	Days away from work (H)	Remained at Work		Enter the number of days the injured or ill worker was:		Check the "Injury" column or choose one type of illness:					
		Job transfer or restriction (I)	Other recordable cases (J)	Away from work (K)	On job transfer or restriction (L)	(M) Injury (1)	Skin disorder (2)	Respiratory condition (3)	Poisoning (4)	Hearing loss (5)	All other illnesses (6)

Page totals ▶

Be sure to transfer these totals to the Summary page (Form 300A) before you post it.

Public reporting burden for this collection of information is estimated to average 14 minutes per response, including time to review the instructions, search and gather the data needed, and complete and review the collection of information. Persons are not required to respond to the collection of information unless it displays a currently valid OMB control number. If you have any comments about these estimates or any other aspects of this data collection, contact: US Department of Labor, OSHA Office of Statistical Analysis, Room N-3644, 200 Constitution Avenue, NW, Washington, DC 20210. Do not send the completed forms to this office.

Page ___ of ___

OSHA's Form 300A (Rev. 01/2004)

Summary of Work-Related Injuries and Illnesses

Year 20___ ___

U.S. Department of Labor
Occupational Safety and Health Administration

Form approved OMB No. 1218-0176

All establishments covered by Part 1904 must complete this Summary page, even if no work-related injuries or illnesses occurred during the year. Remember to review the Log to verify that the entries are complete and accurate before completing this summary.

Using the Log, count the individual entries you made for each category. Then write the totals below, making sure you've added the entries from every page of the Log. If you had no cases, write "0."

Employees, former employees, and their representatives have the right to review the OSHA Form 300 in its entirety. They also have limited access to the OSHA Form 301 or its equivalent. See 29 CFR Part 1904.35, in OSHA's recordkeeping rule, for further details on the access provisions for these forms.

Number of Cases

Total number of deaths

(G)

Total number of cases with days away from work

(H)

Total number of cases with job transfer or restriction

(I)

Total number of other recordable cases

(J)

Number of Days

Total number of days away from work

(K)

Total number of days of job transfer or restriction

(L)

Injury and Illness Types

Total number of . . .
(M)

(1) Injuries ____
(2) Skin disorders ____
(3) Respiratory conditions ____

(4) Poisonings ____
(5) Hearing loss ____
(6) All other illnesses ____

Post this Summary page from February 1 to April 30 of the year following the year covered by the form.

Public reporting burden for this collection of information is estimated to average 50 minutes per response, including time to review the instructions, search and gather the data needed, and complete and review the collection of information. Persons are not required to respond to the collection of information unless it displays a currently valid OMB control number. If you have any comments about these estimates or any other aspects of this data collection, contact: US Department of Labor, OSHA Office of Statistical Analysis, Room N-3644, 200 Constitution Avenue, NW, Washington, DC 20210. Do not send the completed forms to this office.

Establishment information

Your establishment name _____

Street _____

City _____ State _____ ZIP _____

Industry description (e.g., Manufacture of motor truck trailers) _____

Standard Industrial Classification (SIC), if known (e.g., 3715) _____

OR

North American Industrial Classification (NAICS), if known (e.g., 336212) _____

Employment information (If you don't have these figures, see the Worksheet on the back of this page to estimate.)

Annual average number of employees _____

Total hours worked by all employees last year _____

Sign here

Knowingly falsifying this document may result in a fine.

I certify that I have examined this document and that to the best of my knowledge the entries are true, accurate, and complete.

_____ Company executive _____ Title

(___) _____ Phone ___/___/___ Date

OSHA's Form 301

Injury and Illness Incident Report

U.S. Department of Labor
Occupational Safety and Health Administration

Form approved OMB no. 1218-0176

Attention: This form contains information relating to employee health and must be used in a manner that protects the confidentiality of employees to the extent possible while the information is being used for occupational safety and health purposes.

This *Injury and Illness Incident Report* is one of the first forms you must fill out when a recordable work-related injury or illness has occurred. Together with the *Log of Work-Related Injuries and Illnesses* and the accompanying *Summary*, these forms help the employer and OSHA develop a picture of the extent and severity of work-related incidents.

Within 7 calendar days after you receive information that a recordable work-related injury or illness has occurred, you must fill out this form or an equivalent. Some state workers' compensation, insurance, or other reports may be acceptable substitutes. To be considered an equivalent form, any substitute must contain all the information asked for on this form.

According to Public Law 91-596 and 29 CFR 1904, OSHA's recordkeeping rule, you must keep this form on file for 5 years following the year to which it pertains.

If you need additional copies of this form, you may photocopy and use as many as you need.

Information about the employee

1) Full name _____

2) Street _____
   City _____ State _____ ZIP _____

3) Date of birth ___/___/___

4) Date hired ___/___/___

5) ☐ Male   ☐ Female

Information about the physician or other health care professional

6) Name of physician or other health care professional _____

7) If treatment was given away from the worksite, where was it given?
   Facility _____
   Street _____
   City _____ State _____ ZIP _____

8) Was employee treated in an emergency room?
   ☐ Yes   ☐ No

9) Was employee hospitalized overnight as an in-patient?
   ☐ Yes   ☐ No

Completed by _____

Title _____

Phone (___) ___ - ___   Date ___/___/___

Information about the case

10) Case number from the *Log* _____ *(Transfer the case number from the Log after you record the case.)*

11) Date of injury or illness ___/___/___

12) Time employee began work _____ AM / PM

13) Time of event _____ AM / PM   ☐ Check if time cannot be determined

14) **What was the employee doing just before the incident occurred?** Describe the activity, as well as the tools, equipment, or material the employee was using. Be specific. *Examples:* "climbing a ladder while carrying roofing materials"; "spraying chlorine from hand sprayer"; "daily computer key-entry."

15) **What happened?** Tell us how the injury occurred. *Examples:* "When ladder slipped on wet floor, worker fell 20 feet"; "Worker was sprayed with chlorine when gasket broke during replacement"; "Worker developed soreness in wrist over time."

16) **What was the injury or illness?** Tell us the part of the body that was affected and how it was affected; be more specific than "hurt," "pain," or sore." *Examples:* "strained back"; "chemical burn, hand"; "carpal tunnel syndrome."

17) **What object or substance directly harmed the employee?** *Examples:* "concrete floor"; "chlorine"; "radial arm saw." *If this question does not apply to the incident, leave it blank.*

18) **If the employee died, when did death occur?** Date of death ___/___/___

Public reporting burden for this collection of information is estimated to average 22 minutes per response, including time for reviewing instructions, searching existing data sources, gathering and maintaining the data needed, and completing and reviewing the collection of information. Persons are not required to respond to the collection of information unless it displays a currently valid OMB control number. If you have any comments about this estimate or any other aspects of this data collection, including suggestions for reducing this burden, contact: US Department of Labor, OSHA Office of Statistical Analysis, Room N-3644, 200 Constitution Avenue, NW, Washington, DC 20210. Do not send the completed forms to this office.

Chapter 13
WORKING WITH SUBCONTRACTORS

Chapter Survey...

⇨ *Sources for Finding the Right Subcontractor*

⇨ *Creating a Winning Partnership*

⇨ *Site Rules for Contractors*

⇨ *Employee or Independent Contractor: IRS Guidelines*

Subcontractors contract with the general contractor or other subcontractors to complete a portion of a larger project.

It is important to hire the right subcontractors because their work impacts your company's reputation. Just as you want employees who are easy to work with, the same applies to subcontractors.

There are basic criteria you can use to evaluate whether you want to hire a subcontractor:

✓ Do they sell or produce quality products?

✓ Are they reliable? Are they able to complete the project according to the schedule?

✓ Do they have good customer service skills?

✓ Are they able to effectively deal with problems?

✓ Do they give an overall impression of professionalism?

✓ Are they properly licensed and carry appropriate insurance coverage?

✓ Do they remedy situations that involve material defects or failures?

✓ How do they handle change orders?

✓ Are they competitively priced?

Now that you have established your requirements, it is time to find qualified leads.

Sources for Finding the Right Subcontractor

If you have a good reputation, the word travels fast. This also holds true for good subcontractors and suppliers. Some of your best subcontractors can come from referrals. Sources for these referrals might include:

✓ subcontractors in a different field who have worked with other subcontractors on other jobs;

✓ other contractors in your field;

✓ members of your local trade association;

✓ suppliers (for example, electrical supply firms can give referrals on electricians); and

✓ architects or engineers.

Once you come up with credible referrals, you want to make sure that you take extra steps to organize the process.

✓ Keep a list of qualified subcontractors.

✓ Allow sufficient lead time to line up subcontractors for jobs.

✓ Interview subcontractors for their qualifications, even when you are not scheduling them for a job.

✓ Check references if you have not worked with the subcontractor before.

✓ Ensure all subcontractors you work with have proper insurance coverage; request copies of insurance certificates and follow up to ensure coverage is current (as discussed in Chapter 4).

Creating a Winning Partnership

Once you have done all your homework and made your subcontractor selections, you'll want to create a relationship that will set both parties up for success.

✓ Provide an orientation on your policies and procedures.

✓ Be clear on all instructions and solicit questions.

✓ Be open to feedback and suggestions.

✓ Reward good work and provide constructive comments on improvements.

✓ Schedule trades so the job is ready for them and there are minimal barriers for them to complete their job.

✓ Visit the jobsite before the start of your portion of the project to tell other subcontractors your requirements (if it applies).

✓ Complete an IRS W-9 form prior to starting work.

Site Rules for Contractors

As part of an orientation with your subcontractors, you may want to review your site rules. Listed below are some rules to consider:

✓ Keep the jobsite clean and free of debris.

✓ All safety policies and OSHA regulations must be followed.

✓ You must provide your own tools and equipment.

✓ Work must be compliant with all applicable codes.

✓ Keep radios on the jobsite at a moderate listening level and free of offensive content.

✓ Behave professionally and do not use foul language.

✓ Salvage of items is prohibited without permission.

Site rules can be posted at the jobsite so they are visible to everyone and serve as a continual reminder.

Employee or Independent Contractor: IRS Guidelines

The IRS outlines specific guidelines regarding the difference between employees and independent contractors. Make sure you are working within an independent contractor relationship and not an employer-employee basis. If you do have an employer-employee relationship, your company is liable for payroll taxes, workers' compensation and employee benefits for that subcontractor.

To determine whether an individual is an employee or an independent contractor under common law, the relationship of the worker and your company

must be examined. In any employee-independent contractor determination, all information that provides evidence of the degree of control and the degree of independence must be considered.

Evidence of the degree of control and independence falls into three categories: **behavioral control**, **financial control** and the **type of relationship of the parties**.

Behavioral Control

Facts that show whether a business has a right to direct and control how the worker does the task for which the worker is hired include the type and degree of:

✓ **Instruction the business gives to the worker:** An employee is generally subject to the business' instructions about when, where, and how to work. In a subcontractor relationship, the business generally gives up the right to control the details of the worker's performance.

✓ **Training the business gives to the worker:** An employee may be trained to perform services in a particular manner. Independent contractors ordinarily use their own methods.

Financial Control

Facts that show whether the business has a right to control the business aspects of the worker's job include:

✓ **The extent to which the worker has un-reimbursed business expenses:** Independent contractors are more likely to have un-reimbursed expenses than are employees. Fixed ongoing costs that are incurred regardless of whether work is currently being performed are especially important.

✓ **The extent of the worker's investment:** An independent contractor often has a significant investment in the facilities he or she uses in performing services for someone else. However, a significant investment is not necessary for independent contractor status.

✓ **The extent to which the worker makes his or her services available to the relevant market:** An employee is generally guaranteed a regular wage amount for an hourly, weekly, or other period of time for one employer. An independent contractor is usually paid by a flat fee by those which he or she has contracted with. An independent contractor is free to manage multiple contracts.

✓ **The extent to which the worker can realize a profit or loss:** An independent contractor can make a profit or loss.

Type of Relationship

Facts that show the parties' type of relationship include:

✓ **Written contracts describing the relationship the parties intend to create**

✓ **Whether the business provides the worker with employee-type benefits, such as insurance, a pension plan, vacation pay, or sick pay**

✓ **The permanency of the relationship:** If you engage a worker with the expectation that the relationship will continue indefinitely rather than for a specific project or period, this is generally considered an employer-employee relationship.

✓ **The extent to which services performed by the worker are a key aspect of the regular business of the company:** If a worker provides services that are a key aspect of your regular business activity, it is more likely that you will have a right to direct and control his or her activities, indicating an employer-employee relationship.

Now that you know the rules, let's look at a few practical examples to demonstrate how classifications are made.

Example 1: Milton Manning, an experienced tile setter, orally agreed with a corporation to perform full-time services at construction sites. He uses his own tools and performs services in the order designated by the corporation and according to its specifications. The corporation supplies all materials, makes frequent inspections of his work, pays him on a piecework basis, and carries workers' compensation insurance on him.

He does not have a place of business or hold himself out to perform similar services for others. Either party can end the services at any time. Milton Manning is an employee of the corporation.

Example 2: Vera Elm, an electrician, submitted a job estimate to a housing complex for electrical work at $16 per hour for 400 hours. She is to receive $1,280 every two weeks for the next 10 weeks. This is not considered payment by the hour. Even if she works more or less than 400 hours to complete the work, Vera Elm will receive $6,400. She also performs additional electrical installations under contracts with other companies that she obtained through advertisements. Vera is an independent contractor.

Final Inspection...

Sources for Finding the Right Subcontractor: Referrals are a good way to find the right subcontractors. As you collect referrals, develop a process to organize and appropriately schedule them.

Creating a Winning Partnership: Establishing good communication and having clear policies in place set a solid foundation for positive subcontractor relationships.

Site Rules for Contractors: Subcontractors should receive an orientation on your site rules before starting work. Site rules should be posted at the jobsite so they are visible to everyone and serve as a continual reminder.

Employee or Independent Contractor: IRS Guidelines: The IRS uses behavioral control, financial control, and the type of relationship of the parties to make a determination whether someone is an employee or independent contractor.

PART 3
Office
Administration

Chapter 14
FINANCIAL MANAGEMENT

Chapter Survey...

⇨ Bookkeeping

⇨ The Accounting Cycle

⇨ Methods of Accounting

⇨ Contract Accounting

⇨ Cash Management

⇨ Equipment Records and Accounting

⇨ Depreciation Methods

⇨ Accounting Process for Materials

⇨ Payroll Accounting

⇨ Technology Solutions for Accounting

Accounting is important to all businesses because it helps measure the financial fitness of the company. It is a process of collecting, analyzing, and reporting information to develop tools, such as financial statements, that are used to evaluate different financial aspects of the company.

Bookkeeping

The first step in the accounting process is bookkeeping. Bookkeeping involves the accurate recording of all financial transactions that occur in the business. Financial statements are derived from this information.

Here are a few tips to maintain accurate and timely bookkeeping:

✓ Open a separate business checking account and obtain a business credit card to keep business and personal finances separate.

✓ Keep track of all deductible expenses (discussed later in this chapter).

✓ Keep all receipts and identify the source of all receipts so you can separate business from personal receipts and taxable from non-taxable income.

✓ Update business records daily to have quick access to the daily financial position of your business.

✓ Accurately record all information in the checkbook ledger including date, who the check was written to, the amount, and the reason the check was written.

✓ Record expenses when they occur, so you have an accurate picture of your cash situation.

✓ Avoid paying with cash, so you have a "paper trail" of your expenditures.

✓ Balance your checking account monthly. You may want to request month-end bank statements to coordinate with other month-end records.

✓ Keep all financial records for the required amount of time as designated by the IRS.

Bookkeeping involves the clerical side of accounting and requires only minimal knowledge of the entire accounting cycle. You may want to consult with a professional accountant for the more complex financial decision-making of your business.

The Accounting Cycle

The accounting cycle is a series of events that is repeated each reporting period. The cycle begins with a transaction and ends with closing the books and preparing financial statements. Steps in the accounting cycle include

1. **Classifying and recording transactions,**
2. **Posting transactions,**
3. **Preparing a trial balance,**
4. **Preparing an adjusted trial balance,**
5. **Preparing financial statements, and**
6. **Analyzing financial statements.**

STEP 1 — Classify and Record Transactions

The accounting cycle begins with classifying and recording daily transactions. A transaction is an event that either increases or decreases an account balance. A source document is the proof that a transaction took place. Examples of source documents include

- ✓ cash receipts,
- ✓ credit card receipts,
- ✓ customer invoices,
- ✓ purchase orders,
- ✓ materials invoices,
- ✓ deposit slips, and
- ✓ time cards.

Daily transactions are recorded in a set of books called journals. Typical journals that companies keep include:

- ✓ **Cash receipts and sales journal:** This journal is used when cash comes in or a sale is charged to a customer.
- ✓ **Purchases journal:** This journal tracks all purchases made by the company.
- ✓ **Cash disbursements journal:** This journal is used when cash is paid out. Transactions such as loan payments and payments on vendor invoices are recorded here.
- ✓ **Payroll journal:** This journal is used to record a summary of payroll details, such as salaries and wages, deductions, and employer contributions.
- ✓ **General journal:** This journal is used for non-cash transactions.

STEP 2 — Post Transactions

Posting is the process of transferring the transactions recorded in the journals to the appropriate accounts. An **account** is a register of value. Each account can be totaled to determine the balance. For example, cash is an asset account having a specific balance. Most companies use five basic types of accounts:

- ✓ Asset
- ✓ Liability
- ✓ Equity
- ✓ Income
- ✓ Expense

The **chart of accounts** is a numbering system that organizes these account types. A typical chart of accounts is listed below.

1000–1999: Assets

2000–2999: Liabilities

3000–3999: Equity

4000–4999: Revenue

5000–5999: Cost of Goods Sold

6000–6999: Expenses

7000–7999: Other Revenue (i.e., interest income)

8000–8999: Other Expenses (i.e., income taxes)

The accounts are located in the **general ledger**. When you post transactions, you are transferring them from the journal to the general ledger.

STEP 3 — Prepare Trial Balance

When you tally the accounts, you prepare a trial balance. The **trial balance** is a total of all the ledger accounts.

At this point in the accounting cycle, you want to make sure the debits equal the credits.

> **Understanding Debits and Credits:** Every accounting entry in the general ledger contains both a debit and a credit which must equal each other. Depending on what type of account you are dealing with, a debit or credit will either increase or decrease the account balance. The entries that increase or decrease each type of account are listed below.
>
> | Account Type | Debit | Credit |
> | --- | --- | --- |
> | Assets | Increases | Decreases |
> | Liabilities | Decreases | Increases |
> | Equity | Decreases | Increases |
> | Income | Decreases | Increases |
> | Expenses | Increases | Decreases |
>
> For the accounts to balance, there must be a debit in one account and a credit in another. You may hear terms such as the left side or right side of the balance sheet. Something on the left side is simply a debit and the right side is a credit.
>
> If you have any ledger account column totals that do not balance, look for math, posting, and recording errors.

Prepare Adjusted Trial Balance

There are six general types of adjusting entries:

✓ prepaid expense,

✓ accrued expense,

✓ accrued revenue,

✓ unearned revenue,

✓ estimated items, and

✓ inventory adjustment.

When you make adjusting entries, include an explanation as to why the change was made. Once adjusting entries are made, you must go back and tally the account balances where changes were made.

Prepare Financial Statements

Now that you have posted transactions to your accounts and made adjusting entries, you can prepare your financial statements.

The three basic types of financial statements companies use are:

✓ **balance sheet,**

✓ **income statement, and**

✓ **statement of cash flows**.

Financial statements are tools that give insight into the financial health and activities of the company.

Balance Sheet

The balance sheet is one of the basic accounting financial statements. It gives the owner good insight into the growth and stability of the company at a particular point in time.

The balance sheet equation is comprised of assets, liabilities, and owners' equity:

Assets = Liabilities + Owners' Equity

Assets are items of value owned by the business. The cash in your bank account and other assets that can be converted into cash in less than one year are considered **current assets**. They are important because they are used to fund daily operations and can be liquidated easily.

Property and equipment (sometimes referred to as **capital** or **fixed assets**) are assets needed to carry on the business of a company and are not normally consumed in the operation of the business. Land, buildings, equipment, and furniture would all be considered fixed assets.

Other current assets consist of prepaid expenses, such as security deposits, and other miscellaneous assets, such as long-term investments.

Your company may also own **intangible assets**. Examples of these include patents, franchises, and goodwill from the acquisition of another company. It is not as easy to value these assets. Generally, the value of intangible assets is a value both parties agree to when the assets are created.

Liabilities are all debt and obligations owed by the business. Liabilities that will mature and must be paid within one year are called **current liabilities**. Trade credit is usually considered a current liability because it is a short-term debt.

Long-term liabilities are debt obligations that extend beyond one year. Examples of this type of liability include bank loans and deferred taxes.

Owners' equity is made up of the initial investment in the business, plus accumulated net profits not paid out to the owners.

Working capital can also be determined by looking at the balance sheet. The following equation is used to determine working capital.

Current Assets – Current Liabilities = Working Capital

Working capital measures the liquidity of the company's assets. Liquid assets are those that are easily converted to cash. Licensing agencies may look at working capital to determine license limitations.

The balance sheet is usually requested by potential lenders to determine credit limits. The following sample illustrates how the balance sheet equation and accounts are used in the balance sheet.

Quality Construction Compay
Balance Sheet
December 31, 20XX

ASSETS

Current Assets:		
Cash	$ 1,200	
Accounts Receivable	25,200	
Total Current Assets		$ 26,400
Property and Equipment:		
Equipment	$ 53,200	
Building	120,000	
Land	75,000	
Total Property and Equipment		248,200
TOTAL ASSETS		$ 274,600

LIABILITIES AND OWNERS' EQUITY

Current Liabilities:		
Accounts Payable	$ 4,900	
Payroll Taxes Payable	$ 3,300	
Total Current Liabilities		$ 8,200
Long-term Liabilities		
Notes Payable	$ 6,700	
Mortgage Payable	$ 195,000	
Total Long-term Liabilities		201,700
Owners' Equity		64,700
TOTAL LIABILITIES AND OWNERS' EQUITY		$ 274,600

Income Statement

The income statement, sometimes called the profit-and-loss statement, is a summary of the company's revenues and expenses over a given period of time.

The profit equation provides the basis for the income statement and is comprised of the following:

Income - Cost of Goods Sold = Gross Profit

Gross Profit - Expenses = Net Income

Revenues are the income received from the daily operations of the business. Most companies have only a few revenue accounts, but if you have several lines of business, you may want to create an account for each.

Expenses are the monies paid out or owed for goods or services over a given period of time. Most companies have separate accounts for the different types of expenses incurred.

Direct costs are those directly linked with a particular project. On a construction project, your direct costs might include materials, subcontractor fees, permit fees, and labor.

Operating expenses (sometimes called indirect expenses) are the general items that contribute to the cost of operating the business. These expenses can be put into two categories, selling expenses and fixed overhead. **Selling expenses** are the costs incurred to market the business. **Fixed overhead expenses** are those that cannot be linked to a specific project but are necessary for the operation of the business. For example, if you rent warehouse space to store your equipment year round, you would include this item in your bookkeeping under fixed overhead.

Tax provision expenses are the tax liabilities your company has for federal, state, and local taxes. Depending on your business structure, this section of the income statement will vary.

Net profit is the difference between revenues and expenses. Net profit directly contributes to the net worth of the company.

If net profit is on the positive side, those earnings are placed in a retained earnings or equity account.

If net profit is negative, it will reduce the net worth of the company.

The income statement is used by investors or lenders to determine the profitability of the company. The following sample illustrates how the income statement equation and accounts are used in the income statement.

Quality Construction Compay
Income Statement
For the Period Ended December 31, 20XX

REVENUES:		
Construction Sales	$ 545,600	
Less Direct Labor	120,500	
Less Direct Materials	257,000	
Gross Profit		$ 168,100
EXPENSES:		
Selling Expenses:		
Advertising	$ 3,400	
Salaries - Sales	49,500	
Total Selling Expense	$ 52,900	
Administrative Expenses:		
Salaries - Office	$ 34,400	
Telephone	4,800	
Insurance Expenses	29,700	
Total Administrative Expenses	$ 68,900	
Total Expenses		121,800
NET INCOME		$ 46,300

Quality Construction Compay
Statement of Owners' Equity
For the Period Ended December 31, 20XX

Beginning Owners' Equity	$ 92,400
Add Net Income	46,300
Less Distributions to Owners	74,000
Ending Owners' Equity	$ 64,700

Statement of Cash Flows

The statement of cash flows summarizes your current cash position, your cash sources, and use of these funds over a given period of time. This financial statement lists changes in cash based on operating, investing, and financing activities.

The **operating activities** portion of the statement shows the performance of the company to generate a positive or negative cash flow from the operations.

The **investing activities** section lists the cash used or provided to purchase or sell revenue-producing assets.

The **financing activities** section measures the flow of cash between the owners and creditors.

If you want to finance a major project, the lender will likely want to look at your statement of cash flows. This financial statement provides good insight into the company's ability to meet its obligations. The company may appear profitable on other statements, but a lack of cash flow may indicate pending financial problems.

Notes to the Financial Statements

The notes to the financial statements contain important information that is relevant but have no specific place within the financial statement.

✓ **Accounting policies and procedures** important to the company's financial condition and results are disclosed in the notes section.

✓ Detailed information about **current and deferred income taxes** is broken down by federal, state, and local categories. The primary factors that affect the company's tax rate are described.

✓ Specific information about the assets and costs of a **pension plan and other retirement programs** are explained and indicate whether the plans are over- or underfunded.

Anything that affects the financial health of the company that cannot be reflected in the financial statements should be reported in this section.

STEP 6 — Analyze Financial Statements Using Financial Ratios

By using the basic concepts of the balance sheet and income statement, you can analyze them through financial ratios. Ratios can serve as a benchmark for the company's internal performance and as a comparison against industry averages.

Liquidity Ratio

The liquidity ratio (sometimes called the **current ratio**) is calculated by dividing the current liabilities into the current assets.

Current Assets ÷ Current Liabilities = Liquidity (or Current) Ratio

The liquidity ratio determines if the company can pay its current debts. If the ratio is greater than one, the company is in a positive liquidity position. The higher the number, the better liquidity position the company has.

Quick Ratio

The quick ratio (sometimes called the **acid test ratio**) is similar to the liquidity ratio. It is calculated by dividing the current liabilities into the current assets minus inventory.

(Current Assets – Inventory) ÷ Current Liabilities = Quick Ratio

A quick ratio of one or more is generally acceptable by most creditors. A higher number indicates a stronger financial position and a lower number a weaker position.

Activity Ratio

The activity ratio measures how effectively the company manages its credit. The formula for determining the average collection period is as follows:

Revenue ÷ Days in the Business Year = Sales per Day

Current Receivables ÷ Sales per Day = Average Collection Period

The company is in a better position when the average collection period is shorter (or the number is lower). This means that the company is converting credit accounts into cash faster.

Debt Ratio

The debt ratio measures the percent of total funds provided by creditors. The formula is as follows:

Total Debt ÷ Total Assets = Debt Ratio

Companies want to keep their debt ratio relatively low to avoid overextending debt.

Profitability Ratio

The profitability ratio is used to calculate the profit margin of the company. The formula is as follows:

Net Income ÷ Revenues = Profit Margin

The higher the profit margin percentage, the more profitably the company is performing.

Return on Total Assets Ratio

The return on total assets ratio is used to determine if the company's assets are being employed in the best manner. The formula is:

Net Profit (after taxes) ÷ Total Assets = Return on Total Assets

The company is in a favorable position when the percentage return on total assets is high.

Methods of Accounting

An accounting method is a set of rules used to determine when and how income and expenses are reported. There are two basic methods of accounting used to keep track of the company's income and expenses. These are

✓ **Cash method**
✓ **Accrual method**

The primary difference between the methods is in when the transactions are recorded to your accounts.

Cash Method

Using the **cash method of accounting**, you report income in the year you receive it and deduct expenses in the year you paid them. This is the easier of the two accounting methods. Although it is a simpler method, it holds a significant disadvantage. The cash method does not match revenues with the expenses incurred related to that revenue. This gives an inaccurate picture of the company's overall financial situation.

Accrual Method

Using the **accrual method**, you recognize income when the services occur, not when you collect the money. The same principal is applied to expenses, which are recorded when they are incurred, not when you pay for them. Most construction businesses use the accrual method of accounting.

Changing Your Method of Accounting

Once you have set up your accounting method and file your first tax return, you must get IRS approval before you can change to another method. A change in accounting method not only includes a change in your overall system of accounting, but also a change in the treatment of any material item.

Contract Accounting

Most construction businesses use two tax accounting methods; one for their long-term contracts and one overall method for everything else. A long-term contract is defined as any contract that is not completed in the same year it was started.

The choice of your contract accounting method depends on

✓ the type of contracts you have;
✓ your contracts' completion status at the end of your tax year; and
✓ your average annual gross receipts.

Each method discussed assumes that you use a calendar tax year from January 1 to December 31.

Completed Contract Method

Under the completed contract method, income or loss is reported in the year the contract is completed. Direct materials, labor costs, and all indirect costs associated with the contract must be allocated or capitalized to the same account as the income or loss. If the completed contract method is used for long-term contracts (contracts spanning over two calendar years), you may not allocate costs properly and you might overstate deductions.

The advantage of the completed contract method is that it normally achieves maximum deferral of taxes.

The disadvantages of the completed contract method are

✓ the books and records do not show clear information on operations;
✓ income can be bunched into a year when a lot of jobs are completed; and
✓ losses on contracts are not deductible until the contracts are completed.

The completed contract method may be used only by small contractors whose average annual gross receipts do not exceed $10 million for the three tax years preceding the tax year of the contract.

Percentage of Completion Method

The percentage of completion method recognizes income as it is earned during the construction project.

The biggest advantage of using this method for long-term contracts is that it does a better job of matching revenue to the expenses incurred related to that revenue. Accurate matching of revenue to expenses gives you a better picture of your financial position.

The disadvantage of the percentage of completion method is that it relies on estimates. You are estimating the degree of completion on the project, the income and the expenses. The true numbers are not realized until the project is complete.

Percentage of completion is calculated individually by project. To determine the percentage of completion, use the following formula:

Project Costs Incurred ÷ Total Estimated Costs = Percentage of Completion

Once the percentage of completion is calculated, the cumulative earnings can be figured by using the following formula:

Percentage of Completion x Contract Amount = Cumulative Earnings

Adjustments must be made on the balance sheet for billings that are over or under the cumulative earnings. To figure the amount over or under cumulative earnings, use the following formula:

Cumulative Earnings - Amount Billed to Date = Billing Overage/Deficiency

Billings in excess of the cumulative earnings are considered a current liability. Billings less than cumulative earnings are considered a current asset.

Using these formulas, a percentage of completion worksheet example is shown below.

Project Name	Contract Amount	Estimated Cost	Project Cost to Date	Percent Complete	Cumulative Earnings	Amount Billed to Date	Billing Overage/ Deficiency
Project #1	70,000	62,350	35,500	56.94%	39,858	40,150	-292
Project #2	50,000	42,150	12,140	28.80%	14,400	13,500	900
Project #3	30,000	25,110	14,050	55.95%	16,785	15,220	1,565

Cost Comparison Method

The cost comparison method is an approach that combines the completed contract and percentage of completion methods. A 10 percent deferral election is allowed under the cost comparison method. This election allows you to defer recognized revenue on a contract until the total costs incurred equal 10 percent of the estimated contract costs. The initial project costs are capitalized and deferred until costs to date exceed 10 percent of total costs. After exceeding 10 percent, all costs incurred are treated as period costs. Revenue is also fully recognized in that period based on the level of project completion. From that point forward, revenue is calculated using the percentage of completion method until the project is finished.

Cash Management

Cash Flow

As discussed in Chapter 9, it is important to track your incoming cash and expenditures during the construction project to ensure you have enough working capital to complete the job. Balancing incoming progress payments and outgoing expenditures is important to managing the project effectively and should be a consideration when preparing your schedule.

Positive cash flow, meaning more cash is coming in than going out to pay expenses, is an important indicator of the health of your business. Without positive cash flow, your business cannot pay bills and employees. The business will eventually be unable to sustain itself and ultimately fail.

Two important aspects of maintaining a positive cash flow are collecting accounts receivable (money that is owed to your business) and billing and collecting for current projects.

Collecting Accounts Receivable: Collecting accounts receivable should be a systematic process:

✓ Correspondence should look professional, with the services rendered and amount due clearly displayed on the invoice.

✓ Follow-up invoices should be sent on a regular schedule. This will convey that you are serious about receiving prompt payment.

✓ If the account falls delinquent for more than three months, a stern letter outlining the consequences for non-payment should accompany your follow-up invoices.

✓ If you find you are having problems collecting on accounts receivable, you may want to hire a professional collection agency.

Prompt pay and lien laws may also provide additional payment and collection tools.

Billing and Collecting for Current Projects: Prompt billing for current projects is important to receiving timely payments. Once you receive the approval for partial or final payment, you should immediately send an invoice requesting payment. The payment should clearly outline payment terms. For example, if your payment terms are "Net 30," this means that full payment of the invoice is due in 30 days. If amounts due for current projects are not collected in a prompt manner, you may run into cash flow problems.

Bad Debts: When you extend credit to your customers, this debt is recorded in your accounts receivable. Bad debts are uncollected accounts receivable. It is important to monitor accounts receivable regularly. If you notice that the amount of accounts receivable is increasing, you may need to adjust collection procedures. Bad debts affect cash flow and must be kept to a minimum.

According to IRS guidelines, a business deducts its bad debts from gross income when figuring taxable income. Bad debts may be deducted in part or in full. For more information on the specific IRS guidelines on business bad debts, refer to IRS Publication 535, Business Expenses. This publication can be downloaded from the IRS website at www.irs.gov.

Payments

Progress Payments: As discussed in Chapter 8, it is important to address the schedule of progress payments in the contract. Progress payments are partial payments made after specified phases of construction are complete.

To ensure adequate cash flow, it is important to monitor the progress payment schedule closely. You may be required to submit a partial payment estimate to the project architect or engineer prior to the payment due date. The partial payment estimate outlines the work performed and proof of materials and equipment delivery required for the next stage of construction. The architect or engineer certifies each progress payment by confirming the information in the partial payment estimate.

A retainage amount (commonly 10 percent) is usually withheld from progress payments. Retainage is released and paid out to the contractor after all final approvals are obtained at the end of a project.

Calculation of progress payments differs slightly, depending on the type of contract.

Payment for Lump Sum Contracts: Payments for lump sum contracts are calculated by the percentage of work completed. A schedule of estimated costs (sometimes called a schedule of values) is used as a basis to determine the degree of project completion.

Material and subcontractor invoices are compared against the schedule of values to support the degree of project completion.

Payment for Unit Price Contracts: Payments for unit price contracts are based on actual work units completed. The unit price payment request is more detailed and may take longer to complete, but it provides a more accurate picture of the degree of work completion.

Payment for Cost-Plus Contracts: Payments for cost-plus contracts are based on actual costs rather than a percentage of completed work. The schedule of payments should be clearly outlined in the contract. Cost-plus contracts generally include a markup in addition to costs. The payment request should include a markup proportionate to the costs. If payment estimates are required, reconciliation must be done once the actual costs occur to adjust for any amounts that fall over or under the estimate.

Final Payment: Final payment requests should include the final payment amount plus any retainages owed. Final payment is released after final inspection, acceptance by the owner, and submittal of proper documentation.

Prompt Payment Act: The Federal Prompt Payment Act ensures that federal contractors are paid in a timely manner. If late payment is made, interest penalties are charged on the amount due. Prime contractors must receive payment within 14 days after submitting a progress payment invoice. Prime contractors must pay subcontractors within seven days after receiving payment, or they must pay interest penalties.

Utah Prompt Pay Law: The Utah Prompt Pay Act (Utah Code §15-6-1 et. seq.) is intended to insure that contracts with Utah state agencies are paid within a reasonable time after performing public construction projects.

The Prompt Pay Act requires that the state pays for materials and construction services within 60 days of receiving an invoice requesting payment (unless a contract specifies otherwise). Overdue amounts owed to contractors are subject to interest penalties of 2% above the rate paid by the Internal Revenue Service on refund claims. Interest begins to accrue on the first day after payment is due. If payment is delayed due to disputed contract amounts or contract compliance issues, interest penalties do not apply.

After receiving payment from the state, contractors must pay subcontractors and suppliers within 30 days. Payment is considered overdue if it is not received within 45 days after the contractor is paid by the state or as specified in the contract between the contractor and subcontractor or supplier, whichever is later. Overdue amounts are subject to interest penalties of 15.5 percent annual rate which begins to accrue on day 31.

Payment for Private Projects: Payment guidelines for subcontractors and suppliers performing private construction projects are specified under Utah Code §58-55-603. When a contractor receives funds for a project, each subcontractor must then be paid in proportion to the percentage of the work they performed under that billing, unless otherwise agreed by contract. Subcontractors and suppliers must be held at the same retainage rate as the general contractor.

After receiving payment from the owner, general contractors must pay subcontractors and suppliers within 30 days or as specified in the contract between the contractor and subcontractor or supplier, whichever is later. Overdue amounts are subject to interest penalties of 1 percent per month plus attorneys' fees and collection costs. The same rule applies to lower tier subcontractors and suppliers. This law does not mean that there is no duty to pay subcontractors and suppliers until funds are received from a third party.

Petty Cash Fund

Small payments may sometimes be made without writing a check. A petty cash fund is used to make these payments. When you use the petty cash fund, it is important to document your expenditure. A voucher or petty cash disbursement slip should be completed and attached to your receipt as proof of payment.

The petty cash fund should be balanced and replenished monthly.

Equipment Records and Accounting

Options for owning, renting, and leasing equipment were discussed in Chapter 7. Equipment rates were then used to construct the equipment portion of the estimate. For accounting purposes, information on equipment must be tracked. Important information to record includes

- ✓ use rate,
- ✓ use time,
- ✓ maintenance costs,
- ✓ repair costs, and
- ✓ operating costs (i.e., gas, oil, etc.).

A separate record should be prepared for each piece of equipment.

This information is also useful when analyzing the need for future equipment purchases or upgrades.

Depreciation Methods

Depreciation is the process of devaluing a fixed asset as a result of aging, wear and tear, or obsolescence. The asset is depreciated over the course of its "useful life." Depreciation is considered a non-cash expense.

You can depreciate vehicles, office equipment, buildings, and machinery. Land cannot be depreciated, because it does not "wear out" like depreciable items.

To determine the annual depreciation for an item, you must know the initial cost, how many years it will provide value for your business, and the salvage cost of the item when it is fully depreciated. There are two methods to depreciate fixed assets:

✓ **Straight line depreciation**

✓ **Accelerated depreciation**

Using **straight line depreciation**, you simply take the initial cost of the item and subtract the salvage cost. Then you take that total and divide it by the number of "useful life" years.

The calculation is as follows:

Initial Asset Cost – Salvage Cost = Depreciation Cost

Depreciation Cost ÷ Useful Life Years = Yearly Depreciation Amount

Using the **accelerated depreciation** method, the asset is depreciated at a higher rate during the early part of its useful life permitting larger tax deductions. This method is typically used for an asset that will probably be replaced before the end of its useful life. Depreciation percentages are based on the type of asset.

The **modified accelerated cost recovery system (MACRS)** is a depreciation method approved by the IRS. It allows for faster depreciation over longer periods. MACRS divides property into several different classes and takes into account the date the equipment was put in service, cost of equipment, cost recovery period, convention, and depreciation method that applies to your property. Given all these factors, a percentage rate is applied.

For further information, you may refer to the IRS website (www.irs.gov) on how to depreciate property, using MACRS and MACRS's percentage tables.

Accounting Process for Materials

As discussed in Chapter 9, purchase orders are an important project management tool. Purchase orders keep your expenses organized and document exactly what you ordered. They also facilitate the receiving process and timing of deliveries. Purchase orders help track material inventories and related expenses in the accounting system. Invoices should be matched with purchase orders to ensure that the billing is accurate.

Shipping and Delivery Expenses: In addition to the actual material costs, shipping and delivery expenses are factored into the final cost. Shipping and delivery expenses are charged in a few different ways. Two common shipping terms are:

✓ **FOB Freight Prepaid** requires the seller to pay for shipping charges.

✓ **FOB Freight Allowed** requires the buyer to pay shipping charges. A credit for the shipping amount is often given by the seller on the invoice.

It is important to understand the shipping terms ahead of time and note them on the purchase order.

Payment Terms: Payment terms depend on the payment agreement between the buyer and seller. They are generally listed on the seller's invoice. Terms can vary by seller. Listed below are some common terms you may see on your invoices.

✓ Net 10: Payment is due 10 days after receiving the invoice.

✓ Net 30: Payment is due 30 days after receiving the invoice.

✓ Net 60: Payment is due 60 days after receiving the invoice.

✓ COD: Cash payment is due on delivery.

✓ 1/10 Net 30: A 1 percent discount is given to payments received within 10 days; otherwise, payment is due 30 days after receiving the invoice.

✓ EOM: Payment is due at the end of the month.

✓ 1/10 EOM: A 1 percent discount is given to payments received by the 10th of the month following the shipment; otherwise, payment is due at the end of the month following the shipment.

Early payment discounts are a good way to cut costs. Depending on the contract arrangements, project cost savings may be given to the contractor or credited to the overall project budget.

Payroll Accounting

If you have employees, payroll distribution is done on a regular basis. Thorough payroll records are important for several reasons, such as calculating tax liabilities and tracking labor costs. The process for preparing payroll is as follows:

✓ **calculate gross pay for each employee;**
✓ **calculate and deduct applicable taxes and other deductions;**
✓ **calculate net pay and issue checks; and**
✓ **update payroll journal.**

Calculate Gross Pay

Gross pay is determined either by a salary that you set for the employee or based on an hourly wage multiplied by the number of hours worked. Salaried employees are generally paid the same amount each pay period, no matter how many hours they work. Hourly employees generally complete timecards that track the number of hours worked.

Time cards are important documentation if an unemployment benefit dispute arises. Many states require employers to keep timecards. If projects are tracked on the timecard, this information can be used for job costing purposes. The following is a sample time card.

Project Name or Number	Hours Worked								Work Completed	Supervisor Approval
	M	Tu	W	Th	F	Sa	Su	Total		
Total										

Calculate and Deduct Applicable Taxes and Deductions

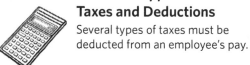

Several types of taxes must be deducted from an employee's pay.

✓ **Federal income tax** is based on the information the employee provided on the W-4 form. Using IRS Publication: Circular E (sample below), you can determine the appropriate deduction.

Wage Bracket Method Tables for Income Tax Withholding

MARRIED Persons—**WEEKLY** Payroll Period

(For Wages Paid through December 31, 2015)

At least	But less than	\multicolumn{11}{}{And the number of withholding allowances claimed is—}										
		0	1	2	3	4	5	6	7	8	9	10
		The amount of income tax to be withheld is—										
$800	$810	$78	$67	$55	$44	$33	$26	$18	$10	$2	$0	$0
810	820	80	68	57	45	34	27	19	11	3	0	0
820	830	81	70	58	47	35	28	20	12	4	0	0
830	840	83	71	60	48	37	29	21	13	5	0	0
840	850	84	73	61	50	38	30	22	14	6	0	0
850	860	86	74	63	51	40	31	23	15	7	0	0
860	870	87	76	64	53	41	32	24	16	8	1	0
870	880	89	77	66	54	43	33	25	17	9	2	0
880	890	90	79	67	56	44	34	26	18	10	3	0
890	900	92	80	69	57	46	35	27	19	11	4	0
900	910	93	82	70	59	47	36	28	20	12	5	0
910	920	95	83	72	60	49	37	29	21	13	6	0
920	930	96	85	73	62	50	39	30	22	14	7	0
930	940	98	86	75	63	52	40	31	23	15	8	0
940	950	99	88	76	65	53	42	32	24	16	9	1
950	960	101	89	78	66	55	43	33	25	17	10	2
960	970	102	91	79	68	56	45	34	26	18	11	3
970	980	104	92	81	69	58	46	35	27	19	12	4
980	990	105	94	82	71	59	48	36	28	20	13	5
990	1,000	107	95	84	72	61	49	37	29	21	14	6
1,000	1,010	108	97	85	74	62	51	39	30	22	15	7
1,010	1,020	110	98	87	75	64	52	40	31	23	16	8
1,020	1,030	111	100	88	77	65	54	42	32	24	17	9
1,030	1,040	113	101	90	78	67	55	43	33	25	18	10
1,040	1,050	114	103	91	80	68	57	45	34	26	19	11
1,050	1,060	116	104	93	81	70	58	46	35	27	20	12
1,060	1,070	117	106	94	83	71	60	48	36	28	21	13
1,070	1,080	119	107	96	84	73	61	49	38	29	22	14
1,080	1,090	120	109	97	86	74	63	51	39	30	23	15
1,090	1,100	122	110	99	87	76	64	52	41	31	24	16
1,100	1,110	123	112	100	89	77	66	54	42	32	25	17
1,110	1,120	125	113	102	90	79	67	55	44	33	26	18
1,120	1,130	126	115	103	92	80	69	57	45	34	27	19
1,130	1,140	128	116	105	93	82	70	58	47	35	28	20
1,140	1,150	129	118	106	95	83	72	60	48	37	29	21
1,150	1,160	131	119	108	96	85	73	61	50	38	30	22
1,160	1,170	132	121	109	98	86	75	63	51	40	31	23
1,170	1,180	134	122	111	99	88	76	64	53	41	32	24
1,180	1,190	135	124	112	101	89	78	66	54	43	33	25
1,190	1,200	137	125	114	102	91	79	67	56	44	34	26
1,200	1,210	138	127	115	104	92	81	69	57	46	35	27
1,210	1,220	140	128	117	105	94	82	70	59	47	36	28
1,220	1,230	141	130	118	107	95	84	72	60	49	37	29
1,230	1,240	143	131	120	108	97	85	73	62	50	39	30
1,240	1,250	144	133	121	110	98	87	75	63	52	40	31
1,250	1,260	146	134	123	111	100	88	76	65	53	42	32
1,260	1,270	147	136	124	113	101	90	78	66	55	43	33
1,270	1,280	149	137	126	114	103	91	79	68	56	45	34
1,280	1,290	150	139	127	116	104	93	81	69	58	46	35
1,290	1,300	152	140	129	117	106	94	82	71	59	48	36
1,300	1,310	153	142	130	119	107	96	84	72	61	49	38
1,310	1,320	155	143	132	120	109	97	85	74	62	51	39
1,320	1,330	156	145	133	122	110	99	87	75	64	52	41
1,330	1,340	158	146	135	123	112	100	88	77	65	54	42
1,340	1,350	159	148	136	125	113	102	90	78	67	55	44
1,350	1,360	161	149	138	126	115	103	91	80	68	57	45
1,360	1,370	162	151	139	128	116	105	93	81	70	58	47
1,370	1,380	164	152	141	129	118	106	94	83	71	60	48
1,380	1,390	165	154	142	131	119	108	96	84	73	61	50
1,390	1,400	167	155	144	132	121	109	97	86	74	63	51
1,400	1,410	168	157	145	134	122	111	99	87	76	64	53
1,410	1,420	170	158	147	135	124	112	100	89	77	66	54
1,420	1,430	171	160	148	137	125	114	102	90	79	67	56
1,430	1,440	173	161	150	138	127	115	103	92	80	69	57
1,440	1,450	174	163	151	140	128	117	105	93	82	70	59
1,450	1,460	176	164	153	141	130	118	106	95	83	72	60
1,460	1,470	177	166	154	143	131	120	108	96	85	73	62
1,470	1,480	179	167	156	144	133	121	109	98	86	75	63
1,480	1,490	180	169	157	146	134	123	111	99	88	76	65

$1,490 and over

✓ **Social Security tax** is calculated at the current prevailing rate. The current tax rate is available online at www.ssa.gov. Employers must pay in an equal amount of Social Security tax but cannot deduct that amount from the employee's payroll.

✓ **Medicare tax** is calculated at the rate of 1.45 percent of gross pay. Employers must pay in an equal amount of Medicare tax but cannot deduct that amount from the employee's payroll.

✓ **Advance earned income credit** needs to be taken, based on the information the employee provided on IRS Form W-5.

✓ **State income tax** should be calculated as it applies to each individual state.

✓ **Other deductions** might include an employee's contribution for medical insurance, 401K, life insurance, etc.

Reporting of payroll taxes is covered in Chapter 15, Tax Basics.

Calculate Net Pay and Issue Checks

Net pay is the payroll amount the employee receives after deductions are taken. Net pay is calculated as:

Gross Pay – Taxes & Deductions = Net Pay

Employees should receive a statement of earnings with their paycheck. The statement of earnings shows how the net pay was calculated. The following is a sample statement of earnings.

				Current	Year to Date
Earnings					
Description	Rate	Hours	Overtime		
		Total Earnings			
Taxes					
Employee Name:		Federal Withholding			
		Social Security			
Employee ID:					
		Medicare			
Pay Period:					
		State Withholding			
Check Date:		Insurance Deductions			
		Total Deductions			
		Net Pay			

Update Payroll Journal

Once checks are issued, the payroll journal must be updated to reflect the new account balance. The payroll journal should contain the same information as the employee statement of earnings. This topic is discussed in the previous section. This information is important to calculating your employer tax liabilities. Instructions on how to pay in employer taxes are covered in Chapter 15, Tax Basics.

Technology Solutions for Accounting

There are many accounting software programs on the market that can help make the accounting process easier.

As with all software, you still need to know the fundamentals, but it will help streamline the process and improve accuracy.

Accounting software can automate the process of posting transactions, creating financial statements, invoicing customers, creating purchase orders, and much more. Think of accounting software as an investment to make you more analytical and help you think strategically about your business.

When choosing the right software, consider what your needs are and how the technology can grow with your company. There are many options. You may want to look at programs that integrate job cost analysis with accounting that have been developed specifically for the construction industry.

Final Inspection...

Bookkeeping: The first step of the accounting process is bookkeeping. Bookkeeping is the accurate recording of all financial transactions that occur in the business.

The Accounting Cycle: The accounting cycle is a process that happens each reporting period, which starts with recording financial transactions and goes through analyzing financial statements.

Methods of Accounting: Cash and accrual are the two main methods of accounting. The primary difference between the two methods is the timing of when you record the transactions to your accounts.

Contract Accounting: The methods for contract accounting include completed contract, percentage of completion, and cost comparison.

Cash Management: Positive cash flow is an important indicator to the health of your business. Collecting on accounts receivable and billing and collecting on current accounts are important to the cash management process.

Equipment Records and Accounting: Depreciation is the process of devaluing a fixed asset as a result of aging, wear and tear, or obsolescence. The two primary methods of depreciation are straight line and accelerated.

Depreciation Methods: Depreciation is the process of devaluing a fixed asset as a result of aging, wear and tear, or obsolescence. The two primary methods of depreciation are straight line and accelerated.

Accounting Process for Materials: Purchase orders help track material inventories and related expenses in the accounting system. Invoices should be matched with purchase orders to ensure that the billing is accurate.

Payroll Accounting: Thorough payroll records are important for such reasons as calculating tax liabilities and tracking labor costs.

Technology Solutions for Accounting: Accounting software can automate the process of posting transactions, creating financial statements, invoicing customers, creating purchase orders, and much more.

Supplemental Forms

Supplemental forms and links are available at **NASCLAforms.org** using access code **UT129354**.

Balance Sheet	Example featured earlier in the chapter that can be modified in Excel
Income Statement	Example featured earlier in the chapter that can be modified in Excel
Time Card	Sample featured earlier in the chapter to track employee time
Earnings Statement	Sample featured earlier in the chapter as a summary to the employee's earnings

Chapter 15
TAX BASICS

Employer Identification Number

Before you become an employer and hire employees, you need a Federal Employer Identification Number (EIN) which is also referred to as a taxpayer identification number.

The only entities that do not need an EIN are:

✓ Sole proprietorships that have no employees and file no excise or pension tax returns; and

✓ LLCs with a single owner (where the owner will file employment tax returns).

In these instances, the owner uses his or her social security number as the taxpayer identification number.

All other types of business entities, including partnerships, are required to obtain an EIN.

The EIN is a 9-digit number that the IRS issues. The digits are arranged as follows: 00-0000000. It is used to identify the tax accounts of employers and certain others who have no employees. Use your EIN on all of the items that you send to the Internal Revenue Service (IRS) and Social Security Administration (SSA).

There are several ways to obtain an EIN through the Internal Revenue Service (IRS).

✓ Call the Business and Specialty Tax Line at 1-800-829-4933.

✓ Fax the completed Form SS-4 application to the fax number designated for your state.

✓ Mail the completed Form SS-4 application.

✓ Apply online at www.irs.gov.

Federal Business Taxes

The form of business you operate determines what taxes you must pay and how you pay them. The following are three general types of business taxes that you may be responsible for.

✓ **Income tax**

✓ **Self-employment tax**

✓ **Employment taxes**

The following table lists the tax responsibilities by business entity type and the corresponding forms to file with the IRS.

Summary of Federal Tax Forms

IF you are a...	Then you may be liable for...	Use Form...
Sole proprietor	Income tax	1040 and Schedule C [1] or C–EZ
	Self-employment tax	1040 and Schedule SE
	Estimated tax	1040–ES
	Employment taxes:	
	• Social security and Medicare taxes and income tax withholding	941
	• Federal unemployment (FUTA) tax	940 or 940–EZ
	• Depositing employment taxes	8109 [2]
	Excise taxes	See *Excise Taxes*
Partnership	Annual return of income	1065
	Employment taxes	Same as sole proprietor
	Excise taxes	See *Excise Taxes*
Partner in a partnership (individual)	Income tax	1040 and Schedule E [3]
	Self-employment tax	1040 and Schedule SE
	Estimated tax	1040–ES
Corporation or S corporation	Income tax	1120 or 1120–A (corporation) [3] 1120S (S corporation) [3]
	Estimated tax	1120–W (corporation only) and 8109 [2]
	Employment taxes	Same as sole proprietor
	Excise taxes	See *Excise Taxes*
S corporation shareholder	Income tax	1040 and Schedule E [3]
	Estimated tax	1040–ES

[1] File a separate schedule for each business.

[2] Do not use if you deposit taxes electronically.

[3] Various other schedules may be needed.

Income Tax

All businesses except partnerships must file an annual income tax return. Partnerships file an information return. The form you use depends on how your business is organized.

Estimated Tax

The federal income tax is a "pay-as-you-go" tax. You must pay the tax as you earn or receive income during the year. If you do not pay your tax through withholding, or do not pay enough tax that way, you might owe estimated tax. If you are not required to make estimated tax payments, you pay any tax due when you file your return.

Sole proprietors, partners, and S corporation shareholders generally have to make estimated tax payments if expected owed tax is $1,000 or more when the income tax return is filed. Form 1040–ES, Estimated Tax for Individuals, is available through the IRS to figure and pay estimated tax.

Corporations generally have to make estimated tax payments if expected owed tax is $500 or more when the income tax return is filed. Form 1120–W, Estimated Tax for Corporations, is available through the IRS to figure the estimated tax. You must deposit the payments electronically, through the mail, or delivery with a payment coupon.

Self-Employment Tax

Self-employment tax (SE tax) is a social security and Medicare tax primarily for individuals who work for themselves. Your payments of SE tax contribute to your coverage under the social security system. Social security coverage provides you with retirement benefits, disability benefits, survivor benefits, and hospital insurance (Medicare) benefits.

You must pay SE tax and file Schedule SE (Form 1040) if your net earnings from self-employment were $400 or more.

You must also pay SE tax on your share of certain partnership income and your guaranteed payments.

A Word About Deductible Expenses...

As defined by the IRS, to be deductible, a business expense must be both ordinary and necessary. An ordinary expense is one that is common and accepted in your industry. A necessary expense is one that is helpful and appropriate for your trade or business.

It is important to distinguish a business expense from a personal expense. Personal expenses would include living or family expenses which would not be considered deductible business expenses. A deductible business expense would include:

✓ Expenses used to figure cost of goods sold, such as cost of product, storage, direct labor, and project overhead; and

✓ Capital expenses, such as business assets and improvements (Although you generally cannot take a current deduction for a capital expense, you may be able to recover the amount you spend through depreciation, amortization, or depletion. These recovery methods allow you to deduct part of your cost each year.)

Federal Employment Taxes

When you have employees, you have certain employment tax responsibilities and forms you must file. Most employers must withhold (except FUTA), deposit, report and pay the following taxes:

✓ **Social security and Medicare taxes (FICA)**

✓ **Federal income tax withholding**

✓ **Federal unemployment (FUTA) tax**

Keep all records of employment taxes for at least four years.

Circular E

The IRS Publication *Circular E: Employer's Tax Guide* is a comprehensive reference providing thorough instructions on calculating, withholding and depositing employee taxes. The Circular E is found on the IRS website at www.irs.gov and at **NASCLAforms.org** using access code **UT129354**.

Social Security and Medicare Taxes (FICA)

 Social security and Medicare taxes pay for benefits that workers and families receive under the Federal Insurance Contributions Act (FICA). Social security tax pays for benefits under the old-age, survivors, and disability insurance part of FICA. Medicare tax pays for benefits under the hospital insurance part of FICA. Medicare is a part of the Social Security Program that provides hospital and medical insurance coverage to persons age 65 and over and those who have permanent kidney failure, or end stage renal disease, and people with other disabilities.

Social Security and Medicare tax is calculated at the current prevailing rate. The current tax rate is available online at www.ssa.gov.

Federal Income Tax Withholding

You generally must withhold federal income tax from your employees' wages. To figure how much to withhold from each wage payment, use the employee's form W-4, Employee's Withholding Allowance Certificate, and the methods described in the previous chapter. The W-4 deductions do not expire unless the employee gives you a new one or if the employee is claiming a tax exemption. A new W-4 form must be completed by February 15 each year from employees claiming a tax withholding exemption.

Form W-2: W-2, Wage and Tax Statement summarizes the employee's previous year's wages and withholding amounts. All employees must be furnished copies of the form W-2 by January 31 for the previous year's wages. Employees should receive copies B, C, and 2.

If employment ends before the end of the year, the W-2 form can be given to the employee at any time but no later than January 31. If an employee asks for the W-2 form, you must furnish copies within 30 days of the request or 30 days of the final payment, whichever is later.

Employers must send Copy A of the W-2 form with the entire page of the W-3 form to the Social Security Administration (SSA) by the last day of February (or last day of March if you file electronically). Send the forms to:

Social Security Administration
Data Operations Center
Wilkes-Barre, PA 18769-0001

Deposit Schedule

There are three deposit schedules, monthly, semiweekly and daily, for determining when you deposit social security, Medicare and withheld income taxes. Prior to the beginning of the calendar year, you must determine which schedule you are required to use.

You are a monthly schedule depositor if your total payroll tax liability for the previous four quarters (July to June) was $50,000 or less. Payments are due on the fifteenth day of the following month after the payments were made. During your first year of business, you are a monthly schedule depositor.

If your total payroll tax liability from the previous four quarters (July to June) is greater than $50,000, you are a semiweekly schedule depositor. The semiweekly deposit schedule depends on your payroll date.

If your payday is on...	Then your deposit date is...
Wednesday, Thursday and/or Friday	Wednesday
Saturday, Sunday, Monday and/or Tuesday	Friday

If your accumulated tax liability is $100,000 or more on any day during a deposit period, you must deposit it on the next banking day. If you are a monthly schedule depositor and accumulate a $100,000 tax liability on any day, you automatically become a semiweekly depositor.

Form 941: If you report less than $2,500 for the quarter, you can use the IRS Form 941, Quarterly Employer's Tax Return to make payments by the due date of the return. If your tax obligation exceeds $2,500 for the quarter, you are subject to payments according to a deposit schedule.

Federal Unemployment Tax (FUTA)

The federal unemployment tax is part of the federal and state program under the Federal Unemployment Tax Act (FUTA) that pays unemployment compensation to workers who lose their jobs.

You report and pay FUTA tax separately from social security and Medicare taxes and withheld income tax. Employers are responsible for FUTA and cannot withhold this amount from the employees' payroll.

You are generally liable for both state and federal unemployment taxes if

✓ you pay wages to employees totaling $1,500, or more, in any quarter of a calendar year, or

✓ you had at least one employee during any day of a week during 20 weeks in a calendar year, regardless of whether or not the weeks were consecutive.

Calculating FUTA: The FUTA tax base and tax rate is calculated at the current prevailing rate. Current tax information is available online at www.irs.gov. Employers who pay the state unemployment tax, on a timely basis, will receive an offset credit to the federal tax. State tax rates are based on requirements of state law.

Deposit Requirements: For deposit purposes, figure FUTA tax quarterly. If your FUTA tax liability is less than $500, you are not required to deposit the tax. Instead, carry it forward and add it to the liability figured in the next quarter to see if you must make a deposit. Use the following schedule to determine when to deposit FUTA taxes.

Quarter	Ending	Due Date
Jan-Feb-Mar	March 31	April 30
Apr-May-June	June 30	July 31
July-Aug-Sept	Sept. 30	Oct. 31
Oct-Nov-Dec	Dec. 31	Jan. 31

Form 940: Report FUTA taxes on Form 940, Employer's Annual Federal Unemployment (FUTA) Tax Return or if you qualify, you can use the simpler Form 940-EZ instead.

Penalties

Accurate and prompt deposits are required to avoid penalties which can range from 2 percent to 100 percent of your tax liability.

Penalties may apply if

✓ you do not make payroll tax deposits on time;

✓ make deposits for less than the required amount; or

✓ do not use the Electronic Federal Tax Payment System (EFTPS) when required.

These penalties are as follows:

2%	Deposits made 1-5 days late.
5%	Deposits made 6-15 days late.
10%	Deposits made more than 16 days late. Also applies to amounts paid within 10 days of the date of the first notice the IRS sent asking for the tax due.
10%	Deposits made at an unauthorized financial institution, paid directly to the IRS, or paid with your tax return.
10%	Amounts subject to electronic deposit requirements but not deposited using EFTPS.
15%	Amounts still unpaid more than 10 days after the date of the first notice that the IRS sent asking for the tax due or the day on which you received notice and demand for immediate payment, whichever is earlier.
100%	Failure to pay "trust fund" taxes defined as withheld income, social security and Medicare taxes. The amount of the penalty is equal to the unpaid balance of the trust fund tax.

Information Returns – 1099-MISC

You may be required to file information returns to report certain types of payments made during the year to persons not treated as employees. Form 1099-MISC, Miscellaneous Income may be used to report payments of $600 or more to independent contractors. Form 1099-MISC must be filed by January 31 for the prior year's payments. Form 1096, Annual Summary and Transmittal of U.S. Information Returns, is used to transmit 1099 forms to the IRS. Form 1096 is due by February 28 for the previous year's 1099s.

Tax Calendar

Listed below are key employment tax deadlines as outlined in the IRS Publication Circular E. IRS Publication 509-Tax Calendar is also a good resource to keep track of other various tax due dates including income and employment taxes.

By January 31	Furnish W-2 Form, Wage and Tax Statement to All Employees
	Furnish Form 1099 to Each Other Payee (for example, independent contractors with payments of $600 or more)
	File Form 940 or 940-EZ, Employer's Annual Federal Unemployment Tax (FUTA) Return
	File Form 945, Annual Return of Withheld Federal Income Tax
By February 15	Request a New W-4 Form from Employees Claiming a Tax Withholding Exemption
On February 16	Exempt W-4 Forms Expire
By February 28	File Copy A of All Forms 1099 with Form 1096, Annual Summary and Transmittal of U.S. Information Returns with the IRS
	File Copy A of W-2 Form, Wage and Tax Statement with W-3 Form, Transmittal of Wage and Tax Statements with the Social Security Administration
By March 31	File Electronic Forms 1099 and 8027 with IRS
	File Electronic W-2 Forms with the Social Security Administration
By April 30, July 31, October 31, and January 31	Deposit FUTA Taxes
	File Form 941, Employer's Quarterly Federal Tax Return and deposit any undeposited income, social security and Medicare taxes
Before December 1	Remind Employees to Submit New W-4 Forms if withholding allowances have changed
On December 31	W-5 Form, Earned Income Credit Advance Payment Certificate Expires

Utah State Tax Specifics

The Utah State Tax Commission is the regulating agency for the state tax program. Forms and helpful links are located on their website at www.tax.utah.gov.

For more information, contact:

Utah State Tax Commission
210 North 1950 West
Salt Lake City, Utah 84134

Phone: (801) 297-2200 or
Toll-free: 1-800-662-4335
TDD: (801) 297-2020
Fax: (801) 297-7699

Website: www.tax.utah.gov

A live chat with a Taxpayer Services Representative is available on the website Monday through Friday from 8:00 a.m. to 5:00 p.m., except state holidays.

The following information and additional publications are available on the Tax Commission website.

Recordkeeping: Tax records should be kept for three years from the date the taxes are due or paid. Businesses must provide the Tax Commission or its authorized agents with access to these records upon request. A taxpayer's license may be revoked for failure to keep adequate records necessary to establish tax liability.

Corporate Franchise Tax

The corporate franchise tax is defined by the tax commission as "a tax on the privilege or right to do business in Utah, and is based on net income". Every corporation is required to file a return and pay the tax each calendar or fiscal year, regardless of whether or not a profit was made or business was conducted.

Estimated Tax: Corporations are required to pay estimated tax on a quarterly basis if the tax liability for the current year or past year is $3,000 or more. A corporation is not subject to the prepayment requirements for the first year that the corporation is required to file a return in Utah, if the corporation makes a payment on or before the due date (without extension) equal to or greater than the minimum $100 tax.

Tax Rate: The quarterly prepayment amounts are based on 90% of the current year's tax or 100% of the prior year's tax.

Due Dates: Payments are due on the fifteenth day of fourth, sixth, ninth, and twelfth month of the corporation's taxable year. Form TC-559, Corporate Franchise and Income Tax Payment Booklet, is used to file and pay estimated tax.

Sales and Use Tax

Sales Tax: Sales tax is defined by the Tax Commission as "a tax on the rental or sale of certain services and all tangible personal property." It is collected by the seller and remitted to the Tax Commission on monthly, quarterly or annual returns. Sales tax is due at the point of the sale.

Publication 42, Sales Tax Information for Sales, Installation and Repair of Tangible Personal Property Attached to Real Property from the Tax Commission provides detailed information for the construction industry on when sales tax due and work that is exempt.

Filing Due Dates: Sales tax returns are due on the last day of the month following each reporting period. If a due date falls on a Saturday, Sunday or legal holiday, the due date is the next business day.

Use Tax: Use tax is defined by the Tax Commission as "a tax on goods or taxable services shipped or delivered from out-of-state locations for use, storage, or consumption in Utah." Use tax applies if sales tax was due but not charged. If items are purchased from an out-of-state retailer for use in Utah and the seller does not collect tax, the consumer must pay the tax directly to the Tax Commission on a sales and use tax return or income tax return.

Filing Guidelines: A sales tax return must be filed whether or not sales or use tax is due. Late returns, underpayments and late payments are subject to penalties and interest. Filing frequency is outlined below and is based upon the amount of annual sales and use tax liability.

Businesses with an annual liability of $96,000 or more are required to pay the tax via electronic funds transfer

(EFT). Discounts are available to those who file and pay monthly sales tax returns by the due date.

Recordkeeping: Sales tax records must include:

✓ Gross receipts from sales or rental payments

✓ All claimed deductions and exemptions

✓ Bills and invoices of tangible personal property purchased for sale, consumption, or lease in Utah

✓ Typical accounting books with supporting documentation

Tax Rates: Sales and use tax rates vary depending on the location of a business. Cities or counties may impose a local tax. Generally, the local tax rate is combined with the state tax rate for collection and reporting to the Utah State Tax Commission. Check with your city or county to determine if local tax is due.

Annual Sales and Use Tax Liability	Filing Status
$0 - $999.99	Annual
$1,000.00 - $49,999.99	Quarterly
$50,000.00 - $95,999.99	Monthly
$96,000.00 or more	Monthly and EFT

Withholding Tax

Employers are required to withhold individual state income tax from the wages and salaries of their employees.

Registering to Withhold Tax: You must submit a completed business registration application, Form TC-69, to obtain a withholding tax identification number. After your application is processed, the Tax Commission will mail information concerning your Utah withholding tax account number and pre-printed forms on which to report and submit your payment of the tax withheld.

Determining Withholding Amounts: Each employee must furnish you with a signed federal W-4 form. You should use these forms along with the tax tables found in Publication 14 to determine how much income tax should be withheld from each employee's paycheck.

Filing Withholding Tax Returns: Withholding tax returns are filed on a quarterly basis.

If you withhold less than $1,000 from employee wages each month, you should file a return and pay the withheld taxes on a quarterly basis. The tax is due the last day of the month following the end of the quarter.

If you withhold more than $1,000 from employee wages each month, you should pay the withheld taxes on a monthly basis and file the return on a quarterly basis. This tax is due on the last day of the following month.

Penalties: There is a penalty of up to 10% for late payment of the tax due. There is also a second penalty if the tax is still due after 90 days of the due date. Penalties are also assessed for failing to timely file reports.

Income Tax Withholding Tables and Instructions: Publication 14 outlines the withholding process in detail and includes the withholding tables needed to withhold the proper amounts for each payroll.

Final Inspection...

Employer Identification Number: An employer identification number is used to identify the tax accounts of employers and certain others who have no employees.

Federal Business Taxes: The form of business you operate determines what taxes you must pay and how you pay them.

Summary of Federal Tax Forms: You must file the specific federal tax forms that correspond to your business entity type.

Income Tax: All businesses except partnerships must file an annual income tax return. Partnerships file an information return.

Self-Employment Tax: Self-employment tax (SE tax) is a social security and Medicare tax primarily for individuals who work for themselves.

Federal Employment Taxes: Federal employment taxes include social security and Medicare (FICA), federal income tax withholding, and federal unemployment tax (FUTA).

Penalties: Accurate and prompt deposits are required to avoid penalties which can range from 2 percent to 100 percent of your tax liability.

Information Returns-1099 MISC: Form 1099-MISC, Miscellaneous Income may be used to report payments of $600 or more to independent contractors.

Tax Calendar: IRS Publication Circular E and Publication 509 provide tax calendars for various taxes that may apply to your business.

Utah State Tax Specifics: Corporate income, franchise, sales and use, and withholding are a few state taxes that may apply to your business.

Supplemental Publications and Forms

Supplemental forms and links are available at **NASCLAforms.org** using access code **UT129354**.

IRS Publication 334	Tax Guide for Small Business
IRS Publication 463	Travel, Entertainment and Gift Expenses
IRS Publication 505	Tax Withholding and Estimated Tax
IRS Publication 509	General Tax Calendar
IRS Publication 533	Self-Employment Tax
IRS Publication 535	Business Expenses
IRS Publication 538	Accounting Periods and Methods
IRS Publication 541	Tax Information on Partnerships
IRS Publication 542	Tax Information on Corporations
IRS Publication 583	Taxpayers Starting a Business
IRS Publication 587	Business Use of Your Home
IRS Publication 946	How to Begin Depreciating Your Property
IRS Publication 1544	Reporting Cash Payments of Over $10,000
IRS Form W-2	Wage and Tax Statement
IRS Form W-3	Tax Reconciliation
IRS Form W-4	Employee Withholding
IRS Form SS-4	Application for Employer Identification Number
IRS Form 940	Employer Annual Federal Unemployment Tax Return
IRS Form 941	Employer's Quarterly Federal Tax Return
IRS Form 1040	U.S. Individual Income Tax Return

IRS Schedule C	Profit or Loss from Business	IRS Form 1120S	U.S. Income Tax Return for an S Corporation Schedule K-1
IRS Schedule-EZ	Net Profit from Business	IRS Form 4562	Depreciation and Amortization
IRS Schedule SE	Self-Employment Tax		
IRS Form 1040-ES	Estimated Tax for Individuals	IRS Form 8300	Report of Cash Payments over $10,000 Received in a Trade or Business
IRS Form 1065	U.S. Partnership Return of Income Schedule K-1, Partner's Share of Income, Credits, Deductions, etc.	Employer's Tax Guide (Circular E)	Publication used to determine federal income tax withholding for employees
IRS Form 1120	U.S. Corporation Income Tax Return		

Chapter 16
UTAH PRECONSTRUCTION AND CONSTRUCTION LIEN LAW

Chapter Survey...

⇨ *What is a Lien?*

⇨ *Who is Entitled to a Lien?*

⇨ *State Construction Registry Program*

⇨ *Notice of Retention*

⇨ *Notice of Commencement*

⇨ *Preliminary Notice*

⇨ *Notice to Subcontractor*

⇨ *Notice of Completion*

⇨ *Conditional Waiver and Release*

⇨ *Waiver and Release Upon Final Payment*

⇨ *Filing a Claim of Lien*

⇨ *Time Limitation for Liens*

⇨ *Priority*

⇨ *Monetary Awards*

⇨ *Bonding Around a Lien*

⇨ *Abuse of Lien Rights*

⇨ *Residence Lien Restriction and Lien Recovery Fund*

What is a Lien?

Contractors' and material suppliers' liens "cloud" the title to real property but can be an effective method (and sometimes the only method) for securing payment for labor or materials used in the improvement of real property. The lien stops the owner from selling the property with a clear title. The lien may be foreclosed in a lawsuit. The court can order that property be sold and the proceeds used to pay the contractor, subcontractor, laborer, or material supplier.

The law governing liens for improvements to real property is found within the Utah Code of Laws, Title 38, Chapter 1a. The state statutes and court opinions establish a strict procedure to perfect and foreclose a lien. It is strongly recommended that a professional be routinely used to record and foreclose on construction liens.

Who is Entitled to a Lien?

The state statutes give lien rights to any person providing labor or performing services or furnishing or renting any materials or equipment used in the construction, alteration, improvement of any building or structure. This includes scheduling, estimating, staking, supervising, managing, materials testing, inspection, observation, and quality control or assurance involved in constructing, altering, or repairing an improvement.

Preconstruction services are defined as means to plan or design, or to assist in the planning or design of, an improvement or a proposed improvement including consulting, conducting a site investigation or assessment, programming, preconstruction cost or quantity estimating, preconstruction scheduling, performing a preconstruction construction feasibility review, procuring construction services, and preparing a study, report, rendering, model, boundary or topographic survey, plat, map, design, plan, drawing, specification, or contract document.

The lien claimant is the person who supplied material, equipment, or labor, did not get paid, and is now claiming a lien.

A lien may apply to preconstruction or construction services. The lien claimant should file a preconstruction service lien or construction service lien accordingly.

Property Subject to Lien: A lien may attach to the property where the building, structure, or improvement is located unless it is covered by the Residence Lien Restriction and Lien Recovery Fund

Act (§38-11-107). For the purposes of assigning property subject to lien, if the building, structure, or improvement occupies two or more lots or subdivisions of land, it is considered as one. Public property is not subject to lien law.

State Construction Registry Program

The State Construction Registry Program serves as a centralized repository for notices of commencement, preliminary notices, and notices of completion for any private and public construction project filings in Utah. The State Construction Registry can accept filings through internet submissions, mail, and fax. A database is maintained with the relevant information from these filings.

Notice of Retention

Within 20 days after commencing preconstruction services, a person performing these services must file a Notice of Retention in order to preserve lien rights.

Notice of Commencement

Within 15 days after a building permit is issued or within 15 days after work commences on the property, the original contractor or owner may file a Notice of Commencement with the State Construction Registry. If duplicate notices are filed by the original contractor and owner, the notices are combined.

Required Information: The Notice of Commencement must include the following information:

✓ Name and address of the project owner;
✓ Name and address of the original contractor;
✓ Name and address of the surety providing any payment bond for the project, or if none exists, a statement that a payment bond was not required for the work being performed;
✓ Name and address of the project; and
✓ Legal description of the property where the project is located.

Optional information in the Notice of Commencement may include:

✓ General description of the project
✓ Lot or parcel number, and any subdivision, development, or other project name

If the information in the Notice of Commencement is inaccurate or not filed in a timely manner, it will be deemed unenforceable.

Government Projects: No later than 15 days after commencement of physical construction work at a government project site, the original contractor, owner, or owner-builder shall file a notice of commencement.

Preliminary Notice

In order to preserve lien rights, any person providing construction services must file a preliminary notice with the State Construction Registry within 20 days after first providing labor, service, equipment, and material to a construction project.

Required Information: The preliminary notice must contain the following information:

✓ Building permit number for the project, or the number assigned to the project by the designated agent;
✓ Name, address, and telephone number of the potential lien claimant;
✓ Name and address of the person who contracted for labor, services, equipment, or materials
✓ Name of project owner
✓ Name of original contractor who contracted with the potential lien claimant; and
✓ Address of the construction project.

If the preliminary notice is not filed in a timely manner, it becomes valid five days after the late filing.

Government Projects: On government projects, all contractors except the person who has a contract with an owner or an owner-builder or a laborer compensated with wages shall file a preliminary notice with the State Construction Registry. The preliminary notice must be given

✓ within 20 days after first providing labor, service, equipment, and material to a construction project; or
✓ within 20 days after the filing of a Notice of Commencement.

Notice to Subcontractor

Within 14 days of a request from a subcontractor, the original contractor must provide a notice informing the subcontractor of all the preliminary notices received for the construction project.

Notice of Completion

Upon completion of a project, a Notice of Completion may be filed by

✓ an owner of a construction project;

✓ an original contractor;

✓ a lender that has provided financing for the construction project;

✓ a surety that has provided bonding for the construction project; or

✓ a title company issuing a title insurance policy on the construction project.

Required Information: The contents of the Notice of Completion must include:

✓ Building permit number or number assigned to the project by the designated agent;

✓ Name, address, and telephone number of the person filing the notice of completion;

✓ Name of the original contractor

✓ Address of the project or a description of the location of the project;

✓ Date on which final completion is alleged to have occurred; and

✓ Method used to determine final completion.

Notification: Once the Notice of Completion is filed, electronic notification is sent out to those who filed notice of commencement for the project, filed preliminary notice for the project, and all interested persons who have requested notices concerning the project.

Conditional Waiver and Release

The claimant may complete a Conditional Waiver and Release form to release any liens prior to final payment for the labor and/or materials provided. The following form must be completed in its entirety for the Interim Waiver and Release to be valid.

UTAH CONDITIONAL WAIVER AND RELEASE UPON PROGRESS PAYMENT

Property Name: _____

Property Location: _____

Undersigned's Customer: _____

Invoice/Payment Application Number: _____

Payment Amount: _____

Payment Period: _____

To the extent provided below, this document becomes effective to release and the undersigned is considered to waive any notice of lien or right under Utah Code Ann., Title 38, Chapter 1a, Preconstruction and Construction Liens, or any bond right under Utah Code Ann., Title 14, Contractors' Bonds, or Section 63G-6-505 related to payment rights the undersigned has on the above described Property once:

(1) the undersigned endorses a check in the above referenced Payment Amount payable to the undersigned; and

(2) the check is paid by the depository institution on which it is drawn.

This waiver and release applies to a progress payment for the work, materials, equipment, or a combination of work, materials, and equipment furnished by the undersigned to the Property or to the Undersigned's Customer which are the subject of the Invoice or Payment Application, but only to the extent of the Payment Amount. This waiver and release does not apply to any retention withheld; any items, modifications, or changes pending approval; disputed items and claims; or items furnished or invoiced after the Payment Period.

The undersigned warrants that the undersigned either has already paid or will use the money the undersigned receives from this progress payment promptly to pay in full all the undersigned's laborers, subcontractors, materialmen, and suppliers for all work, materials, equipment, or combination of work, materials, and equipment that are the subject of this waiver and release.

Dated: _____

_____(Company Name)

_____By:_____

_____Its:_____

Waiver and Release Upon Final Payment

The Waiver and Release Upon Final Payment must follow the Interim Waiver and Release after final payment is received. The following form serves as an Unconditional Waiver and Release.

UTAH WAIVER AND RELEASE UPON FINAL PAYMENT

Property Name: _____

Property Location: _____

Undersigned's Customer: _____

Invoice/Payment Application Number: _____

Payment Amount: _____

To the extent provided below, this document becomes effective to release and the undersigned is considered to waive any notice of lien or right under Utah Code Ann., Title 38, Chapter 1a, Preconstruction and Construction Liens, or any bond right under Utah Code Ann., Title 14, Contractors' Bonds, or Section **63G-6-505** related to payment rights the undersigned has on the above described Property once:

(1)   the undersigned endorses a check in the above referenced Payment Amount payable to the undersigned; and

(2)   the check is paid by the depository institution on which it is drawn.

This waiver and release applies to the final payment for the work, materials, equipment, or combination of work, materials, and equipment furnished by the undersigned to the Property or to the Undersigned's Customer.

The undersigned warrants that the undersigned either has already paid or will use the money the undersigned receives from the final payment promptly to pay in full all the undersigned's laborers, subcontractors, materialmen, and suppliers for all work, materials, equipment, or combination of work, materials, and equipment that are the subject of this waiver and release.

Dated: _____

_____(Company Name)

_____By:_____

_____Its:_____

Filing a Claim of Lien

Time Limitations: A preconstruction service lien must be filed 90 days after completion of the preconstruction service (See U.C.A. §§ 38-1a-402).

The notice to hold and claim a construction services lien must be filed within 180 days after the day of final completion of the original contract if no notice of completion is filed; or 90 days after the notice of completion is filed. (See U.C.A. §§ 38-1a-502).

A general contractor is required to furnish the owner of a project a payment bond to ensure all of the subcontractors are paid if the project is a commercial contract exceeding $50,000. Ninety days after a person supplies labor, services, equipment, or material for the commercial contract, that person can file a claim against the bond if they have not been paid in full.

This action must be commenced within 1 year of the last day on which the person supplied labor, services, equipment, or material. (See U.C.A. § 14-2-1).

*If there is no payment bond, the right of action is against the owner of the project and not against the bond; this does not affect the time limits.

Required Information: The notice of lien claim must contain the following information in order to be valid:

✓ Name of the property owner

✓ Name of the person by whom the lien claimant is employed or to whom the lien claimant furnished the equipment or material

✓ Time when the first and last labor was performed or materials or equipment was furnished

✓ Description of property

✓ Name, current address, and current phone number of lien claimant

✓ Amount of the lien claim

✓ Signature of lien claimant or the lien claimant's authorized agent.

The notice of lien claim must be notarized and properly recorded with the county where the property is located. If the lien is on an owner-occupied residence, the notice of lien claim must contain a statement describing the steps the owner must take to remove the lien as described in §38-1a-701(4).

Notification to Owner: After filing a notice of lien claim, the property owner must receive a copy of the claim of lien within 30 days after filing by registered or certified mail or delivery.

Time Limitation for Liens

In general, a lien claimant shall file an action to enforce the lien within 180 days of filing a written notice to hold and claim a lien under U.C.A. § 38-1a-701.

Priority

Liens against the same property are paid out in the following order:

✓ Subcontractors who are laborers or mechanics working by the day or piece that have not furnished materials

✓ All other subcontractors and all materialmen

✓ Original contractors

Preconstruction service liens relate back and take effect as of the time the Notice of Retention was filed. Construction service liens relate back and take effect as of the time the First Preliminary Notice was filed. Unless a previous agreement is made, a payment to a person claiming or included within a preconstruction service lien and a construction service lien shall be applied first to the preconstruction service lien until paid in full.

Mechanics' and materialmen's liens take priority over any lien, mortgage, or other encumbrances that attach after work commences or materials are delivered, as well as any other encumbrance of which the lien holder had no notice and which was unrecorded.

Monetary Awards

Monetary Redemption: After lien foreclosure and sale of the property, liens and mortgages are subject to the same right of monetary redemption. If the amount after the sale is not sufficient to cover the whole amount of the liens, payment is made in the order of priority as designated in the previous section. Once the amount becomes insufficient to pay a class of lienors, amounts are awarded on a pro rata basis.

Attorneys' Fees: Lienors are entitled to recover reasonable attorneys' fees for the preparation and recording of the notice of lien claim.

Bonding Around a Lien

Filing a Bond: If the owner of the property or any original contractor or subcontractor wants to contest the lien, a bond may be filed with the county recorder where the lien is filed.

The bond must be with an approved surety or cash deposit in the amount of:

✓ 150% of the amount claimed by the lien claimant, if the amount claimed is $25,000 or more;

✓ 175% of the amount claimed by the lien claimant, if the amount claimed is at least $15,000 but less than $25,000; or

✓ 200% of the amount claimed by the lien claimant, if the amount claimed is less than $15,000.

Notification of Bond Filing: If a bond or cash deposit is filed, the lien claimant must be notified within thirty days of filing.

Sufficiency of the Bond: The lien claimant may question the sufficiency of the bond or cash deposit within 90 days of notice. If the lien claimant does not question the sufficiency, the lien is released. If the bond is determined not to be sufficient, the lien is reinstated.

Abuse of Lien Rights

Wrongful lien claims are those claims that contain a greater demand than the sum due

✓ with the intention to cloud the title

✓ to obtain a greater monetary award than is due; or

✓ to gain any unjustified advantage or benefit.

Penalties: Any person who wrongfully files a claim of lien against any property is subject to penalties.

Those who file a wrongful claim may be found guilty of a Class B misdemeanor and have to pay twice the amount by which the wrongful lien exceeds the amount actually due plus damages, or the actual damages incurred by the property owner, whichever is greater.

Lien Recovery Fund

Residence Lien Restriction: In 1994, the Utah Legislature addressed a problem with liens against homeowners. General contractors would not pay their subcontractors and vendors even though the homeowner had paid the general contractor. As a result, the subcontractors and vendors would file mechanics' liens against the homeowner. This meant that the homeowner had to pay for the work twice. To address this problem the Residence Lien Restriction and Lien Recovery Fund Act was passed.

A person who is qualified to file a lien on an owner-occupied residence is barred from filing that lien if:

✓ the homeowner enters into a written contract with a licensed contractor, a contractor exempt from licensure, a factory built housing retailer, or a real estate developer for construction on or the purchase of a single family or duplex residence;

✓ the homeowner has paid the original contractor, factory built housing retailer, or real estate developer in full; and

✓ the homeowner occupies the residence within 180 days of the completion of construction.

Residence Lien Recovery Fund: In order to protect the subcontractor, Utah has established the Residence Lien Recovery Fund. This fund is an alternative payment source for contractors, laborers, or suppliers whose liens are voided because of the Residence Lien Restriction Act.

All contractors are required to join the fund. Any other person or company who provides qualified services (goods and services for residential construction) may join the fund through the Utah Department of Occupational and Professional Licensing: www.dopl.utah.gov/programs/rlrf/index.html.

Department of Occupational and Professional Licensing
Lien Recovery Fund
PO Box 146741
Salt Lake City, Utah 84114-6741

Phone: (801) 530-6104
Toll-free in Utah: (866) 275-3675
Fax: (801) 530-6511

Filing a Claim: Filing a claim with the fund is similar to filing a lien foreclosure action. The following steps must be taken:

✓ File a civil action against the nonpaying party and the homeowner. This must be done within 180 days from when the qualified beneficiary filed a lien, or 270 days from the completion of the original contract, whichever is earlier.

✓ Provide the homeowner with the required application for a Certificate of Compliance. This is available on the DOPL website.

✓ Obtain a judgment against the nonpaying party.

✓ Attempt to collect on the judgment. The claimant must issue a Motion and Order in Supplemental Proceedings and attempt to serve that Motion. If the motion is served, evidence must be provided showing that no assets were located.

✓ Complete and submit the claim application. This application can be found on the DOPL website.

Written Notice: Every contractor who enters into a written contract with a homeowner must provide the following notice:

PROTECTION AGAINST LIENS AND CIVIL ACTION. Notice is hereby provided in accordance with Section 38-11-108 of the Utah Code that under Utah law an "owner" may be protected against liens being maintained against an "owner-occupied residence" and from other civil action being maintained to recover monies owed for "qualified services" performed or provided by suppliers and subcontractors as a part of this contract, if and only if the following conditions are satisfied:

(1) the owner entered into a written contract an original contractor, a factory built housing retailer, or a real estate developer;

(2) the original contractor was properly licensed or exempt from licensure under Title 58, Chapter 55, Utah Construction Trades Licensing Act at the time the contract was executed; and

(3) the owner paid in full the original contractor, factory built housing retailer, or real estate developer or their successors or assigns in accordance with the written contract and any written or oral amendments to the contract.

(4) An owner who has satisfied all of these conditions may perfect his protection from liens by applying for a Certificate of Compliance with the Division of Occupational and Professional Licensing by calling (801) 530-6628 or toll free in Utah only (866) 275-3675 and requesting to speak to the Lien Recovery Fund. (*Utah Administrative Code R156-38a-108*).

This same language must also be included on the face of the Notice of Intent to Hold and Claim Lien.

Final Inspection...

What is a Lien? A lien can be a useful tool in securing payment for labor or materials for improvement on real property.

Who is Entitled to a Lien? The state statutes give lien rights to anyone performing services or furnishing or renting any materials or equipment used in the construction, alteration, improvement of any building or structure. This includes preconstruction services and construction services.

State Construction Registry Program: The State Construction Registry Program serves as a centralized repository for notices of commencement, preliminary notices, and notices of completion for private and public construction project filings in Utah.

Notice of Commencement: A notice of commencement must be filed by the original contractor or owner within 15 days after a building permit is issued or within 15 days after work commences on the property. For government projects, a notice of commencement must be filed within 20 days after first providing labor, service, equipment, and material to a construction project

Preliminary Notice: A preliminary notice on a private project should be filed within 20 days after first providing labor, service, equipment, and material to a construction project. On government projects, the preliminary notice of lien rights should be filed within 20 days after supplying labor and/or materials or 20 days after the notice of commencement was filed.

Notice to Subcontractor: If requested the original contractor must provide a notice informing the subcontractor of all the preliminary notices received within 14 days of the subcontractor's request.

Notice of Completion: Upon completion of a project, a Notice of Completion may be filed by an owner, original contractor, lender that has provided financing for the construction project, surety that has provided bonding for the construction project, or title company issuing a title insurance policy on the construction project.

Conditional Waiver and Release: To release any liens prior to final payment, the lien claimant may complete a conditional waiver and release.

Waiver and Release Upon Final Payment: After final payment is received, an waiver and release upon final payment must be provided if an unconditional waiver and release was received prior to final payment.

Filing a Claim of Lien: A claim of lien must be filed within 90 days after the lienor last provided materials and/or labor for preconstruction services and within 180 days of final completion of the original contract for construction services. The claim of lien must contain specific text by law.

Time Limitation for Liens: In general, a lien claimant shall file an action to enforce the lien within 180 days of filing a written notice to hold and claim a lien.

Priority: Payments on liens are paid in the following order: subcontractors who are laborers or mechanics working by the day or piece that have not furnished materials; all other subcontractors and all materialmen; and original contractors.

Monetary Awards: If the proceeds of a lien foreclosure sale are not sufficient enough to pay lienors, monetary awards are distributed on a pro rata basis.

Bonding Around a Lien: If a bond or cash deposit in the amount of 150 percent of the lien is filed and found sufficient, the lien is released.

Abuse of Lien Rights: Wrongful lien claims are subject to criminal and monetary penalties.

Residence Lien Restriction and Lien Recovery Fund: This act protects homeowners and subcontractors and suppliers from general contractors who do not properly distribute payments for services and materials on residential construction projects.

Appendix A: Glossary

A

Accelerated Depreciation: A method of depreciation where an asset is depreciated at a higher rate during the early part of its useful life permitting larger tax deductions.

Acceptance (Legal): An agreement to an offer made and generally is done by signing the offer. In some cases, a counteroffer is made. A counteroffer is not considered acceptance. It is only when both parties agree to the contract terms that you obtain acceptance.

Accounting Cycle: A process that happens each financial reporting period which starts with recording financial transactions and goes through analysis of financial statements.

Accounts Receivable: Monies that are owed to a business for products and/or services provided.

Accrual Method of Accounting: A method of accounting where income is recognized when the services occur, not when the money is collected. Expenses are recorded when they are incurred, not when they are paid.

Acid Test Ratio: See *Quick Ratio*.

Activity Ratio: A formula that measures how effectively a company manages its credit. It is calculated by dividing sales per day into current receivables.

Addenda or Addendum: Changes made to bid documents after they are issued but before they are due. Addenda ultimately become part of the contract after the bid is accepted.

ADA: The abbreviation for the Americans with Disabilities Act. See *Americans with Disabilities Act*.

AGC: The abbreviation for the Associated General Contractors of America.

Age Discrimination in Employment Act (ADEA): A federal law that prohibits discrimination against individuals who are age 40 or older.

AIA: The abbreviation for the American Institute of Architects.

All-Risk Builders' Risk Insurance: A form of property insurance that covers property owners and builders for buildings under construction typically covering machinery, equipment, materials, supplies, and fixtures that are part of the structure or will become part of the structure. Additional coverage can be added for items, such as temporary structures and scaffolding, used during construction. In general, major construction defects such as poor workmanship and faulty design are not covered.

Allowance: A specified amount designated in an estimate for items that are not specified in the project plans, such as finish materials (carpeting, fixtures, lighting, etc.).

Americans with Disabilities Act (ADA): The Americans with Disabilities Act (ADA) makes it unlawful to discriminate in employment against a qualified individual with a disability.

Arbitration: Arbitration uses a third-party arbitrator or arbitrators to act as a judge or judges to render a decision by which all parties are legally bound. Arbitration is held in a format less formal than a trial.

Asbestos: These naturally occurring, fibrous materials are woven together to create a product with high tensile strength. This material is commonly found in thermal insulation and fireproofing, roofing, and flooring materials.

When these fibers become airborne, they cause a hazard due to their ability to enter the lungs. Diseases associated with asbestos include asbestosis, lung cancer, and mesothelioma.

Asset: Items of value owned by a business.

At-Will Employment: An employment agreement where either the employer or the employee may terminate employment at any time without notice or cause.

Automobile Insurance: A type of insurance providing coverage for liability and physical damage associated with a company vehicle or a fleet of vehicles. All states require vehicle owners to carry some level of liability insurance covering bodily injury and property damage incurred in a vehicle accident.

B

Bad Debt: Uncollectible accounts receivable which is deducted from gross income when figuring taxable income.

Balance Sheet: One of the basic accounting financial statements that shows a company's assets, liabilities, and owners' equity.

Bank Letter of Credit: A cash guarantee that can be converted to a payment to the owner by a bank or lending institution.

Bid: A formal offer to complete a project according to the terms and conditions of the contract for a specified price.

Bid Bond: A type of bond that guarantees the contractor, if awarded the job, will do work at the submitted bid price, enter into a contract with the owner, and furnish the required performance and payment bonds.

Bid Documents: A bid package put together in a competitive bid situation. It may include an invitation to bid, bid instructions, bid sheet, bid schedule, bidder's questionnaire on experience, financial responsibility and capability, copy of the contract, and supplements.

Bid Peddling: An unethical situation where the subcontractor approaches the general contractor after the project is awarded with the intent of lowering the original price submitted on bid day.

Bid Rigging: A form of collusion where contractors coordinate their bids to fix the award outcome of a project.

Bid Shopping: An unethical situation where the general contractor approaches subcontractors other than those who have submitted bids to seek a lower offer than what was quoted in the original bids.

Boilerplate Provisions: Standard language or clauses used in a legal contract that generally appear at the end of the contract. Their purpose is to protect the business in the event of a lawsuit.

Bond: A risk transfer mechanism between a surety bonding company, the contractor, and the project owner. The agreement binds the contractor to comply with the terms and conditions of a contract. If the contractor cannot perform the contract, the surety bonding company assumes the contractor's responsibilities and ensures that the project is completed.

Breach of Contract: When one of the parties involved fails to perform in accordance with any of the terms and conditions of a contract.

Burglary and Theft Insurance: A type of insurance covering loss or damage caused by burglary, theft, larceny, robbery, forgery, fraud, and vandalism.

Business Owner's Policies (BOPs): A type of insurance that bundles property and liability coverage together to eliminate policy gaps or overlaps.

Business Plan: A planning document that outlines business strategies and goals. It is particularly useful for newly-formed or early-stage businesses and companies making major strategic changes. Typical contents are an executive and company summary, products and services description, market analysis, marketing plan, and financial plan.

C

Capital Assets: See *Fixed Assets*.

Cash Method of Accounting: A method of accounting where income is reported in the year it is received and expenses are deducted in the year they are paid.

Certificate of Occupancy: A certificate issued by a building inspector that deems a structure meets all applicable codes and is safe for occupancy.

Certificate of Substantial Completion: A certificate issued by the architect that deems a structure can be used for its intended purpose.

Change Order: A written agreement between the owner and contractor to change the contract. Change orders add to, delete from, or otherwise alter the work set forth in the construction documents.

CFR: The abbreviation for Code of Federal Regulations.

Circular E: An IRS Publication that provides instructions on calculating, withholding and depositing employee taxes and tax tables.

Clean Air Act: A federal law that allows the EPA to set limits on how much of a pollutant is allowed in the air anywhere in the United States.

Clean Water Act: A federal law that establishes the basic structure for regulating discharges of pollutants into the waters of the United States. This act gives the EPA authority to implement pollution control programs, such as setting wastewater standards for the industry and water quality standards for all contaminants in surface waters.

Collaborative Law: A facilitative process wherein all parties agree at the onset to work to identify a solution that is beneficial to all parties involved. In collaborative law, the parties use their advocates, most often their lawyers, to facilitate a mutually beneficial result through the process of negotiation.

Commercial General Liability Insurance (CGL): A basic liability insurance covering bodily injury that results in actual physical damage or loss for individuals who are not employees, damage or loss to property not belonging to the business, personal injury, including slander or damage to reputation, and advertising injury, including charges of negligence that result from promotion of goods or services.

Company Overhead: The expenses that are necessary to keep business operations running but not directly associated with a project (e.g. taxes, legal fees, etc.).

Completed Contract Method: A method of contract accounting where income or loss is reported in the year the contract is completed.

Completed Operations Liability Insurance: A type of liability insurance that provides coverage for loss arising out of completed projects.

Completion Bond: A type of bond that provides assurance to the financial backers of a construction project that it will be completed on time.

Conceptual Estimate: An estimate prepared by the architect using cost models from previous projects.

Consideration (Legal): When both parties give up something of value, typically, services and products in exchange for monetary compensation.

Consolidated Omnibus Budget Act of 1985 (COBRA): A federal law that gives "qualified beneficiaries" (a covered employee's spouse and dependent children) the right to maintain, at their own expense, coverage under their health plan that would be lost due to a "qualifying event," such as termination of employment, at a cost comparable to what it would be if they were still members of the employer's group.

Construction Management (Contracting): A type of contracting where the project owner contracts with a professional construction manager to coordinate and manage a construction project.

Construction Safety Act: See *Contract Work Hours and Safety Standards Act.*

Construction Wrap-Up Liability Insurance: A type of insurance that bundles liability and workers' compensation insurance for general contractors and subcontractors on large construction projects to eliminate gaps in coverage. To qualify for this type of insurance, certain contract cost requirements must be met. These requirements vary by state.

Contingency: A specified amount added to an estimate to protect the contractor if an unanticipated problem or condition arises during the course of the project.

Contract: Legally binding agreement between two or more parties with the main purpose of preventing disputes between parties entering into the agreement. A legally binding contract must have offer and acceptance, consideration, competent parties, and legal purpose.

Contract Work Hours and Safety Standards Act: A federal law that sets overtime standards for service and construction contracts on federal projects. Commonly referred to as the Construction Safety Act.

Contractor's Protective Public and Property Damage Liability Insurance: A type of liability insurance that protects contractors who supervise and subsequently are held liable for actions of subcontractors from claims for personal injury and property damage.

Contractual Liability Insurance: A type of liability insurance that provides contractors with protection for damages that result from their negligence while under written contract.

Corporation (sometimes referred to as C Corporation): A legal business entity that has independent ownership of assets and liabilities from its shareholders. Its existence continues even if one or more shareholders leave.

Cost Comparison Method: A method of contract accounting that combines the completed contract and percentage of completion methods.

Cost-Plus Contract: A type of contract where the contractor is reimbursed for the actual cost of labor and materials and is paid a markup fee for overhead and profit.

Critical Path: The sequence of tasks that determines the duration of the project. Subsequent project tasks cannot begin until a critical path item is complete.

Current Assets: Cash and other assets that can be converted into cash in less than one year.

Current Liabilities: Liabilities that will mature and must be paid within one year.

Current Ratio: See *Liquidity Ratio.*

D

Davis-Bacon Act: The federal law that requires payment of prevailing wage rates and fringe benefits on federally-financed or assisted construction.

Debt Ratio: A formula that measures the percent of total funds provided by creditors. It is calculated by dividing total assets into total debt.

De Minimis Violation: A violation of standards which have no direct or immediate relationship to safety or health.

Depreciation: The process of devaluing a fixed asset as a result of aging, wear and tear, or obsolescence.

Design/Build: A type of contracting where the owner contracts with one company to complete a construction project from start to finish. The company awarded the design/build contract puts together a team of construction professionals, which may include designers, architects, engineers, and contractors.

Direct Costs: Costs directly linked with a particular project.

E

EEOC: Abbreviation for the Equal Employment Opportunity Commission.

Employee Polygraph Protection Act: A federal law that prohibits most private employers from using any type of lie detector test, either for pre-employment screening of job applicants or for testing current employees during the course of employment.

Endangered Species Act (ESA): A federal law that protects threatened or endangered species from further harm.

Entrepreneur: A person engaged in strategic activities that involve the initiation and development of a new business, created to build long-term value and steady cash flow streams.

Equal Pay Act of 1963: A federal law that prohibits employers from paying different wages to men and women who perform essentially the same work under similar working conditions.

Equipment Floater Policy: A type of inland marine insurance covering direct physical loss to equipment and mobile equipment while it is stored on premises, in transit, or at temporary locations or jobsites.

Errors and Omissions Insurance: See *Professional Liability Insurance*.

Expenses: Monies paid out or owed for goods or services.

F

Failure to Abate Prior Violation: A safety violation given when a previous violation has not been corrected.

Fair Labor Standards Act (FLSA): The federal law which prescribes standards for the basic minimum wage and overtime pay and affects most private and public employment. It applies to employers who have one or more employees. FLSA is administered by the Employment Standards Administration's Wage and Hour Division within the U.S. Department of Labor.

Family and Medical Leave Act (FMLA): A federal law that entitles eligible employees of covered employers to take up to 12 weeks of unpaid job-protected leave each year, with the maintenance of group health insurance, for the birth and care of a child, for the placement of a child for adoption or foster care, for the care of a child, spouse, or parent with a serious health condition, or for the employee's serious health condition.

Fast Track Construction: A phased approach where the construction process begins before completion of the contract documents. Generally, the cost is not fixed until after construction documents are complete and some construction commitments have already been made.

Federal Employer Identification Number (EIN): A 9-digit number issued by the IRS, which is used to identify the tax accounts of employers and certain others who have no employees (also referred to as a taxpayer identification number).

Federal Unemployment Tax Act (FUTA): The federal unemployment tax that is part of the federal and state program under which unemployment compensation is paid to workers who lose their jobs.

Fidelity Bond: A type of bond that covers business owners for losses due to dishonest acts by their employees.

Fixed Assets: Assets needed to carry on the business of a company, which are not normally consumed in the operation of the business (sometimes referred to as capital assets).

Foreign Entity: A business originally established in another state or another country.

Foreman: An individual who assists the superintendent with daily project operations and usually supervises specific areas by trade.

For Profit Corporation: A corporation in existence to make a profit for its owners or shareholders. Corporate tax status is determined by the Internal Revenue Service.

FUTA: An abbreviation for Federal Unemployment Tax Act.

H

Health Insurance Portability and Accountability Act of 1996 (HIPAA): A federal law that provides for improved portability and continuity of health insurance coverage connected with employment.

I

I-9 Form: The form required for employers to complete to verify employment eligibility under the Immigration and Nationality Act. I-9 forms must be kept on file for at least three years after the date of hire or for one year after the date employment ends, whichever is later.

Immaterial Breach (Partial Breach): A less serious violation of a contract that usually does not result in termination of the contract. The injured party may only sue for the value of the damages.

Immigration and Nationality Act (INA): A federal law that outlines the conditions for the temporary and permanent employment of aliens in the United States. It includes provisions for all employers that address employment eligibility and employment verification.

Income Statement: A financial statement that provides a summary of the company's revenues and expenses over a given period of time (sometimes called the profit-and-loss statement).

Indemnification: A way to transfer risk and exemption from loss that absolves the indemnified party from any payment for losses and damages incurred by a third party.

Indemnity: A way to transfer risk and exemption from loss incurred by any course of action. Sometimes an insurance payout is called an indemnity.

Indirect Expenses: See *Operating Expenses*.

Inland Marine Insurance (Equipment Theft Insurance): A type of property insurance for your tools and equipment that provides coverage for goods in transit and projects under construction.

Insurance: A protective measure in which coverage is obtained for a specific risk (or set of risks) through a contract. In this contract or policy, one party indemnifies another against specified loss in return for premiums paid.

K

Key Man Insurance: A type of insurance coverage for a specific individual necessary for the continuing success of a business. Key man insurance is available as life insurance, disability insurance, or both.

L

Lead-Based Paint Renovation, Repair and Painting Program: This federal regulation involves those who perform renovations for compensation in residential housing that may contain lead paint. It requires for additional provisions to the Lead PRE regulations. Under the Lead-Based Paint Renovation, Repair and Painting Program, contractors must be certified to perform renovation work that disturbs lead-based paint in homes, child care facilities, and schools built before 1978.

Lead PRE: This federal regulation involves those who perform renovations for compensation in residential housing built before 1978 that may contain lead paint. It requires mandatory notification for owners and occupants of the building being renovated.

Liabilities: All debt and obligations owed by a business.

Liability Insurance: A type of insurance designed to protect against third-party claims that arise from alleged negligence resulting in bodily injury or property damage.

Lien Bond: A type of bond that guarantees liens cannot be placed against the owner's property by contractors for payment of services.

Limited Liability Company (LLC): A legal business entity that has characteristics of both sole proprietorships and corporations. Federal income taxes are paid only on income distributed to members as ordinary income. Members have protection from liability for actions taken by the company or by other members of your company but are not protected from liability for personal actions.

Liquid Assets: Assets that are easily converted to cash.

Liquidity Ratio: A calculation used to determine if a company can pay its current debts. Calculated by dividing current liabilities into the current assets (sometimes called current ratio).

Little Miller Acts: Laws enacted by individual states and local governments regarding required bonds to bid and perform public works projects.

Long-Term Liabilities: Debt obligations that extend beyond one year.

Lump Sum Contract: A contract where the contractor agrees to complete the project for a predetermined, specified price. The contractor essentially assumes all of the risk under this contract agreement because the contractor is responsible for additional costs associated with unforeseen circumstances.

M

Maintenance Bond: A type of bond that guarantees for a stated period, typically for one year, no defective workmanship or material will appear in the completed project.

Marketing: Strategies and techniques used to bring in new customers and retain current customers to ensure a steady flow of leads and customers. This process includes advertising and promotion, pricing strategies, timely distribution, and product design and attributes to meet customer needs.

Marketing Plan: A formal document focusing on a company's marketing strategy by outlining the company's vision, customer base, methods of promotion (e.g. advertising, public relations, online marketing, direct sales, etc.), marketing budget, individual responsible for executing the plan, and industry opportunities and challenges.

MasterFormat: A classification system published by the Construction Specifications Institute that includes numbers and job tasks grouped by major construction activities.

Material Breach: A serious violation of a contract that may void the contract and will most likely end up in litigation.

Material Safety Data Sheet (MSDS): A form that accompanies chemicals and is important to workplace safety. The MSDS contains information such as first aid when contact occurs, disposal, storage, protective equipment required, and spill handling procedures.

Materials Expediter: An individual who supervises the materials procurement process to ensure accurate and timely delivery of materials.

Mechanics' Lien: A legal action that "clouds" the title to real property and serves as an effective method (and sometimes the only method) for securing payment for labor or materials used in the improvement of real property. The lien stops the owner from selling the property with a clear title.

Medicare: Social Security and Medicare taxes pay for benefits that workers and families receive under the Federal Insurance Contributions Act (FICA). Medicare tax pays for benefits under the hospital insurance part of FICA.

Miller Act: The Miller Act requires performance and payment bonds on all federal construction projects valued at greater than $100,000.

Minimum Wage: The minimum amount an employer can pay employees. FLSA and individual state laws designate the minimum pay rate.

Minor: An individual under 18 years of age.

Modified Accelerated Cost Recovery System (MACRS): A depreciation method approved by the IRS that allows for faster depreciation over longer periods.

Motor Truck Cargo Insurance: A type of inland marine insurance protecting the transporter in the event of damaged or lost freight.

N

Named Peril Builders' Risk Insurance: An insurance policy with narrower coverage than all-risk insurance that specifies which perils are covered.

National Environmental Policy Act (NEPA): A federal law that ensures that federal agencies consider environmental impacts in federal planning and decision making and covers construction and post-construction activities.

National Historic Preservation Act (NHPA): A federal law that protects property that is eligible for or included on the National Register of Historic Places (NRHP).

Negotiation (Alternative Dispute Resolution): A dialogue entered into for the purpose of resolving disputes or producing an agreed upon course or courses of action.

Negotiation (Contract): The process where the owner and contractor come to an agreement on the price and terms of the contract.

Net Pay: The payroll amount an employee receives after taxes and deductions are taken out.

Net Profit: The difference between revenues and expenses. Net profit directly contributes to the net worth of the company.

NPDES: The abbreviation for the National Pollutant Discharge Elimination System.

O

Occupational Safety and Health Act (OSHA): Federal law governing safe and healthy working conditions by developing standards, providing assistance, information and training, and conducting research.

Offer: An offer specifically outlines the obligations of the contract, including the work to be done and compensation for this work (e.g. estimate or bid).

Operating Expenses: General items that contribute to the cost of operating the business. These expenses can be put into two categories, selling expenses and fixed overhead (sometimes called indirect expenses).

OSHA: An abbreviation for Occupational Safety and Health Administration; Occupational Safety and Health Act.

OSHA Form 300: An OSHA form that serves as an injury/illness log, with a separate line entry for each recordable injury or illness.

OSHA Form 300A: An OSHA form that includes a summary of the previous year's work-related injuries and illnesses.

OSHA Form 301: An OSHA form that serves as an individual incident report providing details about each specific recordable injury or illness.

Other Than Serious Violation: A safety violation that has a direct relationship to workplace safety and health, but probably would not cause death or serious physical harm.

Overhead: See *Company Overhead; Project Overhead.*

Overtime: The hours an employee works when it exceeds more than 40 hours in a workweek. FLSA designates that eligible employees are paid one-and-one-half-times the regular rate for overtime hours.

Owners' Equity: Consists of the initial investment in a business, plus accumulated net profits not paid out to the owners.

Owner's Representative (Owner's Agent): An appointed representative designated to oversee a project and serve as a liaison to the owner. The owner's representative (agent) may have legal authority to make certain legal decisions on behalf of the owner.

P

Partnership: A business relationship between two or more persons who join to carry on a trade or business. Each person contributes money, property, labor, or skill, and each partner expects to share in the profits and losses of the business.

Payment Bond: A type of bond that guarantees subcontractors and suppliers will be paid for work if they perform properly under the contract.

Percentage of Completion Method: A method of contract accounting that recognizes income as it is earned during the construction project.

Performance Bond: A type of bond that guarantees the contractor will complete a contract within its time frame and conditions.

Petty Cash Fund: A cash fund used to make small payments instead of writing a check.

Positive Cash Flow: A term used to describe when more cash is received than is going out to pay expenses.

Professional Liability Insurance (sometimes called Errors and Omissions Insurance): A type of liability insurance that protects contractors from negligence resulting from errors or omissions of designers and architects.

Profitability Ratio: A formula used to calculate the profit margin of a company. It is calculated by dividing revenues into net income.

Profit-and-Loss Statement: See *Income Statement.*

Progressive Discipline: A method of corrective action where the consequences of the improper behavior become more significant if it continues.

Progress Payments: Partial payments made after completion of specified phases of construction. Payments are generally calculated by taking the difference between the completed work and materials delivered and a predetermined schedule of unit costs.

Project Manager: An individual who plans and coordinates a construction project to meet the overall goals of the project and serves as the main contact with the owner.

Project Overhead: Items necessary to complete the project but not directly associated with labor and materials (e.g. temporary storage, dumpsters, etc.).

Property Insurance: An insurance policy covering property when damage, theft, or loss occurs. Specific risk provisions are often available for occurrences such as fire or theft. Broad-based policies cover a variety of risks (including fire, theft, vandalism, and "acts of God" such as lightning strikes).

Q

Quick Ratio: Similar to the liquidity ratio, it is calculated by dividing the current liabilities into the current assets minus inventory (sometimes called the acid test ratio).

R

Recitals (Legal): Language at the beginning of a contract that provides background to the contract.

Repeated Violation: A safety violation of any standard, regulation, rule, or order where, upon reinspection, a substantially similar violation is found.

Retainage: A specified amount withheld from each progress payment as protection for the owner to ensure completion of the construction project and provide protection against liens, claims, and defaults.

Return on Total Assets Ratio: A formula used to determine if the company's assets are being employed in the best manner. It is calculated by dividing total assets into net profit (after taxes).

Revenues: The income received from the daily operations of the business.

Right-to-Work Laws: Laws passed at the state-level that secure the right of employees to decide for themselves whether or not to join or financially support a union.

Risk Management: An assessment of all areas of a business from operations to administrative functions for the risk of financial loss, lower profit margins, and unnecessary liabilities.

S

S Corporation: A legal business entity formed under the rules of Subchapter S of the Internal Revenue Code. It is taxed like a partnership by passing items of income, loss, deduction, and credits through to its shareholders to be included on their separate returns.

Self-Employment Tax: A social security and Medicare tax primarily for individuals who work for themselves.

Serious Violation: A violation where there is substantial probability that death or serious physical harm could result and that the employer knew, or should have known, of the hazard.

Service Contract Act: The federal act that requires payment of prevailing wage rates and fringe benefits on contracts to provide services to the federal government.

Single Prime Contracting: Traditional form of contracting where the project owner typically hires an architectural firm to design the project and the contractor then performs the work according to the specifications of the project and is responsible for the costs of all materials and labor to obtain project completion.

Social Security Tax: Social Security and Medicare taxes pay for benefits that workers and families receive under the Federal Insurance Contributions Act (FICA). Social Security tax pays for benefits under the old-age, survivors, and disability insurance part of FICA.

Sole Proprietorship: A business that has one individual as the owner (proprietor) who is responsible for 100% of the decisions made on behalf of the business and owns all of the business assets. It can employ others but may just be the owner who works for the business.

Square-Foot Method Estimate: An estimate based on a calculation of the square footage of the project multiplied by a unit cost.

Statement of Cash Flows: A financial statement that summarizes current cash position, cash sources, and use of these funds over a given period of time.

Statute of Limitations: Laws that set a maximum period of time within which a lawsuit or claim may be filed.

Straight Line Depreciation: A method of depreciation where the salvage cost is subtracted from the initial cost of the item.

Subcontractor: An individual or business that contracts with the general contractor or other subcontractors to complete a portion of a larger project.

Subcontractor's Bond: A type of bond that protects the general contractor in the event that the subcontractor does not fully perform the contract and/or pay for labor and materials.

Superintendent: An onsite supervisor responsible for the daily operations.

SUTA Dumping: The transfer of employees between businesses for the purpose of obtaining a lower unemployment compensation tax rate. SUTA dumping is illegal and subject to criminal and/or civil penalties.

T

Taxpayer Identification Number: See *Federal Employer Identification Number.*

Tax Provision Expenses: Tax liabilities owed for federal, state, and local taxes.

Title III of the Consumer Credit Protection Act (CCPA): A federal law that protects employees from being discharged by their employers because their wages have been garnished for any one debt and limits the amount of employees' earnings that may be garnished in any one week.

Title VII of the Civil Rights Act of 1964: A federal law that prohibits discrimination on the basis of race, color, religion, national origin, and sex.

Transportation Floater Insurance: A type of inland marine insurance protecting the transporter against damage that occurs to freight during transport.

Turnkey Construction: Similar to the design/build model, the contractor puts together and manages the construction and design team but also obtains financing and land.

U

Unemployment Insurance: A type of insurance that provides unemployment benefits to eligible workers who become unemployed through no fault of their own and meet certain other eligibility requirements. This program is jointly financed through federal and state employer payroll taxes.

Uniformed Services Employment and Reemployment Rights Act (USERRA): A federal law that protects service members' reemployment rights when returning from a period of service in the uniformed services, including those called up from the reserves or National Guard, and prohibits employer discrimination based on military service or obligation.

Unit-Price Contract: A type of contract where a price per unit is calculated for each item and the contractor is paid according to the actual quantities used.

Unit Price Estimating Method: A method of estimating that bundles all of the cost factors such as labor, materials, equipment, and subcontractors to come up with a unit price for the entire task.

V

Value Engineering: A project management approach with the primary objective of understanding the owner's cost, quality, and time priorities to deliver a product of the highest value.

W

Wage Garnishment Law: A federal law that limits the amount an individual's income may be legally garnished and prohibits firing an employee whose pay is garnished for payment of a single debt.

Walsh-Healey Public Contracts Act: A federal law that requires payment of minimum wage rates and overtime pay on contracts that provide goods to the federal government.

Willful Violation: A safety violation that the employer knowingly commits or commits with plain indifference to the law.

Work Hours: As defined under FLSA, hours that ordinarily include all time during which an employee is required to be on the employer's premises, on duty, or at a prescribed work place.

Worker Adjustment and Retraining Notification Act (WARN): A federal law that offers protection to workers, their families, and communities by requiring employers to provide notice 60 days in advance of covered plant closings and covered mass layoffs.

Workers' Compensation Insurance: A type of insurance providing monetary compensation to employees who are injured or disabled on the job and benefits for dependents of those workers who are killed because of work-related accidents or illnesses. The insurance is purchased by the employer; no part of it should be paid for by employees or deducted from their pay.

Working Capital: The amount of cash available after liabilities or debts are paid. Working capital measures the liquidity of the company's assets.

Workweek: As defined under FLSA, it is a period of 168 hours during seven consecutive 24-hour periods. It may begin on any day of the week and at any hour of the day established by the employer.

Appendix B: Business Plan Template

The following business plan template can be customized for your company. These forms are also located at **NASCLAforms.org** using access code **UT129354** in case you need to modify them on your computer. You may want to work through this plan as you review each chapter, as some of the business plan section topics are covered in more depth.

Business Plan Outline

Section 1: Cover Sheet

1a. Name of Business

1b. Contact Information

Section 2: Executive Summary

2a. Plan Highlights

2b. Keys to Success

Section 3: Company Summary

3a. Vision

3b. Mission

3c. Legal Structure

3d. Management and Personnel Plan

3e. Proposed Location

3f. Facilities Requirements

3g. Operational Hours

Section 4: Products and/or Service

4a. Product and/or Service Description

4b. Vendors

4c. Technology

4d. Expansion Opportunities

Section 5: Market Analysis

5a. Target Market Definition

5b. Market Needs

5c. Market Trends

5d. Market Growth

5e. Competitive Comparison

Section 6: Marketing Strategy

6a. Value Proposition

6b. Competitive Edge

6c. Pricing Strategy

6d. Promotion Strategy

6e. Marketing Programs

Section 7: Financial Plan

7a. Sales Forecast and Assumptions

7b. Profit and Loss Pro Forma

7c. Source of Financing

Note: You may also refer to the Financial Management chapter for additional financial documents such as a balance sheet, income statement, and statement of cash flows. The profit and loss pro forma is a good tool for newly-established businesses to determine how much revenue is needed to break even.

Section 1: Cover Sheet

The cover sheet should contain the name of the business, address, phone number, fax number, e-mail address, and contact name. Some cover sheets also contain a confidentiality statement.

Section 2: Executive Summary

A business plan normally starts with an executive summary, which should be concise and interesting. This summary includes the highlights of your plan and serves as an introduction to the rest of your plan. Topics in your executive summary should include, but not be limited to, the following:

✓ Business name
✓ Business location
✓ Product or service offered
✓ Purpose of the plan
✓ Projected sales
✓ Profitability
✓ Keys to success

The executive summary should only be a page or two long. Although the executive summary appears first in the printed document, most business plan developers do not write it until after the plan is complete.

Section 3: Company Summary

1. **Vision and Mission:** Include a vision and mission statement for your company. The vision should be a short statement about the company's aspirations for the future. The mission describes the company's primary business purpose or goal. These statements outline the business concept and provide a concise definition of where your company fits in the market.

2. **Legal Structure:** Define the legal structure of your company (i.e., sole proprietorship, partnership, corporation, or limited liability company). Explain why you chose this structure and the benefits it will provide to you and your company. Legal structure is covered in Chapter 2.

3. **Management:** Outline the key management personnel needed to run your business. Can you run the business yourself or do you need to hire managers to help run the operations? What are the job responsibilities of these managers?

4. **Employees:** How many employees do you require? What are the job responsibilities of the employees?

5. **Location:** Describe the location of your business. You do not need to provide a specific address if you do not have one, but identify the area (e.g., downtown location, at home, in a rural area). Explain why this location will provide you with the best opportunity for success.

6. **Facility Requirements:** Identify your facility requirements. Do you need office space, a production area, storage space, or mobile storage? You may want to draw a diagram of the space.

7. **Hours of Operation:** What are your hours of operation? Explain how these hours will provide the maximum benefit to your customer. How will you handle emergency situations that arise outside of normal working hours?

Section 4: Product or Service Description

Defining your product or service (or both) may seem simple. You must describe not only your product or service but how you will provide it to your customers. For example, you may be a general contractor, but without reliable subcontractors and suppliers, you may not be able to complete your projects in the time frame promised to the customer.

1. **Product or Service Description:** Write a summary explaining your specialty. For example, are you a general contractor, plumbing contractor, etc.?

2. **Legal Requirements:** Do you have any licensing or registration requirements? Are there any legal requirements for practicing your trade or running your business?

3. **Subcontractors and Suppliers:** Who will be your primary subcontractors and suppliers? What process will you use to evaluate subcontractors and suppliers?

4. **Technology Trends:** Summarize how technology will affect your business. Are there efficiencies that can be gained through technology? For example, can you integrate scheduling or estimating systems into your business processes?

5. **Growth Opportunities:** What expansion opportunities exist in the future after your company is established? Can you offer additional products or services, or expand your customer base to other locations?

Section 5: Market Analysis

A market analysis is often performed as one of the first tasks in researching and formulating a business plan. Understanding your customers, the demand for your work, and your competition is important to the future success of your business.

1. **Target Market:** Define the target market for your product or service. Describe the key characteristics of your customers. For example, do your primary customers include families, retired adults, or businesses?

2. **Product or Service Description:** Describe the need your product or service will be filling for your customers. If you will provide both products and services, describe how these will benefit your customers.

3. **Trends:** Describe how your product or service aligns with the consumer trends of your customers. What are the construction trends for your trade and how do these fit your customer's needs?

4. **Growth Opportunities:** Outline growth opportunities that exist within your target market. For example, if you are a pool builder and your target market is young families, you may want to concentrate on single-family homes rather than commercial projects.

5. **Competition:** List your major competitors. Are they local, regional, or national?

Section 6: Marketing Strategy

A marketing strategy is easily formulated by using the "4 P's": Product, Price, Promotion, and Place. Product is not just your product or service, but how it will benefit your customer. Price refers to your pricing strategy, which can vary based on the market, your goals, and your competition. Promotion deals with marketing in a traditional sense. Your customers will find out about your business through your promotional efforts. Place defines your distribution strategy. In the construction industry, distribution defines the type of customers you want to target. For example, you may decide to differentiate yourself by specializing in certain types of construction.

1. **Value Proposition:** Describe the value that your company will provide your customers. What benefits of using your company will you promote to your customers? For example, you may promote your level of quality or service.

2. **Competitive Edge:** Describe what makes your product or service unique and how you have differentiated yourself from your competitors.

3. **Pricing Strategy:** What pricing strategy will you use? Some options include:
   - ✓ Cost-plus pricing, where you determine a markup percentage and add it to the cost of the job.
   - ✓ Consistency with competition, where your pricing reflects what the competition is charging.
   - ✓ Value pricing, where you try to undercut your competition with lower prices.

4. **Promotion:** How will you familiarize potential customers with your business? Will you promote your product in special venues (i.e., trade shows or special events)? Are there any businesses you can build a co-op relationship with so you can cross-promote each other? For example, you might partner with another trade or supplier to promote each other.

5. **Advertising:** How will you advertise? Will you use media such as radio, TV, newspapers, and the Internet? How often will you advertise?

6. **Sales:** Will you hire sales representatives to promote your company? If so, how many? How will the sales force be divided up? By area or region?

Section 7: Financial Plan

A financial plan can include several aspects of the potential financial health of the company. At a minimum, it should include projected profits over a specific period. This template, for example, shows the first three years of operation. The financial plan should also explain projected cash flow and identify any additional capital required from outside investors or loans.

The profit-and-loss statement is a tabulation of the gross sales income for the company from which all attributed costs must be deducted. A *pro forma* is a "best guess" at these sales numbers and the associated costs. From this pro forma, you can see your profit or loss based on the numbers you projected and adjust your budget accordingly. A blank profit-and-loss form is located at the end of this section, if you are unable to use the form on the **NASCLAforms.org** website. If you use the spreadsheet located on the website, it will automatically calculate gross profit and net income. These calculations were derived from the following formulas:

Income – Cost of Goods Sold = Gross Profit

Gross Profit – Expenses = Net Income

You will learn more about financial calculations in the financial management chapter.

Sales/Income

Use the following points to help you make your sales and expense projections.

You need to determine the average price of the jobs you perform and the number of customers you are projecting for the year. This is your "best guess," but if you have any historical sales data, you may want to use this information in your calculations to determine how your business sales will grow over time.

However you determine your sales, you must list your assumptions so the person reviewing your business plan will understand the numbers presented in your plan.

Projected sales numbers

	Sales (in dollars)
Year 1	
Year 2	
Year 3	

Transfer sales numbers into the profit-and-loss worksheet.

Cost of Goods Sold (COGS)

Cost of goods sold shows the cost of materials and production of the goods a business sells. For each year, enter your inventory cost and the cost to produce the final product for the customer and add together to show the totals. This total represents the cost of goods sold.

	Year 1	Year 2	Year 3
Inventory			
Production Payroll			
Total			

Transfer COGS numbers into the profit-and-loss worksheet.

Management Salaries

Determine how many managers or supervisors you will need to operate your business. A published salary survey will help you estimate what they earn in your type of business and in your region. Determine if you will need to add managers or supervisors in years two and three if you have an increase in business.

	Number of Managers	Manager Annual Salary	Total Management Salaries
Year 1			
Year 2			
Year 3			

Enter the total management salaries in the respective boxes on your spreadsheet.

Payroll Taxes

Payroll taxes are calculated at approximately 13% of the salaries listed on your spreadsheet. A formula has been entered to calculate that amount automatically.

Payroll taxes include the following items:

✓ Social Security, also known as FICA (a set percentage deducted from an employee's check and EMPLOYER MATCHED)

✓ Medicare, also called FICA Medicare (a set percentage deducted from an employee's check and EMPLOYER MATCHED)

✓ FUTA - Federal Unemployment Tax Act, authorizes the IRS to use monies for job service and training funded through the federal employment agency; EMPLOYER PAID ONLY

✓ SUTA - State Unemployment Tax Act, authorizes the state to use monies for job service/training and retraining of displaced workers; EMPLOYER-PAID ONLY

✓ FUI - Federal Unemployment Insurance; EMPLOYER-PAID ONLY

✓ SUI - State Unemployment Insurance; EMPLOYER-PAID ONLY

More details on payroll taxes are provided in Chapter 15.

Outside Services

These services apply to people or businesses who provide services to your company not directly related to the sales or income of the company. They would not appear on your payroll. Estimate your annual expenses for the following outside services. Keep in mind that the cost may be higher in the first year due to start-up needs. The cost may drop in the second year and then level off in the third year.

	Year 1	Year 2	Year 3
Lawyer			
Accountant			
Technology Consultant			
Total			

Enter the year totals into the spreadsheet.

Advertising and Promotion

Consider the type of marketing you will need. If you are creating a radio, newspaper or TV ad, get an estimate on what that would cost. Don't forget to calculate the frequency of advertising you will do. For example, let's say a magazine ad costs $1,000 for a quarter-page ad and the magazine comes out monthly. Your advertising cost would be $12,000 a year. You may want to advertise by printing flyers and mailing them out. Calculate the printing costs as well as the postage to send out the flyers.

	Year 1	Year 2	Year 3
Radio			
TV			
Newspaper			
Magazine			
Flyers			
Direct Mail			
Special Events			
Online Ads			
Other Please Specify:			
Total			

Enter the year totals into the spreadsheet.

Rent

If you rent a facility, determine the rental costs per year. If you have not decided on a location, you may want to look at a few locations and calculate an average rent cost to determine a figure for this category. Keep in mind the square footage requirements that you have set out.

	Annual Rent
Location #1	
Location #2	
Location #3	
Average of all three locations	

If you are going to stay in one location, your rent should remain fixed over three years. If you plan on expanding in years two and three, you may want to increase rent accordingly.

Enter the average of all three locations in the rent column on your spreadsheet.

Office Supplies

Office supplies include items such as paper, pens, printer cartridges, tape, and other materials as well as cleaning supplies. As your business increases, the consumption of these supplies may increase accordingly.

	Year 1	Year 2	Year 3
Office Supplies			
Cleaning Supplies			
Total			

Enter the year totals into the spreadsheet.

Dues, Subscriptions, and Licenses

You may want to join a Chamber of Commerce or trade group or subscribe to trade publications. Your business may also need a license to operate. For example, if you are starting a plumbing company, you may be required to get a contractor's license.

	Year 1	Year 2	Year 3
Chamber of Commerce Membership			
Business Organization Membership (i.e., National Homebuilders Association)			
Magazine/Newspaper Subscriptions			
Business License Fees			
Total			

Enter the year totals into the spreadsheet.

Travel

Does your business require you to travel to meet with customers? Will you travel locally, regionally, or nationally? What are the air travel, rental car, and hotel costs for this travel requirement? Note that the spreadsheet has a separate section for automobile expenses, where you enter costs such as gasoline or repairs. Use the automobile expense section for trips that will be taken in a company or personal vehicle.

	Year 1	Year 2	Year 3
Air Travel			
Rental Cars			
Hotel			
Other			
Please Specify:			
Total			

Enter the year totals into the spreadsheet.

Meals and Entertainment

Determine if you will be providing meals or taking your clients and vendors out for entertainment.

Keep in mind that the IRS allows you to take only a 50 percent deduction on meals and entertainment. It is not considered a 100 percent business expense. Although you enter the full amount on your profit-and-loss statement, your tax accountant will make the proper adjustments on your tax return at the end of the year.

	Year 1	Year 2	Year 3
Meals			
Entertainment			
Total			

Enter the year totals into the spreadsheet.

Automobile Expense

Determine if you will need one or more automobiles or trucks to operate your business. The cost to purchase each vehicle appears under "Assets" on your balance sheet, and the cost to operate the vehicles appears under automobile expense on the profit-and-loss statement.

	Year 1	Year 2	Year 3
Gasoline			
Oil Changes			
Car Washes			
Other			
(Repairs) Please Specify:			
Total			

Enter the annual totals into the spreadsheet.

Utilities and Telephone

Determine what your utilities and telephone costs will be for the first three years your business is operational. To arrive at this estimate, you will need to determine how many telephone lines and cell phones you need. You should also itemize Internet service and record these totals under this line item.

	Year 1	Year 2	Year 3
Electric			
Water			
Garbage			
Telephone			
Internet Service			
Other Please Specify:			
Total			

Enter the annual totals into the spreadsheet.

Auto Insurance

If you have business vehicles, you will need to carry insurance on them. If you increase the number of vehicles in years two and three, insurance expenses will increase as well. Certain vehicles may also cost more to insure than others. For example, if you have delivery trucks, the insurance will probably be more expensive than a mid-size car.

	Year 1	Year 2	Year 3
Vehicle #1			
Vehicle #2			
Vehicle #3			
Total			

Enter the annual totals into the spreadsheet.

Group Medical Insurance

You may want to carry medical, dental, or life insurance for your employees as a benefit and to increase employee retention.

	Year 1	Year 2	Year 3
Medical			
Dental			
Life			
Total			

Enter the annual totals into the spreadsheet.

Business Insurance

By law, businesses are required to carry workers' compensation insurance. Business liability insurance protects your business against accidents such as fire, flooding, burglary, etc. Business liability insurance is not required by law but by contract. For example, most landlords require you to carry business liability insurance, as do banks and governmental agencies with which you have a contract. Insurance and risk management are covered in more detail in the managing risk chapter.

	Year 1	Year 2	Year 3
Workers' Compensation			
Business Liability			
Total			

Enter the annual totals into the spreadsheet.

Worksheet

This is a scratch sheet for entering estimates and data that can then be entered in the spreadsheet.

	Year 1	Year 2	Year 3
Income			
Sales			
Total Income	0.00	0.00	0.00
Cost of Goods Sold			
Inventory Cost			
Production Payroll Cost			
Total COGS	0.00	0.00	0.00
Gross Profit	0.00	0.00	0.00
Expense			
Management Salaries			
Payroll Taxes	0.00	0.00	0.00
Outside Services			
Advertising and Promotion			
Rent			
Office Supplies			
Dues, Subscriptions, and Licenses			
Travel			
Meals and Entertainment			
Automobile Expense			
Utilities/Telephone			
Insurance Auto			
Insurance Group Medical			
Business Insurance			
Total Expense	0.00	0.00	0.00
Net Income	0.00	0.00	0.00

Appendix C: Useful Links

Listed below are website links that relate to each of the chapters. These websites are provided for your reference for more in-depth searches of the topic areas contained in this book.

Chapter 1 – The Plan

American Express Small Business	American Express offers business planning links and an area where you can post questions for a small business advisor.	www.americanexpress.com/us/small-business/openforum/explore
Business Plan Pro	This site offers tools on how to write a business plan including samples and tips to starting a business.	www.bplans.com
Sample Business Plans	These sites provide sample business plans and other valuable business management materials.	www.allbusiness.com www.inc.com/home www.bizmove.com/small-business/business-plan.htm
SBA Business Planning	The SBA has several different links on writing and using your business plan.	www.sba.gov/category/navigation-structure/starting-managing-business

Chapter 2 – Choosing Your Business Structure

IRS Business Structures	The IRS provides a summary of tax considerations by business structure.	www.irs.gov/Businesses/Small-Businesses-&-Self-Employed/Small-Business-and-Self-Employed-Tax-Center-1
SBA Legal Aspects	The SBA has several different links on forms of ownership and licenses.	www.sba.gov/category/navigation-structure/startingmanaging-business/starting-business/establishing-business/business-types
Utah Division of Corporations and Commercial Code	The Utah Division of Corporations and Commercial Code has information on business filings.	www.corporations.utah.gov

Chapter 3 – Becoming a Licensed Contractor

Division of Occupational and Professional Licensing	The Division of Occupational and Professional Licensing regulates contractor licensing in Utah. Their website has useful information on the licensing process and licensing forms.	www.dopl.utah.gov
PSI Exams Online	Licensing candidates can register online for exams and download the Candidate Information Bulletin.	www.psiexams.com

Chapter 4 - Managing Risk

Entrepreneur.com	Entrepreneur.com has links to insurance resources.	www.entrepreneur.com/topic/insurance
Labor Commission of Utah	The Labor Commission of Utah website provides information on the state workers' compensation program.	www.laborcommission.utah.gov
Surety Information Office	This site has resources related to bonding, bank letters of credit and publishes the "Construction Project Owner's Guide to Surety Bond Claims."	www.sio.org
Utah Department of Workforce Services	The Utah Department of Workforce Services website gives information on state unemployment.	jobs.utah.gov/ui/employer/employerhome.aspx

Chapter 5 - Your Business Toolbox

SBA Special Interests	The SBA has several different links for women and minority entrepreneurs.	www.sba.gov/content/minority-owned-businesses
Service Corps of Retired Executives (SCORE)	The SCORE website has useful links for small business and a listing of local SCORE centers.	www.score.org
Small Business Administration (SBA)	The SBA website has resources for small businesses and a link to the Utah District Office website.	www.sba.gov/offices/district/ut/salt-lake-city
Small Business Administration (SBA) Small Disadvantaged Business Certification	The SBA website has resources for small disadvantaged business certifications.	www.sba.gov/sdb
U.S. Minority Business Development Agency (MBDA)	The U.S. MBDA website has links on starting, managing, and financing your business.	www.mbda.gov
U.S. Department of Commerce, Economic Development Administration (EDA)	The U.S. Department of Commerce, EDA division has information on funding opportunities and additional resources.	www.eda.gov
Utah State Government Minority-Owned Business Certifications	The Utah state government website has information on obtaining minority business certifications.	business.utah.gov/partners/sbdcs
Utah State Government Business Resources	The Utah state government website provides information on starting and operating your business in Utah.	www.business.utah.gov

Chapter 6 - Marketing and Sales

Entrepreneur.com Marketing	Entrepreneur.com has several articles on small business marketing.	www.entrepreneur.com/topic/marketing
KnowThis.com Sample Marketing Plans	KnowThis.com has information on writing marketing plans and sample plans.	www.knowthis.com/how-to-write-a-marketing-plan
SBA Marketing Basics	The SBA has several different links on marketing research and writing your marketing plan.	www.sba.gov/content/developing-marketing-plan

Chapter 7 - Bidding and Estimating

Bidshop.com Estimating Software	This site gives a list of software by type of estimating program.	www.bidshop.org
DMOZ.com Estimating Software	This site gives a comprehensive list of estimating software.	www.dmoz.org/Computers/Software/Industry-Specific/Construction/Project_Management/Estimating
U.S. Department of Labor, Bureau of Labor Statistics	The Bureau of Labor Statistics site has helpful information on wages, earnings, and business costs.	www.bls.gov

Chapter 8 - Contract Management

B4UBuild.com	B4UBuild.com has articles on contract law for residential builders.	www.b4ubuild.com/resources/contract/index.shtml
Free Advice.com	Free Advice.com has links to different contract topics.	www.law.freeadvice.com/general_practice/contract_law
Nolo.com	Nolo.com has articles about contract law.	www.nolo.com

Chapter 9 - Scheduling and Project Management

Construction place.com	Constructionplace.com has an informative glossary of terms focused on construction management.	www.constructionplace.com/glossary.asp
Free Download Center.com	Free Download Center.com has project management software downloads.	www.freedownloadscenter.com/Business/Project_Management

Chapter 10 - Customer Relations

Microsoft Small Business Center	The Microsoft site offers helpful customer relations links.	www.microsoft.com/en-us/business
Quicken Small Business Center	The Quicken site offers articles on building excellent customer relations.	www.quicken.intuit.com/all-videos-and-articles.jsp

Chapter 11 – Employee Management

DOL Employment Compliance Guide	The Department of Labor has several links on employment law compliance, a compliance guide, and a compliance advisor.	www.dol.gov/compliance/guide/index.htm www.dol.gov/elaws/
IRS Forms	This site contains IRS forms, such as the W-4 and W-5 that you can download.	www.irs.gov/Forms-&-Pubs
Labor Commission of Utah - Employment Laws	The Labor Commission website gives information on employment laws and resources for employers.	www.laborcommission.utah.gov
Labor Commission of Utah-Workers' Compensation	The Labor Commission of Utah website provides information on the state workers' compensation program.	www.laborcommission.utah.gov/divisions/IndustrialAccidents/index.html
SBA Employment Law	The SBA has several different links on employment law.	www.sba.gov/content/employment-labor-law
U.S. Citizenship and Immigration Services	The I-9 form can be downloaded from this site.	www.uscis.gov
U.S. Equal Employment Opportunity Commission (EEOC)	The EEOC website has information about the Americans with Disabilities Act (ADA).	www.eeoc.gov
Utah New Hire Reporting	The Utah new hire link has information on reporting requirements for new hires.	jobs.utah.gov/employer/index.html
Utah Department of Workforce Services	The Utah Department of Workforce Services website gives information on state unemployment.	jobs.utah.gov/ui/employer/employerhome.aspx

Chapter 12 – Jobsite Safety and Environmental Factors

Common Ground Alliance (CGA)	The Common Ground Alliance is available by calling 811. CGA can connect contractors to One Call Centers to locate underground utilities.	www.call811.com
Construction Industry Compliance Center	The Construction Industry Compliance Center website has information available on environmental regulations including hazardous and non-hazardous waste.	www.cicacenter.org
Energy Star	The Energy Star website has eco-friendly resources for home improvement and residential and commercial construction.	www.energystar.gov
Environmental Protection Agency	The Environmental Protection Agency provides a publication called Managing Your Environmental Responsibilities.	www.epa.gov/nscep

Environmental Protection Agency- Asbestos- Containing Materials List	The Environmental Protection Agency website provides a list of asbestos-containing materials.	www.epa.gov/asbestos
Environmental Protection Agency- Green Building	The Environmental Protection Agency website provides information on components of green building, national, state and local funding opportunities, and publications on various environmental topics.	www.epa.gov/greenbuilding
Environmental Protection Agency- Lead in Paint, Dust, and Soil	The Environmental Protection Agency website provides information on lead hazards.	www.epa.gov/lead
OSHA	The OSHA website has links regarding safety on the job and safety laws and programs.	www.osha.gov
OSHA Compliance Assistance for Construction	The OSHA website has a page with numerous construction compliance assistance links.	www.osha.gov/doc
Labor Commission of Utah-UOSHA	The Labor Commission website has information on the state OSHA program.	laborcommission.utah.gov/divisions/UOSH/index.html
Utah Department of Environmental Quality	The Utah Department of Environmental Quality website provides small business resources for environmental compliance.	www.deq.utah.gov
Utah Department of Environmental Quality, Division of Air Quality	The Utah Department of Environmental Quality, Division of Air Quality website provides information on permitting and the Small Business Assistance Program.	www.airquality.utah.gov
Utah Department of Environmental Quality, Division of Solid and Hazardous Waste	The Utah Department of Environmental Quality, Division of Solid and Hazardous website provides technical assistance on characterizing, storing, treating, and disposing hazardous waste.	www.hazardouswaste.utah.gov
Utah Department of Environmental Quality, Division of Water Quality	The Utah Department of Environmental Quality, Division of Water Quality website provides information on water quality permits and pollution control.	www.waterquality.utah.gov
Utah Safe Digging	Utah's digging safety website and hotline. This site provides information on underground safety and procedures.	www.bluestakes.org

Chapter 13 – Working with Subcontractors

IRS Publication 1779	This IRS publication provides criteria to determine employee versus independent contractor status.	www.irs.gov/pub/irs-pdf/p1779.pdf

Chapter 14 – Financial Management

IRS Publication 15: Circular E	The Circular E, used for federal income tax withholding, is available on the IRS website.	www.irs.gov/publications/p15/index.html
SBA Balance Sheet Template	The SBA has a balance sheet template that you can customize.	www.sba.gov/sites/default/files/balance_sheet.xlt
SBA Income Statement Template	The SBA has an income statement template that you can customize.	www.sba.gov/sites/default/files/income_statement.xlt
SBA Financing Basics	The SBA has several different links on financing and financial statements.	www.sba.gov/category/navigation-structure/starting-managing-business/starting-business/preparing-your-finances/understanding-basics
Social Security Administration	The Social Security Administration website has information on the current social security tax rate.	www.ssa.gov

Chapter 15 – Tax Basics

How to Apply for an EIN	There are several ways to apply for an EIN. The IRS outlines the procedure on their website.	www.irs.gov/Businesses/Small-Businesses-&-Self-Employed/How-to-Apply-for-an-EIN
IRS Service	The IRS site has tax forms, publications, and useful information for small businesses.	www.irs.gov
Tax Basics	The SBA has several different links on federal, state, and local taxes.	www.sba.gov/category/navigation-structure/starting-managing-business/starting-business/establishing-business/taxes
Utah Tax Commission	The Utah Tax Commission website provides helpful information on state taxes.	www.tax.utah.gov

Chapter 16 – Utah Mechanics' Lien Law

Department of Occupational and Professional Licensing, Lien Recovery Fund	This site has information on the Lien Recovery Fund Act and how to register with the Fund.	www.dopl.utah.gov/programs/rlrf/index.html
Find Law.com	Find Law.com has useful articles on lien law.	www.findlaw.com

Trade Links

American Institute of Architects (AIA)	This site has information about the organization and contract documents for purchase.	www.aia.org
American National Standards Institute (ANSI)	The ANSI website has information on membership, accreditation services, and educational resources.	www.ansi.org
American Society of Plumbing Engineers (ASPE)	The ASPE website has information on membership, certifications, and useful resources.	www.aspe.org
American Society of Civil Engineers (ASCE)	The ASCE website has information on membership, conferences, publications, and continuing education.	www.asce.org
American Subcontractors Association (ASA)	This site has information for subcontractors and suppliers in the construction industry.	www.asaonline.com
American Water Works Association (AWWA)	The AWWA website has information on membership, accreditation services, and educational resources.	www.awwa.org
Associated Builders and Contractors (ABC)	The ABC website has information on membership, training, a list of contractors, and links to business development, safety, insurance, and legal resources.	www.abc.org
Associated General Contractors (AGC)	This site has information for construction contractors and industry related companies.	www.agc.org
International Association of Plumbing and Mechanical Officials (IAPMO)	The IAPMO website has information on membership, certification, and educational resources.	www.iapmo.org
National Association of Home Builders (NAHB)	This site is for people interested in homebuilding and the industry.	www.nahb.org
National Association of the Remodeling Industry (NARI)	This site is for people interested in the remodeling industry.	www.nari.org
National Association of State Contractor Licensing Agencies (NASCLA)	This site contains useful information about state licensing agencies and information about the organization.	www.nascla.org

National Association of Women in Construction (NAWIC)	This site has information for women in the construction industry.	www.nawic.org
National Electrical Contractors Association (NECA)	The NECA website has information on membership, codes and standards, industry news, and educational resources.	www.necanet.org
Plumbing, Heating and Cooling Contractors Association (PHCC)	The PHCC website has information on membership, educational resources, and a list of contractors.	www.phccweb.org
Water Quality Association (WQA)	The WQA website has information on membership, certifications, educational resources, and a list of contractors.	www.wqa.org

Appendix D: New Business Checklist

The following is a checklist of steps to starting your business. These steps provide a general overview, but you should check with a professional to determine the legal, financial, and tax obligations specific to your business.

Complete Your Business Plan (covered in Chapter 1 and Appendix B)

- ✓ Establish your business vision and mission.
- ✓ Determine your management structure.
- ✓ Identify your facility requirements and location.
- ✓ Research your market and identify your competitors.
- ✓ Establish a marketing plan and expansion goals.
- ✓ Determine your break-even point and your financial goals.

Choose Your Form of Organization (covered in Chapter 2)

- ✓ Hire a lawyer to prepare organization documents and give legal advice on business issues.
- ✓ Choose a form of organization (i.e., sole proprietorship, partnership, or corporation).
- ✓ Prepare and file business organization documents (i.e., Partnership Agreement, Articles of Organization, Articles of Incorporation, etc.).
- ✓ Register any fictitious names with the proper state and local municipalities.
- ✓ Obtain the required business licenses from state and local municipalities.

Set Up Business Finances

- ✓ Select an accountant to prepare financial documents and give business financial advice.
- ✓ Select a banker and open a business checking account.
- ✓ Apply for business loans (if applicable).
- ✓ Apply for business credit cards and establish a line of credit.

Obtain the Proper Contractor's Licensure (covered in Chapter 3)

- ✓ Obtain the proper application materials and review the process for obtaining licensure.
- ✓ Complete application materials with required documentation.
- ✓ Understand the requirements for maintaining proper licensure.

Assess Your Areas of Risk and Obtain the Proper Insurance Coverage (covered in Chapter 4)

- ✓ Select an insurance company and agent to help assess your risk and coverage requirements.
- ✓ Obtain business insurance (liability, workers' compensation, automobile, etc.).
- ✓ Obtain required bonds.
- ✓ Obtain unemployment insurance registration materials from the proper state agency.

Obtain the Proper Tax Documentation (covered in Chapter 15)

- ✓ Apply for a federal employer identification number (if applicable).
- ✓ Obtain a state employer identification number (if applicable).
- ✓ Obtain the proper federal and state tax forms (i.e., sales and use tax, withholding tax, etc.).

Appendix E:
Utah Construction Trades Licensing Act

EXCERPTS FROM UTAH CODE, TITLE 58, CHAPTER 55

Part 1 - General Provisions

58-55-101. Short title.

This chapter is known as the "Utah Construction Trades Licensing Act."

Renumbered and Amended by Chapter 181, 1994 General Session

58-55-102. Definitions.

In addition to the definitions in Section 58-1-102, as used in this chapter:

(1)   (a)   "Alarm business or company" means a person engaged in the sale, installation, maintenance, alteration, repair, replacement, servicing, or monitoring of an alarm system, except as provided in Subsection (1)(b).

        (b)   "Alarm business or company" does not include:

            (i)   a person engaged in the manufacture or sale of alarm systems unless:

                (A)   that person is also engaged in the installation, maintenance, alteration, repair, replacement, servicing, or monitoring of alarm systems;

                (B)   the manufacture or sale occurs at a location other than a place of business established by the person engaged in the manufacture or sale; or

                (C)   the manufacture or sale involves site visits at the place or intended place of installation of an alarm system; or

            (ii)   an owner of an alarm system, or an employee of the owner of an alarm system who is engaged in installation, maintenance, alteration, repair, replacement, servicing, or monitoring of the alarm system owned by that owner.

(2)   "Alarm company agent":

        (a)   except as provided in Subsection (2)(b), means any individual employed within this state by an alarm business; and

        (b)   does not include an individual who:

            (i)   is not engaged in the sale, installation, maintenance, alteration, repair, replacement, servicing, or monitoring of an alarm system; and

            (ii)   does not, during the normal course of the individual's employment with an alarm business, use or have access to sensitive alarm system information.

(3)   "Alarm system" means equipment and devices assembled for the purpose of:

         (a)   detecting and signaling unauthorized intrusion or entry into or onto certain premises; or

         (b)   signaling a robbery or attempted robbery on protected premises.

(4)   "Apprentice electrician" means a person licensed under this chapter as an apprentice electrician who is learning the electrical trade under the immediate supervision of a master electrician, residential master electrician, a journeyman electrician, or a residential journeyman electrician.

(5)   "Apprentice plumber" means a person licensed under this chapter as an apprentice plumber who is learning the plumbing trade under the immediate supervision of a master plumber, residential master plumber, journeyman plumber, or a residential journeyman plumber.

(6)   "Approved continuing education" means instruction provided through courses under a program established under Subsection 58-55-302.5(2).

(7)   "Board" means the Electrician Licensing Board, Alarm System Security and Licensing Board, or Plumbers Licensing Board created in Section 58-55-201.

(8)   "Combustion system" means an assembly consisting of:

         (a)   piping and components with a means for conveying, either continuously or intermittently, natural gas from the outlet of the natural gas provider's meter to the burner of the appliance;

         (b)   the electric control and combustion air supply and venting systems, including air ducts; and

         (c)   components intended to achieve control of quantity, flow, and pressure.

(9)   "Commission" means the Construction Services Commission created under Section 58-55-103.

(10)   "Construction trade" means any trade or occupation involving:

         (a)   (i)   construction, alteration, remodeling, repairing, wrecking or demolition, addition to, or improvement of any building, highway, road, railroad, dam, bridge, structure, excavation or other project, development, or improvement to other than personal property; and

                (ii)   constructing, remodeling, or repairing a manufactured home or mobile home as defined in Section 15A-1-302; or

         (b)   installation or repair of a residential or commercial natural gas appliance or combustion system.

(11)   "Construction trades instructor" means a person licensed under this chapter to teach one or more construction trades in both a classroom and project environment, where a project is intended for sale to or use by the public and is completed under the direction of the instructor, who has no economic interest in the project.

(12)   (a)   "Contractor" means any person who for compensation other than wages as an employee undertakes any work in the construction, plumbing, or electrical trade for which licensure is required under this chapter and includes:

                (i)   a person who builds any structure on the person's own property for the purpose of sale or who builds any structure intended for public use on the person's own property;

                (ii)   any person who represents that the person is a contractor by advertising or any other means;

                (iii)   any person engaged as a maintenance person, other than an employee, who regularly engages in activities set forth under the definition of "construction trade";

(iv)   any person engaged in any construction trade for which licensure is required under this chapter; or

(v)   a construction manager who performs management and counseling services on a construction project for a fee.

(b)   "Contractor" does not include an alarm company or alarm company agent.

(13)   (a)   "Electrical trade" means the performance of any electrical work involved in the installation, construction, alteration, change, repair, removal, or maintenance of facilities, buildings, or appendages or appurtenances.

(b)   "Electrical trade" does not include:

(i)   transporting or handling electrical materials;

(ii)   preparing clearance for raceways for wiring; or

(iii)   work commonly done by unskilled labor on any installations under the exclusive control of electrical utilities.

(c)   For purposes of Subsection (13)(b):

(i)   no more than one unlicensed person may be so employed unless more than five licensed electricians are employed by the shop; and

(ii)   a shop may not employ unlicensed persons in excess of the five-to-one ratio permitted by this Subsection (13)(c).

(14)   "Elevator" has the same meaning as defined in Section 34A-7-202, except that for purposes of this chapter it does not mean a stair chair, a vertical platform lift, or an incline platform lift.

(15)   "Elevator contractor" means a sole proprietor, firm, or corporation licensed under this chapter that is engaged in the business of erecting, constructing, installing, altering, servicing, repairing, or maintaining an elevator.

(16)   "Elevator mechanic" means an individual who is licensed under this chapter as an elevator mechanic and who is engaged in erecting, constructing, installing, altering, servicing, repairing, or maintaining an elevator under the immediate supervision of an elevator contractor.

(17)   "Employee" means an individual as defined by the division by rule giving consideration to the definition adopted by the Internal Revenue Service and the Department of Workforce Services.

(18)   "Engage in a construction trade" means to:

(a)   engage in, represent oneself to be engaged in, or advertise oneself as being engaged in a construction trade; or

(b)   use the name "contractor" or "builder" or in any other way lead a reasonable person to believe one is or will act as a contractor.

(19)   (a)   "Financial responsibility" means a demonstration of a current and expected future condition of financial solvency evidencing a reasonable expectation to the division and the board that an applicant or licensee can successfully engage in business as a contractor without jeopardy to the public health, safety, and welfare.

(b)   Financial responsibility may be determined by an evaluation of the total history concerning the licensee or applicant including past, present, and expected condition and record of financial solvency and business conduct.

(20)   "Gas appliance" means any device that uses natural gas to produce light, heat, power, steam, hot water, refrigeration, or air conditioning.

(21) (a) "General building contractor" means a person licensed under this chapter as a general building contractor qualified by education, training, experience, and knowledge to perform or superintend construction of structures for the support, shelter, and enclosure of persons, animals, chattels, or movable property of any kind or any of the components of that construction except plumbing, electrical work, mechanical work, work related to the operating integrity of an elevator, and manufactured housing installation, for which the general building contractor shall employ the services of a contractor licensed in the particular specialty, except that a general building contractor engaged in the construction of single-family and multifamily residences up to four units may perform the mechanical work and hire a licensed plumber or electrician as an employee.

      (b) The division may by rule exclude general building contractors from engaging in the performance of other construction specialties in which there is represented a substantial risk to the public health, safety, and welfare, and for which a license is required unless that general building contractor holds a valid license in that specialty classification.

(22) (a) "General engineering contractor" means a person licensed under this chapter as a general engineering contractor qualified by education, training, experience, and knowledge to perform construction of fixed works in any of the following: irrigation, drainage, water, power, water supply, flood control, inland waterways, harbors, railroads, highways, tunnels, airports and runways, sewers and bridges, refineries, pipelines, chemical and industrial plants requiring specialized engineering knowledge and skill, piers, and foundations, or any of the components of those works.

      (b) A general engineering contractor may not perform construction of structures built primarily for the support, shelter, and enclosure of persons, animals, and chattels.

(23) "Immediate supervision" means reasonable direction, oversight, inspection, and evaluation of the work of a person:

      (a) as the division specifies in rule;

      (b) by, as applicable, a qualified electrician or plumber;

      (c) as part of a planned program of training; and

      (d) to ensure that the end result complies with applicable standards.

(24) "Individual" means a natural person.

(25) "Journeyman electrician" means a person licensed under this chapter as a journeyman electrician having the qualifications, training, experience, and knowledge to wire, install, and repair electrical apparatus and equipment for light, heat, power, and other purposes.

(26) "Journeyman plumber" means a person licensed under this chapter as a journeyman plumber having the qualifications, training, experience, and technical knowledge to engage in the plumbing trade.

(27) "Master electrician" means a person licensed under this chapter as a master electrician having the qualifications, training, experience, and knowledge to properly plan, layout, and supervise the wiring, installation, and repair of electrical apparatus and equipment for light, heat, power, and other purposes.

(28) "Master plumber" means a person licensed under this chapter as a master plumber having the qualifications, training, experience, and knowledge to properly plan and layout projects and supervise persons in the plumbing trade.

(29) "Person" means a natural person, sole proprietorship, joint venture, corporation, limited liability company, association, or organization of any type.

(30)   (a)   "Plumbing trade" means the performance of any mechanical work pertaining to the installation, alteration, change, repair, removal, maintenance, or use in buildings, or within three feet beyond the outside walls of buildings of pipes, fixtures, and fittings for:

           (i)   delivery of the water supply;

           (ii)   discharge of liquid and water carried waste; or

           (iii)   the building drainage system within the walls of the building.

       (b)   "Plumbing trade" includes work pertaining to the water supply, distribution pipes, fixtures and fixture traps, soil, waste and vent pipes, and the building drain and roof drains together with their devices, appurtenances, and connections where installed within the outside walls of the building.

(31)   (a)   "Ratio of apprentices" means, for the purpose of determining compliance with the requirements for planned programs of training and electrician apprentice licensing applications, the shop ratio of apprentice electricians to journeyman or master electricians shall be one journeyman or master electrician to one apprentice on industrial and commercial work, and one journeyman or master electrician to three apprentices on residential work.

       (b)   On-the-job training shall be under circumstances in which the ratio of apprentices to supervisors is in accordance with a ratio of one-to-one on nonresidential work and up to three apprentices to one supervisor on residential projects.

(32)   "Residential and small commercial contractor" means a person licensed under this chapter as a residential and small commercial contractor qualified by education, training, experience, and knowledge to perform or superintend the construction of single-family residences, multifamily residences up to four units, and commercial construction of not more than three stories above ground and not more than 20,000 square feet, or any of the components of that construction except plumbing, electrical work, mechanical work, and manufactured housing installation, for which the residential and small commercial contractor shall employ the services of a contractor licensed in the particular specialty, except that a residential and small commercial contractor engaged in the construction of single-family and multifamily residences up to four units may perform the mechanical work and hire a licensed plumber or electrician as an employee.

(33)   "Residential building," as it relates to the license classification of residential journeyman plumber and residential master plumber, means a single or multiple family dwelling of up to four units.

(34)   "Residential journeyman electrician" means a person licensed under this chapter as a residential journeyman electrician having the qualifications, training, experience, and knowledge to wire, install, and repair electrical apparatus and equipment for light, heat, power, and other purposes on buildings using primarily nonmetallic sheath cable.

(35)   "Residential journeyman plumber" means a person licensed under this chapter as a residential journeyman plumber having the qualifications, training, experience, and knowledge to engage in the plumbing trade as limited to the plumbing of residential buildings.

(36)   "Residential master electrician" means a person licensed under this chapter as a residential master electrician having the qualifications, training, experience, and knowledge to properly plan, layout, and supervise the wiring, installation, and repair of electrical apparatus and equipment for light, heat, power, and other purposes on residential projects.

(37)   "Residential master plumber" means a person licensed under this chapter as a residential master plumber having the qualifications, training, experience, and knowledge to properly plan and layout projects and supervise persons in the plumbing trade as limited to the plumbing of residential buildings.

(38)   "Residential project," as it relates to an electrician or electrical contractor, means buildings primarily wired with nonmetallic sheathed cable, in accordance with standard rules and regulations governing this work, including the National Electrical Code, and in which the voltage does not exceed 250 volts line to line and 125 volts to ground.

(39)   "Sensitive alarm system information" means:

    (a)   a pass code or other code used in the operation of an alarm system;

    (b)   information on the location of alarm system components at the premises of a customer of the alarm business providing the alarm system;

    (c)   information that would allow the circumvention, bypass, deactivation, or other compromise of an alarm system of a customer of the alarm business providing the alarm system; and

    (d)   any other similar information that the division by rule determines to be information that an individual employed by an alarm business should use or have access to only if the individual is licensed as provided in this chapter.

(40)   (a)   "Specialty contractor" means a person licensed under this chapter under a specialty contractor classification established by rule, who is qualified by education, training, experience, and knowledge to perform those construction trades and crafts requiring specialized skill, the regulation of which are determined by the division to be in the best interest of the public health, safety, and welfare.

    (b)   A specialty contractor may perform work in crafts or trades other than those in which the specialty contractor is licensed if they are incidental to the performance of the specialty contractor's licensed craft or trade.

(41)   "Unincorporated entity" means an entity that is not:

    (a)   an individual;

    (b)   a corporation; or

    (c)   publicly traded.

(42)   "Unlawful conduct" is as defined in Sections 58-1-501 and 58-55-501.

(43)   "Unprofessional conduct" is as defined in Sections 58-1-501 and 58-55-502 and as may be further defined by rule.

(44)   "Wages" means amounts due to an employee for labor or services whether the amount is fixed or ascertained on a time, task, piece, commission, or other basis for calculating the amount.

Amended by Chapter 81, 2014 General Session

58-55-103. Construction Services Commission created - Functions - Appointment - Qualifications and terms of members - Vacancies - Expenses - Meetings.

(1)   (a)   There is created within the division the Construction Services Commission.

    (b)   The commission shall:

        (i)   with the concurrence of the director, make reasonable rules under Title 63G, Chapter 3, Utah Administrative Rulemaking Act, to administer and enforce this chapter which are consistent with this chapter including:

            (A)   licensing of various licensees;

            (B)   examination requirements and administration of the examinations, to include approving and establishing a passing score for applicant examinations;

            (C)   standards of supervision for students or persons in training to become qualified to obtain a license in the trade they represent; and

            (D)   standards of conduct for various licensees;

      (ii)   approve or disapprove fees adopted by the division under Section 63J-1-504;

      (iii)   except where the boards conduct them, conduct all administrative hearings not delegated to an administrative law judge relating to the licensing of any applicant;

      (iv)   except as otherwise provided in Sections 38-11-207 and 58-55-503, with the concurrence of the director, impose sanctions against licensees and certificate holders with the same authority as the division under Section 58-1-401;

      (v)   advise the director on the administration and enforcement of any matters affecting the division and the construction industry;

      (vi)   advise the director on matters affecting the division budget;

      (vii)   advise and assist trade associations in conducting construction trade seminars and industry education and promotion; and

      (viii)   perform other duties as provided by this chapter.

(2)   (a)   Initially the commission shall be comprised of the five members of the Contractors Licensing Board and two of the three chair persons from the Plumbers Licensing Board, the Alarm System Security and Licensing Board, and the Electricians Licensing Board.

    (b)   The terms of office of the commission members who are serving on the Contractors Licensing Board shall continue as they serve on the commission.

    (c)   Beginning July 1, 2004, the commission shall be comprised of nine members appointed by the executive director with the approval of the governor from the following groups:

      (i)   one member shall be a licensed general engineering contractor;

      (ii)   one member shall be a licensed general building contractor;

      (iii)   two members shall be licensed residential and small commercial contractors;

      (iv)   three members shall be the three chair persons from the Plumbers Licensing Board, the Alarm System Security and Licensing Board, and the Electricians Licensing Board; and

      (v)   two members shall be from the general public, provided, however that the certified public accountant on the Contractors Licensing Board will continue to serve until the current term expires, after which both members under this Subsection (2)(c)(v) shall be appointed from the general public.

(3)   (a)   Except as required by Subsection (3)(b), as terms of current commission members expire, the executive director with the approval of the governor shall appoint each new member or reappointed member to a four-year term ending June 30.

    (b)   Notwithstanding the requirements of Subsection (3)(a), the executive director with the approval of the governor shall, at the time of appointment or reappointment, adjust the length of terms to stagger the terms of commission members so that approximately 1/2 of the commission members are appointed every two years.

    (c)   A commission member may not serve more than two consecutive terms.

(4)   The commission shall elect annually one of its members as chair, for a term of one year.

(5)   When a vacancy occurs in the membership for any reason, the replacement shall be appointed for the unexpired term.

(6)   A member may not receive compensation or benefits for the member's service, but may receive per diem and travel expenses in accordance with:

   (a)   Section 63A-3-106;

   (b)   Section 63A-3-107; and

   (c)   rules made by the Division of Finance pursuant to Sections 63A-3-106 and 63A-3-107.

(7)   (a)   The commission shall meet at least monthly unless the director determines otherwise.

   (b)   The director may call additional meetings at the director's discretion, upon the request of the chair, or upon the written request of four or more commission members.

(8)   (a)   Five members constitute a quorum for the transaction of business.

   (b)   If a quorum is present when a vote is taken, the affirmative vote of commission members present is the act of the commission.

(9)   The commission shall comply with the procedures and requirements of Title 13, Chapter 1, Department of Commerce, and Title 63G, Chapter 4, Administrative Procedures Act, in all of its adjudicative proceedings.

Amended by Chapter 286, 2010 General Session

Part 2 - Board

58-55-201. Board created - Duties.

(1)   There is created a Plumbers Licensing Board, an Alarm System Security and Licensing Board, and an Electricians Licensing Board. Members of the boards shall be selected to provide representation as follows:

   (a)   The Plumbers Licensing Board consists of five members as follows:

      (i)   two members shall be licensed from among the license classifications of master or journeyman plumber;

      (ii)   two members shall be licensed plumbing contractors; and

      (iii)   one member shall be from the public at large with no history of involvement in the construction trades.

   (b)   (i)   The Alarm System Security and Licensing Board consists of five members as follows:

         (A)   three individuals who are officers or owners of a licensed alarm business;

         (B)   one individual from among nominees of the Utah Peace Officers Association; and

         (C)   one individual representing the general public.

      (ii)   The Alarm System Security and Licensing Board shall designate one of its members on a permanent or rotating basis to:

         (A)   assist the division in reviewing complaints concerning the unlawful or unprofessional conduct of a licensee; and

         (B)   advise the division in its investigation of these complaints.

        (iii)   A board member who has, under this Subsection (1)(b)(iii), reviewed a complaint or advised in its investigation is disqualified from participating with the board when the board serves as a presiding officer in an adjudicative proceeding concerning the complaint.

   (c)   The Electricians Licensing Board consists of five members as follows:

        (i)   two members shall be licensed from among the license classifications of master or journeyman electrician, of whom one shall represent a union organization and one shall be selected having no union affiliation;

        (ii)   two shall be licensed electrical contractors of whom one shall represent a union organization and one shall be selected having no union affiliation; and

        (iii)   one member shall be from the public at large with no history of involvement in the construction trades or union affiliation.

(2)   The duties, functions, and responsibilities of each board include the following:

   (a)   recommending to the commission appropriate rules;

   (b)   recommending to the commission policy and budgetary matters;

   (c)   approving and establishing a passing score for applicant examinations;

   (d)   overseeing the screening of applicants for licensing, renewal, reinstatement, and relicensure;

   (e)   assisting the commission in establishing standards of supervision for students or persons in training to become qualified to obtain a license in the occupation or profession it represents; and

   (f)   acting as presiding officer in conducting hearings associated with the adjudicative proceedings and in issuing recommended orders when so authorized by the commission.

Amended by Chapter 215, 2008 General Session

Part 3 - Licensing

58-55-301 License required – License classifications.

(1)   (a)   A person engaged in the construction trades licensed under this chapter, as a contractor regulated under this chapter, as an alarm business or company, or as an alarm company agent, shall become licensed under this chapter before engaging in that trade or contracting activity in this state unless specifically exempted from licensure under Section 58-1-307 or 58-55-305.

   (b)   The license issued under this chapter and the business license issued by the local jurisdiction in which the licensee has its principal place of business shall be the only licenses required for the licensee to engage in a trade licensed by this chapter, within the state.

   (c)   Neither the state nor any of its political subdivisions may require of a licensee any additional business licenses, registrations, certifications, contributions, donations, or anything else established for the purpose of qualifying a licensee under this chapter to do business in that local jurisdiction, except for contract prequalification procedures required by state agencies, or the payment of any fee for the license, registration, or certification established as a condition to do business in that local jurisdiction.

(2)   The division shall issue licenses under this chapter to qualified persons in the following classifications:

   (a)   general engineering contractor;

   (b)   general building contractor;

   (c)   residential and small commercial contractor;

   (d)   elevator contractor;

   (e)   specialty contractor;

   (f)   master plumber;

   (g)   residential master plumber;

   (h)   journeyman plumber;

   (i)   apprentice plumber;

   (j)   residential journeyman plumber;

   (k)   master electrician;

   (l)   residential master electrician;

   (m)   journeyman electrician;

   (n)   residential journeyman electrician;

   (o)   apprentice electrician;

   (p)   construction trades instructor:

      (i)   general engineering classification;

      (ii)   general building classification;

      (iii)   electrical classification;

      (iv)   plumbing classification; and

      (v)   mechanical classification;

   (q)   alarm company;

   (r)   alarm company agent; and

   (s)   elevator mechanic.

(3)   (a)   An applicant may apply for a license in one or more classification or specialty contractor subclassification.

   (b)   A license shall be granted in each classification or subclassification for which the applicant qualifies.

   (c)   A separate application and fee must be submitted for each license classification or subclassification.

Amended by Chapter 227, 2010 General Session

58-55-302 Qualifications for licensure.

(1)   Each applicant for a license under this chapter shall:

   (a)   submit an application prescribed by the division;

   (b)   pay a fee as determined by the department under Section 63J-1-504;

(c)   (i)   meet the examination requirements established by rule by the commission with the concurrence of the director, except for the classifications of apprentice plumber and apprentice electrician for whom no examination is required; or

        (ii)   if required in Section 58-55-304, the individual qualifier must pass the required examination if the applicant is a business entity;

(d)   if an apprentice, identify the proposed supervisor of the apprenticeship;

(e)   if an applicant for a contractor's license:

        (i)   produce satisfactory evidence of financial responsibility, except for a construction trades instructor for whom evidence of financial responsibility is not required;

        (ii)   produce satisfactory evidence of:

            (A)   two years full-time paid employment experience in the construction industry, which experience, unless more specifically described in this section, may be related to any contracting classification; and

            (B)   knowledge of the principles of the conduct of business as a contractor, reasonably necessary for the protection of the public health, safety, and welfare;

        (iii)   except as otherwise provided by rule by the commission with the concurrence of the director, complete a 20-hour course established by rule by the commission with the concurrence of the director, which course may include:

            (A)   construction business practices;

            (B)   bookkeeping fundamentals;

            (C)   mechanics lien fundamentals; and

            (D)   other aspects of business and construction principles considered important by the commission with the concurrence of the director;

        (iv)   (A)   be a licensed master electrician if an applicant for an electrical contractor's license or a licensed master residential electrician if an applicant for a residential electrical contractor's license;

            (B)   be a licensed master plumber if an applicant for a plumbing contractor's license or a licensed master residential plumber if an applicant for a residential plumbing contractor's license; or

            (C)   be a licensed elevator mechanic and produce satisfactory evidence of three years experience as an elevator mechanic if an applicant for an elevator contractor's license; and

        (v)   when the applicant is an unincorporated entity, provide a list of the one or more individuals who hold an ownership interest in the applicant as of the day on which the application is filed that includes for each individual:

            (A)   the individual's name, address, birth date, and Social Security number; and

            (B)   whether the individual will engage in a construction trade; and

(f)   if an applicant for a construction trades instructor license, satisfy any additional requirements established by rule.

(2)   After approval of an applicant for a contractor's license by the applicable board and the division, the applicant shall file the following with the division before the division issues the license:

    (a)   proof of workers' compensation insurance which covers employees of the applicant in accordance with applicable Utah law;

    (b)   proof of public liability insurance in coverage amounts and form established by rule except for a construction trades instructor for whom public liability insurance is not required; and

    (c)   proof of registration as required by applicable law with the:

        (i)   Utah Department of Commerce;

        (ii)   Division of Corporations and Commercial Code;

        (iii)   Unemployment Insurance Division in the Department of Workforce Services, for purposes of Title 35A, Chapter 4, Employment Security Act;

        (iv)   State Tax Commission; and

        (v)   Internal Revenue Service.

(3)   In addition to the general requirements for each applicant in Subsection (1), applicants shall comply with the following requirements to be licensed in the following classifications:

    (a)   (i)   A master plumber shall produce satisfactory evidence that the applicant:

        (A)   has been a licensed journeyman plumber for at least two years and had two years of supervisory experience as a licensed journeyman plumber in accordance with division rule;

        (B)   has received at least an associate of applied science degree or similar degree following the completion of a course of study approved by the division and had one year of supervisory experience as a licensed journeyman plumber in accordance with division rule; or

        (C)   meets the qualifications determined by the division in collaboration with the board to be equivalent to Subsection (3)(a)(i)(A) or (B).

        (ii)   An individual holding a valid Utah license as a journeyman plumber, based on at least four years of practical experience as a licensed apprentice under the supervision of a licensed journeyman plumber and four years as a licensed journeyman plumber, in effect immediately prior to May 5, 2008, is on and after May 5, 2008, considered to hold a current master plumber license under this chapter, and satisfies the requirements of this Subsection (3)(a) for the purpose of renewal or reinstatement of that license under Section 58-55-303.

        (iii)   An individual holding a valid plumbing contractor's license or residential plumbing contractor's license, in effect immediately prior to May 5, 2008, is on or after May 5, 2008:

        (A)   considered to hold a current master plumber license under this chapter if licensed as a plumbing contractor and a journeyman plumber, and satisfies the requirements of this Subsection (3)(a) for purposes of renewal or reinstatement of that license under Section 58-55-303; and

        (B)   considered to hold a current residential master plumber license under this chapter if licensed as a residential plumbing contractor and a residential journeyman plumber, and satisfies the requirements of this

Subsection (3)(a) for purposes of renewal or reinstatement of that license under Section 58-55-303.

(b) A master residential plumber applicant shall produce satisfactory evidence that the applicant:

   (i)   has been a licensed residential journeyman plumber for at least two years and had two years of supervisory experience as a licensed residential journeyman plumber in accordance with division rule; or

   (ii) meets the qualifications determined by the division in collaboration with the board to be equivalent to Subsection (3)(b)(i).

(c) A journeyman plumber applicant shall produce satisfactory evidence of:

   (i)   successful completion of the equivalent of at least four years of full-time training and instruction as a licensed apprentice plumber under supervision of a licensed master plumber or journeyman plumber and in accordance with a planned program of training approved by the division;

   (ii) at least eight years of full-time experience approved by the division in collaboration with the Plumbers Licensing Board; or

   (iii) satisfactory evidence of meeting the qualifications determined by the board to be equivalent to Subsection (3)(c)(i) or (c)(ii).

(d) A residential journeyman plumber shall produce satisfactory evidence of:

   (i)   completion of the equivalent of at least three years of full-time training and instruction as a licensed apprentice plumber under the supervision of a licensed residential master plumber, licensed residential journeyman plumber, or licensed journeyman plumber in accordance with a planned program of training approved by the division;

   (ii) completion of at least six years of full-time experience in a maintenance or repair trade involving substantial plumbing work; or

   (iii) meeting the qualifications determined by the board to be equivalent to Subsection (3)(d)(i) or (d)(ii).

(e) The conduct of licensed apprentice plumbers and their licensed supervisors shall be in accordance with the following:

   (i)   while engaging in the trade of plumbing, a licensed apprentice plumber shall be under the immediate supervision of a licensed master plumber, licensed residential master plumber, licensed journeyman plumber, or a licensed residential journeyman plumber; and

   (ii) a licensed apprentice plumber in the fourth through tenth year of training may work without supervision for a period not to exceed eight hours in any 24-hour period, but if the apprentice does not become a licensed journeyman plumber or licensed residential journeyman plumber by the end of the tenth year of apprenticeship, this nonsupervision provision no longer applies.

(f) A master electrician applicant shall produce satisfactory evidence that the applicant:

   (i)   is a graduate electrical engineer of an accredited college or university approved by the division and has one year of practical electrical experience as a licensed apprentice electrician;

(ii)   is a graduate of an electrical trade school, having received an associate of applied sciences degree following successful completion of a course of study approved by the division, and has two years of practical experience as a licensed journeyman electrician;

(iii)   has four years of practical experience as a journeyman electrician; or

(iv)   meets the qualifications determined by the board to be equivalent to Subsection (3)(f)(i), (ii), or (iii).

(g)   A master residential electrician applicant shall produce satisfactory evidence that the applicant:

(i)   has at least two years of practical experience as a residential journeyman electrician; or

(ii)   meets the qualifications determined by the board to be equivalent to this practical experience.

(h)   A journeyman electrician applicant shall produce satisfactory evidence that the applicant:

(i)   has successfully completed at least four years of full-time training and instruction as a licensed apprentice electrician under the supervision of a master electrician or journeyman electrician and in accordance with a planned training program approved by the division;

(ii)   has at least eight years of full-time experience approved by the division in collaboration with the Electricians Licensing Board; or

(iii)   meets the qualifications determined by the board to be equivalent to Subsection (3)(h)(i) or (ii).

(i)   A residential journeyman electrician applicant shall produce satisfactory evidence that the applicant:

(i)   has successfully completed two years of training in an electrical training program approved by the division;

(ii)   has four years of practical experience in wiring, installing, and repairing electrical apparatus and equipment for light, heat, and power under the supervision of a licensed master, journeyman, residential master, or residential journeyman electrician; or

(iii)   meets the qualifications determined by the division and applicable board to be equivalent to Subsection (3)(i)(i) or (ii).

(j)   The conduct of licensed apprentice electricians and their licensed supervisors shall be in accordance with the following:

(i)   A licensed apprentice electrician shall be under the immediate supervision of a licensed master, journeyman, residential master, or residential journeyman electrician. An apprentice in the fourth year of training may work without supervision for a period not to exceed eight hours in any 24-hour period.

(ii)   A licensed master, journeyman, residential master, or residential journeyman electrician may have under immediate supervision on a residential project up to three licensed apprentice electricians.

(iii)   A licensed master or journeyman electrician may have under immediate supervision on nonresidential projects only one licensed apprentice electrician.

(k)   An alarm company applicant shall:

     (i)   have a qualifying agent who is an officer, director, partner, proprietor, or manager of the applicant who:

          (A)   demonstrates 6,000 hours of experience in the alarm company business;

          (B)   demonstrates 2,000 hours of experience as a manager or administrator in the alarm company business or in a construction business; and

          (C)   passes an examination component established by rule by the commission with the concurrence of the director;

     (ii)   if a corporation, provide:

          (A)   the names, addresses, dates of birth, Social Security numbers, and fingerprint cards of all corporate officers, directors, and those responsible management personnel employed within the state or having direct responsibility for managing operations of the applicant within the state; and

          (B)   the names, addresses, dates of birth, Social Security numbers, and fingerprint cards of all shareholders owning 5% or more of the outstanding shares of the corporation, except this shall not be required if the stock is publicly listed and traded;

     (iii)   if a limited liability company, provide:

          (A)   the names, addresses, dates of birth, Social Security numbers, and fingerprint cards of all company officers, and those responsible management personnel employed within the state or having direct responsibility for managing operations of the applicant within the state; and

          (B)   the names, addresses, dates of birth, Social Security numbers, and fingerprint cards of all individuals owning 5% or more of the equity of the company;

     (iv)   if a partnership, provide the names, addresses, dates of birth, Social Security numbers, and fingerprint cards of all general partners, and those responsible management personnel employed within the state or having direct responsibility for managing operations of the applicant within the state;

     (v)   if a proprietorship, provide the names, addresses, dates of birth, Social Security numbers, and fingerprint cards of the proprietor, and those responsible management personnel employed within the state or having direct responsibility for managing operations of the applicant within the state;

     (vi)   if a trust, provide the names, addresses, dates of birth, Social Security numbers, and fingerprint cards of the trustee, and those responsible management personnel employed within the state or having direct responsibility for managing operations of the applicant within the state;

     (vii)   be of good moral character in that officers, directors, shareholders described in Subsection (3)(k)(ii)(B), partners, proprietors, trustees, and responsible management personnel have not been convicted of a felony, a misdemeanor involving moral turpitude, or any other crime that when considered with the duties and responsibilities of an alarm company is considered by the board to indicate that the best interests of the public are served by granting the applicant a license;

     (viii)   document that none of the applicant's officers, directors, shareholders described in Subsection (3)(k)(ii)(B), partners, proprietors, trustees, and responsible management personnel have been declared by any court of competent jurisdiction incompetent by reason of mental defect or disease and not been restored;

(ix)   document that none of the applicant's officers, directors, shareholders described in Subsection (3)(k)(ii)(B), partners, proprietors, and responsible management personnel are currently suffering from habitual drunkenness or from drug addiction or dependence;

(x)   file and maintain with the division evidence of:

    (A)   comprehensive general liability insurance in form and in amounts to be established by rule by the commission with the concurrence of the director;

    (B)   workers' compensation insurance that covers employees of the applicant in accordance with applicable Utah law; and

    (C)   registration as is required by applicable law with the:

        (I)   Division of Corporations and Commercial Code;

        (II)   Unemployment Insurance Division in the Department of Workforce Services, for purposes of Title 35A, Chapter 4, Employment Security Act;

        (III)   State Tax Commission; and

        (IV)   Internal Revenue Service; and

(xi)   meet with the division and board.

(l)   Each applicant for licensure as an alarm company agent shall:

(i)   submit an application in a form prescribed by the division accompanied by fingerprint cards;

(ii)   pay a fee determined by the department under Section 63J-1-504;

(iii)   be of good moral character in that the applicant has not been convicted of a felony, a misdemeanor involving moral turpitude, or any other crime that when considered with the duties and responsibilities of an alarm company agent is considered by the board to indicate that the best interests of the public are served by granting the applicant a license;

(iv)   not have been declared by any court of competent jurisdiction incompetent by reason of mental defect or disease and not been restored;

(v)   not be currently suffering from habitual drunkenness or from drug addiction or dependence; and

(vi)   meet with the division and board if requested by the division or the board.

(m)   (i)   Each applicant for licensure as an elevator mechanic shall:

    (A)   provide documentation of experience and education credits of not less than three years work experience in the elevator industry, in construction, maintenance, or service and repair; and

    (B)   satisfactorily complete a written examination administered by the division established by rule under Section 58-1-203; or

    (C)   provide certificates of completion of an apprenticeship program for elevator mechanics, having standards substantially equal to those of this chapter and registered with the United States Department of Labor Bureau Apprenticeship and Training or a state apprenticeship council.

        (ii)   (A)   If an elevator contractor licensed under this chapter cannot find a licensed elevator mechanic to perform the work of erecting, constructing, installing, altering, servicing, repairing, or maintaining an elevator, the contractor may:

                (I)   notify the division of the unavailability of licensed personnel; and

                (II)   request the division issue a temporary elevator mechanic license to an individual certified by the contractor as having an acceptable combination of documented experience and education to perform the work described in this Subsection (3)(m)(ii)(A).

            (B)   (I)   The division may issue a temporary elevator mechanic license to an individual certified under Subsection (3)(m)(ii)(A)(II) upon application by the individual, accompanied by the appropriate fee as determined by the department under Section 63J-1-504.

                (II)   The division shall specify the time period for which the license is valid and may renew the license for an additional time period upon its determination that a shortage of licensed elevator mechanics continues to exist.

(4)   In accordance with Title 63G, Chapter 3, Utah Administrative Rulemaking Act, the division may make rules establishing when Federal Bureau of Investigation records shall be checked for applicants as an alarm company or alarm company agent.

(5)   To determine if an applicant meets the qualifications of Subsections (3)(k)(vii) and (3)(l)(iii), the division shall provide an appropriate number of copies of fingerprint cards to the Department of Public Safety with the division's request to:

    (a)   conduct a search of records of the Department of Public Safety for criminal history information relating to each applicant for licensure as an alarm company or alarm company agent and each applicant's officers, directors, shareholders described in Subsection (3)(k)(ii)(B), partners, proprietors, and responsible management personnel; and

    (b)   forward to the Federal Bureau of Investigation a fingerprint card of each applicant requiring a check of records of the Federal Bureau of Investigation for criminal history information under this section.

(6)   The Department of Public Safety shall send to the division:

    (a)   a written record of criminal history, or certification of no criminal history record, as contained in the records of the Department of Public Safety in a timely manner after receipt of a fingerprint card from the division and a request for review of Department of Public Safety records; and

    (b)   the results of the Federal Bureau of Investigation review concerning an applicant in a timely manner after receipt of information from the Federal Bureau of Investigation.

(7)   (a)   The division shall charge each applicant for licensure as an alarm company or alarm company agent a fee, in accordance with Section 63J-1-504, equal to the cost of performing the records reviews under this section.

    (b)   The division shall pay the Department of Public Safety the costs of all records reviews, and the Department of Public Safety shall pay the Federal Bureau of Investigation the costs of records reviews under this section.

(8)   Information obtained by the division from the reviews of criminal history records of the Department of Public Safety and the Federal Bureau of Investigation shall be used or disseminated by the

division only for the purpose of determining if an applicant for licensure as an alarm company or alarm company agent is qualified for licensure.

(9)   (a)   An application for licensure under this chapter shall be denied if:

          (i)   the applicant has had a previous license, which was issued under this chapter, suspended or revoked within one year prior to the date of the applicant's application;

          (ii)   (A)   the applicant is a partnership, corporation, or limited liability company; and

                (B)   any corporate officer, director, shareholder holding 25% or more of the stock in the applicant, partner, member, agent acting as a qualifier, or any person occupying a similar status, performing similar functions, or directly or indirectly controlling the applicant has served in any similar capacity with any person or entity which has had a previous license, which was issued under this chapter, suspended or revoked within one year prior to the date of the applicant's application;

          (iii)   (A)   the applicant is an individual or sole proprietorship; and

                (B)   any owner or agent acting as a qualifier has served in any capacity listed in Subsection (9)(a)(ii)(B) in any entity which has had a previous license, which was issued under this chapter, suspended or revoked within one year prior to the date of the applicant's application; or

          (iv)   (A)   the applicant includes an individual who was an owner, director, or officer of an unincorporated entity at the time the entity's license under this chapter was revoked; and

                (B)   the application for licensure is filed within 60 months after the revocation of the unincorporated entity's license.

    (b)   An application for licensure under this chapter shall be reviewed by the appropriate licensing board prior to approval if:

          (i)   the applicant has had a previous license, which was issued under this chapter, suspended or revoked more than one year prior to the date of the applicant's application;

          (ii)   (A)   the applicant is a partnership, corporation, or limited liability company; and

                (B)   any corporate officer, director, shareholder holding 25% or more of the stock in the applicant, partner, member, agent acting as a qualifier, or any person occupying a similar status, performing similar functions, or directly or indirectly controlling the applicant has served in any similar capacity with any person or entity which has had a previous license, which was issued under this chapter, suspended or revoked more than one year prior to the date of the applicant's application; or

          (iii)   (A)   the applicant is an individual or sole proprietorship; and

                (B)   any owner or agent acting as a qualifier has served in any capacity listed in Subsection (9)(b)(ii)(B) in any entity which has had a previous license, which was issued under this chapter, suspended or revoked more than one year prior to the date of the applicant's application.

(10)   (a)   (i)   A licensee that is an unincorporated entity shall file an ownership status report with the division every 30 days after the day on which the license is issued if the licensee has more than five owners who are individuals who:

    (A) own an interest in the contractor that is an unincorporated entity;

    (B) own, directly or indirectly, less than an 8% interest, as defined by rule made by the division in accordance with Title 63G, Chapter 3, Utah Administrative Rulemaking Act, in the unincorporated entity; and

    (C) engage, or will engage, in a construction trade in the state as owners of the contractor described in Subsection (10)(a)(i)(A).

   (ii) If the licensee has five or fewer owners described in Subsection (10)(a)(i), the licensee shall provide the ownership status report with an application for renewal of licensure.

  (b) An ownership status report required under this Subsection (10) shall:

   (i) specify each addition or deletion of an owner:

    (A) for the first ownership status report, after the day on which the unincorporated entity is licensed under this chapter; and

    (B) for a subsequent ownership status report, after the day on which the previous ownership status report is filed;

   (ii) be in a format prescribed by the division that includes for each owner, regardless of the owner's percentage ownership in the unincorporated entity, the information described in Subsection(1)(e)(v);

   (iii) list the name of:

    (A) each officer or manager of the unincorporated entity; and

    (B) each other individual involved in the operation, supervision, or management of the unincorporated entity; and

   (iv) be accompanied by a fee set by the division in accordance with Section 63J-1-504 if the ownership status report indicates there is a change described in Subsection (10)(b)(i).

  (c) The division may, at any time, audit an ownership status report under this Subsection (10):

   (i) to determine if financial responsibility has been demonstrated or maintained as required under Section 58-55-306; and

   (ii) to determine compliance with Subsection 58-55-501(24), (25), or (27) or Subsection 58-55-502(8) or (9).

(11) (a) An unincorporated entity that provides labor to an entity licensed under this chapter by providing an individual who owns an interest in the unincorporated entity to engage in a construction trade in Utah shall file with the division:

   (i) before the individual who owns an interest in the unincorporated entity engages in a construction trade in Utah, a current list of the one or more individuals who hold an ownership interest in the unincorporated entity that includes for each individual:

    (A) the individual's name, address, birth date, and Social Security number; and

    (B) whether the individual will engage in a construction trade; and

   (ii) every 30 days after the day on which the unincorporated entity provides the list described in Subsection (11)(a)(i), an ownership status report containing the information that would be required under Subsection (10) if the unincorporated entity were a licensed contractor.

(b)   When filing an ownership list described in Subsection (11)(a)(i) or an ownership status report described in Subsection (11)(a)(ii), an unincorporated entity shall pay a fee set by the division in accordance with Section 63J-1-504.

(12)   This chapter may not be interpreted to create or support an express or implied independent contractor relationship between an unincorporated entity described in Subsection (10) or (11) and the owners of the unincorporated entity for any purpose, including income tax withholding.

(13)   A Social Security number provided under Subsection (1)(e)(v) is a private record under Subsection 63G-2-302(1)(i).

Amended by Chapter 258, 2015 General Session

58-55-302.5 Continuing education requirements for contractor licensees – Continuing education courses.

(1)   Each contractor licensee under a license issued under this chapter shall complete six hours of approved continuing education during each two-year renewal cycle established by rule under Subsection 58-55-303(1).

(2)   (a)   The commission shall, with the concurrence of the division, establish by rule a program of approved continuing education for contractor licensees.

        (b)   Beginning on or after June 1, 2015, only courses offered by any of the following may be included in the program of approved continuing education for contractor licensees:

                (i)   the Associated General Contractors of Utah;

                (ii)   Associated Builders and Contractors, Utah Chapter;

                (iii)   the Home Builders Association of Utah;

                (iv)   the National Electrical Contractors Association;

                (v)   the Utah Plumbing & Heating Contractors Association;

                (vi)   the Independent Electrical Contractors of Utah;

                (vii)   the Rocky Mountain Gas Association;

                (viii)   the Utah Mechanical Contractors Association;

                (ix)   the Sheet Metal Contractors Association;

                (x)   the Intermountain Electrical Association;

                (xi)   the Builders Bid Service of Utah;

                (xii)   Utah Roofing Contractors Association;

                (xiii)   a nationally or regionally accredited college or university that has a physical campus in the state; or

                (xiv)   an agency of the state.

        (c)   Each entity listed in Subsections (2)(b)(iv) through (2)(b)(xii) may only offer and market continuing education courses to a licensee who is a member of the entity.

(3)   The division may contract with a person to establish and maintain a continuing education registry to include:

        (a)   a list of courses that the division has approved for inclusion in the program of approved continuing education; and

        (b)   a list of courses that:

                (i)   a contractor licensee has completed under the program of approved continuing education; and

        (ii)   the licensee may access to monitor the licensee's compliance with the continuing education requirement established under Subsection (1).

(4)   The division may charge a fee, as established by the division under Section 63J-1-504, to administer the requirements of this section.

Amended by Chapter 148, 2015 General Session

58-55-302.7 Continuing education requirements for electricians, elevator mechanics, and plumbers.

(1)   As used in this section:

    (a)   "Licensed electrician" means an individual licensed under this chapter as an apprentice electrician, journeyman electrician, master electrician, residential journeyman electrician, or residential master electrician.

    (b)   "Licensed elevator mechanic" means an individual licensed under this chapter as an elevator mechanic.

    (c)   "Licensed plumber" means an individual licensed under this chapter as an apprentice plumber, journeyman plumber, master plumber, residential journeyman plumber, or residential master plumber.

(2)   Beginning December 1, 2010, during each two-year renewal cycle established by rule under Subsection 58-55-303(1):

    (a)   a licensed electrician shall complete 16 hours of continuing education under the continuing education program established under this section;

    (b)   a licensed plumber shall complete 12 hours of continuing education under the continuing education program established under this section; and

    (c)   a licensed elevator mechanic shall complete eight hours of continuing education under the continuing education program established under this section.

(3)   The commission shall, with the concurrence of the division, establish by rule:

    (a)   a continuing education program for licensed electricians;

    (b)   a continuing education program for licensed elevator mechanics; and

    (c)   a continuing education program for licensed plumbers.

(4)   The division may contract with a person to establish and maintain a continuing education registry to include:

    (a)   an online application for a continuing education course provider to apply to the division for approval of the course for inclusion in the continuing education program;

    (b)   a list of courses that the division has approved for inclusion in the continuing education program; and

    (c)   a list of courses that:

        (i)   a licensed electrician, licensed elevator mechanic, or licensed plumber has completed under the continuing education program; and

        (ii)   the licensed electrician, licensed elevator mechanic, or licensed plumber may access to monitor compliance with the continuing education requirement under Subsection (2).

(5)   The division may charge a fee, established by the division under Section 63J-1-504, to administer the requirements of this section.

Amended by Chapter 367, 2011 General Session

58-55-303 Term of license – Expiration – Renewal.

(1) (a) Each license issued under this chapter shall be issued in accordance with a two-year renewal cycle established by rule.

     (b) The division may by rule extend or shorten a renewal period by as much as one year to stagger the renewal cycle it administers.

     (c) (i) Notwithstanding a renewal cycle under Subsection (1)(a) or (b), notwithstanding Title 63G, Chapter 4, Administrative Procedures Act, and subject to Subsection (1)(c)(ii), a license is automatically suspended 60 days after the licensee:

              (A) becomes, after the time of licensing, an unincorporated entity that is subject to the ownership status report filing requirements of Subsection 58-55-302(10)(a)(i); or

              (B) transfers its license to an unincorporated entity that is subject to the ownership status report filing requirements of Subsection 58-55-302(10)(a)(i).

          (ii) An automatic suspension does not occur under Subsection (1)(c)(i) if, before the expiration of the 60-day period in Subsection (1)(c)(i):

              (A) the licensee submits an application for renewal of the license; and

              (B) the division renews the licensee's license pursuant to the licensee's application for renewal.

          (iii) Within 30 days after the effective date of a suspension under Subsection (1)(c)(i), the commission shall, in accordance with Title 63G, Chapter 4, Administrative Procedures Act, make a final determination concerning the suspension.

(2) At the time of renewal, the licensee shall show satisfactory evidence of:

     (a) continuing financial responsibility as required under Section 58-55-306;

     (b) for a contractor licensee, completion of six hours of approved continuing education, as required in Section 58-55-302.5; and

     (c) if the licensee is an apprentice electrician or plumber, journeyman electrician or plumber, master electrician or plumber, residential journeyman electrician or plumber, or residential master electrician or plumber, completion of the number of hours of continuing education specified under Section 58-55-302.7.

(3) Each license automatically expires on the expiration date shown on the license unless the licensee renews the license in accordance with Section 58-1-308.

(4) The requirements of Subsection 58-55-302(9) shall also apply to applicants seeking to renew or reinstate a license.

(5) In addition to any other requirements imposed by law, if a license has been suspended or revoked for any reason, the applicant:

     (a) shall pay in full all fines imposed by the division;

     (b) resolve any outstanding citations or disciplinary actions with the division;

     (c) satisfy any Section 58-55-503 judgment and sentence or nontrial resolution;

     (d) complete a new financial responsibility review as required under Section 58-55-306, using only titled assets; and

     (e) pay in full any reimbursement amount as provided in Title 38, Chapter 11, Residence Lien Restriction and Lien Recovery Fund Act.

Amended by Chapter 57, 2013 General Session

58-55-304 Licensee names – License number use – License qualifier.

(1)   No license may be issued by the division in a name that is identical to or so resembles the name of another licensee that the division determines that it may result in confusion or mistake.

(2)   The contractor's license number shall be made a part of all permit applications, contracts, agreements, or bids when a license is required.

(3)   The division may issue a license in the name of an individual or the name of a business entity for which the individual acts as a qualifier, in accordance with the following:

    (a)   An individual shall:

        (i)   submit an application in the individual's name;

        (ii)   demonstrate the individual's own financial responsibility; and

        (iii)   pass the required examination and meet all other requirements of this chapter.

    (b)   A business entity shall:

        (i)   submit the application in the name of and on behalf of the business entity;

        (ii)   list the individual as the qualifier;

        (iii)   demonstrate financial responsibility of the business entity if applying for a contractor's license;

        (iv)   provide evidence that the individual qualifier has passed the required examination; and

        (v)   meet all other requirements of this chapter.

(4)   A person acting as a qualifier for a business entity licensee must demonstrate to the division that the individual is an owner, officer, or manager within that business entity who exercises material authority in the conduct of that business entity's contracting business by:

    (a)   making substantive technical and administrative decisions relating to the work performed for which a license is required under this chapter;

    (b)   hiring, promoting, transferring, laying off, disciplining, directing, or discharging employees of the licensee either by himself or through others; and

    (c)   not being involved in any other employment or activity which conflicts with the individual's duties and responsibilities to ensure the licensee's performance of work regulated under this chapter does not jeopardize the public health, safety, and welfare.

(5)   (a)   Except as provided in Subsections (5)(b) and (c), it is the duty and responsibility of the licensee and the qualifier to comply with the provisions of this section. Failure to comply with the requirements of this section may be considered unprofessional conduct by the licensee, the qualifier, or both.

    (b)   If a licensee business entity has maintained its license and has not violated the requirements of this chapter or Sections 58-55-101 through 58-55-604 for a period of 10 consecutive years, the business entity may maintain its license under this chapter by recording an active employee name and registration/license number from the applicable trade on the renewal application in order to comply with the individual qualifier requirements of this section. However, this Subsection (5)(b) shall not apply if more than 50% of the ownership of the business entity has been transferred at any time during the ten-year period.

    (c)   If a plumbing or electrical business entity has maintained its license and has not violated the requirements of this chapter or Sections 58-55-101 through 58-55-604 for a period of five consecutive years, the business entity may maintain its license under this chapter by recording an active employee name and registration/license number from the applicable trade on the renewal application in order to comply with the individual qualifier requirements of this section. However, this Subsection (5)(c) shall not apply if more than 50% of the ownership of the business entity has been transferred at any time during the five-year period.

(6)   If an individual qualifying on behalf of a business entity issued a license under this chapter ceases association with that entity as required in Subsection (4), the licensee shall notify the division in writing within 10 days after cessation of association or employment. If notice is given, the license shall remain in force for 60 days after the date of cessation of association or employment. The licensee shall replace the original qualifier with another individual qualifier within the 60-day period or the license shall be automatically suspended.

(7)   Failure to notify the division of cessation of association or employment of a qualifier as required in Subsection (6) may result in immediate suspension of the license upon a finding of good cause.

Amended by Chapter 14, 2004 General Session

58-55-305 Exemptions from licensure.

(1)   In addition to the exemptions from licensure in Section 58-1-307, the following persons may engage in acts or practices included within the practice of construction trades, subject to the stated circumstances and limitations, without being licensed under this chapter:

(a)   an authorized representative of the United States government or an authorized employee of the state or any of its political subdivisions when working on construction work of the state or the subdivision, and when acting within the terms of the person's trust, office, or employment;

(b)   a person engaged in construction or operation incidental to the construction and repair of irrigation and drainage ditches of regularly constituted irrigation districts, reclamation districts, and drainage districts or construction and repair relating to farming, dairying, agriculture, livestock or poultry raising, metal and coal mining, quarries, sand and gravel excavations, well drilling, as defined in Section 73-3-25, hauling to and from construction sites, and lumbering;

(c)   public utilities operating under the rules of the Public Service Commission on work incidental to their own business;

(d)   sole owners of property engaged in building:

(i)   no more than one residential structure per year and no more than three residential structures per five years on their property for their own noncommercial, nonpublic use; except, a person other than the property owner or individuals described in Subsection (1)(e), who engages in building the structure must be licensed under this chapter if the person is otherwise required to be licensed under this chapter; or

(ii)   structures on their property for their own noncommercial, nonpublic use which are incidental to a residential structure on the property, including sheds, carports, or detached garages;

(e)   (i)   a person engaged in construction or renovation of a residential building for noncommercial, nonpublic use if that person:

(A)   works without compensation other than token compensation that is not considered salary or wages; and

(B)   works under the direction of the property owner who engages in building the structure; and

(ii)   as used in this Subsection (1)(e), "token compensation" means compensation paid by a sole owner of property exempted from licensure under Subsection (1)(d) to a person exempted from licensure under this Subsection (1)(e), that is:

        (A)   minimal in value when compared with the fair market value of the services provided by the person;

        (B)   not related to the fair market value of the services provided by the person; and

        (C)   is incidental to the providing of services by the person including paying for or providing meals or refreshment while services are being provided, or paying reasonable transportation costs incurred by the person in travel to the site of construction;

(f)   a person engaged in the sale or merchandising of personal property that by its design or manufacture may be attached, installed, or otherwise affixed to real property who has contracted with a person, firm, or corporation licensed under this chapter to install, affix, or attach that property;

(g)   a contractor submitting a bid on a federal aid highway project, if, before undertaking construction under that bid, the contractor is licensed under this chapter;

(h)   (i)   a person engaged in the alteration, repair, remodeling, or addition to or improvement of a building with a contracted or agreed value of less than $3,000, including both labor and materials, and including all changes or additions to the contracted or agreed upon work; and

     (ii)   notwithstanding Subsection (1)(h)(i) and except as otherwise provided in this section:

        (A)   work in the plumbing and electrical trades on a Subsection (1)(h)(i) project within any six month period of time:

            (I)   must be performed by a licensed electrical or plumbing contractor, if the project involves an electrical or plumbing system; and

            (II)   may be performed by a licensed journeyman electrician or plumber or an individual referred to in Subsection (1)(h)(ii)(A)(I), if the project involves a component of the system such as a faucet, toilet, fixture, device, outlet, or electrical switch;

        (B)   installation, repair, or replacement of a residential or commercial gas appliance or a combustion system on a Subsection (1)(h)(i) project must be performed by a person who has received certification under Subsection 58-55-308(2) except as otherwise provided in Subsection 58-55-308(2)(d) or 58-55-308(3);

        (C)   Installation, repair, or replacement of water-based fire protection systems on a Subsection (1)(h)(i) project must be performed by a licensed fire suppression systems contractor or a licensed journeyman plumber;

        (D)   work as an alarm business or company or as an alarm company agent shall be performed by a licensed alarm business or company or a licensed alarm company agent, except as otherwise provided in this chapter;

        (E)   installation, repair, or replacement of an alarm system on a Subsection (1)(h)(i) project must be performed by a licensed alarm business or company or a licensed alarm company agent;

(F)   installation, repair, or replacement of a heating, ventilation, or air conditioning system (HVAC) on a Subsection (1)(h)(i) project must be performed by an HVAC contractor licensed by the division;

(G)   installation, repair, or replacement of a radon mitigation system or a soil depressurization system must be performed by a licensed contractor; and

(H)   if the total value of the project is greater than $1,000, the person shall file with the division a one-time affirmation, subject to periodic reaffirmation as established by division rule, that the person has:

   (I)   public liability insurance in coverage amounts and form established by division rule; and

   (II)   if applicable, workers compensation insurance which would cover an employee of the person if that employee worked on the construction project;

(i)   a person practicing a specialty contractor classification or construction trade which the director does not classify by administrative rule as significantly impacting the public's health, safety, and welfare;

(j)   owners and lessees of property and persons regularly employed for wages by owners or lessees of property or their agents for the purpose of maintaining the property, are exempt from this chapter when doing work upon the property;

(k)   (i)   a person engaged in minor plumbing work that is incidental, as defined by the division by rule, to the replacement or repair of a fixture or an appliance in a residential or small commercial building, or structure used for agricultural use, as defined in Section 15A-1-202, provided that no modification is made to:

   (A)   existing culinary water, soil, waste, or vent piping; or

   (B)   a gas appliance or combustion system; and

(ii)   except as provided in Subsection (1)(e), installation for the first time of a fixture or an appliance is not included in the exemption provided under Subsection (1)(k)(i);

(l)   a person who ordinarily would be subject to the plumber licensure requirements under this chapter when installing or repairing a water conditioner or other water treatment apparatus if the conditioner or apparatus:

   (i)   meets the appropriate state construction codes or local plumbing standards; and

   (ii)   is installed or repaired under the direction of a person authorized to do the work under an appropriate specialty contractor license;

(m)   a person who ordinarily would be subject to the electrician licensure requirements under this chapter when employed by:

   (i)   railroad corporations, telephone corporations or their corporate affiliates, elevator contractors or constructors, or street railway systems; or

   (ii)   public service corporations, rural electrification associations, or municipal utilities who generate, distribute, or sell electrical energy for light, heat, or power;

(n)   a person involved in minor electrical work incidental to a mechanical or service installation, including the outdoor installation of an above-ground, prebuilt hot tub;

(o)   a person who ordinarily would be subject to the electrician licensure requirements under this chapter but who during calendar years 2009, 2010, or 2011 was issued a specialty contractor license for the electrical work associated with the installation, repair, or maintenance of solar energy panels, may continue the limited electrical work for solar energy panels under a specialty contractor license;

(p) a student participating in construction trade education and training programs approved by the commission with the concurrence of the director under the condition that:

    (i) all work intended as a part of a finished product on which there would normally be an inspection by a building inspector is, in fact, inspected and found acceptable by a licensed building inspector; and

    (ii) a licensed contractor obtains the necessary building permits;

(q) a delivery person when replacing any of the following existing equipment with a new gas appliance, provided there is an existing gas shutoff valve at the appliance:

    (i) gas range;

    (ii) gas dryer;

    (iii) outdoor gas barbeque; or

    (iv) outdoor gas patio heater;

(r) a person performing maintenance on an elevator as defined in Subsection 58-55-102(₁4), if the maintenance is not related to the operating integrity of the elevator; and

(s) an apprentice or helper of an elevator mechanic licensed under this chapter when working under the general direction of the licensed elevator mechanic.

(2) A compliance agency as defined in Section 15A-1-202 that issues a building permit to a person requesting a permit as a sole owner of property referred to in Subsection (1)(d) shall notify the division, in writing or through electronic transmission, of the issuance of the permit.

Amended by Chapter 430, 2013 General Session. Amended by Chapter 449, 2013 General Session

58-55-306 Financial responsibility.

(1) An applicant for licensure as a contractor, and a licensee applying for renewal or reinstatement of a contractor's license shall demonstrate to the division and the commission the applicant's or licensee's financial responsibility before the issuance of or the renewal or reinstatement of a license by:

    (a) (i) completing a questionnaire developed by the division; and

        (ii) signing the questionnaire, certifying that the information provided is true and accurate; or

    (b) submitting a bond in an amount and form determined by the commission with the concurrence of the director.

(2) A licensee, including an individual who holds an ownership interest in an unincorporated entity licensee, shall maintain financial responsibility throughout the period of licensure.

(3) The division may audit the financial responsibility of an applicant or licensee on a random basis or upon finding of a reasonable need.

(4) The burden to demonstrate financial responsibility is upon the applicant, licensee, or owner of an unincorporated entity licensee, as the case may be.

(5) (a) In determining the financial responsibility of an applicant or licensee described in Subsection (1) that is an unincorporated entity, the division:

    (i) shall consider the personal financial information of each individual who holds an ownership interest in the unincorporated entity; and

        (ii)   may, at any time:

              (A)   audit the personal financial information of any individual who holds an ownership interest in the unincorporated entity; or

              (B)   request and obtain a credit report on the individual.

    (b)   If, based on the personal financial information of one or more individuals who hold an ownership interest in the unincorporated entity, the division determines that the applicant or licensee lacks financial responsibility to engage successfully in business as a contractor, the division may:

        (i)   prohibit the individual or individuals from engaging in a construction trade;

        (ii)   prohibit the applicant or licensee from engaging in a construction trade, unless the individual or individuals dissociate from the applicant or licensee within 10 days after the division makes the determination of a lack of financial responsibility; or

        (iii)   require the individual or individuals, applicant, or licensee to submit a bond that is in a form determined by the commission with the concurrence of the director and in an amount that is:

              (A)   determined by the commission with the concurrence of the director; or

              (B)   20% of the annual gross distributions from the unincorporated entity to its owners and that includes coverage for unpaid obligations incurred by the licensee contractor and any failure of the licensee contractor owners to pay income taxes and self-employment taxes on the gross distributions from the unincorporated entity to its owners.

Amended by Chapter 57, 2013 General Session

58-55-307 Confidentiality of records and reports.

    (1)   Credit reports, financial statements, and other information submitted to the division by or at the request and direction of an applicant or licensee for the purpose of supporting a representation of financial responsibility constitute protected records under Title 63G, Chapter 2, Government Records Access and Management Act.

    (2)   Notwithstanding Title 63G, Chapter 2, Government Records Access and Management Act, the records described in Subsection (1) are not open for public inspection and are not subject to discovery in civil or administrative proceedings.

Amended by Chapter 382, 2008 General Session

58-55-308 Scope of practice – Installation, repair, maintenance, cleaning, or replacement of gas appliance or combustion system – Rules.

    (1)   (a)   The commission, with the concurrence of the director, may adopt reasonable rules pursuant to Title 63G, Chapter 3, Utah Administrative Rulemaking Act, to define and limit the scope of practice and operating standards of the classifications and subclassifications licensed under this chapter in a manner consistent with established practice in the relevant industry.

        (b)   The commission and the director may limit the field and scope of operations of a licensee under this chapter in accordance with the rules and the public health, safety, and welfare, based on the licensee's education, training, experience, knowledge, and financial responsibility.

(2)   (a)   The work and scope of practice covered by this Subsection (2) is the installation, repair, maintenance, cleaning, or replacement of a residential or commercial gas appliance or combustion system.

       (b)   The provisions of this Subsection (2) apply to any:

            (i)   licensee under this chapter whose license authorizes the licensee to perform the work described in Subsection (2)(a); and

            (ii)   person exempt from licensure under Subsection 58-55-305(1)(h).

       (c)   Any person described in Subsection (2)(b) that performs work described in Subsection (2)(a):

            (i)   must first receive training and certification as specified in rules adopted by the division; and

            (ii)   shall ensure that any employee authorized under other provisions of this chapter to perform work described in Subsection (2)(a) has first received training and certification as specified in rules adopted by the division.

       (d)   The division may exempt from the training requirements adopted under Subsection (2)(c) a person that has adequate experience, as determined by the division.

(3)   The division may exempt the following individuals from the certification requirements adopted under Subsection (2)(c):

       (a)   a person who has passed a test equivalent to the level of testing required by the division for certification, or has completed an apprenticeship program that teaches the installation of gas line appliances and is approved by the Federal Bureau of Apprenticeship Training; and

       (b)   a person working under the immediate one-to-one supervision of a certified natural gas technician or a person exempt from certification.

(4)   This section does not prohibit a licensed specialty contractor from accepting and entering into a contract involving the use of two or more crafts or trades if the performance of the work in the crafts or trades, other than that in which the contractor is licensed, is incidental and supplemental to the work for which the contractor is licensed.

Amended by Chapter 382, 2008 General Session

58-55-308.1 Definitions – Installation of natural gas facilities – Scope of practice.

(1)   As used in this section:

       (a)   "Gas corporation" is as defined in Section 54-2-1.

       (b)   "Minimum system" means the minimum natural gas facilities necessary to serve each intended consumer, as determined by a gas corporation.

       (c)   (i)   "Natural gas facilities" means:

                (A)   one or more natural gas mains;

                (B)   one or more natural gas service lines; or

                (C)   a combination of Subsections (1)(c)(i)(A) and (B); and

            (ii)   "Natural gas facilities" includes any necessary appurtenant facilities.

       (d)   (i)   "Natural gas main" means a natural gas distribution pipeline that delivers natural gas to another natural gas distribution supply line or to a natural gas service line.

            (ii)   "Natural gas main" does not include a natural gas service line.

     (e)   "Natural gas service line" means a natural gas pipeline that carries natural gas from a natural gas main to a meter for use by the ultimate consumer.

     (f)   "Natural gas tariff specifications" means the standards and specifications:

         (i)   for the construction of natural gas facilities; and

         (ii)   that are:

            (A)   established by a gas corporation; and

            (B)   included in the gas corporation's tariff that is approved by the Public Service Commission.

     (g)   "Qualifying installer" means a person who:

         (i)   a gas corporation approves to install natural gas facilities; and

         (ii)   is:

            (A)   licensed under this chapter; and

            (B)   authorized to install natural gas facilities within the person's scope of practice as established by statute or administrative rule.

(2)   A qualifying installer may install natural gas facilities.

(3)   (a)   Except as provided in Subsections (3)(b) and (c), a qualifying installer shall pay the costs to install natural gas facilities.

     (b)   A gas corporation shall pay the costs of the following services related to natural gas facilities installed by a qualifying installer:

         (i)   engineering;

         (ii)   inspection;

         (iii) mapping; and

         (iv) locating.

     (c)   If a gas corporation requires a qualifying installer to install natural gas facilities that are greater than the minimum system, the gas corporation shall pay any difference in cost between the required natural gas facilities and the minimum system.

(4)   A gas corporation shall inspect and test natural gas facilities that a qualifying installer installs to verify that the natural gas facilities comply with applicable federal, state, and local law and natural gas tariff specifications.

(5)   A gas corporation is not required to supply natural gas to or accept ownership of natural gas facilities until the gas corporation completes all necessary inspections and testing to verify that the natural gas facilities have been installed and tested in compliance with applicable federal, state, and local law and natural gas tariff specifications.

Enacted by Chapter 326, 2014 General Session

58-55-310 Requirements when working for political subdivision or state agency.

Each political subdivision and agency of the state and each board of education which requires the issuance of a permit or license as a precondition to the construction, alteration, improvement, demolition, or other repairs for which a contractor's license is also required under this chapter shall:

    (1)   require that each applicant for a permit or license file a signed statement that the applicant has a current contractor's license with the license number included in the application;

(2)   require that any representation of exemption from the contractor's licensing law be included in the signed statement and that if that exempt person, firm, corporation, association, or other organization intends to hire a contractor to perform any work under the permit or license, that the license number of that contractor be included in the application, but if a contractor has not been selected at the time of the application for a permit or license, the permit or license shall be issued only on the condition that a currently licensed contractor will be selected and that the license number of the contractor will be given to the issuing public body and displayed on the permit or license;

(3)   require that, upon issuance of a permit or license, the contractor affix the contractor's license number to that permit or license for public display; and

(4)   require the contractor to provide proof that the contractor provides workers' compensation insurance, pays into the unemployment insurance fund, provides health insurance as required under federal or state law, and withholds applicable taxes from worker pay.

Amended by Chapter 57, 2013 General Session

58-55-311 Evidence of licensure.

An individual licensed as an alarm company agent shall:

(1)   carry a copy of the individual's license on the individual's person at all times while acting as a licensee;

(2)   display the license upon the request of a peace officer, a representative of the division, or a representative of a customer of the alarm company.

Renumbered and Amended by Chapter 317, 2000 General Session

58-55-312 Interim and temporary permits for alarm company agents.

(1)   Upon receipt of a complete application for licensure in accordance with Section 58-55-302, an applicant for licensure as an alarm company agent may be issued:

(a)   an interim permit; or

(b)   subject to Subsection (3), a temporary permit.

(2)   (a)   Each interim permit shall expire 90 days after it is issued or on the date on which the applicant is issued a license, whichever is earlier.

(b)   The division may reissue an interim permit if the delay in approving a license is beyond the control or influence of the interim permit holder.

(3)   (a)   The division may issue a temporary permit to an applicant for a license as an alarm company agent if:

(i)   the division has received a background check on the applicant from the Bureau of Criminal Identification;

(ii)   (A)   the applicant is or will be employed at a call center, office, or administrative facility of an alarm company; and

(B)   the applicant's only contact with a customer or potential customer of the alarm company is:

(I)   from the call center, office, or administrative facility; and

(II)   by telephone or other remote communication method; and

        (iii)   the alarm company by which the applicant is or will be employed affirms in writing to the division that the applicant, if issued a temporary license, will act only within the scope of the temporary license, as provided in Subsection (3)(a)(ii).

    (b)   A temporary license under this section expires the earliest of:

        (i)   90 days after it is issued;

        (ii)   the date on which the individual to whom the temporary license is issued leaves the employment of the alarm company that employs the individual at the time the temporary license is issued; and

        (iii)   the date on which the division issues a regular license to the applicant or denies the applicant's application.

(4)   An interim permit holder may engage in the scope of an alarm company agent.

Amended by Chapter 387, 2010 General Session

Part 4 - License Denial and Discipline

58-55-401 Grounds for denial of license and disciplinary proceedings.

(1)   In accordance with Section 58-1-401, the division may:

    (a)   refuse to issue a license to an applicant;

    (b)   refuse to renew the license of a licensee;

    (c)   revoke the right of a licensee to recover from the Residence Lien Recovery Fund created by Section 38-11-201;

    (d)   revoke, suspend, restrict, or place on probation the license of a licensee;

    (e)   issue a public or private reprimand to a licensee; and

    (f)   issue a cease and desist order.

(2)   In addition to an action taken under Subsection (1), the division may take an action described in Subsection 58-1-401(2) in relation to a license as a contractor, if:

    (a)   the applicant or licensee is an unincorporated entity; and

    (b)   an individual who holds an ownership interest in the applicant or licensee engages in:

        (i)   unlawful conduct as described in Section 58-55-501; or

        (ii)   unprofessional conduct as described in Section 58-55-502.

Amended by Chapter 413, 2011 General Session

58-55-402 Investigation of regulated activity.

(1)   The division shall be responsible for the investigation of persons and activities in violation of the provisions of this chapter.

(2)   (a)   Investigation by the division shall include investigations of:

        (i)   licensees engaged in unlawful or unprofessional conduct; and

        (ii)   unlicensed persons engaged in the conduct of activity or work regulated under this chapter and for which a license is required.

    (b)   (i)   As used in this Subsection (2)(b), "sign contractor":

          (A)   means a sign installation contractor or nonelectrical outdoor advertising sign contractor, as classified and defined in division rules; and

          (B)   does not include a sign installation contractor or nonelectrical outdoor advertising sign contractor, as classified and defined in division rules, that is subject to Title 72, Chapter 7, Part 5, Utah Outdoor Advertising Act.

      (ii)   The division shall maintain a record of the number of unlicensed persons found to have engaged each year in the conduct of activity or work regulated under this chapter for which a license as a sign contractor is required, including the location where a violation occurred.

(3)   The division shall decline to proceed with investigation of the violation of any provisions of this chapter if the division finds there is no apparent material jeopardy to the public health, safety, and welfare.

(4)   The division shall have no responsibility for the inspection of construction work performed in the state to determine compliance with applicable codes, or industry and workmanship standards, except as provided in Subsections 58-1-501(2)(g), 58-55-502(2), (3), and (4), and 58-55-501(16).

(5)   Authorized representatives of the division shall be permitted to enter upon the premises or site of work regulated under this chapter for the purpose of determining compliance with the provisions of this chapter.

Amended by Chapter 195, 2011 General Session

58-55-403 Minimum time for division action.

The division has at least five working days after receiving an application for licensure to determine whether to issue a license under this chapter.

Amended by Chapter 233, 2000 General Session

Part 5 - Unlawful and Unprofessional Conduct - Penalties

58-55-501 Unlawful conduct.

Unlawful conduct includes:

(1)   engaging in a construction trade, acting as a contractor, an alarm business or company, or an alarm company agent, or representing oneself to be engaged in a construction trade or to be acting as a contractor in a construction trade requiring licensure, unless the person doing any of these is appropriately licensed or exempted from licensure under this chapter;

(2)   acting in a construction trade, as an alarm business or company, or as an alarm company agent beyond the scope of the license held;

(3)   hiring or employing a person who is not licensed under this chapter to perform work on a project, unless the person:

      (a)   is an employee of a person licensed under this chapter for wages; and

      (b)   is not required to be licensed under this chapter;

(4)   applying for or obtaining a building permit either for oneself or another when not licensed or exempted from licensure as a contractor under this chapter;

(5)   issuing a building permit to any person for whom there is no evidence of a current license or exemption from licensure as a contractor under this chapter;

(6)   applying for or obtaining a building permit for the benefit of or on behalf of any other person who is required to be licensed under this chapter but who is not licensed or is otherwise not entitled to obtain or receive the benefit of the building permit;

(7)   failing to obtain a building permit when required by law or rule;

(8)   submitting a bid for any work for which a license is required under this chapter by a person not licensed or exempted from licensure as a contractor under this chapter;

(9)   willfully or deliberately misrepresenting or omitting a material fact in connection with an application to obtain or renew a license under this chapter;

(10)   allowing one's license to be used by another except as provided by statute or rule;

(11)   doing business under a name other than the name appearing on the license, except as permitted by statute or rule;

(12)   if licensed as a specialty contractor in the electrical trade or plumbing trade, journeyman plumber, residential journeyman plumber, journeyman electrician, master electrician, or residential electrician, failing to directly supervise an apprentice under one's supervision or exceeding the number of apprentices one is allowed to have under the speciality contractor's supervision;

(13)   if licensed as a contractor or representing oneself to be a contractor, receiving any funds in payment for a specific project from an owner or any other person, which funds are to pay for work performed or materials and services furnished for that specific project, and after receiving the funds to exercise unauthorized control over the funds by failing to pay the full amounts due and payable to persons who performed work or furnished materials or services within a reasonable period of time;

(14)   employing an unlicensed alarm business or company or an unlicensed individual as an alarm company agent, except as permitted under the exemption from licensure provisions under Section 58-1-307;

(15)   if licensed as an alarm company or alarm company agent, filing with the division fingerprint cards for an applicant which are not those of the applicant, or are in any other way false or fraudulent and intended to mislead the division in its consideration of the applicant for licensure;

(16)   if licensed under this chapter, willfully or deliberately disregarding or violating:

    (a)   the building or construction laws of this state or any political subdivision;

    (b)   the safety and labor laws applicable to a project;

    (c)   any provision of the health laws applicable to a project;

    (d)   the workers' compensation insurance laws of the state applicable to a project;

    (e)   the laws governing withholdings for employee state and federal income taxes, unemployment taxes, Social Security payroll taxes, or other required withholdings; or

    (f)   reporting, notification, and filing laws of this state or the federal government;

(17)   aiding or abetting any person in evading the provisions of this chapter or rules established under the authority of the division to govern this chapter;

(18)   engaging in the construction trade or as a contractor for the construction of residences of up to two units when not currently registered or exempt from registration as a qualified beneficiary under Title 38, Chapter 11, Residence Lien Restriction and Lien Recovery Fund Act;

(19)   failing, as an original contractor, as defined in Section 38-11-102, to include in a written contract the notification required in Section 38-11-108;

(20)   wrongfully filing a preconstruction or construction lien in violation of Section 38-1a-308;

(21)   if licensed as a contractor, not completing the approved continuing education required under Section 58-55-302.5;

(22)   an alarm company allowing an employee with a temporary license under Section 58-55-312 to engage in conduct on behalf of the company outside the scope of the temporary license, as provided in Subsection 58-55-312(3)(a)(ii);

(23)   an alarm company agent under a temporary license under Section 58-55-312 engaging in conduct outside the scope of the temporary license, as provided in Subsection 58-55-312(3)(a) (ii);

(24)   (a)   an unincorporated entity licensed under this chapter having an individual who owns an interest in the unincorporated entity engage in a construction trade in Utah while not lawfully present in the United States; or

          (b)   an unincorporated entity providing labor to an entity licensed under this chapter by providing an individual who owns an interest in the unincorporated entity to engage in a construction trade in Utah while not lawfully present in the United States;

(25)   an unincorporated entity failing to provide the following for an individual who engages, or will engage, in a construction trade in Utah for the unincorporated entity, or for an individual who engages, or will engage, in a construction trade in Utah for a separate entity for which the unincorporated entity provides the individual as labor:

          (a)   workers' compensation coverage:

                  (i)   to the extent required by Title 34A, Chapter 2, Workers' Compensation Act, and Title 34A, Chapter 3, Utah Occupational Disease Act; or

                  (ii)   that would be required under the chapters listed in Subsection (25)(a)(i) if the unincorporated entity were licensed under this chapter; and

          (b)   unemployment compensation in accordance with Title 35A, Chapter 4, Employment Security Act, for an individual who owns, directly or indirectly, less than an 8% interest in the unincorporated entity, as defined by rule made by the division in accordance with Title 63G, Chapter 3, Utah Administrative Rulemaking Act;

(26)   the failure of a sign installation contractor or nonelectrical outdoor advertising sign contractor, as classified and defined in division rules, to:

          (a)   display the contractor's license number prominently on a vehicle that:

                  (i)   the contractor uses; and

                  (ii)   displays the contractor's business name; or

          (b)   carry a copy of the contractor's license in any other vehicle that the contractor uses at a job site, whether or not the vehicle is owned by the contractor;

(27)   (a)   an unincorporated entity licensed under this chapter having an individual who owns an interest in the unincorporated entity engage in a construction trade in the state while the individual is using a Social Security number that does not belong to that individual; or

          (b)   an unincorporated entity providing labor to an entity licensed under this chapter by providing an individual, who owns an interest in the unincorporated entity, to engage in a construction trade in the state while the individual is using a Social Security number that does not belong to that individual;

(28)   a contractor failing to comply with a requirement imposed by a political subdivision, state agency, or board of education under Section 58-55-310; or

(29)   failing to timely comply with the requirements described in Section 58-55-605.

Amended by Chapter 188, 2014 General Session

58-55-502 Unprofessional conduct.

Unprofessional conduct includes:

(1)   failing to establish, maintain, or demonstrate financial responsibility while licensed as a contractor under this chapter;

(2)   disregarding or violating through gross negligence or a pattern of negligence:

     (a)   the building or construction laws of this state or any political subdivision;

     (b)   the safety and labor laws applicable to a project;

     (c)   any provision of the health laws applicable to a project;

     (d)   the workers' compensation insurance laws of this state applicable to a project;

     (e)   the laws governing withholdings for employee state and federal income taxes, unemployment taxes, Social Security payroll taxes, or other required withholdings; or

     (f)   any reporting, notification, and filing laws of this state or the federal government;

(3)   any willful, fraudulent, or deceitful act by a licensee, caused by a licensee, or at a licensee's direction which causes material injury to another;

(4)   contract violations that pose a threat or potential threat to the public health, safety, and welfare including:

     (a)   willful, deliberate, or grossly negligent departure from or disregard for plans or specifications, or abandonment or failure to complete a project without the consent of the owner or the owner's duly authorized representative or the consent of any other person entitled to have the particular project completed in accordance with the plans, specifications, and contract terms;

     (b)   failure to deposit funds to the benefit of an employee as required under any written contractual obligation the licensee has to the employee;

     (c)   failure to maintain in full force and effect any health insurance benefit to an employee that was extended as a part of any written contractual obligation or representation by the licensee, unless the employee is given written notice of the licensee's intent to cancel or reduce the insurance benefit at least 45 days before the effective date of the cancellation or reduction;

     (d)   failure to reimburse the Residence Lien Recovery Fund as required by Section 38-11-207;

     (e)   failure to provide, when applicable, the information required by Section 38-11-108; and

     (f)   willfully or deliberately misrepresenting or omitting a material fact in connection with an application to claim recovery from the Residence Lien Recovery Fund under Section 38-11-204;

(5)   failing as an alarm company to notify the division of the cessation of performance of its qualifying agent, or failing to replace its qualifying agent as required under Section 58-55-304;

(6)   failing as an alarm company agent to carry or display a copy of the licensee's license as required under Section 58-55-311;

(7)   failing to comply with operating standards established by rule in accordance with Section 58-55-308;

(8)   an unincorporated entity licensed under this chapter having an individual who owns an interest in the unincorporated entity engage in a construction trade in Utah while not lawfully present in the United States;

(9)   an unincorporated entity failing to provide the following for an individual who engages, or will engage, in a construction trade in Utah for the unincorporated entity:

    (a)   workers' compensation coverage to the extent required by Title 34A, Chapter 2, Workers' Compensation Act, and Title 34A, Chapter 3, Utah Occupational Disease Act; and

    (b)   unemployment compensation in accordance with Title 35A, Chapter 4, Employment Security Act, for an individual who owns, directly or indirectly, less than an 8% interest in the unincorporated entity, as defined by rule made by the division in accordance with Title 63G, Chapter 3, Utah Administrative Rulemaking Act; or

(10)   the failure of an alarm company or alarm company agent to inform a potential customer, before the customer's purchase of an alarm system or alarm service from the alarm company, of the policy of the county, city, or town within which the customer resides relating to priority levels for responding to an alarm signal transmitted by the alarm system that the alarm company provides the customer.

Amended by Chapter 170, 2011 General Session. Amended by Chapter 413, 2011 General Session

58-55-503 Penalty for unlawful conduct – Citations.

(1)   (a)   (i)   A person who violates Subsection 58-55-308(2), Subsection 58-55-501(1), (2), (3), (4), (5), (6), (7), (9), (10), (12), (14), (15), (22), (23), (24), (25), (26), (27), (28), or (29), or Subsection 58-55-504(2), or who fails to comply with a citation issued under this section after it is final, is guilty of a class A misdemeanor.

            (ii)   As used in this section in reference to Subsection 58-55-504(2), "person" means an individual and does not include a sole proprietorship, joint venture, corporation, limited liability company, association, or organization of any type.

    (b)   A person who violates the provisions of Subsection 58-55-501(8) may not be awarded and may not accept a contract for the performance of the work.

(2)   A person who violates the provisions of Subsection 58-55-501(13) is guilty of an infraction unless the violator did so with the intent to deprive the person to whom money is to be paid of the money received, in which case the violator is guilty of theft, as classified in Section 76-6-412.

(3)   Grounds for immediate suspension of a licensee's license by the division and the commission include:

    (a)   the issuance of a citation for violation of Subsection 58-55-308(2), Section 58-55-501, or Subsection 58-55-504(2); and

    (b)   the failure by a licensee to make application to, report to, or notify the division with respect to any matter for which application, notification, or reporting is required under this chapter or rules adopted under this chapter, including:

            (i)   applying to the division for a new license to engage in a new specialty classification or to do business under a new form of organization or business structure;

            (ii)   filing a current financial statement with the division; and

            (iii)   notifying the division concerning loss of insurance coverage or change in qualifier.

(4)   (a)   If upon inspection or investigation, the division concludes that a person has violated the provisions of Subsection 58-55-308(2), Subsection 58-55-501(1), (2), (3), (9), (10), (12), (14), (19), (21), (22), (23), (24), (25), (26), (27), (28), or (29), Subsection 58-55-504(2), or any rule or order issued with respect to these subsections, and that disciplinary action is appropriate, the director or the director's designee from within the division shall promptly issue a citation to the person according to this chapter and any pertinent rules, attempt

to negotiate a stipulated settlement, or notify the person to appear before an adjudicative proceeding conducted under Title 63G, Chapter 4, Administrative Procedures Act.

    (i)   A person who is in violation of the provisions of Subsection 58-55-308(2), Subsection 58-55-501(1), (2), (3), (9), (10), (12), (14), (19), (21), (22), (23), (24), (25), (26), (27), (28), or (29), or Subsection 58-55-504(2), as evidenced by an uncontested citation, a stipulated settlement, or by a finding of violation in an adjudicative proceeding, may be assessed a fine pursuant to this Subsection (4) and may, in addition to or in lieu of, be ordered to cease and desist from violating Subsection 58-55-308(2), Subsection 58-55-501(1), (2), (3), (9), (10), (12), (14), (19), (21), (24), (25), (26), (27), (28), or (29), or Subsection 58-55-504(2).

    (ii)   Except for a cease and desist order, the licensure sanctions cited in Section 58-55-401 may not be assessed through a citation.

(b)   (i)   A citation shall be in writing and describe with particularity the nature of the violation, including a reference to the provision of the chapter, rule, or order alleged to have been violated.

    (ii)   A citation shall clearly state that the recipient must notify the division in writing within 20 calendar days of service of the citation if the recipient wishes to contest the citation at a hearing conducted under Title 63G, Chapter 4, Administrative Procedures Act.

    (iii)   A citation shall clearly explain the consequences of failure to timely contest the citation or to make payment of any fines assessed by the citation within the time specified in the citation.

(c)   A citation issued under this section, or a copy of a citation, may be served upon a person upon whom a summons may be served:

    (i)   in accordance with the Utah Rules of Civil Procedure;

    (ii)   personally or upon the person's agent by a division investigator or by a person specially designated by the director; or

    (iii)   by mail.

(d)   (i)   If within 20 calendar days after the day on which a citation is served, the person to whom the citation was issued fails to request a hearing to contest the citation, the citation becomes the final order of the division and is not subject to further agency review.

    (ii)   The period to contest a citation may be extended by the division for cause.

(e)   The division may refuse to issue or renew, suspend, revoke, or place on probation the license of a licensee who fails to comply with a citation after it becomes final.

(f)   The failure of an applicant for licensure to comply with a citation after it becomes final is a ground for denial of license.

(g)   A citation may not be issued under this section after the expiration of six months following the occurrence of a violation.

(h)   The director or the director's designee shall assess a fine in accordance with the following:

    (i)   for a first offense handled pursuant to Subsection (4)(a), a fine of up to $1,000;

    (ii)   for a second offense handled pursuant to Subsection (4)(a), a fine of up to $2,000; and

    (iii)   for any subsequent offense handled pursuant to Subsection (4)(a), a fine of up to $2,000 for each day of continued offense.

(i)   (i)   For purposes of issuing a final order under this section and assessing a fine under Subsection (4)(h), an offense constitutes a second or subsequent offense if:

               (A)   the division previously issued a final order determining that a person committed a first or second offense in violation of Subsection 58-55-308(2), Subsection 58-55-501(1), (2), (3), (9), (10), (12), (14), (19), (24), (25), (26), (27), (28), or (29), or Subsection 58-55-504(2); or

               (B)   (I)   the division initiated an action for a first or second offense;

                         (II)   a final order has not been issued by the division in the action initiated under Subsection (4)(i)(i)(B)(I);

                         (III)   the division determines during an investigation that occurred after the initiation of the action under Subsection (4)(i)(i)(B)(I) that the person committed a second or subsequent violation of the provisions of Subsection 58-55-308(2), Subsection 58-55-501(1), (2), (3), (9), (10), (12), (14), (19), (24), (25), (26), (27), (28), or (29), or Subsection 58-55-504(2); and

                         (IV)   after determining that the person committed a second or subsequent offense under Subsection (4)(i)(i)(B)(III), the division issues a final order on the action initiated under Subsection (4)(i)(i)(B)(I).

          (ii)   In issuing a final order for a second or subsequent offense under Subsection (4)(i)(i), the division shall comply with the requirements of this section.

(j)   In addition to any other licensure sanction or fine imposed under this section, the division shall revoke the license of a licensee that violates Subsection 58-55-501(24) or (25) two or more times within a 12-month period, unless, with respect to a violation of Subsection 58-55-501(24), the licensee can demonstrate that the licensee successfully verified the federal legal working status of the individual who was the subject of the violation using a status verification system, as defined in Section 13-47-102.

(k)   For purposes of this Subsection (4), a violation of Subsection 58-55-501(24) or (25) for each individual is considered a separate violation.

(5)   (a)   A penalty imposed by the director under Subsection (4)(h) shall be deposited into the Commerce Service Account created by Section 13-1-2.

          (b)   A penalty that is not paid may be collected by the director by either referring the matter to a collection agency or bringing an action in the district court of the county in which the person against whom the penalty is imposed resides or in the county where the office of the director is located.

          (c)   A county attorney or the attorney general of the state is to provide legal assistance and advice to the director in any action to collect the penalty.

          (d)   In an action brought to enforce the provisions of this section, the court shall award reasonable attorney fees and costs to the prevailing party.

Amended by Chapter 188, 2014 General Session

58-55-504 Crane operators -- Required certification -- Penalty for violation.

(1)   As used in this section:

(a)   "Commercial construction projects" means construction, alteration, repair, demolition, or excavation projects that do not involve:

  (i)   single family detached housing;

  (ii)   multifamily attached housing up to and including a fourplex; or

  (iii)   commercial construction of not more than two stories above ground.

(b) (i)   "Crane operator" means an individual engaged in operating a crane, which for purposes of this section is a power-operated hoisting machine used in construction, demolition, or excavation work that has a power-operated winch, load-line, and boom moving laterally by the rotation of the machine on a carrier.

  (ii)   It does not include operating a fork lift, digger derrick truck, aircraft, bucket truck, knuckle boom, side boom, mechanic's truck, or a vehicle or machine not using a power-operated winch and load-line.

(2) (a)   In order to operate a crane on commercial construction projects, an individual shall be certified as a crane operator by the National Commission for the Certification of Crane Operators or any other organization determined by the division to offer an equivalent testing and certification program that meets the requirements of the American Society of Mechanical Engineers ASME B 30.5 and the accreditation requirements of the National Commission for Certifying Agencies.

  (b)   An individual who violates Subsection (2)(a) is guilty of a class A misdemeanor.

(3)   An individual engaged in construction or operation incidental to petroleum refining or electrical utility construction or maintenance is exempt from the crane operator certification requirement of Subsection (2)(a).

Amended by Chapter 98, 2007 General Session

Part 6 - Payment Provisions

58-55-601 Payment – Account designated.

When making any payment to a materialman, supplier, contractor, or subcontractor with whom he has a running account, or with whom he has more than one contract, or to whom he is otherwise indebted, the contractor shall designate the contract under which the payment is made or the items of account to which it is to be applied. When a payment for materials or labor is made to a subcontractor or materialman, the subcontractor or materialman shall demand of the person making the payment a designation of the account and the items of account to which the payment is to apply. In cases where a lien is claimed for materials furnished or labor performed by a subcontractor or materialman, it is a defense to the claim that a payment was made by the owner to the contractor for the materials and was so designated and paid over to the subcontractor or materialman, if when the payment was received by the subcontractor or materialman, he did not demand a designation of the account and of the items of account to which the payment was to be applied.

Renumbered and Amended by Chapter 181, 1994 General Session

58-55-602 Payment of construction funds – Interest.

(1)   All unpaid construction funds are payable to the contractor as provided in Section 13-8-5.

(2)   On projects involving multiple buildings, each building shall be considered individually in determining the amount to be paid the contractor.

(3)   Partial occupancy of a building requires payment in direct proportion to the value of the part of the building occupied.

(4)   If any payment is retained or withheld, it shall be retained or withheld and released as provided in Section 13-8-5.

Amended by Chapter 365, 1999 General Session

58-55-603 Payment to subcontractors and suppliers.

(1)   When a contractor receives any construction funds from an owner or another contractor for work performed and billed, he shall pay each of his subcontractors and suppliers in proportion to the percentage of the work they performed under that billing, unless otherwise agreed by contract.

(2)   If, under this section and without reasonable cause, or unless otherwise agreed by contract, the contractor fails to pay for work performed by his subcontractors or suppliers within 30 consecutive days after receiving construction funds from the owner or another contractor for work performed and billed, or after the last day payment is due under the terms of the billing, whichever is later, he shall pay to the subcontractor or supplier, in addition to the payment, interest in the amount of 1% per month of the amount due, beginning on the day after payment is due, and reasonable costs of any collection and attorney's fees.

(3)   When a subcontractor receives any construction payment under this section, Subsections (1) and (2) apply to that subcontractor.

Renumbered and Amended by Chapter 181, 1994 General Session

58-55-604 Proof of licensure to maintain or commence action.

A contractor or alarm business or company may not act as agent or commence or maintain any action in any court of the state for collection of compensation for performing any act for which a license is required by this chapter without alleging and proving that the licensed contractor or alarm business or company was appropriately licensed when the contract sued upon was entered into, and when the alleged cause of action arose.

Amended by Chapter 377, 2008 General Session

58-55-605 Pay statement required.

(1)   On the day on which a person licensed under this chapter pays an individual for work that the individual performed, the person shall give the individual a written or electronic pay statement that states:

     (a)   the individual's name;

     (b)   the individual's base rate of pay;

     (c)   the dates of the pay period for which the individual is being paid;

     (d)   if paid hourly, the number of hours the individual worked during the pay period;

     (e)   the amount of and reason for any money withheld in accordance with state or federal law, including:

          (i)   state and federal income tax;

          (ii)   Social Security tax;

          (iii)   Medicare tax; and

          (iv)   court-ordered withholdings; and

     (f)   the total amount paid to the individual for that pay period.

(2)   A person licensed under this chapter shall:

      (a)   comply with the requirements described in Subsection (1) regardless of whether the licensee pays the individual by check, cash, or other means;

      (b)   retain a copy of each pay statement described in Subsection (1) for at least three years after the day on which the person gives a copy of the pay statement to the individual; and

      (c)   upon request, make the pay statement records described in this section available to the division for inspection.

Enacted by Chapter 188, 2014 General Session

Appendix F: Utah Construction Trades Licensing Act Rule

R156-55a-101. Title.

This rule shall be known as the "Utah Construction Trades Licensing Act Rule".

R156-55a-102. Definitions.

In addition to the definitions in Title 58, Chapters 1 and 55, as defined or used in this rule:

(1)   "Construction trades instructor", as used in Subsection 58-55-301(2)(p) is clarified to mean the education facility which is issued the license as a construction trades instructor. It does not mean individuals employed by the facility who may teach classes.

(2)   "Construction trades instruction facility" means the facility which is granted the license as a construction trades instructor as specified in Subsection 58-55-301(2)(p) and as clarified in R156-55a-102(1).

(3)   "Employee", as used in Subsections 58-55-102(12)(a) and 58-55-102(17), means a person providing labor services in the construction trades who works for a licensed contractor, or the substantial equivalent of a licensed contractor as determined by the Division, for compensation who has federal and state taxes withheld and workers' compensation and unemployment insurance provided by the person's employer.

(4)   "Incidental", as used in Subsection 58-55-102(40), means work which:

    (a)   can be safely and competently performed by the specialty contractor; and

    (b)   arises from and is directly related to work performed in the licensed specialty classification and does not exceed 10 percent of the overall contract and does not include performance of any electrical or plumbing work unless specifically included in the specialty classification description under Subsection R156-55a-301(2).

(5)   "Maintenance" means the repair, replacement and refinishing of any component of an existing structure; but, does not include alteration or modification to the existing weight-bearing structural components.

(6)   "Mechanical", as used in Subsections 58-55-102(21) and 58-55-102(32), means the work which may be performed by a S350 HVAC Contractor under Section R156-55a-301.

(7)   "Personal property" means, as it relates to Title 58, Chapter 56, factory built housing and modular construction, a structure which is titled by the Motor Vehicles Division, state of Utah, and taxed as personal property.

(8)   "Qualifier", as used in Title 58, Chapter 55 and this rule, means the individual who demonstrates competence for a contractor or construction trades instruction facility license by passing the examinations, completing the experience requirements or holding the individual licenses that are prerequisite requirements to obtain the contractor or construction trades instruction facility license.

(9)   "School" means a Utah school district, applied technology college, or accredited college.

(10)   "Unprofessional conduct" defined in Title 58, Chapters 1 and 55, is further defined in accordance with Section 58-1-203 in Section R156-55a-501.

R156-55a-103. Authority.

This rule is adopted by the Division under the authority of Subsection 58-1-106(1)(a) to enable the Division to administer Title 58, Chapter 55.

R156-55a-104. Organization - Relationship to Rule R156-1.

The organization of this rule and its relationship to Rule R156-1 is as described in Section R156-1-107.

R156-55a-301. License Classifications - Scope of Practice.

(1)   In accordance with Subsection 58-55-301(2), the classifications of licensure are listed and described in this section. The construction trades or specialty contractor classifications listed are those determined to significantly impact the public health, safety, and welfare. A person who is engaged in work which is included in the items listed in Subsections R156-55a-301(4) and (5) is exempt from licensure in accordance with Subsection 58-55-305(1)(i).

(2)   Licenses shall be issued in the following primary classifications and subclassifications:

E100 - General Engineering Contractor. A General Engineering contractor is a contractor licensed to perform work as defined in Subsection 58-55-102(22).

B100 - General Building Contractor. A General Building contractor is a contractor licensed to perform work as defined in Subsection 58-55-102(21) and pursuant to Subsection 58-55-102(21)(b) is clarified as follows:

(a)   The General Building Contractor scope of practice does not include activities described in this Subsection under specialty classification S202 - Solar Photovoltaic Contractor unless the work is performed under the immediate supervision of an employee who holds a current certificate issued by the North American Board of Certified Energy Practitioners.

(b)   The General Building Contractor scope of practice does not include activities described in this Subsection under specialty classification S354-Radon Mitigation Contractor unless the work is performed under the immediate supervision of an employee who holds a current certificate issued by the National Radon Safety Board (NRSB) or the National Radon Proficiency Program (NEHA-NRPP).

B200 - Modular Unit Installation Contractor. Set up or installation of modular units as defined in Subsection 15A-1-302(8) and constructed in accordance with Section 15A-1-304. The scope of the work permitted under this classification includes construction of the permanent or temporary foundations, placement of the modular unit on a permanent or temporary foundation, securing the units together if required and securing the modular units to the foundations. Work excluded from this classification includes installation of factory built housing and connection of required utilities.

R100 - Residential and Small Commercial Contractor. A Residential and Small Commercial contractor is a contractor licensed to perform work as defined in Subsection 58-55-102(32) and pursuant to Subsection 58-55-102(32) is clarified as follows:

(a)   The Residential and Small Commercial Contractor scope of practice does not include activities described in this Subsection under specialty classification S202-Solar Photovoltaic Contractor unless the work is performed under the immediate supervision of an employee who holds a current certificate issued by the North American Board of Certified Energy Practitioners.

(b)   The Residential and Small Commercial Contractor scope of practice does not include activities described in this Subsection under specialty classification S354-Radon Mitigation Contractor unless the work is performed under the immediate supervision of an employee who holds a current certificate issued by the National Radon Safety Board (NRSB) or the National Radon Proficiency Program (NEHA-NRPP).

R101 - Residential and Small Commercial Non Structural Remodeling and Repair. Remodeling and repair to any existing structure built for support, shelter and enclosure of persons, animals, chattels or movable property of any kind with the restriction that no change is made to the bearing portions of the existing structure, including footings, foundation and weight bearing walls; and the entire project is less than $50,000 in total cost.

R200 - Factory Built Housing Contractor. Disconnection, setup, installation or removal of manufactured housing on a temporary or permanent basis. The scope of the work permitted under this classification includes placement of the manufactured housing on a permanent or temporary foundation, securing the units together if required, securing the manufactured housing to the foundation, and connection of the utilities from the near proximity, such as a meter, to the manufactured housing unit and construction of foundations of less than four feet six inches in height. Work excluded from this classification includes site preparation or finishing, excavation of the ground in the area where a foundation is to be constructed, back filling and grading around the foundation, construction of foundations of more than four feet six inches in height and construction of utility services from the utility source to and including the meter or meters if required or if not required to the near proximity of the manufactured housing unit from which they are connected to the unit.

I101 - General Engineering Trades Instruction Facility. A General Engineering Trades Instruction Facility is a construction trades instruction facility authorized to teach the construction trades and is subject to the scope of practice defined in Subsection 58-55-102(22).

I102 - General Building Trades Instruction Facility. A General Building Trades Instruction Facility is a construction trades instruction facility authorized to teach the construction trades and is subject to the scope of practice defined in Subsections 58-55-102(21) or 58-55-102(32).

I103 - Electrical Trades Instruction Facility. An Electrical Trades Instruction Facility is a construction trades instruction facility authorized to teach the electrical trades and subject to the scope of practice defined in Subsection R156-55a-301(S200).

I104 - Plumbing Trades Instruction Facility. A Plumbing Trades Instruction Facility is a construction trades instruction facility authorized to teach the plumbing trades and subject to the scope of practice defined in Subsection R156-55a-301(S210).

I105 - Mechanical Trades Instruction Facility. A Mechanical Trades Instruction Facility is a construction trades instruction facility authorized to teach the mechanical trades and subject to the scope of practice defined in Subsection R156-55a-301(S350).

S200 - General Electrical Contractor. Fabrication, construction, and/or installation of generators, transformers, conduits, raceways, panels, switch gear, electrical wires, fixtures, appliances, or apparatus which utilizes electrical energy. The General Electrical Contractor scope of practice does not include activities described in this Subsection under specialty classification S354-Radon Mitigation Contractor unless the work is performed under the immediate supervision of an employee who holds a current certificate issued by the National Radon Safety Board (NRSB) or the National Radon Proficiency Program (NEHA-NRPP).

S201 - Residential Electrical Contractor. Fabrication, construction, and/or installation of services, disconnecting means, grounding devices, panels, conductors, load centers, lighting and plug circuits, appliances and fixtures in any residential unit, normally requiring non-metallic sheathed cable, including multiple units up to and including a four-plex, but excluding any work generally recognized in the industry as commercial or industrial.

S202 - Solar Photovoltaic Contractor. Fabrication, construction, installation, and replacement of photovoltaic cell panels and related components. Wiring, connections and wire methods as governed in the National Electrical Code and Subsection R156-55b-102(1) shall only be performed by an S200 General Electrical Contractor or S201 Residential Electrical Contractor. This classification is not required to install stand alone solar systems that do not tie into premises wiring or into the electrical utility, such as signage or street or parking lighting.

A contractor who obtained this classification of licensure between January 1, 2009 and April 25, 2011 and who holds an active license may, in addition to the above, perform the following activities as part of the scope of practice under this subsection: fabrication, construction, installation, and repair of photovoltaic cell panels and related components including battery storage systems, distribution panels, switch gear, electrical wires, inverters, and other electrical apparatus for solar photovoltaic systems. Work excluded from this classification includes work on any alternating current system or system component.

S210 - General Plumbing Contractor. Fabrication and/or installation of material and fixtures to create and maintain sanitary conditions in buildings, by providing a permanent means for a supply of safe and pure water, a means for the timely and complete removal from the premises of all used or contaminated water, fluid and semi-fluid organic wastes and other impurities incidental to life and the occupation of such premises, and provision of a safe and adequate supply of gases for lighting, heating, and industrial purposes. Work permitted under this classification shall include the furnishing of materials, fixtures and labor to extend service from a building out to the main water, sewer or gas pipeline. The General Plumbing Contractor scope of practice does not include activities described in this Subsection under specialty classification S354-Radon Mitigation Contractor unless the work is performed under the immediate supervision of an employee who holds a current certificate issued by the National Radon Safety Board (NRSB) or the National Radon Proficiency Program (NEHA-NRPP).

S211 - Boiler Installation Contractor. Fabrication and/or installation of fire-tube and water-tube power boilers and hot water heating boilers, including all fittings and piping, valves, gauges, pumps, radiators, converters, fuel oil tanks, fuel lines, chimney flues, heat insulation and all other devices, apparatus, and equipment related thereto in a closed system not connected to the culinary water system. Notwithstanding the foregoing, where water delivery for the closed system is connected to the culinary water system and separated from the culinary water system by a backflow prevention device, a contractor licensed under this subsection may connect the closed system to the backflow prevention device, which must be installed by an actively licensed plumber.

S212 - Irrigation Sprinkling Contractor. Layout, fabrication, and/or installation of water distribution system for artificial watering or irrigation.

S213 - Industrial Piping Contractor. Fabrication and/or installation of pipes and piping for the conveyance or transmission of steam, gases, chemicals, and other substances including excavating, trenching, and back-filling related to such work. This classification includes the above work for geo thermal systems.

S214 - Water Conditioning Equipment Contractor. Fabrication and/or installation of water conditioning equipment and only such pipe and fittings as are necessary for connecting the water conditioning equipment to the water supply system within the premises.

S215 - Solar Thermal Systems Contractor. Construction, repair and/or installation of solar thermal systems up to the system shut off valve or where the system interfaces with any other plumbing system.

S216 - Residential Sewer Connection and Septic Tank Contractor. Construction of residential sewer lines including connection to the public sewer line, and excavation and grading related thereto. Excavation, installation and grading of residential septic tanks and their drainage.

S217 - Residential Plumbing Contractor. Fabrication and/or installation of material and fixtures to create and maintain sanitary conditions in residential building, including multiple units up to and including a four-plex by providing a permanent means for a supply of safe and pure water, a means for the timely and complete removal from the premises of all used or contaminated water, fluid and semi-fluid organic wastes and other impurities incidental to life and the occupation of such premises, and provision of a safe and adequate supply of gases for lighting and heating purposes. Work permitted under this classification shall include the furnishing of materials, fixtures and labor to extend service from a residential building out to the main water, sewer or gas pipeline. Excluded is any new construction and service work generally recognized in the industry as commercial or industrial.

S220 - Carpentry Contractor. Fabrication for structural and finish purposes in a structure or building using wood, wood products, metal studs, vinyl materials, or other wood/plastic/metal composites as is by custom and usage accepted in the building industry as carpentry. Incidental work includes the installation of tub liners and wall systems.

S221 - Cabinet, Millwork and Countertop Installation Contractor. On-site construction and/or installation of milled wood products or countertops.

S222 - Overhead and Garage Door Contractor. The installation of overhead and garage doors and door openers.

S230 - Siding Contractor. Fabrication, construction, and/or installation of siding.

S231 - Raingutter Installation Contractor. On-site fabrication and/or installation of rain gutters and drains, roof flashings, gravel stops and metal ridges.

S240 - Glass and Glazing Contractor. Fabrication, construction, installation, and/or removal of all types and sizes of glass, mirrors, substitutes for glass, glass-holding members, frames, hardware, and other incidental related work.

S250 - Insulation Contractor. Installation of any insulating media in buildings and structures for the sole purpose of temperature control, sound control or fireproofing, but shall not include mechanical insulation of pipes, ducts or conduits.

S260 - General Concrete Contractor. Fabrication, construction, mixing, batching, and/or installation of concrete and related concrete products along with the placing and setting of screeds for pavement for flatwork, the construction of forms, placing and erection of steel bars for reinforcing and application of plaster and other cement-related products.

S261 - Concrete Form Setting and Shoring Contractor. Fabrication, construction, and/or installation of forms and shoring material; but, does not include the placement of concrete, finishing of concrete or embedded items such as metal reinforcement bars or mesh.

S262 - Gunnite and Pressure Grouting Contractor. Installation of a concrete product either injected or sprayed under pressure.

S263 - Cementatious Coating Systems Resurfacing and Sealing Contractor. Fabrication, construction, mixing, batching and installation of cementatious coating systems or sealants limited to the resurfacing or sealing of existing surfaces, including the preparation or patching of the surface to be covered or sealed.

S270 - General Drywall and Plastering Contractor. Fabrication, construction, and installation of drywall, gypsum, wallboard panels and assemblies. Preparation of drywall or plaster surfaces for suitable painting or finishing. Application to surfaces of coatings made of plaster, including the preparation of the surface and the provision of abase. This does not include applying stucco to lathe, plaster and other surfaces. Exempted is the plastering of foundations.

S272 - Ceiling Grid Systems, Ceiling Tile and Panel Systems Contractor. Fabrication and/or installation of wood, mineral, fiber, and other types of ceiling tile and panels and the grid systems required for placement.

S273 - Light-weight Metal and Non-bearing Wall Partitions Contractor. Fabrication and/or installation of light-weight metal and other non-bearing wall partitions.

S280 - General Roofing Contractor. Application and/or installation of asphalt, pitch, tar, felt, flax, shakes, shingles, roof tile, slate, and any other material or materials, or any combination of any thereof which use and custom has established as usable for, or which are now used as, water-proof, weatherproof, or watertight seal or membranes for roofs and surfaces; and roof conversion. Incidental work includes the installation of roof clamp ring to the roof drain.

S290 - General Masonry Contractor. Construction by cutting, and/or laying of all of the following brick, block, or forms: architectural, industrial, and refractory brick, all brick substitutes, clay and concrete blocks, terra-cotta, thin set or structural quarry tile, glazed structural tile, gypsum tile, glass block, clay tile, copings, natural stone, plastic refractories, and castables and any incidental works, including the installation of shower pans, as required in construction of the masonry work.

S291 - Stone Masonry Contractor. Construction using natural or artificial stone, either rough or cut and dressed, laid at random, with or without mortar. Incidental work includes the installation of shower pans.

S292 - Terrazzo Contractor. Construction by fabrication, grinding, and polishing of terrazzo by the setting of chips of marble, stone, or other material in an irregular pattern with the use of cement, polyester, epoxy or other common binders. Incidental work includes the installation of shower pans.

S293 - Marble, Tile and Ceramic Contractor. Preparation, fabrication, construction, and installation of artificial marble, burned clay tile, ceramic, encaustic, falence, quarry, semi-vitreous, and other tile, excluding hollow or structural partition tile. Incidental work includes the installation of shower pans.

S294 - Cultured Marble Contractor. Preparation, fabrication and installation of slab and sheet manmade synthetic products including cultured marble, onyx, granite, onice, corian, and corian type products. Incidental work includes the installation of shower pans.

S300 - General Painting Contractor. Preparation of surface and/or the application of all paints, varnishes, shellacs, stains, waxes and other coatings or pigments.

S310 - Excavation and Grading Contractor. Moving of the earth's surface or placing earthen materials on the earth's surface, by use of hand or power machinery and tools, including explosives, in any operation of cut, fill, excavation, grading, trenching, backfilling, or combination thereof as they are generally practiced in the construction trade.

S320 - Steel Erection Contractor. Construction by fabrication, placing, and tying or welding of steel reinforcing bars or erecting structural steel shapes, plates of any profile, perimeter or cross-section that are used to reinforce concrete or as structural members, including riveting, welding, and rigging.

S321 - Steel Reinforcing Contractor. Fabricating, placing, tying, or mechanically welding of reinforcing bars of any profile that are used to reinforce concrete buildings or structures.

S322 - Metal Building Erection Contractor. Erection of pre-fabricated metal structures including concrete foundation and footings, grading, and surface preparation.

S323 - Structural Stud Erection Contractor. Fabrication and installation of metal structural studs and bearing walls.

S330 - Landscaping Contractor.

(a)   grading and preparing land for architectural, horticultural, or decorative treatment;

(b)   arrangement, and planting of gardens, lawns, shrubs, vines, bushes, trees, or other decorative vegetation;

(c)   construction of small decorative pools, tanks, fountains, hothouses, greenhouses, fences, walks, garden lighting of 50 volts or less, or sprinkler systems;

(d)   construction of retaining walls except retaining walls which are intended to hold vehicles, structures, equipment or other non natural fill materials within the area located within a 45 degree angle from the base of the retaining wall to the level of where the additional weight bearing vehicles, structures, equipment or other non natural fill materials are located; or

(e)   patio areas except that:

(i)   no decking designed to support humans or structures shall be included; and

(ii)   no concrete work designed to support structures to be placed upon the patio shall be included.

(f)   This classification does not include running electrical or gas lines to any appliance.

S340 - Sheet Metal Contractor. Layout, fabrication, and installation of air handling and ventilating systems. All architectural sheet metal such as cornices, marquees, metal soffits, gutters, flashings, and skylights and skydomes including both plastic and fiberglass.

S350 - HVAC Contractor. Fabrication and installation of complete warm air heating and air conditioning systems, and complete ventilating systems. The HVAC Contractor scope of practice does not include activities described in this Subsection under specialty classification S354-Radon Mitigation Contractor unless the work is performed under the immediate supervision of an employee who holds a current certificate issued by the National Radon Safety Board (NRSB) or the National Radon Proficiency Program (NEHA-NRPP).

S351 - Refrigerated Air Conditioning Contractor. Fabrication and installation of air conditioning ventilating systems to control air temperatures below 50 degrees.

S352 - Evaporative Cooling Contractor. Fabrication and installation of devices, machinery, and units to cool the air temperature employing evaporation of liquid.

S353 - Warm Air Heating Contractor. Layout, fabrication, and installation of such sheet metal, gas piping, and furnace equipment as necessary for a complete warm air heating and ventilating system.

S354 - Radon Mitigation Contractor. Layout, fabrication, and installation of a radon mitigation system. This classification does not include work on heat recovery ventilation or makeup air components which must be performed by an HVAC Contractor and does not include electrical wiring which must be performed by an Electrical Contractor.

S360 - Refrigeration Contractor. Construction and/or installation of refrigeration equipment including, but not limited to, built-in refrigerators, refrigerated rooms, insulated refrigerated spaces and equipment related thereto; but, the scope of permitted work does not include the installation of gas fuel or electric power services other than connection of electrical devices to a junction box provided for that device and electrical control circuitry not exceeding 50 volts.

S370 - Fire Suppression Systems Contractor. Layout, fabrication, and installation of fire protection systems using water, steam, gas, or chemicals. When a potable sanitary water supply system is used as the source of supply, connection to the water system must be accomplished by a licensed journeyman plumber. Excluded from this classification are persons engaged in the installation of fire suppression systems in hoods above cooking appliances.

S380 - Swimming Pool and Spa Contractor. On-site fabrication, construction and installation of swimming pools, prefabricated pools, spas, and tubs.

S390 - Sewer and Waste Water Pipeline Contractor. Construction of sewer lines, sewage disposal and sewage drain facilities including excavation and grading with respect thereto, and the construction of sewage disposal plants and appurtenances thereto.

S400 - Asphalt Paving Contractor. Construction of asphalt highways, roadways, driveways, parking lots or other asphalt surfaces, which will include but will not be limited to, asphalt overlay, chip seal, fog seal and rejuvenation, micro surfacing, plant mix sealcoat, slurry seal, and the removal of asphalt surfaces by milling. Also included is the excavation, grading, compacting and laying of fill or base-related thereto. Also included in painting on asphalt surfaces including striping, directional and other types of symbols or words.

S410 - Pipeline and Conduit Contractor. Fabrication, construction, and installation of pipes, conduit or cables for the conveyance and transmission from one station to another of such products as water, steam, gases, chemicals, slurries, data or communications. Included are the excavation, cabling, horizontal boring, grading, and backfilling necessary for construction of the system.

S420 - General Fencing, Ornamental Iron and Guardrail Contractor. Fabrication, construction, and installation of fences, guardrails, handrails, and barriers.

S421 - Residential Fencing Contractor. Fabrication and installation of residential fencing up to and including a height of six feet.

S430 - Metal Firebox and Fuel Burning Stove Installer. Fabrication, construction, and installation of metal fireboxes, fireplaces, and wood or coal-burning stoves, including the installation of venting and exhaust systems, provided the individual performing the installation is RMGA certified.

S440 - Sign Installation Contractor. Installation of signs and graphic displays which require installation permits or permission as issued by state or local governmental jurisdictions. Signs and graphic displays shall include signs of all types, both lighted and unlighted, permanent highway marker signs, illuminated awnings, electronic message centers, sculptures or graphic representations including logos and trademarks intended to identify or advertise the user or his product, building trim or lighting with neon or decorative fixtures, or any other animated, moving or stationary device used for advertising or identification purposes. Signs and graphic displays must be fabricated, installed and erected in accordance with professionally engineered specifications and wiring in accordance with the National Electrical Code.

S441 - Non Electrical Outdoor Advertising Sign Contractor. Installation of signs and graphic displays which require installation permits or permission as issued by state and local governmental jurisdictions. Signs and graphics shall include outdoor advertising signs which do not have electrical lighting or other electrical requirements, and in accordance with professionally engineered specifications.

S450 - Mechanical Insulation Contractor. Fabrication, application and installation of insulation materials to pipes, ducts and conduits.

S460 - Wrecking and Demolition Contractor. The raising, cribbing, underpinning, moving, and removal of building and structures.

S470 - Petroleum Systems Contractor. Installation of above and below ground petroleum and petro-chemical storage tanks, piping, dispensing equipment, monitoring equipment and associated petroleum and petro-chemical equipment including excavation, backfilling, concrete and asphalt.

S480 - Piers and Foundations Contractor. The excavation, drilling, compacting, pumping, sealing and other work necessary to construct, alter or repair piers, piles, footings and foundations placed in the earth's subsurface to prevent structural settling and to provide an adequate capacity to sustain or transmit the structural load to the soil or rock below.

S490 - Wood Flooring Contractor. Installation of wood flooring including refinished and unfinished material, sanding, staining and finishing of new and existing wood flooring. Underlayments, non-structural subfloors and other incidental related work.

S491 - Laminate Floor Installation Contractor. Installation of laminate floors including underlayments, non-structural subfloors and other incidental related work, but does not include the installation of sold wood flooring.

S500 - Sports and Athletic Courts, Running Tracks, and Playground Installation Contractor. Installation of sports and athletic courts including but not limited to tennis courts, racquetball courts, handball courts, basketball courts, running tracks, playgrounds, or any combination. Includes nonstructural floor subsurfaces, nonstructural wall surfaces, perimeter walls and perimeter fencing. Includes the installation and attachment of equipment such as poles, basketball standards or other equipment.

S510 - Elevator Contractor. Erecting, constructing, installing, altering, servicing, repairing or maintaining an elevator.

S600 - General Stucco Contractor. Applying stucco to lathe, plaster and other surfaces.

S700 - Specialty License Contractor.

(a)   A specialty license is a license that confines the scope of the allowable contracting work to a specialized area of construction which the Division grants on a case-by-case basis.

(b)   When applying for a specialty license, an applicant, if requested, shall submit to the Division the following:

(i)   a detailed statement of the type and scope of contracting work that the applicant proposes to perform; and

(ii)   any brochures, catalogs, photographs, diagrams, or other material to further clarify the scope of the work that the applicant proposes to perform.

(c)   A contractor issued a specialty license shall confine the contractor's activities to the field and scope of operations as outlined by the Division.

(3)   The scope of practice for the following primary classifications includes the scope of practice stated in the descriptions for the following subclassifications:

TABLE 1

Primary Classification	Included subclassifications
S200	S201, S202
S210	S211, S212, S213, S214, S215, S216, S217
S220	S221, S222
S230	S231
S260	S261, S262, S263
S270	S272, S273
S290	S291, S292, S293, S294
S320	S321, S322, S323
S350	S351, S352, S353, S354
S420	S421
S440	S441
S490	S491

(4)   The following activities are determined to not significantly impact the public health, safety and welfare and therefore do not require a contractors license:

    (a)   sandblasting;

    (b)   pumping services;

    (c)   tree stump or tree removal;

    (d)   installation within a building of communication cables including phone and cable television;

    (e)   installation of low voltage electrical as described in R156-55b-102(1);

    (f)   construction of utility sheds, gazebos or other similar items which are personal property and not attached;

    (g)   building and window washing, including power washing;

    (h)   central vacuum systems installation;

    (i)   concrete cutting;

    (j)   interior decorating;

    (k)   wall paper hanging;

    (l)   drapery and blind installation;

    (m)   welding on personal property which is not attached;

    (n)   chimney sweepers other than repairing masonry;

    (o)   carpet and vinyl floor installation; and

    (p)   artificial turf installation.

(5)   The following activities are those determined to not significantly impact the public health, safety and welfare beyond the regulations by other agencies and therefore do not require a contractors license:

    (a)   lead removal regulated by the Department of Environmental Quality;

    (b)   asbestos removal regulated by the Department of Environmental Quality; and

    (c)   fire alarm installation regulated by the Fire Marshal.

R156-55a-302a. Qualifications for Licensure - Examinations.

(1)   In accordance with Subsection 58-55-302(1)(c), the qualifier for an applicant for licensure as a contractor or the qualifier for an applicant for licensure as a construction trades instruction facility shall pass the following examinations:

    (a)   the Utah Contractor Business - Law Examination; and

    (b)   an approved trade classification specific examination, where required in Subsection (2).

(2)   An approved trade classification specific examination is required for the following contractor license classifications:

    E100 - General Engineering Contractor

    B100 - General Building Contractor

    B200 - Modular Unit Installation Contractor

    R100 - Residential and Small Commercial Contractor

    R101 - Residential and Small Commercial Non Structural Remodeling and Repair Contractor

    R200 - Factory Built Housing Contractor

      I101 - General Engineering Trades Instruction Facility

      I102 - General Building Trades Instruction Facility

      I105 - Mechanical Trades Instruction Facility

      S211 - Boiler Installation Contractor

      S212 - Irrigation Sprinkling Contractor

      S213 - Industrial Piping Contractor

      S215 - Solar Thermal Systems Contractor

      S216 - Residential Sewer Connection and Septic Tank Contractor

      S220 - Carpentry Contractor

      S222 - Overhead and Garage Door Contractor

      S230 - Siding Contractor

      S240 - Glass and Glazing Contractor

      S250 - Insulation Contractor

      S260 - General Concrete Contractor

      S270 - General Drywall and Plastering Contractor

      S280 - General Roofing Contractor

      S290 - General Masonry Contractor

      S293 - Marble, Tile and Ceramic Contractor

      S300 - General Painting Contractor

      S310 - Excavation and Grading Contractor

      S320 - Steel Erection Contractor

      S321 - Steel Reinforcing Contractor

      S330 - Landscaping Contractor

      S340 - Sheet Metal Contractor

      S350 - HVAC Contractor

      S351 - Refrigerated Air Conditioning Contractor

      S353 - Warm Air Heating Contractor

      S360 - Refrigeration Contractor

      S370 - Fire Suppression Systems Contractor

      S380 - Swimming Pool and Spa Contractor

      S390 - Sewer and Waste Water Pipeline Contractor

      S410 - Pipeline and Conduit Contractor

      S440 - Sign Installation Contractor

      S450 - Mechanical Insulation Contractor

      S490 - Wood Flooring Contractor

      S600 - General Stucco Contractor

(3)   The passing score for each examination is 70%.

    (4)   Qualifications to sit for examination.

        (a)   An applicant applying to take any examination specified in this Section must sign an affidavit verifying that an applicant has completed the experience required under Subsection R156-55a-302b.

    (5)   "Approved trade classification specific examination" means a trade classification specific examination:

        (a)   given, currently or in the past, by the Division's contractor examination provider; or

        (b)   given by another state if the Division has determined the examination to be substantially equivalent.

    (6)   An applicant for licensure who fails an examination may retake the failed examination as follows:

        (a)   no sooner than 30 days following any failure up to three failures; and

        (b)   no sooner than six months following any failure thereafter.

R156-55a-302b. Qualifications for Licensure - Experience Requirements.

In accordance with Subsection 58-55-302(1)(e)(ii), the minimum experience requirements are established as follows:

    (1)   Requirements for all license classifications:

        (a)   Unless otherwise provided in this rule, two years of experience shall be lawfully performed within the 10-year period preceding the date of application under the general supervision of a contractor licensed in the classification applied for or a substantially equivalent classification, and shall be subject to the following:

            (i)   If the experience was completed in Utah, it shall be:

                (A)   completed while a W-2 employee of a licensed contractor; or

                (B)   completed while working as an owner of a licensed contractor, which has for all periods of experience claimed, employed a qualifier who performed the duties and served in the capacities specified in Subsection 58-55-304(4) and in Subsection R156-55a-304.

            (ii)   If the experience was completed outside of the state of Utah, it shall be:

                (A)   completed in compliance with the laws of the jurisdiction in which the experience is completed; and

                (B)   completed with supervision that is substantially equivalent to the supervision that is required in Utah.

            (iii)   Experience may be determined to be substantially equivalent if lawfully obtained in a setting which has supervision of qualified persons and an equivalent scope of work, such as performing construction activities in the military where licensure is not required.

        (b)   Unless otherwise provided in this rule, all experience shall be directly related to the scope of practice set forth in Section R156-55a-301 of the classification the applicant is applying for, as determined by the Division.

        (c)   One year of work experience means 2000 hours.

        (d)   No more than 2000 hours of experience during any 12 month period may be claimed.

(e)   Except as described in Subsection (2)b, experience obtained under the supervision of a construction trades instructor as a part of an educational program is not qualifying experience for a contractors license.

(f)   If the applicant's qualifying experience is outdated but has previously been approved in the state of Utah, a passing score on the trade examination and the laws and rules examination obtained within the one-year period preceding the date of application will requalify the applicant's experience.

(2)   Requirements for E100 General Engineering, B100 General Building, R100 Residential and Small Commercial Building license classifications:

(a)   One of the required two years of experience shall be in a supervisory or managerial position.

(b)   A person holding a four year bachelors degree or a two year associates degree in Construction Management may have one year of experience credited towards the supervisory or managerial experience requirement.

(c)   A person holding a Utah professional engineer license may be credited with satisfying one year toward the supervisory or managerial experience required for E100 contractor license.

(3)   Requirements for I101 General Engineering Trades Instruction Facility, I102 General Building Trades Instruction Facility, I103 Electrical Trades Instruction Facility, I104 Plumbing Trades Instruction Facility, I105 Mechanical Trades Instruction Facility license classifications:

An applicant for construction trades instruction facility license shall have the same experience that is required for the license classifications for the construction trade they will instruct.

(4)   Requirements for S202 Solar Photovoltaic Contractor. In addition to the requirements of Subsection (1), an applicant shall hold a current certificate by the North American Board of Certified Energy Practitioners.

(5)   Requirements for S354 Radon Mitigation Contractor. In addition to the requirements of Subsection (1), an applicant shall hold a current certificate issued by the National Radon Safety Board (NRSB) or the National Radon Proficiency Program (NEHA–NRPP). Experience completed prior to the effective date of this rule does not need to be performed under the supervision of a licensed contractor. Experience completed after the effective date of this rule must be performed under the supervision of a licensed contractor who has authority to practice radon mitigation.

R156-55a-302c. Qualifications for Licensure Requiring Licensure in a Prerequisite Classification.

(1)   Beginning at the effective date of this rule, each new applicant as a qualifier for licensure as a I103 Electrical Trades Instruction Facility shall also be licensed as a master electrician or a residential master electrician.

(2)   Beginning at the effective date of this rule, each new applicant as a qualifier for licensure as a I104 Plumbing Trades Instruction Facility shall also be licensed as a master plumber or a residential master plumber.

R156-55a-302d. Qualifications for Licensure - Proof of Insurance and Registrations.

In accordance with the provisions of Subsection 58-55-302(2)(b), an applicant who is approved for licensure shall submit proof of public liability insurance in coverage amounts of at least $100,000 for each incident and $300,000 in total by means of a certificate of insurance naming the Division as a certificate holder.

R156-55a-302e. Additional Requirements for Construction Trades Instructor Classifications.

In accordance with Subsection 58-55-302(1)(f), the following additional requirements for licensure are established:

(1)   Any school that provides instruction to students by building houses for sale to the public is required to become a Utah licensed contractor with a B100 General Building Contractor or R100 Residential and Small Commercial Building Contractor classification or both.

(2)   Any school that provides instruction to students by building houses for sale to the public is also required to be licensed in the appropriate instructor classification.

    (a)   Before being licensed in a construction trades instruction facility classification, the school shall submit the name of an individual person who acts as the qualifier in each of the construction trades instructor classifications in accordance with Section R156-55a-304. The applicant for licensure as a construction trades instructor shall:

        (i)   provide evidence that the qualifier has passed the required examinations established in Section R156-55a-302a; and

        (ii)   provide evidence that the qualifier meets the experience requirement established in Subsection R156-55a-302b(4).

(3)   Each individual employed by a school licensed as a construction trades instruction facility and working with students on a job site shall meet any teacher certification, or other teacher requirements imposed by the school district or college, and be qualified to teach the construction trades instruction facility classification as determined by the qualifier.

R156-55a-302f. Pre-licensure Education - Standards.

(1)   Qualifier Education Requirement. The 20-hour pre-licensure education program required by Subsection 58-55-302(1)(e)(iii) shall be completed by the qualifier for a contractor applicant.

(2)   Program Pre-Approval. A pre-licensure education provider shall submit an application for approval as a provider on the form provided by the Division. The applicant shall demonstrate compliance with Section R156-55a-302f.

(3)   Eligible Providers. The following may be approved to provide pre-licensure education:

    (a)   a nationally or regionally recognized accredited college or university having a physical campus located within the State of Utah; or

    (b)   a non-profit Utah construction trades association involved in the construction trades in the State of Utah representing multiple construction trade classifications whose membership includes at least 250 contractors licensed in Utah.

(4)   Content. The 20-hour program shall include the following topics and hours of education relevant to the practice of the construction trades consistent with the laws and rules of this state:

    (a)   ten hours of financial responsibility instruction that includes the following:

        (i)   record keeping and financial statements;

        (ii)   payroll, including:

            (A)   payroll taxes;

            (B)   worker compensation insurance requirements;

            (C)   unemployment insurance requirements;

            (D)   professional employer organization (employee leasing) alternatives;

            (E)   prohibitions regarding paying employees on 1099 forms as independent contractors, unless licensed or exempted;

            (F)   employee benefits; and

            (G)   Fair Labor Standard Act;

           (iii)   cash flow;

           (iv)   insurance requirements including auto, liability, and health; and

           (v)   independent contractor licensure and exemption requirements;

    (b)   six hours of construction business practices that includes the following:

           (i)   estimating and bidding;

           (ii)   contracts;

           (iii)   project management;

           (iv)   subcontractors; and

           (v)   suppliers;

    (c)   two hours of regulatory requirements that includes the following:

           (i)   licensing laws;

           (ii)   Occupational Safety and Health Administration (OSHA);

           (iii)   Environmental Protection Agency (EPA); and

           (iv)   consumer protection laws; and

    (d)   two hours of mechanic lien fundamentals that include the State Construction Registry.

(5)   Program Schedule.

    (a)   A pre-licensure education provider shall offer programs at least 12 times per year.

    (b)   The pre-licensure education provider is not obligated to provide a course if the provider determines the enrollment is not sufficient to reach breakeven on cost.

(6)   Program Instruction Requirements: The pre-licensure education shall meet the following standards:

    (a)   Time. Each hour of pre-licensure education credit shall consist of 60 minutes of education in the form of live lectures or training sessions. Time allowed for lunches or breaks may not be counted as part of the education time for which education credit is issued.

    (b)   Learning Objectives. The learning objectives of the pre-licensure education shall be reasonably and clearly stated.

    (c)   Teaching Methods. The pre-licensure education shall be presented in a competent and well organized manner consistent with the stated purpose and objective of the program. The student must demonstrate knowledge of the course material and must be given a pass/fail grade.

    (d)   Faculty. The pre-licensure education shall be prepared and presented by individuals who are qualified by education, training or experience.

    (e)   Distance Learning. Distance learning, internet courses, and home study courses are not allowed to meet pre-licensure education requirements.

    (f)   Registration and Attendance. The provider shall have a competent method of registration and verification of attendance of individuals who complete the pre-licensure education.

    (g)   Education Curriculum and Study/Resource Guide. The provider shall be responsible to provide or develop pre-licensure education curriculum and study/resource guide for the pre-licensure education that must be pre-approved by the Commission and the Division prior to use by the provider.

(7)   Certificates of Completion. The pre-licensure education provider shall provide individuals completing the pre-licensure education a certificate that contains the following information:

   (a)   the date of the pre-licensure education;

   (b)   the name of the pre-licensure education provider;

   (c)   the attendee's name;

   (d)   verification of completion of the 20-hour requirement; and

   (e)   the signature of the pre-licensure education provider.

(8)   Reporting of Program Completion. A pre-licensure education provider shall, within seven calendar days, submit directly to the Division verification of attendance and completion on behalf of persons attending and completing the program. This verification shall be submitted on forms provided by the Division.

(9)   Program Monitoring. On a random basis, the Division or Commission may assign monitors at no charge to attend a pre-licensure education course for the purpose of evaluating the education and the instructor(s).

(10)   Documentation Retention. Each provider shall for a period of four years maintain adequate documentation as proof of compliance with this section and shall, upon request, make such documentation available for review by the Division or the Commission. Documentation shall include:

   (a)   the dates of all pre-licensure education courses that have been completed;

   (b)   registration and attendance logs of individuals who completed the pre-licensure education;

   (c)   the name of instructors for each education course provided as a part of the program; and

   (d)   pre-licensure education handouts and materials.

(11)   Disciplinary Proceedings. As provided in Section 58-1-401 and Subsection 58-55-302(1)(e)(iii), the Division may refuse to renew or may revoke, suspend, restrict, place on probation, issue a public reprimand to, or otherwise act upon the approval of any pre-licensure education provider, if the pre-licensure education provider fails to meet any of the requirements of this section or the provider has engaged in other unlawful or unprofessional conduct.

(12)   Exemptions. In accordance with Subsection 58-55-302(1)(e)(iii), the following persons are not required to complete the pre-licensure education program requirements:

   (a)   a person holding a four-year bachelor degree or a two-year associate degree in Construction Management from an accredited program;

   (b)   a person holding an active and unrestricted Utah professional engineer license who is applying for the E100 contractor license classification; or

   (c)   a person who is a qualifier on an existing active and unrestricted contractor license who is:

      (i)   applying to add additional contractor classifications to the license; or

      (ii)   applying to become a qualifier on a new entity that is applying for initial licensure.

R156-55a-303a. Renewal Cycle - Procedures.

(1)   In accordance with Subsection 58-1-308(1), the renewal date for the two year renewal cycle applicable to licensees under Title 58, Chapter 55 is established by rule in Section R156-1-308a(1).

(2)   Renewal procedures shall be in accordance with Section R156-1-308c.

(3)   In accordance with Subsections 58-55-501(21) and 58-1-308(3)(b)(i), there is established a continuing education requirement for license renewal. Each licensee, or the licensee's qualifier, or

an officer, director or supervising individual, as designated by the licensee, shall comply with the continuing education requirements set forth in Section R156-55a-303b.

R156-55a-303b. Continuing Education - Standards.

(1)   Required Hours. Pursuant to Subsection 58-55-302.5, each licensee shall complete a total of six hours of continuing education during each two year license term except that for the renewal term. A minimum of three hours shall be core education. The remaining three hours are to be professional education. Additional core education hours beyond the required amount may be substituted for professional education hours.

    (a)   "Core continuing education" is defined as construction codes, construction laws, OSHA 10 or OSHA 30 safety training, governmental regulations pertaining to the construction trades and employee verification and payment practices.

    (b)   "Professional continuing education" is defined as substantive subjects dealing with the practice of the construction trades, including land development, land use, planning and zoning, energy conservation, professional development, arbitration practices, estimating, finance and bookkeeping, marketing techniques, servicing clients, personal and property protection for the licensee and the licensee's clients and similar topics.

    (c)   The following course subject matter is not acceptable as core education or professional education hours: mechanical office and business skills, such as typing, speed reading, memory improvement and report writing; physical well-being or personal development, such as personal motivation, stress management, time management, dress for success, or similar subjects; presentations by a supplier or a supplier representative to promote a particular product or line of products; and meetings held in conjunction with the general business of the licensee or employer.

    (d)   The Division may defer or waive the continuing education requirements as provided in Section R156-1-308d.

(2)   A continuing education course shall meet the following standards:

    (a)   Time. Each hour of continuing education course credit shall consist of 50 minutes of education in the form of seminars, lectures, conferences, training sessions or distance learning modules. The remaining ten minutes is to allow for breaks.

    (b)   Provider. The course provider shall meet the requirements of this Section and shall be one of the following:

        (i)   a recognized accredited college or university;

        (ii)   a state or federal agency;

        (iii)   a professional association or organization involved in the construction trades; or

        (iv)   a commercial continuing education provider providing a program related to the construction trades.

    (c)   Content. The content of the course shall be relevant to the practice of the construction trades and consistent with the laws and rules of this state.

    (d)   Objectives. The learning objectives of the course shall be reasonably and clearly stated.

    (e)   Teaching Methods. The course shall be presented in a competent, well organized and sequential manner consistent with the stated purpose and objective of the program.

    (f)   Faculty. The course shall be prepared and presented by individuals who are qualified by education, training and experience.

(g)   Distance learning. A course that is provided through Internet or home study may be recognized for continuing education if the course verifies registration and participation in the course by means of a test demonstrating that the participant has learned the material presented. Test questions shall be randomized for each participant. A home study course shall include no fewer than five variations of the final examination, distributed randomly to participants. Home study courses, including the five exam variations, shall be submitted in their entirety to the Division for review.

(h)   Documentation. The course provider shall have a competent method of registration of individuals who actually completed the course, shall maintain records of attendance that are available for review by the Division and shall provide individuals completing the course a certificate that contains the following information:

   (i)   the date of the course;

   (ii)   the name of the course provider;

   (iii)   the name of the instructor;

   (iv)   the course title;

   (v)   the hours of continuing education credit and type of credit (core or professional);

   (vi)   the attendee's name; and

   (vii)   the signature of the course provider.

(3)   On a random basis, the Division may assign monitors at no charge to attend a course for the purpose of evaluating the course and the instructor.

(4)   Each licensee shall maintain adequate documentation as proof of compliance with this section, such as certificates of completion, course handouts and materials. The licensee shall retain this proof for a period of three years from the end of the renewal period for which the continuing education is due. Each licensee shall assure that the course provider has submitted the verification of attendance to the continuing education registry on behalf of the licensee as specified in Subsection (8). Alternatively, the licensee may submit the course for approval and pay any course approval fees and attendance recording fees.

(5)   Licensees who lecture in continuing education courses meeting these requirements shall receive two hours of continuing education for each hour spent lecturing. However, no lecturing or teaching credit is available for participation in a panel discussion.

(6)   The continuing education requirement for electricians, plumbers and elevator mechanics as established in Subsections 58-55-302.7 and 58-55-303(6), which is completed by an employee or owner of a contractor, shall satisfy the continuing education requirement for contractors as established in Subsection 58-55-302.5 and implemented herein. The contractor licensee shall assure that the course provider has submitted the verification of the electrician's attendance on behalf of the licensee to the continuing education registry as specified in Subsection (8).

(7)   A course provider shall submit continuing education courses for approval to the continuing education registry and shall submit verification of attendance and completion on behalf of licensees attending and completing the program directly to the continuing education registry in the format required by the continuing education registry.

(8)   The Division shall review continuing education courses which have been submitted through the continuing education registry and approve only those courses which meet the standards set forth under this Section.

(9)   As provided in Section 58-1-401 and Subsections 58-55-302.5(2) and 58-55-302.7(4)(a), the Division may refuse to renew or may revoke, suspend, restrict, place on probation, issue a public

reprimand to, or otherwise act upon the approval of any course or provider, if the course or provider fails to meet any of the requirements of this section or the provider has engaged in unlawful or unprofessional conduct.

(10) Continuing Education Registry.

    (a) The Division shall designate an entity to act as the Continuing Education Registry under this rule.

    (b) The Continuing Education Registry, in consultation with the Division and the Commission, shall:

        (i) through its internet site electronically receive applications from continuing education course providers and shall submit the application for course approval to the Division for review and approval of only those programs that meet the standards set forth under this Section;

        (ii) publish on their website listings of continuing education programs that have been approved by the Division, and which meet the standards for continuing education credit under this rule;

        (iii) maintain accurate records of qualified continuing education approved;

        (iv) maintain accurate records of verification of attendance and completion, by individual licensee, which the licensee may review for compliance with this rule; and

        (v) make records of approved continuing education programs and attendance and completion available for audit by representatives of the Division.

    (c) Fees. A continuing education registry may charge a reasonable fee to continuing education providers or licensees for services provided for review and approval of continuing education programs.

R156-55a-304. Contractor License Qualifiers.

(1) The capacity and material authority specified in Subsection 58-55-304(4) is clarified as follows:

    (a) Except as allowed in Subsection (b), the qualifier must receive remuneration for work performed for the contractor licensee for not less than 10 hours of work per week.

        (i) If the qualifier is an owner of the business, the remuneration may be in the form of owner's profit distributions or dividends with a minimum ownership of 20 percent of the contractor licensee.

        (ii) If the qualifier is an officer or manager of the contractor licensee, the remuneration must be in the form of W-2 wages.

    (b) The 10 hour minimum in Subsection (a) may be reduced if the total of all hours worked by all owners and employees is less than 50 hours per week, in which case the minimum may not be less than 20 percent of the total hours of work performed by all owners and employees of the contractor.

(2) Construction Trades Instruction Facility Qualifier. In accordance with Subsection 58-55-302(1)(f), the contractor license qualifier requirements in Section 58-55-304 shall also apply to construction trades instruction facilities.

R156-55a-305. Compliance Agency Reporting of Sole Owner Building Permits Issued.

In accordance with Subsection 58-55-305(2), all compliance agencies that issue building permits to sole owners of property must submit information concerning each building permit issued in their jurisdiction within 30 days of the issuance, with the building permit number, date issued, name, address and phone number of the issuing compliance agency, sole owner's full name, home address, phone number, and subdivision and lot number of the building site, to a fax number, email address or written mailing address designated by the Division.

R156-55a-305a. Exempt Contractors Filing Affirmation of Liability and Workers Compensation Insurance.

(1)   Initial affirmation. In accordance with Subsection 58-55-305(1)(h)(ii)(F), any person claiming exemption under Subsection 58-55-305(1)(h) for projects with a value greater than $1,000 but less than $3,000 shall file a registration of exemption with the Division which includes:

        (a)   the identity and address of the person claiming the exemption; and

        (b)   a statement signed by the registrant verifying:

            (i)   that the person has public liability insurance in force which includes the Division being named as a certificate holder, the policy number, the expiration date of the policy, the insurance company name and contact information, and coverage amounts of at least $100,000 for each incident and $300,000 in total; and

            (ii)   that the person has workers compensation insurance in force which names the Division as a certificate holder, includes the policy number, the expiration date of the policy, the insurance company name and contact information; or

            (iii)   that the person does not hire employees and is therefore exempt from the requirement to have workers compensation insurance.

(2)   Periodic reaffirmations required. The affirmation required under Subsection (1) shall be reaffirmed on or before November 30 of each odd numbered year.

R156-55a-306. Contractor Financial Responsibility - Division Audit.

In accordance with Subsections 58-55-302(10)(c), 58-55-306(5), 58-55-306(4)(b), and 58-55-102(19), the Division may consider various relevant factors in conducting a financial responsibility audit of an applicant, licensee, or any owner, including:

(1)   (a)   judgments, tax liens, collection actions, bankruptcy schedules and a history of late payments to creditors, including documentation showing the resolution of each of the above actions;

        (b)   financial statements and tax returns, including the ability to prepare or have prepared competent and current financial statements and tax returns;

        (c)   an acceptable current credit report that meets the following requirements:

            (i)   for individuals:

                (A)   a credit report from each of the three national reporting agencies, TransUnion, Experian, and Equifax; or

                (B)   a merged credit report of the agencies identified in Subsection (A) prepared by the National Association of Credit Managers (NACM); or

            (ii)   for entities, a business credit report such as an Experian Business Credit Report or a Dun and Bradstreet Report;

        (d)   an explanation of the reasons for any financial difficulties and how the financial difficulties were resolved;

        (e)   any of the factors listed in Subsection R156-1-302 that may relate to failure to maintain financial responsibility;

        (f)   each of the factors listed in this Subsection regarding the financial history of the owners of the applicant or licensee;

     (g)   any guaranty agreements provided for the applicant or licensee and any owners; and

     (h)   any history of prior entities owned or operated by the applicant, the licensee, or any owner that have failed to maintain financial responsibility.

R156-55a-308a. Operating Standards for Schools or Colleges Licensed as Contractors.

(1)   Each school licensed as a B100 General Building Contractor or a R100 Residential and Small Commercial Contractor or both shall obtain all required building permits for homes built for resale to the public as part of an educational training program.

(2)   Each employee that works as a teacher for a school licensed as a construction trades instruction facility shall:

     (a)   have on their person a school photo ID card with the trade they are authorized to teach printed on the card; and

     (b)   if instructing in the plumbing or electrical trades, they shall also carry on their person their Utah journeyman or residential journeyman plumber license or Utah journeyman, residential journeyman, master, or residential master electrician license.

(3)   Each school licensed as a construction trades instruction facility shall not allow any teacher or student to work on any portion of the project subcontracted to a licensed contractor unless the teacher or student are lawful employees of the subcontractor.

R156-55a-308b. Natural Gas Technician Certification.

(1)   In accordance with Subsection 58-55-308(1), the scope of practice defined in Subsection 58-55-308(2)(a) requiring certification is further defined as the installation, modifications, maintenance, cleaning, repair or replacement of the gas piping, combustion air vents, exhaust venting system or derating of gas input for altitude of a residential or commercial gas appliance.

(2)   An approved training program shall include the following course content:

     (a)   general gas appliance installation codes;

     (b)   venting requirements;

     (c)   combustion air requirements;

     (d)   gas line sizing codes;

     (e)   gas line approved materials requirements;

     (f)   gas line installation codes; and

     (g)   methods of derating gas appliances for elevation.

(3)   In accordance with Subsection 58-55-308(2)(c)(i), the following programs are approved to provide natural gas technician training, and to issue certificates or documentation of exemption from certification:

     (a)   Federal Bureau of Apprenticeship Training;

     (b)   Utah college apprenticeship program; and

     (c)   Trade union apprenticeship program.

(4)   In accordance with Subsection 58-55-308(3), the approved programs set forth in paragraphs (2)(b) and (2)(c) herein shall require program participants to pass the Rocky Mountain Gas Association Gas Appliance Installers Certification Exam or approved equivalent exams established or adopted by a training program, with a minimum passing score of 80%.

(5)   In accordance with Subsection 58-55-308(3), a person who has not completed an approved training program, but has passed the Rocky Mountain Gas Association Gas Exam or approved equivalent exam established or adopted by an approved training program, with a minimum passing score of 80%, or the Utah licensed Journeyman or Residential Journeyman Plumber Exam, with a minimum passing score of 70%, shall be exempt from the certification requirement set forth in Subsection 58-55-308(2)(c)(i).

(6)   Content of certificates of completion. An approved program shall issue a certificate, including a wallet certificate, to persons who successfully complete their training program containing the following information:

   (a)   name of the program provider;

   (b)   name of the approved program;

   (c)   name of the certificate holder;

   (d)   the date the certification was completed; and

   (e)   signature of an authorized representative of the program provider.

(7)   Documentation of exemption from certification. The following shall constitute documentation of exemption from certification:

   (a)   certification of completion of training issued by the Federal Bureau of Apprenticeship Training;

   (b)   current Utah licensed Journeyman or Residential Journeyman plumber license; or

   (c)   certification from the Rocky Mountain Gas Association or approved equivalent exam which shall include the following:

      (i)   name of the association, school, union, or other organization who administered the exam;

      (ii)   name of the person who passed the exam;

      (iii)   name of the exam;

      (iv)   the date the exam was passed; and

      (v)   signature of an authorized representative of the test administrator.

(8)   Each person engaged in the scope of practice defined in Subsection 58-55-308(2)(a) and as further defined in Subsection (1) herein, shall carry in their possession documentation of certification or exemption.

R156-55a-309. Reinstatement Application Fee.

The application fee for a contractor applicant who is applying for reinstatement more than two years after the expiration of licensure, who has been engaged in unauthorized practice of contracting following the expiration of the applicant's license, shall be the current license application fee normally required for a new application rather than the reinstatement fee provided under R156-1-308g(3)(d).

R156-55a-311. Reorganization - Conversion of Contractor Business Entity.

A reorganization of the business organization or entity under which a licensed contractor is licensed shall require application for a new license under the new form of organization or business structure. The creation of a new legal entity constitutes are organization and includes a change to a new entity under the same form of business entity or a change of the form of business entity between proprietorship, partnership, whether limited or general, joint venture, corporation or any other business form.

Exception: A conversion from one form of entity to another form where "Articles of Conversion" are filed with the Utah Division of Corporations and Commercial Code shall not require a new contractor application.

R156-55a-312. Inactive License.

(1)   The requirements for inactive licensure specified in Subsection R156-1-305(3) shall also include certification that the licensee will not engage in the construction trade(s) for which his license was issued while his license is on inactive status except to identify himself as an inactive licensee.

(2)   A license on inactive status will not be required to meet the requirements of licensure in Subsections 58-55-302(1)(e)(i), 58-55-302(2)(a) and 58-55-302(2)(b).

(3)   The requirements for reactivation of an inactive license specified in Subsection R156-1-305(6) shall also include:

     (a)   documentation that the licensee meets the requirements of Subsections 58-55-302(1)(e)(i), 58-55-302(2)(a) and 58-55-302(2)(b); and

     (b)   documentation that the licensee has taken and passed the business and law examination and the trade examination for the classification for which activation is sought except that the following exceptions shall apply to the reactivation examination requirement:

          (i)   No license shall be in an inactive status for more than six years.

          (ii)   Prior to a license being activated, a licensee shall meet the requirements of renewal.

R156-55a-401. Minimum Penalty for Failure to Maintain Insurance.

(1)   A minimum penalty is hereby established for the violation of Subsection R156-55a-501(2) as follows:

     (a)   For a violation the duration of which is less than 90 days, where the licensee at the time a penalty is imposed documents that the required liability and workers compensation insurance have been reacquired, and provided an insurable loss has not occurred while not insured, a minimum of a 30 day suspension of licensure, stayed indefinitely, automatically executable in addition to any other sanction imposed, upon any subsequent violations of Subsection R156-55a-501(2).

     (b)   For a violation the duration of which is 90 days or longer, or where insurable loss has occurred, where the licensee at the time a penalty is imposed documents that the required insurance have been reacquired, a minimum of 30 days suspension of licensure.

     (c)   For a violation of any duration, where the licensee at the time a penalty is imposed fails to document that the required insurance have been reacquired, a minimum of indefinite suspension. A license which is placed on indefinite suspension may not be reinstated any earlier than 30 days after the licensee documents the required insurance have been reacquired.

     (d)   If insurable loss has occurred and licensee has not paid the damages, the license may be suspended indefinitely until such loss is paid by the licensee.

     (e)   Nothing in this section shall be construed to restrict a presiding officer from imposing more than the minimum penalty for a violation of Subsection R156-55a-501(2) and (3). However, absent extraordinary cause, the presiding officer may not impose less than the minimum penalty.

R156-55a-501. Unprofessional Conduct.

"Unprofessional conduct" includes:

(1)   failing to notify the Division with respect to any matter for which notification is required under this rule or Title 58, Chapter 55, the Construction Trades Licensing Act, including a change in qualifier.

Such failure shall be considered by the Division and the Commission as grounds for immediate suspension of the contractors license;

(2)   failing to continuously maintain insurance and registration as required by Subsection 58-55-302(2), in coverage amounts and form as implemented by this chapter; and

(3)   failing, upon request by the Division, to provide proof of insurance coverage within 30 days.

R156-55a-502. Penalty for Unlawful Conduct.

The penalty for violating Subsection 58-55-501(1) while suspended from licensure shall include the maximum fine allowed by Subsection 58-55-503(4)(i).

R156-55a-503. Administrative Penalties.

(1)   In accordance with Subsection 58-55-503, the following fine schedule shall apply to citations issued under Title 58, Chapter 55:

TABLE II

FINE SCHEDULE

FIRST OFFENSE

Violation	All Licenses Except Electrical or Plumbing	Electrical or Plumbing
58-55-308(2)	$ 500.00	N/A
58-55-501(1)	$ 500.00	$ 500.00
58-55-501(2)	$ 500.00	$ 800.00
58-55-501(3)	$ 800.00	$1,000.00
58-55-501(9)	$ 500.00	$ 500.00
58-55-501(10)	$ 800.00	$1,000.00
58-55-501(12)	N/A	$ 500.00
58-55-501(14)	$ 500.00	N/A
58-55-501(19)	$ 500.00	N/A
58-55-501(21)	$ 500.00	$ 500.00
58-55-501(22)	$ 500.00	N/A
58-55-501(23)	$ 500.00	N/A
58-55-501(24)	$ 500.00	N/A
58-55-501(25)	$ 500.00	N/A
58-55-501(26)	$ 500.00	N/A
58-55-501(27)	$ 500.00	N/A
58-55-501(28)	$ 500.00	N/A
58-55-501(29)	$ 500.00	N/A
58-55-504(2)	$ 500.00	N/A

SECOND OFFENSE

58-55-308(2)	$1,000.00	N/A
58-55-501(1)	$1,000.00	$1,500.00
58-55-501(2)	$1,000.00	$1,500.00
58-55-501(3)	$1,600.00	$2,000.00
58-55-501(9)	$1,000.00	$1,000.00
58-55-501(10)	$1,600.00	$2,000.00
58-55-501(12)	N/A	$1,000.00
58-55-501(14)	$1,000.00	N/A
58-55-501(19)	$1,000.00	N/A
58-55-501(21)	$1,000.00	$1,000.00
58-55-501(22)	$1,000.00	N/A
58-55-501(23)	$1,000.00	N/A
58-55-501(24)	$1,000.00	N/A
58-55-501(25)	$1,000.00	N/A
58-55-501(26)	$1,000.00	N/A
58-55-501(27)	$1,000.00	N/A
58-55-501(28)	$1,000.00	N/A
58-55-501(29)	$1,000.00	N/A
58-55-504(2)	$1,000.00	N/A

THIRD OFFENSE

Double the amount for a second offense with a maximum amount not to exceed the maximum fine allowed under Subsection 58-55-503(4)(h).

(2)   Citations shall not be issued for third offenses, except in extraordinary circumstances approved by the investigative supervisor.

(3)   If multiple offenses are cited on the same citation, the fine shall be determined by evaluating the most serious offense.

(4)   An investigative supervisor may authorize a deviation from the fine schedule based upon the aggravating or mitigating circumstances.

(5)   The presiding officer for a contested citation shall have the discretion, after a review of the aggravating and mitigating circumstances, to increase or decrease the fine amount imposed by an investigator based upon the evidence presented.

R156-55a-504. Crane Operator Certifications.

In accordance with Subsection 58-55-504(2)(a) one of the following certifications is required to operate a crane on commercial construction projects:

(1)   a certification issued by the National Commission for the Certification of Crane Operators;

(2)   a certification issued by the Operating Engineers Certification Program formerly known as the Southern California Crane and Hoisting Certification Program; or

(3)   a certification issued by the Crane Institute of America.

R156-55a-602. Contractor License Bonds.

Pursuant to the provisions of Subsections 58-55-306(1)(b) and 58-55-306(5)(b)(iii), a contractor shall provide a license bond issued by a surety acceptable to the Division in the amount, form, and coverage as follows:

(1)   An acceptable surety is one that is listed in the Department of Treasury, Fiscal Service, Circular 570, entitled "Companies Holding Certificates of Authority as Acceptable Sureties on Federal Bonds and as Acceptable Reinsuring Companies" at the date of the bond.

(2)   The coverage of the license bond shall include losses that may occur as the result of the contractor's violation of the unprofessional or unlawful provisions contained in Title 58, Chapters 1 and 55 and rules R156-1 and R156-55a including the failure to maintain financial responsibility, the failure of the licensee to pay its obligations, and the failure of the owners or a licensed unincorporated entity to pay income taxes or self employment taxes on the gross distributions from the unincorporated entity to its owners.

(3)   The financial history of the applicant, licensee, or any owner, as outlined in Section R156-55a-306, may be reviewed in determining the bond amount required under this section.

(4)   If the licensee is submitting a bond under Subsection 58-55-306(5)(b)(iii)(B), the amount of the bond shall be 20% of the annual gross distributions from the unincorporated entity to its owners. As provided in Subsection 58-55-302(10)(c), the Division, in determining if financial responsibility has been demonstrated, may consider the total number of owners, including new owners added as reported under the provisions of Subsection 58-55-302(10)(a)(i), in setting the amount of the bond required under this subsection.

(5)   If the licensee is submitting a bond under any subsection other than Subsection 58-55-306(5)(b)(iii)(B), the minimum amount of the bond shall be $50,000 for the E100 or B100 classification of licensure; $25,000 for the R100 classification of licensure; or $15,000 for other classifications. A higher amount may be determined by the Division and the Commission as provided in Subsection R156-55a-602(6).

(6)   The amount of the bond specified under Subsection R156-55a-602(5) may be increased by an amount determined by the Commission and Division when the financial history of the applicant, licensee or any owner indicates the bond amount specified in Subsection R156-55a-602(1) is insufficient to reasonably cover risks to the public health, safety and welfare. The financial history of the applicant, licensee or any owner, as outlined in Section R156-55a-306 may be reviewed in determining the bond amount required.

(7)   A contractor may provide a license bond issued by a surety acceptable to the Division in an amount less than the bond amount specified in Subsection R156-55a-602(5) if:

(a)   the contractor demonstrates by clear and convincing evidence that:

(i)   the financial history of the applicant, licensee or any owner indicates the bond amount specified in Subsection R156-55a-602(1) is in excess of what is reasonably necessary to cover risks to the public health, safety and welfare;

(ii)   the contractor's lack of financial responsibility is due to extraordinary circumstances that the contractor could not control as opposed to general financial challenges that all contractors experience; and

(iii)   the contractor's scope of practice will be restricted commensurate with the degree of risk the contract presents to the public health, safety, and welfare; and

(b)   the Commission and Division approve the amount.

KEY: contractors, occupational licensing, licensing

Date of Enactment or Last Substantive Amendment: October 9, 2014

Notice of Continuation: October 4, 2011

Authorizing, and Implemented or Interpreted Law: 58-1-106(1)(a); 58-1-202(1)(a); 58-55-101; 58-55-308(1)(a); 58-55-102(39)(a)

UTAH CONSTRUCTION TRADES LICENSING ACT RULE

R156-55a Utah Administrative Code

Issued October 9, 2014

Disclaimer: The statute/rule above is an unofficial version provided for convenience only and may not be identical to the official versions on the Utah State Legislature (www.le.utah.gov) and the Utah Division of Administrative Rules (www.rules.utah.gov) websites.

Appendix G: General Rule of the Division of Occupational and Professional Licensing

R156-1-101. Title.

This rule is known as the "General Rule of the Division of Occupational and Professional Licensing."

R156-1-102. Definitions.

In addition to the definitions in Title 58, as used in Title 58 or this rule:

(1) "Active and in good standing" means a licensure status which allows the licensee full privileges to engage in the practice of the occupation or profession subject to the scope of the licensee's license classification.

(2) "Aggravating circumstances" means any consideration or factors that may justify an increase in the severity of an action to be imposed upon an applicant or licensee. Aggravating circumstances include:

    (a) prior record of disciplinary action, unlawful conduct, or unprofessional conduct;

    (b) dishonest or selfish motive;

    (c) pattern of misconduct;

    (d) multiple offenses;

    (e) obstruction of the disciplinary process by intentionally failing to comply with rules or orders of the Division;

    (f) submission of false evidence, false statements or other deceptive practices during the disciplinary process including creating, destroying or altering records after an investigation has begun;

    (g) refusal to acknowledge the wrongful nature of the misconduct involved, either to the client or to the Division;

    (h) vulnerability of the victim;

    (i) lack of good faith to make restitution or to rectify the consequences of the misconduct involved;

    (j) illegal conduct, including the use of controlled substances; and

    (k) intimidation or threats of withholding clients' records or other detrimental consequences if the client reports or testifies regarding the unprofessional or unlawful conduct.

(3) "Cancel" or "cancellation" means nondisciplinary action by the Division to rescind, repeal, annul, or void a license:

    (a) issued to a licensee in error, such as where a license is issued to an applicant:

        (i) whose payment of the required application fee is dishonored when presented for payment;

        (ii) who has been issued a conditional license pending a criminal background check and the check cannot be completed due to the applicant's failure to resolve an outstanding warrant or to submit acceptable fingerprint cards;

(iii)   who has been issued the wrong classification of licensure; or

(iv)   due to any other error in issuing a license; or

(b)   not issued erroneously, but where subsequently the licensee fails to maintain the ongoing qualifications for licensure, when such failure is not otherwise defined as unprofessional or unlawful conduct.

(4)   "Charges" means the acts or omissions alleged to constitute either unprofessional or unlawful conduct or both by a licensee, which serve as the basis to consider a licensee for inclusion in the diversion program authorized in Section 58-1-404.

(5)   "Denial of licensure" means action by the Division refusing to issue a license to an applicant for initial licensure, renewal of licensure, reinstatement of licensure or relicensure.

(6)   (a)   "Disciplinary action" means adverse licensure action by the Division under the authority of Subsections 58-1-401(2)(a) through (2)(b).

(b)   "Disciplinary action", as used in Subsection 58-1-401(5), shall not be construed to mean an adverse licensure action taken in response to an application for licensure. Rather, as used in Subsection 58-1-401(5), it shall be construed to mean an adverse action initiated by the Division.

(7)   "Diversion agreement" means a formal written agreement between a licensee, the Division, and a diversion committee, outlining the terms and conditions with which a licensee must comply as a condition of entering in and remaining under the diversion program authorized in Section 58-1-404.

(8)   "Diversion committees" mean diversion advisory committees authorized by Subsection 58-1-404(2)(a)(i) and created under Subsection R156-1-404a.

(9)   "Duplicate license" means a license reissued to replace a license which has been lost, stolen, or mutilated.

(10)   "Emergency review committees" mean emergency adjudicative proceedings review committees created by the Division under the authority of Subsection 58-1-108(2).

(11)   "Expire" or "expiration" means the automatic termination of a license which occurs:

(a)   at the expiration date shown upon a license if the licensee fails to renew the license before the expiration date; or

(b)   prior to the expiration date shown on the license:

(i)   upon the death of a licensee who is a natural person;

(ii)   upon the dissolution of a licensee who is a partnership, corporation, or other business entity; or

(iii)   upon the issuance of a new license which supersedes an old license, including a license which:

(A)   replaces a temporary license;

(B)   replaces a student or other interim license which is limited to one or more renewals or other renewal limitation; or

(C)   is issued to a licensee in an upgraded classification permitting the licensee to engage in a broader scope of practice in the licensed occupation or profession.

(12)   "Inactive" or "inactivation" means action by the Division to place a license on inactive status in accordance with Sections 58-1-305 and R156-1-305.

(13)   "Investigative subpoena authority" means, except as otherwise specified in writing by the director, the Division regulatory and compliance officer, or if the Division regulatory and compliance officer is unable to so serve for any reason, a Department administrative law judge, or if both the Division regulatory and compliance officer and a Department administrative law judge are unable to so serve for any reason, an alternate designated by the director in writing.

(14)   "License" means a right or privilege to engage in the practice of a regulated occupation or profession as a licensee.

(15)   "Limit" or "limitation" means nondisciplinary action placing either terms and conditions or restrictions or both upon a license:

    (a)   issued to an applicant for initial licensure, renewal or reinstatement of licensure, or relicensure; or

    (b)   issued to a licensee in place of the licensee's current license or disciplinary status.

(16)   "Mitigating circumstances" means any consideration or factors that may justify a reduction in the severity of an action to be imposed upon an applicant or licensee.

    (a)   Mitigating circumstances include:

        (i)   absence of prior record of disciplinary action, unlawful conduct or unprofessional conduct;

        (ii)   personal, mental or emotional problems provided such problems have not posed a risk to the health, safety or welfare of the public or clients served such as drug or alcohol abuse while engaged in work situations or similar situations where the licensee or applicant should know that they should refrain from engaging in activities that may pose such a risk;

        (iii)   timely and good faith effort to make restitution or rectify the consequences of the misconduct involved;

        (iv)   full and free disclosure to the client or Division prior to the discovery of any misconduct;

        (v)   inexperience in the practice of the occupation and profession provided such inexperience is not the result of failure to obtain appropriate education or consultation that the applicant or licensee should have known they should obtain prior to beginning work on a particular matter;

        (vi)   imposition of other penalties or sanctions if the other penalties and sanctions have alleviated threats to the public health, safety, and welfare; and

        (vii)   remorse.

    (b)   The following factors may not be considered as mitigating circumstances:

        (i)   forced or compelled restitution;

        (ii)   withdrawal of complaint by client or other affected persons;

        (iii)   resignation prior to disciplinary proceedings;

        (iv)   failure of injured client to complain;

        (v)   complainant's recommendation as to sanction; and

        (vi)   in an informal disciplinary proceeding brought pursuant to Subsection 58-1-501(2)(c) or (d) or Subsections R156-1-501(1) through (5):

(A)   argument that a prior proceeding was conducted unfairly, contrary to law, or in violation of due process or any other procedural safeguard;

(B)   argument that a prior finding or sanction was contrary to the evidence or entered without due consideration of relevant evidence;

(C)   argument that a respondent was not adequately represented by counsel in a prior proceeding; and

(D)   argument or evidence that former statements of a respondent made in conjunction with a plea or settlement agreement are not, in fact, true.

(17)   "Nondisciplinary action" means adverse licensure action by the Division under the authority of Subsections 58-1-401(1) or 58-1-401(2)(c) through (2)(d).

(18)   "Peer committees" mean advisory peer committees to boards created by the legislature in Title 58 or by the Division under the authority of Subsection 58-1-203(1)(f).

(19)   "Probation" means disciplinary action placing terms and conditions upon a license;

(a)   issued to an applicant for initial licensure, renewal or reinstatement of licensure, or relicensure; or

(b)   issued to a licensee in place of the licensee's current license or disciplinary status.

(20)   "Public reprimand" means disciplinary action to formally reprove or censure a licensee for unprofessional or unlawful conduct, with the documentation of the action being classified as a public record.

(21)   "Regulatory authority" as used in Subsection 58-1-501(2)(d) means any governmental entity who licenses, certifies, registers, or otherwise regulates persons subject to its jurisdiction, or who grants the right to practice before or otherwise do business with the governmental entity.

(22)   "Reinstate" or "reinstatement" means to activate an expired license or to restore a license which is restricted, as defined in Subsection (26)(b),or is suspended, or placed on probation, to a lesser restrictive license or an active in good standing license.

(23)   "Relicense" or "relicensure" means to license an applicant who has previously been revoked or has previously surrendered a license.

(24)   "Remove or modify restrictions" means to remove or modify restrictions, as defined in Subsection (25)(a), placed on a license issued to an applicant for licensure.

(25)   "Restrict" or "restriction" means disciplinary action qualifying or limiting the scope of a license:

(a)   issued to an applicant for initial licensure, renewal or reinstatement of licensure, or relicensure in accordance with Section 58-1-304; or

(b)   issued to a licensee in place of the licensee's current license or disciplinary status.

(26)   "Revoke" or "revocation" means disciplinary action by the Division extinguishing a license.

(27)   "Suspend" or "suspension" means disciplinary action by the Division removing the right to use a license for a period of time or indefinitely as indicated in the disciplinary order, with the possibility of subsequent reinstatement of the right to use the license.

(28)   "Surrender" means voluntary action by a licensee giving back or returning to the Division in accordance with Section 58-1-306, all rights and privileges associated with a license issued to the licensee.

(29)   "Temporary license" or "temporary licensure" means a license issued by the Division on a temporary basis to an applicant for initial licensure, renewal or reinstatement of licensure, or relicensure in accordance with Section 58-1-303.

(30)   "Unprofessional conduct" as defined in Title 58 is further defined, in accordance with Subsection 58-1-203(1)(e), in Section R156-1-502.

(31)   "Warning or final disposition letters which do not constitute disciplinary action" as used in Subsection 58-1-108(3) mean letters which do not contain findings of fact or conclusions of law and do not constitute a reprimand, but which may address any or all of the following:

   (a)   Division concerns;

   (b)   allegations upon which those concerns are based;

   (c)   potential for administrative or judicial action; and

   (d)   disposition of Division concerns.

R156-1-102a. Global Definitions of Levels of Supervision.

(1)   Except as otherwise provided by statute or rule, the global definitions of levels of supervision herein shall apply to supervision terminology used in Title 58 and Title R156, and shall be referenced and used, to the extent practicable, in statutes and rules to promote uniformity and consistency.

(2)   Except as otherwise provided by statute or rule, all unlicensed personnel specifically allowed to practice a regulated occupation or profession are required to practice under an appropriate level of supervision defined herein, as specified by the licensing act or licensing act rule governing each occupation or profession.

(3)   Except as otherwise provided by statute or rule, all license classifications required to practice under supervision shall practice under an appropriate level of supervision defined herein, as specified by the licensing act or licensing act rule governing each occupation or profession.

(4)   Levels of supervision are defined as follows:

   (a)   "Direct supervision" and "immediate supervision" mean the supervising licensee is present and available for face-to-face communication with the person being supervised when and where occupational or professional services are being provided.

   (b)   "Indirect supervision" means the supervising licensee:

      (i)   has given either written or verbal instructions to the person being supervised;

      (ii)   is present within the facility in which the person being supervised is providing services; and

      (iii)   is available to provide immediate face-to-face communication with the person being supervised as necessary.

   (c)   "General supervision" means that the supervising licensee:

      (i)   has authorized the work to be performed by the person being supervised;

      (ii)   is available for consultation with the person being supervised by personal face-to-face contact, or direct voice contact by telephone, radio or some other means, without regard to whether the supervising licensee is located on the same premises as the person being supervised; and

      (iii)   can provide any necessary consultation within a reasonable period of time and personal contact is routine.

(5)   "Supervising licensee" means a licensee who has satisfied any requirements to act as a supervisor and has agreed to provide supervision of an unlicensed individual or a licensee in a classification or licensure status that requires supervision in accordance with the provisions of this chapter.

R156-1-103. Authority - Purpose.

This rule is adopted by the Division under the authority of Subsection58-1-106(1)(a) to enable the Division to administer Title 58.

R156-1-106. Division - Duties, Functions, and Responsibilities.

(1)   In accordance with Subsection 58-1-106(2), the following responses to requests for lists of licensees may include multiple licensees per request and may include home telephone numbers, home addresses, and e-mail addresses, subject to the restriction that the addresses and telephone numbers shall only be used by a requester for purposes for which the requester is properly authorized:

     (a)   responses to requests from another governmental entity, government-managed corporation, a political subdivision, the federal government, another state, or a not-for-profit regulatory association to which the Division is a member;

     (b)   responses to requests from an occupational or professional association, private continuing education organizations, trade union, university, or school, for purposes of education programs for licensees;

     (c)   responses to a party to a prelitigation proceeding convened by the Division under Title 78, Chapter 14;

     (d)   responses to universities, schools, or research facilities for the purposes of research;

     (e)   responses to requests from licensed health care facilities or third party credentialing services, for the purpose of verifying licensure status for issuing credentialing or reimbursement purposes; and

     (f)   responses to requests from a person preparing for, participating in, or responding to:

         (i)   a national, state or local emergency;

         (ii)   a public health emergency as defined in Section 26-23b-102; or

         (iii)   a declaration by the President of the United States or other federal official requesting public health-related activities.

(2)   In accordance with Subsection 58-1-106(3)(a) and (b), the Division may deny a request for an address or telephone number of a licensee to an individual who provides proper identification and the reason for the request, in writing, to the Division, if the reason for the request is deemed by the Division to constitute an unwarranted invasion of privacy or a threat to the public health, safety, and welfare.

(3)   In accordance with Subsection 58-1-106(3)(c), proper identification of an individual who requests the address or telephone number of a licensee and the reason for the request, in writing, shall consist of the individual's name, mailing address, and daytime number, if available.

R156-1-107. Organization of Rules -Content, Applicability and Relationship of Rules.

(1)   The rules and sections in Title R156 shall, to the extent practicable, follow the numbering and organizational scheme of the chapters in Title 58.

(2)   Rule R156-1 shall contain general provisions applicable to the administration and enforcement of all occupations and professions regulated in Title 58.

(3)   The provisions of the other rules in Title R156 shall contain specific or unique provisions applicable to particular occupations or professions.

(4)   Specific rules in Title R156 may supplement or alter Rule R156-1unless expressly provided otherwise in Rule R156-1.

R156-1-109. Presiding Officers.

In accordance with Subsection 63G-4-103(1)(h), Sections 58-1-104, 58-1-106, 58-1-109, 58-1-202, 58-1-203, 58-55-103, and 58-55-201, except as otherwise specified in writing by the director, or for Title 58, Chapter 55,the Construction Services Commission, the designation of presiding officers is clarified or established as follows:

(1)   The Division regulatory and compliance officer is designated as the presiding officer for issuance of notices of agency action and for issuance of notices of hearing issued concurrently with a notice of agency action or issued in response to a request for agency action, provided that if the Division regulatory and compliance officer is unable to so serve for any reason, a replacement specified by the director is designated as the alternate presiding officer.

(2)   Subsections 58-1-109(2) and 58-1-109(4) are clarified with regard to defaults as follows. Unless otherwise specified in writing by the director, or with regard to Title 58, Chapter 55, by the Construction Services Commission, the department administrative law judge is designated as the presiding officer for entering an order of default against a party, for conducting any further proceedings necessary to complete the adjudicative proceeding, and for issuing a recommended order to the director or commission, respectively, determining the discipline to be imposed, licensure action to be taken, relief to be granted, etc.

(3)   Except as provided in Subsection (4) or otherwise specified in writing by the director, the presiding officer for adjudicative proceedings before the Division are as follows:

(a)   Director. The director shall be the presiding officer for:

(i)   formal adjudicative proceedings described in Subsections R156-46b-201(1)(b), and R156-46b-201(2)(a) through (c), however resolved, including stipulated settlements and hearings; and

(ii)   informal adjudicative proceedings described in Subsections R156-46b-202(1)(g), (j), (l), (m), (o), (p), and (q), and R156-46b-202(2)(a), (b)(ii), (c), and (d), however resolved, including memoranda of understanding and stipulated settlements.

(b)   Bureau managers or program coordinators. Except for Title 58, Chapter 55, the bureau manager or program coordinator over the occupation or profession or program involved shall be the presiding officer for:

(i)   formal adjudicative proceedings described in Subsection R156-46b-201(1)(c), for purposes of determining whether a request for a board of appeal is properly filed as set forth in Subsections R156-15A-210(1) through (4); and

(ii)   informal adjudicative proceedings described in Subsections R156-46b-202(1)(a) through (d),(f), (h), (j), (n) and R156-46b-202(2)(b)(iii).

(iii)   At the direction of a bureau manager or program coordinator, a licensing technician or program technician may sign an informal order in the name of the licensing technician or program technician provided the wording of the order has been approved in advance by the bureau manager or program coordinator and provided the caption "FOR THE BUREAU MANAGER" or "FOR THE PROGRAM COORDINATOR" immediately precedes the licensing technician's or program technician's signature.

(c)   Citation Hearing Officer. The regulatory and compliance officer or other citation hearing officer designated in writing by the director shall be the presiding officer for the adjudicative proceeding described in SubsectionR156-46b-202(1)(k).

(d)   Uniform Building Code Commission. The Uniform Building Code Commission shall be the presiding officer for the adjudicative proceeding described in Subsection R156-46b-202(1) (e) for convening a board of appeal under Subsection 15A-1-207(3), for serving as fact finder at any evidentiary hearing associated with a board of appeal, and for entering the final order associated with a board of appeal. An administrative law judge shall perform the role specified in Subsection 58-1-109(2).

(e) Residence Lien Recovery Fund Advisory Board. The Residence Lien Recovery Fund Advisory Board shall be the presiding officer for adjudicative proceedings described in Subsection R156-46b-202(1)(f) that exceed the authority of the program coordinator, as delegated by the board, or are otherwise referred by the program coordinator to the board for action.

(4) Unless otherwise specified in writing by the Construction Services Commission, the presiding officers and process for adjudicative proceedings under Title 58, Chapter 55, are established or clarified as follows:

(a) Commission.

(i) The commission shall be the presiding officer for all adjudicative proceedings under Title 58, Chapter 55, except as otherwise delegated by the commission in writing or as otherwise provided in this rule; provided, however, that all orders adopted by the commission as a presiding officer shall require the concurrence of the director.

(ii) Unless otherwise specified in writing by the commission, the commission is designated as the presiding officer:

(A) informal adjudicative proceedings described in Subsections R156-46b-202(1)(l), (m), (o), (p), and (q), and R156-46b-202(2)(b)(i), (c), and (d),however resolved, including memoranda of understanding and stipulated settlements;

(B) to serve as fact finder and adopt orders in formal evidentiary hearings associated with adjudicative proceedings involving persons licensed as or required to be licensed under Title 58, Chapter 55; and

(C) to review recommended orders of a board, an administrative law judge, or other designated presiding officer who acted as the fact finder in an evidentiary hearing involving a person licensed or required to be licensed under Title 58, Chapter 55, and to adopt an order of its own. In adopting its order, the commission may accept, modify or reject the recommended order.

(iii) If the commission is unable for any reason to act as the presiding officer as specified, it shall designate another presiding officer in writing to so act.

(iv) Orders of the commission shall address all issues before the commission and shall be based upon the record developed in an adjudicative proceeding conducted by the commission. In cases in which the commission has designated another presiding officer to conduct an adjudicative proceeding and submit a recommended order, the record to be reviewed by the commission shall consist of the findings of fact, conclusions of law, and recommended order submitted to the commission by the presiding officer based upon the evidence presented in the adjudicative proceeding before the presiding officer.

(v) The commission or its designee shall submit adopted orders to the director for the director's concurrence or rejection within 30 days after it receives a recommended order or adopts an order, whichever is earlier. An adopted order shall be deemed issued and constitute a final order upon the concurrence of the director.

(vi) If the director or his designee refuses to concur in an adopted order of the commission or its designee, the director or his designee shall return the order to the commission or its designee with the reasons set forth in writing for the nonconcurrence therein. The commission or its designee shall reconsider and resubmit an adopted order, whether or not modified, within30 days of the date of the initial or subsequent return, provided that unless the director or his designee and the commission or its designee agree to an extension, any final order must be issued within 90 days of the date of the initial recommended order, or the adjudicative proceeding shall be dismissed. Provided the time frames in this subsection are followed, this subsection shall not preclude an informal resolution such as an executive session of the commission or its designee and the director or his designee to resolve the reasons for the director's refusal to concur in an adopted order.

(vii)   The record of the adjudicative proceeding shall include recommended orders, adopted orders, refusals to concur in adopted orders, and final orders.

(viii)   The final order issued by the commission and concurred in by the director may be appealed by filing a request for agency review with the executive director or his designee within the department.

(ix)   The content of all orders shall comply with the requirements of Subsection 63G-4-203(1)(i) and Sections 63G-4-208 and 63G-4-209.

(b)   Director. The director is designated as the presiding officer for the concurrence role on disciplinary proceedings under Subsections R156-46b-202(2)(b)(i), (c), and (d) as required by Subsection 58-55-103(1)(b)(iv).

(c)   Administrative Law Judge. Unless otherwise specified in writing by the commission, the department administrative law judge is designated as the presiding officer to conduct formal adjudicative proceedings before the commission and its advisory boards, as specified in Subsection 58-1-109(2).

(d)   Bureau Manager. Unless otherwise specified in writing by the commission, the responsible bureau manager is designated as the presiding officer for conducting informal adjudicative proceedings specified in Subsections R156-46b-202(1)(a) through (d),(h), and (n).

(e)   At the direction of a bureau manager, a licensing technician may sign an informal order in the name of the licensing technician provided the wording of the order has been approved in advance by the bureau manager and provided the caption "FOR THE BUREAU MANAGER" immediately precedes the licensing technician's signature.

(f)   Plumbers Licensing Board. Except as set forth in Subsection (c) or as otherwise specified in writing by the commission, the Plumbers Licensing Board is designated as the presiding officer to serve as the fact finder and to issue recommended orders to the commission in formal evidentiary hearings associated with adjudicative proceedings involving persons licensed as or required to be licensed as plumbers.

(g)   Electricians Licensing Board. Except as set forth in Subsection (c) or as otherwise specified in writing by the commission, the Electricians Licensing Board is designated as the presiding officer to serve as the factfinder and to issue recommended orders to the commission in formal evidentiary hearings associated with adjudicative proceedings involving persons licensed as or required to be licensed as electricians.

(h)   Alarm System Security and Licensing Board. Except as set forth in Subsection (c) or as otherwise specified in writing by the commission, the Alarm System Security and Licensing Board is designated as the presiding officer to serve as the fact finder and to issue recommended orders to the commission in formal evidentiary hearings associated with adjudicative proceedings involving persons licensed as or required to be licensed as alarm companies or agents.

R156-1-110. Issuance of Investigative Subpoenas.

(1)   All requests for subpoenas in conjunction with a Division investigation made pursuant to Subsection 58-1-106(1)(c), shall be made in writing to the investigative subpoena authority and shall be accompanied by an original of the proposed subpoena.

    (a)   Requests to the investigative subpoena authority shall contain adequate information to enable the subpoena authority to make a finding of sufficient need, including: the factual basis for the request, the relevance and necessity of the particular person, evidence, documents, etc., to the investigation, and an explanation why the subpoena is directed to the particular person upon whom it is to be served.

    (b)   Approved subpoenas shall be issued under the seal of the Division and the signature of the subpoena authority.

(2)   The person who requests an investigative subpoena is responsible for service of the subpoena.

(3)   (a)   Service may be made:

        (i)   on a person upon whom a summons may be served pursuant to the Utah Rules of Civil Procedure; and

        (ii)   personally or on the agent of the person being served.

    (b)   If a party is represented by an attorney, service shall be made on the attorney.

(4)   (a)   Service may be accomplished by hand delivery or by mail to the last known address of the intended recipient.

    (b)   Service by mail is complete upon mailing.

    (c)   Service may be accomplished by electronic means.

    (d)   Service by electronic means is complete on transmission if transmission is completed during normal business hours at the place receiving the service; otherwise, service is complete on the next business day.

(5)   There shall appear on all investigative subpoenas a certificate of service.

(6)   The investigative subpoena authority may quash or modify an investigative subpoena if it is shown to be unreasonable or oppressive.

    (a)   A motion to quash or modify an investigative subpoena shall be filed with and served upon the subpoena authority no later than ten days after service of the investigative subpoena.

    (b)   A response by the Division to a motion to quash or modify an investigative subpoena shall be filed with and served upon the subpoena authority no later than five business days after receipt of a motion to quash or modify an investigative subpoena.

    (c)   No final reply by the recipient of an investigative subpoena who files a motion to quash or modify shall be permitted.

R156-1-205. Peer or Advisory Committees - Executive Director to Appoint - Terms of Office - Vacancies in Office - Removal from Office - Quorum Requirements - Appointment of Chairman - Division to Provide Secretary - Compliance with Open and Public Meetings Act - Compliance with Utah Administrative Procedures Act - No Provision for Per Diem and Expenses.

(1)   The executive director shall appoint the members of peer or advisory committees established under Title 58 or Title R156.

(2)   Except for ad hoc committees whose members shall be appointed on a case-by-case basis, the term of office of peer or advisory committee members shall be for four years. The executive director

shall, at the time of appointment or reappointment, adjust the length of terms to ensure that the terms of committee members are staggered so that approximately half of the peer or advisory committee is appointed every two years.

(3)   No peer or advisory committee member may serve more than two full terms, and no member who ceases to serve may again serve on the peer or advisory committee until after the expiration of two years from the date of cessation of service.

(4)   If a vacancy on a peer or advisory committee occurs, the executive director shall appoint a replacement to fill the unexpired term. After filling the unexpired term, the replacement may be appointed for only one additional full term.

(5)   If a peer or advisory committee member fails or refuses to fulfill the responsibilities and duties of a peer or advisory committee member, including the attendance at peer committee meetings, the executive director may remove the peer or advisory committee member and replace the member in accordance with this section. After filling the unexpired term, the replacement may be appointed for only one additional full term.

(6)   Committee meetings shall only be convened with the approval of the appropriate board and the concurrence of the Division.

(7)   Unless otherwise approved by the Division, peer or advisory committee meetings shall be held in the building occupied by the Division.

(8)   A majority of the peer or advisory committee members shall constitute a quorum and may act in behalf of the peer or advisory committee.

(9)   Peer or advisory committees shall annually designate one of their members to serve as peer or advisory committee chairman. The Division shall provide a Division employee to act as committee secretary to take minutes of committee meetings and to prepare committee correspondence.

(10)   Peer or advisory committees shall comply with the procedures and requirements of Title 52, Chapter 4, Open and Public Meetings, in their meetings.

(11)   Peer or advisory committees shall comply with the procedures and requirements of Title 63G, Chapter 4, Administrative Procedures Act, in their adjudicative proceedings.

(12)   Peer or advisory committee members shall perform their duties and responsibilities as public service and shall not receive a per diem allowance, or traveling or accommodations expenses incurred in peer or advisory committees business, except as otherwise provided in Title 58 or Title R156.

R156-1-206. Emergency Adjudicative Proceeding Review Committees – Appointment - Terms - Vacancies - Removal - Quorum -Chairman and Secretary - Open and Public Meetings Act -Utah Administrative Procedures Act - Per Diem and Expenses.

(1)   The chairman of the board for the profession of the person against whom an action is proposed may appoint the members of emergency review committees on a case-by-case or period-of-time basis.

(2)   With the exception of the appointment and removal of members and filling of vacancies by the chairman of a board, emergency review committees, committees shall serve in accordance with Subsections R156-1-205(7), and (9) through (12).

R156-1-301. Application for Licensure - Filing Date - Applicable Requirements for Licensure - Issuance Date.

(1)   The filing date for an application for licensure shall be the postmark date of the application or the date the application is received and date stamped by the Division, whichever is earlier.

(2)   Except as otherwise provided by statute, rule or order, the requirements for licensure applicable to an application for licensure shall be the requirements in effect on the filing date of the application.

(3)   The issuance date for a license issued to an applicant for licensure shall be as follows:

    (a)   the date the approval is input into the Division's electronic licensure database for applications submitted and processed manually; or

    (b)   the date printed on the verification of renewal certificate for renewal applications submitted and processed electronically via the Division's Internet Renewal System.

R156-1-302. Consideration of Good Moral Character, Unlawful Conduct, Unprofessional Conduct, or Other Mental or Physical Condition.

Pursuant to the provisions of Subsection 58-1-401(1) and (2), if an applicant or licensee has failed to demonstrate good moral character, has been involved in unlawful conduct, has been involved in unprofessional conduct, or has any other mental or physical condition which conduct or condition, when considered with the duties and responsibilities of the license held or to beheld, demonstrates a threat or potential threat to the public health, safety or welfare, the Division may consider various relevant factors in determining what action to take regarding licensure including the following:

(1)   aggravating circumstances, as defined in Subsection R156-1-102(2);

(2)   mitigating circumstances, as defined in Subsection R156-1-102(16);

(3)   the degree of risk to the public health, safety or welfare;

(4)   the degree of risk that a conduct will be repeated;

(5)   the degree of risk that a condition will continue;

(6)   the magnitude of the conduct or condition as it relates to the harm or potential harm;

(7)   the length of time since the last conduct or condition has occurred;

(8)   the current criminal probationary or parole status of the applicant or licensee;

(9)   the current administrative status of the applicant or licensee;

(10)   results of previously submitted applications, for any regulated profession or occupation;

(11)   results from any action, taken by any professional licensing agency, criminal or administrative agency, employer, practice monitoring group, entity or association;

(12)   evidence presented indicating that restricting or monitoring an individual's practice, conditions or conduct can protect the public health, safety or welfare;

(13)   psychological evaluations; or

(14)   any other information the Division or the board reasonably believes may assist in evaluating the degree of threat or potential threat to the public health, safety or welfare.

R156-1-303. Temporary Licenses in Declared Disaster or Emergency.

(1)   In accordance with Section 53-2a-1203, persons who provide services under this exemption from licensure, shall within 30 days file a notice with the Division as provided under Subsection 53-2a-1205(1) using forms posted on the Division internet site.

(2)   In accordance with Section 53-2a-1205 and Subsection 58-1-303(1), a person who provides services under the exemption from licensure as provided in Section 53-2a-1203 for a declared disaster or emergency shall, after the disaster period ends and before continuing to provide services, meet all the normal requirements for occupational or professional licensure under this title, unless:

(a)   prior to practicing after the declared disaster the person is issued a temporary license under the provisions of Subsection 58-1-303(1)(c); or

(b)   the person qualifies under another exemption from licensure.

R156-1-305. Inactive Licensure.

(1)   In accordance with Section 58-1-305, except as provided in Subsection (2), a licensee may not apply for inactive licensure status.

(2)   The following licenses issued under Title 58 that are active in good standing may be placed on inactive licensure status:

(a)   advanced practice registered nurse;

(b)   architect;

(c)   audiologist;

(d)   certified nurse midwife;

(e)   certified public accountant emeritus;

(f)   certified registered nurse anesthetist;

(g)   certified court reporter;

(h)   certified social worker;

(i)   chiropractic physician;

(j)   clinical mental health counselor;

(k)   clinical social worker;

(l)   contractor;

(m)   deception detection examiner;

(n)   deception detection intern;

(o)   dental hygienist;

(p)   dentist;

(q)   direct-entry midwife;

(r)   dispensing medical practitioner - advanced practice registered nurse;

(s)   dispensing medical practitioner - physician and surgeon;

(t)   dispensing medical practitioner - physician assistant;

(u)   dispensing medical practitioner - osteopathic physician and surgeon;

(v)   dispensing medical practitioner - optometrist;

(w)   dispensing medical practitioner - clinic pharmacy;

(x)   genetic counselor;

(y)   health facility administrator;

(z)   hearing instrument specialist;

(aa)   landscape architect;

(bb)   licensed advanced substance use disorder counselor;

(cc)   marriage and family therapist;

(dd)   naturopath/naturopathic physician;

        (ee)   optometrist;

        (ff)   osteopathic physician and surgeon;

        (gg)   pharmacist;

        (hh)   pharmacy technician;

        (ii)   physical therapist;

        (jj)   physician assistant;

        (kk)   physician and surgeon;

        (ll)   podiatric physician;

        (mm) private probation provider;

        (nn)   professional engineer;

        (oo)   professional land surveyor;

        (pp)   professional structural engineer;

        (qq)   psychologist;

        (rr)   radiology practical technician;

        (ss)   radiologic technologist;

        (tt)   security personnel;

        (uu)   speech-language pathologist;

        (vv)   substance use disorder counselor; and

        (xx)   veterinarian.

(3)   Applicants for inactive licensure shall apply to the Division in writing upon forms available from the Division. Each completed application shall contain documentation of requirements for inactive licensure, shall be verified by the applicant, and shall be accompanied by the appropriate fee.

(4)   If all requirements are met for inactive licensure, the Division shall place the license on inactive status.

(5)   A license may remain on inactive status indefinitely except as otherwise provided in Title 58 or rules which implement Title 58.

(6)   An inactive license may be activated by requesting activation in writing upon forms available from the Division. Unless otherwise provided in Title 58 or rules which implement Title 58, each reactivation application shall contain documentation that the applicant meets current renewal requirements, shall be verified by the applicant, and shall be accompanied by the appropriate fee.

(7)   An inactive licensee whose license is activated during the last 12months of a renewal cycle shall, upon payment of the appropriate fees, be licensed for a full renewal cycle plus the period of time remaining until the impending renewal date, rather than being required to immediately renew their activated license.

(8)   A Controlled Substance license may be placed on inactive status if attached to a primary license listed in Subsection R156-1-305(2) and the primary license is placed on inactive status.

R156-1-308a. Renewal Dates.

(1)   The following standard two-year renewal cycle renewal dates are established by license classification in accordance with the Subsection 58-1-308(1):

TABLE
RENEWAL DATES

(a) Acupuncturist	May 31	even years
(b) Advanced Practice Registered Nurse	January 31	even years
(c) Advanced Practice Registered Nurse-CRNA	January 31	even years
(d) Architect	May 31	even years
(e) Athlete Agent	September 30	even years
(f) Athletic Trainer	May 31	odd years
(g) Audiologist	May 31	odd years
(h) Barber	September 30	odd years
(i) Barber School	September 30	odd years
(j) Building Inspector	November 30	odd years
(k) Burglar Alarm Security	March 31	odd years
(l) C.P.A. Firm	September 30	even years
(m) Certified Court Reporter	May 31	even years
(n) Certified Dietitian	September 30	even years
(o) Certified Medical Language Interpreter	March 31	odd years
(p) Certified Nurse Midwife	January 31	even years
(q) Certified Public Accountant	September 30	even years
(r) Certified Social Worker	September 30	even years
(s) Chiropractic Physician	May 31	even years
(t) Clinical Mental Health Counselor	September 30	even years
(u) Clinical Social Worker	September 30	even years
(v) Construction Trades Instructor	November 30	odd years
(w) Contractor	November 30	odd years
(x) Controlled Substance License	Attached to primary license renewal	
(y) Controlled Substance Precursor	May 31	odd years
(z) Controlled Substance Handler	September 30	odd years
(aa) Cosmetologist/Barber	September 30	odd years
(bb) Cosmetology/Barber School	September 30	odd years
(cc) Deception Detection	November 30	even years
(dd) Dental Hygienist	May 31	even years
(ee) Dentist	May 31	even years
(ff) Direct-entry Midwife	September 30	odd years
(gg) Dispensing Medical Practitioner	September 30	odd years
Advanced Practice Registered Nurse, Optometrist, Osteopathic Physician and Surgeon, Physician and Surgeon, Physician Assistant		
(hh) Dispensing Medical Practitioner	September 30	odd years
Clinic Pharmacy		

(ii) Electrician	November 30	even years
Apprentice, Journeyman, Master, Residential Journeyman, Residential Master		
(jj) Electrologist	September 30	odd years
(kk) Electrology School	September 30	odd years
(ll) Elevator Mechanic	November 30	even years
(mm) Environmental Health Scientist	May 31	odd years
(nn) Esthetician	September 30	odd years
(oo) Esthetics School	September 30	odd years
(pp) Factory Built Housing Dealer	September 30	even years
(qq) Funeral Service Director	May 31	even years
(rr) Funeral Service Establishment	May 31	even years
(ss) Genetic Counselor	September 30	even years
(tt) Health Facility Administrator	May 31	odd years
(uu) Hearing Instrument Specialist	September 30	even years
(vv) Internet Facilitator	September 30	odd years
(ww) Landscape Architect	May 31	even years
(xx) Licensed Advanced Substance Use Disorder Counselor	May 31	odd years
(yy) Licensed Practical Nurse	January 31	even years
(zz) Licensed Substance Use Disorder Counselor	May 31	odd years
(aaa) Marriage and Family Therapist	September 30	even years
(bbb) Massage Apprentice, Therapist	May 31	odd years
(ccc) Master Esthetician	September 30	odd years
(ddd) Medication Aide Certified	March 31	odd years
(eee) Music Therapist	March 31	odd years
(fff) Nail Technologist	September 30	odd years
(ggg) Nail Technology School	September 30	odd years
(hhh) Naturopath/Naturopathic Physician	May 31	even years
(iii) Occupational Therapist	May 31	odd years
(jjj) Occupational Therapy Assistant	May 31	odd years
(kkk) Optometrist	September 30	even years
(lll) Osteopathic Physician and Surgeon, Online Prescriber	May 31	even years
(mmm) Outfitter/Hunting Guide	May 31	even years
(nnn) Pharmacy Class A-B-C-D-E, Online Contract Pharmacy	September 30	odd years
(ooo) Pharmacist	September 30	odd years
(ppp) Pharmacy Technician	September 30	odd years
(qqq) Physical Therapist	May 31	odd years

(rrr) Physical Therapist Assistant	May 31	odd years
(sss) Physician Assistant	May 31	even years
(ttt) Physician and Surgeon, Online Prescriber	January 31	even years
(uuu) Plumber	November 30	even years
Apprentice, Journeyman, Master, Residential Master, Residential Journeyman		
(vvv) Podiatric Physician	September 30	even years
(www) Pre Need Funeral Arrangement Sales Agent	May 31	even years
(xxx) Private Probation Provider	May 31	odd years
(yyy) Professional Engineer	March 31	odd years
(zzz) Professional Geologist	March 31	odd years
(aaaa) Professional Land Surveyor	March 31	odd years
(bbbb) Professional Structural Engineer	March 31	odd years
(cccc) Psychologist	September 30	even years
(dddd) Radiologic Technologist, Radiology Practical Technician	May 31	odd years
Radiologist Assistant		
(eeee) Recreational Therapy	May 31	odd years
Therapeutic Recreation Technician, Therapeutic Recreation Specialist, Master Therapeutic Recreation Specialist		
(ffff) Registered Nurse	January 31	odd years
(gggg) Respiratory Care Practitioner	September 30	even years
(hhhh) Security Personnel	November 30	even years
(iiii) Social Service Worker	September 30	even years
(jjjj) Speech-Language Pathologist	May 31	odd years
(kkkk) Veterinarian	September 30	even years
(llll) Vocational Rehabilitation Counselor	March 31	odd years

(2)   The following non-standard renewal terms and renewal or extension cycles are established by license classification in accordance with Subsection58-1-308(1) and in accordance with specific requirements of the license:

   (a)   Associate Clinical Mental Health Counselor licenses shall be issued for a three year term and may be extended if the licensee presents satisfactory evidence to the Division and the Board that reasonable progress is being made toward passing the qualifying examinations or is otherwise on a course reasonably expected to lead to licensure.

   (b)   Associate Marriage and Family Therapist licenses shall be issued for a three year term and may be extended if the licensee presents satisfactory evidence to the Division and the board that reasonable progress is being made toward passing the qualifying examinations or is otherwise on a course reasonably expected to lead to licensure; but the period of the extension may not exceed two years past the date the minimum supervised experience requirement has been completed.

(c)   Certified Advanced Substance Use Disorder Counselor licenses shall be issued for a period of four years and may be extended if the licensee presents satisfactory evidence to the Division and Board that reasonable progress is being made toward completing the required hours of supervised experience necessary for the next level of licensure.

(d)   Certified Advanced Substance Use Disorder Counselor Intern licenses shall be issued for a period of six months or until the examination is passed whichever occurs first.

(e)   Certified Substance Use Disorder Counselor licenses shall be issued for a period of two years and may be extended if the licensee presents satisfactory evidence to the Division and Board that reasonable progress is being made toward completing the required hours of supervised experience necessary for the next level of licensure.

(f)   Certified Social Worker Intern licenses shall be issued for a period of six months or until the examination is passed whichever occurs first.

(g)   Certified Substance Use Disorder Counselor Intern licenses shall be issued for a period of six months or until the examination is passed, whichever occurs first.

(h)   Dental Educator licenses shall be issued for a two year renewable term, until the date of termination of employment with the dental school as an employee, or until the failure to maintain any of the requirements of Section 58-69-302.5, whichever occurs first.

(i)   Funeral Service Apprentice licenses shall be issued for a two year term and may be extended for an additional two year term if the licensee presents satisfactory evidence to the Division and the board that reasonable progress is being made toward passing the qualifying examinations or is otherwise on a course reasonably expected to lead to licensure.

(j)   Hearing Instrument Intern licenses shall be issued for a three year term and may be extended if the licensee presents satisfactory evidence to the Division and the Board that reasonable progress is being made toward passing the qualifying examination, but a circumstance arose beyond the control of the licensee, to prevent the completion of the examination process.

(k)   Pharmacy technician trainee licenses shall be issued for a period of two years and may be extended if the licensee presents satisfactory evidence to the Division and the Board that reasonable progress is being made toward completing the requirements necessary for the next level of licensure.

(l)   Psychology Resident licenses shall be issued for a two year term and may be extended if the licensee presents satisfactory evidence to the Division and the board that reasonable progress is being made toward passing the qualifying examinations or is otherwise on a course reasonably expected to lead to licensure; but the period of the extension may not exceed two years past the date the minimum supervised experience requirement has been completed.

(m)   Type I Foreign Trained Physician-Educator licenses will be issued initially for a one-year term and thereafter renewed every two years following issuance.

(n)   Type II Foreign Trained Physician-Educator licenses will be issued initially for an annual basis and thereafter renewed annually up to four times following issuance if the licensee continues to satisfy the requirements described in Subsection 58-67-302.7(3) and completes the required continuing education requirements established under Section 58-67-303.

R156-1-308b. Renewal Periods - Adjustment of Renewal Fees for an Extended or Shortened Renewal Period.

(1)   Except as otherwise provided by statute or as required to establish or reestablish a renewal period, each renewal period shall be for a period of two years.

(2)   The renewal fee for a renewal period which is extended or shortened by more than one month to establish or reestablish a renewal period shall increased or decreased proportionately.

R156-1-308c. Renewal of Licensure Procedures.

The procedures for renewal of licensure shall be as follows:

(1)   The Division shall send a renewal notice to each licensee at least 60 days prior to the expiration date shown on the licensee's license. The notice shall include directions for the licensee to renew the license via the Division's website.

(2)   Except as provided in Subsection(4), renewal notices shall be sent by mail deposited in the post office with postage prepaid, addressed to the last mailing address shown on the Division's automated license system.

(3)   In accordance with Subsection 58-1-301.7(1), each licensee is required to maintain a current mailing address with the Division. In accordance with Subsection 58-1-301.7(2), mailing to the last mailing address furnished to the Division constitutes legal notice.

(4)   (If a licensee has authorized the Division to send a renewal notice by email, a renewal notice may be sent by email to the last email address shown on the Division's automated license system. If selected as the exclusive method of receipt of renewal notices, such mailing shall constitute legal notice. It shall be the duty and responsibility of each licensee who authorizes the Division to send a renewal notice by email to maintain a current email address with the Division.

(5)   (Renewal notices shall provide that the renewal requirements are outlined in the online renewal process and that each licensee is required to document or certify that the licensee meets the renewal requirements prior to renewal.

(6)   Renewal notices shall advise each licensee that a license that is not renewed prior to the expiration date shown on the license automatically expires and that any continued practice without a license constitutes a criminal offense under Subsection 58-1-501(1)(a).

(7)   Licensees licensed during the last 12 months of a renewal cycle shall be licensed for a full renewal cycle plus the period of time remaining until the impending renewal date, rather than being required to immediately renew their license.

R156-1-308d. Waiver of Continuing Education Requirements - Renewal Requirements.

(1)   (a)   In accordance with Subsection 58-1-203(1)(g), a licensee may request a waiver of any continuing education requirement established under this title or an extension of time to complete any requirement on the basis that the licensee was unable to complete the requirement due to a medical or related condition, humanitarian or ecclesiastical services, extended presence in a geographical area where continuing education is not available, etc.

        (b)   A request must be submitted no later than the deadline for completing any continuing education requirement.

        (c)   A licensee submitting a request has the burden of proof and must document the reason for the request to the satisfaction of the Division.

        (d)   A request shall include the beginning and ending dates during which the licensee was unable to complete the continuing education requirement and a detailed explanation of the reason why. The explanation shall include the extent and duration of the impediment, extent to which the licensee continued to be engaged in practice of his profession, the nature of the medical condition, the location and nature of the humanitarian services, the geographical area where continuing education is not available, etc.

(e)   The Division may require that a specified number of continuing education hours, courses, or both, be obtained prior to reentering the practice of the profession or within a specified period of time after reentering the practice of the profession, as recommended by the appropriate board, in order to assure competent practice.

(f)   While a licensee may receive a waiver from meeting the minimum continuing education requirements, the licensee shall not be exempted from the requirements of Subsection 58-1-501(2)(i), which requires that the licensee provide services within the competency, abilities and education of the licensee. If a licensee cannot competently provide services, the waiver of meeting the continuing education requirements may be conditioned upon the licensee limiting practice to areas in which the licensee has the required competency, abilities and education.

R156-1-308e. Automatic Expiration of Licensure Upon Dissolution of Licensee.

(1)   A license that automatically expires prior to the expiration date shown on the license due to the dissolution of the licensee's registration with the Division of Corporations, with the registration thereafter being retroactively reinstated pursuant to Section 16-10a-1422, shall:

(a)   upon written application for reinstatement of licensure submitted prior to the expiration date shown on the license, be retroactively reinstated to the date of expiration of licensure; and

(b)   upon written application for reinstatement submitted after the expiration date shown on the current license, be reinstated on the effective date of the approval of the application for reinstatement, rather than relating back retroactively to the date of expiration of licensure.

R156-1-308f. Denial of Renewal of Licensure - Classification of Proceedings - Conditional Renewal of Licensure During Adjudicative Proceedings - Conditional Initial, Renewal, or Reinstatement Licensure During Audit or Investigation.

(1)   When an initial, renewal or reinstatement applicant under Subsections 58-1-301(2) through (3) or 58-1-308(5) or (6)(b) is selected for audit or is under investigation, the Division may conditionally issue an initial license to an applicant for initial licensure, or renew or reinstate the license of an applicant pending the completion of the audit or investigation.

(2)   The undetermined completion of a referenced audit or investigation rather than the established expiration date shall be indicated as the expiration date of a conditionally issued, renewed, or reinstated license.

(3)   A conditional issuance, renewal, or reinstatement shall not constitute an adverse licensure action.

(4)   Upon completion of the audit or investigation, the Division shall notify the initial license, renewal, or reinstatement applicant whether the applicant's license is unconditionally issued, renewed, reinstated, denied, or partially denied or reinstated.

(5)   A notice of unconditional denial or partial denial of licensure to an applicant the Division conditionally licensed, renewed, or reinstated shall include the following:

(a)   that the applicant's unconditional initial issuance, renewal, or reinstatement of licensure is denied or partially denied and the basis for such action;

(b)   the Division's file or other reference number of the audit or investigation; and

(c)   that the denial or partial denial of unconditional initial licensure, renewal, or reinstatement of licensure is subject to review and a description of how and when such review may be requested.

R156-1-308g. Reinstatement of Licensure which was Active and in Good Standing at the Time of Expiration of Licensure - Requirements.

The following requirements shall apply to reinstatement of licensure which was active and in good standing at the time of expiration of licensure:

(1)   In accordance with Subsection 58-1-308(5), if an application for reinstatement is received by the Division between the date of the expiration of the license and 30 days after the date of the expiration of the license, the applicant shall:

    (a)   submit a completed renewal form as furnished by the Division demonstrating compliance with requirements and/or conditions of license renewal; and

    (b)   pay the established license renewal fee and a late fee.

(2)   In accordance with Subsection 58-1-308(5), if an application for reinstatement is received by the Division between 31 days after the expiration of the license and two years after the date of the expiration of the license, the applicant shall:

    (a)   submit a completed renewal form as furnished by the Division demonstrating compliance with requirements and/or conditions of license renewal; and

    (b)   pay the established license renewal fee and reinstatement fee.

(3)   In accordance with Subsection 58-1-308(6)(a), if an application for reinstatement is received by the Division more than two years after the date the license expired and the applicant has not been active in the licensed occupation or profession while in the full-time employ of the United States government or under license to practice that occupation or profession in any other state or territory of the United States during the time the license was expired, the applicant shall:

    (a)   submit an application for licensure complete with all supporting documents as is required of an individual making an initial application for license demonstrating the applicant meets all current qualifications for licensure;

    (b)   provide information requested by the Division and board to clearly demonstrate the applicant is currently competent to engage in the occupation or profession for which reinstatement of licensure is requested; and

    (c)   pay the established license fee for a new applicant for licensure.

(4)   In accordance with Subsection 58-1-308(6)(b), if an application for reinstatement is received by the Division more than two years after the date the license expired but the applicant has been active in the licensed occupation or profession while in the full-time employ of the United States government or under license to practice that occupation or profession in any other state or territory of the United States shall:

    (a)   provide documentation that the applicant has continuously, since the expiration of the applicant's license in Utah, been active in the licensed occupation or profession while in the full-time employ of the United States government or under license to practice that occupation or profession in any other state or territory of the United States;

    (b)   provide documentation that the applicant has completed or is incompliance with any renewal qualifications;

    (c)   provide documentation that the applicant's application was submitted within six months after reestablishing domicile within Utah or terminating full-time government service; and

    (d)   pay the established license renewal fee and the reinstatement fee.

R156-1-308h. Reinstatement of Restricted, Suspended, or Probationary Licensure During Term of Restriction, Suspension, or Probation - Requirements.

(1)   Reinstatement of restricted, suspended, or probationary licensure during the term of limitation, suspension, or probation shall be in accordance with the disciplinary order which imposed the discipline.

(2)   Unless otherwise specified in a disciplinary order imposing restriction, suspension, or probation of licensure, the disciplined licensee may, at reasonable intervals during the term of the disciplinary order, petition for reinstatement of licensure.

(3)   Petitions for reinstatement of licensure during the term of a disciplinary order imposing restriction, suspension, or probation, shall be treated as a request to modify the terms of the disciplinary order, not as an application for licensure.

R156-1-308i. Reinstatement of Restricted, Suspended, or Probationary Licensure After the Specified Term of Suspension of the License or After the Expiration of Licensure in a Restricted, Suspended or Probationary Status - Requirements.

Unless otherwise provided by a disciplinary order, an applicant who applies for reinstatement of a license after the specified term of suspension of the license or after the expiration of the license in a restricted, suspended or probationary status shall:

(1)   submit an application for licensure complete with all supporting documents as is required of an individual making an initial application for license demonstrating the applicant meets all current qualifications for licensure and compliance with requirements and conditions of license reinstatement;

(2)   pay the established license renewal fee and the reinstatement fee;

(3)   provide information requested by the Division and board to clearly demonstrate the applicant is currently competent to be reinstated to engage in the occupation or profession for which the applicant was suspended, restricted, or placed on probation; and

(4)   pay any fines or citations owed to the Division prior to the expiration of license.

R156-1-308j. Relicensure Following Revocation of Licensure - Requirements.

An applicant for relicensure following revocation of licensure shall:

(1)   submit an application for licensure complete with all supporting documents as is required of an individual making an initial application for license demonstrating the applicant meets all current qualifications for licensure and compliance with requirements and/or conditions of license reinstatement;

(2)   pay the established license fee for a new applicant for licensure; and

(3)   provide information requested by the Division and board to clearly demonstrate the applicant is currently competent to be relicensed to engage in the occupation or profession for which the applicant was revoked.

R156-1-308k. Relicensure Following Surrender of Licensure -Requirements.

The following requirements shall apply to relicensure applications following the surrender of licensure:

(1)   An applicant who surrendered a license that was active and in good standing at the time it was surrendered shall meet the requirements for licensure listed in Sections R156-1-308a through R156-1-308l.

(2) An applicant who surrendered a license while the license was active but not in good standing as evidenced by the written agreement supporting the surrender of license shall:

    (a) submit an application for licensure complete with all supporting documents as is required of an individual making an initial application for license demonstrating the applicant meets all current qualifications for licensure and compliance with requirements and/or conditions of license reinstatement;

    (b) pay the established license fee for a new applicant for licensure;

    (c) provide information requested by the Division and board to clearly demonstrate the applicant is currently competent to be relicensed to engage in the occupation or profession for which the applicant was surrendered;

    (d) pay any fines or citations owed to the Division prior to the surrender of license.

R156-1-308l. Reinstatement of Licensure and Relicensure - Term of Licensure.

Except as otherwise governed by the terms of an order issued by the Division, a license issued to an applicant for reinstatement or relicensure issued during the last 12 months of a renewal cycle shall, upon payment of the appropriate fees, be issued for a full renewal cycle plus the period of time remaining until the impending renewal date, rather than requiring the licensee to immediately renew their reinstated or relicensed license.

R156-1-310. Cheating on Examinations.

(1) Policy.

The passing of an examination, when required as a condition of obtaining or maintaining a license issued by the Division, is considered to be a critical indicator that an applicant or licensee meets the minimum qualifications for licensure. Failure to pass an examination is considered to be evidence that an applicant or licensee does not meet the minimum qualifications for licensure. Accordingly, the accuracy of the examination result as a measure of an applicant's or licensee's competency must be assured. Cheating by an applicant or licensee on any examination required as a condition of obtaining a license or maintaining a license shall be considered unprofessional conduct and shall result in imposition of an appropriate penalty against the applicant or licensee.

(2) Cheating Defined.

Cheating is defined as the use of any means or instrumentality by or for the benefit of an examinee to alter the results of an examination in any way to cause the examination results to inaccurately represent the competency of an examinee with respect to the knowledge or skills about which they are examined. Cheating includes:

    (a) communication between examinees inside of the examination room or facility during the course of the examination;

    (b) communication about the examination with anyone outside of the examination room or facility during the course of the examination;

    (c) copying another examinee's answers or looking at another examinee's answers while an examination is in progress;

    (d) permitting anyone to copy answers to the examination;

    (e) substitution by an applicant or licensee or by others for the benefit of an applicant or licensee of another person as the examinee in place of the applicant or licensee;

    (f) use by an applicant or licensee of any written material, audio material, video material or any other mechanism not specifically authorized during the examination for the purpose of assisting an examinee in the examination;

(g)   obtaining, using, buying, selling, possession of or having access to a copy of any portion of the examination prior to administration of the examination.

(3)   Action Upon Detection of Cheating.

(a)   The person responsible for administration of an examination, upon evidence that an examinee is or has been cheating on an examination shall notify the Division of the circumstances in detail and the identity of the examinees involved with an assessment of the degree of involvement of each examinee;

(b)   If cheating is detected prior to commencement of the examination, the examinee may be denied the privilege of taking the examination; or if permitted to take the examination, the examinee shall be notified of the evidence of cheating and shall be informed that the Division may consider the examination to have been failed by the applicant or licensee because of the cheating; or

(c)   If cheating is detected during the examination, the examinee may be requested to leave the examination facility and in that case the examination results shall be the same as failure of the examination; however, if the person responsible for administration of the examination determines the cheating detected has not yet compromised the integrity of the examination, such steps as are necessary to prevent further cheating shall be taken and the examinee may be permitted to continue with the examination.

(d)   If cheating is detected after the examination, the Division shall make appropriate inquiry to determine the facts concerning the cheating and shall thereafter take appropriate action.

(e)   Upon determination that an applicant has cheated on an examination, the applicant may be denied the privilege of retaking the examination for a reasonable period of time, and the Division may deny the applicant a license and may establish conditions the applicant must meet to qualify for a license including the earliest date on which the Division will again consider the applicant for licensure.

R156-1-404a. Diversion Advisory Committees Created.

(1)   There are created diversion advisory committees of at least three members for the professions regulated under Title 58. The diversion committees are not required to be impaneled by the director until the need for the diversion committee arises. Diversion committees may be appointed with representatives from like professions providing a multi-disciplinary committee.

(2)   Committee members are appointed by and serve at the pleasure of the director.

(3)   A majority of the diversion committee members shall constitute a quorum and may act on behalf of the diversion committee.

(4)   Diversion committee members shall perform their duties and responsibilities as public service and shall not receive a per diem allowance, or traveling or accommodations expenses incurred in diversion committees business.

R156-1-404b. Diversion Committees Duties.

The duties of diversion committees shall include:

(1)   reviewing the details of the information regarding licensees referred to the diversion committee for possible diversion, interviewing the licensees, and recommending to the director whether the licensees meet the qualifications for diversion and if so whether the licensees should be considered for diversion;

(2)   recommending to the director terms and conditions to be included in diversion agreements;

(3)   supervising compliance with all terms and conditions of diversion agreements;

(4)   advising the director at the conclusion of a licensee's diversion program whether the licensee has completed the terms of the licensee's diversion agreement; and

(5)   establishing and maintaining continuing quality review of the programs of professional associations and/or private organizations to which licensees approved for diversion may enroll for the purpose of education, rehabilitation or any other purpose agreed to in the terms of a diversion agreement.

R156-1-404c. Diversion - Eligible Offenses.

In accordance with Subsection 58-1-404(4), the unprofessional conduct which may be subject to diversion is set forth in Subsections 58-1-501(2)(e) and (f).

R156-1-404d. Diversion - Procedures.

(1)   Diversion committees shall complete the duties described in Subsections R156-1-404b(1) and (2) no later than 60 days following the referral of a licensee to the diversion committee for possible diversion.

(2)   The director shall accept or reject the diversion committee's recommendation no later than 30 days following receipt of the recommendation.

(3)   If the director finds that a licensee meets the qualifications for diversion and should be diverted, the Division shall prepare and serve upon the licensee a proposed diversion agreement. The licensee shall have a period of time determined by the diversion committee not to exceed 30 days from the service of the proposed diversion agreement to negotiate a final diversion agreement with the director. The final diversion agreement shall comply with Subsections 58-1-404.

(4)   If a final diversion agreement is not reached with the director within 30 days from service of the proposed diversion agreement, the Division shall pursue appropriate disciplinary action against the licensee in accordance with Section 58-1-108.

(5)   In accordance with Subsection 58-1-404(5), a licensee may be represented, at the licensee's discretion and expense, by legal counsel during negotiations for diversion, at the time of execution of the diversion agreement and at any hearing before the director relating to a diversion program.

R156-1-404e. Diversion - Agreements for Rehabilitation, Education or Other Similar Services or Coordination of Services.

(1)   The Division may enter into agreements with professional or occupational organizations or associations, education institutions or organizations, testing agencies, health care facilities, health care practitioners, government agencies or other persons or organizations for the purpose of providing rehabilitation, education or any other services necessary to facilitate an effective completion of a diversion program for a licensee.

(2)   The Division may enter into agreements with impaired person programs to coordinate efforts in rehabilitating and educating impaired professionals.

(3)   Agreements shall be in writing and shall set forth terms and conditions necessary to permit each party to properly fulfill its duties and obligations thereunder. Agreements shall address the circumstances and conditions under which information concerning the impaired licensee will be shared with the Division.

(4)   The cost of administering agreements and providing the services thereunder shall be borne by the licensee benefiting from the services. Fees paid by the licensee shall be reasonable and shall be in proportion to the value of the service provided. Payments of fees shall be a condition of completing the program of diversion.

(5)   In selecting parties with whom the Division shall enter agreements under this section, the Division shall ensure the parties are competent to provide the required services. The Division may limit the number of parties providing a particular service within the limits or demands for the service to permit the responsible diversion committee to conduct quality review of the programs given the committee's limited resources.

R156-1-501. Unprofessional Conduct.

"Unprofessional conduct" includes:

(1)   surrendering licensure to any other licensing or regulatory authority having jurisdiction over the licensee or applicant in the same occupation or profession while an investigation or inquiry into allegations of unprofessional or unlawful conduct is in progress or after a charging document has been filed against the applicant or licensee alleging unprofessional or unlawful conduct;

(2)   practicing a regulated occupation or profession in, through, or with a limited liability company which has omitted the words "limited company," "limited liability company," or the abbreviation "L.C." or "L.L.C." in the commercial use of the name of the limited liability company;

(3)   practicing a regulated occupation or profession in, through, or with a limited partnership which has omitted the words "limited partnership," "limited," or the abbreviation "L.P." or "Ltd." in the commercial use of the name of the limited partnership;

(4)   practicing a regulated occupation or profession in, through, or with a professional corporation which has omitted the words "professional corporation" or the abbreviation "P.C." in the commercial use of the name of the professional corporation;

(5)   using a DBA (doing business as name) which has not been properly registered with the Division of Corporations and with the Division of Occupational and Professional Licensing;

(6)   failing, as a prescribing practitioner, to follow the "Model Policy for the Use of Controlled Substances for the Treatment of Pain", 2004, established by the Federation of State Medical Boards, which is hereby adopted and incorporated by reference;

(7)   failing, as a prescribing practitioner, to follow the "Model Policy on the Use of Opioid Analgesics in the Treatment of Chronic Pain", July 2013, adopted by the Federation of State Medical Boards, which is incorporated by reference; or

(8)   violating any term, condition, or requirement contained in a "diversion agreement", as defined in Subsection 58-1-404(6)(a).

R156-1-502. Administrative Penalties.

(1)   In accordance with Subsection 58-1-401(5) and Section 58-1-502, except as otherwise provided by a specific chapter under Title R156, the following fine schedule shall apply to citations issued under the referenced authority:

TABLE
FINE SCHEDULE
FIRST OFFENSE

Violation	Fine
58-1-501(1)(a)	$ 500.00
58-1-501(1)(c)	$ 800.00
58-1-501(2)(o)	$ 0–$250.00

SECOND OFFENSE

Violation	Fine
58-1-501(1)(a)	$1,000.00
58-1-501(1)(c)	$1,600.00
58-1-501(2)(o)	$251.00–$500.00

THIRD OFFENSE

Double the amount for a second offense with a maximum amount not to exceed the maximum fine allowed under Subsection 58-1-502(2)(j)(iii).

(2)   Citations shall not be issued for third offenses, except in extraordinary circumstances approved by the investigative supervisor.

(3)   If multiple offenses are cited on the same citation, the fine shall be determined by evaluating the most serious offense.

(4)   An investigative supervisor or chief investigator may authorize a deviation from the fine schedule based upon the aggravating or mitigating circumstances.

(5)   The presiding officer for a contested citation shall have the discretion, after a review of the aggravating and mitigating circumstances, to increase or decrease the fine amount imposed by an investigator based upon the evidence reviewed.

R156-1-503. Reporting Disciplinary Action.

The Division may report disciplinary action to other state or federal governmental entities, state and federal data banks, the media, or any other person who is entitled to such information under the Government Records Access and Management Act.

R156-1-506. Supervision of Cosmetic Medical Procedures.

The 80 hours of documented education and experience required under Subsection 58-1-506(2)(f)(iii) to maintain competence to perform nonablative cosmetic medical procedures is defined to include the following:

(1)   the appropriate standards of care for performing nonablative cosmetic medical procedures;

(2)   physiology of the skin;

(3)   skin typing and analysis;

(4)   skin conditions, disorders, and diseases;

(5)   pre and post procedure care;

(6)   infection control;

(7)   laser and light physics training;

(8)   laser technologies and applications;

(9)   safety and maintenance of lasers;

(10)   cosmetic medical procedures an individual is permitted to perform under this title;

(11)   recognition and appropriate management of complications from a procedure; and

(12)   current cardio-pulmonary resuscitation (CPR) certification for health care providers from one of the following organizations:

    (a)   American Heart Association;

    (b)   American Red Cross or its affiliates; or

    (c)   American Safety and Health Institute.

KEY: diversion programs, licensing, supervision, evidentiary restrictions

Date of Enactment or Last Substantive Amendment: August 21, 2014

Notice of Continuation: January 5, 2012

Authorizing, and Implemented or Interpreted Law: 58-1-106(1)(a); 58-1-308; 58-1-501(2)

GENERAL RULE OF THE DIVISION OF OCCUPATIONAL AND PROFESSIONAL LICENSING

R156-1

Utah Administrative Code Issued August 21, 2014

Disclaimer: The statute/rule above is an unofficial version provided for convenience only and may not be identical to the official versions on the Utah State Legislature (www.le.utah.gov) and the Utah Division of Administrative Rules (www.rules.utah.gov) websites.

Appendix H:
Utah Workers' Compensation Law

34A-2-101. Title.

This chapter shall be known as the "Workers' Compensation Act."

34A-2-102.   Definition of terms.

As used in this chapter:

(1)   "Average weekly wages" means the average weekly wages as determined under Section 34A-2-409.

(2)   "Award" means a final order of the commission as to the amount of compensation due:

    (a)   any injured employee; or

    (b)   the dependents of any deceased employee.

(3)   "Compensation" means the payments and benefits provided for in this chapter or Chapter 3, Utah Occupational Disease Act.

(4)   "Decision" means the ruling of an administrative law judge or, in accordance with Section 34A-2-801, the commissioner or Appeals Board and may include:

    (a)   an award or denial of medical, disability, death, or other related benefits under this chapter or Chapter 3, Utah Occupational Disease Act; or

    (b)   another adjudicative ruling in accordance with this chapter or Chapter 3, Utah Occupational Disease Act.

(5)   "Director" means the director of the division, unless the context requires otherwise.

(6)   "Disability" means an administrative determination that may result in an entitlement to compensation as a consequence of becoming medically impaired as to function. Disability can be total or partial, temporary or permanent, industrial or nonindustrial.

(7)   "Division" means the Division of Industrial Accidents.

(8)   "Impairment" is a purely medical condition reflecting any anatomical or functional abnormality or loss. Impairment may be either temporary or permanent, industrial or nonindustrial.

(9)   "Order" means an action of the commission that determines the legal rights, duties, privileges, immunities, or other interests of one or more specific persons, but not a class of persons.

(10)   (a)   "Personal injury by accident arising out of and in the course of employment" includes any injury caused by the willful act of a third person directed against an employee because of the employee's employment.

    (b)   "Personal injury by accident arising out of and in the course of employment" does not include a disease, except as the disease results from the injury.

(11)   "Safe" and "safety," as applied to any employment or place of employment, means the freedom from danger to the life or health of employees reasonably permitted by the nature of the employment.

(12) "Workers' Compensation Fund" means the nonprofit, quasipublic corporation created in Title 31A, Chapter 33, Workers' Compensation Fund.

34A-2-103. Employers enumerated and defined — Regularly employed — Statutory employers.

(1) (a) The state, and each county, city, town, and school district in the state are considered employers under this chapter and Chapter 3, Utah Occupational Disease Act.

    (b) For the purposes of the exclusive remedy in this chapter and Chapter 3, Utah Occupational Disease Act prescribed in Sections 34A-2-105 and 34A-3-102, the state is considered to be a single employer and includes any office, department, agency, authority, commission, board, institution, hospital, college, university, or other instrumentality of the state.

(2) (a) Except as provided in Subsection (4), each person, including each public utility and each independent contractor, who regularly employs one or more workers or operatives in the same business, or in or about the same establishment, under any contract of hire, express or implied, oral or written, is considered an employer under this chapter and Chapter 3, Utah Occupational Disease Act.

    (b) As used in this Subsection (2):

        (i) "Independent contractor" means any person engaged in the performance of any work for another who, while so engaged, is:

            (A) independent of the employer in all that pertains to the execution of the work;

            (B) not subject to the routine rule or control of the employer;

            (C) engaged only in the performance of a definite job or piece of work; and

            (D) subordinate to the employer only in effecting a result in accordance with the employer's design.

        (ii) "Regularly" includes all employments in the usual course of the trade, business, profession, or occupation of the employer, whether continuous throughout the year or for only a portion of the year.

(3) (a) The client under a professional employer organization agreement regulated under Title 31A, Chapter 40, Professional Employer Organization Licensing Act:

        (i) is considered the employer of a covered employee; and

        (ii) ubject to Section 31A-40-209, shall secure workers' compensation benefits for a covered employee by complying with Subsection 34A-2-201(1) or (2) and commission rules.

    (b) The division shall promptly inform the Insurance Department if the division has reason to believe that a professional employer organization is not in compliance with Subsection 34A-2-201(1) or (2) and commission rules.

(4) A domestic employer who does not employ one employee or more than one employee at least 40 hours per week is not considered an employer under this chapter and Chapter 3, Utah Occupational Disease Act.

(5) (a) As used in this Subsection (5):

        (i) (A) "agricultural employer" means a person who employs agricultural labor as defined in Subsections 35A-4-206(1) and (2) and does not include employment as provided in Subsection 35A-4-206(3); and

(B)   notwithstanding Subsection (5)(a)(i)(A), only for purposes of determining who is a member of the employer's immediate family under Subsection (5)(a)(ii), if the agricultural employer is a corporation, partnership, or other business entity, "agricultural employer" means an officer, director, or partner of the business entity;

(ii)   "employer's immediate family" means:

    (A)   an agricultural employer's:

        (I)   spouse;

        (II)   grandparent;

        (III)   parent;

        (IV)   sibling;

        (V)   child;

        (VI)   grandchild;

        (VII)   nephew; or

        (VIII) niece;

    (B)   a spouse of any person provided in Subsection (5)(a)(ii)(A)(II) through (VIII); or

    (C)   an individual who is similar to those listed in Subsection (5)(a)(ii)(A) or (B) as defined by rules of the commission; and

(iii) "nonimmediate family" means a person who is not a member of the employer's immediate family.

(b)   For purposes of this chapter and Chapter 3, Utah Occupational Disease Act, an agricultural employer is not considered an employer of a member of the employer's immediate family.

(c)   For purposes of this chapter and Chapter 3, Utah Occupational Disease Act, an agricultural employer is not considered an employer of a nonimmediate family employee if:

    (i)   for the previous calendar year the agricultural employer's total annual payroll for all nonimmediate family employees was less than $8,000; or

    (ii)   (A)   for the previous calendar year the agricultural employer's total annual payroll for all nonimmediate family employees was equal to or greater than $8,000 but less than $50,000; and

        (B)   the agricultural employer maintains insurance that covers job-related injuries of the employer's nonimmediate family employees in at least the following amounts:

            (I) $300,000 liability insurance, as defined in Section 31A-1-301; and

            (II) $5,000 for health care benefits similar to benefits under health care insurance as defined in Section 31A-1-301.

(d)   For purposes of this chapter and Chapter 3, Utah Occupational Disease Act, an agricultural employer is considered an employer of a nonimmediate family employee if:

    (i)   for the previous calendar year the agricultural employer's total annual payroll for all nonimmediate family employees is equal to or greater than $50,000; or

        (ii)   (A)   for the previous year the agricultural employer's total payroll for nonimmediate family employees was equal to or exceeds $8,000 but is less than $50,000; and

                  (B)   the agricultural employer fails to maintain the insurance required under Subsection (5)(c)(ii)(B).

(6)   An employer of agricultural laborers or domestic servants who is not considered an employer under this chapter and Chapter 3, Utah Occupational Disease Act, may come under this chapter and Chapter 3, Utah Occupational Disease Act, by complying with:

     (a)   this chapter and Chapter 3, Utah Occupational Disease Act; and

     (b)   the rules of the commission.

(7)   (a)   (i)   As used in this Subsection (7)(a), "employer" includes any of the following persons that procures work to be done by a contractor notwithstanding whether or not the person directly employs a person:

                  (A)   a sole proprietorship;

                  (B)   a corporation;

                  (C)   a partnership;

                  (D)   a limited liability company; or

                  (E)   a person similar to one described in Subsections (7)(a)(i)(A) through (D).

            (ii)   If an employer procures any work to be done wholly or in part for the employer by a contractor over whose work the employer retains supervision or control, and this work is a part or process in the trade or business of the employer, the contractor, all persons employed by the contractor, all subcontractors under the contractor, and all persons employed by any of these subcontractors, are considered employees of the original employer for the purposes of this chapter and Chapter 3, Utah Occupational Disease Act.

     (b)   Any person who is engaged in constructing, improving, repairing, or remodelling a residence that the person owns or is in the process of acquiring as the person's personal residence may not be considered an employee or employer solely by operation of Subsection (7)(a).

     (c)   A partner in a partnership or an owner of a sole proprietorship is not considered an employee under Subsection (7)(a) if the employer who procures work to be done by the partnership or sole proprietorship obtains and relies on either:

            (i)   a valid certification of the partnership's or sole proprietorship's compliance with Section 34A-2-201 indicating that the partnership or sole proprietorship secured the payment of workers' compensation benefits pursuant to Section 34A-2-201; or

            (ii)   if a partnership or sole proprietorship with no employees other than a partner of the partnership or owner of the sole proprietorship, a workers' compensation coverage waiver issued pursuant to Part 10, Workers' Compensation Coverage Waivers Act, stating that:

                  (A)   the partnership or sole proprietorship is customarily engaged in an independently established trade, occupation, profession, or business; and

                  (B)   the partner or owner personally waives the partner's or owner's entitlement to the benefits of this chapter and Chapter 3, Utah Occupational Disease Act, in the operation of the partnership or sole proprietorship.

(d)   A director or officer of a corporation is not considered an employee under Subsection (7)(a) if the director or officer is excluded from coverage under Subsection 34A-2-104(4).

(e)   A contractor or subcontractor is not an employee of the employer under Subsection (7)(a), if the employer who procures work to be done by the contractor or subcontractor obtains and relies on either:

   (i)   a valid certification of the contractor's or subcontractor's compliance with Section 34A-2-201; or

   (ii)   if a partnership, corporation, or sole proprietorship with no employees other than a partner of the partnership, officer of the corporation, or owner of the sole proprietorship, a workers' compensation coverage waiver issued pursuant to Part 10, Workers' Compensation Coverage Waivers Act, stating that:

      (A)   the partnership, corporation, or sole proprietorship is customarily engaged in an independently established trade, occupation, profession, or business; and

      (B)   the partner, corporate officer, or owner personally waives the partner's, corporate officer's, or owner's entitlement to the benefits of this chapter and Chapter 3, Utah Occupational Disease Act, in the operation of the partnership's, corporation's, or sole proprietorship's enterprise under a contract of hire for services.

(f)   (i)   For purposes of this Subsection (7)(f), "eligible employer" means a person who:

      (A)   is an employer; and

      (B)   procures work to be done wholly or in part for the employer by a contractor, including:

         (I)   all persons employed by the contractor;

         (II)   all subcontractors under the contractor; and

         (III)   all persons employed by any of these subcontractors.

   (ii)   Notwithstanding the other provisions in this Subsection (7), if the conditions of Subsection (7)(f)(iii) are met, an eligible employer is considered an employer for purposes of Section 34A-2-105 of the contractor, subcontractor, and all persons employed by the contractor or subcontractor described in Subsection (7)(f)(i)(B).

   (iii) Subsection (7)(f)(ii) applies if the eligible employer:

      (A)   under Subsection (7)(a) is liable for and pays workers' compensation benefits as an original employer under Subsection (7)(a) because the contractor or subcontractor fails to comply with Section 34A-2-201;

      (B)   (I)   secures the payment of workers' compensation benefits for the contractor or subcontractor pursuant to Section 34A-2-201;

             (II)   procures work to be done that is part or process of the trade or business of the eligible employer; and

             (II)   does the following with regard to a written workplace accident and linjury reduction program that meets the requirements of Subsection 34A-2-111(3)(d):

                     (Aa)   adopts the workplace accident and injury reduction program;

      (Bb) posts the workplace accident and injury reduction program at the work site at which the eligible employer procures work; and

      (Cc) enforces the workplace accident and injury reduction program according to the terms of the workplace accident and injury reduction program; or

    (C) (I) obtains and relies on:

      (Aa) a valid certification described in Subsection (7)(c)(i) or (7)(e)(i);

      (Bb) a workers' compensation coverage waiver described in Subsection (7)(c)(ii) or (7)(e)(ii); or

      (Cc) proof that a director or officer is excluded from coverage under Subsection 34A-2-104(4);

     (II) is liable under Subsection (7)(a) for the payment of workers' compensation benefits if the contractor or subcontractor fails to comply with Section 34A-2-201;

     (III) procures work to be done that is part or process in the trade or business of the eligible employer; and

     (IV) does the following with regard to a written workplace accident and injury reduction program that meets the requirements of Subsection 34A-2-111(3)(d):

      (Aa) adopts the workplace accident and injury reduction program;

      (Bb) posts the workplace accident and injury reduction program at the work site at which the eligible employer procures work; and

      (Cc) enforces the workplace accident and injury reduction program according to the terms of the workplace accident and injury reduction program.

(8) (a) For purposes of this Subsection (8), "unincorporated entity" means an entity organized or doing business in the state that is not:

   (i) an individual;

   (ii) a corporation; or

   (iii) publicly traded.

  (b) For purposes of this chapter and Chapter 3, Utah Occupational Disease Act, an unincorporated entity that is required to be licensed under Title 58, Chapter 55, Utah Construction Trades Licensing Act, is presumed to be the employer of each individual who holds, directly or indirectly, an ownership interest in the unincorporated entity. Notwithstanding Subsection (7)(c) and Subsection 34A-2-104(3), the unincorporated entity shall provide the individual who holds the ownership interest workers' compensation coverage under this chapter and Chapter 3, Utah Occupational Disease Act, unless the presumption is rebutted under Subsection (8)(c).

  (c) Pursuant to rules made by the commission in accordance with Title 63G, Chapter 3, Utah Administrative Rulemaking Act, an unincorporated entity may rebut the presumption under

Subsection (8)(b) for an individual by establishing by clear and convincing evidence that the individual:

    (i)   is an active manager of the unincorporated entity;

    (ii)   directly or indirectly holds at least an 8% ownership interest in the unincorporated entity; or

    (iii)   is not subject to supervision or control in the performance of work by:

        (A)   the unincorporated entity; or

        (B)   a person with whom the unincorporated entity contracts.

(d)   As part of the rules made under Subsection (8)(c), the commission may define:

    (i)   "active manager";

    (ii)   "directly or indirectly holds at least an 8% ownership interest"; and

    (iii)   "subject to supervision or control in the performance of work."

34A-2-104. "Employee," "worker," and "operative" defined — Specific circumstances — Exemptions.

(1)   As used in this chapter and Chapter 3, Utah Occupational Disease Act, "employee," "worker," and "operative" mean:

    (a)   (i)   an elective or appointive officer and any other person:

        (A)   in the service of:

            (I)   the state;

            (II)   a county, city, or town within the state; or

            (III)   a school district within the state;

        (B)   serving the state, or any county, city, town, or school district under:

            (I)   an election;

            (II)   appointment; or

            (III)   any contract of hire, express or implied, written or oral; and

        (ii)   including:

        (A)   an officer or employee of the state institutions of learning; and

        (B)   a member of the National Guard while on state active duty; and

    (b)   a person in the service of any employer, as defined in Section 34A-2-103, who employs one or more workers or operatives regularly in the same business, or in or about the same establishment:

        (i)   under any contract of hire:

        (A)   express or implied; and

        (B)   oral or written;

        (ii)   including aliens and minors, whether legally or illegally working for hire; and

        (iii)   not including any person whose employment:

        (A)   is casual; and

        (B)   not in the usual course of the trade, business, or occupation of the employee's employer.

(2) (a) Unless a lessee provides coverage as an employer under this chapter and Chapter 3, Utah Occupational Disease Act, any lessee in mines or of mining property and each employee and sublessee of the lessee shall be:

      (i) covered for compensation by the lessor under this chapter and Chapter 3, Utah Occupational Disease Act;

      (ii) subject to this chapter and Chapter 3, Utah Occupational Disease Act; and

      (iii) entitled to the benefits of this chapter and Chapter 3, Utah Occupational Disease Act, to the same extent as if the lessee, employee, or sublessee were employees of the lessor drawing the wages paid employees for substantially similar work.

    (b) The lessor may deduct from the proceeds of ores mined by the lessees an amount equal to the insurance premium for that type of work.

(3) (a) A partnership or sole proprietorship may elect to include any partner of the partnership or owner of the sole proprietorship as an employee of the partnership or sole proprietorship under this chapter and Chapter 3, Utah Occupational Disease Act.

    (b) If a partnership or sole proprietorship makes an election under Subsection (3)(a), the partnership or sole proprietorship shall serve written notice upon its insurance carrier naming the persons to be covered.

    (c) A partner of a partnership or owner of a sole proprietorship may not be considered an employee of the partner's partnership or the owner's sole proprietorship under this chapter or Chapter 3, Utah Occupational Disease Act, until the notice described in Subsection (3)(b) is given.

    (d) For premium rate making, the insurance carrier shall assume the salary or wage of the partner or sole proprietor electing coverage under Subsection (3)(a) to be 100% of the state's average weekly wage.

(4) (a) A corporation may elect not to include any director or officer of the corporation as an employee under this chapter and Chapter 3, Utah Occupational Disease Act.

    (b) If a corporation makes an election under Subsection (4)(a), the corporation shall serve written notice upon its insurance carrier naming the persons to be excluded from coverage.

    (c) A director or officer of a corporation is considered an employee under this chapter and Chapter 3, Utah Occupational Disease Act until the notice described in Subsection (4)(b) is given.

(5) As used in this chapter and Chapter 3, Utah Occupational Disease Act, "employee," "worker," and "operative" do not include:

    (a) a sales agent or associate broker, as defined in Section 61-2f-102, who performs services in that capacity for a principal broker if:

      (i) substantially all of the sales agent's or associate broker's income for services is from real estate commissions; and

      (ii) the sales agent's or associate broker's services are performed under a written contract that provides that:

        (A) the real estate agent is an independent contractor; and

        (B) the sales agent or associate broker is not to be treated as an employee for federal income tax purposes;

(b)   an offender performing labor under Section 64-13-16 or 64-13-19, except as required by federal statute or regulation;

(c)   an individual who for an insurance producer, as defined in Section 31A-1-301, solicits, negotiates, places or procures insurance if:

(i)   substantially all of the individual's income from those services is from insurance commissions; and

(ii)   the services of the individual are performed under a written contract that states that the individual:

(A)   is an independent contractor;

(B)   is not to be treated as an employee for federal income tax purposes; and

(C)   can derive income from more than one insurance company;

(d)   notwithstanding Subsection 34A-2-103(4), an individual who provides domestic work for a person if:

(i)   the person for whom the domestic work is being provided receives or is eligible to receive the domestic work under a state or federal program designed to pay the costs of domestic work to prevent the person from being placed in:

(A)   an institution; or

(B)   a more restrictive placement than where that person resides at the time the person receives the domestic work;

(ii)   the individual is paid by a person designated by the Secretary of the Treasury in accordance with Section 3504, Internal Revenue Code, as a fiduciary, agent, or other person that has the control, receipt, custody, or disposal of, or pays the wages of the individual; and

(iii)   the domestic work is performed under a written contract that notifies the individual that the individual is not an employee under this chapter or Chapter 3, Utah Occupational Disease Act; or

(e)   subject to Subsections (6) and (7), an individual who:

(i)   (A)   owns a motor vehicle; or

(B)   leases a motor vehicle to a motor carrier;

(ii)   personally operates the motor vehicle described in Subsection (5)(e)(i);

(iii)   operates the motor vehicle described in Subsection (5)(e)(i) under a written agreement with the motor carrier that states that the individual operates the motor vehicle as an independent contractor; and

(iv)   (A)   provides to the motor carrier at the time the written agreement described in Subsection (5)(e)(iii) is executed or as soon after the execution as provided by the commission, a copy of a workers' compensation coverage waiver issued pursuant to Part 10, Workers' Compensation Coverage Waivers Act, to the individual; and

(B)   provides to the motor carrier at the time the written agreement described in Subsection (5)(e)(iii) is executed or as soon after the execution as provided by an insurer, proof that the individual is covered by occupational accident related insurance with the coverage and benefit limits listed in Subsection (7)(c).

(6)   An individual described in Subsection (5)(d) or (e) may become an employee under this chapter and Chapter 3, Utah Occupational Disease Act, if the employer of the individual complies with:

    (a)   this chapter and Chapter 3, Utah Occupational Disease Act; and

    (b)   commission rules.

(7)   For purposes of Subsection (5)(e):

    (a)   "Motor carrier" means a person engaged in the business of transporting freight, merchandise, or other property by a commercial vehicle on a highway within this state.

    (b)   "Motor vehicle" means a self-propelled vehicle intended primarily for use and operation on the highways, including a trailer or semitrailer designed for use with another motorized vehicle.

    (c)   "Occupational accident related insurance" means insurance that provides the following coverage at a minimum aggregate policy limit of $1,000,000 for all benefits paid, including medical expense benefits, for an injury sustained in the course of working under a written agreement described in Subsection (5)(e)(iii):

        (i)   disability benefits;

        (ii)   eath benefits;

        (iii)   medical expense benefits, which include:

            (A)   hospital coverage;

            (B)   surgical coverage;

            (C)   prescription drug coverage; and

            (D)   dental coverage.

34A-2-105. Exclusive remedy against employer, and officer, agent, or employee of employer — Employee leasing arrangements.

(1)   The right to recover compensation pursuant to this chapter for injuries sustained by an employee, whether resulting in death or not, shall be the exclusive remedy against the employer and shall be the exclusive remedy against any officer, agent, or employee of the employer and the liabilities of the employer imposed by this chapter shall be in place of any and all other civil liability whatsoever, at common law or otherwise, to the employee or to the employee's spouse, widow, children, parents, dependents, next of kin, heirs, personal representatives, guardian, or any other person whomsoever, on account of any accident or injury or death, in any way contracted, sustained, aggravated, or incurred by the employee in the course of or because of or arising out of the employee's employment, and no action at law may be maintained against an employer or against any officer, agent, or employee of the employer based upon any accident, injury, or death of an employee. Nothing in this section, however, shall prevent an employee, or the employee's dependents, from filing a claim for compensation in those cases in accordance with Chapter 3, Utah Occupational Disease Act.

(2)   The exclusive remedy provisions of this section apply to both the client company and the employee leasing company in an employee leasing arrangement under Title 58, Chapter 59, Professional Employer Organization Registration Act.

(3)   (a)   For purposes of this section:

        (i)   "Temporary employee" means an individual who for temporary work assignment is:

            (A)   an employee of a temporary staffing company; or

(B)   registered by or otherwise associated with a temporary staffing company.

(ii)   "Temporary staffing company" means a company that engages in the assignment of individuals as temporary fulltime or parttime employees to fill assignments with a finite ending date to another independent entity.

(b)   If the temporary staffing company secures the payment of workers' compensation in accordance with Section 34A-2-201 for all temporary employees of the temporary staffing company, the exclusive remedy provisions of this section apply to both the temporary staffing company and the client company and its employees and provide the temporary staffing company the same protection that a client company and its employees has under this section for the acts of any of the temporary staffing company's temporary employees on assignment at the client company worksite.

34A-2-106. Injuries or death caused by wrongful acts of persons other than employer, officer, agent, or employee of employer — Rights of employer or insurance carrier in cause of action — Maintenance of action — Notice of intention to proceed against third party — Right to maintain action not involving employeeemployer relationship — Disbursement of proceeds of recovery — Exclusive remedy.

(1)   When any injury or death for which compensation is payable under this chapter or Chapter 3, Utah Occupational Disease Act is caused by the wrongful act or neglect of a person other than an employer, officer, agent, or employee of the employer:

(a)   the injured employee, or in case of death, the employee's dependents, may claim compensation; and

(b)   the injured employee or the employee's heirs or personal representative may have an action for damages against the third person.

(2)   (a)   If compensation is claimed and the employer or insurance carrier becomes

obligated to pay compensation, the employer or insurance carrier:

(i)   shall become trustee of the cause of action against the third party; and

(ii)   may bring and maintain the action either in its own name or in the name of the injured employee, or the employee's heirs or the personal representative of the deceased.

(b)   Notwithstanding Subsection (2)(a), an employer or insurance carrier may not settle and release a cause of action of which it is a trustee under Subsection (2)(a) without the consent of the commission.

(3)   (a)   Before proceeding against a third party, to give a person described in Subsections (3)(a) (i) and (ii) a reasonable opportunity to enter an appearance in the proceeding, the injured employee or, in case of death, the employee's heirs, shall give written notice of the intention to bring an action against the third party to:

(i)   the carrier; and

(ii)   any other person obligated for the compensation payments.

(b)   The injured employee, or, in case of death, the employee's heirs, shall give written notice to the carrier and other person obligated for the compensation payments of any known attempt to attribute fault to the employer, officer, agent, or employee of the employer:

(i)   by way of settlement; or

(ii)   in a proceeding brought by the injured employee, or, in case of death, the employee's heirs.

(4)   For the purposes of this section and notwithstanding Section 34A-2-103, the injured employee or the employee's heirs or personal representative may also maintain an action for damages against any of the following persons who do not occupy an employeeemployer relationship with the injured or deceased employee at the time of the employee's injury or death:

    (a)   a subcontractor;

    (b)   a general contractor;

    (c)   an independent contractor;

    (d)   a property owner; or

    (e)   a lessee or assignee of a property owner.

(5)   If any recovery is obtained against a third person, it shall be disbursed in accordance with Subsections (5)(a) through (c).

    (a)   The reasonable expense of the action, including attorneys' fees, shall be paid and charged proportionately against the parties as their interests may appear. Any fee chargeable to the employer or carrier is to be a credit upon any fee payable by the injured employee or, in the case of death, by the dependents, for any recovery had against the third party.

    (b)   The person liable for compensation payments shall be reimbursed, less the proportionate share of costs and attorneys' fees provided for in Subsection (5)(a), for the payments made as follows:

        (i)   without reduction based on fault attributed to the employer, officer, agent, or employee of the employer in the action against the third party if the combined percentage of fault attributed to persons immune from suit is determined to be less than 40% prior to any reallocation of fault under Subsection 782739(2); or

        (ii)   less the amount of payments made multiplied by the percentage of fault attributed to the employer, officer, agent, or employee of the employer in the action against the third party if the combined percentage of fault attributed to persons immune from suit is determined to be 40% or more prior to any reallocation of fault under Subsection 782739(2).

    (c)   The balance shall be paid to the injured employee, or the employee's heirs in case of death, to be applied to reduce or satisfy in full any obligation thereafter accruing against the person liable for compensation.

(6)   The apportionment of fault to the employer in a civil action against a third party is not an action at law and does not impose any liability on the employer. The apportionment of fault does not alter or diminish the exclusiveness of the remedy provided to employees, their heirs, or personal representatives, or the immunity provided employers pursuant to Section 34A-2-105 or 34A3102 for injuries sustained by an employee, whether resulting in death or not. Any court in which a civil action is pending shall issue a partial summary judgment to an employer with respect to the employer's immunity as provided in Section 34A-2-105 or 34A3102, even though the conduct of the employer may be considered in allocating fault to the employer in a third party action in the manner provided in Sections 782737 through 782743.

34A-2-107. Appointment of workers' compensation advisory council — Composition — Terms of members — Duties — Compensation.

(1)   The commissioner shall appoint a workers' compensation advisory council composed of:

    (a)   the following voting members:

        (i)   five employer representatives; and

           (ii)   five employee representatives; and

    (b)   the following nonvoting members:

           (i)   a representative of the Workers' Compensation Fund;

           (ii)   a representative of a private insurance carrier;

           (iii)   a representative of health care providers;

           (iv)   the Utah insurance commissioner or the insurance commissioner's designee; and

           (v)   the commissioner or the commissioner's designee.

(2)   Employers and employees shall consider nominating members of groups who historically may have been excluded from the council, such as women, minorities, and individuals with disabilities.

(3)   (a)   Except as required by Subsection (3)(b), as terms of current council members expire, the commissioner shall appoint each new member or reappointed member to a two-year term beginning July 1 and ending June 30.

    (b)   Notwithstanding the requirements of Subsection (3)(a), the commissioner shall, at the time of appointment or reappointment, adjust the length of terms to ensure that the terms of council members are staggered so that approximately half of the council is appointed every two years.

(4)   (a)   When a vacancy occurs in the membership for any reason, the replacement shall be appointed for the unexpired term.

    (b)   The commissioner shall terminate the term of a council member who ceases to be representative as designated by the member's original appointment.

(5)   (a)   The council shall confer at least quarterly for the purpose of advising the commission, the division, and the Legislature on:

           (i)   the Utah workers' compensation and occupational disease laws;

           (ii)   the administration of the laws described in Subsection (5)(a)(i);

           (iii)   rules related to the laws described in Subsection (5)(a)(i); and

           (iv)   advising the Legislature in accordance with Subsection (5)(b).

    (b)   (i)   The council and the commission shall jointly study during 2009 the premium assessment under Section **59-9-101** on an admitted insurer writing workers' compensation insurance in this state and on a self-insured employer under Section **34A-2-202** as to:

                (A)   whether or not the premium assessment should be changed; or

                (B)   whether or not changes should be made to how the premium assessment is used.

           (ii)   The council and commission shall jointly report the results of the study described in this Subsection to the Business and Labor Interim Committee by no later than the 2009 November interim meeting.

(6)   Regarding workers' compensation, rehabilitation, and reemployment of employees who acquire a disability because of an industrial injury or occupational disease the council shall:

    (a)   offer advice on issues requested by:

           (i)   the commission;

           (ii)   the division; and

              (iii)   the Legislature; and

     (b)   make recommendations to:

              (i)   the commission; and

              (ii)   the division.

(7)   The commissioner or the commissioner's designee shall serve as the chair of the council and call the necessary meetings.

(8)   The commission shall provide staff support to the council.

(9)   A member may not receive compensation or benefits for the member's service, but may receive per diem and travel expenses in accordance with:

     (a)   Section **63A-3-106**;

     (b)   Section **63A-3-107**; and

     (c)   rules made by the Division of Finance pursuant to Sections **63A-3-106** and **63A-3-107**.

34A-2-108. Void agreements between employers and employees.

(1)   Except as provided in Section 34A-2-420, an agreement by an employee to waive the employee's rights to compensation under this chapter or Chapter 3, Utah Occupational Disease Act, is not valid.

(2)   An agreement by an employee to pay any portion of the premium paid by his employer is not valid.

(3)   Any employer who deducts any portion of the premium from the wages or salary of any employee entitled to the benefits of this chapter or Chapter 3, Utah Occupational Disease Act:

     (a)   is guilty of a misdemeanor; and

     (b)   shall be fined not more than $100 for each such offense.

34A-2-109. Interstate and intrastate commerce.

(1)   Except as provided in Subsection (2), this chapter and Chapter 3, Utah Occupational Disease Act, apply to employers and their employees engaged in:

     (a)   intrastate commerce;

     (b)   interstate commerce; and

     (c)   foreign commerce.

(2)   If a rule of liability or method of compensation is established by the Congress of the United States as to interstate or foreign commerce, this chapter and Chapter 3 apply only to the extent that:

     (a)   this chapter and Chapter 3 has a mutual connection with intrastate work; and

     (b)   the connection to intrastate work is clearly separable and distinguishable from interstate or foreign commerce.

34A-2-110. Workers' compensation insurance fraud — Elements — Penalties — Notice.

(1)   As used in this section:

     (a)   "Corporation" has the same meaning as in Section **76-2-201**.

     (b)   "Intentionally" has the same meaning as in Section **76-2-103**.

     (c)   "Knowingly" has the same meaning as in Section **76-2-103**.

     (d)   "Person" has the same meaning as in Section **76-1-601**.

(e) "Recklessly" has the same meaning as in Section **76-2-103**.

(f) "Thing of value" means one or more of the following obtained under this chapter or Chapter 3, Utah Occupational Disease Act:

(i) workers' compensation insurance coverage;

(ii) disability compensation;

(iii) a medical benefit;

(iv) a good;

(v) a professional service;

(vi) a fee for a professional service; or

(vii) anything of value.

(2) (a) A person is guilty of workers' compensation insurance fraud if that person intentionally, knowingly, or recklessly:

(i) devises a scheme or artifice to do the following by means of a false or fraudulent pretense, representation, promise, or material omission:

(A) obtain a thing of value under this chapter or Chapter 3;

(B) avoid paying the premium that an insurer charges, for an employee on the basis of the underwriting criteria applicable to that employee, to obtain a thing of value under this chapter or Chapter 3; or

(C) deprive an employee of a thing of value under this chapter or Chapter 3; and

(ii) communicates or causes a communication with another in furtherance of the scheme or artifice.

(b) A violation of this Subsection (2) includes a scheme or artifice to:

(i) make or cause to be made a false written or oral statement with the intent to obtain insurance coverage as mandated by this chapter or Chapter 3 at a rate that does not reflect the risk, industry, employer, or class code actually covered by the insurance coverage;

(ii) form a business, reorganize a business, or change ownership in a business with the intent to:

(A) obtain insurance coverage as mandated by this chapter or Chapter 3 at a rate that does not reflect the risk, industry, employer, or class code actually covered by the insurance coverage;

(B) misclassify an employee as described in Subsection (2)(b)(iii); or

(C) deprive an employee of workers' compensation coverage as required by Subsection **34A-2-103**(8);

(iii) misclassify an employee as one of the following so as to avoid the obligation to obtain insurance coverage as mandated by this chapter or Chapter 3:

(A) an independent contractor;

(B) a sole proprietor;

(C) an owner;

(D) a partner;

(E) an officer; or

     (F) a member in a limited liability company;

   (iv) use a workers' compensation coverage waiver issued under Part 10, Workers' Compensation Coverage Waivers Act, to deprive an employee of workers' compensation coverage under this chapter or Chapter 3; or

   (v) collect or make a claim for temporary disability compensation as provided in Section **34A-2-410** while working for gain.

(3) (a) Workers' compensation insurance fraud under Subsection (2) is punishable in the manner prescribed in Subsection (3)(c).

  (b) A corporation or association is guilty of the offense of workers' compensation insurance fraud under the same conditions as those set forth in Section **76-2-204**.

  (c) (i) In accordance with Subsection (3)(c)(ii), the determination of the degree of an offense under Subsection (2) shall be measured by the following on the basis of which creates the greatest penalty:

    (A) the total value of all property, money, or other things obtained or sought to be obtained by the scheme or artifice described in Subsection (2); or

    (B) the number of individuals not covered under this chapter or Chapter 3 because of the scheme or artifice described in Subsection (2).

   (ii) A person is guilty of:

    (A) a class A misdemeanor:

     (I) if the value of the property, money, or other thing of value described in Subsection (3)(c)(i)(A) is less than $1,000; or

     (II) for each individual described in Subsection (3)(c)(i)(B), if the number of individuals described in Subsection (3)(c)(i)(B) is less than five;

    (B) a third degree felony:

     (I) if the value of the property, money, or other thing of value described in Subsection (3)(c)(i)(A) is equal to or greater than $1,000, but is less than $5,000; or

     (II) for each individual described in Subsection (3)(c)(i)(B), if the number of individuals described in Subsection (3)(c)(i)(B) is equal to or greater than five, but is less than 50; and

    (C) a second degree felony:

     (I) if the value of the property, money, or other thing of value described in Subsection (3)(c)(i)(A) is equal to or greater than $5,000; or

     (II) for each individual described in Subsection (3)(c)(i)(B), if the number of individuals described in Subsection (3)(c)(i)(B) is equal to or greater than 50.

(4) The following are not a necessary element of an offense described in Subsection (2):

  (a) reliance on the part of a person;

  (b) the intent on the part of the perpetrator of an offense described in Subsection (2) to permanently deprive a person of property, money, or anything of value; or

  (c) an insurer or self-insured employer giving written notice in accordance with Subsection (5) that workers' compensation insurance fraud is a crime.

(5)　(a)　An insurer or self-insured employer who, in connection with this chapter or Chapter 3, Utah Occupational Disease Act, prints, reproduces, or furnishes a form described in Subsection (5)(b) shall cause to be printed or displayed in comparative prominence with other content on the form the statement: "Any person who knowingly presents false or fraudulent underwriting information, files or causes to be filed a false or fraudulent claim for disability compensation or medical benefits, or submits a false or fraudulent report or billing for health care fees or other professional services is guilty of a crime and may be subject to fines and confinement in state prison."

　　　　(b)　Subsection (5)(a) applies to a form upon which a person:

　　　　　　(i)　applies for insurance coverage;

　　　　　　(ii)　applies for a workers' compensation coverage waiver issued under Part 10, Workers' Compensation Coverage Waivers Act;

　　　　　　(iii)　reports payroll;

　　　　　　(iv)　makes a claim by reason of accident, injury, death, disease, or other claimed loss; or

　　　　　　(v)　makes a report or gives notice to an insurer or self-insured employer.

　　　　(c)　An insurer or self-insured employer who issues a check, warrant, or other financial instrument in payment of compensation issued under this chapter or Chapter 3 shall cause to be printed or displayed in comparative prominence above the area for endorsement a statement substantially similar to the following: "Workers' compensation insurance fraud is a crime punishable by Utah law."

　　　　(d)　This Subsection (5) applies only to the legal obligations of an insurer or a self-insured employer.

　　　　(e)　A person who violates Subsection (2) is guilty of workers' compensation insurance fraud, and the failure of an insurer or a self-insured employer to fully comply with this Subsection (5) is not:

　　　　　　(i)　a defense to violating Subsection (2); or

　　　　　　(ii)　grounds for suppressing evidence.

(6)　In the absence of malice, a person, employer, insurer, or governmental entity that reports a suspected fraudulent act relating to a workers' compensation insurance policy or claim is not subject to civil liability for libel, slander, or another relevant cause of action.

(7)　In an action involving workers' compensation, this section supersedes Title 31A, Chapter 31, Insurance Fraud Act.

34A-2-111. Managed health care programs — Other safety programs.

(1)　As used in this section:

　　　　(a)　(i)　"Health care provider" means a person who furnishes treatment or care to persons who have suffered bodily injury.

　　　　　　(ii)　"Health care provider" includes:

　　　　　　　　(A)　a hospital;

　　　　　　　　(B)　a clinic;

　　　　　　　　(C)　an emergency care center;

　　　　　　　　(D)　a physician;

                  (E)   a nurse;

                  (F)   a nurse practitioner;

                  (G)   a physician's assistant;

                  (H)   a paramedic; or

                  (I)   an emergency medical technician.

(b)   "Physician" means any health care provider licensed under:

    (i)   Title 58, Chapter 5a, Podiatric Physician Licensing Act;

    (ii)   Title 58, Chapter 24b, Physical Therapy Practice Act;

    (iii)   Title 58, Chapter 67, Utah Medical Practice Act;

    (iv)   Title 58, Chapter 68, Utah Osteopathic Medical Practice Act;

    (v)(Title 58, Chapter 69, Dentist and Dental Hygienist Practice Act;

    (vi)   Title 58, Chapter 70a, Physician Assistant Act;

    (vii) Title 58, Chapter 71, Naturopathic Physician Practice Act;

    (viii) Title 58, Chapter 72, Acupuncture Licensing Act; and

    (ix)   Title 58, Chapter 73, Chiropractic Physician Practice Act.

(c)   "Preferred health care facility" means a facility:

    (i)   that is a health care facility as defined in Section **26-21-2**; and

    (ii)   designated under a managed health care program.

(d)   "Preferred provider physician" means a physician designated under a managed health care program.

(e)   "Self-insured employer" is as defined in Section **34A-2-201.5**.

(2)   (a)   A self-insured employer and insurance carrier may adopt a managed health care program to provide employees the benefits of this chapter or Chapter 3, Utah Occupational Disease Act, beginning January 1, 1993. The plan shall comply with this Subsection (2).

    (b)   (i)   A preferred provider program may be developed if the preferred provider program allows a selection by the employee of more than one physician in the health care specialty required for treating the specific problem of an industrial patient.

         (ii)   (A)   Subject to the requirements of this section, if a preferred provider program is developed by an insurance carrier or self-insured employer, an employee is required to use:

              (I)   preferred provider physicians; and

              (II)   preferred health care facilities.

           (B)   If a preferred provider program is not developed, an employee may have free choice of health care providers.

         (iii)   The failure to do the following may, if the employee has been notified of the preferred provider program, result in the employee being obligated for any charges in excess of the preferred provider allowances:

           (A)   use a preferred health care facility; or

           (B)   initially receive treatment from a preferred provider physician.

(iv) Notwithstanding the requirements of Subsections (2)(b)(i) through (iii), a self-insured employer or other employer may:

    (A) (I) (Aa) have its own health care facility on or near its worksite or premises; and

           (Bb) continue to contract with other health care providers; or

      (II) operate a health care facility; and

    (B) require employees to first seek treatment at the provided health care or contracted facility.

(v) An employee subject to a preferred provider program or employed by an employer having its own health care facility may procure the services of any qualified health care provider:

    (A) for emergency treatment, if a physician employed in the preferred provider program or at the health care facility is not available for any reason;

    (B) for conditions the employee in good faith believes are nonindustrial; or

    (C) when an employee living in a rural area would be unduly burdened by traveling to:

      (I) a preferred provider physician; or

      (II) preferred health care facility.

(c) (i) (A) An employer, insurance carrier, or self-insured employer may enter into contracts with the following for the purposes listed in Subsection (2)(c)(i)(B):

    (I) health care providers;

    (II) medical review organizations; or

    (III) vendors of medical goods, services, and supplies including medicines.

    (B) A contract described in Subsection (1)(c)(i)(A) may be made for the following purposes:

      (I) insurance carriers or self-insured employers may form groups in contracting for managed health care services with health care providers;

      (II) peer review;

      (III) methods of utilization review;

      (IV) use of case management;

      (V) discounted purchasing; and

      (VI) the establishment of a reasonable health care treatment protocol program including the implementation of medical treatment and quality care guidelines that are:

        (Aa) scientifically based;

        (Bb) peer reviewed; and

        (Cc) consistent with standards for health care treatment protocol programs that the commission shall establish by rules made in accordance with Title 63G, Chapter 3, Utah Administrative Rulemaking Act, including the authority of the commission to approve a health care treatment protocol program before it is used or disapprove a health care treatment protocol program that does not comply with this Subsection (2)(c)(i)(B)(VII).

  (ii) An insurance carrier may make any or all of the factors in Subsection (2)(c)(i) a condition of insuring an entity in its insurance contract.

(3) (a) In addition to a managed health care program, an insurance carrier may require an employer to establish a work place safety program if the employer:

  (i) has an experience modification factor of 1.00 or higher, as determined by the National Council on Compensation Insurance; or

  (ii) is determined by the insurance carrier to have a three-year loss ratio of 100% or higher.

 (b) A workplace safety program may include:

  (i) a written workplace accident and injury reduction program that:

   (A) promotes safe and healthful working conditions; and

   (B) is based on clearly stated goals and objectives for meeting those goals; and

  (ii) a documented review of the workplace accident and injury reduction program each calendar year delineating how procedures set forth in the program are met.

 (c) A written workplace accident and injury reduction program permitted under Subsection (3)(b)(i) should describe:

  (i) how managers, supervisors, and employees are responsible for implementing the program;

  (ii) how continued participation of management will be established, measured, and maintained;

  (iii) the methods used to identify, analyze, and control new or existing hazards, conditions, and operations;

  (iv) how the program will be communicated to all employees so that the employees are informed of work-related hazards and controls;

  (v) how workplace accidents will be investigated and corrective action implemented; and

  (vi) how safe work practices and rules will be enforced.

 (d) For the purposes of a workplace accident and injury reduction program of an eligible employer described in Subsection **34A-2-103**(7)(f), the workplace accident and injury reduction program shall:

  (i) include the provisions described in Subsections (3)(b) and (c), except that the employer shall conduct a documented review of the workplace accident and injury reduction program at least semiannually delineating how procedures set forth in the workplace accident and injury reduction program are met; and

  (ii) require a written agreement between the employer and all contractors and subcontractors on a project that states that:

   (A) the employer has the right to control the manner or method by which the work is executed;

       (B)   if a contractor, subcontractor, or any employee of a contractor or subcontractor violates the workplace accident and injury reduction program, the employer maintains the right to:

           (I)   terminate the contract with the contractor or subcontractor;

           (II)   remove the contractor or subcontractor from the work site; or

           (III)   require that the contractor or subcontractor not permit an employee that violates the workplace accident and injury reduction program to work on the project for which the employer is procuring work; and

       (C)   the contractor or subcontractor shall provide safe and appropriate equipment subject to the right of the employer to:

           (I)   inspect on a regular basis the equipment of a contractor or subcontractor; and

           (II)   require that the contractor or subcontractor repair, replace, or remove equipment the employer determines not to be safe or appropriate.

(4)   The premiums charged to any employer who fails or refuses to establish a workplace safety program pursuant to Subsection (3)(b)(i) or (ii) may be increased by 5% over any existing current rates and premium modifications charged that employer.

34A-2-112. Administration of this chapter and Chapter 3.

(1)   Administration of this chapter and Chapter 3, Utah Occupational Disease Act, is vested in the commission to be administered through the division, the Division of Adjudication, and for administrative appeals through the commissioner and the Appeals Board.

(2)   The commission:

       (a)   has jurisdiction over every workplace in the state and may administer this chapter and Chapter 3, Utah Occupational Disease Act, and any rule or order issued under these chapters, to ensure that every employee in this state has a safe workplace in which employers have secured the payment of workers' compensation benefits for their employees in accordance with this chapter and Chapter 3, Utah Occupational Disease Act;

       (b)   through the division under the supervision of the director, has the duty and full authority to take any administrative action authorized under this chapter or Chapter 3, Utah Occupational Disease Act; and

       (c)   through the Division of Adjudication, commissioner, and Appeals Board, provide for the adjudication and review of an administrative action, decision, or order of the commission in accordance with this title.

34A-2-113. Designated agent required.

Each workers' compensation insurance carrier writing insurance in this state shall maintain a designated agent in this state that is:

(1)   registered with the division; and

(2)   authorized to receive on behalf of the workers' compensation insurance carrier all notices or orders provided for under this chapter or Chapter 3, Utah Occupational Disease Act.

34A-2-201. Employers to secure workers' compensation benefits for employees — Methods.

An employer shall secure the payment of workers' compensation benefits for its employees by:

(1) insuring, and keeping insured, the payment of this compensation with the Workers' Compensation Fund;

(2) insuring, and keeping insured, the payment of this compensation with any stock corporation or mutual association authorized to transact the business of workers' compensation insurance in this state; or

(3) obtaining approval from the division in accordance with Section 34A-2-201.5 to pay direct compensation as a self-insured employer in the amount, in the manner, and when due as provided for in this chapter or Chapter 3, Utah Occupational Disease Act.

34A-2-201.3. Direct payments prohibited except by self-insured employer.

(1) An employer who is not a self-insured employer, as defined in Section **34A-2-201.5**, may not pay a benefit provided for under this chapter and Chapter 3, Utah Occupational Disease Act, directly:

(a)   to an employee; or

(b)   for the employee.

(2) (a)   Subject to Title 63G, Chapter 4, Administrative Procedures Act, if the division finds that an employer is violating or has violated Subsection (1), the division shall send written notice to the employer of the requirements of this section and Section **34A-2-201**.

(b)   The division shall send the notice described in Subsection (2)(a) to the last address on the records of the commission for the employer.

(3) (a)   If, after the division mails the notice required by Subsection (2) to an employer, the employer again violates Subsection (1), the division may impose a penalty against the employer of up to $1,000 for each violation.

(b)   If, after the division imposes a penalty under Subsection (3)(a) against the employer, the employer again violates Subsection (1), the division may impose a penalty of up to $5,000 for each violation.

(4) (a)   The division shall deposit a penalty imposed under Subsection (3) into the Uninsured Employers' Fund created by Section **34A-2-704** to be used for the purposes of the Uninsured Employers' Fund specified in Section **34A-2-704**.

(b)   The administrator of the Uninsured Employers' Fund shall collect money required to be deposited into the Uninsured Employers' Fund under this Subsection (4) in accordance with Section **34A-2-704**.

(5) A penalty under this section is in addition to any other penalty imposed under this chapter or Chapter 3, Utah Occupational Disease Act, against an employer who fails to comply with Section **34A-2-201**.

(6) In accordance with Title 63G, Chapter 3, Utah Administrative Rulemaking Act, the commission shall adopt rules to implement this section.

34A-2-201.5. Self-insured employer — Acceptable security — Procedures.

(1) As used in this section:

(a)   "Acceptable security" means one or more of the following:

(i)   cash;

(ii)   a surety bond issued:

           (A)   by a person acceptable to the division; and

           (B)   in a form approved by the division;

      (iii)   an irrevocable letter of credit issued:

           (A)   by a depository institution acceptable to the division; and

           (B)   in a form approved by the division;

      (iv)   a United States Treasury Bill;

      (v)   a deposit in a depository institution that:

           (A)   has an office located in Utah; and

           (B)   is insured by the Federal Deposit Insurance Corporation; or

      (vi)   a certificate of deposit in a depository institution that:

           (A)   has an office located in Utah; and

           (B)   is insured by the Federal Deposit Insurance Corporation.

(b)   "Compensation" is as defined in Section 34A-2-102.

(c)   "Depository institution" is as defined in Section 71103.

(d)   "Member of a public agency insurance mutual" means a political subdivision or public agency that is included within a public agency insurance mutual.

(e)   "Public agency insurance mutual" is as defined in Section 31A1103.

(f)   "Self-insured employer" means one of the following that is authorized by the division to pay direct workers' compensation benefits under Subsection (2):

      (i)   an employer; or

      (ii)   a public agency insurance mutual.

(2)   (a)   If approved by the division as a self-insured employer in accordance with this section:

      (i)   an employer may directly pay compensation in the amount, in the manner, and when due as provided for in this chapter and Chapter 3, Utah Occupational Disease Act; and

      (ii)   a public agency insurance mutual may directly pay compensation:

           (A)   on behalf of the members of the public agency insurance mutual; and

           (B)   in the amount, in the manner, and when due as provided in this chapter and Chapter 3, Utah Occupational Disease Act.

(b)   If an employer's or a public agency insurance mutual's application to directly pay compensation as a self-insured employer is approved by the division, the application is considered acceptance:

      (i)   of the conditions, liabilities, and responsibilities imposed by this chapter and Chapter 3, Utah Occupational Disease Act, including the liability imposed pursuant to Subsection 34A-2-704(14);

      (ii)   by:

           (A)   the employer; or

           (B)   (I)   the public agency insurance mutual; and

                 (II)   the members of the public agency insurance mutual.

(c)   The division's denial under this Subsection (2) of an application to directly pay compensation as a self-insured employer becomes a final order of the commission 30 calendar days from the date of the denial unless within that 30 days the employer or the public agency insurance mutual that filed the application files an application for a hearing in accordance with Part 8, Adjudication.

(3)   To qualify as a self-insured employer, an employer or a public agency insurance mutual shall:

(a)   submit a written application requesting to directly pay compensation as a self-insured employer;

(b)   annually provide the division proof of the employer's or the public agency insurance mutual's ability to directly pay compensation in the amount, manner, and time provided by this chapter and Chapter 3, Utah Occupational Disease Act; and

(c)   if requested by the division, deposit acceptable security in the amounts determined by the division to be sufficient to secure the employer's or the public agency insurance mutual's liabilities under this chapter and Chapter 3, Utah Occupational Disease Act.

(4)   (a)   Acceptable security deposited by a self-insured employer in accordance with Subsection (3)(c) shall be:

(i)   deposited on behalf of the division by the self-insured employer with the state treasurer; and

(ii)   withdrawn only upon written order of the division.

(b)   The self-insured employer has no right, title, interest in, or control over acceptable security that is deposited in accordance with this section.

(c)   If the division determines that the amount of acceptable security deposited in accordance with this section is in excess of that needed to secure payment of the self-insured employer's liability under this chapter and Chapter 3, Utah Occupational Disease Act, the division shall return the amount that is determined to be excess to the self-insured employer.

(5)   (a)   The division may at any time require a self-insured employer to:

(i)   increase or decrease the amount of acceptable security required to be deposited under Subsection (3)(c); or

(ii)   modify the type of acceptable security to be deposited under Subsection (3)(c).

(b)   (i)   If the division requires a self-insured employer to take an action described in Subsection (5)(a), a perfected security interest is created in favor of the division in the assets of the self-insured employer to the extent necessary to pay any amount owed by the self-insured employer under this chapter and Chapter 3, Utah Occupational Disease Act, that cannot be paid by acceptable security deposited in accordance with this section.

(ii)   The perfected security interest created in Subsection (5)(b)(i) ends when the self-insured employer complies with the division's request under Subsection (5)(a) to the satisfaction of the division.

(6)   (a)   If an employer or a public agency insurance mutual is approved under Subsection (2) to directly pay compensation as a self-insured employer, the division may revoke the employer's or the public agency insurance mutual's approval.

(b)   The division's revocation of the employer's or the public agency insurance mutual's approval under Subsection (6)(a) becomes a final order of the commission 30 calendar days from the date of the revocation unless within that 30 days the employer or the public agency insurance mutual files an application for a hearing in accordance with Part 8, Adjudication.

(7)   If the division finds that a self-insured employer has failed to pay compensation that the self-insured employer was liable to pay under this chapter or Chapter 3, Utah Occupational Disease Act, the division may use the acceptable security deposited and any interest earned on the acceptable security to pay:

    (a)   the self-insured employer's liability under this chapter and Chapter 3, Utah Occupational Disease Act; and

    (b)   any costs, including legal fees, associated with the administration of the compensation incurred by:

        (i)   the division;

        (ii)   a surety;

        (iii)   an adjusting agency; or

        (iv)   the Uninsured Employers' Fund.

(8)   (a)   If the division determines that the acceptable security deposited under Subsection (3)(c) should be available for payment of the self-insured employer's liabilities under Subsection (7), the division shall:

        (i)   determine the method of claims administration, which may include administration by:

            (A)   a surety;

            (B)   an adjusting agency;

            (C)   the Uninsured Employers' Fund; or

            (D)   any combination of Subsections (8)(a)(i)(A) through (C); and

        (ii)   audit the self-insured employer's liabilities under this chapter and Chapter 3, Utah Occupational Disease Act.

    (b)   The following shall cooperate in the division's audit under Subsection (8)(a)(ii) and provide any relevant information in its possession:

        (i)   the self-insured employer;

        (ii)   if the self-insured employer is a public agency insurance mutual, a member of the public agency insurance mutual;

        (iii)   any excess insurer;

        (iv)   any adjusting agency;

        (v)   a surety;

        (vi)   an employee of a self-insured employer if the employee makes a claim for compensation under this chapter or Chapter 3, Utah Occupational Disease Act; and

        (vii)   an employee of a member of a public agency insurance mutual that is approved as a self-insured employer under this section, if the employee makes a claim for compensation under this chapter or Chapter 3, Utah Occupational Disease Act.

(9)   (a)   Payment by a surety is a full release of the surety's liability under the bond to the extent of that payment, and entitles the surety to full reimbursement by the principal or the principal's estate including reimbursement of:

(i)   necessary attorney's fees; and

(ii)   other costs and expenses.

(b)   A payment, settlement, or administration of benefits made in good faith pursuant to this section by a surety, an adjusting agency, the Uninsured Employers' Fund, or this division is valid and binding as between:

    (i)   (A)   the surety;

          (B)   adjusting agency;

          (C)   the Uninsured Employers' Fund; or

          (D)   the division;

    (ii)   the self-insured employer; and

    (iii)   if the self-insured employer is a public agency insurance mutual, the members of the public agency insurance mutual.

(10)   (a)   The division shall resolve any dispute concerning:

    (i)   the depositing, renewal, termination, exoneration, or return of all or any portion of acceptable security deposited under this section;

    (ii)   any liability arising out of the depositing or failure to deposit acceptable security;

    (iii)   the adequacy of the acceptable security; or

    (iv)   the reasonableness of administrative costs under Subsection (7)(b), including legal fees.

(b)   The division's decision under Subsection (10)(a) becomes a final order of the commission 30 calendar days from the date of the decision, unless within that 30 days the employer or public agency insurance mutual files an application for hearing in accordance with Part 8, Adjudication.

34A-2-202. Assessment on self-insured employers including the state, counties, cities, towns, or school districts paying compensation direct.

(1)   (a)   (i)   A self-insured employer, including a county, city, town, or school district, shall pay annually, on or before March 31, an assessment in accordance with this section and rules made by the commission under this section.

        (ii)   For purposes of this section, "self-insured employer" is as defined in Section **34A-2-201.5**, except it includes the state if the state self-insures under Section **34A-2-203**.

   (b)   The assessment required by Subsection (1)(a) is:

        (i)   to be collected by the State Tax Commission;

        (ii)   paid by the State Tax Commission into the state treasury as provided in Subsection **59-9-101**(2); and

        (iii) subject to the offset provided in Section **34A-2-202.5**.

   (c)   The assessment under Subsection (1)(a) shall be based on a total calculated premium multiplied by the premium assessment rate established pursuant to Subsection **59-9-101**(2).

   (d)   The total calculated premium, for purposes of calculating the assessment under Subsection (1)(a), shall be calculated by:

        (i)   multiplying the total of the standard premium for each class code calculated in Subsection (1)(e) by the self-insured employer's experience modification factor; and

        (ii)   multiplying the total under Subsection (1)(d)(i) by a safety factor determined under Subsection (1)(g).

(e)   A standard premium shall be calculated by:

        (i)   multiplying the prospective loss cost for the year being considered, as filed with the insurance department pursuant to Section **31A-19a-406**, for each applicable class code by 1.10 to determine the manual rate for each class code; and

        (ii)   multiplying the manual rate for each class code under Subsection (1)(e)(i) by each $100 of the self-insured employer's covered payroll for each class code.

(f)   (i)   Each self-insured employer paying compensation direct shall annually obtain the experience modification factor required in Subsection (1)(d)(i) by using:

           (A)   the rate service organization designated by the insurance commissioner in Section **31A-19a-404**; or

           (B)   or a self-insured employer that is a public agency insurance mutual, an actuary approved by the commission.

        (ii)   If a self-insured employer's experience modification factor under Subsection (1)(f)(i) is less than 0.50, the self-insured employer shall use an experience modification factor of 0.50 in determining the total calculated premium.

(g)   To provide incentive for improved safety, the safety factor required in Subsection (1)(d)(ii) shall be determined based on the self-insured employer's experience modification factor as follows:

EXPERIENCE MODIFICATION FACTOR	SAFETY FACTOR
Less than or equal to 0.90	0.56
Greater than 0.90 but less than or equal to 1.00	0.78
Greater than 1.00 but less than or equal to 1.10	1.00
Greater than 1.10 but less than or equal to 1.20	1.22
Greater than 1.20	1.44

(h)   (i)   A premium or premium assessment modification other than a premium or premium assessment modification under this section may not be allowed.

        (ii)   If a self-insured employer paying compensation direct fails to obtain an experience modification factor as required in Subsection (1)(f)(i) within the reasonable time period established by rule by the State Tax Commission, the State Tax Commission shall use an experience modification factor of 2.00 and a safety factor of 2.00 to calculate the total calculated premium for purposes of determining the assessment.

        (iii)   Prior to calculating the total calculated premium under Subsection (1)(h)(ii), the State Tax Commission shall provide the self-insured employer with written notice that failure to obtain an experience modification factor within a reasonable time period, as established by rule by the State Tax Commission:

           (A)   shall result in the State Tax Commission using an experience modification factor of 2.00 and a safety factor of 2.00 in calculating the total calculated premium for purposes of determining the assessment; and

(B)   may result in the division revoking the self-insured employer's right to pay compensation direct.

(I)   The division may immediately revoke a self-insured employer's certificate issued under Sections **34A-2-201** and **34A-2-201.5** that permits the self-insured employer to pay compensation direct if the State Tax Commission assigns an experience modification factor and a safety factor under Subsection because the self-insured employer failed to obtain an experience modification factor.

(2)   Notwithstanding the annual payment requirement in Subsection (1)(a), a self-insured employer whose total assessment obligation under Subsection (1)(a) for the preceding year was $10,000 or more shall pay the assessment in quarterly installments in the same manner provided in Section **59-9-104** and subject to the same penalty provided in Section **59-9-104** for not paying or underpaying an installment.

(3)   (a)   The State Tax Commission shall have access to all the records of the division for the purpose of auditing and collecting any amounts described in this section.

(b)   Time periods for the State Tax Commission to allow a refund or make an assessment shall be determined in accordance with Title 59, Chapter 1, Part 14, Assessment, Collections, and Refunds Act.

(4)   (a)   A review of appropriate use of job class assignment and calculation methodology may be conducted as directed by the division at any reasonable time as a condition of the self-insured employer's certification of paying compensation direct.

(b)   The State Tax Commission shall make any records necessary for the review available to the commission.

(c)   The commission shall make the results of any review available to the State Tax Commission.

34A-2-202.5.   Offset for occupational health and safety related donations.

(1)   As used in this section:

(a)   "Occupational health and safety center" means the Rocky Mountain Center for Occupational and Environmental Health created in Title 53B, Chapter 17, Part 8, Rocky Mountain Center for Occupational and Environmental Health.

(b)   "Qualified donation" means a donation that is:

(i)   cash;

(ii)   given directly to an occupational health and safety center; and

(iii)   given exclusively for the purpose of:

(A)   supporting graduate level education and training in fields of:

(I)   safety and ergonomics;

(II)   industrial hygiene;

(III)   occupational health nursing; and

(IV)   occupational medicine;

(B)   providing continuing education programs for employers designed to promote workplace safety; and

(C)   paying reasonable administrative, personnel, equipment, and overhead costs of the occupational health and safety center.

(c) "Self-insured employer" is a self-insured employer as defined in Section 34A-2-201.5 that is required to pay the assessment imposed under Section 34A-2-202.

(2) (a) A self-insured employer may offset against the assessment imposed under Section 34A-2-202 an amount equal to the lesser of:

(i) the total of qualified donations made by the self-insured employer in the calendar year for which the assessment is calculated; and

(ii) .10% of the self-insured employer's total calculated premium calculated under Subsection 34A-2-202(1)(d) for the calendar year for which the assessment is calculated.

(b) The offset provided under this Subsection (2) shall be allocated to the restricted account and funds described in Subsection 599101(2)(c) in proportion to the rates provided in Subsection 599101(2)(c).

(3) An occupational health and safety center shall:

(a) provide a self-insured employer a receipt for any qualified donation made by the self-insured employer to the occupational health and safety center;

(b) expend monies received by a qualified donation:

(i) for the purposes described in Subsection (1)(b)(iii); and

(ii) in a manner that can be audited to ensure that the monies are expended for the purposes described in Subsection (1)(b)(iii); and

(c) in conjunction with the report required by Section 599102.5, report to the Legislature through the Office of the Legislative Fiscal Analyst by no later than July 1 of each year:

(i) the qualified donations received by the occupational health and safety center in the previous calendar year; and

(ii) the expenditures during the previous calendar year of qualified donations received by the occupational health and safety center.

34A-2-202.5. Offset for occupational health and safety related donations.

(1) As used in this section:

(a) "Occupational health and safety center" means the Rocky Mountain Center for Occupational and Environmental Health created in Title 53B, Chapter 17, Part 8, Rocky Mountain Center for Occupational and Environmental Health.

(b) "Qualified donation" means a donation that is:

(i) cash;

(ii) given directly to an occupational health and safety center; and

(iii) given exclusively for the purpose of:

(A) supporting graduate level education and training in fields of:

(I) safety and ergonomics;

(II) industrial hygiene;

(III) occupational health nursing; and

(IV) occupational medicine;

(B) providing continuing education programs for employers designed to promote workplace safety; and

(C)   paying reasonable administrative, personnel, equipment, and overhead costs of the occupational health and safety center.

(c)   "Self-insured employer" is a self-insured employer as defined in Section **34A-2-201.5** that is required to pay the assessment imposed under Section **34A-2-202**.

(2)   (a)   A self-insured employer may offset against the assessment imposed under Section **34A-2-202** an amount equal to the lesser of:

(i)   the total of qualified donations made by the self-insured employer in the calendar year for which the assessment is calculated; and

(ii)   .10% of the self-insured employer's total calculated premium calculated under Subsection **34A-2-202**(1)(d) for the calendar year for which the assessment is calculated.

(b)   The offset provided under this Subsection (2) shall be allocated in proportion to the percentages provided in Subsection **59-9-101**(2)(c).

(3)   An occupational health and safety center shall:

(a)   provide a self-insured employer a receipt for any qualified donation made by the self-insured employer to the occupational health and safety center;

(b)   expend money received by a qualified donation:

(i)   for the purposes described in Subsection (1)(b)(iii); and

(ii)   in a manner that can be audited to ensure that the money is expended for the purposes described in Subsection (1)(b)(iii); and

(c)   in conjunction with the report required by Section **59-9-102.5**, report to the Legislature through the Office of the Legislative Fiscal Analyst by no later than July 1 of each year:

(i)   the qualified donations received by the occupational health and safety center in the previous calendar year; and

(ii)   the expenditures during the previous calendar year of qualified donations received by the occupational health and safety center.

34A-2-203 (Superseded 05/01/13). Payment of premiums for workers' compensation.

(1)   Until June 30, 2007, a department, commission, board, or other agency of the state shall pay the insurance premium on its employees direct to the Workers' Compensation Fund.

(2)   Beginning July 1, 2007, the state shall secure the payment of workers' compensation benefits for its employees:

(a)   by:

(i)   insuring, and keeping insured, the payment of this compensation with the Workers' Compensation Fund;

(ii)   insuring, and keeping insured, the payment of this compensation with any stock corporation or mutual association authorized to transact the business of workers' compensation insurance in this state; or

(iii)   paying direct compensation as a self-insured employer in the amount, in the manner, and when due as provided for in this chapter or Chapter 3, Utah Occupational Disease Act;

(b)   in accordance with Title 63A, Chapter 4, Risk Management; and

(c)   subject to Subsection (3).

(3)   (a)   If the state determines to secure the payment of workers' compensation benefits for its employees by paying direct compensation as a self-insured employer in the amount, in the manner, and due as provided for in this chapter or Chapter 3, Utah Occupational Disease Act, the state is:

        (i)   exempt from Section 34A-2-202.5 and Subsection 34A-2-704(14); and

        (ii)   required to pay a premium assessment as provided in Section 34A-2-202.

    (b)   If the state chooses to pay workers' compensation benefits for its employees through insuring under Subsection (2)(a)(i) or (ii), the state shall obtain that insurance in accordance with Title 63, Chapter 56, Utah Procurement Code.

34A-2-203 (Effective 05/01/13). Payment of premiums for workers' compensation.

(1)   Until June 30, 2007, a department, commission, board, or other agency of the state shall pay the insurance premium on its employees direct to the Workers' Compensation Fund.

(2)   Beginning July 1, 2007, the state shall secure the payment of workers' compensation benefits for its employees:

    (a)   by:

        (iii)   insuring, and keeping insured, the payment of this compensation with the Workers' Compensation Fund;

        (iv)   insuring, and keeping insured, the payment of this compensation with any stock corporation or mutual association authorized to transact the business of workers' compensation insurance in this state; or

        (v)   paying direct compensation as a self-insured employer in the amount, in the manner, and when due as provided for in this chapter or Chapter 3, Utah Occupational Disease Act;

    (b)   in accordance with Title 63A, Chapter 4, Risk Management; and

    (c)   subject to Subsection (3).

(3)   (a)   If the state determines to secure the payment of workers' compensation benefits for its employees by paying direct compensation as a self-insured employer in the amount, in the manner, and due as provided for in this chapter or Chapter 3, Utah Occupational Disease Act, the state is:

        (i)   exempt from Section 34A-2-202.5 and Subsection 34A-2-704(14); and

        (ii)   required to pay a premium assessment as provided in Section 34A-2-202.

    (b)   If the state chooses to pay workers' compensation benefits for its employees through insuring under Subsection (2)(a)(i) or (ii), the state shall obtain that insurance in accordance with Title 63G, Chapter 6a, Utah Procurement Code.

34A-2-204. Compliance with chapter — Notice to employees.

(1)   Each employer providing insurance, or electing directly to pay compensation to the employer's injured workers, or the dependents of the employer's killed employees, in accordance with this chapter and Chapter 3, Utah Occupational Disease Act, shall post in conspicuous places about the employer's place of business typewritten or printed notices stating, that:

    (a)   the employer has complied with this chapter and Chapter 3, Utah Occupational Disease Act, and all the rules of the commission made under this chapter and Chapter 3, Utah Occupational Disease Act; and

(b)   if such is the case, the employer has been authorized by the division directly to compensate the employees or dependents.

(2)   The notice required in Subsection (1) when posted in accordance with Subsection (1), shall constitute sufficient notice to the employer's employees of the fact that the employer has complied with the law as to securing compensation to the employer's employees and their dependents.

34A-2-205. Notification of workers' compensation insurance coverage to division — Cancellation requirements — Penalty for violation.

(1)   (a)   An insurance carrier writing workers' compensation insurance coverage in this state or for this state, regardless of the state in which the policy is written, shall file notification of that coverage with the division or the division's designee within 30 days after the inception date of the policy in the form prescribed by the division.

(b)   A policy described in Subsection (1)(a) is in effect from inception until canceled by filing with the division or the division's designee a notification of cancellation in the form prescribed by the division within 10 days after the cancellation of a policy.

(c)   Failure to notify the division or its designee under Subsection (1)(b) results in the continued liability of the carrier until the date that notice of cancellation is received by the division or the division's designee.

(d)   An insurance carrier described in this Subsection (1) shall make a filing within 30 days of:

    (i)   the reinstatement of a policy;

    (ii)   the changing or addition of a name or address of the insured; or

    (iii)   the merger of an insured with another entity.

(e)   A filing under this section shall include:

    (i)   the name of the insured;

    (ii)   the principal business address;

    (iii)   any and all assumed name designations;

    (iv)   the address of all locations within this state where business is conducted; and

    (v)   all federal employer identification numbers or federal tax identification numbers.

(2)   Noncompliance with this section is grounds for revocation of an insurance carrier's certificate of authority in addition to the grounds specified in Title 31A, Insurance Code.

(3)   (a)   The division may assess an insurer up to $150 if the insurer fails to comply with this section.

(b)   The division shall deposit an amount assessed under Subsection (3)(a) into the Uninsured Employers' Fund created in Section **34A-2-704** to be used for the purposes of the Uninsured Employer's Fund specified in Section **34A-2-704**.

(c)   The administrator of the Uninsured Employers' Fund shall collect money required to be deposited into the Uninsured Employers' Fund under this Subsection (3) in accordance with Section **34A-2-704**.

(4)   (a)   The notification of workers' compensation insurance coverage required to be filed under Subsection (1) is a protected record under Section **63G-2-305**.

(b)   The commission or any of its divisions may not disclose the information described in Subsection (4)(a) except as provided in:

    (i)   Title 63G, Chapter 2, Government Records Access and Management Act, for a protected record; or

           (ii)   Subsection (4)(c), notwithstanding whether Title 63G, Chapter 2, Government Records Access and Management Act, permits disclosure.

    (c)   The commission may disclose the information described in Subsection (4)(a) if:

           (i)   the information is disclosed on an individual case basis related to a single employer;

           (ii)   the information facilitates the:

                (A)   coverage of subcontractors by identifying the insurance carrier providing workers' compensation coverage for an employer;

                (B)   filing of a claim by an employee; or

                (C)   payment of services rendered on an employee's claim by a medical practitioner; and

           (iii)   promotes the purposes of this chapter or Chapter 3, Utah Occupational Disease Act.

    (d)   In accordance with Title 63G, Chapter 3, Utah Administrative Rulemaking Act, the commission shall make rules concerning when information may be disclosed under Subsection (4)(c).

34A-2-206. Furnishing information to division — Employers' annual report — Rights of division — Examination of employers under oath — Penalties.

(1)   (a)   Every employer shall furnish the division, upon request, all information required by it to carry out the purposes of this chapter and Chapter 3, Utah Occupational Disease Act.

    (b)   In the month of July of each year every employer shall prepare and mail to the division a statement containing the following information:

           (i)   the number of persons employed during the preceding year from July 1, to June 30, inclusive;

           (ii)   the number of the persons employed at each kind of employment;

           (iii)   the scale of wages paid in each class of employment, showing the minimum and maximum wages paid; and

           (iv)   the aggregate amount of wages paid to all employees.

(2)   (a)   The information required under Subsection (1) shall be furnished in the form prescribed by the division.

    (b)   Every employer shall:

           (i)   answer fully and correctly all questions and give all the information sought by the division under Subsection (1); or

           (ii)   if unable to comply with Subsection (2)(b)(i), give to the division, in writing, good and sufficient reasons for the failure.

(3)   (a)   The division may require the information required to be furnished by this chapter or Chapter 3, Utah Occupational Disease Act, to be made under oath and returned to the division within the period fixed by it or by law.

    (b)   The division, or any person employed by the division for that purpose, shall have the right to examine, under oath, any employer, or the employer's agents or employees, for the purpose of ascertaining any information that the employer is required by this chapter or Chapter 3, Utah Occupational Disease Act, to furnish to the division.

(4)   (a)   The division may seek a penalty of not to exceed $500 for each offense to be recovered in a civil action brought by the commission or the division on behalf of the commission against an employer who:

      (i)   within a reasonable time to be fixed by the division and after the receipt of written notice signed by the director or the director's designee specifying the information demanded and served by certified mail, refuses to furnish to the division:

            (A)   the annual statement required by this section; or

            (B)   other information as may be required by the division under this section; or

      (ii) willfully furnishes a false or untrue statement.

      (b)   All penalties collected under Subsection (4)(a) shall be paid into the Employers' Reinsurance Fund created in Section 34A-2-702.

34A-2-207. Noncompliance — Civil action by employees.

(1)   (a)   Employers who fail to comply with Section 34A-2-201 are not entitled to the benefits of this chapter or Chapter 3, Utah Occupational Disease Act, during the period of noncompliance, but shall be liable in a civil action to their employees for damages suffered by reason of personal injuries arising out of or in the course of employment caused by the wrongful act, neglect, or default of the employer or any of the employer's officers, agents, or employees, and also to the dependents or personal representatives of such employees when death results from such injuries.

      (b)   In any action described in Subsection (1)(a), the defendant may not avail himself of any of the following defenses:

      (i)   the fellowservant rule;

      (ii) assumption of risk; or

      (iii) contributory negligence.

(2)   Proof of the injury shall constitute prima facie evidence of negligence on the part of the employer and the burden shall be upon the employer to show freedom from negligence resulting in the injury.

(3)   An employer who fails to comply with Section 34A-2-201 is subject to Sections 34A-2-208 and 34A-2-212.

(4)   In any civil action permitted under this section against the employer, the employee shall be entitled to necessary costs and a reasonable attorney fee assessed against the employer.

34A-2-209. Employer's penalty for violation — Notice of noncompliance — Proof required — Admissible evidence — Criminal prosecution.

(1)   (a)   (i)   An employer who fails to comply, and every officer of a corporation or association that fails to comply, with Section **34A-2-201** is guilty of a class B misdemeanor.

            (ii) Each day's failure to comply with Subsection (1)(a)(i) is a separate offense.

      (b)   If the division sends written notice of noncompliance by certified mail to the last-known address of an employer, a corporation, or an officer of a corporation or association, and the employer, corporation, or officer does not within 10 days of the day on which the notice is delivered provide to the division proof of compliance, the notice and failure to provide proof constitutes prima facie evidence that the employer, corporation, or officer is in violation of this section.

(2)   (a)   If the division has reason to believe that an employer is conducting business without securing the payment of compensation in a manner provided in Section **34A-2-201**, the division may give notice of noncompliance by certified mail to the following at the last-known address of the following:

            (i)   the employer; or

            (ii)   if the employer is a corporation or association:

                    (A)   the corporation or association; or

                    (B)   the officers of the corporation or association.

        (b)   If an employer, corporation, or officer described in Subsection (2)(a) does not, within 10 days of the day on which the notice is delivered, provide to the division proof of compliance, the employer and every officer of an employer corporation or association is guilty of a class B misdemeanor.

        (c)   Each day's failure to comply with Subsection (2)(a) is a separate offense.

(3)   A fine, penalty, or money collected or assessed under this section shall be:

        (a)   deposited in the Uninsured Employers' Fund created by Section **34A-2-704**;

        (b)   used for the purposes of the Uninsured Employers' Fund specified in Section **34A-2-704**; and

        (c)   collected by the Uninsured Employers' Fund administrator in accordance with Section **34A-2-704**.

(4)   A form or record kept by the division or its designee pursuant to Section **34A-2-205** is admissible as evidence to establish noncompliance under this section.

(5)   The commission or division on behalf of the commission may prosecute or request the attorney general or district attorney to prosecute a criminal action in the name of the state to enforce this chapter or Chapter 3, Utah Occupational Disease Act.

34A-2-210. Power to bring suit for noncompliance.

(1)   (a)   The commission or the division on behalf of the commission may maintain a suit in any court of the state to enjoin any employer, within this chapter or Chapter 3, Utah Occupational Disease Act, from further operation of the employer's business, when the employer fails to provide for the payment of benefits in one of the three ways provided in Section 34A-2-201.

        (b)   Upon a showing of failure to provide for the payment of benefits, the court shall enjoin the further operation of the employer's business until the payment of these benefits has been secured by the employer as required by Section 34A-2-201. The court may enjoin the employer without requiring bond from the commission or division.

(2)   If the division has reason to believe that an employer is conducting a business without securing the payment of compensation in one of the three ways provided in Section 34A-2-201, the division may give the employer five days written notice by registered mail of the noncompliance and if the employer within the five days written notice does not remedy the default:

        (a)   the commission or the division on behalf of the commission may file suit under Subsection (1); and

        (b)   the court may, ex parte, issue without bond a temporary injunction restraining the further operation of the employer's business.

34A-2-211. Notice of noncompliance to employer — Enforcement power of division — Penalty.

(1)   (a)   In addition to the remedies specified in Section **34A-2-210**, if the division has reason to believe that an employer is conducting business without securing the payment of benefits in a manner provided in Section **34A-2-201**, the division may give that employer written notice of the noncompliance by certified mail to the last-known address of the employer.

       (b)   If the employer does not remedy the default within 15 days after the day on which the notice is delivered, the division may issue an order requiring the employer to appear before the division and show cause why the employer should not be ordered to comply with Section **34A-2-201**.

       (c)   If the division finds that an employer has failed to provide for the payment of benefits in a manner provided in Section **34A-2-201**, the division may require the employer to comply with Section **34A-2-201**.

(2)   (a)   Notwithstanding Subsection (1), the division may impose a penalty against the employer under this Subsection (2):

           (i)   subject to Title 63G, Chapter 4, Administrative Procedures Act; and

           (ii)   if the division believes that an employer of one or more employees is conducting business without securing the payment of benefits in a manner provided in Section **34A-2-201**.

       (b)   The penalty imposed under Subsection (2)(a) shall be the greater of:

           (i) $1,000; or

           (ii)   three times the amount of the premium the employer would have paid for workers' compensation insurance based on the rate filing of the Workers' Compensation Fund, during the period of noncompliance.

       (c)   For purposes of Subsection (2)(b)(ii):

           (i)   the premium is calculated by applying rates and rate multipliers to the payroll basis under Subsection (2)(c)(ii), using the highest rated employee class code applicable to the employer's operations; and

           (ii)   the payroll basis is 150% of the state's average weekly wage multiplied by the highest number of workers employed by the employer during the period of the employer's noncompliance multiplied by the number of weeks of the employer's noncompliance up to a maximum of 156 weeks.

(3)   A penalty imposed under Subsection (2) shall be:

       (a)   deposited in the Uninsured Employers' Fund created by Section **34A-2-704**;

       (b)   used for the purposes of the Uninsured Employers' Fund specified in Section **34A-2-704**; and

       (c)   collected by the Uninsured Employers' Fund administrator in accordance with Section **34A-2-704**.

(4)   (a)   An employer who disputes a determination, imposition, or amount of a penalty imposed under Subsection (2) shall request a hearing before an administrative law judge within 30 days of the date of issuance of the administrative action imposing the penalty or the administrative action becomes a final order of the commission.

(b)   An employer's request for a hearing under Subsection (4)(a) shall specify the facts and grounds that are the basis of the employer's objection to the determination, imposition, or amount of the penalty.

(c)   An administrative law judge's decision under this Subsection (4) may be reviewed pursuant to Part 8, Adjudication.

(5)   An administrative action issued by the division under this section shall:

(a)   be in writing;

(b)   be sent by certified mail to the last-known address of the employer;

(c)   state the findings and administrative action of the division; and

(d)   specify its effective date, which may be:

(i)   immediate; or

(ii)   at a later date.

(6)   A final order of the commission under this section, upon application by the commission made on or after the effective date of the order to a court of general jurisdiction in any county in this state, may be enforced by an order to comply:

(a)   entered ex parte; and

(b)   without notice by the court.

34A-2-212. Docketing awards in district court — Enforcing judgment.

(1)   (a)   An abstract of any final order providing an award may be filed under this chapter or Chapter 3, Utah Occupational Disease Act, in the office of the clerk of the district court of any county in the state.

(b)   The abstract shall be docketed in the judgment docket of the district court where the abstract is filed. The time of the receipt of the abstract shall be noted on the abstract by the clerk of the district court and entered in the docket.

(c)   When filed and docketed under Subsections (1)(a) and (b), the order shall constitute a lien from the time of the docketing upon the real property of the employer situated in the county, for a period of eight years from the date of the order unless the award provided in the final order is satisfied during the eightyear period.

(d)   Execution may be issued on the lien within the same time and in the same manner and with the same effect as if said award were a judgment of the district court.

(2)   (a)   If the employer was uninsured at the time of the injury, the county attorney for the county in which the applicant or the employer resides, depending on the district in which the final order is docketed, shall enforce the judgment when requested by the commission or division on behalf of the commission.

(b)   In an action to enforce an order docketed under Subsection (1), reasonable attorney's fees and court costs shall be allowed in addition to the award.

34A-2-301. Places of employment to be safe — Willful neglect Penalty.

(1)   An employer may not:

(a)   construct, occupy, or maintain any place of employment that is not safe;

(b)   require or knowingly permit any employee to be in any employment or place of employment that is not safe;

(c)   fail to provide and use safety devices and safeguards;

(d)   remove, disable, or bypass safety devices and safeguards;

(e)   fail to obey orders of the commission;

(f)   fail to obey rules of the commission;

(g)   fail to adopt and use methods and processes reasonably adequate to render the employment and place of employment safe; or

(h)   fail or neglect to do every other thing reasonably necessary to protect the life, health, and safety of the employer's employees.

(2)   Compensation as provided in this chapter shall be increased 15%, except in case of injury resulting in death, when injury is caused by the willful failure of an employer to comply with:

(a)   the law;

(b)   a rule of the commission;

(c)   any lawful order of the commission; or

(d)   the employer's own written workplace safety program.

34A-2-302. Employee's willful misconduct — Penalty.

(1)   For purposes of this section:

(a)   "controlled substance" is as defined in Section 58372;

(b)   "local government employee" is as defined in Section 3441101;

(c)   "local governmental entity" is as defined in Section 3441101;

(d)   "state institution of higher education" is as defined in Section 3441101; and

(e)   "valid prescription" is a prescription, as defined in Section 58372, that:

(i)   is prescribed for a controlled substance for use by the employee for whom it was prescribed; and

(ii)   has not been altered or forged.

(2)   An employee may not:

(a)   remove, displace, damage, destroy, or carry away any safety device or safeguard provided for use in any employment or place of employment;

(b)   interfere in any way with the use of a safety device or safeguard described in Subsection (2)(a) by any other person;

(c)   interfere with the use of any method or process adopted for the protection of any employee in the employer's employment or place of employment; or

(d)   fail or neglect to follow and obey orders and to do every other thing reasonably necessary to protect the life, health, and safety of employees.

(3)   Except in case of injury resulting in death:

(a)   compensation provided for by this chapter shall be reduced 15% when injury is caused by the willful failure of the employee:

(i)   to use safety devices when provided by the employer; or

(ii)   to obey any order or reasonable rule adopted by the employer for the safety of the employee; and

(b)   except when the employer permitted, encouraged, or had actual knowledge of the conduct described in Subsection (3)(b)(i) through (iii), disability compensation may not be awarded under this chapter or Title 34A, Chapter 3, Utah Occupational Disease Act, to an employee when the major contributing cause of the employee's injury is the employee's:

    (i)   use of a controlled substance that the employee did not obtain under a valid prescription;

    (ii)   intentional abuse of a controlled substance that the employee obtained under a valid prescription if the employee uses the controlled substance intentionally:

        (A)   in excess of prescribed therapeutic amounts; or

        (B)   in an otherwise abusive manner; or

    (iii)   intoxication from alcohol with a blood or breath alcohol concentration of .08 grams or greater as shown by a chemical test.

(4)   (a)   For purposes of Subsection (3), as shown by a chemical test that conforms to scientifically accepted analytical methods and procedures and includes verification or confirmation of any positive test result by gas chromatography, gas chromatographymass spectroscopy, or other comparably reliable analytical method, before the result of the test may be used as a basis for the presumption, it is presumed that the major contributing cause of the employee's injury is the employee's conduct described in Subsections (3)(b)(i) through (iii) if at the time of the injury:

    (i)   the employee has in the employee's system:

        (A)   any amount of a controlled substance or its metabolites if the employee did not obtain the controlled substance under a valid prescription; or

        (B)   a controlled substance the employee obtained under a valid prescription or the metabolites of the controlled substance if the amount in the employee's system is consistent with the employee using the controlled substance intentionally:

            (I)   in excess of prescribed therapeutic amounts; or

            (II)   in an otherwise abusive manner;

    (ii)   the employee has a blood or breath alcohol concentration of .08 grams or greater.

(b)   The presumption created under Subsection (4)(a) may be rebutted by evidence showing that:

    (i)   the chemical test creating the presumption is inaccurate because the employer failed to comply with:

        (A)   Sections 34384 through 34386; or

        (B)   if the employer is a local governmental entity or state institution of higher education, Section 3441104 and Subsection 3441103(5);

    (ii)   the employee did not engage in the conduct described in Subsections (3)(b)(i) through (iii);

    (iii)   the test results do not exclude the possibility of passive inhalation of marijuana because the concentration of total urinary cannabinoids is less than 50 nanograms/ml as determined by a test conducted in accordance with:

        (A)   Sections 34384 through 34386; or

        (B)   if the employer is a local governmental entity or state institution of higher education, Section 3441104 and Subsection 3441103(5);

             (iv)   a competent medical opinion from a physician verifies that the amount in the employee's system of the following does not support a finding that the conduct described in Subsections (3)(b)(i) through (iii) was the major contributing cause of the employee's injury:

                  (A)   any amount of a controlled substance or its metabolites if the employee did not obtain the controlled substance under a valid prescription; or

                  (B)   a controlled substance the employee obtained under a valid prescription or the metabolites of the controlled substance if the amount in the employee's system is consistent with the employee using the controlled substance intentionally:

                      (I)   in excess of prescribed therapeutic amounts; or

                      (II)   in an otherwise abusive manner;

                  (C)   alcohol; or

                  (D)   a combination of Subsections (4)(b)(iii)(A) through (C); or

             (iii)   the conduct described in Subsections (3)(b)(i) through (iii) was not the major contributing cause of the employee's injury.

        (c)   (i)   Except as provided in Subsections (4)(c)(ii) and (iii), if a chemical test that creates the presumption under Subsection (4)(a) is taken at the request of the employer, the employer shall comply with:

                  (A)   Title 34, Chapter 38, Drug and Alcohol Testing; or

                  (B)   if the employee is a local governmental employee or an employee of a state institution of higher education, Title 34, Chapter 41, Local Governmental Entity DrugFree Workplace Policies.

             (i)   Notwithstanding Section 343813, the results of a test taken under Title 34, Chapter 38, may be disclosed to the extent necessary to establish or rebut the presumption created under Subsection (4)(a).

             (ii)   Notwithstanding Section 3441103, the results of a test taken under Title 34, Chapter 41, may be disclosed to the extent necessary to establish or rebut the presumption created under Subsection (4)(a).

    (5)   If any provision of this section, or the application of any provision of this section to any person or circumstance, is held invalid, the remainder of this section shall be given effect without the invalid provision or application.

34A-2-401. Compensation for industrial accidents to be paid.

    (1)   An employee described in Section 34A-2-104 who is injured and the dependents of each such employee who is killed, by accident arising out of and in the course of the employee's employment, wherever such injury occurred, if the accident was not purposely selfinflicted, shall be paid:

        (a)   compensation for loss sustained on account of the injury or death;

        (b)   the amount provided in this chapter for:

             (i)   medical, nurse, and hospital services;

             (ii)   medicines; and

             (iii)   in case of death, the amount of funeral expenses.

(2)   The responsibility for compensation and payment of medical, nursing, and hospital services and medicines, and funeral expenses provided under this chapter shall be:

    (a)   on the employer and the employer's insurance carrier; and

    (b)   not on the employee.

(3)   Payment of benefits provided by this chapter or Chapter 3, Utah Occupational Disease Act, shall commence within 30 calendar days after any final award by the commission.

34A-2-402. Mental stress claims.

(1)   Physical, mental, or emotional injuries related to mental stress arising out of and in the course of employment shall be compensable under this chapter only when there is a sufficient legal and medical causal connection between the employee's injury and employment.

(2)   (a)   Legal causation requires proof of extraordinary mental stress from a sudden stimulus arisir.g predominantly and directly from employment.

    (b)   The extraordinary and sudden nature of the alleged mental stress is judged according to an objective standard in comparison with contemporary national employment and nonemployment life.

(3)   Medical causation requires proof that the physical, mental, or emotional injury was medically caused by the mental stress that is the legal cause of the physical, mental, or emotional injury.

(4)   Good faith employer personnel actions including disciplinary actions, work evaluations, job transfers, layoffs, demotions, promotions, terminations, or retirements, may not form the basis of compensable mental stress claims under this chapter.

(5)   Alleged discrimination, harassment, or unfair labor practices otherwise actionable at law may not form the basis of compensable mental stress claims under this chapter.

(6)   An employee who alleges a compensable industrial accident involving mental stress bears the burden of proof to establish legal and medical causation by a preponderance of the evidence.

34A-2-403. Dependents Presumption.

(1)   The following persons shall be presumed to be wholly dependent for support upon a deceased employee:

    (a)   a child under 18 years of age, or over if the child is physically or mentally incapacitated and dependent upon the parent, with whom the child is living at the time of the death of the parent, or who is legally bound for the child's support; and

    (b)   for purposes of payments to be made under Subsection 34A-2-702(5)(a)(i), a surviving spouse with whom the deceased employee lived at the time of the employee's death.

(2)   (a)   In a case not provided for in Subsection (1), the question of dependency, in whole or in part, shall be determined in accordance with the facts in each particular case existing at the time of the injury or death of an employee, except for purposes of dependency reviews under Subsection 34A-2-702(5)(a)(iv).

    (b)   A person may not be considered as a dependent unless that person is:

        (i)   a member of the family of the deceased employee;

        (ii)   the spouse of the deceased employee;

        (iii)   a lineal descendant or ancestor of the deceased employee; or

        (iv)   brother or sister of the deceased employee.

(3)   As used in this chapter and Chapter 3, Utah Occupational Disease Act:

    (a)   "brother or sister" includes a half brother or sister; and

    (b)   "child" includes:

        (i)   a posthumous child; or

        (ii)   a child legally adopted prior to the injury.

34A-2-404. Injuries to minors.

(1)   A minor is considered sui juris for the purposes of this chapter and Chapter 3, Utah Occupational Disease Act, and no other person shall have any cause of action or right to compensation for an injury to the minor employee.

(2)   Notwithstanding Subsection (1), in the event of the award of a lump sum of compensation to a minor employee, the sum shall be paid only to the minor's legally appointed guardian.

34A-2-405. Employee injured outside state Entitled to compensation Limitation of time.

(1)   Except as provided in Subsection (2), if an employee who has been hired or is regularly employed in this state receives personal injury by accident arising out of and in the course of employment outside of this state, the employee, or the employee's dependents in case of the employee's death, shall be entitled to compensation according to the law of this state.

(2)   This section applies only to those injuries received by the employee within six months after leaving this state, unless prior to the expiration of the sixmonth period the employer has filed with the division notice that the employer has elected to extend such coverage a greater period of time.

34A-2-406. Exemptions from chapter for employees temporarily in state Conditions Evidence of insurance.

(1)   Any employee who has been hired in another state and the employee's employer are exempt from this chapter and Chapter 3, Utah Occupational Disease Act, while the employee is temporarily within this state doing work for the employee's employer if:

    (a)   the employer has furnished workers' compensation insurance coverage under the workers' compensation or similar laws of the other state;

    (b)   the coverage covers the employee's employment while in this state; and

    (c)   (i)   the extraterritorial provisions of this chapter and Chapter 3 are recognized in the other state and employers and employees who are covered in this state are likewise exempted from the application of the workers' compensation or similar laws of the other state; or

        (ii)   the Workers' Compensation Fund:

            (A)   is an admitted insurance carrier in the other state; or

            (B)   has agreements with a carrier and is able to furnish workers' compensation insurance or similar coverage to Utah employers and their subsidiaries or affiliates doing business in the other state.

(2)   The benefits under the workers' compensation or similar laws of the other state are the exclusive remedy against an employer for any injury, whether resulting in death or not, received by an employee while working for the employer in this state.

(3)   A certificate from an authorized officer of the industrial commission or similar department of the other state certifying that the employer is insured in the other state and has provided extraterritorial coverage insuring the employer's employees while working in this state is prima facie evidence that the employer carries compensation insurance.

34A-2-407. Reporting of industrial injuries — Regulation of health care providers — Funeral expenses.

(1)   As used in this section, "physician" is as defined in Section 34A-2-111.

(2)   (a)   An employee sustaining an injury arising out of and in the course of employment shall provide notification to the employee's employer promptly of the injury.

        (b)   If the employee is unable to provide the notification required by Subsection (2)(a), the following may provide notification of the injury to the employee's employer:

            (i)   the employee's next-of-kin; or

            (ii)   the employee's attorney.

        (c)   An employee claiming benefits under this chapter, or Chapter 3, Utah Occupational Disease Act, shall comply with rules adopted by the commission regarding disclosure of medical records of the employee medically relevant to the industrial accident or occupational disease claim.

(3)   (a)   An employee is barred for any claim of benefits arising from an injury if the employee fails to notify within the time period described in Subsection (3)(b):

            (i)   the employee's employer in accordance with Subsection (2); or

            (ii)   the division.

        (b)   The notice required by Subsection (3)(a) shall be made within:

            (i)   180 days of the day on which the injury occurs; or

            (ii)   in the case of an occupational hearing loss, the time period specified in Section 34A-2-506.

(4)   The following constitute notification of injury required by Subsection (2):

        (a)   an employer's or physician's injury report filed with:

            (i)   the division;

            (ii)   the employer; or

            (iii)   the employer's insurance carrier; or

        (b)   the payment of any medical or disability benefits by:

            (i)   the employer; or

            (ii)   the employer's insurance carrier.

(5)   (a)   In the form prescribed by the division, an employer shall file a report with the division of a:

            (i)   work-related fatality; or

            (ii)   work-related injury resulting in:

                (A)   medical treatment;

                (B)   loss of consciousness;

                (C)   loss of work;

                (D)   restriction of work; or

                (E)   transfer to another job.

        (b)   The employer shall file the report required by Subsection (5)(a) within seven days after:

            (i)   the occurrence of a fatality or injury;

            (ii)   the employer's first knowledge of a fatality or injury; or

              (iii)   the employee's notification of a fatality or injury.

    (c)   (i)   An employer shall file a subsequent report with the division of a previously reported injury that later results in death.

           (ii)   The subsequent report required by this Subsection (5)(c) shall be filed with the division within seven days following:

                (A)   the death; or

                (B)   the employer's first knowledge or notification of the death.

    (d)   A report is not required to be filed under this Subsection (5) for a minor injury, such as a cut or scratch that requires first-aid treatment only, unless:

           (i)   a treating physician files a report with the division in accordance with Subsection (9); or

           (ii)   a treating physician is required to file a report with the division in accordance with Subsection (9).

(6)   An employer required to file a report under Subsection (5) shall provide the employee with:

    (a)   a copy of the report submitted to the division; and

    (b)   a statement, as prepared by the division, of the employee's rights and responsibilities related to the industrial injury.

(7)   An employer shall maintain a record in a manner prescribed by the commission by rule of all:

    (a)   work-related fatalities; or

    (b)   work-related injuries resulting in:

           (i)   medical treatment;

           (ii)   loss of consciousness;

           (iii)   loss of work;

           (iv)   restriction of work; or

           (v)   transfer to another job.

(8)   (a)   Except as provided in Subsection (8)(b), an employer who refuses or neglects to make a report, maintain a record, or file a report with the division as required by this section is:

           (i)   guilty of a class C misdemeanor; and

           (ii)   subject to a civil assessment:

                (A)   imposed by the division, subject to the requirements of Title 63G, Chapter 4, Administrative Procedures Act; and

                (B)   that may not exceed $500.

    (b)   An employer is not subject to the civil assessment or guilty of a class C misdemeanor under this Subsection (8) if:

           (i)   the employer submits a report later than required by this section; and

           (ii)   the division finds that the employer has shown good cause for submitting a report later than required by this section.

    (c)   (i)   A civil assessment collected under this Subsection (8) shall be deposited into the Uninsured Employers' Fund created in Section 34A-2-704 to be used for a purpose specified in Section 34A-2-704.

    (ii)   The administrator of the Uninsured Employers' Fund shall collect money required to be deposited into the Uninsured Employers' Fund under this Subsection (8)(c) in accordance with Section 34A-2-704.

(9)   (a)   A physician attending an injured employee shall comply with rules established by the commission regarding:

    (i)   fees for physician's services;

    (ii)   disclosure of medical records of the employee medically relevant to the employee's industrial accident or occupational disease claim; and

    (iii)   reports to the division regarding:

        (A)   the condition and treatment of an injured employee; or

        (B)   any other matter concerning industrial cases that the physician is treating.

    (b)   A physician who is associated with, employed by, or bills through a hospital is subject to Subsection (9)(a).

    (c)   A hospital providing services for an injured employee is not subject to the requirements of Subsection (9)(a) except for rules made by the commission that are described in Subsection (9)(a)(ii) or (iii).

    (d)   The commission's schedule of fees may reasonably differentiate remuneration to be paid to providers of health services based on:

    (i)   the severity of the employee's condition;

    (ii)   the nature of the treatment necessary; and

    (iii)   the facilities or equipment specially required to deliver that treatment.

    (e)   This Subsection (9) does not prohibit a contract with a provider of health services relating to the pricing of goods and services.

(10)   A copy of the initial report filed under Subsection (9)(a)(iii) shall be furnished to:

    (a)   the division;

    (b)   the employee; and

    (c)   (i)   the employer; or

        (ii)   the employer's insurance carrier.

(11)   (a)   Subject to appellate review under Section **34A-1-303**, the commission has exclusive jurisdiction to hear and determine:

    (i)   whether goods provided to or services rendered to an employee are compensable pursuant to this chapter or Chapter 3, Utah Occupational Disease Act, including:

        (A)   medical, nurse, or hospital services;

        (B)   medicines; and

        (C)   artificial means, appliances, or prosthesis;

    (ii)   the reasonableness of the amounts charged or paid for a good or service described in Subsection (11)(a)(i); and

    (iii)   collection issues related to a good or service described in Subsection (11)(a)(i).

    (b)   Except as provided in Subsection (11)(a), Subsection 34A-2-211 (6), or Section 34A-2-212, a person may not maintain a cause of action in any forum within this state other than the commission for collection or payment for goods or services described in Subsection (11)(a) that are compensable under this chapter or Chapter 3, Utah Occupational Disease Act.

34A-2-408. Compensation — None for first three days after injury unless disability extended.

(1)   (a)   Except as provided in Subsections (1)(b) and (2), compensation may not be allowed for the first three days after the injury is received.

        (b)   The disbursements authorized in this chapter or Chapter 3, Utah Occupational Disease Act, for medical, nurse and hospital services, and for medicines and funeral expenses are payable for the first three days after the injury is received.

(2)   If the period of total temporary disability lasts more than 14 days, compensation shall also be payable for the first three days after the injury is received.

34A-2-409. Average weekly wage — Basis of computation.

(1)   Except as otherwise provided in this chapter or Chapter 3, Utah Occupational Disease Act, the average weekly wage of the injured employee at the time of the injury is the basis upon which to compute the weekly compensation rate and shall be determined as follows:

    (a)   if at the time of the injury the wages are fixed by the year, the average weekly wage shall be that yearly wage divided by 52;

    (b)   if at the time of the injury the wages are fixed by the month, the average weekly wage shall be that monthly wage divided by 41/3;

    (c)   if at the time of the injury the wages are fixed by the week, that amount shall be the average weekly wage;

    (d)   if at the time of the injury the wages are fixed by the day, the weekly wage shall be determined by multiplying the daily wage by the greater of:

        (i)   the number of days and fraction of days in the week during which the employee under a contract of hire was working at the time of the accident, or would have worked if the accident had not intervened; or

        (ii)   three days;

    (e)   if at the time of the injury the wages are fixed by the hour, the average weekly wage shall be determined by multiplying the hourly rate by the greater of:

        (i)   the number of hours the employee would have worked for the week if the accident had not intervened; or

        (ii)   20 hours;

    (f)   if at the time of the injury the hourly wage has not been fixed or cannot be ascertained, the average weekly wage for the purpose of calculating compensation shall be the usual wage for similar services where those services are rendered by paid employees;

    (g)   (i)   if at the time of the injury the wages are fixed by the output of the employee, the average weekly wage shall be the wage most favorable to the employee computed by dividing by 13 the wages, not including overtime or premium pay, of the employee earned through that employer in the first, second, third, or fourth period of 13 consecutive calendar weeks in the 52 weeks immediately preceding the injury; or

        (iii)   if the employee has been employed by that employer less than 13 calendar weeks immediately preceding the injury, the employee's average weekly wage shall be computed as under Subsection (1)(g)(i), presuming the wages, not including overtime or premium pay, to be the amount the employee would have earned had the employee been so employed for the full 13 calendar weeks immediately preceding the injury and had worked, when work was available to other employees, in a similar occupation.

(2) If none of the methods in Subsection (1) will fairly determine the average weekly wage in a particular case, the commission shall use such other method as will, based on the facts presented, fairly determine the employee's average weekly wage.

(3) When the average weekly wage of the injured employee at the time of the injury is determined in accordance with this section, it shall be taken as the basis upon which to compute the weekly compensation rate. After the weekly compensation is computed, it shall be rounded to the nearest dollar.

(4) If it is established that the injured employee was of such age and experience when injured that under natural conditions the employee's wages would be expected to increase, that fact may be considered in arriving at the employee's average weekly wage.

34A-2-410. Temporary disability — Amount of payments — State average weekly wage defined.

(1) (a) In case of temporary disability, so long as the disability is total, the employee shall receive 662/3% of that employee's average weekly wages at the time of the injury but:

   (i) not more than a maximum of 100% of the state average weekly wage at the time of the injury per week; and

   (ii) not less than a minimum of $45 per week plus $5 for a dependent spouse and $5 for each dependent child under the age of 18 years, up to a maximum of four dependent children, not to exceed the average weekly wage of the employee at the time of the injury, but not to exceed 100% of the state average weekly wage at the time of the injury per week.

(b) In no case shall the compensation benefits exceed 312 weeks at the rate of 100% of the state average weekly wage at the time of the injury over a period of 12 years from the date of the injury.

(2) In the event a light duty medical release is obtained prior to the employee reaching a fixed state of recovery, and when no light duty employment is available to the employee from the employer, temporary disability benefits shall continue to be paid.

(3) The "state average weekly wage" as referred to in this chapter and Chapter 3, Utah Occupational Disease Act, shall be determined by the commission as follows:

(a) On or before June 1 of each year, the total wages reported on contribution reports to the Unemployment Insurance Division for the preceding calendar year shall be divided by the average monthly number of insured workers determined by dividing the total insured workers reported for the preceding year by 12.

(b) The average annual wage obtained under Subsection (3)(a) shall be divided by 52.

(c) The average weekly wage determined under Subsection (3)(b) is rounded to the nearest dollar.

(4) The state average weekly wage determined under Subsection (3) shall be used as the basis for computing the maximum compensation rate for:

(a) injuries or disabilities arising from occupational disease that occurred during the twelvemonth period commencing July 1 following the June 1 determination; and

(b) any death resulting from the injuries or disabilities arising from occupational disease.

34A-2-411. Temporary partial disability — Amount of payments.

(1)   If the injury causes temporary partial disability for work, the employee shall receive weekly compensation equal to:

(a)   662/3% of the difference between the employee's average weekly wages before the accident and the weekly wages the employee is able to earn after the accident, but not more than 100% of the state average weekly wage at the time of injury; plus

(b) $5 for a dependent spouse and $5 for each dependent child under the age of 18 years, up to a maximum of four such dependent children, but only up to a total weekly compensation that does not exceed 100% of the state average weekly wage at the time of injury.

(2)   The commission may order an award for temporary partial disability for work at any time prior to 12 years after the date of the injury to an employee:

(a)   whose physical condition resulting from the injury is not finally healed and fixed 12 years after the date of injury; and

(b)   who files an application for hearing under Section 34A-2-417.

(3)   The duration of weekly payments may not exceed 312 weeks nor continue more than 12 years after the date of the injury. Payments shall terminate when the disability ends or the injured employee dies.

34A-2-412. Permanent partial disability — Scale of payments.

(1)   An employee who sustained a permanent impairment as a result of an industrial accident and who files an application for hearing under Section 34A-2-417 may receive a permanent partial disability award from the commission.

(2)   Weekly payments may not in any case continue after the disability ends, or the death of the injured person.

(3)   (a)   In the case of the injuries described in Subsections (4) through (6), the compensation shall be 662/3% of that employee's average weekly wages at the time of the injury, but not more than a maximum of 662/3% of the state average weekly wage at the time of the injury per week and not less than a minimum of $45 per week plus $5 for a dependent spouse and $5 for each dependent child under the age of 18 years, up to a maximum of four dependent children, but not to exceed 662/3% of the state average weekly wage at the time of the injury per week.

(b)   The compensation determined under Subsection (3)(a) shall be:

(iii)   paid in routine pay periods not to exceed four weeks for the number of weeks provided for in this section; and

(iv)   in addition to the compensation provided for temporary total disability and temporary partial disability.

(4)   For the loss of: Number of Weeks

(a)   Upper extremity

(v)   Arm

(A)   Arm and shoulder (forequarter amputation)   218

(B)   Arm at shoulder joint, or above deltoid insertion   187

(C)   Arm between deltoid insertion and elbow joint, at   178
elbow joint, or below elbow joint proximal to insertion
of biceps tendon

(D)   Forearm below elbow joint distal to insertion of biceps   168
tendon

    (vi) Hand
(A)	At wrist or midcarpal or midmetacarpal amputation	168
(B)	All fingers except thumb at metacarpophalangeal joints	101

    (vii) Thumb
(A)	At metacarpophalangeal joint or with resection of carpometacarpal bone	67
(B)	At interphalangeal joint	50

    (viii) Index finger
(A)	At metacarpophalangeal joint or with resection of metacarpal bone	42
(B)	At proximal interphalangeal joint	34
(C)	At distal interphalangeal joint	18

    (ix) Middle finger
(A)	At metacarpophalangeal joint or with resection of metacarpal bone	34
(B)	At proximal interphalangeal joint	27
(C)	At distal interphalangeal joint	15

    (x) Ring finger
(D)	At metacarpophalangeal joint or with resection of metacarpal bone	17
(E)	At proximal interphalangeal joint	13
(F)	At distal interphalangeal joint	8

    (xi) Little finger
(A)	At metacarpophalangeal joint or with resection of metacarpal bone	8
(B)	At proximal interphalangeal joint	6
(C)	At distal interphalangeal joint	4

(b) Lower extremity

    (i) Leg
(A)	Hemipelvectomy (leg, hip and pelvis)	156
(B)	Leg at hip joint or three inches or less below tuberosity of ischium	125
(C)	Leg above knee with functional stump, at knee joint or GrittiStokes amputation or below knee with short stump (three inches or less below intercondylar notch)	112
(D)	Leg below knee with functional stump	88

    (ii) Foot
(A)	Foot at ankle	88
(B)	Foot partial amputation (Chopart's)	66
(C)	Foot midmetatarsal amputation	44

    (iii) Toes
(A)	Great toe		
	(I)	With resection of metatarsal bone	26
	(II)	At metatarsophalangeal joint	16
	(III)	At interphalangeal joint	12
(B)	Lesser toe (2nd 5th)		
	(I)	With resection of metatarsal bone	4
	(II)	At metatarsophalangeal joint	3

		(III)	At proximal interphalangeal joint	2
		(IV)	At distal interphalangeal joint	1
	(C)		All toes at metatarsophalangeal joints	26

(v) Miscellaneous

	(A)	One eye by enucleation	120
	(B)	Total blindness of one eye	100
	(C)	Total loss of binaural hearing	109

(5)   Permanent and complete loss of use shall be deemed equivalent to loss of the member. Partial loss or partial loss of use shall be a percentage of the complete loss or loss of use of the member. This Subsection (5) does not apply to the items listed in Subsection (4)(b)(iv).

(6)   (a)   For any permanent impairment caused by an industrial accident that is not otherwise provided for in the schedule of losses in this section, permanent partial disability compensation shall be awarded by the commission based on the medical evidence.

      (b)   Compensation for any impairment described in Subsection (6)(a) shall, as closely as possible, be proportionate to the specific losses in the schedule set forth in this section.

      (c)   Permanent partial disability compensation may not:

            (vi) exceed 312 weeks, which shall be considered the period of compensation for permanent total loss of bodily function; and

            (i)   be paid for any permanent impairment that existed prior to an industrial accident.

(7)   The amounts specified in this section are all subject to the limitations as to the maximum weekly amount payable as specified in this section, and in no event shall more than a maximum of 662/3% of the state average weekly wage at the time of the injury for a total of 312 weeks in compensation be required to be paid.

34A-2-413. Permanent total disability — Amount of payments — Rehabilitation.

(1)   (a)   In the case of a permanent total disability resulting from an industrial accident or occupational disease, the employee shall receive compensation as outlined in this section.

      (b)   To establish entitlement to permanent total disability compensation, the employee shall prove by a preponderance of evidence that:

            (i)   the employee sustained a significant impairment or combination of impairments as a result of the industrial accident or occupational disease that gives rise to the permanent total disability entitlement;

            (ii)   the employee has a permanent, total disability; and

            (iii) the industrial accident or occupational disease is the direct cause of the employee's permanent total disability.

      (c)   To establish that an employee has a permanent, total disability the employee shall prove by a preponderance of the evidence that:

            (i)   the employee is not gainfully employed;

            (ii)   the employee has an impairment or combination of impairments that limit the employee's ability to do basic work activities;

            (iii) the industrial or occupationally caused impairment or combination of impairments prevent the employee from performing the essential functions of the work activities for which the employee has been qualified until the time of the industrial accident or occupational disease that is the basis for the employee's permanent total disability claim; and

(iv)   the employee cannot perform other work reasonably available, taking into consideration the employee's:

        (A)   age;

        (B)   education;

        (C)   past work experience;

        (D)   medical capacity; and

        (E)   residual functional capacity.

(d)   Evidence of an employee's entitlement to disability benefits other than those provided under this chapter and Chapter 3, Utah Occupational Disease Act, if relevant:

    (i)   may be presented to the commission;

    (ii)   is not binding; and

    (iii)   creates no presumption of an entitlement under this chapter and Chapter 3, Utah Occupational Disease Act.

(e)   In determining under Subsections (1)(b) and (c) whether an employee cannot perform other work reasonably available, the following may not be considered:

    (i)   whether the employee is incarcerated in a facility operated by or contracting with a federal, state, county, or municipal government to house a criminal offender in either a secure or nonsecure setting; or

    (ii)   whether the employee is not legally eligible to be employed because of a reason unrelated to the impairment or combination of impairments.

(2)   For permanent total disability compensation during the initial 312-week entitlement, compensation is 66-2/3% of the employee's average weekly wage at the time of the injury, limited as follows:

(a)   compensation per week may not be more than 85% of the state average weekly wage at the time of the injury;

(b)   (i)   subject to Subsection (2)(b)(ii), compensation per week may not be less than the sum of $45 per week and:

        (A) $5 for a dependent spouse; and

        (B) $5 for each dependent child under the age of 18 years, up to a maximum of four dependent minor children; and

    (ii)   the amount calculated under Subsection (2)(b)(i) may not exceed:

        (A)   the maximum established in Subsection (2)(a); or

        (B)   the average weekly wage of the employee at the time of the injury; and

(c)   after the initial 312 weeks, the minimum weekly compensation rate under Subsection (2)(b) is 36% of the current state average weekly wage, rounded to the nearest dollar.

(3)   This Subsection (3) applies to claims resulting from an accident or disease arising out of and in the course of the employee's employment on or before June 30, 1994.

(a)   The employer or its insurance carrier is liable for the initial 312 weeks of permanent total disability compensation except as outlined in Section **34A-2-703** as in effect on the date of injury.

(b)   The employer or its insurance carrier may not be required to pay compensation for any combination of disabilities of any kind, as provided in this section and Sections **34A-2-410** through **34A-2-412** and Part 5, Industrial Noise, in excess of the amount of compensation payable over the initial 312 weeks at the applicable permanent total disability compensation rate under Subsection (2).

(c)   The Employers' Reinsurance Fund shall for an overpayment of compensation described in Subsection (3)(b), reimburse the overpayment:

    (i)   to the employer or its insurance carrier; and

    (ii)   out of the Employers' Reinsurance Fund's liability to the employee.

(d)   After an employee receives compensation from the employee's employer, its insurance carrier, or the Employers' Reinsurance Fund for any combination of disabilities amounting to 312 weeks of compensation at the applicable permanent total disability compensation rate, the Employers' Reinsurance Fund shall pay all remaining permanent total disability compensation.

(e)   Employers' Reinsurance Fund payments shall commence immediately after the employer or its insurance carrier satisfies its liability under this Subsection (3) or Section **34A-2-703**.

(4)   This Subsection (4) applies to claims resulting from an accident or disease arising out of and in the course of the employee's employment on or after July 1, 1994.

(a)   The employer or its insurance carrier is liable for permanent total disability compensation.

(b)   The employer or its insurance carrier may not be required to pay compensation for any combination of disabilities of any kind, as provided in this section and Sections **34A-2-410** through **34A-2-412** and Part 5, Industrial Noise, in excess of the amount of compensation payable over the initial 312 weeks at the applicable permanent total disability compensation rate under Subsection (2).

(c)   The employer or its insurance carrier may recoup the overpayment of compensation described in Subsection (4) by reasonably offsetting the overpayment against future liability paid before or after the initial 312 weeks.

(5)   (a)   A finding by the commission of permanent total disability is not final, unless otherwise agreed to by the parties, until:

    (i)   an administrative law judge reviews a summary of reemployment activities undertaken pursuant to Chapter 8a, Utah Injured Worker Reemployment Act;

    (ii)   the employer or its insurance carrier submits to the administrative law judge:

        (A)   a reemployment plan as prepared by a qualified rehabilitation provider reasonably designed to return the employee to gainful employment; or

        (B)   notice that the employer or its insurance carrier will not submit a plan; and

    (iii)   the administrative law judge, after notice to the parties, holds a hearing, unless otherwise stipulated, to:

        (A)   consider evidence regarding rehabilitation; and

        (B)   review any reemployment plan submitted by the employer or its insurance carrier under Subsection (5)(a)(ii).

(b)   Before commencing the procedure required by Subsection (5)(a), the administrative law judge shall order:

(i)   the initiation of permanent total disability compensation payments to provide for the employee's subsistence; and

(ii) the payment of any undisputed disability or medical benefits due the employee.

(c)   Notwithstanding Subsection (5)(a), an order for payment of benefits described in Subsection (5)(b) is considered a final order for purposes of Section **34A-2-212**.

(d)   The employer or its insurance carrier shall be given credit for any disability payments made under Subsection (5)(b) against its ultimate disability compensation liability under this chapter or Chapter 3, Utah Occupational Disease Act.

(e)   An employer or its insurance carrier may not be ordered to submit a reemployment plan. If the employer or its insurance carrier voluntarily submits a plan, the plan is subject to Subsections (5)(e)(i) through (iii).

(i)   The plan may include, but not require an employee to pay for:

(A) retraining;

(B) education;

(C) medical and disability compensation benefits;

(D) job placement services; or

(E) incentives calculated to facilitate reemployment.

(ii) The plan shall include payment of reasonable disability compensation to provide for the employee's subsistence during the rehabilitation process.

(iii) The employer or its insurance carrier shall diligently pursue the reemployment plan. The employer's or insurance carrier's failure to diligently pursue the reemployment plan is cause for the administrative law judge on the administrative law judge's own motion to make a final decision of permanent total disability.

(f)   If a preponderance of the evidence shows that successful rehabilitation is not possible, the administrative law judge shall order that the employee be paid weekly permanent total disability compensation benefits.

(g)   If a preponderance of the evidence shows that pursuant to a reemployment plan, as prepared by a qualified rehabilitation provider and presented under Subsection (5)(e), an employee could immediately or without unreasonable delay return to work but for the following, an administrative law judge shall order that the employee be denied the payment of weekly permanent total disability compensation benefits:

(i)   incarceration in a facility operated by or contracting with a federal, state, county, or municipal government to house a criminal offender in either a secure or nonsecure setting; or

(ii) not being legally eligible to be employed because of a reason unrelated to the impairment or combination of impairments.

(6) (a)   The period of benefits commences on the date the employee acquired the permanent, total disability, as determined by a final order of the commission based on the facts and evidence, and ends:

(i)   with the death of the employee; or

(ii) when the employee is capable of returning to regular, steady work.

(b)   An employer or its insurance carrier may provide or locate for a permanently totally disabled employee reasonable, medically appropriate, part-time work in a job earning at least minimum wage, except that the employee may not be required to accept the work to the extent that it would disqualify the employee from Social Security disability benefits.

(c)   An employee shall:

    (iii)   fully cooperate in the placement and employment process; and

    (iv)   accept the reasonable, medically appropriate, part-time work.

(d)   In a consecutive four-week period when an employee's gross income from the work provided under Subsection (6)(b) exceeds $500, the employer or insurance carrier may reduce the employee's permanent total disability compensation by 50% of the employee's income in excess of $500.

(e)   If a work opportunity is not provided by the employer or its insurance carrier, an employee with a permanent, total disability may obtain medically appropriate, part-time work subject to the offset provisions of Subsection (6)(d).

(f)   (i)   The commission shall establish rules regarding the part-time work and offset.

    (ii)   The adjudication of disputes arising under this Subsection (6) is governed by Part 8, Adjudication.

(g)   The employer or its insurance carrier has the burden of proof to show that medically appropriate part-time work is available.

(h)   The administrative law judge may:

    (i)   excuse an employee from participation in any work:

        (A)   that would require the employee to undertake work exceeding the employee's:

            (I)   medical capacity; or

            (II)   residual functional capacity; or

        (B)   for good cause; or

    (ii)   allow the employer or its insurance carrier to reduce permanent total disability benefits as provided in Subsection (6)(d) when reasonable, medically appropriate, part-time work is offered, but the employee fails to fully cooperate.

(7)   When an employee is rehabilitated or the employee's rehabilitation is possible but the employee has some loss of bodily function, the award shall be for permanent partial disability.

(8)   As determined by an administrative law judge, an employee is not entitled to disability compensation, unless the employee fully cooperates with any evaluation or reemployment plan under this chapter or Chapter 3, Utah Occupational Disease Act. The administrative law judge shall dismiss without prejudice the claim for benefits of an employee if the administrative law judge finds that the employee fails to fully cooperate, unless the administrative law judge states specific findings on the record justifying dismissal with prejudice.

(9)   (a)   The loss or permanent and complete loss of the use of the following constitutes total and permanent disability that is compensated according to this section:

    (i)   both hands;

    (ii)   both arms;

    (iii)   both feet;

    (iv)   both legs;

              (v)   both eyes; or

              (vi)   any combination of two body members described in this Subsection (9)(a).

     (b)   A finding of permanent total disability pursuant to Subsection (9)(a) is final.

(10)   (a)   An insurer or self-insured employer may periodically reexamine a permanent total disability claim, except those based on Subsection (9), for which the insurer or self-insured employer had or has payment responsibility to determine whether the employee continues to have a permanent, total disability.

     (b)   Reexamination may be conducted no more than once every three years after an award is final, unless good cause is shown by the employer or its insurance carrier to allow more frequent reexaminations.

     (c)   The reexamination may include:

              (i)   the review of medical records;

              (ii)   employee submission to one or more reasonable medical evaluations;

              (iii)   employee submission to one or more reasonable rehabilitation evaluations and retraining efforts;

              (iv)   employee disclosure of Federal Income Tax Returns;

              (v)   employee certification of compliance with Section **34A-2-110**; and

              (vi)   employee completion of one or more sworn affidavits or questionnaires approved by the division.

     (d)   The insurer or self-insured employer shall pay for the cost of a reexamination with appropriate employee reimbursement pursuant to rule for reasonable travel allowance and per diem as well as reasonable expert witness fees incurred by the employee in supporting the employee's claim for permanent total disability benefits at the time of reexamination.

     (e)   If an employee fails to fully cooperate in the reasonable reexamination of a permanent total disability finding, an administrative law judge may order the suspension of the employee's permanent total disability benefits until the employee cooperates with the reexamination.

     (f)   (i)   If the reexamination of a permanent total disability finding reveals evidence that reasonably raises the issue of an employee's continued entitlement to permanent total disability compensation benefits, an insurer or self-insured employer may petition the Division of Adjudication for a rehearing on that issue. The insurer or self-insured employer shall include with the petition, documentation supporting the insurer's or self-insured employer's belief that the employee no longer has a permanent, total disability.

              (ii)   If the petition under Subsection (10)(f)(i) demonstrates good cause, as determined by the Division of Adjudication, an administrative law judge shall adjudicate the issue at a hearing.

              (iii)   Evidence of an employee's participation in medically appropriate, part-time work may not be the sole basis for termination of an employee's permanent total disability entitlement, but the evidence of the employee's participation in medically appropriate, part-time work under Subsection (6) may be considered in the reexamination or hearing with other evidence relating to the employee's status and condition.

     (g)   In accordance with Section **34A-1-309**, the administrative law judge may award reasonable attorney fees to an attorney retained by an employee to represent the employee's interests with respect to reexamination of the permanent total disability finding, except if the employee does not prevail, the attorney fees shall be set at $1,000. The attorney fees awarded shall be paid by the employer or its insurance carrier in addition to the permanent total disability compensation benefits due.

(h)   During the period of reexamination or adjudication, if the employee fully cooperates, each insurer, self-insured employer, or the Employers' Reinsurance Fund shall continue to pay the permanent total disability compensation benefits due the employee.

(11)   If any provision of this section, or the application of any provision to any person or circumstance, is held invalid, the remainder of this section is given effect without the invalid provision or application.

34A-2-414. Benefits in case of death Distribution of award to dependents — Death of dependents — Remarriage of surviving spouse.

(1)   (a)   The benefits in case of death shall be paid to one or more of the dependents of the decedent for the benefit of all the dependents, as may be determined by an administrative law judge.

(b)   The administrative law judge may apportion the benefits among the dependents in the manner that the administrative law judge considers just and equitable.

(c)   Payment to a dependent subsequent in right may be made, if the administrative law judge considers it proper, and shall operate to discharge all other claims.

(2)   The dependents, or persons to whom benefits are paid, shall apply the same to the use of the several beneficiaries thereof in compliance with the finding and direction of the administrative law judge.

(3)   In all cases of death when:

(a)   the dependents are a surviving spouse and one or more minor children, it shall be sufficient for the surviving spouse to make application to the Division of Adjudication on behalf of that individual and the minor children; and

(b)   all of the dependents are minors, the application shall be made by the guardian or next friend of the minor dependents.

(4)   The administrative law judge may, for the purpose of protecting the rights and interests of any minor dependents the administrative law judge considers incapable of doing so, provide a method of safeguarding any payments due the minor dependents.

(5)   Should any dependent of a deceased employee die during the period covered by weekly payments authorized by this section, the right of the deceased dependent to compensation under this chapter or Chapter 3, Utah Occupational Disease Act, shall cease.

(6)   (a)   If a surviving spouse, who is a dependent of a deceased employee and who is receiving the benefits of this chapter or Chapter 3 remarries, that individual's sole right after the remarriage to further payments of compensation shall be the right to receive in a lump sum the lesser of:

(i)   the balance of the weekly compensation payments unpaid from the time of remarriage to the end of six years or 312 weeks from the date of the injury from which death resulted; or

(ii)   an amount equal to 52 weeks of compensation at the weekly compensation rate the surviving spouse was receiving at the time of such remarriage.

(b)   (i)   If there are other dependents remaining at the time of remarriage, benefits payable under this chapter or Chapter 3, Utah Occupational Disease Act, shall be paid to such person as an administrative law judge may determine, for the use and benefit of the other dependents.

(ii) The weekly benefits to be paid under Subsection (6)(b)(i) shall be paid at intervals of not less than four weeks.

34A-2-415. Increase of award to children and dependent spouse — Effect of death, marriage, majority, or termination of dependency of children — Death, divorce, or remarriage of spouse.

If an award is made to, or increased because of a dependent spouse or dependent minor child or children, as provided in this chapter or Chapter 3, Utah Occupational Disease Act, the award or increase in amount of the award shall cease at:

(1) the death, marriage, attainment of the age of 18 years, or termination of dependency of the minor child or children; or

(2) upon the death, divorce, or remarriage of the spouse of the employee, subject to the provisions in Section 34A-2-414 relative to the remarriage of a spouse.

34A-2-416. Additional benefits in special cases.

(1) An administrative law judge may extend indefinitely benefits received by a wholly dependent person under this chapter or Chapter 3, Utah Occupational Disease Act, if at the termination of the benefits:

(a) the wholly dependent person is still in a dependent condition; and

(b) under all reasonable circumstances the wholly dependent person should be entitled to additional benefits.

(2) If benefits are extended under Subsection (1):

(a) the liability of the employer or insurance carrier involved may not be extended; and

(b) the additional benefits allowed shall be paid out of the Employers' Reinsurance Fund created in Subsection 34A-2-702(1).

34A-2-417. Claims and benefits — Time limits for filing — Burden of proof.

(1) (a) Except with respect to prosthetic devices or in a permanent total disability case, an employee is entitled to be compensated for a medical expense if:

(i) the medical expense is:

(A) reasonable in amount; and

(B) necessary to treat the industrial accident; and

(ii) the employee submits or makes a reasonable attempt to submit the medical expense:

(A) to the employee's employer or insurance carrier for payment; and

(B) within one year from the later of:

(I) the day on which the medical expense is incurred; or

(II) the day on which the employee knows or in the exercise of reasonable diligence should have known that the medical expense is related to the industrial accident.

(b) For an industrial accident that occurs on or after July 1, 1988, and is the basis of a claim for a medical expense, an employee is entitled to be compensated for the medical expense if the employee meets the requirements of Subsection (1)(a).

(2)   (a)   A claim described in Subsection (2)(b) is barred, unless the employee:

           (i)   files an application for hearing with the Division of Adjudication no later than six years from the date of the accident; and

           (ii)   by no later than 12 years from the date of the accident, is able to meet the employee's burden of proving that the employee is due the compensation claimed under this chapter.

      (b)   Subsection (2)(a) applies to a claim for compensation for:

           (i)   temporary total disability benefits;

           (ii)   temporary partial disability benefits;

           (iii) permanent partial disability benefits; or

           (iv) permanent total disability benefits.

      (c)   The commission may enter an order awarding or denying an employee's claim for compensation under this chapter within a reasonable time period beyond 12 years from the date of the accident, if:

           (i)   the employee complies with Subsection (2)(a); and

           (ii)   12 years from the date of the accident:

                (C)   (I)   the employee is fully cooperating in a commission approved reemployment plan; and

                     (II) the results of that commission approved reemployment plan are not known; or

                (D)   the employee is actively adjudicating issues of compensability before the commission.

(3)   A claim for death benefits is barred unless an application for hearing is filed within one year of the date of death of the employee.

(4)   (a)   (i)   Subject to Subsections (2)(c) and (4)(b), after an employee files an application for hearing within six years from the date of the accident, the Division of Adjudication may enter an order to show cause why the employee's claim should not be dismissed because the employee has failed to meet the employee's burden of proof to establish an entitlement to compensation claimed in the application for hearing.

           (ii)   The order described in Subsection (4)(a)(i) may be entered on the motion of the:

                (A)   Division of Adjudication;

                (B)   employee's employer; or

                (C)   employer's insurance carrier.

      (b)   Under Subsection (4)(a), the Division of Adjudication may dismiss a claim:

           (i)   without prejudice; or

            (ii)   with prejudice only if:

                (A)   the Division of Adjudication adjudicates the merits of the employee's entitlement to the compensation claimed in the application for hearing; or

                (B)   the employee fails to comply with Subsection (2)(a)(ii).

      (c)   If a claim is dismissed without prejudice under Subsection (4)(b), the employee is subject to the time limits under Subsection (2)(a) to claim compensation under this chapter.

(5)   A claim for compensation under this chapter is subject to a claim or lien for recovery under Section **26-19-5**.

34A-2-418. Awards Medical, nursing, hospital, and burial expenses — Artificial means and appliances.

(1)   In addition to the compensation provided in this chapter or Chapter 3, Utah Occupational Disease Act, the employer or the insurance carrier shall pay reasonable sums for medical, nurse, and hospital services, for medicines, and for artificial means, appliances, and prostheses necessary to treat the injured employee.

(2)   If death results from the injury, the employer or the insurance carrier shall pay the burial expenses in ordinary cases as established by rule.

(3)   If a compensable accident results in the breaking of or loss of an employee's artificial means or appliance including eyeglasses, the employer or insurance carrier shall provide a replacement of the artificial means or appliance.

(4)   An administrative law judge may require the employer or insurance carrier to maintain the artificial means or appliances or provide the employee with a replacement of any artificial means or appliance for the reason of breakage, wear and tear, deterioration, or obsolescence.

(5)   An administrative law judge may, in unusual cases, order, as the administrative law judge considers just and proper, the payment of additional sums:

    (a)   for burial expenses; or

    (b)   to provide for artificial means or appliances.

34A-2-419. Agreements in addition to compensation and benefits.

(1)   (a)   Subject to the approval of the division, any employer securing the payment of workers' compensation benefits for its employees under Section 34A-2-201 may enter into or continue any agreement with the employer's employees to provide compensation or other benefits in addition to the compensation and other benefits provided by this chapter or Chapter 3, Utah Occupational Disease Act.

    (b)   An agreement may not be approved if it requires contributions from the employees, unless it confers benefits in addition to those provided under this chapter or Chapter 3, Utah Occupational Disease Act, at least commensurate with the contributions.

    (c)   An agreement for additional benefits may be terminated by the division if:

        (i)   it appears that the agreement is not fairly administered;

        (ii)   its operation discloses defects threatening its solvency; or

        (iii)   for any substantial reason it fails to accomplish the purposes of this chapter or Chapter 3, Utah Occupational Disease Act.

    (d)   If the agreement is terminated, the division shall determine the proper distribution of any remaining assets.

    (e)   The termination under Subsection (1)(c) becomes a final order of the commission effective 30 days from the date the division terminates the agreement, unless within the 30 days either the employer or employee files an application for hearing with the Division of Adjudication in accordance with Part 8, Adjudication. The application for hearing may contest:

        (i)   the recommendation to terminate the agreement;

        (ii)   the distribution of remaining assets after termination; or

        (iii)   both the recommendation to terminate and the distribution of remaining assets.

(2)   (a)   Any employer who makes a deduction from the wages or salary of any employee to pay for the statutory benefits of this chapter or Chapter 3, Utah Occupational Disease Act, is guilty of a class A misdemeanor.

(b)   Subject to the supervision of the division, nothing in this chapter or Chapter 3, Utah Occupational Disease Act, may be construed as preventing the employer and the employer's employees from entering into mutual contracts and agreements respecting hospital benefits and accommodations, medical and surgical services, nursing, and medicines to be furnished to the employees as provided in this chapter or Chapter 3, Utah Occupational Disease Act, if no direct or indirect profit is made by any employer as a result of the contract or agreement.

(3)   The purpose and intent of this section is that, where hospitals are maintained and medical and surgical services and medicines furnished by the employer from payments by, or assessments on, the employer's employees, the payments or assessments may not be more or greater than necessary to make these benefits selfsupporting for the care and treatment of the employer's employees. Money received or retained by the employer from the employees for the purpose of these benefits shall be paid and applied to these services. Any hospitals so maintained in whole or in part by payments or assessment of employees are subject to the inspection and supervision of the division as to services and treatment rendered to the employees.

34A-2-420. Continuing jurisdiction of commission — No authority to change statutes of limitation — Authority to destroy records Interest on award — Authority to approve final settlement claims.

(1)   (a)   The powers and jurisdiction of the commission over each case shall be continuing.

(b)   After notice and hearing, the Division of Adjudication, commissioner, or Appeals Board in accordance with Part 8, Adjudication, may from time to time modify or change a former finding or order of the commission.

(c)   This section may not be interpreted as modifying in any respect the statutes of limitations contained in other sections of this chapter or Chapter 3, Utah Occupational Disease Act.

(d)   The commission may not in any respect change the statutes of limitation referred to in Subsection (1)(c).

(2)   Records pertaining to cases that have been closed and inactive for ten years, other than cases of total permanent disability or cases in which a claim has been filed as in Section 34A-2-417, may be destroyed at the discretion of the commission.

(3)   Awards made by a final order of the commission shall include interest at the rate of 8% per annum from the date when each benefit payment would have otherwise become due and payable.

(4)   Notwithstanding Subsection (1) and Section 34A-2-108, an administrative law judge shall review and may approve the agreement of the parties to enter into a full and final:

(a)   compromise settlement of disputed medical, disability, or death benefit entitlements under this chapter or Chapter 3, Utah Occupational Disease Act; or

(b)   commutation and settlement of reasonable future medical, disability, or death benefit entitlements under this chapter or Chapter 3 by means of a lump sum payment, structured settlement, or other appropriate payout.

34A-2-421. Lumpsum payments.

An administrative law judge, under special circumstances and when the same is deemed advisable, may commute periodic benefits to one or more lumpsum payments.

34A-2-422.   Compensation exempt from execution — Transfer of payment rights.

(1)   For purposes of this section:

    (a)   "Payment rights under workers' compensation" means the right to receive compensation under this chapter or Chapter 3, Utah Occupational Disease Act, including the payment of a workers' compensation claim, award, benefit, or settlement.

    (b)   (i)   Subject to Subsection (1)(b)(ii), "transfer" means:

        (A)   a sale;

        (B)   an assignment;

        (C)   a pledge;

        (D)   an hypothecation; or

        (E)   other form of encumbrance or alienation for consideration.

       (iv)   "Transfer" does not include the creation or perfection of a security interest in a right to receive a payment under a blanket security agreement entered into with an insured depository institution, in the absence of any action to:

        (A)   redirect the payments to:

           (I)   the insured depository institution; or

           (II)   an agent or successor in interest to the insured depository institution; or

        (B)   otherwise enforce a blanket security interest against the payment rights.

(2)   Compensation before payment:

    (a)   is exempt from:

       (i)   all claims of creditors; and

       (ii)   attachment or execution; and

    (b)   shall be paid only to employees or their dependents, except as provided in Sections 26195 and 34A-2-417.

(3)   (a)   Subject to Subsection (3)(b), beginning April 30, 2007, a person may not:

       (i)   transfer payment rights under workers' compensation; or

       (ii)   accept or take any action to provide for a transfer of payment rights under workers' compensation.

    (b)   A person may take an action prohibited under Subsection (3)(a) if the commission approves the transfer of payment rights under workers' compensation:

       (i)   before the transfer of payment rights under workers' compensation takes effect; and

       (ii)   upon a determination by the commission that:

        (A)   the person transferring the payment rights under workers' compensation received before executing an agreement to transfer those payment rights:

           (I)   adequate notice that the transaction involving the transfer of payment rights under workers' compensation involves the transfer of those payment rights; and

           (II)   an explanation of the financial consequences of and alternatives to the transfer of payment rights under workers' compensation in sufficient detail that the person transferring the payment rights under workers' compensation made an informed decision to transfer those payment rights; and

    (B)   the transfer of payment rights under workers' compensation is in the best interest of the person transferring the payment rights under workers' compensation taking into account the welfare and support of that person's dependents.

(c)   The approval by the commission of the transfer of a person's payment rights under workers' compensation is a full and final resolution of the person's payment rights under workers' compensation that are transferred:

    (i)   if the commission approves the transfer of the payment rights under workers' compensation in accordance with Subsection (3)(b); and

    (ii)   once the person no longer has a right to appeal the decision in accordance with this title.

34A-2-423. Survival of claim in case of death.

(1)   As used in this section:

    (a)   "Estate" is as defined in Section 751201.

    (b)   "Personal representative" is as defined in Section 751201.

(2)   The personal representative of the estate of an employee may adjudicate an employee's claim for compensation under this chapter if in accordance with this chapter, the employee files a claim:

    (a)   before the employee dies; and

    (b)   for compensation for an industrial accident or occupational disease for which compensation is payable under this chapter or Chapter 3, Utah Occupational Disease Act.

(3)   If the commission finds that the employee is entitled to compensation under this chapter for the claim described in Subsection (2)(a), the commission shall order that compensation be paid for the period:

    (a)   beginning on the day on which the employee is entitled to receive compensation under this chapter; and

    (b)   ending on the day on which the employee dies.

(4)   (a)   Compensation awarded under Subsection (3) shall be paid to:

        (i)   if the employee has one or more dependents on the day on which the employee dies, to the dependents of the employee; or

        (ii)   if the employee has no dependents on the day on which the employee dies, to the estate of the employee.

    (b)   The commission may apportion any compensation paid to dependents under this Subsection (4) in the manner that the commission considers just and equitable.

(5)   If an employee that files a claim under this chapter dies from the industrial accident or occupational disease that is the basis of the employee's claim, the compensation awarded under this section shall be in addition to death benefits awarded in accordance with Section 34A-2-414.

34A-2-501. Definitions.

    (1)   "Harmful industrial noise" means:

        (a)   sound that results in acoustic trauma such as sudden instantaneous temporary noise or impulsive or impact noise exceeding 140 dB peak sound pressure levels; or

        (b)   the sound emanating from equipment and machines during employment exceeding the following permissible sound levels, dBA slow response, and corresponding durations per day, in hours:

Sound level	Duration
90	8
92	6
95	4
97	3
100	2
102	1.5
105	1.0
110	0.5
115	0.25 or less

    (2)   "Loss of hearing" means binaural hearing loss measured in decibels with frequencies of 500, 1,000, 2,000, and 3,000 cycles per second (Hertz). If the average decibel loss at 500, 1,000, 2,000, and 3,000 cycles per second (Hertz) is 25 decibels or less, usually no hearing impairment exists.

34A-2-502. Intensity tests.

    (1)   The commission may conduct tests to determine the intensity of noise at places of employment.

    (2)   An administrative law judge may consider tests conducted by the commission, and any other tests taken by authorities in the field of sound engineering, as evidence of harmful industrial noise.

34A-2-503. Loss of hearing — Occupational hearing loss due to noise to be compensated.

    (1)   Permanent hearing loss caused by exposure to harmful industrial noise or by direct head injury shall be compensated according to the terms and conditions of this chapter or Chapter 3, Utah Occupational Disease Act.

    (2)   A claim for compensation for hearing loss for harmful industrial noise may not be paid under this chapter or Chapter 3, Utah Occupational Disease Act, unless it can be demonstrated by a professionally controlled sound test that the employee has been exposed to harmful industrial noise as defined in Section 34A-2-501 while employed by the employer against whom the claim is made.

34A-2-504. Loss of hearing — Extent of employer's liability.

    (1)   An employer is liable only for the hearing loss of an employee that arises out of and in the course of the employee's employment for that employer.

    (2)   If previous occupational hearing loss or nonoccupational hearing impairment is established by competent evidence, the employer may not be liable for the prior hearing loss so established, whether or not compensation has previously been paid or awarded. The employer is liable only for the difference between the percentage of hearing loss presently established and that percentage of prior hearing loss established by preemployment audiogram or other competent evidence.

(3)   The date for compensation for occupational hearing loss shall be determined by the date of direct head injury or the last date when harmful industrial noise contributed substantially in causing the hearing loss.

34A-2-505.   Loss of hearing — Compensation for permanent partial disability.

(1)   Compensation for permanent partial disability for binaural hearing loss shall be determined by multiplying the percentage of binaural hearing loss by 109 weeks of compensation benefits as provided in this chapter or Chapter 3, Utah Occupational Disease Act.

(2)   When an employee files one or more claims for hearing loss the percentage of hearing loss previously found to exist shall be deducted from any subsequent award by the commission.

(3)   In no event shall compensation benefits be paid for total or 100% binaural hearing loss exceeding 109 weeks of compensation benefits.

34A-2-506.   Loss of hearing — Time for filing claim.

An employee's occupational hearing loss shall be reported to the employer pursuant to Section 34A-2-407 within 180 days of the date the employee:

(1)   first suffered altered hearing; and

(2)   knew, or in the exercise of reasonable diligence should have known, that the hearing loss was caused by employment.

34A-2-507.   Measuring hearing loss.

(1)   The degree of hearing loss shall be established, no sooner than six weeks after termination of exposure to the harmful industrial noise, by audiometric determination of hearing threshold level performed by medical or paramedical professionals recognized by the commission, as measured from 0 decibels on an audiometer calibrated to ANSIS3.61969, American National Standard "Specifications for Audiometers" (1969).

(2)   (a)   In any evaluation of occupational hearing loss, only hearing levels at frequencies of 500, 1,000, 2,000, and 3,000 cycles per second (Hertz) shall be considered. The individual measurements for each ear shall be added together and then shall be divided by four to determine the average decibel loss in each ear.

        (b)   To determine the percentage of hearing loss in each ear, the average decibel loss for each decibel of loss exceeding 25 decibels shall be multiplied by 1.5% up to the maximum of 100% which is reached at 91.7 decibels.

(3)   Binaural hearing loss or the percentage of binaural hearing loss is determined by:

        (a)   multiplying the percentage of hearing loss in the better ear by five;

        (b)   adding the amount under Subsection (3)(a) with the percentage of hearing loss in the poorer ear; and

        (c)   dividing the number calculated under Subsection (3)(b) by six.

34A-2-601.   Medical panel, director, or consultant — Findings and reports — Objections to report — Hearing — Expenses.

(1)   (a)   The Division of Adjudication may refer the medical aspects of a case described in this Subsection (1)(a) to a medical panel appointed by an administrative law judge:

                (i)   upon the filing of a claim for compensation arising out of and in the course of employment for:

(A)   disability by accident; or

(B)   death by accident; and

(ii)   if the employer or the employer's insurance carrier denies liability.

(b)   An administrative law judge may appoint a medical panel upon the filing of a claim for compensation based upon disability or death due to an occupational disease.

(c)   A medical panel appointed under this section shall consist of one or more physicians specializing in the treatment of the disease or condition involved in the claim.

(d)   As an alternative method of obtaining an impartial medical evaluation of the medical aspects of a controverted case, the division may employ a medical director or one or more medical consultants:

(i)   on a full-time or part-time basis; and

(ii)   for the purpose of:

(A)   evaluating medical evidence; and

(B)   advising an administrative law judge with respect to the administrative law judge's ultimate fact-finding responsibility.

(e)   If all parties agree to the use of a medical director or one or more medical consultants, the medical director or one or more medical consultants is allowed to function in the same manner and under the same procedures as required of a medical panel.

(2)   (a)   A medical panel, medical director, or medical consultant may do the following to the extent the medical panel, medical director, or medical consultant determines that it is necessary or desirable:

(i)   conduct a study;

(ii)   take an x-ray;

(iii)   perform a test; or

(iv)   if authorized by an administrative law judge, conduct a post-mortem examination.

(b)   A medical panel, medical director, or medical consultant shall make:

(i)   a report in writing to the administrative law judge in a form prescribed by the Division of Adjudication; and

(ii)   additional findings as the administrative law judge may require.

(c)   In an occupational disease case, in addition to the requirements of Subsection (2)(b), a medical panel, medical director, or medical consultant shall certify to the administrative law judge:

(i)   the extent, if any, of the disability of the claimant from performing work for remuneration or profit;

(ii)   whether the sole cause of the disability or death, in the opinion of the medical panel, medical director, or medical consultant results from the occupational disease; and

(iii)   (A)   whether any other cause aggravated, prolonged, accelerated, or in any way contributed to the disability or death; and

(B)   if another cause contributed to the disability or death, the extent in percentage to which the other cause contributed to the disability or death.

(d)   (i)   An administrative law judge shall promptly distribute full copies of a report submitted to the administrative law judge under this Subsection (2) by mail to:

      (A)   the applicant;

      (B)   the employer;

      (C)   the employer's insurance carrier; and

      (D)   an attorney employed by a person listed in Subsections (2)(d)(i)(A) through (C).

   (ii)   Within 20 days after the report described in Subsection (2)(d)(i) is deposited in the United States post office, the following may file with the administrative law judge a written objection to the report:

      (A)   the applicant;

      (B)   the employer; or

      (C)   the employer's insurance carrier.

   (iv)   If no written objection is filed within the period described in Subsection (2)(d)(ii), the report is considered admitted in evidence.

(e)   (i)   An administrative law judge may base the administrative law judge's finding and decision on the report of:

      (A)   a medical panel;

      (B)   the medical director; or

      (C)   one or more medical consultants.

   (ii)   Notwithstanding Subsection (2)(e)(i), an administrative law judge is not bound by a report described in Subsection (2)(e)(i) if other substantial conflicting evidence in the case supports a contrary finding.

(f)   (i)   If a written objection to a report is filed under Subsection (2)(d), the administrative law judge may set the case for hearing to determine the facts and issues involved.

   (ii)   At a hearing held pursuant to this Subsection (2)(f), any party may request the administrative law judge to have any of the following present at the hearing for examination and cross-examination:

      (A)   the chair of the medical panel;

      (B)   the medical director; or

      (C)   the one or more medical consultants.

   (iii)   For good cause shown, an administrative law judge may order the following to be present at the hearing for examination and cross-examination:

      (A)   a member of a medical panel, with or without the chair of the medical panel;

      (B)   the medical director; or

      (C)   a medical consultant.

(g)   (i)   A written report of a medical panel, medical director, or one or more medical consultants may be received as an exhibit at a hearing described in Subsection (2)(f).

   (ii)   Notwithstanding Subsection (2)(g)(i), a report received as an exhibit under Subsection (2)(g)(i) may not be considered as evidence in the case except as far as the report is sustained by the testimony admitted.

(h) For a claim referred under Subsection (1) to a medical panel, medical director, or medical consultant before July 1, 1997, the commission shall pay out of the Employers' Reinsurance Fund established in Section **34A-2-702**:

  (i) expenses of a study or report of the medical panel, medical director, or medical consultant; and

  (ii) the expenses of the medical panel's, medical director's, or medical consultant's appearance before an administrative law judge.

(i) (i) For a claim referred under Subsection (1) to a medical panel, medical director, or medical consultant on or after July 1, 1997, the commission shall pay out of the Uninsured Employers' Fund established in Section **34A-2-704** the expenses of:

    (A) a study or report of the medical panel, medical director, or medical consultant; and

    (B) the medical panel's, medical director's, or medical consultant's appearance before an administrative law judge.

  (ii) Notwithstanding Section **34A-2-704**, the expenses described in Subsection (2)(i)(i) shall be paid from the Uninsured Employers' Fund whether or not the employment relationship during which the industrial accident or occupational disease occurred is localized in Utah as described in Subsection **34A-2-704**(20).

34A-2-602. Physical examinations.

(1) The division or an administrative law judge may require an employee claiming the right to receive compensation under this chapter to submit to a medical examination at any time, and from time to time, at a place reasonably convenient for the employee, and as may be provided by the rules of the commission.

(2) If an employee refuses to submit to an examination under Subsection (1), or obstructs the examination, the employee's right to have the employee's claim for compensation considered, if the employee's claim is pending before an administrative law judge, commissioner, or Appeals Board, or to receive any payments for compensation theretofore granted by a final order of the commission, shall be suspended during the period of the refusal or obstruction.

34A-2-603. Autopsy in death cases — Certified pathologist — Attending physicians — Penalty for refusal to permit — Liability.

(1) (a) On the filing of a claim for compensation for death under this chapter or Chapter 3, Utah Occupational Disease Act, when, in the opinion of the commissioner or the commissioner's designee it is necessary to accurately and scientifically ascertain the cause of death, an autopsy may be ordered by the commissioner or the commissioner's designee.

  (b) The commissioner or the commissioner's designee shall:

    (i) designate the certified pathologist to make the autopsy; and

    (ii) determine who shall pay the charge of the certified pathologist making the autopsy.

(2) Any person interested may designate a duly licensed physician to attend the autopsy ordered under Subsection (1).

(3) The findings of the certified pathologist performing the autopsy shall be filed with the commission.

(4) All proceedings for compensation shall be suspended upon refusal of a claimant or claimants to permit such autopsy when ordered under Subsection (1).

(5)   When an autopsy has been performed pursuant to an order of the commissioner or the commissioner's designee no cause of action shall lie against any person, firm, or corporation for participating in or requesting the autopsy.

34A-2-604. Employee leaving place of treatment.

(1)   An injured employee who desires to leave the locality in which the employee has been employed during the treatment of the employee's injury, or to leave this state, shall:

    (a)   report to the employee's attending physician for examination;

    (b)   notify the division in writing of the intention to leave; and

    (c)   accompany the notice with a certificate from the attending physician setting forth:

        (i)   the exact nature of the injury;

        (ii)   the condition of the employee; and

        (iii)   a statement of the probable length of time disability will continue.

(2)   An employee may leave the locality in which the employee was employed only after:

    (a)   complying with Subsection (1); and

    (b)   receiving the written consent of the division.

(3)   If an employee does not comply with this section, compensation may not be allowed during the absence.

34A-2-701. Premium assessment restricted account for safety.

(1)   There is created in the General Fund a restricted account known as the "Workplace Safety Account."

(2)   (a)   An amount equal to 0.25% of the premium income remitted to the state treasurer pursuant to Subsection **59-9-101**(2)(c)(ii) shall be deposited in the Workplace Safety Account in the General Fund for use as provided in this section.

    (b)   Beginning with fiscal year 2008-09, if the balance in the Workplace Safety Account exceeds $500,000 at the close of a fiscal year, the excess shall be transferred to the Employers' Reinsurance Fund, created under Subsection **34A-2-702**(1).

(3)   The Legislature shall appropriate from the restricted account money to one or both of the following:

    (a)   money to the commission for use by the commission to:

        (i)   improve safety consultation services available to Utah employers; or

        (ii)   provide for electronic or print media advertising campaigns designed to promote workplace safety; and

    (b)   subject to Subsection (7), money known as the "Eddie P. Mayne Workplace Safety and Occupational Health Funding Program":

        (i)   to an institution within the state system of higher education, as defined in Section **53B-1-102**; and

        (ii)   to be expended by an education and research center that is:

            (A)   affiliated with the institution described in Subsection (3)(b)(i); and

            (B)   designated as an education and research center by the National Institute for Occupational Safety and Health.

(4)   From money appropriated by the Legislature from the restricted account to the commission for use by the commission, the commission may fund other safety programs or initiatives recommended to it by its state workers' compensation advisory council created under Section **34A-2-107**.

(5)   (a)   The commission shall annually report to the governor, the Legislature, and its state council regarding:

        (i)   the use of the money appropriated to the commission under Subsection (3) or (4); and

        (ii)   the impact of the use of the money on the safety of Utah's workplaces.

    (b)   By no later than August 15 following a fiscal year in which an education and research center receives money from an appropriation under Subsection (3)(b), the education and research center shall report:

        (i)   to:

            (A)   the governor;

            (B)   the Legislature;

            (C)   the commission; and

            (D)   the state workers' compensation advisory council created under Section **34A-2-107**; and

        (ii)   regarding:

            (A)   the use of the money appropriated under Subsection (3)(b); and

            (B)   the impact of the use of the money on the safety of Utah's workplaces.

(6)   The money deposited in the restricted account:

    (a)   shall be:

        (i)   used only for the activities described in Subsection (3) or (4); and

        (ii)   expended according to processes that can be verified by audit; and

    (b)   may not be used by the commission for:

        (i)   administrative costs unrelated to the restricted account; or

        (ii)   any activity of the commission other than the activities of the commission described in Subsection (3) or (4).

(7)   The total of appropriations under Subsection (3)(b) may not exceed for a fiscal year an amount equal to 20% of the premium income remitted to the state treasurer pursuant to Subsection **59-9-101**(2)(c) and deposited in the Workplace Safety Account during the previous fiscal year.

34A-2-702.   Employers' Reinsurance Fund — Injury causing death — Burial expenses — Payments to dependents.

(1)   (a)   There is created an Employers' Reinsurance Fund for the purpose of making payments for industrial accidents or occupational diseases occurring on or before June 30, 1994. The payments shall be made in accordance with this chapter or Chapter 3, Utah Occupational Disease Act. The Employers' Reinsurance Fund shall have no liability for industrial accidents or occupational diseases occurring on or after July 1, 1994.

    (b)   The Employers' Reinsurance Fund shall succeed to all monies previously held in the "Special Fund," the "Combined Injury Fund," or the "Second Injury Fund."

    (c)   The commissioner shall appoint an administrator of the Employers' Reinsurance Fund.

(d)   The state treasurer shall be the custodian of the Employers' Reinsurance Fund, and the administrator shall make provisions for and direct its distribution.

(e)   Reasonable costs of administering the Employers' Reinsurance Fund or other fees may be paid from the fund.

(2)   The state treasurer shall:

(a)   receive workers' compensation premium assessments from the State Tax Commission; and

(b)   invest the Employers' Reinsurance Fund to ensure maximum investment return for both long and short term investments in accordance with Section 51712.5.

(3)   The administrator may employ, retain, or appoint counsel to represent the Employers' Reinsurance Fund in proceedings brought to enforce claims against or on behalf of the fund. If requested by the commission, the attorney general shall aid in representation of the fund.

(4)   The liability of the state, its departments, agencies, instrumentalities, elected or appointed officials, or other duly authorized agents, with respect to payment of any compensation benefits, expenses, fees, medical expenses, or disbursement properly chargeable against the Employers' Reinsurance Fund, is limited to the cash or assets in the Employers' Reinsurance Fund, and they are not otherwise, in any way, liable for the operation, debts, or obligations of the Employers' Reinsurance Fund.

(5)   If injury causes death within a period of 312 weeks from the date of the accident, the employer or insurance carrier shall pay the burial expenses of the deceased as provided in Section 34A-2-418, and further benefits in the amounts and to the persons in accordance with Subsections (5)(a) through (c).

(a)

    (i)   If there are wholly dependent persons at the time of the death, the payment by the employer or its insurance carrier shall be 662/3% of the decedent's average weekly wage at the time of the injury, but not more than a maximum of 85% of the state average weekly wage at the time of the injury per week and not less than a minimum of $45 per week, plus $5 for a dependent spouse, plus $5 for each dependent minor child under the age of 18 years, up to a maximum of four such dependent minor hildren, but not exceeding the average weekly wage of the employee at the time of the injury, and not exceeding 85% of the state average weekly wage at the time of the injury per week.

    (ii)   Compensation shall continue during dependency for the remainder of the period between the date of the death and the expiration of 312 weeks after the date of the injury.

    (iii)   The payment by the employer or its insurance carrier to wholly dependent persons during dependency following the expiration of the first 312-week period described in Subsection (5)(a)(i) shall be an amount equal to the weekly benefits paid to those wholly dependent persons during that initial 312-week period, reduced by 50% of any weekly federal Social Security death benefits paid to those wholly dependent persons.

    (iv)   The issue of dependency shall be subject to review by an administrative law judge at the end of the initial 312-week period and annually after the initial 312-week period. If in any review it is determined that, under the facts and circumstances existing at that time, the applicant is no longer a wholly dependent person, the applicant may be considered a partly dependent or nondependent person and shall be paid such benefits as the administrative law judge may determine under Subsection (5)(b)(iii).

(v)   For purposes of any dependency determination, a surviving spouse of a deceased employee shall be conclusively presumed to be wholly dependent for a 312-week period from the date of death of the employee. This presumption shall not apply after the initial 312-week period and, in determining the then existing annual income of the surviving spouse, the administrative law judge shall exclude 50% of any federal Social Security death benefits received by that surviving spouse.

(b)

(i)   If there are partly dependent persons at the time of the death, the payment shall be 662/3% of the decedent's average weekly wage at the time of the injury, but not more than a maximum of 85% of the state average weekly wage at the time of the injury per week and not less than a minimum of $45 per week.

(ii)   Compensation shall continue during dependency for the remainder of the period between the date of death and the expiration of 312 weeks after the date of injury as the administrative law judge in each case may determine. Compensation may not amount to more than a maximum of $30,000.

(iii)   The benefits provided for in this subsection shall be in keeping with the circumstances and conditions of dependency existing at the date of injury, and any amount awarded by the administrative law judge under this subsection shall be consistent with the general provisions of this chapter and Chapter 3, Utah Occupational Disease Act.

(iv)   Benefits to persons determined to be partly dependent under Subsection (5)(a) (v) shall be determined by the administrative law judge in keeping with the circumstances and conditions of dependency existing at the time of the dependency review and may be paid in an amount not exceeding the maximum weekly rate that partly dependent persons would receive if wholly dependent.

(v)   Payments under this section shall be paid to such persons during their dependency by the employer or its insurance carrier.

(c)   If there are wholly dependent persons and also partly dependent persons at the time of death, the administrative law judge may apportion the benefits as the administrative law judge considers just and equitable; provided, that the total benefits awarded to all parties concerned do not exceed the maximum provided for by law.

(6)   The Employers' Reinsurance Fund:

(a)   shall be:

(i)   used only in accordance with Subsection (1) for:

(A)   the purpose of making payments for industrial accidents or occupational diseases occurring on or before June 30, 1994, in accordance with this section and Section 34A-2-703; and

(B)   payment of:

(I)   reasonable costs of administering the Employers' Reinsurance Fund; or

(II)   fees required to be paid by the Employers' Reinsurance Fund;

(i)   expended according to processes that can be verified by audit; and

(b)   may not be used for:

(ii)   administrative costs unrelated to the fund; or

(iii)   any activity of the commission other than an activity described in Subsection (6)(a).

34A-2-703. Payments from Employers' Reinsurance Fund.

If an employee, who has at least a 10% whole person permanent impairment from any cause or origin, subsequently incurs an additional impairment by an accident arising out of and in the course of the employee's employment during the period of July 1, 1988, to June 30, 1994, inclusive, and if the additional impairment results in permanent total disability, the employer or its insurance carrier and the Employers' Reinsurance Fund are liable for the payment of benefits as follows:

(1)   The employer or its insurance carrier is liable for the first $20,000 of medical benefits and the initial 156 weeks of permanent total disability compensation as provided in this chapter or Chapter 3, Utah Occupational Disease Act.

(2)   Reasonable medical benefits in excess of the first $20,000 shall be paid in the first instance by the employer or its insurance carrier. Then, as provided in Subsection (5), the Employers' Reinsurance Fund shall reimburse the employer or its insurance carrier for 50% of those expenses.

(3)   After the initial 156-week period under Subsection (1), permanent total disability compensation payable to an employee under this chapter or Chapter 3, Utah Occupational Disease Act, becomes the liability of and shall be paid by the Employers' Reinsurance Fund.

(4)   If it is determined that the employee is permanently and totally disabled, the employer or its insurance carrier shall be given credit for all prior payments of temporary total, temporary partial, and permanent partial disability compensation made as a result of the industrial accident. Any overpayment by the employer or its insurance carrier shall be reimbursed by the Employers' Reinsurance Fund under Subsection (5).

(5)   (a)   Upon receipt of a duly verified petition, the Employers' Reinsurance Fund shall reimburse the employer or its insurance carrier for the Employers' Reinsurance Fund's share of medical benefits and compensation paid to or on behalf of an employee. A request for Employers' Reinsurance Fund reimbursements shall be accompanied by satisfactory evidence of payment of the medical or disability compensation for which the reimbursement is requested. Each request is subject to review as to reasonableness by the administrator. The administrator may determine the manner of reimbursement.

        (b)   A decision of the administrator under Subsection (5)(a) may be appealed in accordance with Part 8, Adjudication.

(6)   If, at the time an employee is determined to have a permanent, total disability, the employee has other actionable workers' compensation claims, the employer or insurance carrier that is liable for the last industrial accident resulting in permanent total disability shall be liable for the benefits payable by the employer as provided in this section and Section **34A-2-413**. The employee's entitlement to benefits for prior actionable claims shall then be determined separately on the facts of those claims. Any previous permanent partial disability arising out of those claims shall then be considered to be impairments that may give rise to Employers' Reinsurance Fund liability under this section.

34A-2-704. Uninsured Employers' Fund.

(1)   (a)   There is created an Uninsured Employers' Fund. The Uninsured Employers' Fund has the purpose of assisting in the payment of workers' compensation benefits to a person entitled to the benefits, if:

                (i)   that person's employer:

                        (A)   is individually, jointly, or severally liable to pay the benefits; and

                        (B)   (I)   becomes or is insolvent;

                                (II)   appoints or has appointed a receiver; or

          (III)   otherwise does not have sufficient funds, insurance, sureties, or other security to cover workers' compensation liabilities; and

    (ii)   the employment relationship between that person and the person's employer is localized within the state as provided in Subsection (20).

(b)   The Uninsured Employers' Fund succeeds to money previously held in the Default Indemnity Fund.

(c)   If it becomes necessary to pay benefits, the Uninsured Employers' Fund is liable for the obligations of the employer set forth in this chapter and Chapter 3, Utah Occupational Disease Act, with the exception of a penalty on those obligations.

(2)   (a)   Money for the Uninsured Employers' Fund shall be deposited into the Uninsured Employers' Fund in accordance with this chapter and Subsection **59-9-101**(2).

    (b)   The commissioner shall appoint an administrator of the Uninsured Employers' Fund.

    (c)   (i)   The state treasurer is the custodian of the Uninsured Employers' Fund.

        (ii)   The administrator shall make provisions for and direct distribution from the Uninsured Employers' Fund.

(3)   Reasonable costs of administering the Uninsured Employers' Fund or other fees required to be paid by the Uninsured Employers' Fund may be paid from the Uninsured Employers' Fund.

(4)   The state treasurer shall:

    (a)   receive workers' compensation premium assessments from the State Tax Commission; and

    (b)   invest the Uninsured Employers' Fund to ensure maximum investment return for both long and short term investments in accordance with Section **51-7-12.5**.

(5)   (a)   The administrator may employ, retain, or appoint counsel to represent the Uninsured Employers' Fund in a proceeding brought to enforce a claim against or on behalf of the Uninsured Employers' Fund.

    (b)   If requested by the commission, the following shall aid in the representation of the Uninsured Employers' Fund:

        (i)   the attorney general; or

        (ii)   the city attorney, or county attorney of the locality in which:

            (A)   an investigation, hearing, or trial under this chapter or Chapter 3, Utah Occupational Disease Act, is pending;

            (B)   the employee resides; or

            (C)   an employer:

                (I)   resides; or

                (II)   is doing business.

    (c)   (i)   Notwithstanding Title 63A, Chapter 3, Part 5, Office of State Debt Collection, the administrator shall provide for the collection of money required to be deposited in the Uninsured Employers' Fund under this chapter and Chapter 3, Utah Occupational Disease Act.

        (ii)   To comply with Subsection (5)(c)(i), the administrator may:

            (A)   take appropriate action, including docketing an award in a manner consistent with Section **34A-2-212**; and

            (B)   employ counsel and other personnel necessary to collect the money described in Subsection (5)(c)(i).

(6)   To the extent of the compensation and other benefits paid or payable to or on behalf of an employee or the employee's dependents from the Uninsured Employers' Fund, the Uninsured Employers' Fund, by subrogation, has the rights, powers, and benefits of the employee or the employee's dependents against the employer failing to make the compensation payments.

(7)   (a)   The receiver, trustee, liquidator, or statutory successor of an employer meeting a condition listed in Subsection (1)(a)(i)(B) is bound by a settlement of a covered claim by the Uninsured Employers' Fund.

        (b)   A court with jurisdiction shall grant a payment made under this section a priority equal to that to which the claimant would have been entitled in the absence of this section against the assets of the employer meeting a condition listed in Subsection (1)(a)(i)(B).

        (c)   The expenses of the Uninsured Employers' Fund in handling a claim shall be accorded the same priority as the liquidator's expenses.

(8)   (a)   The administrator shall periodically file the information described in Subsection (8)(b) with the receiver, trustee, or liquidator of:

                (i)   an employer that meets a condition listed in Subsection (1)(a)(i)(B);

                (ii)   a public agency insurance mutual, as defined in Section **31A-1-103**, that meets a condition listed in Subsection (1)(a)(i)(B); or

                (iii)   an insolvent insurance carrier.

        (b)   The information required to be filed under Subsection (8)(a) is:

                (i)   a statement of the covered claims paid by the Uninsured Employers' Fund; and

                (ii)   an estimate of anticipated claims against the Uninsured Employers' Fund.

        (c)   A filing under this Subsection (8) preserves the rights of the Uninsured Employers' Fund for claims against the assets of the employer that meets a condition listed in Subsection (1)(a)(i)(B).

(9)   When an injury or death for which compensation is payable from the Uninsured Employers' Fund has been caused by the wrongful act or neglect of another person not in the same employment, the Uninsured Employers' Fund has the same rights as allowed under Section **34A-2-106**.

(10)   The Uninsured Employers' Fund, subject to approval of the administrator, shall discharge its obligations by:

        (a)   adjusting its own claims; or

        (b)   contracting with an adjusting company, risk management company, insurance company, or other company that has expertise and capabilities in adjusting and paying workers' compensation claims.

(11)   (a)   For the purpose of maintaining the Uninsured Employers' Fund, an administrative law judge, upon rendering a decision with respect to a claim for workers' compensation benefits in which an employer that meets a condition listed in Subsection (1)(a)(i)(B) is duly joined as a party, shall:

                (i)   order the employer that meets a condition listed in Subsection (1)(a)(i)(B) to reimburse the Uninsured Employers' Fund for the benefits paid to or on behalf of an injured employee by the Uninsured Employers' Fund along with interest, costs, and attorney fees; and

           (ii)   impose a penalty against the employer that meets a condition listed in Subsection (1)(a)(i)(B):

                  (A)   of 15% of the value of the total award in connection with the claim; and

                  (B)   that shall be deposited into the Uninsured Employers' Fund.

     (b)   An award under this Subsection (11) shall be collected by the administrator in accordance with Subsection (5)(c).

(12)   The state, the commission, and the state treasurer, with respect to payment of compensation benefits, expenses, fees, or disbursement properly chargeable against the Uninsured Employers' Fund:

     (a)   are liable only to the assets in the Uninsured Employers' Fund; and

     (b)   are not otherwise in any way liable for the making of a payment.

(13)   The commission may make reasonable rules for the processing and payment of a claim for compensation from the Uninsured Employers' Fund.

(14)   (a)   (i)   If it becomes necessary for the Uninsured Employers' Fund to pay benefits under this section to an employee described in Subsection (14)(a)(ii), the Uninsured Employers' Fund may assess all other self-insured employers amounts necessary to pay:

                  (A)   the obligations of the Uninsured Employers' Fund subsequent to a condition listed in Subsection (1)(a)(i)(B) occurring;

                  (B)   the expenses of handling covered a claim subsequent to a condition listed in Subsection (1)(a)(i)(B) occurring;

                  (C)   the cost of an examination under Subsection (15); and

                  (D)   other expenses authorized by this section.

           (iii)   This Subsection (14) applies to benefits paid to an employee of:

                  (A)   a self-insured employer, as defined in Section **34A-2-201.5**, that meets a condition listed in Subsection (1)(a)(i)(B); or

                  (B)   if the self-insured employer that meets a condition described in Subsection (1)(a)(i)(B) is a public agency insurance mutual, a member of the public agency insurance mutual.

     (b)   The assessments of a self-insured employer shall be in the proportion that the manual premium of the self-insured employer for the preceding calendar year bears to the manual premium of all self-insured employers for the preceding calendar year.

     (c)   A self-insured employer shall be notified of the self-insured employer's assessment not later than 30 days before the day on which the assessment is due.'

     (d)   (i)   A self-insured employer may not be assessed in any year an amount greater than 2% of that self-insured employer's manual premium for the preceding calendar year.

           (ii)   If the maximum assessment does not provide in a year an amount sufficient to make all necessary payments from the Uninsured Employers' Fund for one or more self-insured employers that meet a condition listed in Subsection (1)(a)(i)(B), the unpaid portion shall be paid as soon as money becomes available.

(e)   A self-insured employer is liable under this section for a period not to exceed three years after the day on which the Uninsured Employers' Fund first pays benefits to an employee described in Subsection (14)(a)(ii) for the self-insured employer that meets a condition listed in Subsection (1)(a)(i)(B).

(f)   This Subsection (14) does not apply to a claim made against a self-insured employer that meets a condition listed in Subsection (1)(a)(i)(B) if the condition listed in Subsection (1)(a)(i)(B) occurred before July 1, 1986.

(15)   (a)   The following shall notify the division of any information indicating that any of the following may be insolvent or in a financial condition hazardous to its employees or the public:

(i)   a self-insured employer; or

(ii)   if the self-insured employer is a public agency insurance mutual, a member of the public agency insurance mutual.

(b)   Upon receipt of the notification described in Subsection (15)(a) and with good cause appearing, the division may order an examination of:

(i)   that self-insured employer; or

(ii)   if the self-insured employer is a public agency insurance mutual, a member of the public agency mutual.

(c)   The cost of the examination ordered under Subsection (15)(b) shall be assessed against all self-insured employers as provided in Subsection (14).

(d)   The results of the examination ordered under Subsection (15)(b) shall be kept confidential.

(16)   (a)   In a claim against an employer by the Uninsured Employers' Fund, or by or on behalf of the employee to whom or to whose dependents compensation and other benefits are paid or payable from the Uninsured Employers' Fund, the burden of proof is on the employer or other party in interest objecting to the claim.

(b)   A claim described in Subsection (16)(a) is presumed to be valid up to the full amount of workers' compensation benefits claimed by the employee or the employee's dependents.

(c)   This Subsection (16) applies whether the claim is filed in court or in an adjudicative proceeding under the authority of the commission.

(17)   A partner in a partnership or an owner of a sole proprietorship may not recover compensation or other benefits from the Uninsured Employers' Fund if:

(a)   the person is not included as an employee under Subsection **34A-2-104**(3); or

(b)   the person is included as an employee under Subsection **34A-2-104**(3), but:

(i)   the person's employer fails to insure or otherwise provide adequate payment of direct compensation; and

(ii)   the failure described in Subsection (17)(b)(i) is attributable to an act or omission over which the person had or shared control or responsibility.

(18)   A director or officer of a corporation may not recover compensation or other benefits from the Uninsured Employers' Fund if the director or officer is excluded from coverage under Subsection **34A-2-104**(4).

(19)   The Uninsured Employers' Fund:

    (a)   shall be:

        (i)   used in accordance with this section only for:

            (A)   the purpose of assisting in the payment of workers' compensation benefits in accordance with Subsection (1); and

            (B)   in accordance with Subsection (3), payment of:

                (I)   reasonable costs of administering the Uninsured Employers' Fund; or

                (II)   fees required to be paid by the Uninsured Employers' Fund; and

        (iii)   expended according to processes that can be verified by audit; and

    (b)   may not be used for:

        (i)   administrative costs unrelated to the Uninsured Employers' Fund; or

        (ii)   an activity of the commission other than an activity described in Subsection (19)(a).

(20)   (a)   For purposes of Subsection (1), an employment relationship is localized in the state if:

        (i)   (A)   the employer who is liable for the benefits has a business premise in the state; and

            (B)   (I)   the contract for hire is entered into in the state; or

                (II)   the employee regularly performs work duties in the state for the employer who is liable for the benefits; or

        (ii)   the employee is:

            (A)   a resident of the state; and

            (B)   regularly performs work duties in the state for the employer who is liable for the benefits.

    (b)   In accordance with Title 63G, Chapter 3, Utah Administrative Rulemaking Act, the commission shall by rule define what constitutes regularly performing work duties in the state.

34A-2-705. Industrial Accident Restricted Account.

(1)   As used in this section:

    (a)   "Account" means the Industrial Accident Restricted Account created by this section.

    (b)   "Advisory council" means the state workers' compensation advisory council created under Section **34A-2-107**.

(2)   There is created in the General Fund a restricted account known as the "Industrial Accident Restricted Account."

(3)   (a)   The account is funded from:

        (i)   .5% of the premium income remitted to the state treasurer and credited to the account pursuant to Subsection **59-9-101**(2)(c)(iv); and

        (ii)   amounts deposited under Section **34A-2-1003**.

    (b)   If the balance in the account exceeds $500,000 at the close of a fiscal year, the excess shall be transferred to the Uninsured Employers' Fund created under Section **34A-2-704**.

(4)   (a)   From money appropriated by the Legislature from the account to the commission and subject to the requirements of this section, the commission may fund:

            (i)   the activities of the Division of Industrial Accidents described in Section **34A-1-202**;

            (ii)   the activities of the Division of Adjudication described in Section **34A-1-202**; and

            (iii)   the activities of the commission described in Section **34A-2-1005**.

        (b)   The money deposited in the account may not be used for a purpose other than a purpose described in this Subsection (4), including an administrative cost or another activity of the commission unrelated to the account.

(5)   (a)   Each year before the public hearing required by Subsection **59-9-101**(2)(d)(i), the commission shall report to the advisory council regarding:

            (i)   the commission's budget request to the governor for the next fiscal year related to:

                (A)   the Division of Industrial Accidents; and

                (B)   the Division of Adjudication;

            (ii)   the expenditures of the commission for the fiscal year in which the commission is reporting related to:

                (A)   the Division of Industrial Accidents; and

                (B)   the Division of Adjudication;

            (iii)   revenues generated from the premium assessment under Section **59-9-101** on an admitted insurer writing workers' compensation insurance in this state and on a self-insured employer under Section **34A-2-202**; and

            (iv)   money deposited under Section **34A-2-1003**.

        (b)   The commission shall annually report to the governor and the Legislature regarding:

            (i)   the use of the money appropriated to the commission under this section;

            (ii)   revenues generated from the premium assessment under Section **59-9-101** on an admitted insurer writing workers' compensation insurance in this state and on a self-insured employer under Section **34A-2-202**; and

            (iii)   money deposited under Section **34A-2-1003**.

34A-2-801. Initiating adjudicative proceedings — Procedure for review of administrative action.

(1)   (a)   To contest an action of the employee's employer or its insurance carrier concerning a compensable industrial accident or occupational disease alleged by the employee or a dependent any of the following shall file an application for hearing with the Division of Adjudication:

            (i)   the employee;

            (ii)   a representative of the employee, the qualifications of whom are defined in rule by the commission; or

            (iii)   a dependent as described in Section **34A-2-403**.

        (b)   To appeal the imposition of a penalty or other administrative act imposed by the division on the employer or its insurance carrier for failure to comply with this chapter or Chapter 3, Utah Occupational Disease Act, any of the following shall file an application for hearing with the Division of Adjudication:

(i)   the employer;

(ii)   the insurance carrier; or

(iii)   a representative of either the employer or the insurance carrier, the qualifications of whom are defined in rule by the commission.

(c)   A person providing goods or services described in Subsections **34A-2-407**(11) and **34A-3-108**(12) may file an application for hearing in accordance with Section **34A-2-407** or **34A-3-108**.

(d)   An attorney may file an application for hearing in accordance with Section **34A-1-309**.

(2)   Unless a party in interest appeals the decision of an administrative law judge in accordance with Subsection (3), the decision of an administrative law judge on an application for hearing filed under Subsection (1) is a final order of the commission 30 days after the day on which the decision is issued.

(3)   (a)   A party in interest may appeal the decision of an administrative law judge by filing a motion for review with the Division of Adjudication within 30 days of the date the decision is issued.

(b)   Unless a party in interest to the appeal requests under Subsection (3)(c) that the appeal be heard by the Appeals Board, the commissioner shall hear the review.

(c)   A party in interest may request that an appeal be heard by the Appeals Board by filing the request with the Division of Adjudication:

(i)   as part of the motion for review; or

(ii)   if requested by a party in interest who did not file a motion for review, within 20 days of the day on which the motion for review is filed with the Division of Adjudication.

(d)   A case appealed to the Appeals Board shall be decided by the majority vote of the Appeals Board.

(4)   All records on appeals shall be maintained by the Division of Adjudication. Those records shall include an appeal docket showing the receipt and disposition of the appeals on review.

(5)   Upon appeal, the commissioner or Appeals Board shall make its decision in accordance with Section **34A-1-303**.

(6)   The commissioner or Appeals Board shall promptly notify the parties to a proceeding before it of its decision, including its findings and conclusions.

(7)   The decision of the commissioner or Appeals Board is final unless within 30 days after the date the decision is issued further appeal is initiated under the provisions of this section or Title 63G, Chapter 4, Administrative Procedures Act.

(8)   (a)   Within 30 days after the day on which the decision of the commissioner or Appeals Board is issued, an aggrieved party may secure judicial review by commencing an action in the court of appeals against the commissioner or Appeals Board for the review of the decision of the commissioner or Appeals Board.

(b)   In an action filed under Subsection (8)(a):

(i)   any other party to the proceeding before the commissioner or Appeals Board shall be made a party; and

(ii)   the commission shall be made a party.

(c)   A party claiming to be aggrieved may seek judicial review only if the party exhausts the party's remedies before the commission as provided by this section.

(d)   At the request of the court of appeals, the commission shall certify and file with the court all documents and papers and a transcript of all testimony taken in the matter together with the decision of the commissioner or Appeals Board.

34A-2-802. Rules of evidence and procedure before commission — Admissible evidence.

(1)   The commission, the commissioner, an administrative law judge, or the Appeals Board, is not bound by the usual common law or statutory rules of evidence, or by any technical or formal rules or procedure, other than as provided in this section or as adopted by the commission pursuant to this chapter and Chapter 3, Utah Occupational Disease Act. The commission may make its investigation in such manner as in its judgment is best calculated to ascertain the substantial rights of the parties and to carry out justly the spirit of the chapter.

(2)   The commission may receive as evidence and use as proof of any fact in dispute all evidence considered material and relevant including the following:

(a)   depositions and sworn testimony presented in open hearings;

(b)   reports of attending or examining physicians, or of pathologists;

(c)   reports of investigators appointed by the commission;

(d)   reports of employers, including copies of time sheets, book accounts, or other records; or

(e)   hospital records in the case of an injured or diseased employee.

34A-2-803. Violation of judgments, orders, decrees, or provisions of chapter — Grade of offense.

(1)   An employer, employee, or other person is guilty of a misdemeanor if that employer, employee, or other person violates this chapter or Chapter 3, Utah Occupational Disease Act, including:

(a)   doing any act prohibited by this chapter or Chapter 3, Utah Occupational Disease Act;

(b)   failing or refusing to perform any duty lawfully imposed under this chapter or Chapter 3, Utah Occupational Disease Act;

(c)   failing, neglecting, or refusing to obey any lawful order given or made by the commission, or any judgment or decree made by any court in connection with the provisions of this chapter or Chapter 3, Utah Occupational Disease Act.

(2)   Every day during which any person fails to observe and comply with any order of the commission, or to perform any duty imposed by this chapter or Chapter 3, Utah Occupational Disease Act, shall constitute a separate and distinct offense.

34A-2-901. Workers' compensation presumption for emergency medical services providers.

(1)   An emergency medical services provider who claims to have contracted a disease, as defined by Section 7829101, as a result of a significant exposure in the performance of his duties as an emergency medical services provider, is presumed to have contracted the disease by accident during the course of his duties as an emergency medical services provider if:

(a)   his employment or service as an emergency medical services provider in this state commenced prior to July 1, 1988, and he tests positive for a disease during the tenure of his employment or service, or within three months after termination of his employment or service; or

(b)   the individual's employment or service as an emergency medical services provider in this state commenced on or after July 1, 1988, and he tests negative for any disease at the time his employment or service commenced, and again three months later, and he subsequently tests positive during the tenure of his employment or service, or within three months after termination of his employment or service.

(2)   Each emergency medical services agency shall inform the emergency medical services providers that it employs or utilizes of the provisions and benefits of this section at commencement of and termination of employment or service.

34A-2-902. Workers' compensation claims by emergency medical services providers — Time limits.

(1)   For all purposes of establishing a workers' compensation claim, the "date of accident" is presumed to be the date on which an emergency medical services provider first tests positive for a disease, as defined in Section **78B-8-401**. However, for purposes of establishing the rate of workers' compensation benefits under Subsection **34A-2-702**(5), if a positive test for a disease occurs within three months after termination of employment, the last date of employment is presumed to be the "date of accident."

(2)   The time limits prescribed by Section **34A-2-417** do not apply to an employee whose disability is due to a disease, so long as the employee who claims to have suffered a significant exposure in the service of his employer gives notice, as required by Section **34A-3-108**, of the "date of accident."

(3)   Any claim for workers' compensation benefits or medical expenses shall be filed with the Division of Adjudication of the Labor Commission within one year after the date on which the employee first acquires a disability or requires medical treatment for a disease, or within one year after the termination of employment as an emergency medical services provider, whichever occurs later.

34A-2-903. Failure to be tested — Time limit for death benefits.

(1)   An emergency medical services provider who refuses or fails to be tested in accordance with Section **34A-2-901** is not entitled to any of the presumptions provided by this part.

(2)   Death benefits payable under Section **34A-2-702** are payable only if it can be established by competent evidence that death was a consequence of or result of the disease and, notwithstanding Subsection **34A-2-702**(5), that death occurred within six years from the date the employee first acquired a disability or required medical treatment for the disease that caused the employee's death.

34A-2-904. Volunteer emergency medical services providers — Workers' compensation premiums.

(1)   For purposes of receiving workers' compensation benefits, any person performing the services of an emergency medical services provider is considered an employee of the entity for whom it provides those services.

(2)   (a)   With regard to emergency medical services providers who perform those services for minimal or no compensation on a volunteer basis, and who are primarily employed other than as emergency medical services providers, the amount of workers' compensation benefits shall be based on that primary employment. Any excess premiums necessary for workers' compensation shall be paid by the entity that utilized that individual as an emergency medical services provider.

(b)   With regard to emergency medical services providers who perform those services for minimal or no compensation or on a volunteer basis, and who have no other employment, the amount of workers' compensation benefits shall be the minimum benefit. Any premium necessary for workers' compensation shall be paid by the entity that utilizes that individual as an emergency medical services provider.

(3)   Workers' compensation benefits are the exclusive remedy for all injuries and occupational diseases, as provided by Title 34A, Chapters 2 and 3. However, emergency medical services providers described in Subsection (2) are not precluded from utilizing insurance benefits provided by a primary employer, or any other insurance benefits, in addition to workers' compensation benefits.

34A-2-905.   Rulemaking authority — Rebuttable presumption.

(1)   The Labor Commission has authority to establish rules necessary for the purposes of this part.

(2)   The presumption provided by this part is a rebuttable presumption.

Appendix I:
Utah Occupational Disease Act

34A-3-101. Title — Definitions.

(1)   This chapter is known as the "Utah Occupational Disease Act."

(2)   For purposes of this chapter, "division" means the Division of Industrial Accidents.

34A-3-102. Chapter to be administered by commission — Exclusive remedy.

(1)   The commission shall administer this chapter through the division, the Division of Adjudication, and the Appeals Board in accordance with Section **34A-2-112**.

(2)   Subject to the limitations provided in this chapter and, unless otherwise noted, all provisions of Chapter 2, Workers' Compensation Act, and Chapter 8a, Utah Injured Worker Reemployment Act, are incorporated into this chapter and shall be applied to occupational disease claims.

(3)   The right to recover compensation under this chapter for diseases or injuries to health sustained by a Utah employee is the exclusive remedy as outlined in Section **34A-2-105**.

34A-3-103. Occupational diseases.

For purposes of this chapter, a compensable occupational disease means any disease or illness that arises out of and in the course of employment and is medically caused or aggravated by that employment.

34A-3-104. Employer liability for compensation.

(1)   Every employer is liable for the payment of disability and medical benefits to every employee who acquires a disability, or death benefits to the dependents of any employee who dies, by reason of an occupational disease under the terms of this chapter.

(2)   Compensation may not be paid when the last day of injurious exposure of the employee to the hazards of the occupational disease occurred before 1941.

34A-3-105. Last employer liable — Exception.

(1)   To the extent compensation is payable under this chapter for an occupational disease which arises out of and in the course of an employee's employment for more than one employer, the only employer liable shall be the employer in whose employment the employee was last injuriously exposed to the hazards of the disease if:

     (a)   the employee's exposure in the course of employment with that employer was a substantial contributing medical cause of the alleged occupational disease; and

     (b)   the employee was employed by that employer for at least 12 consecutive months.

(2)   Should the conditions of Subsection (1) not be met, liability for disability, death, and medical benefits shall be apportioned between employers based on the involved employers' causal contribution to the occupational disease.

34A-3-106. Mental stress claims.

(1)   Physical, mental, or emotional diseases related to mental stress arising out of and in the course of employment shall be compensable under this chapter only when there is a sufficient legal and medical causal connection between the employee's disease and employment.

(2)   (a)   Legal causation requires proof of extraordinary mental stress arising predominantly and directly from employment.

        (b)   The extraordinary nature of the alleged mental stress is judged according to an objective standard in comparison with contemporary national employment and nonemployment life.

(3)   Medical causation requires proof that the physical, mental, or emotional disease was medically caused by the mental stress that is the legal cause of the physical, mental, or emotional disease.

(4)   Good faith employer personnel actions including disciplinary actions, work evaluations, job transfers, layoffs, demotions, promotions, terminations, or retirements, may not form the basis of compensable mental stress claims under this chapter.

(5)   Alleged discrimination, harassment, or unfair labor practices otherwise actionable at law may not form the basis of compensable mental stress claims under this chapter.

(6)   An employee who alleges a compensable occupational disease involving mental stress bears the burden of proof to establish legal and medical causation by a preponderance of the evidence.

34A-3-107. Benefits — Disability compensation, death, medical, hospital, and burial expenses — Procedure and payments.

(1)   The benefits to which an employee with a disability or the employee's dependents are entitled under this chapter shall be based upon the employee's average weekly wage at the time the cause of action arises and shall be computed in accordance with and in all ways shall be equivalent to the benefits for disability and death provided in Chapter 2, Workers' Compensation Act.

(2)   The employee with a disability is entitled to medical, hospital, and burial expenses equivalent to those provided in Chapter 2.

(3)   The procedure and payment of benefits under this chapter shall be equivalent to and consistent with Chapter 2, including Section **34A-2-703**.

34A-3-108. Reporting of occupational diseases — Regulation of health care providers.

(1)   An employee sustaining an occupational disease, as defined in this chapter, arising out of and in the course of employment shall provide notification to the employee's employer promptly of the occupational disease. If the employee is unable to provide notification, the employee's next-of-kin or attorney may provide notification of the occupational disease to the employee's employer.

(2)   (a)   An employee who fails to notify the employee's employer or the division within 180 days after the cause of action arises is barred from a claim of benefits arising from the occupational disease.

        (b)   The cause of action is considered to arise on the date the employee first:

                (i)   suffers disability from the occupational disease; and

                (ii)   knows or in the exercise of reasonable diligence should have known, that the occupational disease is caused by employment.

(3)   The following constitute notification of an occupational disease:

        (a)   an employer's or physician's injury report filed with the:

                (i)   division;

           (ii)   employer; or

           (iii)   insurance carrier; or

    (b)   the payment of any medical or disability benefit by the employer or the employer's insurance carrier.

(4)   (a)   In the form prescribed by the division, an employer shall file a report with the division of any occupational disease resulting in:

           (i)   medical treatment;

           (ii)   loss of consciousness;

           (iii)   loss of work;

           (iv)   restriction of work; or

           (v)   transfer to another job.

    (b)   The report required under Subsection (4)(a), shall be filed within seven days after:

           (i)   the occurrence of an occupational disease;

           (ii)   the employer's first knowledge of an occupational disease; or

           (iii)   the employee's notification of an occupational disease.

    (c)   An employer shall file a subsequent report with the division of a previously reported occupational disease that later resulted in death. The subsequent report shall be filed with the division within seven days following:

           (i)   the death; or

           (ii)   the employer's first knowledge or notification of the death.

    (d)   A report is not required for:

           (i)   a minor injury that requires first-aid treatment only, unless a treating physician files, or is required to file, the Physician's Initial Report of Work Injury or Occupational Disease with the division;

           (ii)   occupational diseases that manifest after the employee is no longer employed by the employer with which the exposure occurred; or

           (iii)   when the employer is not aware of an exposure occasioned by the employment that results in an occupational disease as defined by Section **34A-3-103**.

(5)   An employer shall provide the employee with:

    (a)   a copy of the report submitted to the division; and

    (b)   a statement, as prepared by the division, of the employee's rights and responsibilities related to the occupational disease.

(6)   An employer shall maintain a record in a manner prescribed by the division of occupational diseases resulting in:

    (a)   medical treatment;

    (b)   loss of consciousness;

    (c)   loss of work;

    (d)   restriction of work; or

    (e)   transfer to another job.

(7)   An employer who refuses or neglects to make a report, maintain a record, or file a report with the division as required by this section is guilty of a class C misdemeanor and subject to citation under Section **34A-6-302** and a civil assessment as provided under Section **34A-6-307**, unless the division finds that the employer has shown good cause for submitting a report later than required by this section.

(8)   (a)   Except as provided in Subsection (8)(c), a physician, surgeon, or other health care provider attending an occupationally diseased employee shall:

        (i)   comply with the rules, including the schedule of fees, for services as adopted by the commission; and

        (ii)   make reports to the division at any and all times as required as to the condition and treatment of an occupationally diseased employee or as to any other matter concerning industrial cases being treated.

        (b)   A physician, as defined in Section **34A-2-111**, who is associated with, employed by, or bills through a hospital is subject to Subsection (8)(a).

        (c)   A hospital is not subject to the requirements of Subsection (8)(a) except a hospital is subject to rules made by the commission under Subsections **34A-2-407**(9)(a)(ii) and (iii).

        (d)   The commission's schedule of fees may reasonably differentiate remuneration to be paid to providers of health services based on:

        (i)   the severity of the employee's condition;

        (ii)   the nature of the treatment necessary; and

        (iii)   the facilities or equipment specially required to deliver that treatment.

        (e)   This Subsection (8) does not prohibit a contract with a provider of health services relating to the pricing of goods and services.

(9)   A copy of the physician's initial report shall be furnished to the:

        (a)   division;

        (b)   employee; and

        (c)   employer or its insurance carrier.

(10)   A person subject to reporting under Subsection (8)(a)(ii) or Subsection **34A-2-407**(9)(a)(iii) who refuses or neglects to make a report or comply with this section is guilty of a class C misdemeanor for each offense, unless the division finds that there is good cause for submitting a late report.

(11)   (a)   An application for a hearing to resolve a dispute regarding an occupational disease claim shall be filed with the Division of Adjudication.

        (b)   After the filing, a copy shall be forwarded by mail to:

        (i)   (A)   the employer; or

                (B)   the employer's insurance carrier;

        (ii)   the applicant; and

        (iii)   the attorneys for the parties.

(12)   (a)   Subject to appellate review under Section **34A-1-303**, the commission has exclusive jurisdiction to hear and determine:

        (i)   whether goods provided to or services rendered to an employee is compensable pursuant to this chapter and Chapter 2, Workers' Compensation Act, including the following:

    (A) medical, nurse, or hospital services;

    (B) medicines; and

    (C) artificial means, appliances, or prosthesis;

   (ii) the reasonableness of the amounts charged or paid for a good or service described in Subsection (12)(a)(i); and

   (iii) collection issues related to a good or service described in Subsection (12)(a)(i).

  (b) Except as provided in Subsection (12)(a), Subsection **34A-2-211**(6), or Section **34A-2-212**, a person may not maintain a cause of action in any forum within this state other than the commission for collection or payment of goods or services described in Subsection (12)(a) that are compensable under this chapter or Chapter 2, Workers' Compensation Act.

34A-3-109. Limitations — Rights barred if not filed within limits — Burden of proof.

 (1) The limitation of rights regarding medical benefits provided in Subsection 34A2417(1) does not apply to compensable occupational diseases under the terms of this chapter.

 (2) (a) A claim described in Subsection (2)(b) is barred, unless the employee:

   (i) files an application for hearing with the Division of Adjudication no later than six years from the date the employee's cause of action arose; and

   (ii) by no later than 12 years from the date on which the employee's cause of action arose, is able to meet the employee's burden of proving that the employee is due the compensation claimed under this chapter.

  (b) Subsection (2)(a) applies to a claim for compensation for:

   (i) temporary total disability benefits;

   (ii) temporary partial disability benefits;

   (iii) permanent partial disability benefits; or

   (iv) permanent total disability benefits.

  (c) The commission may enter an order awarding or denying an employee's claim for compensation under this chapter within a reasonable time period beyond 12 years from the date on which the employee's cause of action arose, if:

   (i) the employee complies with Subsections (2)(a)(i) and (ii); and

   (ii) 12 years from the date on which the employee's cause of action arose:

    (A) (I) the employee is fully cooperating in a commission approved reemployment plan; and

     (II) the results of that commission approved reemployment plan are not known; or

    (B) the employee is actively adjudicating issues of compensability before the commission.

 (3) (a) Subject to Subsection (3)(b), a claim for death benefits is barred unless an application for hearing is filed within one year of the date the deceased employee's dependents knew, or in the exercise of reasonable diligence should have known, that the employee's death was caused by an occupational disease.

  (b) A dependents' claim for death benefits may not be actionable more than six years after the employee's cause of action arises.

(4)   (a)   (i)   Subject to Subsections (2)(c) and (4)(b), after an employee files an application for hearing within six years from the date on which the cause of action arose, the Division of Adjudication may enter an order to show cause why the employee's claim should not be dismissed because the employee has failed to meet the employee's burden of proof to establish an entitlement to compensation claimed in the application for hearing.

              (ii)   The order described in Subsection (4)(a)(i) may be entered on the motion of the:

                    (A)   Division of Adjudication;

                    (B)   employee's employer; or

                    (C)   employer's insurance carrier.

      (b)   Under Subsection (4)(a), the Division of Adjudication may dismiss a claim in an application for hearing:

              (i)   without prejudice; or

               (ii)   with prejudice only if:

                    (A)   the Division of Adjudication adjudicates the merits of the employee's entitlement to the compensation claimed in the application for hearing; or

                    (B)   the employee fails to comply with Subsection (2)(a)(ii).

      (c)   If a claim is dismissed without prejudice under Subsection (4)(b), the employee is subject to the time limits under Subsection (2)(a) to claim compensation under this chapter.

34A-3-110.   Occupational disease aggravated by other diseases.

The compensation payable under this chapter shall be reduced and limited to the proportion of the compensation that would be payable if the occupational disease were the sole cause of disability or death, as the occupational disease as a causative factor bears to all the causes of the disability or death when the occupational disease, or any part of the disease:

    (1)   is causally related to employment with a nonUtah employer not subject to commission jurisdiction;

    (2)   is of a character to which the employee may have had substantial exposure outside of employment or to which the general public is commonly exposed;

    (3)   is aggravated by any other disease or infirmity not itself compensable; or

    (4)   when disability or death from any other cause not itself compensable is aggravated, prolonged, accelerated, or in any way contributed to by an occupational disease.

34A-3-111.   Compensation not additional to that provided for accidents.

The compensation provided under this chapter is not in addition to compensation that may be payable under Chapter 2, and in all cases when injury results by reason of an accident arising out of and in the course of employment and compensation is payable for the injury under Chapter 2, compensation under this chapter may not be payable.

34A-3-112.   Employee's willful misconduct.

    (1)   Notwithstanding anything contained in this chapter, an employee or dependent of any employee is not entitled to receive compensation for disability or death from an occupational disease when the disability or death, wholly or in part, was caused by the purposeful selfexposure of the employee.

    (2)   Except in cases resulting in death:

(a)   Compensation provided for in this chapter shall be reduced 15% when the occupational disease is caused by the willful failure of the employee:

   (i)   to use safety devices when provided by the employer; or

   (ii)   to obey any order or reasonable rule adopted by the employer for the safety of the employee.

(b)   Except when the employer permitted, encouraged, or had actual knowledge of the conduct described in Subsections (2)(b)(i) through (iii), disability compensation may not be awarded under this chapter to an employee when the major contributing cause of the employee's disease is the employee's:

   (i)   use of illegal substances;

   (ii)   intentional abuse of drugs in excess of prescribed therapeutic amounts; or

   (iii) intoxication from alcohol with a blood or breath alcohol concentration of .08 grams or greater as shown by a chemical test.

Appendix J: Utah Injured Worker Reemployment Act

34A-8a-101. Title — Intent statement.

(1) This chapter is known as the "Utah Injured Worker Reemployment Act."

(2) This chapter is intended to promote and monitor the state's and the employer's capacity to assist the injured worker in returning to the work force by evaluating the effectiveness of the voluntary efforts of employers under this chapter.

34A-8a-102. Definitions.

(1) "Division" means the Division of Industrial Accidents.

(2) (a) "Gainful employment" means employment that:

    (i) is reasonably attainable in view of an industrial injury or occupational disease; and

    (ii) offers to an injured worker, as reasonably feasible, an opportunity for earnings.

  (b) Factors considered in determining gainful employment include an injured worker's:

    (i) education;

    (ii) experience; and

    (iii) physical and mental impairment and condition.

(3) "Initial written report" means a report required under Section **34A-8a-301**.

(4) "Injured worker" means an employee who sustains an industrial injury or occupational disease for which benefits are provided under Chapter 2, Workers' Compensation Act, or Chapter 3, Utah Occupational Disease Act.

(5) "Injured worker with a disability" means an injured worker who:

  (a) because of the injury or disease that is the basis of the employee being an injured worker:

    (i) is or will be unable to return to work in the injured worker's usual and customary occupation; or

    (ii) is unable to perform work for which the injured worker has previous training and experience; and

  (b) reasonably can be expected to attain gainful employment after an evaluation provided for in accordance with this chapter.

(6) "Parties" means:

  (a) an injured worker with a disability;

  (b) the employer of the injured worker with a disability;

  (c) the employer's workers' compensation insurance carrier; and

  (d) a rehabilitation or reemployment professional for the employer or the employer's workers' compensation insurance carrier.

(7)   "Reemployment plan" means a written:

    (a)   description or rationale for the manner and means by which it is proposed an injured worker with a disability may return to gainful employment; and

    (b)   definition of the voluntary responsibilities of:

        (i)   the injured worker with a disability;

        (ii)   the employer; and

        (iii)   one or more other parties involved with the implementation of the reemployment plan.

34A-8a-104. Application.

This chapter applies only to an industrial injury or occupational disease that occurs on or after July 1, 1990.

34A-8a-105. Duties of Utah State Office of Rehabilitation not affected.

This chapter does not affect the duties and responsibilities of the Utah State Office of Rehabilitation.

34A-8a-201. Chapter administration.

The commission shall administer this chapter:

(1)   through the division; and

(2)   in conjunction with the commission's administration of Chapter 2, Workers' Compensation Act, and Chapter 3, Utah Occupational Disease Act.

34A-8a-202. Rulemaking authority.

The commission may provide for the administration of this chapter by rule in accordance with Title 63G, Chapter 3, Utah Administrative Rulemaking Act.

34A-8a-203. Reporting.

(1)   As used in this section, "reporting entity" means one of the following that provides benefits under Chapter 2, Workers' Compensation Act, or Chapter 3, Utah Occupational Disease Act:

    (a)   a self-insured employer as defined in Section **34A-2-201.5**; or

    (b)   a workers' compensation insurance carrier.

(2)   Subject to the requirements of this section, a reporting entity shall quarterly report to the commission the following information for the previous quarter beginning with reporting for the quarter that begins July 1, 2009:

    (a)   the total number of injured workers for whom a reporting entity is required during the quarter to file an initial report under Section **34A-8a-301**;

    (b)   the number of injured workers reported in Subsection (2)(a) for whom the reporting entity made a referral in accordance with Section **34A-8a-302**;

    (c)   the number of injured workers reported in Subsection (2)(a) for whom the reporting entity did not make a referral in accordance with Section **34A-8a-302** because:

        (i)   the injured worker was not medically stable during the quarter;

        (ii)   the injured worker's physical capacity had not been determined during the quarter; or

        (iii)   liability for the injured worker's claim was under review during the quarter;

(d)   the number of injured workers reported in Subsection (2)(a) for whom a referral or reemployment plan described in Section **34A-8a-302** was not necessary because:

      (i)   the injured worker returned to work in the same job, a new job, or a modified job:

          (A)   with the same employer; or

          (B)   a new employer;

      (ii)   the injured worker became self-employed;

      (iii)   the injured worker returned to work as a result of vocational rehabilitation support services, as defined by rule by the commission made in accordance with Title 63G, Chapter 3, Utah Administrative Rulemaking Act; or

      (iv)   the injured worker's disability was too severe to return to work; and

(e)   other information that the commission requires by rule, made in accordance with Title 63G, Chapter 3, Utah Administrative Rulemaking Act, regarding the voluntary efforts of employers under this chapter for the number of injured workers reported in Subsection (2)(a).

(3)   In addition to the rulemaking authority under Subsection (2), the commission shall make rules in accordance with Title 63G, Chapter 3, Utah Administrative Rulemaking Act, regarding:

    (a)   the form of a report required under this section; and

    (b)   the procedure for filing a report required under this section.

(4)   (a)   If a reporting entity fails to make a report as required by this section, the commission shall, pursuant to Title 63G, Chapter 4, Administrative Procedures Act, impose a civil assessment of up to $500 for each quarter that a reporting entity fails to make a report.

    (b)   (i)   The commission shall deposit a civil assessment imposed under this Subsection (4) into the Uninsured Employers' Fund created by Section **34A-2-704** to be used for the purposes of the Uninsured Employers' Fund specified in Section **34A-2-704**.

          (ii)   The administrator of the Uninsured Employers' Fund shall collect money required to be deposited into the Uninsured Employers' Fund under this Subsection (4) in accordance with Section **34A-2-704**.

34A-8a-204. Administrative review.

An employer or an injured worker may apply to the Division of Adjudication for resolution of an issue of law or fact arising under this chapter in accordance with Title 63G, Chapter 4, Administrative Procedures Act.

34A-8a-301. Initial report on injured worker.

(1)   An employer or the employer's workers' compensation insurance carrier shall prepare an initial written report assessing an injured worker's need or lack of need for vocational assistance in reemployment if:

    (a)   it appears that the injured worker is or will be an injured worker with a disability; or

    (b)   the period of the injured worker's temporary total disability compensation period exceeds 90 days.

(2)   (a)   Subject to Subsection (2)(b), an employer or the employer's workers' compensation insurance carrier shall:

          (i)   serve the initial written report required by Subsection (1) on the injured worker; and

          (ii)   file the initial written report required by Subsection (1) with the division.

      (b)   An employer or the employer's workers' compensation insurance carrier shall comply with Subsection (2)(a) by no later than 30 days after the earlier of the day on which:

           (i)   it appears that the injured worker is or will be an injured worker with a disability; or

           (ii)   the 90-day period described in Subsection (1)(b) ends.

(3)   With the initial written report required by Subsection (1), an employer or the employer's workers' compensation insurance carrier shall provide an injured worker information regarding reemployment.

34A-8a-302. Evaluation of injured worker — Reemployment plan.

(1)   Subject to the other provisions of this section, if an injured worker is an injured worker with a disability, the employer or the employer's workers' compensation insurance carrier shall, within 10 days after the day on which the employer or workers' compensation insurance carrier serves the initial written report on the injured worker, refer the injured worker with a disability to:

      (a)   the Utah State Office of Rehabilitation; or

      (b)   at the employer's or workers' compensation insurance carrier's option, a private rehabilitation or reemployment service.

(2)   An employer or the employer's workers' compensation insurance carrier shall make the referral required by Subsection (1) for the purpose of:

      (a)   providing an evaluation; and

      (b)   developing a reemployment plan.

(3)   The commission may authorize an employer or the employer's workers' compensation insurance carrier to:

      (a)   not make a referral required by Subsection (1); or

      (b)   make a referral during a different time period than required by Subsection (1).

34A-8a-303. Reemployment objectives.

(1)   The commission through the division shall administer this chapter with the objective of assisting in returning an injured worker with a disability to gainful employment in the following order of employment priority:

      (a)   same job, same employer;

      (b)   modified job, same employer;

      (c)   same job, new employer;

      (d)   modified job, new employer;

      (e)   new job, new employer; or

      (f)   retraining in a new occupation.

(2)   Nothing in this chapter or its application is intended to:

      (a)   modify or in any way affect an existing employee-employer relationship; or

      (b)   provide an employee with a guarantee or right to employment or continued employment with an employer.

34A-8a-304. Rehabilitation counselor.

A rehabilitation counselor to whom a referral is made under Section **34A-8a-302** shall have the same or comparable qualifications as those established by the Utah State Office of Rehabilitation for personnel assigned to rehabilitation and evaluation duties.

Appendix K: Utah Preconstruction and Construction Lien Law

38-1a-101. Title.

This chapter is known as "Preconstruction and Construction Liens."

38-1a-102. Definitions.

As used in this chapter:

(1)　"Alternate means" means a method of filing a legible and complete notice or other document with the registry other than electronically, as established by the division by rule.

(2)　"Anticipated improvement" means the improvement:

    (a)　for which preconstruction service is performed; and

    (b)　that is anticipated to follow the performing of preconstruction service.

(3)　"Applicable county recorder" means the office of the recorder of each county in which any part of the property on which a claimant claims or intends to claim a preconstruction or construction lien is located.

(4)　"Bona fide loan" means a loan to an owner or owner-builder by a lender in which the owner or owner-builder has no financial or beneficial interest greater than 5% of the voting shares or other ownership interest.

(5)　"Claimant" means a person entitled to claim a preconstruction or construction lien.

(6)　"Compensation" means the payment of money for a service rendered or an expense incurred, whether based on:

    (a)　time and expense, lump sum, stipulated sum, percentage of cost, cost plus fixed or percentage fee, or commission; or

    (b)　a combination of the bases listed in Subsection (6)(a).

(7)　"Construction lien" means a lien under this chapter for construction work.

(8)　"Construction loan" does not include a consumer loan secured by the equity in the consumer's home.

(9)　"Construction project" means construction work provided under an original contract.

(10)　"Construction work":

    (a)　means labor, service, material, or equipment provided for the purpose and during the process of constructing, altering, or repairing an improvement; and

    (b)　includes scheduling, estimating, staking, supervising, managing, materials testing, inspection, observation, and quality control or assurance involved in constructing, altering, or repairing an improvement.

(11)　"Contestable notice" means a notice of retention under Section 38-1a-401, a preliminary notice under Section 38-1a-501, or a notice of completion under Section 38-1a-506.

(12)　"Contesting person" means an owner, original contractor, subcontractor, or other interested person.

(13)   "Designated agent" means the third party the division contracts with as provided in Section 38-1a-202 to create and maintain the registry.

(14)   "Division" means the Division of Occupational and Professional Licensing created in Section 58-1-103.

(15)   "Entry number" means the reference number that:

     (a)   the designated agent assigns to each notice or other document filed with the registry; and

     (b)   is unique for each notice or other document.

(16)   "Final completion" means:

     (a)   the date of issuance of a permanent certificate of occupancy by the local government entity having jurisdiction over the construction project, if a permanent certificate of occupancy is required;

     (b)   the date of the final inspection of the construction work by the local government entity having jurisdiction over the construction project, if an inspection is required under a state-adopted building code applicable to the construction work, but no certificate of occupancy is required;

     (c)   unless the owner is holding payment to ensure completion of construction work, the date on which there remains no substantial work to be completed to finish the construction work under the original contract, if a certificate of occupancy is not required and a final inspection is not required under an applicable state-adopted building code; or

     (d)   the last date on which substantial work was performed under the original contract, if, because the original contract is terminated before completion of the construction work defined by the original contract, the local government entity having jurisdiction over the construction project does not issue a certificate of occupancy or perform a final inspection.

(17)   "First preliminary notice filing" means the filing of a preliminary notice that is:

     (a)   the earliest preliminary notice filed on a construction project;

     (b)   filed on or after August 1, 2011;

     (c)   not filed on a project that, according to the law in effect before August 1, 2011, commenced before August 1, 2011;

     (d)   not canceled under Section 38-1a-307; and

     (e)   not withdrawn under Subsection 38-1a-501(5).

(18)   "Government project-identifying information" has the same meaning as defined in Section 38-1b-102.

(19)   "Improvement" means:

     (a)   a building, infrastructure, utility, or other human-made structure or object constructed on or for and affixed to real property; or

     (b)   a repair, modification, or alteration of a building, infrastructure, utility, or object referred to in Subsection (19)(a).

(20)   "Interested person" means a person who may be affected by a construction project.

(21)   "Notice of commencement" means a notice required under Section 38-1b-201 for a government project, as defined in Section 38-1b-102.

(22)   "Original contract":

    (a)   means a contract between an owner and an original contractor for preconstruction service or construction work; and

    (b)   does not include a contract between an owner-builder and another person.

(23)   "Original contractor" means a person who contracts with an owner, other than an owner-builder, to provide preconstruction service or construction work.

(24)   "Owner" means the person who owns the project property.

(25)   "Owner-builder" means an owner who:

    (a)   contracts with one or more other persons for preconstruction service or construction work for an improvement on the owner's real property; and

    (b)   obtains a building permit for the improvement.

(26)   "Preconstruction service":

    (a)   means to plan or design, or to assist in the planning or design of, an improvement or a proposed improvement:

        (i)   before construction of the improvement commences; and

        (ii)   for compensation separate from any compensation paid or to be paid for construction work for the improvement; and

    (b)   includes consulting, conducting a site investigation or assessment, programming, preconstruction cost or quantity estimating, preconstruction scheduling, performing a preconstruction construction feasibility review, procuring construction services, and preparing a study, report, rendering, model, boundary or topographic survey, plat, map, design, plan, drawing, specification, or contract document.

(27)   "Preconstruction lien" means a lien under this chapter for a preconstruction service.

(28)   "Prelender claimant" means a person whose construction lien is made subject to a construction lender's mortgage or trust deed, as provided in Section 38-1a-503, by the person's acceptance of payment in full and the person's withdrawal of the person's preliminary notice.

(29)   "Private project" means a construction project that is not a government project.

(30)   "Project property" means the real property on or for which preconstruction service or construction work is or will be provided.

(31)   "Refiled preliminary notice" means a preliminary notice that a prelender claimant files with the registry on a construction project after withdrawing a preliminary notice that the claimant previously filed for the same project.

(32)   "Registry" means the State Construction Registry under Part 2, State Construction Registry.

(33)   "Required notice" means:

    (a)   a notice of retention under Section 38-1a-401;

    (b)   a preliminary notice under Section 38-1a-501 or Section 38-1b-202;

    (c)   a notice of commencement;

    (d)   a notice of construction loan under Section 38-1a-601;

    (e)   a notice under Section 38-1a-602 concerning a construction loan default;

    (f)   a notice of intent to obtain final completion under Section 38-1a-506; or

    (g)   a notice of completion under Section 38-1a-507.

(34)   "Subcontractor" means a person who contracts to provide preconstruction service or construction work to:

    (a)   a person other than the owner; or

    (b)   the owner, if the owner is an owner-builder.

(35)   "Substantial work" does not include repair work or warranty work.

(36)   "Supervisory subcontractor" means a person who:

    (a)   is a subcontractor under contract to provide preconstruction service or construction work; and

    (b)   contracts with one or more other subcontractors for the other subcontractor or subcontractors to provide preconstruction service or construction work that the person is under contract to provide.

38-1a-103. Government projects not subject to chapter — Exception.

Except as provided in Section 38-1a-102, Part 2, State Construction Registry, and Chapter 1b, Government Construction Projects, this chapter does not apply to a government project, as defined in Section 38-1b-102.

38-1a-104. Owner-builder original contract — Owner-builder as original contractor.

For purposes of this chapter:

(1)   an original contract is considered to exist between an owner-builder as owner and the owner-builder as original contractor; and

(2)   in addition to being an owner, an owner-builder is considered to be an original contractor.

38-1a-105. No waiver of rights — Exception.

(1)   (a)   A right or privilege under this chapter may not be waived or limited by contract.

    (b)   A provision of a contract purporting to waive or limit a right or privilege under this chapter is void.

(2)   Notwithstanding Subsection (1), a claimant may waive or limit, in whole or in part, a lien right under this chapter in consideration of payment as provided in Section 38-1a-802.

38-1a-201. Establishment of State Construction Registry — Filing index.

(1)   Subject to receiving adequate funding through a legislative appropriation and contracting with an approved third party vendor as provided in Section 38-1a-202, the division shall establish and maintain the State Construction Registry to:

    (a)   (i)   assist in protecting public health, safety, and welfare; and

        (ii)   promote a fair working environment;

    (b)   be overseen by the division with the assistance of the designated agent;

    (c)   provide a central repository for all required notices;

    (d)   make accessible, by way of an Internet website:

        (i)   the filing and review of required notices; and

        (ii)   the transmitting of building permit information under Subsection 38-1a-205(1) and the reviewing of that information;

    (e)   accommodate:

        (i)   electronic filing of required notices and electronic transmitting of building permit information described in Subsection (1)(d)(ii); and

> > (ii) the filing of required notices by alternate means, including United States mail, telefax, or any other method as the division provides by rule;
>
> (f) (i) provide electronic notification for up to three email addresses for each interested person who requests to receive notification under Section 38-1a-204 from the designated agent; and
>
> > (ii) provide alternate means of providing notification to a person who makes a filing by alternate means, including United States mail, telefax, or any other method as the division prescribes by rule; and
>
> (g) provide hard-copy printing of electronic receipts for an individual filing evidencing the date and time of the individual filing and the content of the individual filing.

(2) The designated agent shall index filings in the registry by:

> (a) the name of the owner;
>
> (b) the name of the original contractor;
>
> (c) subdivision, development, or other project name, if any;
>
> (d) lot or parcel number;
>
> (e) the address of the project property;
>
> (f) entry number;
>
> (g) the name of the county in which the project property is located;
>
> (h) for construction projects that are not government projects:
>
> > (i) the tax parcel identification number of each parcel included in the project property; and
> >
> > (ii) the building permit number;
>
> (i) for government projects, the government project-identifying information; and
>
> (j) any other identifier that the division considers reasonably appropriate in collaboration with the designated agent.

38-1a-202 (Effective 05/01/13). Contract to establish and maintain registry — Designated agent — Rules — Duties of designated agent — Limit of liability.

(1) (a) The division shall contract, in accordance with Title 63G, Chapter 6a, Utah Procurement Code, with a third party to establish and maintain the registry for the purposes established under this part.

> (b) The designated agent is not an agency, instrumentality, or political subdivision of the state.

(2) (a) The third party under contract under this section is the division's designated agent, and shall develop and maintain a registry from the information provided by:

> > (i) local government entities issuing building permits;
> >
> > (ii) original contractors;
> >
> > (iii) subcontractors;
> >
> > (iv) construction lenders; and
> >
> > (v) other interested persons.
>
> (b) The registry shall accommodate filings by third parties on behalf of clients.

(3)   (a)   The division shall make rules and develop procedures for:

             (i)   the division to oversee and enforce this chapter and Chapter 1b, Government Construction Projects;

             (ii)   the designated agent to administer this chapter and Chapter 1b, Government Construction Projects; and

             (iii)   the form of submission of a filing by alternate means, which may include procedures for rejecting an illegible or incomplete filing.

        (b)   If this chapter directs or authorizes the division to make a rule or adopt a procedure to implement the provisions of this chapter or Chapter 1b, Government Construction Projects, the division shall make the rule or adopt the procedure in accordance with Title 63G, Chapter 3, Utah Administrative Rulemaking Act.

(4)   (a)   The designated agent shall archive computer data files at least semiannually for auditing purposes.

        (b)   The division shall make rules to allow the designated agent to periodically archive projects from the registry.

        (c)   The designated agent may not archive a project earlier than:

             (i)   one year after the day on which a notice of completion is filed for a construction project;

             (ii)   if no notice of completion is filed, two years after the last filing activity for a project; or

             (iii)   one year after the day on which a contestable notice is cancelled under Section 38-1a-307.

        (d)   The division may audit the designated agent's administration of the registry as often as the division considers necessary.

(5)   The designated agent shall carry errors and omissions insurance in the amounts that the division establishes by rule.

(6)   (a)   The designated agent shall make reasonable efforts to assure the accurate entry into the registry of information provided by alternate means.

        (b)   The designated agent shall meet or exceed standards established by the division for the accuracy of data entry for information on documents filed by alternate means.

(7)   The designated agent is not liable for the correctness of the information contained in a document filed by alternate means which the registered agent enters into the database.

38-1a-202 (Superseded 05/01/13). Contract to establish and maintain registry — Designated agent — Rules — Duties of designated agent — Limit of liability.

(1)   (a)   The division shall contract, in accordance with Title 63G, Chapter 6, Utah Procurement Code, with a third party to establish and maintain the registry for the purposes established under this part.

        (b)   The designated agent is not an agency, instrumentality, or political subdivision of the state.

(2)   (a)   The third party under contract under this section is the division's designated agent, (i) local government entities issuing building permits;

             (i)   original contractors;

             (ii)   subcontractors;

            (iii)   construction lenders; and

            (iv)   other interested persons.

    (b)   The registry shall accommodate filings by third parties on behalf of clients.

(3)   (a)   The division shall make rules and develop procedures for:

        (i)   the division to oversee and enforce this chapter and Chapter 1b, Government Construction Projects;

        (ii)   the designated agent to administer this chapter and Chapter 1b, Government Construction Projects; and

        (iii)   the form of submission of a filing by alternate means, which may include procedures for rejecting an illegible or incomplete filing.

    (b)   If this chapter directs or authorizes the division to make a rule or adopt a procedure to implement the provisions of this chapter or Chapter 1b, Government Construction Projects, the division shall make the rule or adopt the procedure in accordance with Title 63G, Chapter 3, Utah Administrative Rulemaking Act.

(4)   (a)   The designated agent shall archive computer data files at least semiannually for auditing purposes.

    (b)   The division shall make rules to allow the designated agent to periodically archive projects from the registry.

    (c)   The designated agent may not archive a project earlier than:

        (i)   one year after the day on which a notice of completion is filed for a construction project;

        (ii)   if no notice of completion is filed, two years after the last filing activity for a project; or

        (iii)   one year after the day on which a contestable notice is cancelled under Section 38-1a-307.

    (d)   The division may audit the designated agent's administration of the registry as often as the division considers necessary.

(5)   The designated agent shall carry errors and omissions insurance in the amounts that the division establishes by rule.

(6)   (a)   The designated agent shall make reasonable efforts to assure the accurate entry into the registry of information provided by alternate means.

    (b)   The designated agent shall meet or exceed standards established by the division for the accuracy of data entry for information on documents filed by alternate means.

(7)   The designated agent is not liable for the correctness of the information contained in a document filed by alternate means which the registered agent enters into the database.

38-1a-203. Filings with the registry.

(1)   The division and the designated agent need not determine the timeliness of any notice before filing the notice in the registry.

(2)   A notice filed by a third party on behalf of another is considered to be filed by the person on whose behalf the notice is filed.

(3)   A person filing a notice of commencement, preliminary notice, or notice of completion is responsible for verifying the accuracy of information entered into the registry, whether the person files electronically, by alternate means, or through a third party.

(4)   Each notice or other document submitted for inclusion in the registry and for which this chapter does not specify information required to be included in the notice or other document shall contain:

(a)   the name of the county in which the project property to which the notice or other document applies is located;

(b)   for a private project:

(i)   the tax parcel identification number of each parcel included in the project property; or

(ii)   the number of the building permit for the construction project on the project property; and

(c)   for a government project, the government project-identifying information.

38-1a-204. Notification of filings with the registry.

(1)   The designated agent shall provide notification of the filing of a required notice relating to an anticipated improvement or construction project to:

(a)   the person filing the required notice, unless the person indicates to the division or designated agent that the person does not want to receive notification; and

(b)   each person who requests notification of the filing of a required notice for that anticipated improvement or construction project.

(2)   (a)   A person may request the designated agent to provide the person notification of the filing of a required notice for any anticipated improvement or construction project.

(b)   A person requesting notification under Subsection (2)(a) is responsible:

(i)   to provide an email address, mailing address, or telefax number to which notification may be sent; and

(ii)   for the accuracy of the email address, mailing address, or telefax number.

(c)   A person is considered to have requested notification under Subsection (2)(a) if the person files, with respect to the same anticipated improvement or construction project that relates to the required notice that is the subject of the notification:

(i)   a notice of retention;

(ii)   a notice of commencement;

(iii)   a preliminary notice;

(iv)   a notice of construction loan; or

(v)   a notice of completion.

(3)   The designated agent fulfills the notification requirement under Subsection (1) by sending the notification to the email address, mailing address, or telefax number that the person provides to the designated agent, whether or not the person actually receives the notification.

38-1a-205. Building permit — Transmission to registry — Posting at project site.

(1)   (a)   A county, city, or town issuing a building permit for a private project:

(i)   shall, no later than 15 days after issuing the permit, input the building permit application and transmit the building permit information to the registry electronically by way of the Internet or computer modem or by any other means; and

        (ii)   may collect a building permit fee related to the issuance of the building permit, but may not spend or otherwise use the building permit fee until the county, city, or town complies with Subsection (1)(a)(i) with respect to the building permit for which the fee is charged.

    (b)   The person to whom a building permit, filed under Subsection (1)(a), is issued is responsible for the accuracy of the information in the building permit.

    (c)   For the purposes of classifying a record under Title 63G, Chapter 2, Government Records Access and Management Act, the division shall classify in the registry building permit information transmitted from a county, city, or town to the registry notwithstanding the classification of the building permit information by the county, city, or town.

(2)   At the time a building permit is obtained, each original contractor for construction service shall conspicuously post at the project site a copy of the building permit obtained for the project.

38-1a-206. Registry fees.

(1)   In accordance with the process required by Section 63J-1-504, the division shall establish the fees for:

    (a)   required notices, whether filed electronically or by alternate means;

    (b)   a request for notification under Section 38-1a-204;

    (c)   providing notification of a required notice, whether electronically or by alternate means;

    (d)   a duplicate receipt of a filing; and

    (e)   account setup for a person who wishes to be billed periodically for filings with the registry.

(2)   The fees allowed under Subsection (1) may not in the aggregate exceed the amount reasonably necessary to create and maintain the registry.

(3)   The fees established by the division may vary by method of filing if one form or means of filing is more costly to process than another form or means of filing.

(4)   The division may provide by contract that the designated agent may retain all fees collected by the designated agent, except that the designated agent shall remit to the division the cost of the division's oversight.

(5)   (a)   A person who is delinquent on the payment of a fee established under this section may not file a notice with the registry.

    (b)   The division shall make a determination whether a person is delinquent on the payment of a fee for filing established under this section in accordance with Title 63G, Chapter 4, Administrative Procedures Act.

    (c)   Any order that the division issues in a proceeding described in Subsection (5)(b) may prescribe the method of that person's payment of fees for filing notices with the registry after issuance of the order.

38-1a-207. Registry classification.

(1)   The registry is classified as a public record under Title 63G, Chapter 2, Government Records Access and Management Act, unless the division classifies it otherwise.

(2)   A request for information submitted to the designated agent is not subject to Title 63G, Chapter 2, Government Records Access and Management Act.

(3)   A person desiring information contained in a public record in the registry shall request the information from the designated agent.

(4)   The designated agent may charge a commercially reasonable fee allowed by the designated agent's contract with the division for providing information under Subsection (3).

(5)   Notwithstanding Title 63G, Chapter 2, Government Records Access and Management Act, if information is available in a public record contained in the registry, a person may not request the information from the division.

(6)   (a)   A person may request information that is not a public record contained in the registry from the division in accordance with Title 63G, Chapter 2, Government Records Access and Management Act.

        (b)   The division shall inform the designated agent of how to direct an inquiry made to the designated agent for information that is not a public record contained in the registry.

38-1a-208. Actions that are not adjudicative proceedings.

None of the following is an adjudicative proceeding under Title 63G, Chapter 4, Administrative Procedures Act:

(1)   the filing of a notice permitted or required by this chapter;

(2)   the rejection of a filing permitted or required by this chapter; or

(3)   other action by the designated agent in connection with a filing of any notice permitted or required by this chapter.

38-1a-209. Abuse of registry — Penalty.

(1)   As used in this section, "third party" means an owner, an original contractor, a subcontractor, or any interested party.

(2)   A person abuses the registry if that person files a notice in the registry:

        (a)   without a good faith basis for doing so;

        (b)   with the intent to exact more than is due from the owner or any other interested party; or

        (c)   to procure an unjustified advantage or benefit.

(3)   A person who abuses the registry as described in Subsection (2) is liable to a third party who is affected by the notice for twice the amount of the actual damages incurred by the third party or $2,000, whichever is greater.

38-1a-210. Limitation of liability.

(1)   The state and the state's agencies, instrumentalities, political subdivisions, and an employee of a governmental entity are immune from suit for any injury resulting from the registry.

(2)   The designated agent and its principals, agents, and employees are not liable to any person for the accuracy, coherence, suitability, completeness, or legal effectiveness of information filed or searched in the registry if the designated agent:

        (a)   develops and maintains the registry in compliance with reliability, availability, and security standards established by the division; and

        (b)   meets data entry accuracy standards established by the division under Subsection 38-1a-202(6)(b).

(3)   The designated agent and its principals, agents, and employees are not liable for their inability to perform obligations under this chapter to the extent performance of those obligations is prevented by:

(a)   a storm, earthquake, or other act of God;

(b)   a fire;

(c)   an accident;

(d)   governmental interference; or

(e)   any other event or cause beyond the designated agent's control.

38-1a-211. Limit on notice effect of document filing in the registry.

The filing of a document in the registry is not intended to give notice to all persons of the content of the document within the meaning of Section 57-3-102 and does not constitute constructive notice of matters relating to real property to purchasers for value and without knowledge.

38-1a-301. Those entitled to lien — What may be attached.

(1)   Except as provided in Section 38-11-107, a person who provides preconstruction service or construction work on or for a project property has a lien on the project property for the reasonable value of the preconstruction service or construction work, respectively, as provided in this chapter.

(2)   A person may claim a preconstruction lien and a separate construction lien on the same project property.

(3)   (a)   A construction lien may include an amount claimed for a preconstruction service.

        (b)   A preconstruction lien may not include an amount claimed for construction work.

(4)   A preconstruction or construction lien attaches only to the interest that the owner has in the project property that is the subject of the lien.

38-1a-302. Land covered by lien — Multiple lots occupied by improvement — What a lien attaches to.

(1)   A preconstruction or construction lien extends to and covers as much of the land on which the improvement is made as necessary for the convenient use and occupation of the land.

(2)   If an improvement occupies two or more lots or other subdivisions of land, the lots or subdivisions are considered as one for the purposes of this chapter.

(3)   A preconstruction or construction lien attaches to all franchises, privileges, appurtenances, machinery, and fixtures pertaining to or used in connection with the improvement.

38-1a-303. Limits on attachment, garnishment, and execution levy — Subcontractor lien not affected by payments, debts, offsets, and counterclaims involving other parties.

(1)   An assignment, attachment, or garnishment of or encumbrance or execution levy on money that an owner owes to an original contractor is not valid as against a subcontractor's preconstruction or construction lien.

(2)   An assignment, attachment, or garnishment of or encumbrance or execution levy on money that an original contractor owes to a subcontractor is not valid as against a lien of a laborer employed by the day or piece.

(3)   The preconstruction or construction lien of a subcontractor may not be diminished, impaired, or otherwise affected by:

        (a)   a payment, whether in cash or in-kind, to the original contractor or another subcontractor;

        (b)   a debt owed by the original contractor to the owner;

        (c)   a debt owed by another subcontractor to the original contractor or to a third subcontractor; or

(d)   an offset or counterclaim in favor of the owner against the original contractor, or in favor of the original contractor against another subcontractor, or in favor of another subcontractor against a third subcontractor.

38-1a-304. Liens on multiple properties in one claim.

(1)   A claimant may claim a preconstruction or construction lien against two or more improvements owned by the same person.

(2)   If a claimant claims a preconstruction or construction lien against two or more improvements owned by the same person, the claimant shall designate the amount claimed to be due on each of the improvements.

38-1a-305. Payments applied first to preconstruction lien.

Unless an agreement waiving or limiting a right under a preconstruction or construction lien expressly provides that a payment is required to be applied to a specific lien, mortgage, or encumbrance, a payment to a person claiming both a preconstruction lien and a construction lien shall be applied first to the preconstruction lien until paid in full.

38-1a-306. Substantial compliance.

(1)   Substantial compliance with the requirements of this chapter is sufficient to claim, as applicable, a preconstruction lien or a construction lien.

(2)   Subsection (1) may not be construed to excuse compliance with or affect the requirement to file:

(a)   a notice of retention as provided in Section 38-1a-401 in order to claim a preconstruction lien; or

(b)   a preliminary notice as provided in Section 38-1a-501 in order to claim a construction lien.

38-1a-307. Contesting certain notices.

(1)   A contesting person who believes that a contestable notice lacks proper basis and is therefore invalid may request from the person who filed the notice evidence establishing the validity of the notice.

(2)   Within 10 days after receiving a request under Subsection (1), the person who filed the contestable notice shall provide the requesting person evidence that the notice is valid.

(3)   If the person who filed the notice does not provide timely evidence of the validity of the contestable notice, the person who filed the notice shall immediately cancel the notice from the registry in the manner prescribed by the division by rule.

38-1a-308. Intentional submission of excessive lien notice — Criminal and civil liability.

(1)   A person is guilty of a class B misdemeanor if:

(a)   the person intentionally submits for recording a notice of preconstruction lien or notice of construction lien against any property containing a greater demand than the sum due; and

(b)   by submitting the notice, the person intends:

(i)   to cloud the title;

(ii)   to exact from the owner or person liable by means of the excessive notice of preconstruction or construction lien more than is due; or

(iii)   to procure any unjustified advantage or benefit.

(2)   (a)   As used in this Subsection (2), "third party" means an owner, original contractor, or subcontractor.

      (b)   In addition to any criminal penalty under Subsection (1), a person who submits a notice of preconstruction lien or notice of construction lien as described in Subsection (1) is liable to a third party who is affected by the lien for twice the amount by which the excessive lien notice exceeds the amount actually due or the actual damages incurred by the owner, original contractor, or subcontractor, whichever is greater.

38-1a-309. Interest rate on lien.

Unless otherwise specified in a lawful contract between the owner-builder and the person claiming a lien under this chapter, the interest rate applicable to the lien is the rate described in Subsection 15-1-1(2).

38-1a-401. Notice of retention.

(1)   (a)   A person who desires to claim a preconstruction lien on real property shall file a notice of retention with the registry no later than 20 days after the person commences providing preconstruction service for the anticipated improvement on the real property.

      (b)   A person who fails to file a timely notice of retention as required in this section may not claim a valid preconstruction lien.

      (c)   A timely filed notice of retention is effective as to each preconstruction service that the person filing the notice provides for the anticipated improvement under a single original contract, including preconstruction service that the person provides to more than one supervising subcontractor under that original contract.

      (d)   A notice of retention filed for preconstruction service provided or to be provided under an original contract for an anticipated improvement on real property is not valid for preconstruction service provided or to be provided under a separate original contract for an anticipated improvement on the same real property.

      (e)   A notice of retention that is timely filed with the database with respect to an anticipated improvement is considered to have been filed at the same time as the earliest timely filed notice of retention for that anticipated improvement.

      (f)   A notice of retention shall include:

          (i)   the name, address, telephone number, and email address of the person providing the preconstruction service;

          (ii)   the name, address, telephone number, and email address of the person who employed the person providing the preconstruction service;

          (iii)   a general description of the preconstruction service the person provided or will provide;

          (iv)   the name of the record or reputed owner;

          (v)   the name of the county in which the property on which the anticipated improvement will occur is located;

          (vi)   (A)   the tax parcel identification number of each parcel included in that property; or

                (B)   the entry number of a previously filed notice of retention that includes the tax parcel identification number of each parcel included in that property; and

          (vii)   a statement that the person filing the notice intends to claim a preconstruction lien if the person is not paid for the preconstruction service the person provides.

      (g)   (i)   A claimant who is an original contractor or a supervisory subcontractor may include in a notice of retention the name, address, and telephone number of each subcontractor who is under contract with the claimant to provide preconstruction service that the claimant is under contract to provide.

           (ii) claimant is not a substitute for the subcontractor's own submission of a notice of retention.

(2)   The burden is on the person filing the notice of retention to prove that the person has substantially complied with the requirements of this section.

(3)   (a)   Subject to Subsection (3)(b), a person required by this section to file a notice of retention is required to give only one notice for each anticipated improvement.

      (b)   A person who provides preconstruction service under more than one original contract for the same anticipated improvement and desires to claim a preconstruction lien for preconstruction service provided under each original contract shall file a separate notice of retention for preconstruction service provided under each original contract.

(4)   A person filing a notice of retention by alternate means is responsible for verifying and changing any incorrect information in the notice of retention before the expiration of the period during which the notice is required to be filed.

38-1a-402. Notice of preconstruction lien — Requirements.

(1)   Within 90 days after completing a preconstruction service for which a claimant is not paid in full, a claimant who desires to claim a preconstruction lien shall submit for recording with each applicable county recorder a notice of preconstruction lien.

(2)   A claimant who fails to submit a notice of preconstruction lien as provided in Subsection (1) may not claim a preconstruction lien.

(3)   (a)   A notice of preconstruction service lien shall include:

           (i)   the claimant's name, mailing address, and telephone number;

           (ii)   a statement that the claimant claims a preconstruction lien;

           (iii)   the date the claimant's notice of retention was filed;

           (iv)   the name of the person who employed the claimant;

           (v)   a general description of the preconstruction service provided by the claimant;

           (vi)   the date that the claimant last provided preconstruction service;

           (vii) the name, if known, of the reputed owner or, if not known, the name of the record owner;

           (viii) a description of the project property sufficient for identification;

           (ix)   the principal amount, excluding interest, costs, and attorney fees, claimed by the claimant;

           (x)   the claimant's signature or the signature of the claimant's authorized agent;

           (xi)   an acknowledgment or certificate as required under Title 57, Chapter 3, Recording of Documents; and

           (xii) if the lien is against an owner-occupied residence, as defined in Section 38-11-102, a statement meeting the requirements that the division has established by rule, describing the steps the owner of the owner-occupied residence may take to require a claimant to remove the lien as provided in Section 38-11-107.

(b)   (i)   A claimant who is an original contractor or a supervising subcontractor may include in a notice of preconstruction lien the name, address, and telephone number of each subcontractor who is under contract with the claimant to provide preconstruction service that the claimant is under contract to provide.

           (ii)   The inclusion of a subcontractor in a notice of preconstruction lien filed by another claimant is not a substitute for the subcontractor's own submission of a notice of preconstruction lien.

(4)   (a)   A county recorder:

           (i)   shall record each notice of preconstruction lien in an index maintained for that purpose; and

           (ii)   need not verify that a valid notice of retention is filed with respect to the claimed preconstruction lien.

    (b)   All persons are considered to have notice of a notice of preconstruction lien from the time it is recorded.

(5)   (a)   Within 30 days after a claimant's notice of preconstruction lien is recorded, the claimant shall send by certified mail a copy of the notice to the reputed or record owner.

    (b)   If the record owner's address is not readily available to the claimant, the claimant may mail a copy of the notice to the owner's last-known address as it appears on the last completed assessment roll of the county in which the property is located.

    (c)   A claimant's failure to mail a copy of the notice as required in this Subsection (5) precludes the claimant from being awarded costs and attorney fees against the reputed or record owner in an action to enforce the lien.

(6)   Nothing in this section may be construed to prohibit a claimant from recording a notice of preconstruction lien before completing the preconstruction service the claimant contracted to provide.

38-1a-403. Effective time and priority of preconstruction lien — Subordination to bona fide loan.

(1)   Except as otherwise provided in this chapter, a preconstruction lien:

    (a)   relates back to and takes effect as of the time of filing of the earliest timely filed notice of retention under Section 38-1a-401 for the anticipated improvement for which the preconstruction lien is claimed; and

    (b)   has priority over:

           (i)   any lien, mortgage, or other encumbrance that attaches after the earliest timely filed notice of retention is filed; and

           (ii)   any lien, mortgage, or other encumbrance of which the claimant had no notice and that was unrecorded at the time the earliest timely filed notice of retention is filed.

(2)   A preconstruction lien is subordinate to an interest securing a bona fide loan if and to the extent that the lien covers preconstruction service provided after the interest securing a bona fide loan is recorded.

38-1a-404. When preconstruction service considered complete.

Preconstruction service is considered complete for any project, project phase, or bid package as of the date that construction work for that project, project phase, or bid package, respectively, commences.

38-1a-501. Preliminary notice.

(1) (a) (i) A person who desires to claim a construction lien on real property shall file a preliminary notice with the registry no later than 20 days after the person commences providing construction work on the real property.

  (ii) A prelender claimant who provides construction work to a construction project after the recording of a construction lender's mortgage or trust deed on the project property and who desires to claim a construction lien for that construction work shall file a preliminary notice with the registry no later than 20 days after the recording of the mortgage or trust deed.

  (b) Subject to Subsection (1)(c), a preliminary notice is effective as to all construction work that the person filing the notice provides to the construction project under a single original contract, including construction work that the person provides to more than one supervisory subcontractor under that original contract.

  (c) (i) A person who desires to claim a construction lien on real property but fails to file a timely preliminary notice within the period specified in Subsection (1)(a) may, subject to Subsection (1)(d), file a preliminary notice with the registry after the period specified in Subsection (1)(a).

  (ii) A person who files a preliminary notice under Subsection (1)(c)(i) may not claim a construction lien for construction work the person provides to the construction project before the date that is five days after the preliminary notice is filed.

  (d) Notwithstanding Subsections (1)(a) and (c), a preliminary notice has no effect if it is filed more than 10 days after the filing of a notice of completion under Section 38-1a-507 for the construction project for which the preliminary notice is filed.

  (e) A person who fails to file a preliminary notice as required in this section may not claim a construction lien.

  (f) (i) Except as provided in Subsection (1)(f)(ii), a preliminary notice that is filed with the registry as provided in this section is considered to be filed at the time of the first preliminary notice filing.

  (ii) A timely filed preliminary notice that is a refiled preliminary notice is considered to be filed immediately after the recording of a mortgage or trust deed of the construction lender that paid the pre-lender claimant in full for construction work the claimant provided before the recording of the mortgage or trust deed.

  (g) If a preliminary notice filed with the registry includes the tax parcel identification number of a parcel not previously associated in the registry with a construction project, the designated agent shall promptly notify the person who filed the preliminary notice that:

  (i) the preliminary notice includes a tax parcel identification number of a parcel not previously associated in the registry with a construction project; and

  (ii) the likely explanation is that:

  (A) the preliminary notice is the first filing for the project; or

  (B) the tax parcel identification number is incorrectly stated in the preliminary notice.

  (h) A preliminary notice shall include:

  (i) the name, address, telephone number, and email address of the person providing the construction work for which the preliminary notice is filed;

        (ii)   the name and address of the person who contracted with the claimant for the construction work;

        (iii)   the name of the record or reputed owner;

        (iv)   the name of the original contractor for construction work under which the claimant is providing or will provide construction work;

        (v)   the address of the project property or a description of the location of the project;

        (vi)   the name of the county in which the project property is located; and

        (vii)   (A)   the tax parcel identification number of each parcel included in the project property;

              (B)   the entry number of a previously filed notice of construction loan under Section 38-1a-601 on the same project;

              (C)   the entry number of a previously filed preliminary notice on the same project that includes the tax parcel identification number of each parcel included in the project property; or

              (D)   the entry number of the building permit issued for the project.

    (i)   A preliminary notice may include:

        (i)   the subdivision, development, or other project name applicable to the construction project for which the preliminary notice is filed; and

        (ii)   the lot or parcel number of each lot or parcel that is included in the project property.

(2)   (a)   The burden is upon the person filing the preliminary notice to prove that the person has substantially complied with the requirements of this section.

    (b)   Substantial compliance with the requirements of Subsections (1)(h)(iii) through (vii) may be established by a person's reasonable reliance on information in the registry provided by a previously filed:

        (i)   notice of construction loan under Section 38-1a-601;

        (ii)   preliminary notice; or

        (iii)   building permit.

(3)   (a)   Subject to Subsection (3)(b), a person required by this section to give preliminary notice is required to give only one notice for each construction project.

    (b)   If the construction work is provided pursuant to contracts under more than one original contract for construction work, the notice requirements shall be met with respect to the construction work provided under each original contract.

(4)   A person filing a preliminary notice by alternate means is responsible for verifying and changing any incorrect information in the preliminary notice before the expiration of the time period during which the notice is required to be filed.

(5)   (a)   A person who files a preliminary notice before the recording of a construction lender's mortgage or trust deed may withdraw the preliminary notice by filing with the registry a notice of withdrawal as provided in Subsection (5)(b).

    (b)   A notice of withdrawal shall include:

        (i)   the information required for a preliminary notice under Subsection (1)(g); and

        (ii)   the entry number of the preliminary notice being withdrawn.

(6)   A person who files a preliminary notice that contains inaccurate or incomplete information may not be held liable for damages suffered by any other person who relies on the inaccurate or incomplete information in filing a preliminary notice.

38-1a-502. Notice of construction lien — Contents — Recording — Service on owner.

(1)   (a)   A person who desires to claim a construction lien shall submit for recording in the office of each applicable county recorder a notice of construction lien no later than, except as provided in Subsection (1)(b):

(i)   180 days after the date on which final completion of the original contract occurs, if no notice of completion is filed under Section 38-1a-507; or

(ii)   90 days after the date on which a notice of completion is filed under Section 38-1a-507, but not later than 180 days after the date on which final completion of the original contract occurs.

(b)   A subcontractor who provides substantial work after a certificate of occupancy is issued or a required final inspection is completed and desires to claim a construction lien shall submit for recording in the office of each applicable county recorder a notice of construction lien no later than 180 days after final completion of that subcontractor's work.

(2)   A notice of construction lien shall contain:

(a)   the name of the reputed owner if known or, if not known, the name of the record owner;

(b)   the name of the person by whom the claimant was employed or to whom the claimant provided construction work;

(c)   the time when the claimant first and last provided construction work;

(d)   a description of the project property, sufficient for identification;

(e)   the name, current address, and current phone number of the claimant;

(f)   the amount claimed under the construction lien;

(g)   the signature of the claimant or the claimant's authorized agent;

(h)   an acknowledgment or certificate as required under Title 57, Chapter 3, Recording of Documents; and

(i)   if the construction lien is on an owner-occupied residence, as defined in Section 38-11-102, a statement describing what steps an owner, as defined in Section 38-11-102, may take to require a lien claimant to remove the lien in accordance with Section 38-11-107.

(3)   (a)   A county recorder:

(i)   shall record each notice of construction lien in an index maintained for that purpose; and

(ii)   need not verify that a valid preliminary notice is filed with respect to the claimed construction lien.

(b)   All persons are considered to have notice of a notice of construction lien from the time it is recorded.

(4)   (a)   Within 30 days after filing a notice of construction lien, the claimant shall deliver or mail by certified mail a copy of the notice to the reputed owner or the record owner.

(b)   If the record owner's current address is not readily available to the claimant, the claimant may mail a copy of the notice to the last known address of the record owner, using the names and addresses appearing on the last completed real property assessment rolls of the county where the project property is located.

(c) Failure to deliver or mail the notice of lien to the reputed owner or record owner precludes the claimant from an award of costs and attorney fees against the reputed owner or record owner in an action to enforce the construction lien.

(5) The division shall make rules governing the form of the statement required under Subsection (2)(i).

38-1a-503. Relation back and priority of liens.

(1) A construction lien relates back to, and takes effect as of, the time of the first preliminary notice filing.

(2) (a) Subject to Subsection (2)(b), a construction lien has priority over:

   (i) any lien, mortgage, or other encumbrance that attaches after the first preliminary notice filing; and

   (ii) any lien, mortgage, or other encumbrance of which the claimant had no notice and which was unrecorded at the time of the first preliminary notice filing.

(b) A recorded mortgage or trust deed of a construction lender has priority over a construction lien of a claimant who files a preliminary notice in accordance with Section **38-1a-501** before the mortgage or trust deed is recorded if the claimant:

   (i) accepts payment in full for construction work that the claimant provides to the construction project before the mortgage or trust deed is recorded; and

   (ii) withdraws the claimant's preliminary notice by filing a notice of withdrawal under Subsection **38-1a-501**(5).

38-1a-504. Construction liens on equal footing.

(1) Construction liens on a project property are on an equal footing with one another, regardless of when the notices of construction lien relating to the construction liens are submitted for recording and regardless of when construction work for which the liens are claimed is provided.

(2) Subsection (1) relates to the relationship between claimants' construction liens and does not affect the priority of a construction lender's mortgage or trust deed, as established under this chapter.

38-1a-505. Materials for a construction project not subject to process —Exception.

(1) Materials provided for use in a construction project are not subject to attachment, execution, or other legal process to enforce a debt owed by the purchaser of the materials, if the materials are in good faith about to be applied to the construction, alteration, or repair of an improvement that is the subject of the construction project.

(2) Subsection (1) does not apply to an attachment, execution, or other legal process to enforce a debt incurred to purchase the materials described in Subsection (1).

38-1a-506. Notice of intent to obtain final completion.

(1) An owner, as defined in Section 14-2-1, of a nonresidential construction project that is registered with the registry, or an original contractor of a commercial nonresidential construction project that is registered with the registry under Section 38-1a-501, shall file with the registry a notice of intent to obtain final completion as provided in this section if:

(a) the completion of performance time under the original contract for construction work is greater than 120 days;

(b) the total original construction contract price exceeds $500,000; and

(c) the original contractor or owner has not obtained a payment bond in accordance with Section 14-2-1.

(2)   The notice of intent described in Subsection (1) shall be filed at least 45 days before the day on which the owner or original contractor of a commercial nonresidential construction project files or could have filed a notice of completion under Section 38-1a-507.

(3)   A person who provides construction work to an owner or original contractor who files a notice of intent in accordance with Subsection (1) shall file an amendment to the person's preliminary notice previously filed by the person as required in Section 38-1a-501:

    (a)   that includes:

        (i)   a good faith estimate of the total amount remaining due to complete the contract, purchase order, or agreement relating to the person's approved construction work;

        (ii)   the identification of each original contractor or subcontractor with whom the person has a contract or contracts for providing construction work; and

        (iii)   a separate statement of all known amounts or categories of work in dispute; and

    (b)   no later than 20 days after the day on which the owner or contractor files a notice of intent.

(4)   (a)   A person described in Subsection (3) may demand a statement of adequate assurance from the owner, contractor, or subcontractor with whom the person has privity of contract no later than 10 days after the day on which the person files a balance statement in accordance with Subsection (3) from an owner, contractor, or subcontractor who is in privity of contract with the person.

    (b)   A demand for adequate assurance as described in Subsection (4)(a) may include a request for a statement from the owner, contractor, or subcontractor that the owner, contractor, or subcontractor has sufficient funds dedicated and available to pay for all sums due to the person filing for the adequate assurances or that will become due in order to complete a construction project.

    (c)   A person who demands adequate assurance under Subsection (4)(a) shall deliver copies of the demand to the owner and contractor:

        (i)   by hand delivery with a responsible party's acknowledgment of receipt;

        (ii)   by certified mail with a return receipt; or

        (iii)   as provided under Rule 4, Utah Rules of Civil Procedure.

(5)   (a)   A person described in Subsection (3) may bring a legal action against a party with whom the person is in privity of contract, including a request for injunctive or declaratory relief, to determine the adequacy of the funds of the owner, contractor, or subcontractor with whom the demanding person contracted if, after the person demands adequate assurance in accordance with the requirements of this section:

        (i)   the owner, contractor, or subcontractor fails to provide adequate assurance that the owner, contractor, or subcontractor has sufficient available funds, or access to financing or other sufficient available funds, to pay for the completion of the demanding person's approved work on the construction project; or

        (ii)   the parties disagree, in good faith, as to whether there are adequate funds, or access to financing or other sufficient available funds, to pay for the completion of the demanding person's approved work on the construction project.

    (b)   If a court finds that an owner, contractor, or subcontractor has failed to provide adequate assurance in accordance with Subsection (4)(a), the court may require the owner, contractor, or subcontractor to post adequate security with the court sufficient to assure timely payment of the remaining contract balance for the approved work of the person seeking adequate assurance, including:

(i)   cash;

(ii)   a bond;

(iii)   an irrevocable letter of credit;

(iv)   property;

(v)   financing; or

(vi)   another form of security approved by the court.

(6)   (a)   A person is subject to the civil penalty described in Subsection (6)(b), if the person files a balance statement described in Subsection (3) that misrepresents the amount due under the contract with the intent to:

            (i)   charge an owner, contractor, or subcontractor more than the actual amount due; or

            (ii)   procure any other unfair advantage or benefit on the person's behalf.

        (b)   The civil penalty described in Subsection (6)(a) is the greater of:

            (i)   twice the amount by which the balance statement filed under Subsection (3) exceeds the amount actually remaining due under the contract for completion of construction; and

            (ii)   the actual damages incurred by the owner, contractor, or subcontractor.

(7)   A court shall award reasonable attorney fees to a prevailing party for an action brought under this section.

(8)   Failure to comply with the requirements established in this section does not affect any other requirement or right under this chapter.

(9)   A person who has not filed a preliminary notice as required under Section 38-1a-501 is not entitled to a right or a remedy provided in this section.

(10)   This section does not create a cause of action against a person with whom the demanding party is not in privity of contract.

38-1a-507. Notice of completion.

(1)   (a)   Upon final completion of a construction project, a notice of completion may be filed with the registry by:

            (i)   an owner;

            (ii)   an original contractor for construction work;

            (iii)   a lender that has provided financing for the construction project;

            (iv)   a surety that has provided bonding for the construction project; or

            (v)   a title company issuing a title insurance policy on the construction project.

        (b)   A notice of completion shall include:

            (i)   the name, address, telephone number, and email address of the person filing the notice of completion;

            (ii)   the name of the county in which the project property is located;

            (iii)   for a private project:

                (A)   the tax parcel identification number of each parcel included in the project property;

           (B)   the entry number of a preliminary notice on the same project that includes the tax parcel identification number of each parcel included in the project property; or

           (C)   the entry number of the building permit issued for the project;

       (iv)   for a government project, the government project-identifying information;

       (v)   the date on which final completion is alleged to have occurred; and

       (vi)   the method used to determine final completion.

(2)   A person filing a notice of completion by alternate means is responsible for verifying and changing any incorrect information in the notice of completion before the expiration of the time period during which the notice is required to be filed.

38-1a-601. Notice of construction loan.

(1)   After recording a mortgage or trust deed securing a construction loan on a private project, the construction lender on the loan shall promptly, in conjunction with the closing of the construction loan, file with the registry a notice of construction loan.

(2)   A notice under Subsection (1) shall accurately state:

      (a)   the lender's name, address, and telephone number;

      (b)   the name of the trustor on the trust deed securing the loan;

      (c)   the tax parcel identification number of each parcel included or to be included in the construction project for which the loan was given;

      (d)   the address of the project property; and

      (e)   the name of the county in which the project property is located.

(3)   A construction lender that files a notice of construction loan containing incomplete or inaccurate information may not be held liable for damages suffered by any other person who relies on the inaccurate or incomplete information in filing a preliminary notice.

38-1a-602. Notice concerning construction loan default.

(1)   Within five business days after a notice of default is filed for recording under Section **57-1-24** with respect to a trust deed on the project property securing a construction loan, the construction lender under the loan shall file a notice with the registry.

(2)   A notice under Subsection (1) shall:

      (a)   include:

         (i)   the information required to be included in a notice of construction loan under Subsection 38-1a-601(2); and

         (ii)   the entry number of the notice of construction loan;

      (b)   state that a notice of default with respect to the construction loan has been recorded; and

      (c)   state the date that the notice of default was recorded.

38-1a-701. Action to enforce lien — Time for filing action — Notice of pendency of action — Action involving a residence.

(1)   As used in this section:

      (a)   "Owner" has the same meaning as defined in Section 38-11-102.

      (b)   "Residence" has the same meaning as defined in Section 38-11-102.

(2)   In order to enforce a preconstruction lien or construction lien, a claimant shall file an action to enforce the lien:

    (a)   except as provided in Subsection (2)(b), within 180 days after the day on which the claimant files:

        (i)   a notice of preconstruction lien under Section 38-1a-402, for a preconstruction lien; or

        (ii)   a notice of construction lien under Section 38-1a-502, for a construction lien; or

    (b)   if an owner files for protection under the bankruptcy laws of the United States before the expiration of the 180-day period under Subsection (2)(a), within 90 days after the automatic stay under the bankruptcy proceeding is lifted or expires.

(3)   (a)   (i)   Within the time period provided in Subsection (2) for filing an action, a claimant shall file for record with each applicable county recorder a notice of the pendency of the action, in the manner provided for actions affecting the title or right to possession of real property.

        (ii)   If a claimant fails to file for record a notice of the pendency of the action, as required in Subsection (3)(a)(i), the preconstruction lien or construction lien, as applicable, is void, except as to persons who have been made parties to the action and persons having actual knowledge of the commencement of the action.

    (b)   The burden of proof is upon the claimant and those claiming under the claimant to show actual knowledge under Subsection (3)(a)(ii).

(4)   (a)   A preconstruction lien or construction lien is automatically and immediately void if an action to enforce the lien is not filed within the time required by this section.

    (b)   Notwithstanding Section 78B-2-111, a court has no subject matter jurisdiction to adjudicate a preconstruction or construction lien that becomes void under Subsection (4)(a).

(5)   This section may not be interpreted to impair or affect the right of any person to whom a debt may be due for any preconstruction service or construction work to maintain a personal action to recover the debt.

(6)   (a)   If a claimant files an action to enforce a preconstruction or construction lien involving a residence, the claimant shall include with the service of the complaint on the owner of the residence:

        (i)   instructions to the owner of the residence relating to the owner's rights under Title 38, Chapter 11, Residence Lien Restriction and Lien Recovery Fund Act; and

        (ii)   a form to enable the owner of the residence to specify the grounds upon which the owner may exercise available rights under Title 38, Chapter 11, Residence Lien Restriction and Lien Recovery Fund Act.

    (b)   The instructions and form required by Subsection (6)(a) shall meet the requirements established by the division by rule.

    (c)   If a claimant fails to provide to the owner of the residence the instructions and form required by Subsection (6)(a), the claimant is barred from maintaining or enforcing the preconstruction or construction lien upon the residence.

    (d)   A court shall stay an action to determine the rights and liabilities of an owner of a residence under this chapter, Title 38, Chapter 11, Residence Lien Restriction and Lien Recovery Fund Act, and Title 14, Chapter 2, Private Contracts, until after the owner is given a reasonable period of time to:

        (i)   establish compliance with Subsections 38-11-204(4)(a) and (4)(b) through an informal proceeding, as set forth in Title 63G, Chapter 4, Administrative Procedures Act, commenced at the division within 30 days after the owner is served with summons in the foreclosure action; and

        (ii)   obtain a certificate of compliance or denial of certificate of compliance, as defined in Section 38-11-102.

(e)   An owner applying for a certificate of compliance under Subsection (6)(d) shall send by certified mail to all claimants:

        (i)   a copy of the application for a certificate of compliance; and

        (ii)   all materials filed in connection with the application.

(f)   The division shall notify all claimants listed in an owner's application for a certificate of compliance under Subsection (6)(d) of the issuance or denial of a certificate of compliance.

38-1a-702. Parties — Consolidation of separate actions.

(1)   In an action under this part, subject to the time restrictions under Subsection **38-1a-701**(2):

    (a)   a claimant who is not contesting the claim of another claimant may join as a plaintiff;

    (b)   a claimant who fails or refuses to become a plaintiff may be made a defendant; and

    (c)   a claimant who is not made a party may intervene at any time before the final hearing.

(2)   If separate actions are commenced under this part to enforce preconstruction or construction liens on the same property, the court may consolidate the actions and make all claimants parties to the consolidated action.

38-1a-703. Order of satisfaction if multiple liens on same property.

If liens are claimed against the same property the decree shall provide for their satisfaction in the following order:

(1)   subcontractors who are laborers or mechanics working by the day or piece, but who have not furnished materials;

(2)   all other subcontractors and all materialmen; and

(3)   original contractors.

38-1a-704. Sale of property — Redemption — Disposition of proceeds.

(1)   The court shall cause the property to be sold in satisfaction of the liens and costs as in the case of a foreclosure of a mortgage, subject to the same right of redemption.

(2)   If the proceeds of sale after the payment of costs are not sufficient to satisfy the whole amount of liens included in the decree, then the proceeds shall be paid in the order designated in Section **38-1a-703**, and pro rata to the persons claiming in each class if the sum realized is insufficient to pay the persons of the class in full.

(3)   Any excess sale proceeds remaining after the payment of all liens and costs shall be paid to the owner.

38-1a-705. Deficiency judgment.

A claimant whose preconstruction or construction lien is not paid in full through an enforcement action as provided in this part may:

(1)   have judgment for the unpaid balance entered against the person liable; and

(2)   execute on the judgment in the same manner as execution on judgments generally.

38-1a-706. Apportionment of costs — Costs and attorney fees to subcontractor.

(1)   Except as provided in Section 38-11-107, the court shall apportion costs between the owner and original contractor according to the right of the case.

(2)   The court shall award a subcontractor with a valid preconstruction or construction lien:

    (a)   all of the subcontractor's costs, including the costs of preparing and recording the notice of preconstruction or construction lien; and

    (b)   the subcontractor's reasonable attorney fees incurred in preparing and recording the notice of preconstruction or construction lien.

38-1a-707. Attorney fees — Offer of judgment.

(1)   Except as provided in Section 38-11-107 and in Subsection (2), in any action brought to enforce any lien under this chapter the successful party shall be entitled to recover reasonable attorney fees, to be fixed by the court, which shall be taxed as costs in the action.

(2)   A person who files a wrongful lien as provided in Section 38-1a-308 may not recover attorney fees under Subsection (1).

(3)   (a)   A person against whom an action is brought to enforce a preconstruction or construction lien may make an offer of judgment pursuant to Rule 68 of the Utah Rules of Civil Procedure.

    (b)   If the offer is not accepted and the judgment finally obtained by the offeree is not more favorable than the offer, the offeree shall pay the costs and attorney fees incurred by the offeror after the offer was made.

38-1a-801. Preconstruction and construction liens assignable — Action by assignee to enforce lien.

(1)   A preconstruction lien or construction lien is assignable as any other chose in action.

(2)   An assignee of a preconstruction lien or construction lien may, in the assignee's own name, commence and prosecute an action on the lien as provided in Part 7, Enforcement of Preconstruction and Construction Liens.

38-1a-802 (Effective 05/01/13). Waiver or limitation of a lien right — Forms — Scope.

(1)   As used in this section:

    (a)   "Check" means a payment instrument on a depository institution including:

        (i)   a check;

        (ii)   a draft;

        (iii)   an order; or

        (iv)   other instrument.

    (b)   "Depository institution" is as defined in Section 7-1-103.

    (c)   "Receives payment" means, in the case of a restrictive endorsement, a payee has endorsed a check and the check is presented to and paid by the depository institution on which it is drawn.

(2)   Notwithstanding Section 38-1a-105, a claimant's written consent that waives or limits the claimant's lien rights is enforceable only if the claimant:

    (a)   (i)   executes a waiver and release that is signed by the claimant or the claimant's authorized agent; or

                (ii)   for a restrictive endorsement on a check, includes a restrictive endorsement on a check that is:

                        (A)   signed by the claimant or the claimant's authorized agent; and

                        (B)   in substantially the same form set forth in Subsection (4)(d); and

    (b)   receives payment of the amount identified in the waiver and release or check that includes the restrictive endorsement:

                (i)   including payment by a joint payee check; and

                (ii)   for a progress payment, only to the extent of the payment.

(3)   (a)   Notwithstanding the language of a waiver and release described in Subsection (2), Subsection (3)(b) applies if:

                (i)   the payment given in exchange for any waiver and release of lien is made by check; and

                (ii)   the check fails to clear the depository institution on which it is drawn for any reason.

    (b)   If the conditions of Subsection (3)(a) are met:

                (i)   the waiver and release described in Subsection (3)(a) is void; and

                (ii)   the following will not be affected by the claimant's execution of the waiver and release:

                        (A)   any lien;

                        (B)   any lien right;

                        (C)   any bond right;

                        (D)   any contract right; or

                        (E)   any other right to recover payment afforded to the claimant in law or equity.

(4)   (a)   A waiver and release given by a claimant meets the requirements of this section if it is in substantially the form provided in this Subsection (4) for the circumstance provided in this Subsection (4).

    (b)   A waiver and release may be in substantially the following form if the claimant is required to execute a waiver and release in exchange for or to induce the payment of a progress billing:

"UTAH CONDITIONAL WAIVER AND RELEASE UPON PROGRESS PAYMENT

Property Name: _____

Property Location: _____

Undersigned's Customer: _____

Invoice/Payment Application Number: _____

Payment Amount: _____

Payment Period: _____

To the extent provided below, this document becomes effective to release and the undersigned is considered to waive any notice of lien or right under Utah Code Ann., Title 38, Chapter 1a, Preconstruction and Construction Liens, or any bond right under Utah Code Ann., Title 14, Contractors' Bonds, or Section 63G-6a-1103 related to payment rights the undersigned has on the above described Property once:

(1)   the undersigned endorses a check in the above referenced Payment Amount payable to the undersigned; and

(2)   the check is paid by the depository institution on which it is drawn.

This waiver and release applies to a progress payment for the work, materials, equipment, or a combination of work, materials, and equipment furnished by the undersigned to the Property or to the Undersigned's Customer which are the subject of the Invoice or Payment Application, but only to the extent of the Payment Amount. This waiver and release does not apply to any retention withheld; any items, modifications, or changes pending approval; disputed items and claims; or items furnished or invoiced after the Payment Period.

The undersigned warrants that the undersigned either has already paid or will use the money the undersigned receives from this progress payment promptly to pay in full all the undersigned's laborers, subcontractors, materialmen, and suppliers for all work, materials, equipment, or combination of work, materials, and equipment that are the subject of this waiver and release.

Dated: _____

_____(Company Name)

_____By:_____

_____Its:_____"

(c)   A waiver and release may be in substantially the following form if the lien claimant is required to execute a waiver and release in exchange for or to induce the payment of a final billing:

"UTAH WAIVER AND RELEASE UPON FINAL PAYMENT

Property Name: _____

Property Location: _____

Undersigned's Customer: _____

Invoice/Payment Application Number: _____

Payment Amount: _____

To the extent provided below, this document becomes effective to release and the undersigned is considered to waive any notice of lien or right under Utah Code Ann., Title 38, Chapter 1a, Preconstruction and Construction Liens, or any bond right under Utah Code Ann., Title 14, Contractors' Bonds, or Section 63G-6a-1103 related to payment rights the undersigned has on the above described Property once:

(1)   the undersigned endorses a check in the above referenced Payment Amount payable to the undersigned; and

(2)   the check is paid by the depository institution on which it is drawn.

This waiver and release applies to the final payment for the work, materials, equipment, or combination of work, materials, and equipment furnished by the undersigned to the Property or to the Undersigned's Customer.

The undersigned warrants that the undersigned either has already paid or will use the money the undersigned receives from the final payment promptly to pay in full all the undersigned's laborers, subcontractors, materialmen, and suppliers for all work, materials, equipment, or combination of work, materials, and equipment that are the subject of this waiver and release.

Dated: _____

_____(Company Name)

_____By:_____

_____Its:_____ "

(d)   A restrictive endorsement placed on a check to effectuate a waiver and release described in this Subsection (4) meets the requirements of this section if it is in substantially the following form:

"This check is a progress/ final payment for property described on this check sufficient for identification. Endorsement of this check is an acknowledgment by the endorser that the waiver and release to which the payment applies is effective to the extent provided in Utah Code Ann. Subsection **38-1a-802**(4)(b) or (c) respectively."

(e)   (i)   If using a restrictive endorsement under Subsection (4)(d), the person preparing the check shall indicate whether the check is for a progress payment or a final payment by circling the word "progress" if the check is for a progress payment, or the word "final" if the check is for a final payment.

(ii)   If a restrictive endorsement does not indicate whether the check is for a progress payment or a final payment, it is considered to be for a progress payment.

(5)   (a)   If the conditions of Subsection (5)(b) are met, this section does not affect the enforcement of:

        (i)   an accord and satisfaction regarding a bona fide dispute; or

        (ii)   an agreement made in settlement of an action pending in any court or arbitration.

    (b)   Pursuant to Subsection (5)(a), this section does not affect enforcement of an accord and satisfaction or settlement described in Subsection (5)(a) if the accord and satisfaction or settlement:

        (i)   is in a writing signed by the claimant; and

        (ii)   specifically references the lien rights waived or impaired.

38-1a-802 (Superseded 05/01/13). Waiver or limitation of a lien right — Forms — Scope.

(1)   As used in this section:

    (a)   "Check" means a payment instrument on a depository institution including:

        (i)   a check;

        (ii)   a draft;

        (iii)   an order; or

        (iv)   other instrument.

    (b)   "Depository institution" is as defined in Section 7-1-103.

    (c)   "Receives payment" means, in the case of a restrictive endorsement, a payee has endorsed a check and the check is presented to and paid by the depository institution on which it is drawn.

(2)   Notwithstanding Section 38-1a-105, a claimant's written consent that waives or limits the claimant's lien rights is enforceable only if the claimant:

    (a)   (i)   executes a waiver and release that is signed by the claimant or the claimant's authorized agent; or

        (ii)   for a restrictive endorsement on a check, includes a restrictive endorsement on a check that is:

            (A)   signed by the claimant or the claimant's authorized agent; and

            (B)   in substantially the same form set forth in Subsection (4)(d); and

    (b)   receives payment of the amount identified in the waiver and release or check that includes the restrictive endorsement:

        (i)   including payment by a joint payee check; and

        (ii)   for a progress payment, only to the extent of the payment.

(3)   (a)   Notwithstanding the language of a waiver and release described in Subsection (2), Subsection (3)(b) applies if:

        (i)   the payment given in exchange for any waiver and release of lien is made by check; and

        (ii)   the check fails to clear the depository institution on which it is drawn for any reason.

    (b)   If the conditions of Subsection (3)(a) are met:

        (i)   the waiver and release described in Subsection (3)(a) is void; and

        (ii)   the following will not be affected by the claimant's execution of the waiver and release:

            (A)   any lien;

           (B)   any lien right;

           (C)   any bond right;

           (D)   any contract right; or

           (E)   any other right to recover payment afforded to the claimant in law or equity.

(4)   (a)   A waiver and release given by a claimant meets the requirements of this section if it is in substantially the form provided in this Subsection (4) for the circumstance provided in this Subsection (4).

      (b)   A waiver and release may be in substantially the following form if the claimant is required to execute a waiver and release in exchange for or to induce the payment of a progress billing:

"UTAH CONDITIONAL WAIVER AND RELEASE UPON PROGRESS PAYMENT

Property Name: _____

Property Location: _____

Undersigned's Customer: _____

Invoice/Payment Application Number: _____

Payment Amount: _____

Payment Period: _____

To the extent provided below, this document becomes effective to release and the undersigned is considered to waive any notice of lien or right under Utah Code Ann., Title 38, Chapter 1a, Preconstruction and Construction Liens, or any bond right under Utah Code Ann., Title 14, Contractors' Bonds, or Section 63G-6-505 related to payment rights the undersigned has on the above described Property once:

(1)   the undersigned endorses a check in the above referenced Payment Amount payable to the undersigned; and

(2)   the check is paid by the depository institution on which it is drawn.

This waiver and release applies to a progress payment for the work, materials, equipment, or a combination of work, materials, and equipment furnished by the undersigned to the Property or to the Undersigned's Customer which are the subject of the Invoice or Payment Application, but only to the extent of the Payment Amount. This waiver and release does not apply to any retention withheld; any items, modifications, or changes pending approval; disputed items and claims; or items furnished or invoiced after the Payment Period.

The undersigned warrants that the undersigned either has already paid or will use the money the undersigned receives from this progress payment promptly to pay in full all the undersigned's laborers, subcontractors, materialmen, and suppliers for all work, materials, equipment, or combination of work, materials, and equipment that are the subject of this waiver and release.

Dated: _____

_____(Company Name)

_____By:_____

_____Its:_____"

(c) A waiver and release may be in substantially the following form if the lien claimant is required to execute a waiver and release in exchange for or to induce the payment of a final billing:

"UTAH WAIVER AND RELEASE UPON FINAL PAYMENT

Property Name: _____

Property Location: _____

Undersigned's Customer: _____

Invoice/Payment Application Number: _____

Payment Amount: _____

To the extent provided below, this document becomes effective to release and the undersigned is considered to waive any notice of lien or right under Utah Code Ann., Title 38, Chapter 1a, Preconstruction and Construction Liens, or any bond right under Utah Code Ann., Title 14, Contractors' Bonds, or Section **63G-6-505** related to payment rights the undersigned has on the above described Property once:

(1) the undersigned endorses a check in the above referenced Payment Amount payable to the undersigned; and

(2) the check is paid by the depository institution on which it is drawn.

This waiver and release applies to the final payment for the work, materials, equipment, or combination of work, materials, and equipment furnished by the undersigned to the Property or to the Undersigned's Customer.

The undersigned warrants that the undersigned either has already paid or will use the money the undersigned receives from the final payment promptly to pay in full all the undersigned's laborers, subcontractors, materialmen, and suppliers for all work, materials, equipment, or combination of work, materials, and equipment that are the subject of this waiver and release.

Dated: _____

_____(Company Name)

_____By:_____

_____Its:_____"

(d) A restrictive endorsement placed on a check to effectuate a waiver and release described in this Subsection (4) meets the requirements of this section if it is in substantially the following form:

"This check is a progress/ final payment for property described on this check sufficient for identification. Endorsement of this check is an acknowledgment by the endorser that the waiver and release to which the payment applies is effective to the extent provided in Utah Code Ann. Subsection 38-1a-802(4)(b) or (c) respectively."

(e) (i) If using a restrictive endorsement under Subsection (4)(d), the person preparing the check shall indicate whether the check is for a progress payment or a final payment by circling the word "progress" if the check is for a progress payment, or the word "final" if the check is for a final payment.

(ii) If a restrictive endorsement does not indicate whether the check is for a progress payment or a final payment, it is considered to be for a progress payment.

(5)   (a)   If the conditions of Subsection (5)(b) are met, this section does not affect the enforcement of:

              (i)   an accord and satisfaction regarding a bona fide dispute; or

              (ii)   an agreement made in settlement of an action pending in any court or arbitration.

       (b)   Pursuant to Subsection (5)(a), this section does not affect enforcement of an accord and satisfaction or settlement described in Subsection (5)(a) if the accord and satisfaction or settlement:

              (i)   is in a writing signed by the claimant; and

              (ii)   specifically references the lien rights waived or impaired.

38-1a-803. Cancellation of preconstruction or construction lien — Penalty for failure to cancel timely.

(1)   After the full amount owing under a preconstruction or construction lien, including costs and cancellation fees, has been paid, a person interested in the property that is the subject of the lien may request the claimant to submit for recording with the office of each applicable county recorder a cancellation of the lien.

(2)   Within 10 days after receiving a request under Subsection (1), the claimant shall submit to the office of each applicable county recorder a cancellation of the preconstruction or construction lien, as applicable.

(3)   A claimant who fails to submit a cancellation within the time prescribed in Subsection (2) is liable to the person who requested the cancellation for $100 for each day after the time prescribed in Subsection (2) that the cancellation is not submitted, or the person's actual damages, whichever is greater.

38-1a-804. Notice of release of lien and substitution of alternate security.

(1)   The owner of any interest in a project property that is subject to a recorded preconstruction or construction lien, or any original contractor or subcontractor affected by the lien, who disputes the correctness or validity of the lien may submit for recording a notice of release of lien and substitution of alternate security:

       (a)   that meets the requirements of Subsection (2);

       (b)   in the office of each applicable county recorder where the lien was recorded; and

       (c)   at any time before the date that is 90 days after the first summons is served in an action to foreclose the preconstruction or construction lien for which the notice under this section is submitted for recording.

(2)   A notice of release of lien and substitution of alternate security recorded under Subsection (1) shall:

       (a)   meet the requirements for the recording of documents in Title 57, Chapter 3, Recording of Documents;

       (b)   reference the preconstruction or construction lien sought to be released, including the applicable entry number, book number, and page number; and

       (c)   have as an attachment a surety bond or evidence of a cash deposit that:

              (i)   (A)   if a surety bond, is executed by a surety company that is treasury listed, A-rated by AM Best Company, and authorized to issue surety bonds in this state; or

                     (B)   if evidence of a cash deposit, meets the requirements established by rule by the Department of Commerce in accordance with Title 63G, Chapter 3, Utah Administrative Rulemaking Act;

         (ii)   is in an amount equal to:

               (A)   150% of the amount claimed by the claimant under the preconstruction or construction lien or as determined under Subsection (7), if the lien claim is for $25,000 or more;

               (B)   175% of the amount claimed by the claimant under the preconstruction or construction lien or as determined under Subsection (7), if the lien claim is for at least $15,000 but less than $25,000; or

               (C)   200% of the amount claimed by the claimant under the preconstruction or construction lien or as determined under Subsection (7), if the lien claim is for less than $15,000;

         (i)   is made payable to the claimant;

         (ii)   is conditioned for the payment of:

               (A)   the judgment that would have been rendered, or has been rendered against the project property in the action to enforce the lien; and

               (B)   any costs and attorney fees awarded by the court; and

         (iii)   has as principal:

               (A)   the owner of the interest in the project property; or

               (B)   the original contractor or subcontractor affected by the lien.

(3)   (a)   Upon the recording of the notice of release of lien and substitution of alternate security under Subsection (1), the real property described in the notice shall be released from the preconstruction lien or construction lien to which the notice applies.

       (b)   A recorded notice of release of lien and substitution of alternate security is effective as to any amendment to the preconstruction or construction lien being released if the bond amount remains enough to satisfy the requirements of Subsection (2)(c)(ii).

(4)   (a)   Upon the recording of a notice of release of lien and substitution of alternate security under Subsection (1), the person recording the notice shall serve a copy of the notice, together with any attachments, within 30 days upon the claimant.

       (b)   If a suit is pending to foreclose the preconstruction or construction lien at the time the notice is served upon the claimant under Subsection (4)(a), the claimant shall, within 90 days after the receipt of the notice, institute proceedings to add the alternate security as a party to the lien foreclosure suit.

(5)   The alternate security attached to a notice of release of lien shall be discharged and released upon:

       (a)   the failure of the claimant to commence a suit against the alternate security within the same time as an action to enforce the lien under Section 38-1a-701;

       (b)   the failure of the lien claimant to institute proceedings to add the alternate security as a party to a lien foreclosure suit within the time required by Subsection (4)(b);

       (c)   the dismissal with prejudice of the lien foreclosure suit or suit against the alternate security as to the claimant; or

       (d)   the entry of judgment against the claimant in:

         (i)   a lien foreclosure suit; or

         (ii)   suit against the alternate security.

(6)   If a copy of the notice of release of lien and substitution of alternate security is not served upon the claimant as provided in Subsection (4)(a), the claimant has six months after the discovery

of the notice to commence an action against the alternate security, except that no action may be commenced against the alternate security after two years from the date the notice was recorded.

(7)   (a)   The owner of any interest in a project property that is subject to a recorded preconstruction or construction lien, or an original contractor or subcontractor affected by the lien, who disputes the amount claimed under a preconstruction or construction lien may petition the district court in the county in which the notice of lien is recorded for a summary determination of the correct amount owing under the lien for the sole purpose of providing alternate security.

(b)   A petition under this Subsection (7) shall:

   (i)   state with specificity the factual and legal bases for disputing the amount claimed under the preconstruction or construction lien; and

   (ii)   be supported by a sworn affidavit and any other evidence supporting the petition.

(c)   A petitioner under Subsection (7)(a) shall, as provided in Utah Rules of Civil Procedure, Rule 4, serve on the claimant:

   (i)   a copy of the petition; and

   (ii)   a notice of hearing if a hearing is scheduled.

(d)   If a court finds a petition under Subsection (7)(a) insufficient, the court may dismiss the petition without a hearing.

(e)   If a court finds a petition under Subsection (7)(a) sufficient, the court shall schedule a hearing within 10 days to determine the correct amount claimed under the preconstruction or construction lien for the sole purpose of providing alternate security.

(f)   A claimant may:

   (i)   attend a hearing held under this Subsection (7); and

   (ii)   contest the petition.

(g)   A determination under this section is limited to a determination of the amount claimed under a preconstruction or construction lien for the sole purpose of providing alternate security and does not conclusively establish:

   (i)   the amount to which the claimant is entitled;

   (ii)   the validity of the claim; or

   (iii)   any person's right to any other legal remedy.

(h)   If a court, in a proceeding under this Subsection (7), determines that the amount claimed under a preconstruction or construction lien is excessive, the court shall set the amount for the sole purpose of providing alternate security.

(i)   In an order under Subsection (7)(h), the court shall include a legal description of the project property.

(j)   A petitioner under this Subsection (7) may record a certified copy of any order issued under this Subsection (7) in the county in which the lien is recorded.

(k)   A court may not award attorney fees for a proceeding under this Subsection (7), but shall consider those attorney fees in any award of attorney fees under any other provision of this chapter.

38-1b-101. Title.

This chapter is known as "Government Construction Projects."

38-1b-102. Definitions.

As used in this chapter:

(1) "Alternate means" has the same meaning as defined in Section **38-1a-102**.

(2) "Construction project" has the same meaning as defined in Section **38-1a-102**.

(3) "Construction work" has the same meaning as defined in Section **38-1a-102**.

(4) "Designated agent" has the same meaning as defined in Section **38-1a-102**.

(5) "Division" means the Division of Occupational and Professional Licensing created in Section **58-1-103**.

(6) "Government project" means a construction project undertaken by or for:

    (a) the state, including a department, division, or other agency of the state; or

    (b) a county, city, town, school district, local district, special service district, community development and renewal agency, or other political subdivision of the state.

(7) "Government project-identifying information" means:

    (a) the lot or parcel number of each lot included in the project property that has a lot or parcel number; or

    (b) the unique project number assigned by the designated agent.

(8) "Original contractor" has the same meaning as defined in Section **38-1a-102**.

(9) "Owner" has the same meaning as defined in Section **38-1a-102**.

(10) "Owner-builder" has the same meaning as defined in Section **38-1a-102**.

(11) "Private project" means a construction project that is not a government project.

(12) "Project property" has the same meaning as defined in Section **38-1a-102**.

(13) "Registry" has the same meaning as defined in Section **38-1a-102**.

38-1b-201. Notice of commencement for a government project.

(1) No later than 15 days after commencement of physical construction work at a government project site, the original contractor, owner, or owner-builder shall file a notice of commencement with the registry.

(2) An original contractor, owner, or owner-builder on a government project may file a notice of commencement with the designated agent before the commencement of physical construction work on the project property.

(3) (a) If duplicate notices of commencement are filed, they shall be combined into one notice for each government project, and any notices filed relate back to the date of the earliest-filed notice of commencement for the project.

    (b) A duplicate notice of commencement that is untimely filed relates back under Subsection (3)(a) if the earlier filed notice of commencement is timely filed.

    (c) Duplicate notices of commencement shall be automatically linked by the designated agent.

(4) The designated agent shall assign each government project a unique project number that:

    (a) identifies the project; and

    (b) can be associated with all notices of commencement, preliminary notices, and notices of completion filed in connection with the project.

(5)   A notice of commencement is effective only as to any construction work that is provided after the notice of commencement is filed.

(6)   (a)   A notice of commencement shall include:

        (i)   the name, address, and email address of the owner;

        (ii)   the name, address, and email address of the original contractor;

        (iii)   the name, address, and email address of the surety providing any payment bond for the project or, if none exists, a statement that a payment bond was not required for the work being performed;

        (iv)   (A)   the address of the project property if the project property can be reasonably identified by an address; or

            (B)   the name and general description of the location of the project property, if the project property cannot be reasonably identified by an address; and

        (v)   the government project-identifying information.

    (b)   A notice of commencement may include a general description of the project.

(7)   If a notice of commencement for a government project is not filed within the time set forth in Subsection (1), then Section **38-1b-202** and Section **38-1b-203**, with respect to the filing of a notice of completion, do not apply.

(8)   (a)   The burden is upon any person seeking to enforce a notice of commencement to verify the accuracy of information in the notice of commencement and prove that the notice of commencement is filed timely and meets all of the requirements of this section.

    (b)   A substantial inaccuracy in a notice of commencement renders the notice of commencement invalid.

    (c)   A person filing a notice of commencement by alternate means is responsible for verifying and changing any incorrect information in the notice of commencement before the expiration of the time period during which the notice is required to be filed.

38-1b-202. Preliminary notice on government project.

(1)   (a)   Except for a person who has a contract with an owner or an owner-builder or a laborer compensated with wages, a subcontractor on a government project shall file a preliminary notice with the registry by the later of:

        (i)   20 days after the subcontractor commences providing construction work to the construction project; and

        (ii)   20 days after the filing of a notice of commencement, if the subcontractor's work commences before the filing of the first notice of commencement.

    (b)   Subsection (1) does not exempt the following from complying with the requirements of this section:

        (i)   a temporary labor service company or organization;

        (ii)   a professional employer company or organization; or

        (iii)   any other entity that provides labor.

(2)   A preliminary notice filed within the period described in Subsection (1) is effective as to all construction work that the subcontractor provides to the construction project, including construction work that the subcontractor provides to more than one contractor or subcontractor.

(3)   (a)   If more than one notice of commencement is filed for a project, a person may attach a preliminary notice to any notice of commencement filed for the project.

       (b)   A preliminary notice attached to an untimely notice of commencement is valid if there is also a valid and timely notice of commencement for the project.

(4)   A preliminary notice filed after the period prescribed by Subsection (1) becomes effective on the date that is five days after the date on which the preliminary notice is filed.

(5)   Except as provided in Subsection (8), failure to file a preliminary notice within the period required by Subsection (1) precludes a person from maintaining any claim for compensation earned for construction work provided to the construction project before the the date that is five days after the preliminary notice was filed, except as against the person with whom the person contracted.

(6)   A preliminary notice on a government project shall include:

       (a)   the government project-identifying information;

       (b)   the name, address, and telephone number of the person providing the construction work;

       (c)   the name and address of the person who contracted with the claimant for the providing of construction work;

       (d)   the name of the record or reputed owner;

       (e)   the name of the original contractor under which the claimant is performing or will perform its work; and

       (f)   the address of the project property or a description of the location of the project property.

(7)   Upon request, an original contractor shall provide a subcontractor with the number assigned to the project by the designated agent.

(8)   A person who provides construction work before the filing of a notice of commencement need not file a preliminary notice to maintain any right the person would otherwise have, if the notice of commencement is filed more than 15 days after the day on which the person begins work on the project.

(9)   The burden is upon the person filing a preliminary notice to prove that the person has substantially complied with the requirements of this section.

(10)   Subsections 38-1a-501(1)(e) and (f) and (3) apply to a preliminary notice on a government project under this section to the same extent that those subsections apply under Section 38-1a-501 to a preliminary notice on a project that is not a government project.

38-1b-203. Notice of intent to obtain final completion and notice of completion.

Sections 38-1a-506 and 38-1a-507 apply to a government project to the same extent as those sections apply to a construction project that is subject to Chapter 1a, Preconstruction and Construction Liens.

Appendix L: Residence Lien Restriction and Lien Recovery Fund Act

Part 1 - General Provisions

38-11-101.   Title.

This chapter is known as the "Residence Lien Restriction and Lien Recovery Fund Act."

Enacted by Chapter 308, 1994 General Session

38-11-102.   Definitions.

(1)   "Board" means the Residence Lien Recovery Fund Advisory Board established under Section 38-11-104.

(2)   "Certificate of compliance" means an order issued by the director to the owner finding that the owner is in compliance with the requirements of Subsections 38-11-204(4)(a) and (4)(b) and is entitled to protection under Section 38-11-107.

(3)   "Construction on an owner-occupied residence" means designing, engineering, constructing, altering, remodeling, improving, repairing, or maintaining a new or existing residence.

(4)   "Department" means the Department of Commerce.

(5)   "Director" means the director of the Division of Occupational and Professional Licensing.

(6)   "Division" means the Division of Occupational and Professional Licensing.

(7)   "Duplex" means a single building having two separate living units.

(8)   "Encumbered fund balance" means the aggregate amount of outstanding claims against the fund. The remainder of the money in the fund is unencumbered funds.

(9)   "Executive director" means the executive director of the Department of Commerce.

(10)   "Factory built housing" is as defined in Section 15A-1-302.

(11)   "Factory built housing retailer" means a person that sells factory built housing to consumers.

(12)   "Fund" means the Residence Lien Recovery Fund established under Section 38-11-201.

(13)   "Laborer" means a person who provides services at the site of the construction on an owner-occupied residence as an employee of an original contractor or other qualified beneficiary performing qualified services on the residence.

(14)   "Licensee" means any holder of a license issued under Title 58, Chapter 3a, Architects Licensing Act; Chapter 22, Professional Engineers and Professional Land Surveyors Licensing Act; Chapter 53, Landscape Architects Licensing Act; and Chapter 55, Utah Construction Trades Licensing Act.

(15)   "Nonpaying party" means the original contractor, subcontractor, or real estate developer who has failed to pay the qualified beneficiary making a claim against the fund.

(16)   "Original contractor" means a person who contracts with the owner of real property or the owner's agent to provide services, labor, or material for the construction of an owner-occupied residence.

(17)   "Owner" means a person who:

      (a)   contracts with a person who is licensed as a contractor or is exempt from licensure under Title 58, Chapter 55, Utah Construction Trades Licensing Act, for the construction on an owner-occupied residence upon real property that the person:

          (i)   owns; or

          (ii)   purchases after the person enters into a contract described in this Subsection (17)(a) and before completion of the owner-occupied residence;

      (b)   contracts with a real estate developer to buy a residence upon completion of the construction on the owner-occupied residence; or

      (c)   purchases a residence from a real estate developer after completion of the construction on the owner-occupied residence.

(18)   "Owner-occupied residence" means a residence that is, or after completion of the construction on the residence will be, occupied by the owner or the owner's tenant or lessee as a primary or secondary residence within 180 days after the day on which the construction on the residence is complete.

(19)   "Qualified beneficiary" means a person who:

      (a)   provides qualified services;

      (b)   pays necessary fees or assessments required under this chapter; and

      (c)   registers with the division:

          (i)   as a licensed contractor under Subsection 38-11-301(1) or (2), if that person seeks recovery from the fund as a licensed contractor; or

          (ii)   as a person providing qualified services other than as a licensed contractor under Subsection 38-11-301(3) if the person seeks recovery from the fund in a capacity other than as a licensed contractor.

(20)   (a)   "Qualified services" means the following performed in construction on an owner-occupied residence:

          (i)   contractor services provided by a contractor licensed or exempt from licensure under Title 58, Chapter 55, Utah Construction Trades Licensing Act;

          (ii)   architectural services provided by an architect licensed under Title 58, Chapter 3a, Architects Licensing Act;

          (iii)   engineering and land surveying services provided by a professional engineer or land surveyor licensed or exempt from licensure under Title 58, Chapter 22, Professional Engineers and Professional Land Surveyors Licensing Act;

          (iv)   landscape architectural services by a landscape architect licensed or exempt from licensure under Title 58, Chapter 53, Landscape Architects Licensing Act;

          (v)   design and specification services of mechanical or other systems;

          (vi)   other services related to the design, drawing, surveying, specification, cost estimation, or other like professional services;

          (vii)   providing materials, supplies, components, or similar products;

          (viii)   renting equipment or materials;

          (ix)   labor at the site of the construction on the owner-occupied residence; and

          (x)   site preparation, set up, and installation of factory built housing.

      (b)   "Qualified services" does not include the construction of factory built housing in the factory.

(21)   "Real estate developer" means a person having an ownership interest in real property who:

     (a)   contracts with a person who is licensed as a contractor or is exempt from licensure under Title 58, Chapter 55, Utah Construction Trades Licensing Act, for the construction of a residence that is offered for sale to the public; or

     (b)   is a licensed contractor under Title 58, Chapter 55, Utah Construction Trades Licensing Act, who engages in the construction of a residence that is offered for sale to the public.

(22)   (a)   "Residence" means an improvement to real property used or occupied, to be used or occupied as, or in conjunction with:

         (i)   a primary or secondary detached single-family dwelling; or

         (ii)   a multifamily dwelling up to and including duplexes.

     (b)   "Residence" includes factory built housing.

(23)   "Subsequent owner" means a person who purchases a residence from an owner within 180 days after the day on which the construction on the residence is completed.

Amended by Chapter 108, 2014 General Session

38-11-103.   Administration.

This chapter shall be administered by the Division of Occupational and Professional Licensing pursuant to the provisions of this chapter and consistent with Title 58, Chapter 1, Division of Occupational and Professional Licensing Act.

Amended by Chapter 172, 1995 General Session

38-11-104.   Board.

(1)   There is created the Residence Lien Recovery Fund Advisory Board consisting of:

     (a)   three individuals licensed as a contractor who are actively engaged in construction on owner-occupied residences;

     (b)   three individuals who are employed in responsible management positions with major suppliers of materials or equipment used in the construction on owner-occupied residences; and

     (c)   one member from the general public who has no interest in the construction on owner-occupied residences, or supply of materials used in the construction on owner-occupied residences.

(2)   The board shall be appointed and members shall serve their respective terms in accordance with Section 58-1-201.

(3)   The duties and responsibilities of the board shall be to:

     (a)   advise the division with respect to informal adjudication of any claim for payment from the fund and any request for a certificate of compliance received by the division;

     (b)   act as the presiding officer, as defined by rule, in formal adjudicative proceedings held before the division with respect to any claim made for payment from the fund;

     (c)   advise the division with respect to:

         (i)   the general operation of the fund;

         (ii)   the amount and frequency of any assessment under this chapter;

         (iii)   the amount of any fees required under this chapter;

(iv)   the availability and advisability of using funds for purchase of surety bonds to guarantee payment to qualified beneficiaries; and

(v)   the limitation on the fund balance under Section 38-11-206; and

(d)   review the administrative expenditures made by the division pursuant to Subsection 38-11-201(4) and report its findings regarding those expenditures to the executive director on or before the first Monday of December of each year.

(4)   The attorney general shall render legal assistance as requested by the board.

Amended by Chapter 42, 2004 General Session

38-11-105.   Procedures established by rule.

In compliance with Title 63G, Chapter 4, Administrative Procedures Act, the division shall establish procedures by rule by which claims for compensation from the fund and requests for certificates of compliance shall be adjudicated and by which assessments shall be collected.

Amended by Chapter 382, 2008 General Session

38-11-106.   State not liable.

The state and the state's agencies, instrumentalities, and political subdivisions are not liable for:

(1)   issuance or denial of any certificate of compliance;

(2)   any claims made against the fund; or

(3)   failure of the fund to pay any amounts ordered by the director to be paid from the fund.

Amended by Chapter 42, 2004 General Session

38-11-107.   Restrictions upon maintaining a lien against residence or owner's interest in the residence.

(1)   (a)   A person qualified to file a lien upon an owner-occupied residence and the real property associated with that residence under Chapter 1a, Preconstruction and Construction Liens, who provides qualified services under an agreement, other than directly with the owner, is barred from maintaining a lien upon that residence and real property or recovering a judgment in any civil action against the owner or the owner-occupied residence to recover money owed for qualified services provided by that person if:

(i)   an owner meets the conditions described in Subsections 38-11-204(4)(a) and (b); or

(ii)   (A)   a subsequent owner purchases a residence from an owner;

(B)   the subsequent owner who purchased the residence under Subsection (1)(a)(ii)(A) occupies the residence as a primary or secondary residence within 180 days from the date of transfer or the residence is occupied by the subsequent owner's tenant or lessee as a primary or secondary residence within 180 days from the date of transfer; and

(C)   the owner from whom the subsequent owner purchased the residence met the conditions described in Subsections 38-11-204(4)(a) and (b).

(b)   (i)   As used in this Subsection (1)(b):

(A)   "Contract residence":

(I)   means the owner-occupied residence for which a subcontractor provides service, labor, or materials; and

(II) includes the real property associated with that owner-occupied residence.

(B) "General contract" means an oral or written contract between an owner and an original contractor for providing service, labor, or materials for construction on an owner-occupied residence.

(C) "Subcontractor" means a person who provides service, labor, or materials for construction on an owner-occupied residence under an agreement other than directly with the owner.

(ii) A subcontractor qualified to file a lien upon a contract residence under Chapter 1a, Preconstruction and Construction Liens, is barred from maintaining a lien upon that contract residence or from recovering a judgment in a civil action against the owner, the contract residence, or, as provided in Subsection (1)(b)(iii), a subsequent owner to recover for service, labor, or materials provided by the subcontractor:

(A) if the amount of the general contract under which the subcontractor provides service, labor, or materials totals no more than $5,000; and

(B) whether or not the original contractor is licensed under Title 58, Chapter 55, Utah Construction Trades Licensing Act.

(iii) A subsequent owner is protected under Subsection (1)(b)(ii) to the same extent as an owner if:

(A) the subsequent owner purchases the contract residence from the owner; and

(B) (I) the subsequent owner occupies the residence as a primary or secondary residence within 180 days after the date of transfer; or

(II) the subsequent owner's tenant or lessee occupies the residence as a primary or secondary residence within 180 days after the date of the transfer.

(2) If a residence is constructed under conditions that do not meet all of the provisions of Subsection (1)(a) or (b), that residence and the real property associated with that residence as provided in Section 38-1a-302 is subject to any lien as provided in Section 38-1a-301.

(3) A lien claimant who files a preconstruction or construction lien under Chapter 1a, Preconstruction and Construction Liens, or a foreclosure action upon an owner-occupied residence is not liable for costs and attorney fees under Sections 38-1a-706 and 38-1a-707 or for any damages arising from a civil action related to the lien filing or foreclosure action if the lien claimant removes the lien within 15 days from the date the owner obtains a certificate of compliance and mails a copy of the certificate of compliance by certified mail to the lien claimant at the address provided for by Subsection 38-1a-502(2)(e). The 15-day period begins accruing from the date postmarked on the certificate of compliance sent to the lien claimant.

Amended by Chapter 278, 2012 General Session

38-11-108. Notification of rights under chapter.

(1) Beginning July 1, 1995, the original contractor or real estate developer shall state in the written contract with the owner what actions are necessary for the owner to be protected under Section 38-11-107 from the maintaining of a mechanic's lien or other civil action against the owner or the owner-occupied residence to recover money owed for qualified services.

(2)　　In accordance with Title 63G, Chapter 3, Utah Administrative Rulemaking Act, the division may issue rules providing for the form and content of the information required by Subsection (1).

Amended by Chapter 382, 2008 General Session

38-11-109.　Severability clause.

If any provision of this chapter is held invalid or unconstitutional by a court of competent jurisdiction, the invalidity shall not affect the other provisions of this chapter which can be given effect without the invalid or unconstitutional provision.

Enacted by Chapter 193, 1999 General Session

38-11-110.　Issuance of certificates of compliance.

(1)　(a)　The director may issue a certificate of compliance only after determining through an informal proceeding, as set forth in Title 63G, Chapter 4, Administrative Procedures Act:

　　　(i)　that the owner is in compliance with Subsections 38-11-204(4)(a) and (b); or

　　　(ii)　subject to Subsection (2), that the owner is entitled to protection under Subsection 38-11-107(1)(b).

　(b)　If the director determines through an informal proceeding under Subsection (1)(a) that an owner seeking the issuance of a certificate of compliance under Subsection (1)(a)(i) is not in compliance as provided in Subsection (1)(a)(i), the director may not issue a certificate of compliance.

(2)　(a)　An owner seeking the issuance of a certificate of compliance under Subsection (1)(a)(ii) shall submit an affidavit, as defined by the division by rule, affirming that the owner is entitled to protection under Subsection 38-11-107(1)(b).

　(b)　If an owner's affidavit under Subsection (2)(a) is disputed, the owner may file a complaint in small claims court or district court to resolve the dispute.

　(c)　The director may issue a certificate of compliance to an owner seeking issuance of a certificate under Subsection (1)(a)(ii) if:

　　　(i)　the owner's affidavit under Subsection (2)(a) is undisputed; or

　　　(ii)　a small claims court or district court resolves any dispute over the owner's affidavit in favor of the owner.

Amended by Chapter 31, 2010 General Session

Part 2 - Residence Lien Recovery Fund

38-11-201.　Residence Lien Recovery Fund.

(1)　There is created an expendable special revenue fund called the "Residence Lien Recovery Fund."

(2)　(a)　The fund consists of all amounts collected by the division in accordance with Section 38-11-202.

　(b)　(i)　The division shall deposit the funds in an account with the state treasurer.

　　　(ii)　The division shall record the funds in the Residence Lien Recovery Fund.

　(c)　The fund shall earn interest.

(3)   The division shall employ personnel and resources necessary to administer the fund and shall use fund money in accordance with Sections 38-11-203 and 38-11-204 and to pay the costs charged to the fund by the attorney general.

(4)   Costs incurred by the division for administering the fund shall be paid out of fund money.

(5)   The Division of Finance shall report annually to the Legislature, the division, and the board. The report shall state:

    (a)   amounts received by the fund;

    (b)   disbursements from the fund;

    (c)   interest earned and credited to the fund; and

    (d)   the fund balance.

(6)   (a)   For purposes of establishing and assessing fees under Section 63J-1-504, the provisions of this chapter are considered a new program for fiscal year 1995-96.

    (b)   The department shall submit its fee schedule to the Legislature for its approval at the 1996 Annual General Session.

Amended by Chapter 400, 2013 General Session

38-11-202.   Payments to the fund.

The Residence Lien Recovery Fund shall be supported solely from:

(1)   initial and special assessments collected by the division from licensed contractors registered as qualified beneficiaries in accordance with Subsections 38-11-301(1) and (2) and Section 38-11-206;

(2)   initial and special assessments collected by the division from other qualified beneficiaries registering with the division in accordance with Subsection 38-11-301(3) and Section 38-11-206;

(3)   fees determined by the division under Section 63J-1-504 collected from laborers under Subsection 38-11-204(7) when the laborers obtain a recovery from the fund;

(4)   amounts collected by subrogation under Section 38-11-205 on behalf of the fund following a payment from the fund;

(5)   application fees determined by the division under Section 63J-1-504 collected from:

    (a)   qualified beneficiaries or laborers under Subsection 38-11-204(1)(b) when qualified beneficiaries or laborers make a claim against the fund; or

    (b)   owners or agents of the owners seeking to obtain a certificate of compliance for the owner;

(6)   registration fees determined by the division under Section 63J-1-504 collected from other qualified beneficiaries registering with the department in accordance with Subsection 38-11-301(3)(a)(iii);

(7)   reinstatement fees determined by the division under Section 63J-1-504 collected from registrants in accordance with Subsection 38-11-302(5)(b);

(8)   civil fines authorized under Subsection 38-11-205(2) collected by the attorney general for failure to reimburse the fund; and

(9)   any interest earned by the fund.

Amended by Chapter 183, 2009 General Session

38-11-203.   Disbursements from the fund — Limitations.

(1)   A payment of any claim upon the fund by a qualified beneficiary shall be made only upon an order issued by the director finding that:

    (a)   the claimant was a qualified beneficiary during the construction on a residence;

      (b)   the claimant complied with the requirements of Section 38-11-204; and

      (c)   there is adequate money in the fund to pay the amount ordered.

(2)   A payment of a claim upon the fund by a laborer shall be made only upon an order issued by the director finding that:

      (a)   the laborer complied with the requirements of Subsection 38-11-204(7); and

      (b)   there is adequate money in the fund to pay the amount ordered.

(3)   (a)   An order under this section may be issued only after the division has complied with the procedures established by rule under Section 38-11-105.

      (b)   The director shall order payment of the qualified services as established by evidence, or if the claimant has obtained a judgment, then in the amount awarded for qualified services in the judgment to the extent the qualified services are attributable to the owner-occupied residence at issue in the claim.

      (c)   The director shall order payment of interest on amounts claimed for qualified services based on the current prime interest rate at the time payment was due to the date the claim is approved for payment except for delays attributable to the claimant but not more than 10% per annum.

      (d)   The rate shall be the Prime Lending Rate as published in the Wall Street Journal on the first business day of each calendar year adjusted annually.

      (e)   The director shall order payment of costs in the amount stated in the judgment. If the judgment does not state a sum certain for costs, or if no judgment has been obtained, the director shall order payment of reasonable costs as supported by evidence. The claim application fee as established by the division pursuant to Subsection 38-11-204(1)(b) is not a reimbursable cost.

      (f)   If a judgment has been obtained with attorneys' fees, notwithstanding the amount stated in a judgment, or if no judgment has been obtained but the contract provides for attorneys' fees, the director shall order payment of attorneys' fees not to exceed 15% of qualified services. If the judgment does not state a sum for attorneys' fees, no attorneys' fees will be paid by the director.

(4)   (a)   Payments made from the fund may not exceed $75,000 per construction project to qualified beneficiaries and laborers who have claim against the fund for that construction project.

      (b)   If claims against the fund for a construction project exceed $75,000, the $75,000 shall be awarded proportionately so that each qualified beneficiary and laborer awarded compensation from the fund for qualified services shall receive an identical percentage of the qualified beneficiary's or laborer's award.

(5)   Subject to the limitations of Subsection (4), if on the day the order is issued there are inadequate funds to pay the entire claim and the director determines that the claimant has otherwise met the requirements of Subsection (1) or (2), the director shall order additional payments once the fund meets the balance limitations of Section 38-11-206.

Amended by Chapter 42, 2004 General Session

38-11-204. Claims against the fund — Requirement to make a claim — Qualifications to receive compensation — Qualifications to receive a certificate of compliance.

(1)   To claim recovery from the fund a person shall:

      (a)   meet the requirements of Subsection (4) or (6);

(b)   pay an application fee determined by the division under Section 63J-1-504; and

(c)   file with the division a completed application on a form provided by the division accompanied by supporting documents establishing:

    (i)   that the person meets the requirements of Subsection (4) or (6);

    (ii)   that the person was a qualified beneficiary or laborer during the construction on the owner-occupied residence; and

    (iii)   the basis for the claim.

(2)   To recover from the fund, the application required by Subsection (1) shall be filed no later than one year:

(a)   from the date the judgment required by Subsection (4)(d) is entered;

(b)   from the date the nonpaying party filed bankruptcy, if the claimant is precluded from obtaining a judgment or from satisfying the requirements of Subsection (4)(d) because the nonpaying party filed bankruptcy within one year after the entry of judgment; or

(c)   from the date the laborer, trying to recover from the fund, completed the laborer's qualified services.

(3)   The issuance of a certificate of compliance is governed by Section 38-11-110.

(4)   To recover from the fund, regardless of whether the residence is occupied by the owner, a subsequent owner, or the owner or subsequent owner's tenant or lessee, a qualified beneficiary shall establish that:

(a)   (i)   the owner of the owner-occupied residence or the owner's agent entered into a written contract with an original contractor licensed or exempt from licensure under Title 58, Chapter 55, Utah Construction Trades Licensing Act:

    (A)   for the performance of qualified services;

    (B)   to obtain the performance of qualified services by others; or

    (C)   for the supervision of the performance by others of qualified services in construction on that residence;

    (ii)   the owner of the owner-occupied residence or the owner's agent entered into a written contract with a real estate developer for the purchase of an owner-occupied residence; or

    (iii)   the owner of the owner-occupied residence or the owner's agent entered into a written contract with a factory built housing retailer for the purchase of an owner-occupied residence;

(b)   the owner has paid in full the original contractor, licensed or exempt from licensure under Title 58, Chapter 55, Utah Construction Trades Licensing Act, real estate developer, or factory built housing retailer under Subsection (4)(a) with whom the owner has a written contract in accordance with the written contract and any amendments to the contract;

(c)   (i)   the original contractor, licensed or exempt from licensure under Title 58, Chapter 55, Utah Construction Trades Licensing Act, the real estate developer, or the factory built housing retailer subsequently failed to pay a qualified beneficiary who is entitled to payment under an agreement with that original contractor or real estate developer licensed or exempt from licensure under Title 58, Chapter 55, Utah Construction Trades Licensing Act, for services performed or materials supplied by the qualified beneficiary;

(ii)   a subcontractor who contracts with the original contractor, licensed or exempt from licensure under Title 58, Chapter 55, Utah Construction Trades Licensing Act, the real estate developer, or the factory built housing retailer failed to pay a qualified beneficiary who is entitled to payment under an agreement with that subcontractor or supplier; or

(iii)   a subcontractor who contracts with a subcontractor or supplier failed to pay a qualified beneficiary who is entitled to payment under an agreement with that subcontractor or supplier;

(d)   (i)   unless precluded from doing so by the nonpaying party's bankruptcy filing within the applicable time, the qualified beneficiary filed an action against the nonpaying party to recover money owed to the qualified beneficiary within the earlier of:

   (A)   180 days from the date the qualified beneficiary filed a notice of claim under Section 38-1a-502; or

   (B)   270 days from the completion of the original contract pursuant to Subsection 38-1a-502(1);

   (ii)   the qualified beneficiary has obtained a judgment against the nonpaying party who failed to pay the qualified beneficiary under an agreement to provide qualified services for construction of that owner-occupied residence;

   (iii)   (A)   the qualified beneficiary has:

      (I)   obtained from a court of competent jurisdiction the issuance of an order requiring the judgment debtor, or if a corporation any officer of the corporation, to appear before the court at a specified time and place to answer concerning the debtor's or corporation's property;

      (II)   received return of service of the order from a person qualified to serve documents under the Utah Rules of Civil Procedure, Rule 4(b); and

      (III)   made reasonable efforts to obtain asset information from the supplemental proceedings; and

   (C)   if assets subject to execution are discovered as a result of the order required under Subsection (4)(d)(iii)(A) or for any other reason, to obtain the issuance of a writ of execution from a court of competent jurisdiction; or

   (iv)   the qualified beneficiary timely filed a proof of claim where permitted in the bankruptcy action, if the nonpaying party has filed bankruptcy;

(e)   the qualified beneficiary is not entitled to reimbursement from any other person; and

(f)   the qualified beneficiary provided qualified services to a contractor, licensed or exempt from licensure under Title 58, Chapter 55, Utah Construction Trades Licensing Act.

(5)   The requirements of Subsections (4)(d)(ii) and (iii) need not be met if the qualified beneficiary is prevented from compliance because the nonpaying party files bankruptcy.

(6)   To recover from the fund a laborer shall:

(a)   establish that the laborer has not been paid wages due for the work performed at the site of a construction on an owner-occupied residence; and

(b)   provide any supporting documents or information required by rule by the division.

(7)   A fee determined by the division under Section 63J-1-504 shall be deducted from any recovery from the fund received by a laborer.

(8)   The requirements of Subsections (4)(a) and (b) may be satisfied if an owner or agent of the owner establishes to the satisfaction of the director that the owner of the owner-occupied residence or the owner's agent entered into a written contract with an original contractor who:

   (a)   was a business entity that was not licensed under Title 58, Chapter 55, Utah Construction Trades Licensing Act, but was solely or partly owned by an individual who was licensed under Title 58, Chapter 55, Utah Construction Trades Licensing Act; or

   (b)   was a natural person who was not licensed under Title 58, Chapter 55, Utah Construction Trades Licensing Act, but who was the sole or partial owner and qualifier of a business entity that was licensed under Title 58, Chapter 55, Utah Construction Trades Licensing Act.

(9)   The director shall have equitable power to determine if the requirements of Subsections (4)(a) and (b) have been met, but any decision by the director under this chapter shall not alter or have any effect on any other decision by the division under Title 58, Occupations and Professions.

Amended by Chapter 278, 2012 General Session

38-11-205.   Subrogation.

(1)   (a)   (i)   The state, on behalf of the fund, has the right of subrogation only to the extent of payments made from the fund.

                 (ii)   Upon payment from the fund to a claimant, any payment to the claimant that was the basis of the claimant's claim against the fund shall be assigned to the fund for the enforcement of subrogation rights by the attorney general.

                 (iii)   A claimant's judgment or bankruptcy claim against the nonpaying party shall be automatically assigned to the state, to the extent paid by the fund on a particular residence, upon the state's filing of the director's order of payment of claim with the appropriate court.

        (b)   The state's right of subrogation under Subsection (1)(a) has priority over any rights of the qualified beneficiary under the judgment or any civil penalties imposed.

        (c)   The state shall be awarded attorney's fees and court costs incurred in recovering claims paid from the fund.

(2)   (a)   The attorney general shall enforce all subrogation claims and may contract with private attorneys as necessary to adequately enforce subrogation claims.

        (b)   (i)   In addition to the subrogation claims the attorney general may seek a civil fine of $5,000 per residence for failure to reimburse the Residence Lien Recovery Fund within 90 days after any disbursement from the fund resulting from the registrant's failure to pay qualified beneficiaries under this chapter.

                 (ii)   All claims under the judgment have priority over the civil penalty.

(3)   The attorney general may charge the fund for costs incurred by the attorney general under this chapter.

Amended by Chapter 193, 1999 General Session

38-11-206.   Limitations on fund balance — Payment of special assessments.

(1)   (a)   If on June 30 of any year the balance in the fund is less than $1,500,000, the division shall make a special assessment against all qualified beneficiaries in an amount that will restore the unencumbered fund balance to not less than $2,000,000 or more than $2,500,000.

(b)   The amount of the special assessment shall be determined by the division under Section 63J-1-504 after consultation with the board.

(2)   Special assessments made under this section shall be due and payable on December 1 following assessment.

(3)   The fund balance limitations set forth in Subsection (1)(a) shall be used by the division only for the purpose of determining the amount of any special assessment and do not prohibit the fund balance from exceeding $2,500,000 or falling below $2,000,000.

Amended by Chapter 367, 2011 General Session

38-11-207.   Reimbursement to the fund.

(1)   If the director disburses money from the fund as a result of a person licensed under Title 58, Chapter 55, Utah Construction Trades Licensing Act, or a qualified beneficiary failing to pay qualified beneficiaries:

(a)   the division shall issue a notice of the disbursement from the fund and the obligation to reimburse the fund to the licensee or qualified beneficiary; and

(b)   the licensee or qualified beneficiary shall reimburse the fund within 20 days from the issuance of the notice required by Subsection (1)(a).

(2)   The notice required by Subsection (1)(a) shall meet the requirements established by rule by the division in accordance with Title 63G, Chapter 3, Utah Administrative Rulemaking Act.

(3)   (a)   A finding of fact in an administrative action that a payment of any amount has been made from the fund in settlement of a claim arising from the act, representation, transaction, or conduct of a person licensed under Title 58, Chapter 55, Utah Construction Trades Licensing Act, in violation of Section 58-55-603 shall result in the immediate suspension of that person's license without further compliance with Title 63G, Chapter 4, Administrative Procedures Act.

(b)   The finding of fact for Subsection (3)(a) may be made in the same administrative action as the related claim and may be included in the findings required by Section 38-11-203.

(c)   The suspension required by Subsection (3)(a) shall remain in effect until the person applies for reinstatement and is issued a license in accordance with Sections 58-1-308 and 58-55-303.

Amended by Chapter 382, 2008 General Session

Part 3 - Registration

38-11-301.   Registration as a qualified beneficiary — Initial regular assessment — Affidavit.

(1)   A person licensed as of July 1, 1995, as a contractor under the provisions of Title 58, Chapter 55, Utah Construction Trades Licensing Act, in license classifications that regularly engage in providing qualified services shall be automatically registered as a qualified beneficiary upon payment of the initial assessment.

(2)   A person applying for licensure as a contractor after July 1, 1995, in license classifications that regularly engage in providing qualified services shall be automatically registered as a qualified beneficiary upon issuance of a license and payment of the initial assessment.

(3)   (a)   After July 1, 1995, any person providing qualified services as other than a contractor as provided in Subsection (1) or any person exempt from licensure under the provisions of Title 58, Chapter 55, Utah Construction Trades Licensing Act, may register as a qualified beneficiary by:

        (i)   submitting an application in a form prescribed by the division;

        (ii)   demonstrating registration with the Division of Corporations and Commercial Code as required by state law;

        (iii)   paying a registration fee determined by the division under Section 63J-1-504; and

        (iv)   paying the initial assessment established under Subsection (4), and any special assessment determined by the division under Subsection 38-11-206(1).

    (b)   A person who does not register under Subsection (1), (2), or (3)(a) shall be prohibited from recovering under the fund as a qualified beneficiary for work performed as qualified services while not registered with the fund.

(4)   (a)   An applicant shall pay an initial assessment determined by the division under Section 63J-1-504.

    (b)   The initial assessment to qualified registrants under Subsection (1) shall be made not later than July 15, 1995, and shall be paid no later than November 1, 1995.

    (c)   The initial assessment to qualified registrants under Subsections (2) and (3) shall be paid at the time of application for license or registration, however, beginning on May 1, 1996, only one initial assessment or special assessments thereafter shall be required for persons having multiple licenses under this section.

(5)   A person shall be considered to have been registered as a qualified beneficiary on January 1, 1995, for purposes of meeting the requirements of Subsection 38-11-204(1)(c)(ii) if the person:

    (a)   (i)   is licensed on or before July 1, 1995, as a contractor under the provisions of Title 58, Chapter 55, Utah Construction Trades Licensing Act, in license classifications that regularly engage in providing qualified services; or

        (ii)   provides qualified services after July 1, 1995, as other than a contractor as provided in Subsection (5)(a)(i) or is exempt from licensure under the provisions of Title 58, Chapter 55, Utah Construction Trades Licensing Act; and

    (b)   registers as a qualified beneficiary under Subsection (1) or (3) on or before November 1, 1995.

Amended by Chapter 183, 2009 General Session   .

38-11-302.   Effective date and term of registration — Penalty for failure to pay assessments — Reinstatement.

(1)   (a)   A registration as a qualified beneficiary under this chapter is effective on the date the division receives the initial assessment of the qualified beneficiary.

    (b)   A registrant shall be required to renew the registrant's registration upon imposition of a special assessment under Subsection 38-11-206(1).

(2)   A registration automatically expires if a registrant fails to renew the registrant's registration as required under Subsection (1).

(3)   The division shall notify a qualified beneficiary in accordance with procedures established by rule when renewal of registration is required in connection with a special assessment.

(4)   The license renewal notice to a contractor shall notify the licensee that failure to renew the license will result in automatic expiration of the licensee's registration as a qualified beneficiary and of the limitations set forth in Subsection (6) on qualified beneficiaries whose registration has expired to make a claim upon the fund.

(5)   Registration may be reinstated by:

    (a)   submitting an application for reinstatement in a form prescribed by the division;

    (b)   paying a reinstatement fee determined by the division under Section 63J-1-504; and

    (c)   paying all unpaid assessments that were assessed during the period of the person's registration and all assessments made upon qualified beneficiaries during the period the applicant's registration was expired.

(6)   (a)   A qualified beneficiary whose registration expires loses all rights to make a claim upon the fund or receive compensation from the fund resulting from providing qualified service during the period of expiration.

    (b)   Except as provided by Section 58-55-401, a qualified beneficiary whose registration expires may make a claim upon the fund or receive compensation from the fund for qualified services provided during the period the qualified beneficiary was part of the fund.

Amended by Chapter 183, 2009 General Session

Appendix M: Residence Lien Restriction and Lien Recovery Fund Rule

R156-38a-101. Title.

This rule is known as the "Residence Lien Restriction and Lien Recovery Fund Act Rule."

R156-38a-102. Definitions.

In addition to the definitions in Title 38, Chapter 11, Residence Lien Restriction and Lien Recovery Fund Act; Title 58, Chapter 1, Division of Occupational and Professional Licensing Act; and Rule R156-1, General Rule of the Division of Occupational and Professional Licensing, which shall apply to this rule, as used in this rule:

    (1)   "Affidavit", as required by Subsection 38-11-110(2)(a), means a form affidavit approved by the Division and posted on the Division's website or otherwise made available for public inspection, that establishes the following:

        (a)   the applicant is an owner as defined in Subsection 38-11-102(17);

        (b)   the residence is an owner-occupied residence as defined in Subsection 38-11-102(18);

        (c)   the amount of the general contract as defined in Subsection 38-11-107(1)(b)(i)(B) and clarified in Subsection R156-38a-102(14);

        (d)   the original contractor as defined in Subsection 38-11-102(16);

        (e)   the location of the residence; and

        (f)   any other information necessary to establish eligibility for the issuance of a certificate of compliance under Subsection 38-11-110(2)(a), as determined by the Division.

    (2)   "Affidavit of Compliance" means the affidavit submitted by the owner seeking issuance of a certificate of compliance under Subsection 38-11-110(1)(a)(ii).

    (3)   "Applicant" means either a claimant, as defined in Subsection (4), or a homeowner, as defined in Subsection (8), who submits an application for a certificate of compliance.

    (4)   "Claimant" means a person who submits an application or claim for payment from the fund.

    (5)   "Construction project", as used in Subsection 38-11-203(4), means all qualified services related to the written contract required by Subsection 38-11-204(4)(a).

    (6)   "Contracting entity" means an original contractor, a factory built housing retailer, or a real estate developer that contracts with a homeowner.

    (7)   "During the construction", as used in Subsection 38-11-204(1)(c)(ii), means beginning at the time the claimant first provides qualified services and throughout the time frame the claimant provides qualified services.

    (8)   "Homeowner" means the owner of an owner-occupied residence.

    (9)   "Licensed or exempt from licensure", as used in Subsection 38-11-204(4) means that, on the date the written contract was entered into, the contractor held a valid, active license issued by the Division pursuant to Title 58, Chapter 55 of the Utah Code in any classification or met any of the exemptions to licensure given in Title 58, Chapters 1 and 55.

    (10)   "Necessary party" includes the Division, on behalf of the fund, and the applicant.

(11)   "Owner", as defined in Subsection 38-11-102(17), does not include any person or developer who builds residences that are offered for sale to the public.

(12)   "Permissive party" includes:

    (a)   with respect to claims for payment: the nonpaying party, the homeowner, and any entity who may be required to reimburse the fund if a claimant's claim is paid from the fund;

    (b)   with respect to an application for a certificate of compliance: the original contractor and any entity who has demanded from the homeowner payment for qualified services.

(13)   "Qualified services", as used in Subsection 38-11-102(20) do not include:

    (a)   services provided by the claimant to cure a breach of the contract between the claimant and the nonpaying party; or

    (b)   services provided by the claimant under a warranty or similar arrangement.

(14)   "Totals no more", as used in Subsection 38-11-107(1)(b)(ii)(A), means the inclusion of all changes or additions.

(15)   "Written contract", as used in Subsection 38-11-204(4)(a)(i), means one or more documents for the same construction project which collectively contain all of the following:

    (a)   an offer or agreement conveyed for qualified services that will be performed in the future;

    (b)   an acceptance of the offer or agreement conveyed prior to the commencement of any qualified services; and

    (c)   identification of the residence, the parties to the agreement, the qualified services that are to be performed, and an amount to be paid for the qualified services that will be performed.

R156-38a-103a. Authority - Purpose - Organization.

(1)   This rule is adopted by the Division under the authority of Section 38-11-103 to enable the Division to administer Title 38, Chapter 11, the Residence Lien Restriction and Lien Recovery Fund Act.

(2)   The organization of this rule is patterned after the organization of Title 38, Chapter 11.

R156-38a-103b. Duties, Functions, and Responsibilities of the Division.

The duties, functions and responsibilities of the Division with respect to the administration of Title 38, Chapter 11, shall, to the extent applicable and not in conflict with the Act or this rule, be in accordance with Section 58-1-106.

R156-38a-104. Board.

Board meetings shall comply with the requirements set forth in Section R156-1-205.

R156-38a-105a. Adjudicative Proceedings.

(1)   The classification of adjudicative proceedings initiated under Title 38, Chapter 11 is set forth at Sections R156-46b-201 and R156-46b-202.

(2)   The identity and role of presiding officers for adjudicative proceedings initiated under Title 38, Chapter 11, is set forth in Sections 58-1-109 and R156-1-109.

(3)   Issuance of investigative subpoenas under Title 38, Chapter 11 shall be in accordance with Subsection R156-1-110.

(4)   Adjudicative proceedings initiated under Title 38, Chapter 11, shall be conducted in accordance with Title 63G, Chapter 4, Utah Administrative Procedures Act, and Rules R151-46b and R156-46b, Utah Administrative Procedures Act Rules for the Department of Commerce and the Division of

Occupational and Professional Licensing, respectively, except as otherwise provided by Title 38, Chapter 11 or this rule.

(5) Claims for payment and applications for a certificate of compliance shall be filed with the Division and served upon all necessary and permissive parties.

(6) Service of claims, applications for a certificate of compliance, or other pleadings by mail to a qualified beneficiary of the fund addressed to the address shown on the Division's records with a certificate of service as required by R151-46b-8, shall constitute proper service. It shall be the responsibility of each applicant or registrant to maintain a current address with the Division.

(7) A permissive party is required to file a response to a claim or application for certificate of compliance within 30 days of notification by the Division of the filing of the claim or application for certificate of compliance, to perfect the party's right to participate in the adjudicative proceeding to adjudicate the claim or application. The response of a permissive party seeking to dispute an owner's affidavit of compliance shall clearly state the basis for the dispute.

(8) (a) For claims wherein the claimant has had judgment entered against the nonpaying party, findings of fact and conclusions of law entered by a civil court or state agency submitted in support of or in opposition to a claim against the fund shall not be subject to readjudication in an adjudicative proceeding to adjudicate the claim.

(b) For claims wherein the nonpaying party's bankruptcy filing precluded the claimant from having judgment entered against the nonpaying party, a claim or issue resolved by a prior judgment, order, findings of fact, or conclusions of law entered in by a civil court or a state agency submitted in support of or in opposition to a claim against the fund shall not be subject to readjudication with respect to the parties to the judgment, order, findings of fact, or conclusions of law.

(9) A party to the adjudication of a claim against the fund may be granted a stay of the adjudicative proceeding during the pendency of a judicial appeal of a judgment entered by a civil court or the administrative or judicial appeal of an order entered by an administrative agency provided:

(a) the administrative or judicial appeal is directly related to the adjudication of the claim; and

(b) the request for the stay of proceedings is filed with the presiding officer conducting the adjudicative proceeding and concurrently served upon all parties to the adjudicative proceeding, no later than the deadline for filing the appeal.

(10) Notice pursuant to Subsection 38-1a-701(6)(f) shall be accomplished by sending a copy of the Division's order by first class, postage paid United States Postal Service mail to each lien claimant listed on the application for certificate of compliance. The address for the lien claimant shall be:

(a) if the lien claimant is a licensee of the Division or a registrant of the fund, the notice shall be mailed to the current mailing address shown on the Division's records; or

(b) if the lien claimant is not a licensee of the Division or a registrant of the fund, the notice shall be mailed to the registered agent address shown on the records of the Division of Corporations and Commercial Code.

R156-38a-105b. Notices of Denial - Notices of Incomplete Application - Conditional Denial of Claims - Extensions of Time to Correct Claims - Prolonged Status.

(1) (a) A written notice of denial of a claim or certificate of compliance shall be provided to an applicant who submits a complete application if the Division determines that the application does not meet the requirements of Section 38-11-204 or Subsection 38-11-110(1)(a), respectively.

(b)   A written notice of incomplete application shall be provided to an applicant who submits an incomplete application. The notice shall advise the applicant that the application is incomplete and that the application will be denied, unless the applicant corrects the deficiencies within the time period specified in the notice and the application otherwise meets all qualifications for approval.

(2)   An applicant may upon written request receive a single 30 day extension of the time period specified in the notice of incomplete application.

(3)   (a)   A claimant may for any reason be granted a single request for prolonged status;

        (b)   A homeowner seeking issuance of a certificate of compliance may be granted prolonged status if the homeowner submits a written request documenting that the homeowner:

            (i)   can be reasonably expected to complete the application if an additional extension is granted; or

            (ii)   has filed a pending action in small claims or district court to resolve a dispute of the affidavit of compliance.

        (c)   An application under (3)(a) or (3)(b) that is granted prolonged status shall be inactive for a period of one year or until reactivated by the applicant, whichever comes first.

        (d)   At the end of the one year period, the applicant under (3)(a) or (3)(b) shall be required to either complete the application or demonstrate reasonable cause for prolonged status to be renewed for another one year period. The following shall constitute valid causes for renewing prolonged status:

            (i)   continuing litigation the outcome of which will affect whether the applicant can demonstrate compliance with Section 38-11-110 or 38-11-204;

            (ii)   ongoing bankruptcy proceedings involving the nonpaying party or contracting entity that would prevent the applicant from complying with Section 38-11-204;

            (iii)   continuing compliance by the nonpaying party with a payment agreement between the claimant and the nonpaying party; or

            (iv)   other reasonable cause as determined by the presiding officer.

        (e)   Upon expiration of the one year prolonged status of an application, the Division shall issue to the applicant an updated notice of incomplete application pursuant to Subsection (1)(b). Included with that notice shall be a form that provides the applicant an opportunity to:

            (i)   reactivate the application;

            (ii)   withdraw the application; or

            (iii)   request prolonged status be renewed pursuant to Subsection (3)(d).

        (f)   A request for renewal of prolonged status made under Subsection (3)(d) shall include evidence sufficient to demonstrate the validity of the reasons given as justification for renewal.

        (g)   If an applicant's request for prolonged status or renewal of prolonged status is denied, the applicant may request agency review.

        (h)   An application which has been reactivated from prolonged status may not be again prolonged unless the applicant can establish compliance with the requirements of Subsection (3)(d)

R156-38a-107. Application of Requirements under Subsection 38-11-107(1)(b).

The provisions of Subsection 38-11-107(1)(b) shall apply only to general contracts entered into after May 10, 2010.

R156-38a-108. Notification of Rights under Title 38, Chapter 11.

A notice in substantially the following form shall prominently appear in an easy-to-read type style and size in every contract between an original contractor and homeowner and in every notice of intent to hold and claim lien filed under Section 38-1a-502 against a homeowner or against an owner-occupied residence:

"X. PROTECTION AGAINST LIENS AND CIVIL ACTION. Notice is hereby provided in accordance with Section 38-11-108 of the Utah Code that under Utah law an "owner" may be protected against liens being maintained against an "owner-occupied residence" and from other civil action being maintained to recover monies owed for "qualified services" performed or provided by suppliers and subcontractors as a part of this contract, if either section (1) or (2) is met:

(1) (a) the owner entered into a written contract with an original contractor, a factory built housing retailer, or a real estate developer;

(b) the original contractor was properly licensed or exempt from licensure under Title 58, Chapter 55, Utah Construction Trades Licensing Act at the time the contract was executed; and

(c) the owner paid in full the contracting entity in accordance with the written contract and any written or oral amendments to the contract; or

(2) the amount of the general contract between the owner and the original contractor totals no more than $5,000."

(3) An owner who can establish compliance with either section (1) or (2) may perfect the owner's protection by applying for a Certificate of Compliance with the Division of Occupational and Professional Licensing. The application is available at www.dopl.utah.gov/rlrf.

R156-38a-109. Format for Instruction and Form Required under Subsection 38-1a-701(6).

The instructions and form required under Subsection 38-1a-701(6) shall be the Homeowner's Application for Certificate of Compliance prepared by the Division.

R156-38a-110a. Applications by Homeowners seeking issuance of Certificate of Compliance under Subsection 38-11-110(1)(a)(i) - Supporting Documents and Information.

The following supporting documents shall, at a minimum, accompany each homeowner application for a certificate of compliance seeking protection under Subsection 38-11-110(1)(a)(i):

(1) a copy of the written contract between the homeowner and the contracting entity;

(2) (a) if the homeowner contracted with an original contractor, documentation issued by the Division that the original contractor was licensed or exempt from licensure under Title 58, Chapter 55, Utah Construction Trades Licensing Act, on the date the contract was entered into;

(b) if the homeowner contracted with a real estate developer:

(i) a copy of the contract between the real estate developer and the licensed contractor with whom the real estate developer contracted for construction of the residence or other credible evidence showing the existence of such a contract and setting forth a description of the services provided to the real estate developer by the contractor;

(ii) credible evidence that the real estate developer offered the residence for sale to the public; and

(iii)   documentation issued by the Division that the contractor with whom the real estate developer contracted for construction of the residence was licensed or exempt from licensure under Title 58, Chapter 55, Utah Construction Trades Licensing Act, on the date the contract was entered into;

(c)   if the real estate developer is a licensed contractor under Title 58, Chapter 55, Utah Construction Trades Licensing Act, who engages in the construction of a residence that is offered for sale to the public:

      (i)   a copy of the contract between the homeowner and the contractor real estate developer;

      (ii)   credible evidence that the contractor real estate developer offered the residence for sale to the public; and

      (iii)   documentation issued by the Division showing that the contractor real estate developer with whom the homeowner contracted for construction of the residence was licensed or exempt from licensure under Title 58, Chapter 55, Utah Construction Trades Licensing Act, on the date the contract was entered into;

(d)   if the homeowner contracted with a manufactured housing retailer, a copy of the completed retail purchase contract;

(3)   one of the following:

(a)   except as provided in Subsection (7), an affidavit from the contracting entity acknowledging that the homeowner paid the contracting entity in full in accordance with the written contract and any amendments to the contract; or

(b)   other credible evidence establishing that the homeowner paid the contracting entity in full in accordance with the written contract and any amendments to the contract; and

(4)   credible evidence establishing ownership of the incident residence on the date the written contract between the owner and the contracting entity was entered;

(5)   one of the following:

(a)   a copy of the certificate of occupancy issued by the local government entity having jurisdiction over the incident residence;

(b)   if no occupancy permit was required by the local government entity but a final inspection was required, a copy of the final inspection approval issued by the local government entity; or

(c)   if neither Subsection (5)(a) nor (b) applies, an affidavit from the homeowner or other credible evidence establishing the date on which the original contractor substantially completed the written contract;

(6)   (a)   an affidavit from the homeowner establishing that the residence is an owner-occupied residence as defined in Subsection 38-11-102(18); or

      (b)   other credible evidence establishing that the residence if an owner-occupied residence as defined in Subsection 38-11-102(18).

(7)   If any of the following apply, the affidavit described in Subsection (3)(a) shall not be accepted as evidence of payment in full unless that affidavit is accompanied by independent, credible evidence substantiating the statements made in the affidavit:

(a)   the affiant is the homeowner;

(b)   the homeowner is an owner, member, partner, shareholder, employee, or qualifier of the contracting entity;

(c)   the homeowner has a familial relationship with an owner, member, partner, shareholder, employee, or qualifier of the contracting entity;

(d)   the homeowner has a familial relationship with the affiant;

(e)   an owner, member, partner, shareholder, employee, or qualifier of the contracting entity is also an owner, member, partner, shareholder, employee, or qualifier of the homeowner;

(f)   the contracting entity is an owner, member, partner, shareholder, employee, or qualifier of the homeowner; or

(g)   the affiant stands to benefit in any way from approval of the claim or application for certificate of compliance.

R156-38a-110b. Applications by Homeowners seeking issuance of a Certificate of Compliance under Subsection 38-11-110(1)(a)(ii) - Supporting Documents and Information.

The following supporting documents shall, at a minimum, accompany each homeowner application for a certificate of compliance seeking protection under Subsection 38-11-110(1)(a)(ii):

(1)   (a)   the original affidavit of compliance; and

        (b)   a list of known subcontractors who provided service, labor, or materials under the general contractor.

(2)   When an affidavit of compliance is disputed, the owner must submit evidence demonstrating compliance with the requirements specified in Subsection 38-11-110(2)(c)(ii).

R156-38a-202a. Initial Assessment Procedures.

The initial assessment shall be a flat or identical assessment levied against all qualified beneficiaries to create the fund.

R156-38a-202b. Special Assessment Procedures.

(1)   Special assessments shall take into consideration the claims history against the fund.

(2)   The amount of special assessments shall be established by the Division and Board in accordance with the procedures set forth in Section 38-11-206.

R156-38a-203. Limitation on Payment of Claims.

(1)   Claims may be paid prior to the pro-rata adjustment required by Subsection 38-11-203(4)(b) if the Division determines that a pro-rata payment will likely not be required.

(2)   If any claims have been paid before the Division determines a pro-rata payment will likely be required, the Division will notify the claimants of the likely adjustment and that the claimants will be required to reimburse the Division when the final pro-rata amounts are determined.

(3)   The pro-rata payment amount required by Subsection 38-11-203(4)(b) shall be calculated as follows:

        (a)   determine the total claim amount each claimant would be entitled to without consideration of the limit set in Subsection 38-11-203(4)(b);

        (b)   sum the amounts each claimant would be entitled to without consideration of the limit to determine the total amount payable to all claimants without consideration of the limit;

        (c)   divide the limit amount by the total amount payable to all claimants without consideration of the limit to find the claim allocation ratio; and

        (d)   for each claim, multiply the total claim amount without consideration of the limit by the claim allocation ratio to find the net payment for each claim.

R156-38a-204a. Claims Against the Fund by Nonlaborers - Supporting Documents and Information.

The following supporting documents shall, at a minimum, accompany each nonlaborer claim for recovery from the fund:

    (1)   one of the following:

        (a)   a copy of the certificate of compliance issued by the Division establishing that the owner is in compliance with Subsection 38-11-204(4)(a) and (b) for the residence at issue in the claim;

        (b)   the documents required in Section R156-38a-110a; or

        (c)   a copy of a civil judgment containing findings of fact that:

            (i)   the homeowner entered a written contract in compliance with Subsection 38-11-204(4)(a);

            (ii)   the contracting entity was licensed or exempt from licensure under Title 58, Chapter 55, Utah Construction Trades Licensing Act;

            (iii)   the homeowner paid the contracting entity in full in accordance with the written contract and any amendments to the contract; and

            (iv)   the homeowner is an owner as defined in Subsection 38-11-102(17) and the residence is an owner-occupied residence as defined in Subsection 38-11-102(18);

    (2)   if the applicant recorded a notice of claim under Section 38-1a-502, a copy of that notice establishing the date that notice was filed.

    (3)   one of the following as applicable:

        (a)   a copy of an action date stamped by a court of competent jurisdiction filed by the claimant against the nonpaying party to recover monies owed for qualified services performed on the owner-occupied residence; or

        (b)   documentation that a bankruptcy filing by the nonpaying party prevented the claimant from satisfying Subsection (a);

    (4)   one of the following:

        (a)   a copy of a civil judgment entered in favor of the claimant against the nonpaying party containing a finding that the nonpaying party failed to pay the claimant pursuant to their contract; or

        (b)   documentation that a bankruptcy filing by the nonpaying party prevented the claimant from obtaining a civil judgment, including a copy of the proof of claim filed by the claimant with the bankruptcy court, together with credible evidence establishing that the nonpaying party failed to pay the claimant pursuant to their contract;

    (5)   one or more of the following as applicable:

        (a)   a copy of a supplemental order issued following the civil judgment entered in favor of the claimant and a copy of the return of service of the supplemental order indicating either that service was accomplished on the nonpaying party or that said nonpaying party could not be located or served;

        (b)   a writ of execution issued if any assets are identified through the supplemental order or other process, which have sufficient value to reasonably justify the expenditure of costs and legal fees which would be incurred in preparing, issuing, and serving execution papers and in holding an execution sale; or

(c)   documentation that a bankruptcy filing or other action by the nonpaying party prevented the claimant from satisfying Subparagraphs (a) and (b);

(6)   certification that the claimant is not entitled to reimbursement from any other person at the time the claim is filed and that the claimant will immediately notify the presiding officer if the claimant becomes entitled to reimbursement from any other person after the date the claim is filed; and

(7)   one or more of the following:

    (a)   a copy of invoices setting forth a description of, the location of, the performance dates of, and the value of the qualified services claimed;

    (b)   a copy of a civil judgment containing a finding setting forth a description of, the location of, the performance dates of, and the value of the qualified services claimed; or

    (c)   credible evidence setting forth a description of, the location of, the performance dates of, and the value of the qualified services claimed.

(8)   If the claimant is requesting payment of costs and attorney fees other than those specifically enumerated in the judgment against the nonpaying party, the claim shall include documentation of those costs and fees adequate for the Division to apply the requirements set forth in Section R156-38a-204d.

(9)   In claims in which the presiding officer determines that the claimant has made a reasonable but unsuccessful effort to produce all documentation specified under this rule to satisfy any requirement to recover from the fund, the presiding officer may elect to accept the evidence submitted by the claimant if the requirements to recover from the fund can be established by that evidence.

(10)   A separate claim must be filed for each residence and a separate filing fee must be paid for each claim.

R156-38a-204b. Claims Against the Fund by Laborers - Supporting Documents.

(1)   The following supporting documents shall, at a minimum, accompany each laborer claim for recovery from the fund:

    (a)   one of the following:

        (i)   a copy of a wage claim assignment filed with the Employment Standards Bureau of the Antidiscrimination and Labor Division of the Labor Commission of Utah for the amount of the claim, together with all supporting documents submitted in conjunction therewith; or

        (ii)   a copy of an action filed by claimant against claimant's employer to recover wages owed;

    (b)   one of the following:

        (i)   a copy of a final administrative order for payment issued by the Employment Standards Bureau of the Antidiscrimination and Labor Division of the Labor Commission of Utah containing a finding that the claimant is an employee and that the claimant has not been paid wages due for work performed at the site of construction on an owner-occupied residence;

        (ii)   a copy of a civil judgment entered in favor of claimant against the employer containing a finding that the employer failed to pay the claimant wages due for work performed at the site of construction on an owner-occupied residence; or

        (iii)   a copy of a bankruptcy filing by the employer which prevented the entry of an order or a judgment against the employer;

      (c)   one of the following:

            (i)   a copy of the certificate of compliance issued by the Division establishing that the owner is in compliance with Subsection 38-11-204(4)(a) and (b) for the residence at issue in the claim;

            (ii)   an affidavit from the homeowner establishing that he is an owner as defined in Subsection 38-11-102(17) and that the residence is an owner-occupied residence as defined by Subsection 38-11-102(18);

            (iii)   a copy of a civil judgment containing a finding that the homeowner is an owner as defined by Subsection 38-11-102(17) and that the residence is an owner-occupied residence as defined by Subsection 38-11-102(18); or

            (iv)   other credible evidence establishing that the owner is an owner as defined by Subsection 38-11-102(17) and that the residence is an owner-occupied residence as defined by Subsection 38-11-102(18).

(2)   When a laborer makes claim on multiple residences as a result of a single incident of nonpayment by the same employer, the Division must require payment of at least one application fee required under Section 38-11-204(1)(b) and at least one registration fee required under Subsection 38-11-204(7), but may waive additional application and registration fees for claims for the additional residences, where no legitimate purpose would be served by requiring separate filings.

R156-38a-204c. Calculation of Costs, Attorney Fees and Interest for Payable Claims.

(1)   Payment for qualified services, costs, attorney fees, and interest shall be made as specified in Section 38-11-203.

(2)   When a claimant provides qualified service on multiple properties, irrespective of whether those properties are owner-occupied residences, and files claim for payment on some or all of those properties and the claims are supported by a single judgment or other common documentation and the judgment or documentation does not differentiate costs and attorney fees by property, the amount of costs and attorney fees shall be allocated among the related properties using the following formula: (Qualified services attributable to the owner-occupied residence at issue in the claim divided by Total qualified services awarded as judgment principal or total documented qualified services) x Total costs or total attorney fees.

(3)   (a)   For claims wherein the claimant has had judgment entered against the nonpaying party, post-judgment costs shall be limited to those costs allowable by a district court, such as costs of service, garnishments, or executions, and shall not include postage, copy expenses, telephone expenses, or other costs related to the preparation and filing of the claim application.

      (b)   For claims wherein the nonpaying party's bankruptcy filing precluded the claimant from having judgment entered against the nonpaying party, total costs shall be limited to those costs that would have been allowable by the district court had judgment been entered, such as, but not limited to, costs of services, garnishments, or executions, and shall not include postage, copy expenses, telephone expenses, or other costs related to the preparation and filing of the claim application.

(4)   The interest rate or rates applicable to a claim shall be the rate for the year or years in which payment for the qualified services was due.

(5)   If the evidence submitted in fulfillment of Subsection R156-38a-204b(7) does not specify the date or dates upon which payment was due, the Division shall assume payment was due 30 calendar days after the date on which the claimant billed the nonpaying party for the qualified services.

(6)   If the qualified services at issue in a claim were billed in two or more installments and payment was due on two or more dates, the claimant shall provide documentation sufficient for the Division to determine each payment due date and the attendant portion of qualified services for which payment was due on that date. If the claimant does not provide sufficient documentation, the Division shall assume the nonpaying party's debt accrued evenly throughout the period so an equal portion of the qualified services balance shall be applied to each billing installment.

(7)   If a claimant receives partial payment for qualified services between the time judgment is entered and the claim is filed, the Division shall calculate payment amounts by accruing costs, attorney fees and interest to the date of the payment then reducing the individual balances of first interest, then costs, then attorney fees, and finally qualified services to a zero balance until the entire payment is applied. The Division shall then make payment of the remaining balances plus additional accrued interest on the remaining qualified services balance.

R156-38a-301a. Contractor Registration as a Qualified Beneficiary - All License Classifications Required to Register Unless Specifically Exempted - Exempted Classifications.

(1)   All license classifications of contractors are determined to be regularly engaged in providing qualified services for purposes of automatic registration as a qualified beneficiary, as set forth in Subsections 38-11-301(1) and (2), with the exception of the following license classifications:

TABLE II

Primary Classification Number	Subclassification Number	Classification
E100		General Engineering Contractor
	S211	Boiler Installation Contractor
	S213	Industrial Piping Contractor
	S262	Gunnite and Pressure Grouting Contractor
S320		Steel Erection Contractor
	S321	Steel Reinforcing Contractor
	S322	Metal Building Erection Contractor
	S323	Structural Stud Erection Contractor
S340		Sheet Metal Contractor
S360		Refrigeration Contractor
S440		Sign Installation Contractor
	S441	Non Electrical Outdoor Advertising Sign Contractor
S450		Mechanical Insulation Contractor
S470		Petroleum System Contractor
S480		Piers and Foundations Contractor
I101		General Engineering Trades Instructor
I102		General Building Trades Instructor
I103		General Electrical Trades Instructor
I104		General Plumbing Trades Instructor
I105		General Mechanical Trades Instructor
I105		General Mechanical Trades Instructor

(2)   A licensee with a license classification that requires registration in the fund whose license is on inactive status on the assessment date of any special assessment of the fund, is not required to pay the special assessment during the time the license remains on inactive status.

(3)   Before a licensee can reactivate the license, the licensee must pay any special assessment or assessments within the two years prior to the reactivation date.

R156-38a-301b. Event Necessitating Registration - Name Change by Qualified Beneficiary - Reorganization of Registrant's Business Type - Transferability of Registration.

(1)   Any change in entity status by a registrant requires registration with the Fund by the new or surviving entity before that entity is a qualified beneficiary.

(2)   The following constitute a change of entity status for purposes of Subsection (1):

    (a)   creation of a new legal entity as a successor or related-party entity of the registrant;

    (b)   change from one form of legal entity to another by the registrant; or

    (c)   merger or other similar transaction wherein the existing registrant is acquired by or assumed into another entity and no longer conducts business as its own legal entity.

(3)   A qualified beneficiary registrant shall notify the Division in writing of a name change within 30 days of the change becoming effective. The notice shall provide the following:

    (a)   the registrant's prior name;

    (b)   the registrant's new name;

    (c)   the registrant's registration number; and

    (d)   proof of registration with the Division of Corporations and Commercial Code as required by state law.

(4)   A registration shall not be transferred, lent, borrowed, sold, exchanged for consideration, assigned, or made available for use by any entity other than the registrant for any reason.

(5)   A claimant shall not be considered a qualified beneficiary registrant merely by virtue of owning or being owned by an entity that is a qualified beneficiary.

R156-38a-302. Renewal and Reinstatement Procedures.

(1)   Renewal notices required in connection with a special assessment shall be sent to each registrant at least 30 days prior to the expiration date for the existing registration established in the renewal notice. Unless the registrant pays the special assessment by the expiration date shown on the renewal notice, the registrant's registration in the fund automatically expires on the expiration date.

(2)   (a)   Renewal notices shall be sent by letter deposited in the post office with postage prepaid, addressed to the last address shown on the Division's records. Such mailing shall constitute legal notice. It shall be the duty and responsibility of the registrant to maintain a current mailing address with the Division; or

    (b)   If a registrant has authorized the Division to send a renewal notice by email, the email shall be sent to the last email address shown on the Division's records. Such mailing shall constitute legal notice. It shall be the duty and responsibility of the registrant to maintain a current email address with the Division.

(3)   Renewal notices shall specify the amount of the special assessment, the application requirement, and other renewal requirements, if any; shall require that each registrant document or certify that the registrant meets the renewal requirements; and shall advise the registrant of the consequences of failing to renew a registration.

(4)   Renewal applications must be received by the Division in its ordinary course of business on or before the renewal application due date in order to be processed as a renewal application. Late applications will be processed as reinstatement applications.

(5)   A registrant whose registration has expired may have the registration reinstated by complying with the requirements and procedures specified in Subsection 38-11-302(5).

R156-38a-401. Requirements for a Letter of Credit and/or Evidence of a Cash Deposit as Alternate Security for Mechanics' Lien.

To qualify as alternate security under Subsection 38-1a-804(2)(c)(i)(B) "evidence of a cash deposit" must be an account at a federally insured depository institution that is pledged to the protected party and is payable to the protected party upon the occurrence of specified conditions in a written agreement.

KEY: licensing, contractors, liens

Date of Enactment or Last Substantive Amendment: September 9, 2010

Notice of Continuation: December 9, 2014

Authorizing, and Implemented or Interpreted Law: 38-11-101; 58-1-106(1)(a); 58-1-202(1)(a)

RESIDENCE LIEN RESTRICTION AND LIEN RECOVERY FUND RULE

R156-38a

Utah Administrative Code

Issued September 9, 2010

Appendix N: Division of Occupational and Professional Licensing Act

Part 1 - Division Administration

58-1-101 Short title.

This chapter is known as the "Division of Occupational and Professional Licensing Act."

Renumbered and Amended by Chapter 297, 1993 General Session

58-1-102 Definitions.

For purposes of this title:

(1) "Ablative procedure" is as defined in Section 58-67-102.

(2) "Cosmetic medical procedure":

  (a) is as defined in Section 58-67-102; and

  (b) except for Chapter 67, Utah Medical Practice Act, and Chapter 68, Utah Osteopathic Medical Practice Act, does not apply to the scope of practice of an individual licensed under this title if the individual's scope of practice includes the authority to operate or perform surgical procedures.

(3) "Department" means the Department of Commerce.

(4) "Director" means the director of the Division of Occupational and Professional Licensing.

(5) "Division" means the Division of Occupational and Professional Licensing created in Section 58-1-103.

(6) "Executive director" means the executive director of the Department of Commerce.

(7) "Licensee" includes any holder of a license, certificate, registration, permit, student card, or apprentice card authorized under this title.

(8) (a) (i) "Nonablative procedure" means a procedure that is expected or intended to alter living tissue, but not intended or expected to excise, vaporize, disintegrate, or remove living tissue.

    (ii) Notwithstanding Subsection (8)(a)(i), nonablative procedure includes hair removal.

  (b) "Nonablative procedure" does not include:

    (i) a superficial procedure;

    (ii) the application of permanent make-up; or

    (iii) the use of photo therapy and lasers for neuromusculoskeletal treatments that are performed by an individual licensed under this title who is acting within their scope of practice.

(9) "Superficial procedure" means a procedure that is expected or intended to temporarily alter living skin tissue and may excise or remove stratum corneum but have no appreciable risk of damage to any tissue below the stratum corneum.

(10)   "Unlawful conduct" has the meaning given in Subsection 58-1-501(1).

(11)   "Unprofessional conduct" has the meaning given in Subsection 58-1-501(2).

Amended by Chapter 362, 2012 General Session

58-1-103 Division created to administer licensing laws.

There is created within the Department of Commerce the Division of Occupational and Professional Licensing. The division shall administer and enforce all licensing laws of Title 58, Occupations and Professions.

Renumbered and Amended by Chapter 297, 1993 General Session

58-1-104 Director of division—Appointment—Duties.

(1)   The division shall be under the supervision, direction, and control of a director. The director shall be appointed by the executive director with the approval of the governor. The director shall hold office at the pleasure of the governor.

(2)   The director shall perform all duties, functions, and responsibilities assigned to the division by law or rule and, where provided, with the collaboration and assistance of the boards established under this title.

Renumbered and Amended by Chapter 297, 1993 General Session

58-1-105 Employment of staff.

The director, with the approval of the executive director, may employ necessary staff, including specialists and professionals, to assist him in performing the duties, functions, and responsibilities of the division.

Renumbered and Amended by Chapter 297, 1993 General Session

58-1-106 Division—Duties, functions, and responsibilities.

(1)   The duties, functions, and responsibilities of the division include the following:

(a)   prescribing, adopting, and enforcing rules to administer this title;

(b)   investigating the activities of any person whose occupation or profession is regulated or governed by the laws and rules administered and enforced by the division;

(c)   subpoenaing witnesses, taking evidence, and requiring by subpoena duces tecum the production of any books, papers, documents, records, contracts, recordings, tapes, correspondence, or information relevant to an investigation upon a finding of sufficient need by the director or by the director's designee;

(d)   taking administrative and judicial action against persons in violation of the laws and rules administered and enforced by the division, including the issuance of cease and desist orders;

(e)   seeking injunctions and temporary restraining orders to restrain unauthorized activity;

(f)   giving public notice of board meetings;

(g)   keeping records of board meetings, proceedings, and actions and making those records available for public inspection upon request;

(h)   issuing, refusing to issue, revoking, suspending, renewing, refusing to renew, or otherwise acting upon any license;

(i)   preparing and submitting to the governor and the Legislature an annual report of the division's operations, activities, and goals;

(j)   preparing and submitting to the executive director a budget of the expenses for the division;

(k)   establishing the time and place for the administration of examinations; and

(l)   preparing lists of licensees and making these lists available to the public at cost upon request unless otherwise prohibited by state or federal law.

(2)   The division may not include home telephone numbers or home addresses of licensees on the lists prepared under Subsection (1)(l), except as otherwise provided by rules of the division made in accordance with Title 63G, Chapter 3, Utah Administrative Rulemaking Act.

(3)   (a)   The division may provide the home address or home telephone number of a licensee on a list prepared under Subsection (1) upon the request of an individual who provides proper identification and the reason for the request, in writing, to the division.

(b)   A request under Subsection (3)(a) is limited to providing information on only one licensee per request.

(c)   The division shall provide, by rule, what constitutes proper identification under Subsection (3)(a).

Amended by Chapter 382, 2008 General Session

58-1-107 Applicability—Relationship to specific chapters under title.

The provisions of this chapter uniformly apply to the administration and enforcement of this title. However, unless expressly prohibited in this chapter, any provision of this chapter may be supplemented or altered by specific chapters of this title.

Enacted by Chapter 297, 1993 General Session

58-1-108 Adjudicative proceedings.

(1)   The division and all boards created under the authority of this title shall comply with the procedures and requirements of Title 13, Chapter 1, Department of Commerce, and Title 63G, Chapter 4, Administrative Procedures Act, in all of their adjudicative proceedings as defined by Subsection 63G-4-103(1).

(2)   Before proceeding under Section 63G-4-502, the division shall review the proposed action with a committee of no less than three licensees appointed by the chairman of the licensing board created under this title for the profession of the person against whom the action is proposed.

(3)   Notwithstanding Title 63G, Chapter 4, Administrative Procedures Act, a warning or final disposition letter which does not constitute disciplinary action against the addressee, issued in response to a complaint of unprofessional or unlawful conduct under this title, does not constitute an adjudicative proceeding.

Amended by Chapter 382, 2008 General Session

58-1-109 Presiding officers—Content of orders—Recommended orders—Final orders—Appeal of orders.

(1)   Unless otherwise specified by statute or rule, the presiding officer for adjudicative proceedings before the division shall be the director. However, pursuant to Title 63G, Chapter 4, Administrative Procedures Act, the director may designate in writing an individual or body of individuals to act as presiding officer to conduct or to assist the director in conducting any part or all of an adjudicative proceeding.

(2)   Unless otherwise specified by the director, an administrative law judge shall be designated as the presiding officer to conduct formal adjudicative proceedings in accordance with Subsection 63G-4-102(4), Sections 63G-4-204 through 63G-4-207, and 63G-4-209.

(3)   Unless otherwise specified by the director, the licensing board of the occupation or profession that is the subject of the proceedings shall be designated as the presiding officer to serve as fact finder at the evidentiary hearing in a formal adjudicative proceeding.

(4)   At the close of an evidentiary hearing in an adjudicative proceeding, unless otherwise specified by the director, the presiding officer who served as the fact finder at the hearing shall issue a recommended order based upon the record developed at the hearing determining all issues pending before the division.

(5)   (a)   The director shall issue a final order affirming the recommended order or modifying or rejecting all or any part of the recommended order and entering new findings of fact, conclusions of law, statement of reasons, and order based upon the director's personal attendance at the hearing or a review of the record developed at the hearing. Before modifying or rejecting a recommended order, the director shall consult with the presiding officer who issued the recommended order.

      (b)   If the director issues a final order modifying or rejecting a recommended order, the licensing board of the occupation or profession that is the subject of the proceeding may, by a two-thirds majority vote of all board members, petition the executive director or designee within the department to review the director's final order. The executive director's decision shall become the final order of the division. This subsection does not limit the right of the parties to appeal the director's final order by filing a request for agency review under Subsection (8).

(6)   If the director is unable for any reason to rule upon a recommended order of a presiding officer, the director may designate another person within the division to issue a final order.

(7)   If the director or the director's designee does not issue a final order within 20 calendar days after the date of the recommended order of the presiding officer, the recommended order becomes the final order of the director or the director's designee.

(8)   The final order of the director may be appealed by filing a request for agency review with the executive director or the executive director's designee within the department.

(9)   The content of all orders shall comply with the requirements of Subsection 63G-4-203(1)(i) and Sections 63G-4-208 and 63G-4-209.

Amended by Chapter 382, 2008 General Session

58-1-110 Legislative review in Title 58, Occupations and Professions.

Legislation proposing the licensing or regulation of an occupation or profession under Title 58, Occupations and Professions, that is not currently subject to licensing or regulation under Title 58, Occupations and Professions:

(1)   may not be enacted by the Legislature unless:

      (a)   a proposal to license or regulate the occupation or profession has been reviewed by the Occupational and Professional Licensure Review Committee as described in Title 36, Chapter 23, Occupational and Professional Licensure Review Committee Act; or

      (b)   the proposed legislation contains a provision that expressly exempts the legislation from the review requirement of Subsection (1)(a);

(2)   is subject to a reauthorization schedule as described in Title 63I, Chapter 1, Legislative Oversight and Sunset Act; and

(3)   shall include a repeal date in Section 63I-1-258 that is no later than 10 years after the effective date of the legislation.

Enacted by Chapter 323, 2013 General Session

Part 2 - Boards

58-1-201 Boards—Appointment—Membership—Terms—Vacancies—Quorum—Per diem and expenses—Chair—Financial interest or faculty position in professional school that teaches continuing education prohibited.

(1)   (a)   (i)   The executive director shall appoint the members of the boards established under this title.

                   (ii)   In appointing these members the executive director shall give consideration to recommendations by members of the respective occupations and professions and by their organizations.

        (b)   Each board shall be composed of five members, four of whom shall be licensed or certified practitioners in good standing of the occupation or profession the board represents, and one of whom shall be a member of the general public, unless otherwise provided under the specific licensing chapter.

        (c)   (i)   The name of each person appointed to a board shall be submitted to the governor for confirmation or rejection.

                   (ii)   If an appointee is rejected by the governor, the executive director shall appoint another person in the same manner as set forth in Subsection (1)(a).

(2)   (a)   (i)   Except as required by Subsection (2)(b), as terms of current board members expire, the executive director shall appoint each new member or reappointed member to a four-year term.

                   (ii)   Upon the expiration of the term of a board member, the board member shall continue to serve until a successor is appointed, but for a period not to exceed six months from the expiration date of the member's term.

        (b)   Notwithstanding the requirements of Subsection (2)(a), the executive director shall, at the time of appointment or reappointment, adjust the length of terms to ensure that the terms of board members are staggered so that approximately half of the board is appointed every two years.

        (c)   A board member may not serve more than two consecutive terms, and a board member who ceases to serve on a board may not serve again on that board until after the expiration of a two-year period beginning from that cessation of service.

        (d)   (i)   When a vacancy occurs in the membership for any reason, the replacement shall be appointed for the unexpired term.

                   (ii)   After filling that term, the replacement member may be appointed for only one additional full term.

        (e)   The director, with the approval of the executive director, may remove a board member and replace the member in accordance with this section for the following reasons:

                   (i)   the member fails or refuses to fulfill the responsibilities and duties of a board member, including attendance at board meetings;

                   (ii)   the member engages in unlawful or unprofessional conduct; or

                   (iii)   if appointed to the board position as a licensed member of the board, the member fails to maintain a license that is active and in good standing.

(3)   A majority of the board members constitutes a quorum. A quorum is sufficient authority for the board to act.

    (4)   A member may not receive compensation or benefits for the member's service, but may receive per diem and travel expenses in accordance with:

        (a)   Section 63A-3-106;

        (b)   Section 63A-3-107; and

        (c)   rules made by the Division of Finance pursuant to Sections 63A-3-106 and 63A-3-107.

    (5)   Each board shall annually designate one of its members to serve as chair for a one-year period.

    (6)   A board member may not be a member of the faculty of, or have a financial interest in, a vocational or professional college or school that provides continuing education to any licensee if that continuing education is required by statute or rule.

Amended by Chapter 262, 2013 General Session

58-1-202 Boards—Duties, functions, and responsibilities.

    (1)   The duties, functions, and responsibilities of each board include the following:

        (a)   recommending to the director appropriate rules;

        (b)   recommending to the director policy and budgetary matters;

        (c)   approving and establishing a passing score for applicant examinations;

        (d)   screening applicants and recommending licensing, renewal, reinstatement, and relicensure actions to the director in writing;

        (e)   assisting the director in establishing standards of supervision for students or persons in training to become qualified to obtain a license in the occupation or profession it represents;

        (f)   acting as presiding officer in conducting hearings associated with adjudicative proceedings and in issuing recommended orders when so designated by the director; and

        (g)   in accordance with Subsection (3), each board may recommend to the appropriate legislative committee whether the board supports a change to the licensing act.

    (2)   Subsection (1) does not apply to boards created in Title 58, Chapter 55, Utah Construction Trades Licensing Act.

    (3)   (a)   This Subsection (3) applies to the following:

            (i)   Chapter 5a, Podiatric Physician Licensing Act;

            (ii)   Chapter 16a, Utah Optometry Practice Act;

            (iii)   Chapter 17b, Pharmacy Practice Act;

            (iv)   Chapter 24b, Physical Therapy Practice Act;

            (v)   Chapter 28, Veterinary Practice Act;

            (vi)   Chapter 31b, Nurse Practice Act;

           (vii)   Chapter 40a, Athletic Trainer Licensing Act;

          (viii)   Chapter 44a, Nurse Midwife Practice Act;

            (ix)   Chapter 67, Utah Medical Practice Act;

            (x)   Chapter 68, Utah Osteopathic Medical Practice Act;

           (xi)   Chapter 69, Dentist and Dental Hygienist Practice Act;

          (xii)   Chapter 70a, Physician Assistant Act;

	(xiii)	Chapter 71, Naturopathic Physician Practice Act; and
	(xiv)	Chapter 73, Chiropractic Physician Practice Act.
(b)		Subsection (1)(g) does not:
	(i)	require a board's approval to amend a practice act; and
	(ii)	apply to technical or clarifying amendments to a practice act.

Amended by Chapter 259, 2012 General Session

58-1-203 Duties, functions, and responsibilities of division in collaboration with board—Construction Services Commission.

(1) The following duties, functions, and responsibilities of the division shall be performed by the division with the collaboration and assistance of the appropriate board:

    (a) defining which schools, colleges, universities, departments of universities, military educational and training programs, or other institutions of learning are reputable and in good standing with the division;

    (b) prescribing license qualifications;

    (c) prescribing rules governing applications for licenses;

    (d) providing for a fair and impartial method of examination of applicants;

    (e) defining unprofessional conduct, by rule, to supplement the definitions under this chapter or other licensing chapters;

    (f) establishing advisory peer committees to the board and prescribing their scope of authority; and

    (g) establishing conditions for reinstatement and renewal of licenses.

(2) Notwithstanding Subsection (1), the duties, functions, and responsibilities of the division outlined in Subsection (1) shall, instead, be performed by the Construction Services Commission for all purposes of Title 58, Chapter 55, Utah Construction Trades Licensing Act.

Amended by Chapter 181, 2011 General Session

Part 3 - Licensing

58-1-301 License application—Licensing procedure.

(1)   (a) Each license applicant shall apply to the division in writing upon forms available from the division. Each completed application shall contain documentation of the particular qualifications required of the applicant, shall include the applicant's Social Security number, shall be verified by the applicant, and shall be accompanied by the appropriate fees.

    (b) An applicant's Social Security number is a private record under Subsection 63G-2-302(1)(i).

(2)   (a) A license shall be issued to an applicant who submits a complete application if the division determines that the applicant meets the qualifications of licensure.

    (b) A written notice of additional proceedings shall be provided to an applicant who submits a complete application, but who has been, is, or will be placed under investigation by the division for conduct directly bearing upon the applicant's qualifications for licensure, if the outcome of additional proceedings is required to determine the division's response to the application.

(c)   A written notice of denial of licensure shall be provided to an applicant who submits a complete application if the division determines that the applicant does not meet the qualifications of licensure.

(d)   A written notice of incomplete application and conditional denial of licensure shall be provided to an applicant who submits an incomplete application. This notice shall advise the applicant that the application is incomplete and that the application is denied, unless the applicant corrects the deficiencies within the time period specified in the notice and otherwise meets all qualifications for licensure.

(3)   Before any person is issued a license under this title, all requirements for that license as established under this title and by rule shall be met.

(4)   If all requirements are met for the specific license, the division shall issue the license.

Amended by Chapter 426, 2013 General Session

58-1-301.5 Division access to Bureau of Criminal Identification records.

(1)   The division shall have direct access to criminal background information maintained by the Bureau of Criminal Identification under Title 53, Chapter 10, Part 2, Bureau of Criminal Identification, for background screening of persons who are applying for licensure, licensure renewal, licensure reinstatement, or relicensure, as required in:

(a)   Section 58-17b-307 of Title 58, Chapter 17b, Pharmacy Practice Act;

(b)   Section 58-31b-302 of Title 58, Chapter 31b, Nurse Practice Act;

(c)   Section 58-47b-302 of Title 58, Chapter 47b, Massage Therapy Practice Act;

(d)   Section 58-55-302 of Title 58, Chapter 55, Utah Construction Trades Licensing Act, as it applies to alarm companies and alarm company agents;

(e)   Section 58-63-302 of Title 58, Chapter 63, Security Personnel Licensing Act; and

(f)   Section 58-64-302 of Title 58, Chapter 64, Deception Detection Examiners Licensing Act.

(2)   The division's access to criminal background information under this section:

(a)   shall meet the requirements of Section 53-10-108; and

(b)   includes convictions, pleas of nolo contendere, pleas of guilty or nolo contendere held in abeyance, dismissed charges, and charges without a known disposition.

Amended by Chapter 262, 2013 General Session

58-1-301.7 Change of information.

(1)   (a)   An applicant, licensee, or certificate holder shall send the division a signed statement, in a form required by the division, notifying the division within 10 business days of a change in mailing address.

(b)   When providing a mailing address, the individual may provide a post office box or other mail drop location.

(c)   In addition to providing a mailing address, an applicant, licensee, or certificate holder may provide to the division, in a form required by the division, an email address and may designate email as the preferred method of receiving notifications from the division.

(2)   An applicant, licensee, or certificate holder is considered to have received a notification that has been sent to the most recent:

(a)   mailing address provided to the division by the applicant, licensee, or certificate holder; or

  (b)   email address furnished to the division by the applicant, licensee, or certificate holder, if email has been designated by the applicant, licensee, or certificate holder as the preferred method of receiving notifications from the division.

Amended by Chapter 262, 2013 General Session

58-1-302 License by endorsement.

(1)   The division may issue a license without examination to a person who has been licensed in a state, district, or territory of the United States, or in a foreign country, where the education, experience, and examination requirements are, or were at the time the license was issued, substantially equal to the requirements of this state.

(2)   Before a person may be issued a license under this section, the person shall produce satisfactory evidence of the person's identity, qualifications, and good standing in the occupation or profession for which licensure is sought.

Amended by Chapter 262, 2013 General Session

58-1-303 Temporary license.

(1)   (a)   The division may issue a temporary license to a person who has met all license requirements except the passing of an examination. In this case:

             (i)   the licensee shall take the next available examination; and

             (ii)   the temporary license automatically expires upon release of official examination results if the applicant fails the examination.

       (b)   The division may issue a temporary license to a person licensed in another state or country who is in Utah temporarily to teach or assist a Utah resident licensed to practice an occupation or profession under this title.

       (c)   The division may issue a temporary license to a person licensed in another state who met the requirements for licensure in that state, which were equal to or greater than the requirements for licensure of this state at the time the license was obtained in the other state, upon a finding by the division, in collaboration with the appropriate board, that the issuance of a temporary license is necessary to or justified by:

             (i)   a local or national emergency or any governmental action causing an unusual circumstance that might be reasonably considered to materially jeopardize the public health, safety, or welfare if a temporary license is not issued;

             (ii)   a lack of necessary available services in any community or area of the state from an occupation or profession licensed under this title, if the lack of services might be reasonably considered to materially jeopardize the public health, safety, or welfare if a temporary license is not issued; or

             (iii) a need to first observe an applicant for licensure in this state in a monitored or supervised practice of the applicant's occupation or profession before a decision is made by the division either to grant or deny the applicant a regular license.

(2)   The division may not issue a temporary license to a person who qualifies for one under Subsection (1)(a) more than three consecutive times within the three-year period immediately following the issuance of the first temporary license.

(3)   The division may not issue a temporary license to a person solely because there is a competitive advantage enjoyed or a competitive disadvantage suffered by any party caused by the absence of a

licensed person, unless in addition there is or will be a material risk presented to the public health, safety, or welfare.

Renumbered and Amended by Chapter 297, 1993 General Session

58-1-304 Restricted license.

(1)   The division may issue a restricted or probationary license to an applicant for licensure, renewal, or reinstatement of licensure if:

(a)   the applicant appears to meet the qualifications for licensure, but has engaged in unlawful, unprofessional, or other conduct bearing upon the applicant's qualifications; and

(b)   the division determines the need to observe the applicant in a monitored or supervised practice of the applicant's occupation or profession or to attach other reasonable restrictions or conditions upon the applicant in order to accommodate licensure, while protecting the public health, safety, and welfare.

(2)   Issuance of a restricted or probationary license is considered a partial denial of licensure that is subject to agency review.

Amended by Chapter 262, 2013 General Session

58-1-305 Inactive license.

(1)   The division may adopt rules permitting inactive licensure. The rules shall specify the requirements and procedures for placing a license on inactive status, the length of time a license may remain on inactive status, and the requirements and procedures to activate an inactive license.

(2)   Except as otherwise specified by rule, an inactive licensee has no right or privilege to engage in the practice of the licensed occupation or profession.

Enacted by Chapter 297, 1993 General Session

58-1-306 Surrender of license.

(1)   The division may, by written agreement, accept the voluntary surrender of a license.

(2)   Unless otherwise stated in the written agreement, tender and acceptance of a voluntary surrender of a license does not foreclose the division from pursuing additional disciplinary or other action authorized under this title or in rules adopted under this title.

(3)   Unless otherwise stated in the written agreement, tender and acceptance of a voluntary surrender of a license terminates all rights and privileges associated with the license.

(4)   Unless otherwise stated in the written agreement, the surrendered rights and privileges of licensure may be reacquired only by reapplying for licensure and meeting the requirements for a new or reinstated license set forth under this title or in rules adopted under this title.

(5)   Unless otherwise stated in the written agreement, documentation of tender and acceptance of a voluntary surrender of a license is a public record.

(6)   Unless otherwise stated in the written agreement, when a tender and acceptance of a voluntary surrender of a license occurs while adjudicative proceedings are pending against the licensee for unprofessional or unlawful conduct, the division may report the surrender of license to appropriate state and federal agencies and licensing data banks.

Enacted by Chapter 297, 1993 General Session

58-1-307 Exemptions from licensure.

(1)   Except as otherwise provided by statute or rule, the following individuals may engage in the practice of their occupation or profession, subject to the stated circumstances and limitations, without being licensed under this title:

(a)   an individual serving in the armed forces of the United States, the United States Public Health Service, the United States Department of Veterans Affairs, or other federal agencies while engaged in activities regulated under this chapter as a part of employment with that federal agency if the individual holds a valid license to practice a regulated occupation or profession issued by any other state or jurisdiction recognized by the division;

(b)   a student engaged in activities constituting the practice of a regulated occupation or profession while in training in a recognized school approved by the division to the extent the activities are supervised by qualified faculty, staff, or designee and the activities are a defined part of the training program;

(c)   an individual engaged in an internship, residency, preceptorship, postceptorship, fellowship, apprenticeship, or on-the-job training program approved by the division while under the supervision of qualified individuals;

(d)   an individual residing in another state and licensed to practice a regulated occupation or profession in that state, who is called in for a consultation by an individual licensed in this state, and the services provided are limited to that consultation;

(e)   an individual who is invited by a recognized school, association, society, or other body approved by the division to conduct a lecture, clinic, or demonstration of the practice of a regulated occupation or profession if the individual does not establish a place of business or regularly engage in the practice of the regulated occupation or profession in this state;

(f)   an individual licensed under the laws of this state, other than under this title, to practice or engage in an occupation or profession, while engaged in the lawful, professional, and competent practice of that occupation or profession;

(g)   an individual licensed in a health care profession in another state who performs that profession while attending to the immediate needs of a patient for a reasonable period during which the patient is being transported from outside of this state, into this state, or through this state;

(h)   an individual licensed in another state or country who is in this state temporarily to attend to the needs of an athletic team or group, except that the practitioner may only attend to the needs of the athletic team or group, including all individuals who travel with the team or group in any capacity except as a spectator;

(i)   an individual licensed and in good standing in another state, who is in this state:

(i)   temporarily, under the invitation and control of a sponsoring entity;

(ii)   for a reason associated with a special purpose event, based upon needs that may exceed the ability of this state to address through its licensees, as determined by the division; and

(iii)   for a limited period of time not to exceed the duration of that event, together with any necessary preparatory and conclusionary periods;

(j)   a law enforcement officer, as defined under Section 53-13-103, who:

(i)   is operating a voice stress analyzer in the course of the officer's full-time employment with a federal, state, or local law enforcement agency;

        (ii)   has completed the manufacturer's training course and is certified by the manufacturer to operate that voice stress analyzer; and

        (iii)   is operating the voice stress analyzer in accordance with Section 58-64-601, regarding deception detection instruments; and

   (k)   the spouse of an individual serving in the armed forces of the United States while the individual is stationed within this state, provided:

        (i)   the spouse holds a valid license to practice a regulated occupation or profession issued by any other state or jurisdiction recognized by the division; and

        (ii)   the license is current and the spouse is in good standing in the state of licensure.

(2)   (a)   A practitioner temporarily in this state who is exempted from licensure under Subsection (1) shall comply with each requirement of the licensing jurisdiction from which the practitioner derives authority to practice.

   (b)   Violation of a limitation imposed by this section constitutes grounds for removal of exempt status, denial of license, or other disciplinary proceedings.

(3)   An individual who is licensed under a specific chapter of this title to practice or engage in an occupation or profession may engage in the lawful, professional, and competent practice of that occupation or profession without additional licensure under other chapters of this title, except as otherwise provided by this title.

(4)   Upon the declaration of a national, state, or local emergency, a public health emergency as defined in Section 26-23b-102, or a declaration by the President of the United States or other federal official requesting public health-related activities, the division in collaboration with the board may:

   (a)   suspend the requirements for permanent or temporary licensure of individuals who are licensed in another state for the duration of the emergency while engaged in the scope of practice for which they are licensed in the other state;

   (b)   modify, under the circumstances described in this Subsection (4) and Subsection (5), the scope of practice restrictions under this title for individuals who are licensed under this title as:

        (i)   a physician under Chapter 67, Utah Medical Practice Act, or Chapter 68, Utah Osteopathic Medical Practice Act;

        (ii)   a nurse under Chapter 31b, Nurse Practice Act, or Chapter 31c, Nurse Licensure Compact;

        (iii)   a certified nurse midwife under Chapter 44a, Nurse Midwife Practice Act;

        (iv)   a pharmacist, pharmacy technician, or pharmacy intern under Chapter 17b, Pharmacy Practice Act;

        (v)   a respiratory therapist under Chapter 57, Respiratory Care Practices Act;

        (vi)   a dentist and dental hygienist under Chapter 69, Dentist and Dental Hygienist Practice Act; and

        (vii)   a physician assistant under Chapter 70a, Physician Assistant Act;

   (c)   suspend the requirements for licensure under this title and modify the scope of practice in the circumstances described in this Subsection (4) and Subsection (5) for medical services personnel or paramedics required to be certified under Section 26-8a-302;

   (d)   suspend requirements in Subsections 58-17b-620(3) through (6) which require certain prescriptive procedures;

      (e)   exempt or modify the requirement for licensure of an individual who is activated as a member of a medical reserve corps during a time of emergency as provided in Section 26A-1-126; and

      (f)   exempt or modify the requirement for licensure of an individual who is registered as a volunteer health practitioner as provided in Title 26, Chapter 49, Uniform Emergency Volunteer Health Practitioners Act.

(5)   Individuals exempt under Subsection (4)(c) and individuals operating under modified scope of practice provisions under Subsection (4)(b):

      (a)   are exempt from licensure or subject to modified scope of practice for the duration of the emergency;

      (b)   must be engaged in the distribution of medicines or medical devices in response to the emergency or declaration; and

      (c)   must be employed by or volunteering for:

            (i)   a local or state department of health; or

            (ii)   a host entity as defined in Section 26-49-102.

(6)   In accordance with the protocols established under Subsection (8), upon the declaration of a national, state, or local emergency, the Department of Health or a local health department shall coordinate with public safety authorities as defined in Subsection 26-23b-110(1) and may:

      (a)   use a vaccine, antiviral, antibiotic, or other prescription medication that is not a controlled substance to prevent or treat a disease or condition that gave rise to, or was a consequence of, the emergency; or

      (b)   distribute a vaccine, antiviral, antibiotic, or other prescription medication that is not a controlled substance:

            (i)   if necessary, to replenish a commercial pharmacy in the event that the commercial pharmacy's normal source of the vaccine, antiviral, antibiotic, or other prescription medication is exhausted; or

            (ii)   for dispensing or direct administration to treat the disease or condition that gave rise to, or was a consequence of, the emergency by:

                  (A)   a pharmacy;

                  (B)   a prescribing practitioner;

                  (C)   a licensed health care facility;

                  (D)   a federally qualified community health clinic; or

                  (E)   a governmental entity for use by a community more than 50 miles from a person described in Subsections (6)(b)(ii)(A) through (D).

(7)   In accordance with protocols established under Subsection (8), upon the declaration of a national, state, or local emergency, the Department of Health shall coordinate the distribution of medications:

      (a)   received from the strategic national stockpile to local health departments; and

      (b)   from local health departments to emergency personnel within the local health departments' geographic region.

(8)   The Department of Health shall establish by rule, made in accordance with Title 63G, Chapter 3, Utah Administrative Rulemaking Act, protocols for administering, dispensing, and distributing

a vaccine, an antiviral, an antibiotic, or other prescription medication that is not a controlled substance in the event of a declaration of a national, state, or local emergency. The protocol shall establish procedures for the Department of Health or a local health department to:

(a)   coordinate the distribution of:

(i)   a vaccine, an antiviral, an antibiotic, or other prescription medication that is not a controlled substance received by the Department of Health from the strategic national stockpile to local health departments; and

(ii)   a vaccine, an antiviral, an antibiotic, or other non-controlled prescription medication received by a local health department to emergency personnel within the local health department's geographic region;

(b)   authorize the dispensing, administration, or distribution of a vaccine, an antiviral, an antibiotic, or other prescription medication that is not a controlled substance to the contact of a patient, as defined in Section 26-6-2, without a patient-practitioner relationship, if the contact's condition is the same as that of the physician's patient; and

(c)   authorize the administration, distribution, or dispensing of a vaccine, an antiviral, an antibiotic, or other non-controlled prescription medication to an individual who:

(i)   is working in a triage situation;

(ii)   is receiving preventative or medical treatment in a triage situation;

(iii)   does not have coverage for the prescription in the individual's health insurance plan;

(iv)   is involved in the delivery of medical or other emergency services in response to the declared national, state, or local emergency; or

(v)   otherwise has a direct impact on public health.

(9)   The Department of Health shall give notice to the division upon implementation of the protocol established under Subsection (8).

Amended by Chapter 150, 2012 General Session

58-1-308 Term of license—Expiration of license—Renewal of license—Reinstatement of license—Application procedures.

(1)   (a)   Each license issued under this title shall be issued in accordance with a two-year renewal cycle established by rule.

(b)   A renewal period may be extended or shortened by as much as one year to maintain established renewal cycles or to change an established renewal cycle.

(2)   (a)   The expiration date of a license shall be shown on the license.

(b)   A license that is not renewed prior to the expiration date shown on the license automatically expires.

(c)   A license automatically expires prior to the expiration date shown on the license upon the death of a licensee who is a natural person, or upon the dissolution of a licensee that is a partnership, corporation, or other business entity.

(d)   If the existence of a dissolved partnership, corporation, or other business entity is reinstated prior to the expiration date shown upon the entity's expired license issued by the division, the division shall, upon written application, reinstate the applicant's license, unless it finds that the applicant no longer meets the qualifications for licensure.

(e)   Expiration of licensure is not an adjudicative proceeding under Title 63G, Chapter 4, Administrative Procedures Act.

(3)   (a)   The division shall notify each licensee in accordance with procedures established by rule that the licensee's license is due for renewal and that unless an application for renewal is received by the division by the expiration date shown on the license, together with the appropriate renewal fee and documentation showing completion of or compliance with renewal qualifications, the license will not be renewed.

        (b)   Examples of renewal qualifications which by statute or rule the division may require the licensee to document completion of or compliance with include:

            (i)   continuing education;

            (ii)   continuing competency;

            (iii)   quality assurance;

            (iv)   utilization plan and protocol;

            (v)   financial responsibility;

            (vi)   certification renewal; and

            (vii)   calibration of equipment.

(4)   (a)   (i)   An application for renewal that complies with Subsection (3) is complete.

            (ii)   A renewed license shall be issued to applicants who submit a complete application, unless it is apparent to the division that the applicant no longer meets the qualifications for continued licensure.

        (b)   (i)   The division may evaluate or verify documentation showing completion of or compliance with renewal requirements on an entire population or a random sample basis, and may be assisted by advisory peer committees.

            (ii)   If necessary, the division may complete its evaluation or verification subsequent to renewal and, if appropriate, pursue action to suspend or revoke the license of a licensee who no longer meets the qualifications for continued licensure.

        (c)   The application procedures specified in Subsection 58-1-301(2), apply to renewal applications to the extent they are not in conflict with this section.

(5)   (a)   Any license that is not renewed may be reinstated at any time within two years after nonrenewal upon submission of an application for reinstatement, payment of the renewal fee together with a reinstatement fee determined by the department under Section 63J-1-504, and upon submission of documentation showing completion of or compliance with renewal qualifications.

        (b)   The application procedures specified in Subsection 58-1-301(2) apply to the reinstatement applications to the extent they are not in conflict with this section.

        (c)   Except as otherwise provided by rule, a license that is reinstated no later than 120 days after it expires shall be retroactively reinstated to the date it expired.

(6)   (a)   If not reinstated within two years, the holder may obtain a license only if the holder meets requirements provided by the division by rule or by statute for a new license.

        (b)   Each licensee under this title who has been active in the licensed occupation or profession while in the full-time employ of the United States government or under license to practice that occupation or profession in any other state or territory of the United States may reinstate the licensee's license without taking an examination by submitting an application for reinstatement, paying the current annual renewal fee and the reinstatement fee, and submitting documentation showing completion of or compliance with any renewal qualifications at any time within six months after reestablishing domicile within Utah or terminating full-time government service.

Amended by Chapter 183, 2009 General Session

58-1-309 Laws and rules examination.

In addition to qualifications for licensure or renewal of licensure enumerated in specific practice acts under this title, the division may by rule require an applicant to pass an examination of the laws and rules relevant to the occupation or profession to ensure familiarity with these laws and rules.

Enacted by Chapter 297, 1993 General Session

Part 4 - License Denial

58-1-401 Grounds for denial of license—Disciplinary proceedings—Time limitations—Sanctions.

(1)   The division shall refuse to issue a license to an applicant and shall refuse to renew or shall revoke, suspend, restrict, place on probation, or otherwise act upon the license of a licensee who does not meet the qualifications for licensure under this title.

(2)   The division may refuse to issue a license to an applicant and may refuse to renew or may revoke, suspend, restrict, place on probation, issue a public reprimand to, or otherwise act upon the license of a licensee for the following reasons:

    (a)   the applicant or licensee has engaged in unprofessional conduct, as defined by statute or rule under this title;

    (b)   the applicant or licensee has engaged in unlawful conduct as defined by statute under this title;

    (c)   the applicant or licensee has been determined to be mentally incompetent by a court of competent jurisdiction; or

    (d)   the applicant or licensee is unable to practice the occupation or profession with reasonable skill and safety because of illness, drunkenness, excessive use of drugs, narcotics, chemicals, or other type of material, or as a result of a mental or physical condition, when the condition demonstrates a threat or potential threat to the public health, safety, or welfare.

(3)   A licensee whose license to practice an occupation or profession regulated by this title has been suspended, revoked, placed on probation, or restricted may apply for reinstatement of the license at reasonable intervals and upon compliance with conditions imposed upon the licensee by statute, rule, or terms of the license suspension, revocation, probation, or restriction.

(4)   The division may issue cease and desist orders to:

    (a)   a licensee or applicant who may be disciplined under Subsection (1) or (2);

    (b)   a person who engages in or represents that the person is engaged in an occupation or profession regulated under this title; and

    (c)   a person who otherwise violates this title or a rule adopted under this title.

(5)   The division may impose an administrative penalty in accordance with Section 58-1-502.

(6)   (a)   The division may not take disciplinary action against a person for unprofessional or unlawful conduct under this title, unless the division enters into a stipulated agreement or initiates an adjudicative proceeding regarding the conduct within four years after the conduct is reported to the division, except under Subsection (6)(b).

(b)   The division may not take disciplinary action against a person for unprofessional or unlawful conduct more than 10 years after the occurrence of the conduct, unless the proceeding is in response to a civil or criminal judgment or settlement and the proceeding is initiated within one year following the judgment or settlement.

Amended by Chapter 262, 2013 General Session

58-1-402 Administrative review—Special appeals boards.

(1)   (a)   Any applicant who has been denied a license to practice on the basis of credentials, character, or failure to pass a required examination, or who has been refused renewal or reinstatement of a license to practice on the basis that the applicant does not meet qualifications for continued licensure in any occupation or profession under the jurisdiction of the division may submit a request for agency review to the executive director within 30 days following notification of the denial of a license or refusal to renew or reinstate a license.

(b)   The executive director shall determine whether the circumstances for denying an application for an initial license or for renewal or reinstatement of a license would justify calling a special appeals board under Subsection (2). The executive director's decision is not subject to agency review.

(2)   A special appeals board shall consist of three members appointed by the executive director as follows:

(a)   one member from the occupation or profession in question who is not on the board of that occupation or profession;

(b)   one member from the general public who is neither an attorney nor a practitioner in an occupation or profession regulated by the division; and

(c)   one member who is a resident lawyer currently licensed to practice law in this state who shall serve as chair of the special appeals board.

(3)   The special appeals board shall comply with the procedures and requirements of Title 63G, Chapter 4, Administrative Procedures Act, in its proceedings.

(4)   (a)   Within a reasonable amount of time following the conclusion of a hearing before a special appeals board, the board shall enter an order based upon the record developed at the hearing. The order shall state whether a legal basis exists for denying the application for an initial license or for renewal or reinstatement of a license that is the subject of the appeal. The order is not subject to further agency review.

(b)   The division or the applicant may obtain judicial review of the decision of the special appeals board in accordance with Sections 63G-4-401 and 63G-4-403.

(5)   A member may not receive compensation or benefits for the member's service, but may receive per diem and travel expenses in accordance with:

(a)   Section 63A-3-106;

(b)   Section 63A-3-107; and

(c)   rules made by the Division of Finance pursuant to Sections 63A-3-106 and 63A-3-107.

(6)   If an applicant under Subsection (1) is not given a special appeals board, the applicant shall be given agency review under the ordinary agency review procedures specified by rule.

Amended by Chapter 286, 2010 General Session

58-1-403 Minimum 90-day suspension.

A license may not be reinstated subsequent to action taken under Section 58-1-401 within 90 days after the action has been taken, unless the division in collaboration with the appropriate board imposes other conditions.

Renumbered and Amended by Chapter 297, 1993 General Session

58-1-404 Diversion—Procedure.

(1)   As used in this section, "diversion" means suspending action to discipline a licensee who is or could be charged in a Notice of Agency Action with certain offenses within the category of unprofessional or unlawful conduct on the condition that the licensee agrees to participate in an educational or rehabilitation program or fulfill some other condition.

(2)   (a)   (i)   The director may establish a diversion advisory committee for each occupation or profession or similar groups of occupations or professions licensed by the division.

            (ii)   The committees shall assist the director in the administration of this section.

        (b)   (i)   Each committee shall consist of at least three licensees from the same or similar occupation or profession as the person whose conduct is the subject of the committee's consideration.

            (ii)   The director shall appoint the members of a diversion advisory committee from nominations submitted by the corresponding board established for the same or similar occupation or profession under Section 58-1-201 or from other qualified nominees developed by or submitted to the division.

            (iii)   Committee members may not serve concurrently as members of the corresponding board.

            (iv)   Committee members shall serve voluntarily without remuneration.

            (v)   The director may:

                (A)   dissolve a diversion advisory committee;

                (B)   remove or request the replacement of a member of a committee; and

                (C)   establish procedures that are necessary and proper for a committee's administration.

(3)   The director may, after consultation with the appropriate diversion advisory committee and by written agreement with the licensee, divert the licensee to a diversion program:

        (a)   at any time after receipt by the division of a complaint against the licensee when no adjudicative proceeding has been commenced;

        (b)   at any time prior to the conclusion of a hearing under Section 63G-4-206 when an adjudicative proceeding has been commenced against the licensee; or

        (c)   after a self-referral by a licensee who is not the subject of a current investigation, complaint, or adjudicative proceeding.

(4)   (a)   In accordance with Title 63G, Chapter 3, Utah Administrative Rulemaking Act, the division shall define by rule the particular offenses within the category of unprofessional or unlawful conduct that may be subject to diversion.

        (b)   A licensee may be eligible for a diversion program only once for the same or similar offense, whether the diversion program was in this state or another jurisdiction, and is not eligible if previously disciplined by the division, by a licensing agency of another state, or by a federal government agency for the same or a similar offense.

(c)   The term of a diversion agreement shall be five years or less, but may be extended for an additional period of time as agreed to by the parties in writing.

(d)   A decision by the director not to divert a licensee is not subject to appeal or judicial review.

(5)   A licensee may be represented by counsel:

(a)   during the negotiations for diversion;

(b)   at the time of the execution of the diversion agreement; and

(c)   at each hearing before the director relating to a diversion program.

(6)   (a)   As used in this section, "diversion agreement" means a written agreement between the division, through its director, and the licensee, which specifies formal terms and conditions the licensee must fulfill in order to comply with the diversion program.

(b)   (i)   A diversion agreement shall contain a full detailed statement of the requirements agreed to by the licensee and a full detailed stipulation of the facts upon which the diversion agreement is premised.

(ii)   The facts stipulated in the diversion agreement shall constitute binding admissions of the licensee:

(A)   in a proceeding under Subsection (6)(c) or (6)(d) to terminate the diversion agreement and impose disciplinary sanctions against the licensee; and

(B)   in a disciplinary proceeding based on unprofessional or unlawful conduct that is not the basis of the diversion agreement.

(c)   The diversion agreement shall provide that if the licensee makes an intentional material misrepresentation of fact in the stipulation of facts contained in the diversion agreement, the director shall initiate the procedures set forth in Subsection (13) to terminate the diversion agreement and issue an order of license revocation.

(d)   (i)   The diversion agreement shall provide that if the licensee fails to comply with its terms, the director shall initiate the procedures set forth in Subsection (14) to terminate the diversion agreement and issue an order of license suspension, which shall be stayed in favor of an order of probation having the same terms as those that comprised the diversion agreement.

(ii)   The division may waive and not include as probationary requirements each term of the diversion agreement it does not consider necessary to protect the public.

(iii)   The term of the order of probation shall be as provided in Subsection (14)(c)(ii).

(e)   The division director may not approve a diversion agreement unless the licensee, as part of the diversion agreement:

(i)   knowingly and intelligently waives the right to a hearing under Title 63G, Chapter 4, Administrative Procedures Act, for the conduct upon which the diversion agreement was premised;

(ii)   agrees to be subject to the procedures and remedies set forth in this section;

(iii)   acknowledges an understanding of the consequences of making an intentional misrepresentation of fact in the stipulation of facts contained in the diversion agreement; and

(iv)   acknowledges an understanding of the consequences of failing to comply with the terms of the diversion agreement.

(7)   (a)   If the division and the licensee enter into a diversion agreement after the division has commenced an adjudicative proceeding against the licensee, the director shall stay that proceeding pending completion of the diversion agreement.

        (b)   The order staying the adjudicative proceeding shall be filed in that proceeding and may reference the diversion agreement.

(8)   (a)   Upon successful completion of a diversion agreement, the director shall dismiss each charge under the director's jurisdiction of unprofessional or unlawful conduct that was filed against the licensee.

        (b)   Whether or not an adjudicative proceeding had been commenced against the licensee, the division may not thereafter subject the licensee to disciplinary action for the conduct that formed the basis of the completed diversion agreement.

        (c)   Neither the execution of a diversion agreement nor the dismissal of filed charges constitute disciplinary action, and no report of either may be made to disciplinary databases.

        (d)   The division may consider the completion of a diversion program and the contents of the diversion agreement in determining the appropriate disciplinary action if the licensee is charged in the future with the same or similar conduct.

        (e)   The order of dismissal shall be filed in the adjudicative proceeding in which the misconduct was charged and may reference the diversion agreement.

(9)   (a)   Acceptance of the licensee into diversion does not preclude the division from investigating or continuing to investigate the licensee for unlawful or unprofessional conduct committed before, during, or after participation in the diversion program.

        (b)   Acceptance of the licensee into diversion does not preclude the division from taking disciplinary action or continuing to take disciplinary action against the licensee for unlawful or unprofessional conduct committed before, during, or after participation in the diversion program, except for that conduct that formed the basis for the diversion agreement.

        (c)   A licensee terminated from the diversion program for failure to comply with the diversion agreement is subject to disciplinary action by the division for acts committed before, during, and after participation in the diversion program, including violations identified in the diversion agreement.

(10)   The classification, retention, and disclosure of records relating to a licensee's participation in the diversion program is governed by Title 63G, Chapter 2, Government Records Access and Management Act, except that a provision in the diversion agreement that addresses access to or release of diversion records regarding the licensee shall govern the access to and release of those records.

(11)   Notwithstanding any other provision of this section, the fact that the licensee completed a diversion program and the contents of the diversion agreement itself may be considered by the division in determining the appropriate disciplinary action if the licensee is charged in the future with the same or similar conduct.

(12)   Meetings regarding the diversion program are not subject to Title 52, Chapter 4, Open and Public Meetings Act.

(13)   (a)   If, during the course of the diversion agreement, information is brought to the attention of the director that the licensee made an intentional material misrepresentation of fact in the stipulation of facts contained in the diversion agreement, the director shall cause to be served upon the licensee an order to show cause specifying the information relied upon by the director and setting a time and place for a hearing to determine whether or

not the licensee made the intentional material misrepresentation of fact and whether the agreement should be terminated on that ground.

(b)   Proceedings to terminate a diversion agreement on the grounds that the licensee made an intentional material misrepresentation of fact in the stipulation of facts contained in the diversion agreement and to issue an order of license revocation shall comply with Title 63G, Chapter 4, Administrative Procedures Act, except as follows:

    (i)   the notice of agency action shall be in the form of an order to show cause, which shall contain all of the information specified in Subsection 63G-4-201(2), except a statement that a written response to the order to show cause is required;

    (ii)   no written response to the order to show cause is required;

    (iii)   discovery is prohibited, but the division may issue subpoenas or other orders to compel production of necessary evidence on behalf of either party and all parties shall have access to information contained in the division's diversion file to the extent permitted by law;

    (iv)   the hearing shall be held only after timely notice to all parties; and

    (v)   an agency review or reconsideration of an order terminating a diversion agreement or of an order of license revocation pursuant to this Subsection (13) shall be limited to the division director's findings of fact, conclusions of law, and order that arose out of the order to show cause proceeding.

(c)   Upon finding the licensee made an intentional material misrepresentation of fact in the stipulation of facts contained in the diversion agreement and that terminating the agreement is in the best interest of the public, and issuing an order to that effect, the director shall issue an order of license revocation, revoking the licensee's professional license.

(d)   The order terminating the diversion agreement and the order of license revocation shall include findings of fact and conclusions of law as determined by the director following the hearing or as otherwise stipulated and agreed to by the parties.

(e)   If the diversion agreement being terminated was entered into after the division had commenced an adjudicative proceeding against the licensee, that adjudicative proceeding shall be considered to be merged into the order of license revocation and it may not constitute a basis for a separate disciplinary action against the licensee.

(f)   The order terminating the diversion agreement and the order of license revocation shall notify the licensee of the right to request agency review or reconsideration.

(14)   (a)   If, during the course of the diversion agreement, information is brought to the attention of the director that the licensee has violated the diversion agreement and if it appears in the best interest of the public to proceed with charges, the director, after consultation with the diversion advisory committee, shall cause to be served upon the licensee an order to show cause specifying the facts relied upon by the director and setting a time and place for a hearing to determine whether or not the licensee has violated the diversion agreement and whether the agreement should be terminated.

    (b)   Proceedings to terminate a diversion agreement as described in Subsection (14)(c) shall comply with Title 63G, Chapter 4, Administrative Procedures Act, except as follows:

        (i)   the notice of agency action shall be in the form of an order to show cause, which shall contain all of the information specified in Subsection 63G-4-201(2), except a statement that a written response to the order to show cause is required;

(ii)   no written response to the order to show cause shall be required;

(iii)   discovery is prohibited, but the division may issue subpoenas or other orders to compel production of necessary evidence on behalf of either party and all parties shall have access to information contained in the division's diversion file to the extent permitted by law;

(iv)   the hearing shall be held only after timely notice to all parties; and

(v)   an agency review or reconsideration of an order terminating a diversion agreement or of an order of license suspension and probation pursuant to this Subsection (14) shall be limited to the division director's findings of fact, conclusions of law, and order that arose out of the order to show cause proceeding.

(c)   (i)   Upon finding the licensee has violated the diversion agreement by conduct that is entirely the same or similar to the conduct upon which the diversion agreement is premised, or by violating a compliance provision contained in the diversion agreement, and further finding that terminating the agreement is in the best interest of the public, and after issuing an order to that effect, the director shall issue an order of probation, consisting of the same terms as those which comprised the diversion agreement.

(ii)   Upon finding that the licensee has violated the diversion agreement by conduct that includes conduct that is not the same or similar to the conduct upon which the diversion agreement is premised, and further finding that terminating the agreement is in the best interest of the public, and after issuing an order to that effect, the director shall, after notice of opportunity to be heard is provided to the licensee, issue an order imposing each disciplinary sanction the division deems appropriate, including suspension, public reprimand, a fine, probation, or revocation of licensure.

(iii)   The period of probation shall be the time period which remained under the diversion agreement, or five years from the date of the order of license suspension and probation, whichever is longer, unless otherwise agreed by the parties.

(iv)   The period of probation is tolled during the time the licensee does not have an active license in the state.

(d)   (i)   The order terminating the diversion agreement and the order of license suspension and probation shall include findings of fact and conclusions of law as determined by the director following the hearing or as otherwise stipulated and agreed to by the parties.

(ii)   The findings of fact may include those facts to which the licensee stipulated in the diversion agreement and additional facts as the director may determine in the course of the hearing.

(e)   If the diversion agreement being terminated was entered into after the division had commenced an adjudicative proceeding against the licensee, that adjudicative proceeding shall be considered to be merged into the order of license suspension and probation and it may not constitute a basis for separate disciplinary action against the licensee.

(f)   The order terminating the diversion agreement and the order of license suspension and probation shall notify the licensee of the right to request agency review or reconsideration.

(g)   (i)   The terms and conditions of the order of license suspension and probation may be amended by order of the director, pursuant to motion or stipulation of the parties.

(ii)   The order of the director on the motion shall not be subject to agency review, but is subject to agency reconsideration under Section 63G-4-302.

(h) (i) If, during the course of probation, the director has reason to believe the licensee has violated the order of probation, the director shall cause to be served upon the licensee an order to show cause why the probation should not be terminated and why each additional disciplinary sanction the division deems appropriate should not be imposed, including suspension, public reprimand, a fine, or revocation of licensure.

(ii) The order to show cause shall specify the facts relied upon by the director and shall set a time and place for hearing before the director to determine whether or not the licensee has violated the order of probation, whether that order should be terminated, and why each additional disciplinary sanction the division deems appropriate should not be imposed, including suspension, public reprimand, a fine, or revocation of licensure.

(15) (a) Nothing in this section precludes the division from issuing an emergency order pursuant to Section 63G-4-502.

(b) If the division issues an emergency order against a licensee who is subject to a diversion agreement with the division, that diversion agreement shall be immediately and automatically terminated upon the issuance of the emergency order, without requiring compliance with the provisions of Title 63G, Chapter 4, Administrative Procedures Act.

(c) (i) A licensee whose diversion agreement has been terminated pursuant to Subsection (15)(b) is entitled, upon request, to a posttermination hearing to challenge the termination of the diversion agreement.

(ii) The request shall be considered a request for agency action and shall comply with the requirements of Subsection 63G-4-201(3).

(iii) The division shall uphold the termination of the diversion agreement if it finds that:

(A) the licensee violated the diversion agreement; and

(B) it is in the best interest of the public to terminate the diversion agreement.

(16) The administrative statute of limitations for taking disciplinary action described in Subsection 58-1-401(6) shall be tolled during a diversion program.

Amended by Chapter 262, 2013 General Session

58-1-405 Provisions of volunteer health or veterinary services—Division authority.

In accordance with Section 26-49-205, the division may pursue actions against a volunteer health practitioner operating under Title 26, Chapter 49, Uniform Emergency Volunteer Health Practitioners Act.

Enacted by Chapter 242, 2008 General Session

Part 5 - Unlawful and Unprofessional Conduct - Penalties

58-1-501 Unlawful and unprofessional conduct.

(1) "Unlawful conduct" means conduct, by any person, that is defined as unlawful under this title and includes:

(a) practicing or engaging in, representing oneself to be practicing or engaging in, or attempting to practice or engage in any occupation or profession requiring licensure under this title if the person is:

(i) not licensed to do so or not exempted from licensure under this title; or

      (ii)   restricted from doing so by a suspended, revoked, restricted, temporary, probationary, or inactive license;

  (b)   (i)   impersonating another licensee or practicing an occupation or profession under a false or assumed name, except as permitted by law; or

      (ii)   for a licensee who has had a license under this title reinstated following disciplinary action, practicing the same occupation or profession using a different name than the name used before the disciplinary action, except as permitted by law and after notice to, and approval by, the division;

  (c)   knowingly employing any other person to practice or engage in or attempt to practice or engage in any occupation or profession licensed under this title if the employee is not licensed to do so under this title;

  (d)   knowingly permitting the person's authority to practice or engage in any occupation or profession licensed under this title to be used by another, except as permitted by law;

  (e)   obtaining a passing score on a licensure examination, applying for or obtaining a license, or otherwise dealing with the division or a licensing board through the use of fraud, forgery, or intentional deception, misrepresentation, misstatement, or omission; or

  (f)   (i)   issuing, or aiding and abetting in the issuance of, an order or prescription for a drug or device to a person located in this state:

        (A)   without prescriptive authority conferred by a license issued under this title, or by an exemption to licensure under this title; or

        (B)   with prescriptive authority conferred by an exception issued under this title or a multistate practice privilege recognized under this title, if the prescription was issued without first obtaining information, in the usual course of professional practice, that is sufficient to establish a diagnosis, to identify underlying conditions, and to identify contraindications to the proposed treatment; and

      (ii)   Subsection (1)(f)(i) does not apply to treatment rendered in an emergency, on-call or cross coverage situation, provided that the person who issues the prescription has prescriptive authority conferred by a license under this title, or is exempt from licensure under this title.

(2)   "Unprofessional conduct" means conduct, by a licensee or applicant, that is defined as unprofessional conduct under this title or under any rule adopted under this title and includes:

  (a)   violating, or aiding or abetting any other person to violate, any statute, rule, or order regulating an occupation or profession under this title;

  (b)   violating, or aiding or abetting any other person to violate, any generally accepted professional or ethical standard applicable to an occupation or profession regulated under this title;

  (c)   engaging in conduct that results in conviction, a plea of nolo contendere, or a plea of guilty or nolo contendere which is held in abeyance pending the successful completion of probation with respect to a crime of moral turpitude or any other crime that, when considered with the functions and duties of the occupation or profession for which the license was issued or is to be issued, bears a reasonable relationship to the licensee's or applicant's ability to safely or competently practice the occupation or profession;

  (d)   engaging in conduct that results in disciplinary action, including reprimand, censure, diversion, probation, suspension, or revocation, by any other licensing or regulatory authority having jurisdiction over the licensee or applicant in the same occupation or profession if the conduct would, in this state, constitute grounds for denial of licensure or disciplinary proceedings under Section 58-1-401;

(e)   engaging in conduct, including the use of intoxicants, drugs, narcotics, or similar chemicals, to the extent that the conduct does, or might reasonably be considered to, impair the ability of the licensee or applicant to safely engage in the occupation or profession;

(f)   practicing or attempting to practice an occupation or profession regulated under this title despite being physically or mentally unfit to do so;

(g)   practicing or attempting to practice an occupation or profession regulated under this title through gross incompetence, gross negligence, or a pattern of incompetency or negligence;

(h)   practicing or attempting to practice an occupation or profession requiring licensure under this title by any form of action or communication which is false, misleading, deceptive, or fraudulent;

(i)   practicing or attempting to practice an occupation or profession regulated under this title beyond the scope of the licensee's competency, abilities, or education;

(j)   practicing or attempting to practice an occupation or profession regulated under this title beyond the scope of the licensee's license;

(k)   verbally, physically, mentally, or sexually abusing or exploiting any person through conduct connected with the licensee's practice under this title or otherwise facilitated by the licensee's license;

(l)   acting as a supervisor without meeting the qualification requirements for that position that are defined by statute or rule;

(m)   issuing, or aiding and abetting in the issuance of, an order or prescription for a drug or device:

    (i)   without first obtaining information in the usual course of professional practice, that is sufficient to establish a diagnosis, to identify conditions, and to identify contraindications to the proposed treatment; or

    (ii)   with prescriptive authority conferred by an exception issued under this title, or a multi-state practice privilege recognized under this title, if the prescription was issued without first obtaining information, in the usual course of professional practice, that is sufficient to establish a diagnosis, to identify underlying conditions, and to identify contraindications to the proposed treatment;

(n)   violating a provision of Section 58-1-501.5; or

(o)   violating the terms of an order governing a license.

Amended by Chapter 408, 2014 General Session

58-1-501.3 Health professional prescribing exceptions for expedited partner therapy for sexually transmitted diseases.

(1)   For purposes of this section:

    (a)   "Drug to treat a sexually transmitted disease" means a drug:

        (i)   as defined in Section 58-17b-102; and

        (ii)   that is:

            (A)   an antibiotic; and

            (B)   prescribed in accordance with guidelines from the Centers for Disease Control and Prevention for patient delivered expedited partner therapy in the management of sexually transmitted disease.

    (b)   "Partner" means a person:

        (i)   with whom a practitioner does not have a bonafide practitioner-patient relationship; and

        (ii)   who is identified as, or claims to be a sexual partner of a patient.

    (c)   "Patient" means a person who:

        (i)   has a sexually transmitted disease; and

        (ii)   has a bonafide practitioner-patient relationship with a practitioner.

    (d)   "Sexually transmitted disease" means:

        (i)   gonorrhea; or

        (ii)   chlamydia.

(2)   This section does not require a practitioner or a licensee under this chapter to prescribe or dispense a drug to treat a sexually transmitted disease for patient delivered expedited partner therapy. A practitioner's or licensee's decision to use expedited partner therapy as allowed by this section is voluntary.

(3)   Notwithstanding Sections 58-1-501, 58-17b-501, and 58-17b-502, it is not unlawful conduct or unprofessional conduct, and it does not violate the provisions of this chapter if:

    (a)   a practitioner, in accordance with this Subsection (3):

        (i)   issues a prescription for a drug to treat a sexually transmitted disease to a partner by:

            (A)   writing "partner of (patient name)" on the prescription order; and

            (B)   giving the partner's prescription to the patient for subsequent use by the partner; or

        (ii)   notwithstanding Section 58-17b-610, dispenses a drug sample to treat a sexually transmitted disease to the patient for the subsequent use of the partner; or

    (b)   a pharmacist, in accordance with this Subsection (3), dispenses a prescription drug for the treatment of a sexually transmitted disease to:

        (i)   a person who:

            (A)   claims to be a partner; and

            (B)   presents a prescription for the drug to the pharmacist which is written for the unnamed partner of a named patient;

        (ii)   the patient for the subsequent use by the unnamed partner; or

        (iii)   an agent of the patient or partner.

(4)   (a)   For purposes of Subsection (3), and notwithstanding Section 58-17b-602:

        (i)   the partner does not have to be identified on the prescription order by information that would disclose the identity of the partner; and

        (ii)   when dispensing a drug to treat a sexually transmitted disease directly to the partner, the patient's identifying information may, but does not need to, be included on the partner's drug label.

(b) Information provided by a pharmacist to a patient or the patient's agent for subsequent use by a partner satisfies the requirements of patient counseling for both the patient and the partner under Section 58-17b-613.

(5) (a) The Legislature finds that the prevention and treatment of sexually transmitted diseases in the state is a compelling public health issue.

(b) A practitioner or licensee under this chapter is not liable for a medical malpractice action if the use of expedited partner therapy is in compliance with this section, except for those acts which are grossly negligent or willful and wanton.

Enacted by Chapter 151, 2009 General Session

58-1-501.5 Anatomic pathology services—Billing violations.

(1) As used in this section, the following definitions apply:

(a) (i) "Anatomic pathology services" including "technical or professional component of anatomic pathology services" means:

(A) histopathology or surgical pathology, meaning the gross examination of, histologic processing of, or microscopic examination of human organ tissue performed by a physician or under the supervision of a physician;

(B) cytopathology, meaning the examination of human cells, from fluids, aspirates, washings, brushings, or smears, including the pap test examination performed by a physician or under the supervision of a physician;

(C) hematology, meaning the microscopic evaluation of human bone marrow aspirates and biopsies performed by a physician or under the supervision of a physician and peripheral human blood smears when the attending or treating physician or other practitioner of the healing arts or a technologist requests that a blood smear be reviewed by a pathologist;

(D) subcellular pathology and molecular pathology; and

(E) blood bank services performed by a pathologist.

(ii) "Anatomic pathology services" including "technical or professional component of anatomic pathology services" does not include the initial collection or packaging of a sample for transport.

(b) "Clinical laboratory" or "laboratory" means a facility for the biological, microbiological, serological, chemical, immunohematological, hematological, biophysical, cytological, pathological, or other examination of materials derived from the human body for the purpose of providing information for the diagnosis, prevention, or treatment of any disease or impairment of human beings or the assessment of the health of human beings.

(c) "Health care facility" has the meaning provided in Section 26-21-2.

(d) "Health care provider" includes:

(i) an advanced practice registered nurse licensed under Chapter 31b, Nurse Practice Act;

(ii) a chiropractic physician licensed under Chapter 73, Chiropractic Physician Practice Act;

(iii) a dentist licensed under Chapter 69, Dentist and Dental Hygienist Practice Act;

(iv) a nurse midwife licensed under Chapter 44a, Nurse Midwife Practice Act;

           (v)   an optometrist licensed under Chapter 16a, Utah Optometry Practice Act;

           (vi)   an osteopathic physician and surgeon licensed under Chapter 68, Utah Osteopathic Medical Practice Act;

           (vii)   a podiatric physician licensed under Chapter 5a, Podiatric Physician Licensing Act;

           (viii)   a physician and surgeon licensed under Chapter 67, Utah Medical Practice Act; and

           (ix)   a physician assistant licensed under Chapter 70a, Physician Assistant Act.

      (e)   "Insurer" includes:

           (i)   any entity offering accident and health insurance as defined in Section 31A-1-301;

           (ii)   workers' compensation benefits;

           (iii)   a health maintenance organization; or

           (iv)   any self-insurance, as defined in Section 31A-1-301, that offers health care insurance or benefits.

(2)   (a)   A health care provider who orders anatomic pathology services for a patient from an independent physician or laboratory may not directly or indirectly mark up, charge a commission, or make a profit on the anatomic pathology service provided by the independent physician or laboratory.

      (b)   Nothing in Subsection (2)(a):

           (i)   restricts the ability of a health care provider, who has not performed or supervised either the technical or professional component of the anatomic pathology service, to obtain payment for services related solely to the collection and packaging of a sample and administrative billing costs; or

           (ii)   restricts the ability of the lab function in the Department of Health to bill for services.

(3)   A health care provider when billing a patient directly for anatomic pathology services provided by an independent physician or laboratory shall furnish an itemized bill which conforms with the billing practices of the American Medical Association that conspicuously discloses the charge for each anatomic pathology service, physician or laboratory name, and address for each anatomic pathology service rendered to the patient by the physician or laboratory that performed the anatomic pathology service.

(4)   The disclosure to be made under Subsection (3) shall not be required when the anatomic pathology service is being ordered by a hospital, a laboratory performing either the professional or technical component of the service, or a physician performing either the professional or technical component of the service, a public health clinic, or a state or federal agency.

(5)   Failure to comply with the requirements of this section shall be considered to be unprofessional conduct.

Amended by Chapter 250, 2008 General Session

58-1-501.6 Health care provider advertisements and disclosure—Unprofessional conduct.

For purposes of this section:

(1)   (a)   "Advertisement" includes:

           (i)   billboards;

           (ii)   written documents such as:

               (A)   brochures;

               (B)   pamphlets;

(C)   direct mail solicitations;

(D)   radio, television, and telephone solicitation scripts; and

(E)   telephone directories;

(iii)   media, including television, radio, and Internet websites; and

(iv)   any other means of promotion intended to directly or indirectly induce a person to enter into an agreement for services with a health care provider.

(b)   "Advertisement" does not include materials that provide information about health care provider networks established by health insurance carriers.

(2)   "Health care provider" means a natural person who is:

(a)   defined as a health care provider in Section 78B-3-403; and

(b)   licensed under this title.

(3)   (a)   This section does not provide authority for a health care provider to advertise the services offered by the health care provider.

(b)   If a health care provider's licensing authority and professional ethics permit the health care provider to advertise, the provisions of this section apply to any advertisement for the health care provider's services, on or after July 1, 2011.

(4)   An advertisement for a health care provider's services that includes the health care provider's name shall identify the license type, as used by the division, under which the health care provider is practicing.

(5)   (a)   A physician licensed under Chapter 67, Utah Medical Practice Act, may comply with the requirements of this section by using any one of the designations in the definitions of "practice of medicine" in Section 58-67-102.

(b)   A physician licensed under Chapter 68, Utah Osteopathic Medical Practice Act, may comply with this section by using any of the designations in the definition of "practice of osteopathic medicine" in Section 58-68-102.

(6)   It is unprofessional conduct if a health care provider violates this section.

Enacted by Chapter 139, 2011 General Session

58-1-501.7 Standards of conduct for prescription drug education—Academic and commercial detailing.

(1)   For purposes of this section:

(a)   "Academic detailing":

(i)   means a health care provider who is licensed under this title to prescribe or dispense a prescription drug and employed by someone other than a pharmaceutical manufacturer:

(A)   for the purpose of countering information provided in commercial detailing; and

(B)   to disseminate educational information about prescription drugs to other health care providers in an effort to better align clinical practice with scientific research; and

(ii)   does not include a health care provider who:

(A)   is disseminating educational information about a prescription drug as part of teaching or supervising students or graduate medical education students at an institution of higher education or through a medical residency program;

                (B)   is disseminating educational information about a prescription drug to a patient or a patient's representative; or

                (C)   is acting within the scope of practice for the health care provider regarding the prescribing or dispensing of a prescription drug.

(b)   "Commercial detailing" means an educational practice employed by a pharmaceutical manufacturer in which clinical information and evidence about a prescription drug is shared with health care professionals.

(c)   "Manufacture" is as defined in Section 58-37-2.

(d)   "Pharmaceutical manufacturer" is a person who manufactures a prescription drug.

(2)   (a)   Except as provided in Subsection (3), the provisions of this section apply to an academic detailer beginning July 1, 2013.

      (b)   An academic detailer and a commercial detailer who educate another health care provider about prescription drugs through written or oral educational material is subject to federal regulations regarding:

            (i)   false and misleading advertising in 21 C.F.R., Part 201 (2007);

            (ii)   prescription drug advertising in 21 C.F.R., Part 202 (2007); and

            (iii)   the federal Office of the Inspector General's Compliance Program Guidance for Pharmaceutical Manufacturers issued in April 2003, as amended.

      (c)   A person who is injured by a violation of this section has a private right of action against a person engaged in academic detailing, if:

            (i)   the actions of the person engaged in academic detailing, that are a violation of this section, are:

                (A)   the result of gross negligence by the person; or

                (B)   willful and wanton behavior by the person; and

            (ii)   the damages to the person are reasonable, foreseeable, and proximately caused by the violations of this section.

(3)   (a)   For purposes of this Subsection, "accident and health insurer":

            (i)   is as defined in Section 31A-1-301; and

            (ii)   includes a self-funded health benefit plan and an administrator for a self-funded health benefit plan.

      (b)   This section does not apply to a person who engages in academic detailing if that person is engaged in academic detailing on behalf of:

            (i)   an accident and health insurer, including when an accident and health insurer contracts with or offers:

                (A)   the state Medicaid program, including the Primary Care Network within the state's Medicaid program;

                (B)   the Children's Health Insurance Program created in Section 26-40-103;

                (C)   the state's high risk insurance program created in Section 31A-29-104;

                (D)   a Medicare plan; and

                (E)   a Medicare supplement plan;

        (ii)   a hospital as defined in Section 26-21-2;

        (iii)   any class of pharmacy as defined in Section 58-17b-102, including any affiliated pharmacies;

        (iv)   an integrated health system as defined in Section 13-5b-102; or

        (v)   a medical clinic.

    (c)   This section does not apply to communicating or disseminating information about a prescription drug for the purpose of conducting research using prescription drugs at a health care facility as defined in Section 26-21-2, or a medical clinic.

Enacted by Chapter 100, 2013 General Session

58-1-501.8 Occupational and professional identification of health care providers—Unlawful and unprofessional conduct—Penalties.

(1)   For purposes of this section:

    (a)   "Badge" means a tag or badge in plain view:

        (i)   attached to a health care provider's clothing; or

        (ii)   hanging from a lanyard around a health care provider's neck.

    (b)   "Clothing" means a health care provider's outermost article of clothing that is visible to others.

    (c)   "Deceptive or misleading conduct" means any affirmative communication or representation that falsely states, describes, holds out, or details an individual's licensure, training, education, or profession.

    (d)   "Health care provider" means a natural person who is:

        (i)   defined as a health care provider in Section 78B-3-403; and

        (ii)   licensed under this title.

    (e)   "Identification" means a badge or stitching, or permanent writing in plain view on clothing that:

        (i)   includes the health care provider's name;

        (ii)   includes the license type held by the health care provider;

        (iii)   is worn in a manner that is visible and apparent to others; and

        (iv)   contains the information required by Subsections (1)(e)(i) and (ii):

           (A)   in a manner and of sufficient size that can be easily read; and

           (B)   on both sides of the badge, unless the badge or tag is attached to clothing in a way that prevents the badge from rotating.

    (f)   "License type" means a designation of the license type that satisfies the requirements of Section 58-1-501.6.

    (g)   "Patient encounter" means an interaction in a health care facility, health care clinic, or office in which a patient can see a health care provider delivering services directly to a patient.

(2)   Beginning January 1, 2015, except as provided in Subsections (3) and (4), a health care provider shall wear identification during any patient encounter.

(3)   A health care provider's identification may be covered if required under sterilization or isolation protocols.

(4)   A health care provider is not required to wear identification:

(a)   if wearing identification would jeopardize the health care provider's safety; or

(b)   (i)   in an office in which:

(A)   the license type and names of all health care providers working in the office are displayed on the office door; or

(B)   each health care provider working in the office has the health care provider's license posted prominently in the office and readily visible to a patient; and

(ii)   if the office is an office:

(A)   of a solo health care provider; or

(B)   of a single type of health care provider.

(5)   An individual who is a student or is in training to obtain a license as a health care provider shall:

(a)   wear identification during patient encounters that identifies the person as in training, or a student, for the particular license type; and

(b)   otherwise comply with the provisions of this section.

(6)   It is unprofessional conduct if a health care provider violates this section.

(7)   It is unlawful conduct if an individual:

(a)   wears identification in a patient encounter that suggests that the individual is practicing or engaging in an occupation or profession that the individual may not lawfully practice or engage in under this title; or

(b)   engages in deceptive or misleading conduct.

(8)   An individual who violates this section is subject to Section 58-1-502.

Enacted by Chapter 99, 2014 General Session

58-1-502 Unlawful and unprofessional conduct—Penalties.

(1)   Unless otherwise specified in this title, a person who violates the unlawful conduct provisions defined in this title is guilty of a class A misdemeanor.

(2)   (a)   In addition to any other statutory penalty for a violation related to a specific occupation or profession regulated by this title, if upon inspection or investigation, the division concludes that a person has violated Subsection 58-1-501(1)(a), (1)(c), or (2)(o), or a rule or order issued with respect to those subsections, and that disciplinary action is appropriate, the director or the director's designee from within the division shall promptly:

(i)   issue a citation to the person according to this section and any pertinent rules;

(ii)   attempt to negotiate a stipulated settlement; or

(iii)   notify the person to appear before an adjudicative proceeding conducted under Title 63G, Chapter 4, Administrative Procedures Act.

(b)   (i)   The division may assess a fine under this Subsection (2) against a person who violates Subsection 58-1-501(1)(a), (1)(c), or (2)(o), or a rule or order issued with respect to those subsections, as evidenced by:

(A)   an uncontested citation;

(B)   a stipulated settlement; or

(C)   a finding of a violation in an adjudicative proceeding.

          (ii)   The division may, in addition to or in lieu of a fine under Subsection (2)(b)(i), order the person to cease and desist from violating Subsection 58-1-501(1)(a), (1)(c), or (2)(o), or a rule or order issued with respect to those subsections.

(c)   Except for a cease and desist order, the division may not assess the licensure sanctions cited in Section 58-1-401 through a citation.

(d)   A citation shall:

          (i)   be in writing;

          (ii)   describe with particularity the nature of the violation, including a reference to the provision of the chapter, rule, or order alleged to have been violated;

          (iii)   clearly state that the recipient must notify the division in writing within 20 calendar days of service of the citation if the recipient wishes to contest the citation at a hearing conducted under Title 63G, Chapter 4, Administrative Procedures Act; and

          (iv)   clearly explain the consequences of failure to timely contest the citation or to make payment of a fine assessed by the citation within the time specified in the citation.

(e)   The division may issue a notice in lieu of a citation.

(f)   (i)   If within 20 calendar days from the service of the citation, the person to whom the citation was issued fails to request a hearing to contest the citation, the citation becomes the final order of the division and is not subject to further agency review.

          (ii)   The period to contest a citation may be extended by the division for cause.

(g)   The division may refuse to issue or renew, suspend, revoke, or place on probation the license of a licensee who fails to comply with a citation after it becomes final.

(h)   The failure of an applicant for licensure to comply with a citation after it becomes final is a ground for denial of license.

(i)   The division may not issue a citation under this section after the expiration of six months following the occurrence of a violation.

(j)   The director or the director's designee shall assess fines according to the following:

          (i)   for the first offense handled pursuant to Subsection (2)(a), a fine of up to $1,000;

          (ii)   for a second offense handled pursuant to Subsection (2)(a), a fine of up to $2,000; and

          (iii)   for each subsequent offense handled pursuant to Subsection (2)(a), a fine of up to $2,000 for each day of continued offense.

(3)   (a)   An action for a first or second offense that has not yet resulted in a final order of the division may not preclude initiation of a subsequent action for a second or subsequent offense during the pendency of a preceding action.

      (b)   The final order on a subsequent action is considered a second or subsequent offense, respectively, provided the preceding action resulted in a first or second offense, respectively.

(4)   (a)   The director may collect a penalty that is not paid by:

          (i)   either referring the matter to a collection agency; or

          (ii)   bringing an action in the district court of the county where the person against whom the penalty is imposed resides or in the county where the office of the director is located.

(b)   A county attorney or the attorney general of the state shall provide legal assistance and advice to the director in an action to collect the penalty.

(c)   A court may award reasonable attorney fees and costs to the division in an action brought by the division to enforce the provisions of this section.

Amended by Chapter 262, 2013 General Session

58-1-503 Maximum civil penalty for violation of court order.

(1)   If any written order issued under this title or if an injunction or temporary restraining order issued by a court of competent jurisdiction relating to this title is violated, the court may impose a civil penalty of not more than $2,000 for each day the written order, injunction, or temporary restraining order is violated, if the person in violation has received notice of the written order, injunction, or temporary restraining order.

(2)   All penalties ordered under this section shall be deposited into the General Fund.

Renumbered and Amended by Chapter 297, 1993 General Session

58-1-504 Court-ordered discipline.

The division shall promptly withhold, suspend, restrict, or reinstate the use of a license issued under this title if so ordered by a court.

Enacted by Chapter 232, 1997 General Session

58-1-505 Cosmetic medical procedure supervisor.

(1)   For purposes of this section and Section 58-1-506:

(a)   "Cosmetic medical facility" means a physician's office or a facility that has a supervisor who performs the supervision required in Section 58-1-506.

(b)   "Supervisor" means:

(i)   a physician with an unrestricted license under Chapter 67, Utah Medical Practice Act, or Chapter 68, Utah Osteopathic Medical Practice Act, who is acting within the scope of the practice of medicine, as defined in Section 58-67-102; and

(ii)   an advanced practice registered nurse with an unrestricted license under Chapter 31b, Nurse Practice Act, who is acting within the scope of practice of advanced practice registered nursing, as defined in Section 58-31b-102.

(2)   (a)   An individual authorized by this title to perform a cosmetic medical procedure shall be supervised by a supervisor when performing a medical procedure.

(b)   Cosmetic medical procedures may only be performed in a cosmetic medical facility.

(c)   A supervisor may delegate the supervisory role only to another individual who is qualified as a supervisor.

Enacted by Chapter 362, 2012 General Session

58-1-506 Supervision of cosmetic medical procedures.

(1)   For purposes of this section:

(a)   "Delegation group A" means the following who are licensed under this title, acting within their respective scope of practice, and qualified under Subsections (2)(f)(i) and (iii):

(i) a physician assistant, if acting under the supervision of a physician and the procedure is included in the delegation of services agreement as defined in Section 58-70a-102;

(ii) a registered nurse;

(iii) a master esthetician; and

(iv) an electrologist, if evaluating for or performing laser hair removal.

(b) "Delegation group B" means:

(i) a practical nurse or an esthetician who is licensed under this title, acting within their respective scope of practice, and qualified under Subsections (2)(f)(i) and (iii); and

(ii) a medical assistant who is qualified under Subsections (2)(f)(i) and (iii).

(c) "Direct cosmetic medical procedure supervision" means the supervisor:

(i) has authorized the procedure to be done on the patient by the supervisee; and

(ii) is present and available for a face-to-face communication with the supervisee when and where a cosmetic medical procedure is performed.

(d) "General cosmetic medical procedure supervision" means the supervisor:

(i) has authorized the procedure to be done on the patient by the supervisee;

(ii) is available in a timely and appropriate manner in person to evaluate and initiate care for a patient with a suspected adverse reaction or complication; and

(iii) is located within 60 minutes or 60 miles of the cosmetic medical facility.

(e) "Indirect cosmetic medical procedure supervision" means the supervisor:

(i) has authorized the procedure to be done on the patient by the supervisee;

(ii) has given written instructions to the person being supervised;

(iii) is present within the cosmetic medical facility in which the person being supervised is providing services; and

(iv) is available to:

(A) provide immediate face-to-face communication with the person being supervised; and

(B) evaluate the patient, as necessary.

(f) "Hair removal review" means:

(i) conducting an in-person, face-to-face interview of a patient based on the responses provided by the patient to a detailed medical history assessment that was prepared by the supervisor;

(ii) evaluating for contraindications and conditions that are part of the treatment plan; and

(iii) if the patient history or patient presentation deviates in any way from the treatment plan, referring the patient to the supervisor and receiving clearance from the supervisor before starting the treatment.

(2) A supervisor supervising a nonablative cosmetic medical procedure for hair removal shall:

(a) have an unrestricted license to practice medicine or advanced practice registered nursing in the state;

(b)   develop the medical treatment plan for the procedure;

(c)   conduct a hair removal review, or delegate the hair removal review to a member of delegation group A, of the patient prior to initiating treatment or a series of treatments;

(d)   personally perform the nonablative cosmetic medical procedure for hair removal, or authorize and delegate the procedure to a member of delegation group A or B;

(e)   during the nonablative cosmetic medical procedure for hair removal provide general cosmetic medical procedure supervision to individuals in delegation group A performing the procedure, except physician assistants, who shall be supervised as provided in Chapter 70a, Physician Assistant Act, and indirect cosmetic medical procedure supervision to individuals in delegation group B performing the procedure; and

(f)   verify that a person to whom the supervisor delegates an evaluation under Subsection (2)(c) or delegates a procedure under Subsection (2)(d) or (3)(b)(ii):

    (i)   has received appropriate training regarding the medical procedures developed under Subsection (2)(b);

    (ii)   has an unrestricted license under this title or is performing under the license of the supervising physician and surgeon; and

    (iii)   has maintained competence to perform the nonablative cosmetic medical procedure through documented education and experience of at least 80 hours, as further defined by rule, regarding:

        (A)   the appropriate standard of care for performing nonablative cosmetic medical procedures;

        (B)   physiology of the skin;

        (C)   skin typing and analysis;

        (D)   skin conditions, disorders, and diseases;

        (E)   pre and post procedure care;

        (F)   infection control;

        (G)   laser and light physics training;

        (H)   laser technologies and applications;

        (I)   safety and maintenance of lasers;

        (J)   cosmetic medical procedures an individual is permitted to perform under this title;

        (K)   recognition and appropriate management of complications from a procedure; and

        (L)   cardio-pulmonary resuscitation (CPR).

(3)   For a nonablative cosmetic medical procedure other than hair removal under Subsection (2):

    (a)   (i)   except as provided in Subsection (3)(a)(ii) and (iii), a physician who has an unrestricted license to practice medicine shall:

        (A)   develop a treatment plan for the nonablative cosmetic medical procedure; and

        (B)   conduct an in-person face-to-face evaluation of the patient prior to the initiation of a treatment protocol or series of treatments;

(ii)   a nurse practitioner who has an unrestricted license for advanced practice registered nursing may perform the evaluation and develop the treatment plan under Subsection (3)(a) (i) for nonablative medical procedures other than tattoo removal; or

(iii)   a physician assistant acting under the supervision of a physician, with the procedure included in the delegation of service agreement as defined in Section 58-70a-102, may perform the evaluation under Subsection (3)(a)(i)(B) for nonablative medical procedures other than tattoo removal; and

(b)   the supervisor supervising the procedure shall:

    (i)   have an unrestricted license to practice medicine or advanced practice registered nursing;

    (ii)   personally perform the nonablative cosmetic medical procedure or:

        (A)   authorize and provide general cosmetic medical procedure supervision for the nonablative cosmetic medical procedure that is performed by a registered nurse or a master esthetician;

        (B)   authorize and provide supervision as provided in Chapter 70a, Physician Assistant Act, for the nonablative cosmetic medical procedure that is performed by a physician assistant, if the procedure is included in the delegation of services agreement; or

        (C)   authorize and provide direct cosmetic medical procedure supervision for the nonablative cosmetic medical procedure that is performed by an esthetician; and

    (iii)   verify that a person to whom the supervisor delegates a procedure under Subsection (3)(b):

        (A)   has received appropriate training regarding the medical procedures to be performed;

        (B)   has an unrestricted license and is acting within their scope of practice under this title; and

        (C)   is qualified under Subsection (2)(f)(iii).

(4)   A supervisor performing or supervising a cosmetic medical procedure under Subsection (2) or (3) shall ensure that:

    (a)   the supervisor's name is prominently posted at the cosmetic medical facility identifying the supervisor;

    (b)   a copy of the supervisor's license is displayed on the wall of the cosmetic medical facility;

    (c)   the patient receives written information with the name and licensing information of the supervisor who is supervising the nonablative cosmetic medical procedure and the person who is performing the nonablative cosmetic medical procedure;

    (d)   the patient is provided with a telephone number that is answered within 24 hours for follow-up communication; and

    (e)   the cosmetic medical facility's contract with a master esthetician who performs a nonablative cosmetic medical procedure at the facility is kept on the premises of the facility.

(5)   Failure to comply with the provisions of this section is unprofessional conduct.

(6)   A chiropractic physician licensed under Chapter 73, Chiropractic Physician Practice Act is not subject to the supervision requirements in this section for a nonablative cosmetic medical procedure for hair removal if the chiropractic physician is acting within the scope of practice of a chiropractic physician and with training specific to nonablative hair removal.

Enacted by Chapter 362, 2012 General Session

58-1-507 Cosmetic medical procedure—Truth in advertising.

Beginning July 1, 2013, a facility that performs a cosmetic medical procedure as defined in Section 58-67-102 may not advertise or hold itself out to the public as a "medical spa," "medical facility," or "medical clinic" unless the facility has an individual on the premises while a cosmetic medical procedure is performed who is licensed under:

(1)   Chapter 31b, Nurse Practice Act, as an advanced practice registered nurse, practicing as a nurse practitioner;

(2)   Chapter 67, Utah Medical Practice Act; or

(3)   Chapter 68, Utah Osteopathic Medical Practice Act.

Enacted by Chapter 362, 2012 General Session

Appendix O: State Construction Code Administration and Adoption of Approved State Construction Code Rule

R156-15A-101. Title.

This rule is known as the "State Construction Code Administration and Adoption of Approved State Construction Code Rule".

R156-15A-102. Definitions.

In addition to the definitions in Title 15A, as used in Title 15A or this rule:

(1)   "Building permit" means, for the purpose of determining the building permit surcharge under Subsection 15A-1-209(5)(a), a warrant, license or authorization to build or construct a building or structure or any part thereof.

(2)   "Building permit fee" means, for the purpose of determining the building permit surcharge under Subsection 15A-1-209(5)(a), fees assessed by a state agency or state political subdivision for the issuance of permits for construction, alteration, remodeling, repair, and installation, including building, electrical, mechanical and plumbing components.

(3)   "Permit number", as used in Section 15A-1-209, means the standardized building permit number described below in Sections R156-15A-220 and R156-15A-221.

(4)   "Refuses to establish a method of appeal" means, with respect to Subsection 15A-1-207(3)(b), that a compliance agency does not in fact adopt a formal written method of appealing uniform building standard matters in accordance with generally recognized standards of due process; or, that the compliance agency does not convene an appeals board and render a decision in the matter within ninety days from the date on which the appeal is properly filed with the compliance agency.

R156-15A-103. Authority.

This rule is adopted by the Division under the authority of Subsection 15A-1-204(6), Section 15A-1-205 and Subsection 58-1-106(1)(a) to enable the Division to administer Title 15A.

R156-15A-201. Advisory Peer Committees Created - Membership - Duties.

(1)   There is created in accordance with Subsections 58-1-203(1)(f) and 15A-1-203(10)(d), the following advisory peer committees to the Uniform Building Codes Commission:

(a)   the Education Advisory Committee consisting of ten members, which shall include a factory built housing dealer, a design professional, a general contractor, an electrical contractor, a mechanical or plumbing contractor, an educator, and four inspectors (one from each of the specialties of plumbing, electrical, mechanical and general building);

(b)   the Plumbing and Health Advisory Committee consisting of nine members;

(c)   the Structural Advisory Committee consisting of seven members;

(d)   the Architectural Advisory Committee consisting of seven members;

     (e)   the Fire Protection Advisory Committee consisting of five members;

        (i)   This committee shall join together with the Fire Advisory and Code Analysis Committee of the Utah Fire Prevention Board to form the Unified Code Analysis Council.

        (ii)   The Unified Code Analysis Council shall meet as directed by the Utah Fire Prevention Board, or as directed by the Uniform Building Code Commission, or as needed to review fire prevention and building code issues that require definitive and specific analysis.

        (iii)   The Unified Code Analysis Council shall select one of its members to act as chair and another to act as vice chair. The chair and vice chair shall serve for one-year terms on a calendar year basis. Elections for chair and vice chair shall occur at the meeting conducted in the last quarter of the calendar year.

        (iv)   The chair or vice chair shall report to the Utah Fire Prevention Board or Uniform Building Code Commission recommendations of the council with regard to the review of fire and building codes;

     (f)   the Mechanical Advisory Committee consisting of seven members; and

     (g)   the Electrical Advisory Committee consisting of seven members.

(2)   The committees shall be appointed and serve in accordance with Subsection 15A-1-203(10)(d). The membership of each committee shall be made up of individuals who have direct knowledge or involvement in the area of code involved in the title of that committee.

(3)   The duties and responsibilities of the committees shall include:

     (a)   reviewing codes proposed for adoption or approval as assigned by the Division in collaboration with the Commission;

     (b)   reviewing requests for amendments to the adopted codes or approved codes as assigned to each committee by the Division with the collaboration of the Commission; and

     (c)   submitting recommendations concerning the reviews made under Subsection (a) and (b).

(4)   The duties and responsibilities of the Education Advisory Committee shall include:

     (a)   reviewing and making recommendations regarding funding requests that are submitted; and

     (b)   reviewing and making recommendations regarding budget, revenue and expenses of the education fund established pursuant to Subsection 15A-1-209(5).

R156-15A-202. Code Amendment Process.

In accordance with Section 15A-1-206, the procedure and manner under which requests for amendments to codes shall be filed with the Division and recommended or declined for adoption are as follows:

(1)   All requests for amendments to any of the adopted codes or approved codes shall be submitted to the Division on forms specifically prepared by the Division for that purpose.

(2)   The processing of requests for code amendments shall be in accordance with Division policies and procedures.

R156-15A-210. Compliance with Codes - Appeals.

If the Commission is required to act as an appeals board in accordance with the provisions of Subsection 15A-1-207(3)(b), the following shall regulate the convening and conduct of the appeals board:

(1)   If a compliance agency refuses to establish a method of appeal regarding a uniform building standard issue, the appellant may petition the Commission to act as the appeals board.

(2)   The appellant shall file the request to convene the Commission as an appeals board in accordance with the requirements for a request for agency action, as set forth in Subsection 63G-4-201(3)(a) and Section R151-4-201. A request by other means shall not be considered and shall be returned to the appellant with appropriate instructions.

(3)   A copy of the final written decision of the compliance agency interpreting or applying a code which is the subject of the dispute shall be submitted as an attachment to the request. If the appellant requests, but does not receive a timely final written decision, the appellant shall submit an affidavit to this effect in lieu of including a copy of the final written decision with the request.

(4)   The request shall be filed with the Division no later than 30 days following the issuance of the compliance agency's disputed written decision.

(5)   The compliance agency shall file a written response to the request not later than 20 days after the filing of the request. The request and response shall be provided to the Commission in advance of any hearing in order to properly frame the disputed issues.

(6)   Except with regard to the time period specified in Subsection (7), the time periods specified in this section may, upon a showing of good cause, be modified by the presiding officer conducting the proceeding.

(7)   The Commission shall convene as an appeals board within 45 days after a request is properly filed.

(8)   Upon the convening of the Commission as an appeals board, the board members shall review the issue to be considered to determine if a member of the board has a conflict of interest which would preclude the member from fairly hearing and deciding the appeal. If it is determined that a conflict does exist, the member shall be excused from participating in the proceeding.

(9)   The hearing shall be a formal hearing held in accordance with the Utah Administrative Procedures Act, Title 63G, Chapter 4.

(10)   Decisions relating to the application and interpretation of the code made by a compliance agency board of appeals shall be binding for the specific individual case and shall not require Commission approval.

R156-15A-220. Standardized Building Permit Number.

As provided in Section 15A-1-209, any agency issuing a permit for construction within the state of Utah shall use the standardized building permit numbering system in a form adopted by rule. There are no additional requirements to those specified in Subsection 15A-1-209.

R156-15A-230. Building Code Training Fund Fees.

In accordance with Subsection 15A-1-209(5)(a), on April 30, July 31, October 31 and January 31 of each year, each state agency and each state political subdivision that assesses a building permit fee shall file with the Division a report of building fees and surcharge for the immediately preceding calendar quarter; and, shall remit 80% of the amount of the surcharge collected to the Division.

R156-15A-231. Administration of Building Code Training Fund and Factory Built Housing Fees Account.

In accordance with Subsection 15A-1-209(5)(c), the Division shall use monies received under Subsection 15A-1-209(5)(a) to provide education regarding codes and code amendments to building inspectors and individuals engaged in construction-related trades or professions. In accordance with Subsection 58-56-17.5(2)(c), the Division shall use a portion of the monies received under Subsection 58-56-17.5(1) to provide education for factory built housing. The following procedures, standards, and policies are established to apply to the administration of these separate funds:

(1)   The Division shall not approve or deny education grant requests from the Building Code Training Fund or from the Factory Built Housing Fees Account until the Uniform Building Code

Commission (UBCC) Education Advisory Committee ("the Committee"), created in accordance with Subsections 58-1-203(1)(f) and R156-15A-201(1)(a), has considered and made its recommendations on the requests.

(2)   Appropriate funding expenditure categories include:

    (a)   grants in the form of reimbursement funding to the following organizations that administer code related or factory built housing educational events, seminars or classes:

        (i)   schools, colleges, universities, departments of universities, or other institutions of learning;

        (ii)   professional associations or organizations; and

        (iii)   governmental agencies.

    (b)   costs or expenses incurred as a result of educational events, seminars, or classes directly administered by the Division;

    (c)   expenses incurred for the salary, benefits or other compensation and related expenses resulting from the employment of a Board Secretary;

    (d)   office equipment and associated administrative expenses required for the performance of the duties of the Board Secretary, including but not limited to computer equipment, telecommunication equipment and costs and general office supplies; and

    (e)   other related expenses as determined by the Division.

(3)   The following procedure shall be used for submission, review and payment of funding grants:

    (a)   A funding grant applicant shall submit a completed "Application for Building Code Training Funds Grant" or a "Factory Built Housing Education Grant Application" a minimum of 15 days prior to the meeting at which the request is to be considered and prior to the training event on forms provided for that purpose by the Division. Applications received less than 15 days prior to a meeting may be denied.

    (b)   Payment of approved funding grants will be made as reimbursement after the approved event, class, or seminar has been held and the required receipts, invoices and supporting documentation, including proof of payment, if requested by the Division or Committee, have been submitted to the Division.

    (c)   Approved funding grants shall be reimbursed only for eligible expenditures which have been executed in good faith with the intent to ensure the best reasonable value.

    (d)   A Request for Reimbursement of an approved funding grant shall be submitted to the Division within 60 days following the approved event, class, or seminar unless an extenuating circumstance occurs. Written notice must be given to the Division of such an extenuating circumstance. Failure to submit a Request for Reimbursement within 60 days shall result in non-payment of approved funds, unless an extenuating circumstance has been reviewed and accepted by the Division.

(4)   The Committee shall consider the following in determining whether to recommend approval of a proposed funding request to the Division:

    (a)   the fund balance available and whether the proposed request meets the overall training objectives of the fund, including but not limited to:

        (i)   the need for training on the subject matter;

        (ii)   the need for training in the geographical area where the training is offered; and

        (iii)   the need for training on new codes being considered for adoption;

      (b)   the prior record of the program sponsor in providing codes training including:

            (i)   whether the subject matter taught was appropriate;

            (ii)   whether the instructor was appropriately qualified and prepared; and

            (iii)   whether the program sponsor followed appropriate and adequate procedures and requirements in providing the training and submitting requests for funding;

      (c)   costs of the facility including:

            (i)   the location of a facility or venue, or the type of event, seminar or class;

            (ii)   the suitability of said facility or venue with regard to the anticipated attendance at or in connection with additional non-funded portions of an event or conference;

            (iii)   the duration of the proposed educational event, seminar, or class; and

            (iv)   whether the proposed cost of the facility is reasonable compared to the cost of alternative available facilities;

      (d)   the estimated cost for instructor fees including:

            (i)   a reimbursement rate not to exceed $150 per instruction hour without further review and approval by the Committee;

            (ii)   the experience or expertise of the instructor in the proposed training area;

            (iii)   the quality of training based upon events, seminars or classes that have been previously taught by the instructor;

            (iv)   the drawing power of the instructor, meaning the ability to increase the attendance at the proposed educational event, seminar or class;

            (v)   travel expenses; and

            (vi)   whether the proposed cost for the instructor or instructors is reasonable compared to the costs of similar educational events, seminars, or classes;

      (e)   the estimated cost of advertising materials, brochures, registration and agenda materials, including:

            (i)   printing costs that may include creative or design expenses; and

            (ii)   delivery or mailing costs;

      (f)   other reasonable and comparable cost alternatives for each proposed expense item;

      (g)   other information the Committee reasonably believes may assist in evaluating a proposed expenditure; and

      (h)   a total reimbursement rate of the lesser of $10 per student hour or the cost of all approved actual expenditures.

(5)   The Division, after consideration and recommendation of the Committee, based upon the criteria in Subsection (4), may reimburse the following items in addition to the lesser of $10 per student hour or the cost of all approved actual expenditures:

      (a)   text books, code books, or code update books;

      (b)   cost of one Division licensee mailing list per provider per two-year renewal period;

      (c)   cost incurred to upload continuing education hours into the Division's online registry for contractors, plumbers, electricians or elevator mechanics; and

            (d)   reasonable cost of advertising materials, brochures, registration and agency materials, including:

                  (i)   printing costs that may include creative or design expenses; and

                  (ii)   delivery or mailing costs.

(6)   Joint function.

            (a)   "Joint function" means a proposed event, class, seminar, or program that provides code or code related or factory built housing education and education or activities in other areas.

            (b)   Only the prorated portions of a joint function that are code and code related or factory built housing education are eligible for a funding grant.

            (c)   In considering a proposed funding request that involves a joint function, the Committee shall consider whether:

                  (i)   the expenses subject to funding are reasonably prorated for the costs directly related to the code and code amendment or factory built housing education; and

                  (ii)   the education being proposed will be reasonable and successful in the training objective in the context of the entire program or event.

(7)   Advertising materials, brochures and agenda or training materials for a Building Code Training funded educational event, seminar, or class shall include a statement that acknowledges that partial funding of the training program has been provided by the Utah Division of Occupational and Professional Licensing from the 1% surcharge funds on all building permits.

(8)   Advertising materials, brochures and agenda or training materials for a Factory Built Housing Fees Account funded educational event, seminar, or class shall include a statement that acknowledges that partial funding of the training program has been provided by the Utah Division of Occupational and Professional Licensing from surcharge fees on factory built housing sales.

(9)   If an approved event or joint event is not held, no amount is reimbursable with the exception of the costs described in Subsection (5)(d).

R156-15A-301. Factory Built Housing Dispute Resolution.

In accordance with Subsection 15A-1-306(1)(f)(i), the dispute resolution program is defined and clarified as follows:

(1)   Persons with manufactured housing disputes may file a complaint with the Division.

(2)   The Division shall investigate such complaints and as part of the investigation may take any of the following actions:

            (a)   negotiate an informal resolution with the parties involved;

            (b)   take any informal or formal action allowed by any applicable statute, including but not limited to:

                  (A)   pursuing disciplinary proceedings under Section 58-1-401;

                  (B)   assessing civil penalties under Subsection 15A-1-306(2); and

                  (C)   referring matters to appropriate criminal prosecuting agencies and cooperating or assisting with the investigation and prosecution of cases by such agencies.

(3)   In addition, persons with manufactured housing disputes may pursue a civil remedy.

R156-15A-401. Adoption - Approved Codes.

Approved Codes. In accordance with Subsection 15A-1-204(6)(a), and subject to the limitations contained in Subsection 15A-1-204(6)(b), the following codes or standards are hereby incorporated by reference and approved for use and adoption by a compliance agency as the construction standards which may be applied to existing buildings in the regulation of building alteration, remodeling, repair, removal, seismic evaluation, and rehabilitation in the state:

(1)   the 1997 edition of the Uniform Code for the Abatement of Dangerous Buildings (UCADB) promulgated by the International Code Council;

(2)   the 2012 edition of the International Existing Building Code (IEBC), including its appendix chapters, promulgated by the International Code Council;

(3)   ASCE 31-03, Seismic Evaluation of Existing Buildings, promulgated by the American Society of Civil Engineers;

(4)   ASCE/SEI 41-06, the Seismic Rehabilitation of Existing Buildings, promulgated by the American Society of Civil Engineers, 2007 edition.

R156-15A-402. Statewide Amendments to the IEBC.

The following are adopted as amendments to the IEBC to be applicable statewide:

(1)   In Section 202 the definition for existing buildings is deleted and replaced with the following:

EXISTING BUILDING. A building lawfully erected under a prior adopted code, or one which is deemed a legal non-conforming building by the code official, and one which is not a dangerous building.

(2)   In Section 301.1 the exception is deleted.

(3)   In Section 705.1, Exception number 3, the following is added at the end:

"This exception does not apply if the existing facility is undergoing a change of occupancy classification."

(4)   Section 706.2.1 is deleted and replaced with the following:

706.2.1 Parapet bracing, wall anchors, and other appendages. Buildings constructed prior to 1975 shall have parapet bracing, wall anchors, and appendages such as cornices, spires, towers, tanks, signs, statuary, etc. evaluated by a licensed engineer when said building is undergoing reroofing, or alteration of or repair to said feature. Such parapet bracing, wall anchors, and appendages shall be evaluated in accordance with the reduced International Building Code level seismic forces as specified in IEBC Section 301.1.4.2 and design procedures of Section 301.1.4. When found to be deficient because of design or deteriorated condition, the engineer's recommendations to anchor, brace, reinforce, or remove the deficient feature shall be implemented.

EXCEPTIONS:

1. Group R-3 and U occupancies.

2. Unreinforced masonry parapets need not be braced according to the above stated provisions provided that the maximum height of an unreinforced masonry parapet above the level of the diaphragm tension anchors or above the parapet braces shall not exceed one and one-half times the thickness of the parapet wall. The parapet height may be a maximum of two and one-half times its thickness in other than Seismic Design Categories D, E, or F.

(5)   Section 1007.3.1 is deleted and replaced with the following:

1007.3.1 Compliance with the International Building Code Level Seismic Forces. When a building or portion thereof is subject to a change of occupancy such that a change in the nature of the occupancy results in a higher risk category based on Table 1604.5 of the International Building Code; or where such change of occupancy results in a reclassification of a building to a higher hazard category as shown in Table 1012.4; or where a change of a Group M occupancy to a Group A, E, F, I-1, R-1, R-2, or R-4 occupancy with two-thirds or more of the floors involved in Level 3 alteration work; or when such change of occupancy results in a design occupant load increase of 100% or more, the building shall conform to the seismic requirements of the International Building Code for the new risk category.

Exceptions 1-4 remain unchanged.

5. Where the design occupant load increase is less than 25 occupants and the occupancy category does not change.

(6)   In Section 1012.7.3 exception 2 is deleted.

(7)   In Section 1012.8.2 number 7 is added as follows:

7. When a change of occupancy in a building or portion of a building results in a Group R-2 occupancy, not less than 20 percent of the dwelling or sleeping units shall be Type B dwelling or sleeping units. These dwelling or sleeping units may be located on any floor of the building provided with an accessible route. Two percent, but not less than one unit, of the dwelling or sleeping units shall be Type A dwelling units.

R156-15A-403. Local Amendment to the IEBC.

The following are adopted as amendments to the IEBC to be applicable to the following jurisdictions: None.

KEY: contractors, building codes, building inspections, licensing

Date of Enactment or Last Substantive Amendment: October 23, 2014

Authorizing, and Implemented or Interpreted Law: 58-1-106(1)(a); 58-1-202(1)(a); 15A-1-204(6); 15A-1-205

Appendix P: State Construction and Fire Codes Act

Chapter 1 - General Chapter

Part 1 - General Provisions

15A-1-101 Titles.

    (1)   This title is known as the "State Construction and Fire Codes Act."

    (2)   This chapter is known as "General Chapter."

Enacted by Chapter 14, 2011 General Session

15A-1-102 Definitions.

As used in this title:

    (1)   "Board" means the Utah Fire Prevention Board created in Section 53-7-203.

    (2)   "Division" means the Division of Occupational and Professional Licensing created in Section 58-1-103, except as provided in:

          (a)   Part 4, State Fire Code Administration Act; and

          (b)   Chapter 5, State Fire Code Act.

    (3)   "State Construction Code" means the State Construction Code adopted by:

          (a)   Chapter 2, Adoption of State Construction Code;

          (b)   Chapter 3, Statewide Amendments Incorporated as Part of State Construction Code; and

          (c)   Chapter 4, Local Amendments Incorporated as Part of State Construction Code.

    (4)   "State Fire Code" means the State Fire Code adopted by Chapter 5, State Fire Code Act.

    (5)   "Utah Code" means the Utah Code Annotated (1953), as amended.

Enacted by Chapter 14, 2011 General Session

15A-1-103 Formatting powers.

    (1)   As part of the division's compliance with Section 15A-1-205, the division may modify the format of the State Construction Code to provide accessibility to users of the State Construction Code.

    (2)   Consistent with Part 4, State Fire Code Administration Act, and Title 53, Chapter 7, Utah Fire Prevention and Safety Act, the State Fire Marshall Division under the direction of the board may modify the format of the State Fire Code to provide accessibility to users of the State Fire Code.

Enacted by Chapter 14, 2011 General Session

15A-1-104 Permit approval required — Certificate of occupancy valid.

(1)   As used in this section:

(a)   "Compliance agency" is as defined in Section 15A-1-202.

(b)   "Project" is as defined in Section 15A-1-209.

(2)   A compliance agency for a political subdivision may not reject a permit, or otherwise withhold approval of a project whenever approval is required, for failure to comply with the applicable provisions of this title unless the compliance agency:

(a)   cites with specificity the applicable provision with which the project has failed to comply; and

(b)   describes how the project has failed to comply.

(3)   If a compliance agency or a representative of a compliance agency issues a certificate of occupancy, the compliance agency may not withdraw the certificate of occupancy or exert additional jurisdiction over the elements of the project for which the certificate was issued unless additional changes or modifications requiring a building permit are made to elements of the project after the certificate was issued.

Enacted by Chapter 197, 2014 General Session

Part 2 - State Construction Code Administration Act

15A-1-201 Title.

This part is known as the "State Construction Code Administration Act."

Enacted by Chapter 14, 2011 General Session

15A-1-202 Definitions.

As used in this chapter:

(1)   "Agricultural use" means a use that relates to the tilling of soil and raising of crops, or keeping or raising domestic animals.

(2)   (a)   "Approved code" means a code, including the standards and specifications contained in the code, approved by the division under Section 15A-1-204 for use by a compliance agency.

(b)   "Approved code" does not include the State Construction Code.

(3)   "Building" means a structure used or intended for supporting or sheltering any use or occupancy and any improvements attached to it.

(4)   "Code" means:

(a)   the State Construction Code; or

(b)   an approved code.

(5)   "Commission" means the Uniform Building Code Commission created in Section 15A-1-203.

(6)   "Compliance agency" means:

(a)   an agency of the state or any of its political subdivisions which issues permits for construction regulated under the codes;

(b)   any other agency of the state or its political subdivisions specifically empowered to enforce compliance with the codes; or

(c)   any other state agency which chooses to enforce codes adopted under this chapter by authority given the agency under a title other than this part and Part 3, Factory Built Housing and Modular Units Administration Act.

(7)   "Construction code" means standards and specifications published by a nationally recognized code authority for use in circumstances described in Subsection 15A-1-204(1), including:

(a)   a building code;

(b)   an electrical code;

(c)   a residential one and two family dwelling code;

(d)   a plumbing code;

(e)   a mechanical code;

(f)   a fuel gas code;

(g)   an energy conservation code; and

(h)   a manufactured housing installation standard code.

(8)   "Legislative action" includes legislation that:

(a)   adopts a new State Construction Code;

(b)   amends the State Construction Code; or

(c)   repeals one or more provisions of the State Construction Code.

(9)   "Local regulator" means a political subdivision of the state that is empowered to engage in the regulation of construction, alteration, remodeling, building, repair, and other activities subject to the codes.

(10)   "Not for human occupancy" means use of a structure for purposes other than protection or comfort of human beings, but allows people to enter the structure for:

(a)   maintenance and repair; and

(b)   the care of livestock, crops, or equipment intended for agricultural use which are kept there.

(11)   "Opinion" means a written, nonbinding, and advisory statement issued by the commission concerning an interpretation of the meaning of the codes or the application of the codes in a specific circumstance issued in response to a specific request by a party to the issue.

(12)   "State regulator" means an agency of the state which is empowered to engage in the regulation of construction, alteration, remodeling, building, repair, and other activities subject to the codes adopted pursuant to this chapter.

Enacted by Chapter 14, 2011 General Session

15A-1-203 Uniform Building Code Commission — Unified Code Analysis Council.

(1)   There is created a Uniform Building Code Commission to advise the division with respect to the division's responsibilities in administering the codes.

(2)   The commission shall consist of 11 members as follows:

(a)   one member shall be from among candidates nominated by the Utah League of Cities and Towns and the Utah Association of Counties;

(b)   one member shall be a licensed building inspector employed by a political subdivision of the state;

(c)   one member shall be a licensed professional engineer;

       (d)   one member shall be a licensed architect;

       (e)   one member shall be a fire official;

       (f)   three members shall be contractors licensed by the state, of which one shall be a general contractor, one an electrical contractor, and one a plumbing contractor;

       (g)   two members shall be from the general public and have no affiliation with the construction industry or real estate development industry; and

       (h)   one member shall be from the Division of Facilities Construction Management of the Department of Administrative Services.

(3)   (a)   The executive director shall appoint each commission member after submitting a nomination to the governor for confirmation or rejection.

       (b)   If the governor rejects a nominee, the executive director shall submit an alternative nominee until the governor confirms the nomination. An appointment is effective after the governor confirms the nomination.

(4)   (a)   Except as required by Subsection (4)(b), as terms of commission members expire, the executive director shall appoint each new commission member or reappointed commission member to a four-year term.

       (b)   Notwithstanding the requirements of Subsection (4)(a), the executive director shall, at the time of appointment or reappointment, adjust the length of terms to ensure that the terms of commission members are staggered so that approximately half of the commission is appointed every two years.

(5)   When a vacancy occurs in the commission membership for any reason, the executive director shall appoint a replacement for the unexpired term.

(6)   (a)   A commission member may not serve more than two full terms.

       (b)   A commission member who ceases to serve may not again serve on the commission until after the expiration of two years from the date of cessation of service.

(7)   A majority of the commission members constitute a quorum and may act on behalf of the commission.

(8)   A commission member may not receive compensation or benefits for the commission member's service, but may receive per diem and travel expenses in accordance with:

       (a)   Section 63A-3-106;

       (b)   Section 63A-3-107; and

       (c)   rules made by the Division of Finance pursuant to Sections 63A-3-106 and 63A-3-107.

(9)   (a)   The commission shall annually designate one of its members to serve as chair of the commission.

       (b)   The division shall provide a secretary to facilitate the function of the commission and to record the commission's actions and recommendations.

(10)   The commission shall:

       (a)   in accordance with Section 15A-1-204, report to the Business and Labor Interim Committee;

       (b)   offer an opinion regarding the interpretation of or the application of a code if a person submits a request for an opinion;

       (c)   act as an appeals board as provided in Section 15A-1-207;

(d)   establish advisory peer committees on either a standing or ad hoc basis to advise the commission with respect to matters related to a code, including a committee to advise the commission regarding health matters related to a plumbing code; and

(e)   assist the division in overseeing code-related training in accordance with Section 15A-1-209.

(11)   A person requesting an opinion under Subsection (10)(b) shall submit a formal request clearly stating:

(a)   the facts in question;

(b)   the specific citation at issue in a code; and

(c)   the position taken by the persons involved in the facts in question.

(12)   (a)   In a manner consistent with Subsection (10)(d), the commission shall jointly create with the Utah Fire Prevention Board an advisory peer committee known as the "Unified Code Analysis Council" to review fire prevention and construction code issues that require definitive and specific analysis.

(b)   The commission and Utah Fire Prevention Board shall jointly, by rule made in accordance with Title 63G, Chapter 3, Utah Administrative Rulemaking Act, provide for:

(i)   the appointment of members to the Unified Code Analysis Council; and

(ii)   procedures followed by the Unified Code Analysis Council.

Enacted by Chapter 14, 2011 General Session

15A-1-204 Adoption of State Construction Code — Amendments by commission — Approved codes — Exemptions.

(1)   (a)   The State Construction Code is the construction codes adopted with any modifications in accordance with this section that the state and each political subdivision of the state shall follow.

(b)   A person shall comply with the applicable provisions of the State Construction Code when:

(i)   new construction is involved; and

(ii)   the owner of an existing building, or the owner's agent, is voluntarily engaged in:

(A)   the repair, renovation, remodeling, alteration, enlargement, rehabilitation, conservation, or reconstruction of the building; or

(B)   changing the character or use of the building in a manner that increases the occupancy loads, other demands, or safety risks of the building.

(c)   On and after July 1, 2010, the State Construction Code is the State Construction Code in effect on July 1, 2010, until in accordance with this section:

(i)   a new State Construction Code is adopted; or

(ii)   one or more provisions of the State Construction Code are amended or repealed in accordance with this section.

(d)   A provision of the State Construction Code may be applicable:

(i)   to the entire state; or

(ii)   within a county, city, or town.

(2)   (a)   The Legislature shall adopt a State Construction Code by enacting legislation that adopts a construction code with any modifications.

(b)   Legislation enacted under this Subsection shall state that it takes effect on the July 1 after the day on which the legislation is enacted, unless otherwise stated in the legislation.

(c)   Subject to Subsection (5), a State Construction Code adopted by the Legislature is the State Construction Code until, in accordance with this section, the Legislature adopts a new State Construction Code by:

(i)   adopting a new State Construction Code in its entirety; or

(ii)   amending or repealing one or more provisions of the State Construction Code.

(3)   (a)   The commission shall by no later than November 30 of each year recommend to the Business and Labor Interim Committee whether the Legislature should:

(i)   amend or repeal one or more provisions of a State Construction Code; or

(ii)   in a year of a regularly scheduled update of a nationally recognized code, adopt a construction code with any modifications.

(b)   The commission may recommend legislative action related to the State Construction Code:

(i)   on its own initiative;

(ii)   upon the recommendation of the division; or

(iii)   upon the receipt of a request by one of the following that the commission recommend legislative action related to the State Construction Code:

(A)   a local regulator;

(B)   a state regulator;

(C)   a state agency involved with the construction and design of a building;

(D)   the Construction Services Commission;

(E)   the Electrician Licensing Board;

(F)   the Plumbers Licensing Board; or

(G)   a recognized construction-related association.

(4)   If the Business and Labor Interim Committee decides to recommend legislative action to the Legislature, the Business and Labor Interim Committee shall prepare legislation for consideration by the Legislature in the next general session that, if passed by the Legislature, would:

(a)   adopt a new State Construction Code in its entirety; or

(b)   amend or repeal one or more provisions of the State Construction Code.

(5)   (a)   Notwithstanding Subsection (3), the commission may, in accordance with Title 63G, Chapter 3, Utah Administrative Rulemaking Act, amend the State Construction Code if the commission determines that waiting for legislative action in the next general legislative session would:

(i)   cause an imminent peril to the public health, safety, or welfare; or

(ii)   place a person in violation of federal or other state law.

(b)   If the commission amends the State Construction Code in accordance with this Subsection (5), the commission shall file with the division:

(i)   the text of the amendment to the State Construction Code; and

(ii)   an analysis that includes the specific reasons and justifications for the commission's findings.

(c)   If the State Construction Code is amended under this Subsection (5), the division shall:

    (i)   publish the amendment to the State Construction Code in accordance with Section 15A-1-205; and

    (ii)   notify the Business and Labor Interim Committee of the amendment to the State Construction Code, including a copy of the commission's analysis described in Subsection (5)(b).

(d)   If not formally adopted by the Legislature at its next annual general session, an amendment to the State Construction Code under this Subsection is repealed on the July 1 immediately following the next annual general session that follows the adoption of the amendment.

(6)   (a)   The division, in consultation with the commission, may approve, without adopting, one or more approved codes, including a specific edition of a construction code, for use by a compliance agency.

    (b)   If the code adopted by a compliance agency is an approved code described in Subsection (a), the compliance agency may:

        (i)   adopt an ordinance requiring removal, demolition, or repair of a building;

        (ii)   adopt, by ordinance or rule, a dangerous building code; or

        (iii)   adopt, by ordinance or rule, a building rehabilitation code.

(7)   (a)   Except as provided in Subsection (7)(b), a structure used solely in conjunction with agriculture use, and not for human occupancy, is exempt from the permit requirements of the State Construction Code.

    (b)   (i)   Unless exempted by a provision other than Subsection (7)(a), a plumbing, electrical, and mechanical permit may be required when that work is included in a structure described in Subsection (7)(a).

        (ii)   Unless located in whole or in part in an agricultural protection area created under Title 17, Chapter 41, Agriculture and Industrial Protection Areas, a structure described in Subsection (7)(a) is not exempt from a permit requirement if the structure is located on land that is:

            (A)   within the boundaries of a city or town, and less than five contiguous acres; or

            (B)   within a subdivision for which the county has approved a subdivision plat under Title 17, Chapter 27a, Part 6, Subdivisions, and less than two contiguous acres.

(8)   A structure that is no more than 1,000 square feet and is used solely for the type of sales described in Subsection 59-12-104is exempt from the permit requirements described in:

    (a)   Chapter 2, Adoption of State Construction Code;

    (b)   Chapter 3, Statewide Amendments Incorporated as Part of State Construction Code; and

    (c)   Chapter 4, Local Amendments Incorporated as Part of State Construction Code.

Amended by Chapter 178, 2014 General Session

Amended by Chapter 189, 2014 General Session

15A-1-205 Division duties.

(1)   (a)   The division shall administer the codes adopted or approved under Section 15A-1-204 pursuant to this chapter.

(b)   Notwithstanding Subsection (1)(a), the division has no responsibility to:

(i)   conduct inspections to determine compliance with the codes;

(ii)   issue permits; or

(iii)   assess building permit fees.

(2)   As part of the administration of the codes, the division shall:

(a)   comply with Section 15A-1-206;

(b)   schedule appropriate hearings;

(c)   maintain and publish for reference:

(i)   the current State Construction Code; and

(ii)   any approved code; and

(d)   publish the opinions of the commission with respect to interpretation and application of the codes.

Enacted by Chapter 14, 2011 General Session

15A-1-206 Code amendment process.

(1)   The division, in consultation with the commission, shall establish by rule the procedure under which a request that the commission recommend legislative action is to be:

(a)   filed with the division;

(b)   reviewed by the commission; and

(c)   addressed by the commission in the commission's report to the Business and Labor Interim Committee required by Section 15A-1-204.

(2)   The division shall accept a request that the commission recommend legislative action in accordance with Section 15A-1-204 from:

(a)   a local regulator;

(b)   a state regulator;

(c)   a state agency involved with the construction and design of a building;

(d)   the Construction Services Commission;

(e)   the Electrician Licensing Board;

(f)   the Plumbers Licensing Board; or

(g)   a recognized construction-related association.

(3)   (a)   If one or more requests are received in accordance with this section, the division shall hold at least one public hearing before the commission concerning the requests.

(b)   The commission shall conduct a public hearing under this Subsection in accordance with the rules of the commission, which may provide for coordinating the public hearing with a meeting of the commission.

(c)   After a public hearing described in this Subsection (3), the commission shall prepare a written report of its recommendations made on the basis of the public hearing. The commission shall include the information in the written report prepared under this Subsection (3)(c) in the commission's report to the Business and Labor Interim Committee under Section 15A-1-204.

(4)   In making rules required by this chapter, the division shall comply with Title 63G, Chapter 3, Utah Administrative Rulemaking Act.

Enacted by Chapter 14, 2011 General Session

15A-1-207 Compliance with codes — Responsibility for inspections — Appeals.

(1)   The compliance agency having jurisdiction over the project and the applicable codes has the responsibility for inspection of construction projects and enforcement of compliance with the codes.

(2)   A compliance agency shall furnish in writing to the division a finding by the compliance agency that a licensed contractor, electrician, or plumber has materially violated a code in a manner to jeopardize the public health, safety, and welfare and failed to comply with corrective orders of the compliance agency. A compliance agency shall conduct a primary investigation to determine that, in fact, there has been a material violation of a code jeopardizing the public interest and provide the report of investigation to the division.

(3)   (a)   A compliance agency shall establish a method of appeal by which a person disputing the application and interpretation of a code may appeal and receive a timely review of the disputed issues in accordance with the codes.

        (b)   If a compliance agency refuses to establish a method of appeal, the commission shall act as the appeals board and conduct a hearing within 45 days. The findings of the commission are binding.

(4)   An appeals board established under this section may not:

        (a)   interpret the administrative provisions of a code; or

        (b)   waive a requirement of a code.

Enacted by Chapter 14, 2011 General Session

15A-1-208 Standards for specialized buildings.

(1)   This chapter may not be implied to repeal or otherwise affect the authority granted to a state agency to make or administer standards for specialized buildings, as provided in:

        (a)   Title 26, Chapter 21, Health Care Facility Licensing and Inspection Act;

        (b)   Title 26, Chapter 39, Utah Child Care Licensing Act;

        (c)   Title 62A, Chapter 2, Licensure of Programs and Facilities;

        (d)   Title 64, Chapter 13, Department of Corrections - State Prison; or

        (e)   another statute that grants a state agency authority to make or administer other special standards.

(2)   If a special standard conflicts with a code, the special standard prevails.

(3)   This chapter does not apply to the administration of the statutes described in Subsection (1).

Enacted by Chapter 14, 2011 General Session

15A-1-209 Building permit requirements.

(1)   As used in this section, "project" means a "construction project" as defined in Section 38-1a-102.

(2)   (a)   The division shall develop a standardized building permit numbering system for use by any compliance agency in the state that issues a permit for construction.

(b)   The standardized building permit numbering system described under Subsection (2)(a) shall include a combination of alpha or numeric characters arranged in a format acceptable to the compliance agency.

(c)   A compliance agency issuing a permit for construction shall use the standardized building permit numbering system described under Subsection (2)(a).

(d)   A compliance agency may not use a numbering system other than the system described under Subsection (2)(a) to define a building permit number.

(3)   (a)   In accordance with Title 63G, Chapter 3, Utah Administrative Rulemaking Act, the division shall adopt a standardized building permit form by rule.

        (b)   The standardized building permit form created under this Subsection shall include fields for indicating the following information:

            (i)   the name and address of the owner of each parcel of property on which the project will occur;

            (ii)   the name and address of the contractor for the project;

            (iii)   (A)   the address of the project; or

                      (B)   a general description of the project;

            (iv)   the county in which the property on which the project will occur is located;

            (v)   the tax parcel identification number of each parcel of the property; and

            (vi)   whether the permit applicant is an original contractor or owner-builder.

        (c)   The standardized building permit form created under this Subsection may include any other information the division considers useful.

        (d)   A compliance agency shall issue a permit for construction only on a standardized building permit form approved by the division.

        (e)   A permit for construction issued by a compliance agency under Subsection (3)(d) shall print the standardized building permit number assigned under Subsection in the upper right-hand corner of the building permit form in at least 12-point font.

        (f)   (i)   Except as provided in Subsection (3)(f)(ii), a compliance agency may not issue a permit for construction if the information required by Subsection (3)(b) is not completed on the building permit form.

            (ii)   If a compliance agency does not issue a separate permit for different aspects of the same project, the compliance agency may issue a permit for construction without the information required by Subsection (3)(b)(vi).

        (g)   A compliance agency may require additional information for the issuance of a permit for construction.

(4)   A local regulator issuing a single-family residential building permit application shall include in the application or attach to the building permit the following notice prominently placed in at least 14-point font: "Decisions relative to this application are subject to review by the chief executive officer of the municipal or county entity issuing the single-family residential building permit and appeal under the International Residential Code as adopted by the Legislature."

(5)   (a)   A compliance agency shall:

            (i)   charge a 1% surcharge on a building permit it issues; and

            (ii)   transmit 80% of the amount collected to the division to be used by the division in accordance with Subsection (5)(c).

(b)   The portion of the surcharge transmitted to the division shall be deposited as a dedicated credit.

(c)   The division shall use the money received under this Subsection to provide education:

(i)   regarding the codes and code amendments that under Section 15A-1-204 are adopted, approved, or being considered for adoption or approval; and

(ii)   to:

(A)   building inspectors; and

(B)   individuals engaged in construction-related trades or professions.

Amended by Chapter 278, 2012 General Session

15A-1-210 Review of building inspection.

(1)   As used in this section, "International Residential Code" means the International Residential Code as adopted under the State Construction Code.

(2)   Subject to Subsection (3), a city or county shall, by ordinance, provide for review of an inspection conducted by the city's or county's building inspector for a single-family residential building permit.

(3)   Upon request by a person seeking a single-family residential building permit, a chief executive officer of the municipality or county issuing the single-family residential building permit, or the chief executive officer's designee, shall, with reasonable diligence, review an inspection described in Subsection to determine whether the inspection constitutes a fair administration of the State Construction Code.

(4)   A review described in this section:

(a)   is separate and unrelated to an appeal under the International Residential Code;

(b)   may not be used to review a matter that may be brought by appeal under the International Residential Code;

(c)   may not result in the waiver or modification of an International Residential Code requirement or standard;

(d)   may not conflict with an appeal, or the result of an appeal, under the International Residential Code; and

(e)   does not prohibit a person from bringing an appeal under the International Residential Code.

(5)   A person who seeks a review described in this section may not be prohibited by preclusion, estoppel, or otherwise from raising an issue or bringing a claim in an appeal under the International Residential Code on the grounds that the person raised the issue or brought the claim in the review described in this section.

Enacted by Chapter 14, 2011 General Session

Part 3 - Factory Built Housing and Modular Units Administration Act

15A-1-301 Title.

This part is known as "Factory Built Housing and Modular Units Administration Act."

Enacted by Chapter 14, 2011 General Session

15A-1-302 Definitions.

As used in this part:

(1)   "Compliance agency" is as defined in Section 15A-1-202.

(2)   "Factory built housing" means a manufactured home or mobile home.

(3)   "Factory built housing set-up contractor" means an individual licensed by the division to set up or install factory built housing on a temporary or permanent basis.

(4)   "HUD Code" means the National Manufactured Housing Construction and Safety Standards Act, 42 U.S.C. Sec. 5401 et seq.

(5)   "Local regulator" is as defined in Section 15A-1-202.

(6)   "Manufactured home" means a transportable factory built housing unit constructed on or after June 15, 1976, according to the HUD Code, in one or more sections, that:

    (a)   in the traveling mode, is eight body feet or more in width or 40 body feet or more in length, or when erected on site, is 400 or more square feet; and

    (b)   is built on a permanent chassis and designed to be used as a dwelling with or without a permanent foundation when connected to the required utilities, and includes the plumbing, heating, air-conditioning, and electrical systems.

(7)   "Mobile home" means a transportable factory built housing unit built before June 15, 1976, in accordance with a state mobile home code which existed prior to the HUD Code.

(8)   "Modular unit" means a structure:

    (a)   built from sections that are manufactured in accordance with the State Construction Code and transported to a building site; and

    (b)   the purpose of which is for human habitation, occupancy, or use.

(9)   "State regulator" is as defined in Section 15A-1-202.

Enacted by Chapter 14, 2011 General Session

15A-1-303 Factory built housing units.

(1)   (a)   A manufactured home constructed, sold, or setup in the state shall be constructed in accordance with the HUD Code.

    (b)   A manufactured home setup in the state shall be installed in accordance with the provisions of the State Construction Code applicable to manufactured housing installation.

    (c)   A local regulator subdivision has the authority and responsibility to issue a building permit for the modification or setup of a manufactured home within that political subdivision.

    (d)   A local regulator shall conduct the inspection of a modification to or the setup of a manufactured home and give an approval within the political subdivision in which the modification or setup takes place.

    (e)   A manufactured home constructed on or after June 15, 1976, shall be identifiable by the manufacturer's data plate bearing the date the unit was manufactured and a HUD label attached to the exterior of the home certifying the home was manufactured to HUD standards.

(2)   (a)   A mobile home sold or setup in the state shall be constructed in accordance with the portions of the State Construction Code applicable to a mobile home at the time the mobile home was constructed.

(b)   A mobile home setup in the state shall be installed in accordance with the portions of the State Construction Code applicable to manufactured housing installation.

(c)   A local regulator has the authority and responsibility to issue a building permit for the setup of a mobile home within that political subdivision.

(d)   A local regulator shall conduct the inspection of a modification to or the setup of a mobile home and give the approvals given by the local regulator within the political subdivision in which the modification or setup takes place.

Enacted by Chapter 14, 2011 General Session

15A-1-304 Modular units.

Modular unit construction, setup, issuance of permits for construction or setup, and setup shall be in accordance with the following:

(1)   Construction and setup of a modular unit shall be in accordance with the State Construction Code.

(2)   A local regulator has the responsibility and authority for plan review and issuance of permits for construction, modification, or setup for the political subdivision in which the modular unit is to be setup;

(3)   An inspection of the construction, modification of, or setup of a modular unit shall conform with this chapter.

(4)   A local regulator has the responsibility to issue an approval for the political subdivision in which a modular unit is to be setup or is setup.

(5)   Nothing in this section precludes:

(a)   a local regulator from contracting with a qualified third party for the inspection or plan review provided in this section; or

(b)   the state from entering into an interstate compact for third party inspection of the construction of a modular unit.

Enacted by Chapter 14, 2011 General Session

15A-1-305 Modification of factory built housing units and modular units.

(1)   A modification to a factory built housing unit shall be made in accordance with the following:

(a)   Modification to a manufactured home or mobile home before installation or setup of the unit for habitation shall be made in accordance with the HUD Code.

(b)   (i)   Modification to a manufactured home or mobile home after installation or setup of the unit for habitation shall be made in accordance with the HUD Code if the modification does not include the addition of any space to the existing unit or the attachment of any structure to the existing unit.

(ii)   If a modification to a manufactured home or mobile home after installation or setup for the unit for habitation includes the addition of any space to the existing unit or the attachment of any structure to the unit, the modification shall be made as follows:

(A)   modifications to the existing unit shall be in accordance with the HUD Code; and

(B)   additional structure outside of the existing unit shall be in accordance with this chapter.

(2)   A modification to a modular housing unit shall be made in accordance with this chapter.

Enacted by Chapter 14, 2011 General Session

15A-1-306 Factory built housing and modular units — Division responsibility — Unlawful conduct.

(1) The division:

    (a) shall maintain current information on the HUD Code and the portions of the State Construction Code relevant to manufactured housing installation and will provide at reasonable cost the information to compliance agencies, local regulators, or state regulators requesting such information;

    (b) shall provide qualified personnel to advise compliance agencies, local regulators, and state regulators regarding the standards for construction and setup, construction and setup inspection, and additions or modifications to factory built housing;

    (c) is designated as the state administrative agency for purposes of the HUD Code;

    (d) may inspect factory built housing units in the state during the construction process to determine compliance of the manufacturer with this chapter for those units to be installed within the state, and upon a finding of substantive deficiency, issue a corrective order to the manufacturer and provide a copy of the order to the local regulator in the state's political subdivision where the unit is to be installed;

    (e) shall have rights of entry and inspection as specified under the HUD Code; and

    (f) shall implement by rule a continuing education requirement for manufactured housing installation contractors.

(2) The division may assess civil penalties payable to the state for violation of the HUD Code in an amount identical to those set forth in Section 611 of the National Manufactured Housing Construction and Safety Standards Act of 1974, 42 U.S.C. Sec. 5410.

(3) The state may impose criminal sanctions for violations of the HUD Code identical to those set forth in Section 611 of the National Manufactured Housing Construction and Safety Standards Act of 1974, 42 U.S.C. Sec. 5410, provided that if the criminal sanction is a fine, the fine shall be payable to the state.

Amended by Chapter 262, 2013 General Session

Part 4 - State Fire Code Administration Act

15A-1-401 Title.

This part is known as the "State Fire Code Administration Act."

Enacted by Chapter 14, 2011 General Session

15A-1-402 Definitions.

As used in this part:

(1) "Division" means the State Fire Marshal Division created in Section 53-7-103.

(2) "Legislative action" includes legislation that:

    (a) adopts a State Fire Code;

    (b) amends a State Fire Code; or

    (c) repeals one or more provisions of a State Fire Code.

Enacted by Chapter 14, 2011 General Session

15A-1-403 Adoption of State Fire Code.

(1)   (a)   The State Fire Code is:

(i)   a code promulgated by a nationally recognized code authority that is adopted by the Legislature under this section with any modifications; and

(ii)   a code to which cities, counties, fire protection districts, and the state shall adhere in safeguarding life and property from the hazards of fire and explosion.

(b)   On and after July 1, 2010, the State Fire Code is the State Fire Code in effect on July 1, 2010, until in accordance with this section:

(i)   a new State Fire Code is adopted; or

(ii)   one or more provisions of the State Fire Code are amended or repealed in accordance with this section.

(c)   A provision of the State Fire Code may be applicable:

(i)   to the entire state; or

(ii)   within a city, county, or fire protection district.

(2)   (a)   The Legislature shall adopt a State Fire Code by enacting legislation that adopts a nationally recognized fire code with any modifications.

(b)   Legislation enacted under this Subsection (2) shall state that it takes effect on the July 1 after the day on which the legislation is enacted, unless otherwise stated in the legislation.

(c)   Subject to Subsection (5), a State Fire Code adopted by the Legislature is the State Fire Code until in accordance with this section the Legislature adopts a new State Fire Code by:

(i)   adopting a new State Fire Code in its entirety; or

(ii)   amending or repealing one or more provisions of the State Fire Code

(3)   (a)   The board shall, by no later than November 30 of each year, recommend to the Business and Labor Interim Committee whether the Legislature should:

(i)   amend or repeal one or more provisions of the State Fire Code; or

(ii)   in a year of a regularly scheduled update of a nationally recognized fire code, adopt with any modifications the nationally recognized fire code.

(b)   The board may recommend legislative action related to the State Fire Code:

(i)   on its own initiative; or

(ii)   upon the receipt of a request by a city, county, or fire protection district that the board recommend legislative action related to the State Fire Code.

(c)   Within 45 days after receipt of a request under Subsection (3)(b), the board shall direct the division to convene an informal hearing concerning the request.

(d)   The board shall conduct a hearing under this section in accordance with the rules of the board.

(e)   The board shall decide whether to include in the report required under Subsection (3)(a) whether to recommend the legislative action raised by a request.

(f)   Within 15 days following the completion of a hearing of the board under this Subsection (3), the board shall direct the division to notify the entity that made the request of the board's decision regarding the request. The division shall provide the notice:

(i)   in writing; and

(ii)   in a form prescribed by the board.

(4)   If the Business and Labor Interim Committee decides to recommend legislative action to the Legislature, the Business and Labor Interim Committee shall prepare legislation for consideration by the Legislature in the next general session that, if passed by the Legislature, would:

    (a)   adopt a new State Fire Code in its entirety; or

    (b)   amend or repeal one or more provisions of the State Fire Code.

(5)   (a)   Notwithstanding Subsection (3), the board may, in accordance with Title 63G, Chapter 3, Utah Administrative Rulemaking Act, amend a State Fire Code if the board determines that waiting for legislative action in the next general legislative session would:

        (i)   cause an imminent peril to the public health, safety, or welfare; or

        (ii)   place a person in violation of federal or other state law.

    (b)   If the board amends a State Fire Code in accordance with this Subsection (5), the board shall:

        (i)   publish the State Fire Code with the amendment; and

        (ii)   notify the Business and Labor Interim Committee of the adoption, including a copy of an analysis by the board identifying specific reasons and justifications for its findings.

    (c)   If not formally adopted by the Legislature at its next annual general session, an amendment to a State Fire Code adopted under this Subsection (5) is repealed on the July 1 immediately following the next annual general session that follows the adoption of the amendment.

(6)   (a)   A legislative body of a political subdivision may enact an ordinance that is more restrictive in its fire code requirements than the State Fire Code:

        (i)   in order to meet a public safety need of the political subdivision; and

        (ii)   subject to the requirements of this Subsection (6).

    (b)   A legislative body of a political subdivision that enacts an ordinance under this section on or after July 1, 2010 shall:

        (i)   notify the board in writing at least 30 days before the day on which the legislative body enacts the ordinance and include in the notice a statement as to the proposed subject matter of the ordinance; and

        (ii)   after the legislative body enacts the ordinance, report to the board before the board makes the report required under Subsection (6)(c), including providing the board:

            (A)   a copy of the ordinance enacted under this Subsection (6); and

            (B)   a description of the public safety need that is the basis of enacting the ordinance.

    (c)   The board shall submit to the Business and Labor Interim Committee each year with the recommendations submitted in accordance with Subsection (3):

        (i)   a list of the ordinances enacted under this Subsection (6) during the fiscal year immediately proceeding the report; and

        (ii)   recommendations, if any, for legislative action related to an ordinance enacted under this Subsection (6).

      (d)   (i)   The state fire marshal shall keep an indexed copy of an ordinance enacted under this Subsection (6).

            (iii)   The state fire marshal shall make a copy of an ordinance enacted under this Subsection (6) available on request.

      (e)   The board may make rules in accordance with Title 63G, Chapter 3, Utah Administrative Rulemaking Act, to establish procedures for a legislative body of a political subdivision to follow to provide the notice and report required under this Subsection (6).

Enacted by Chapter 14, 2011 General Session

Chapter 2 - Adoption of State Construction Code

Part 1 - General Provisions

15A-2-101 Title - Adoption of code.

    (1)   This chapter is known as the "Adoption of State Construction Code."

    (2)   In accordance with Chapter 1, Part 2, State Construction Code Administration Act, the Legislature repeals the State Construction Code in effect on July 1, 2010, and adopts the following as the State Construction Code:

      (a)   this chapter;

      (b)   Chapter 3, Statewide Amendments Incorporated as Part of State Construction Code; and

      (c)   Chapter 4, Local Amendments Incorporated as Part of State Construction Code.

Enacted by Chapter 14, 2011 General Session

15A-2-102 Definitions.

As used in this chapter and Chapter 3, Statewide Amendments Incorporated as Part of State Construction Code, and Chapter 4, Local Amendments Incorporated as Part of State Construction Code:

    (1)   "HUD Code" means the Federal Manufactured Housing Construction and Safety Standards Act, as issued by the Department of Housing and Urban Development and published in 24 C.F.R. Parts 3280 and 3282 (as revised April 1, 1990).

    (2)   "IBC" means the edition of the International Building Code adopted under Section 15A-2-103.

    (3)   "IECC" means the edition of the International Energy Conservation Code adopted under Section 15A-2-103.

    (4)   "IFGC" means the edition of the International Fuel Gas Code adopted under Section 15A-2-103.

    (5)   "IMC" means the edition of the International Mechanical Code adopted under Section 15A-2-103.

    (6)   "IPC" means the edition of the International Plumbing Code adopted under Section 15A-2-103.

    (7)   "IRC" means the edition of the International Residential Code adopted under Section 15A-2-103.

    (8)   "NEC" means the edition of the National Electrical Code adopted under Section 15A-2-103.

    (9)   "UWUI" means the edition of the Utah Wildland Urban Interface Code adopted under Section 15A-2-103.

Amended by Chapter 189, 2014 General Session

15A-2-103 Specific editions adopted of construction code of a nationally recognized code authority.

(1)   Subject to the other provisions of this part, the following construction codes are incorporated by reference, and together with the amendments specified in Chapter 3, Part 3, Statewide Amendments to International Plumbing Code, and Chapter 4, Local Amendments Incorporated as Part of State Construction Code, are the construction standards to be applied to building construction, alteration, remodeling, and repair, and in the regulation of building construction, alteration, remodeling, and repair in the state:

   (a)   the 2012 edition of the International Building Code, including Appendix J, issued by the International Code Council;

   (b)   the 2012 edition of the International Residential Code, issued by the International Code Council;

   (c)   the 2012 edition of the International Plumbing Code, issued by the International Code Council;

   (d)   the 2012 edition of the International Mechanical Code, issued by the International Code Council;

   (e)   the 2012 edition of the International Fuel Gas Code, issued by the International Code Council;

   (f)   the 2011 edition of the National Electrical Code, issued by the National Fire Protection Association;

   (g)   the 2012 edition of the International Energy Conservation Code, issued by the International Code Council;

   (h)   subject to Subsection 15A-2-104(2), the HUD Code;

   (i)   subject to Subsection 15A-2-104(1), Appendix E of the 2012 edition of the International Residential Code, issued by the International Code Council; and

   (j)   subject to Subsection 15A-2-104(1), the 2005 edition of the NFPA 225 Model Manufactured Home Installation Standard, issued by the National Fire Protection Association.

(2)   Consistent with Title 65A, Chapter 8, Management of Forest Lands and Fire Control, the Legislature adopts the 2006 edition of the Utah Wildland Urban Interface Code, issued by the International Code Council, with the alternatives or amendments approved by the Utah Division of Forestry, as a construction code that may be adopted by a local compliance agency by local ordinance or other similar action as a local amendment to the codes listed in this section.

Amended by Chapter 258, 2015 General Session

15A-2-104 Installation standards for manufactured housing.

(1)   The following are the installation standards for manufactured housing for new installations or for existing manufactured or mobile homes that are subject to relocation, building alteration, remodeling, or rehabilitation in the state:

   (a)   The manufacturer's installation instruction for the model being installed is the primary standard.

   (b)   If the manufacturer's installation instruction for the model being installed is not available or is incomplete, the following standards apply:

      (i)   Appendix E of the 2012 edition of the IRC, as issued by the International Code Council for installations defined in Section AE101 of Appendix E; or

      (ii)   if an installation is beyond the scope of the 2012 edition of the IRC as defined in Section AE101 of Appendix E, the 2005 edition of the NFPA 225 Model Manufactured Home Installation Standard, issued by the National Fire Protection Association.

(c)   A manufacturer, dealer, or homeowner is permitted to design for unusual installation of a manufactured home not provided for in the manufacturer's standard installation instruction, Appendix E of the 2012 edition of the IRC, or the 2005 edition of the NFPA 225, if the design is approved in writing by a professional engineer or architect licensed in Utah.

(d)   For a mobile home built before June 15, 1976, the mobile home shall also comply with the additional installation and safety requirements specified in Chapter 3, Part 8, Installation and Safety Requirements for Mobile Homes Built Before June 15, 1976.

(2)   Pursuant to the HUD Code Section 604(d), a manufactured home may be installed in the state that does not meet the local snow load requirements as specified in Chapter 3, Part 2, Statewide Amendments to International Residential Code, except that the manufactured home shall have a protective structure built over the home that meets the IRC and the snow load requirements under Chapter 3, Part 2, Statewide Amendments to International Residential Code.

Amended by Chapter 189, 2014 General Session

15A-2-105 Scope of application.

(1)   To the extent that a construction code adopted under Section 15A-2-103 establishes a local administrative function or establishes a method of appeal which pursuant to Section 15A-1-207 is designated to be established by the compliance agency:

(a)   that provision of the construction code is not included in the State Construction Code; and

(b)   a compliance agency may establish provisions to establish a local administrative function or a method of appeal.

(2)   (a)   To the extent that a construction code adopted under Subsection (1) establishes a provision, standard, or reference to another code that by state statute is designated to be established or administered by another state agency, or a local city, town, or county jurisdiction:

(i)   that provision of the construction code is not included in the State Construction Code; and

(ii)   the state agency or local government has authority over that provision of the construction code.

(b)   Provisions excluded under this Subsection (2) include:

(i)   the International Property Maintenance Code;

(ii)   the International Private Sewage Disposal Code, authority over which is reserved to the Department of Health and the Department of Environmental Quality;

(iii)   the International Fire Code, authority over which is reserved to the board, pursuant to Section 15A-1-403;

(iv)   a day care provision that is in conflict with Title 26, Chapter 39, Utah Child Care Licensing Act, authority over which is designated to the Utah Department of Health; and

(v)   a wildland urban interface provision that goes beyond the authority under Section 15A-1-204, for the State Construction Code, authority over which is designated to the Utah Division of Forestry or to a local compliance agency.

(3)   If a construction code adopted under Subsection 15A-2-103(1) establishes a provision that exceeds the scope described in Chapter 1, Part 2, State Construction Code Administration Act, to the extent the scope is exceeded, the provision is not included in the State Construction Code.

Enacted by Chapter 14, 2011 General Session

Chapter 3 - Statewide Amendments Incorporated as Part of State Construction Code

Part 1 - Statewide Amendments to International Building Code

15A-3-101 General provision.

The amendments in this part are adopted as amendments to the IBC to be applicable statewide.

Enacted by Chapter 14, 2011 General Session

15A-3-102 Amendments to Chapters 1 through 3 of IBC.

(1)   IBC, Section 106, is deleted.

(2)   (a)   In IBC, Section 110, a new section is added as follows: "110.3.5, Weather-resistant exterior wall envelope. An inspection shall be made of the weather-resistant exterior wall envelope as required by Section 1403.2, and flashing as required by Section 1405.4 to prevent water from entering the weather-resistive barrier."

        (b)   The remaining sections of IBC, Section 110, are renumbered as follows: 110.3.6, Lath or gypsum board inspection; 110.3.7, Fire- and smoke-resistant penetrations; 110.3.8, Energy efficiency inspections; 110.3.9, Other inspections; 110.3.10, Special inspections; and 110.3.11, Final inspection.

(3)   IBC, Section 115.1, is deleted and replaced with the following: "115.1 Authority. Whenever the building official finds any work regulated by this code being performed in a manner either contrary to the provisions of this code or other pertinent laws or ordinances or is dangerous or unsafe, the building official is authorized to stop work."

(4)   In IBC, Section 202, the following definition is added for Ambulatory Surgical Center: "AMBULATORY SURGICAL CENTER. A building or portion of a building licensed by the Utah Department of Health where procedures are performed that may render patients incapable of self preservation where care is less than 24 hours. See Utah Administrative Code R432-13."

(5)   In IBC, Section 202, the definition for Foster Care Facilities is modified by changing the word "Foster" to "Child."

(6)   In IBC, Section 202, the definition for "[F]Record Drawings" is modified by deleting the words "a fire alarm system" and replacing them with "any fire protection system".

(7)   In IBC, Section 202, the following definition is added for Residential Treatment/Support Assisted Living Facility: "RESIDENTIAL TREATMENT/SUPPORT ASSISTED LIVING FACILITY. See Section 308.1.2."

(8)   In IBC, Section 202, the following definition is added for Type I Assisted Living Facility: "TYPE I ASSISTED LIVING FACILITY. See Section 308.1.2."

(9)   In IBC, Section 202, the following definition is added for Type II Assisted Living Facility: "TYPE II ASSISTED LIVING FACILITY. See Section 308.1.2."

(10)   In the list in IBC, Section 304.1, the following words are added after the words "Ambulatory care facilities": "where four or more care recipients are rendered incapable of self preservation."

(11)   In IBC, Section 305.2, the words "child care centers," are inserted after the word "supervision," and the following sentence is added at the end of the paragraph: "See Section 425 for special requirements for Day Care."

(12)   In IBC, Section 305.2.2 and 305.2.3, the word "five" is deleted and replaced with the word "four" in both places.

(13)   A new IBC Section 305.2.4 is added as follows: "305.2.4 Child Day Care — Residential Certificate or a Family License. Areas used for child day care purposes with a Residential Certificate R430-50 or a Family License, as defined in Utah Administrative Code, R430-90, Licensed Family Child Care, may be located in a Group R-2 or R-3 occupancy as provided in Section 310.5 or shall comply with the International Residential Code in accordance with Section R101.2."

(14)   A new IBC Section 305.2.5 is added as follows: "305.2.5 Child Care Centers. Areas used for Hourly Child Care Centers, as defined in Utah Administrative Code, R430-60, Child Care Center as defined in Utah Administrative Code, R430-100, or Out of School Time Programs, as defined in Utah Administrative Code, R430-70, may be classified as accessory occupancies."

(15)   A new IBC Section 308.2.1 is added as follows: "308.2.1 Assisted living facilities and related occupancies. The following words and terms shall, for the purposes of this section and as used elsewhere in this code, have the meanings shown herein.

TYPE I ASSISTED LIVING FACILITY. A residential facility licensed by the Utah Department of Health that provides a protected living arrangement for ambulatory, non-restrained persons who are capable of achieving mobility sufficient to exit the facility without the assistance of another person.

Occupancies. Limited capacity, type I assisted living facilities with two to five residents shall be classified as R-3 occupancies. Small, type I assisted living facilities with six to sixteen residents shall be classified as R-4 occupancies. Large, type I assisted living facilities with over sixteen residents shall be classified as I-1 occupancies.

TYPE II ASSISTED LIVING FACILITY. A residential facility licensed by the Utah Department of Health that provides an array of coordinated supportive personal and health care services to residents who meet the definition of semi-independent.

Semi-Independent. A person who is:

A.   Physically disabled but able to direct his or her own care; or

B.   Cognitively impaired or physically disabled but able to evacuate from the facility with the physical assistance of one person.

Occupancies. Limited capacity, type II assisted living facilities with two to five residents shall be classified as R-4 occupancies. Small, type II assisted living facilities with six to sixteen residents shall be classified as I-1 occupancies. Large, type II assisted living facilities with over sixteen residents shall be classified as I-2 occupancies.

RESIDENTIAL TREATMENT/SUPPORT ASSISTED LIVING FACILITY. A residential treatment/support assisted living facility which creates a group living environment for four or more residents licensed by the Utah Department of Human Services, and provides a protected living arrangement for ambulatory, non-restrained persons who are capable of achieving mobility sufficient to exit the facility without the physical assistance of another person."

(16)   In IBC, Section 308.3, the words "(see Section 308.2.1)" are added after the words "assisted living facilities".

(17)   In IBC, Section 308.3.1, all of the words after the first International Residential Code are deleted.

(18)   In IBC, Section 308.4, the following changes are made:

    (a)   The words "five persons" are deleted and replaced with the words "three persons."

    (b)   The words "foster care facilities" are deleted and replaced with "child care facilities."

    (c)   The words "(both intermediate care facilities and skilled nursing facilities)" are added after "nursing homes."

    (d)   The words "Ambulatory Surgical Centers with five or more operating rooms" are added to the list.

(19)   In IBC, Section 308.4.1, the word "five" is deleted and replaced with the word "three" in both places.

(20)   In IBC, Section 308.6, the word "five" is deleted and replaced with the word "four".

(21)   In IBC, Section 308.6.1, the following changes are made:

    (a)   The word "five" is deleted and replaced with the word "four".

    (b)   The words "2-1/2 years or less of age" are deleted and replaced with "under the age of two".

    (c)   The following sentence is added at the end: "See Section 425 for special requirements for Day Care."

(22)   In IBC, Sections 308.6.3 and 308.6.4, the word "five" is deleted and replaced with the word "four" in both places and the following sentence is added at the end: "See Section 425 for special requirements for Day Care."

(23)   In IBC, Section 310.5, the words "and single family dwellings complying with the IRC" are added after "Residential occupancies".

(24)   In IBC, Section 310.5.1, the words "other than Child Care" are inserted after the word "dwelling" in the first sentence and the following sentence is added at the end: "See Section 425 for special requirements for Child Day Care."

(25)   A new IBC Section 310.5.2 is added as follows: "310.5.2 Child Care. Areas used for child care purposes may be located in a residential dwelling unit under all of the following conditions and Section 425:

    1.   Compliance with Utah Administrative Code, R710-8, Day Care Rules, as enacted under the authority of the Utah Fire Prevention Board.

    2.   Use is approved by the Utah Department of Health, as enacted under the authority of the Utah Code, Title 26, Chapter 39, Utah Child Care Licensing Act, and in any of the following categories:

        a.   Utah Administrative Code, R430-50, Residential Certificate Child Care.

        b.   Utah Administrative Code, R430-90, Licensed Family Child Care.

    3.   Compliance with all zoning regulations of the local regulator."

(26)   In IBC, Section 310.6, the words "(see Section 308.2.1)" are added after "assisted living facilities".

Amended by Chapter 297, 2013 General Session

15A-3-103 Amendments to Chapters 4 through 6 of IBC.

(1)   IBC Section 403.5.5 is deleted.

(2)   IBC Section (F)406.5.8 is deleted and replaced with the following: "(F)406.5.8 Standpipe system. An open parking garage shall be equipped with an approved Class I manual standpipe system when fire department access is not provided for firefighting operations to within 150 feet of all portions of the open parking garage as measured from the approved fire department vehicle access. Exception: Open parking garages equipped throughout with an automatic sprinkler system in accordance with Section 903.3.1.1 and a standpipe system is not required by Section 905.3.1."

(3)   A new IBC Section (F)406.5.8.1 is added as follows: "(F)406.5.8.1 Installation requirements. Class I manual standpipe shall be designed and installed in accordance with Section 905 and NFPA 14. Class I manual standpipe shall be accessible throughout the parking garage such that all portions of the parking structure are protected within 150 feet of a hose connection."

(4)   In IBC, Section 422.2, a new paragraph is added as follows: "422.2 Separations: Ambulatory care facilities licensed by the Utah Department of Health shall be separated from adjacent tenants with a fire barrier having a minimum one hour fire-resistance rating. Any level below the level of exit discharge shall be separated from the level of exit discharge by a horizontal assembly having a minimum one hour fire-resistance rating. Exception: A fire barrier is not required to separate the level of exit discharge when:

    1. Such levels are under the control of the Ambulatory Care Facility.

    2. Any hazardous spaces are separated by horizontal assembly having a minimum one hour fire-resistance rating."

(5)   A new IBC Section 425, Day Care, is added as follows:

"425.1 Detailed Requirements. In addition to the occupancy and construction requirements in this code, the additional provisions of this section shall apply to all Day Care in accordance with Utah Administrative Code R710-8 Day Care Rules.

425.2 Definitions.

425.2.1 Authority Having Jurisdiction (AHJ): State Fire Marshal, his duly authorized deputies, or the local fire enforcement authority code official.

425.2.2 Day Care Facility: Any building or structure occupied by clients of any age who receive custodial care for less than 24 hours by individuals other than parents, guardians, relatives by blood, marriage or adoption.

425.2.3 Day Care Center: Providing care for five or more clients in a place other than the home of the person cared for. This would also include Child Care Centers, Out of School Time or Hourly Child Care Centers licensed by the Department of Health.

425.2.4 Family Day Care: Providing care for clients listed in the following two groups:

425.2.4.1 Type 1: Services provided for five to eight clients in a home. This would also include a home that is certified by the Department of Health as Residential Certificate Child Care or licensed as Family Child Care.

425.2.4.2 Type 2: Services provided for nine to sixteen clients in a home with sufficient staffing. This would also include a home that is licensed by the Department of Health as Family Child Care.

425.2.5 R710-8: Utah Administrative Code, R710-8, Day Care Rules, as enacted under the authority of the Utah Fire Prevention Board.

425.3. Family Day Care.

425.3.1 Family Day Care units shall have on each floor occupied by clients, two separate means of egress, arranged so that if one is blocked the other will be available.

425.3.2 Family Day Care units that are located in the basement or on the second story shall be provided with two means of egress, one of which shall discharge directly to the outside.

425.3.2.1 Residential Certificate Child Care and Licensed Family Child Care with five to eight clients in a home, located on the ground level or in a basement, may use an emergency escape or rescue window as allowed in IFC, Chapter 10, Section 1029.

425.3.3 Family Day Care units shall not be located above the second story.

425.3.4 In Family Day Care units, clients under the age of two shall not be located above or below the first story.

425.3.4.1 Clients under the age of two may be housed above or below the first story where there is at least one exit that leads directly to the outside and complies with IFC, Section 1009 or Section 1010 or Section 1026.

425.3.5 Family Day Care units located in split entry/split level type homes in which stairs to the lower level and upper level are equal or nearly equal, may have clients housed on both levels when approved by the AHJ.

425.3.6 Family Day Care units shall have a portable fire extinguisher on each level occupied by clients, which shall have a classification of not less than 2A:10BC, and shall be serviced in accordance with NFPA, Standard 10, Standard for Portable Fire Extinguishers.

425.3.7 Family Day Care units shall have single station smoke detectors in good operating condition on each level occupied by clients. Battery operated smoke detectors shall be permitted if the facility demonstrates testing, maintenance, and battery replacement to insure continued operation of the smoke detectors.

425.3.8 Rooms in Family Day Care units that are provided for clients to sleep or nap, shall have at least one window or door approved for emergency escape.

425.3.9 Fire drills shall be conducted in Family Day Care units quarterly and shall include the complete evacuation from the building of all clients and staff. At least annually, in Type I Family Day Care units, the fire drill shall include the actual evacuation using the escape or rescue window, if one is used as a substitute for one of the required means of egress.

425.4 Day Care Centers.

425.4.1 Day Care Centers shall comply with either I-4 requirements or E requirements of the IBC, whichever is applicable for the type of Day Care Center.

425.4.2 Emergency Evacuation Drills shall be completed as required in IFC, Chapter 4, Section 405.

425.4.3 Location at grade. Group E child day care centers shall be located at the level of exit discharge.

425.4.3.1 Child day care spaces for children over the age of 24 months may be located on the second floor of buildings equipped with automatic fire protection throughout and an automatic fire alarm system.

425.4.4 Egress. All Group E child day care spaces with an occupant load of more than 10 shall have a second means of egress. If the second means of egress is not an exit door leading directly to the exterior, the room shall have an emergency escape and rescue window complying with Section 1029.

425.4.5 All Group E Child Day Care Centers shall comply with Utah Administrative Code, R430-100 Child Care Centers, R430-60 Hourly Child Care Centers, and R430-70 Out of School Time.

425.5 Requirements for all Day Care.

425.5.1 Heating equipment in spaces occupied by children shall be provided with partitions, screens, or other means to protect children from hot surfaces and open flames.

425.5.2 A fire escape plan shall be completed and posted in a conspicuous place. All staff shall be trained on the fire escape plan and procedure."

(6)   In IBC, Section 504.2, a new section is added as follows: "504.2.1 Notwithstanding the exceptions to Section 504.2, Group I-2 Assisted Living Facilities shall be allowed to be two stories of Type V-A construction when all of the following apply:

1.   All secured units are located at the level of exit discharge in compliance with Section 1008.1.9.3 as amended;

2.   The total combined area of both stories shall not exceed the total allowable area for a one-story building; and

3.   All other provisions that apply in Section 407 have been provided."

Amended by Chapter 297, 2013 General Session

15A-3-104 Amendments to Chapters 7 through 9 of IBC.

(1)   IBC, Section (F)901.8, is deleted and replaced with the following: "(F)901.8 Pump and riser room size. Fire pump and automatic sprinkler system riser rooms shall be designed with adequate space for all installed equipment necessary for the installation and to provide sufficient working space around the stationary equipment. Clearances around equipment shall be in accordance with manufacturer requirements and not less than the following minimum elements:

901.8.1 A minimum clear and unobstructed distance of 12-inches shall be provided from the installed equipment to the elements of permanent construction.

901.8.2 A minimum clear and unobstructed distance of 12-inches shall be provided between all other installed equipment and appliances.

901.8.3 A clear and unobstructed width of 36-inches shall be provided in front of all installed equipment and appliances, to allow for inspection, service, repair or replacement without removing such elements of permanent construction or disabling the function of a required fire-resistance-rated assembly.

901.8.4 Automatic sprinkler system riser rooms shall be provided with a clear and unobstructed passageway to the riser room of not less than 36-inches, and openings into the room shall be clear and unobstructed, with doors swinging in the outward direction from the room and the opening providing a clear width of not less than 34-inches and a clear height of the door opening shall not be less than 80-inches.

901.8.5 Fire pump rooms shall be provided with a clear and unobstructed passageway to the fire pump room of not less than 72-inches, and openings into the room shall be clear, unobstructed and large enough to allow for the removal of the largest piece of equipment, with doors swinging in the outward direction from the room and the opening providing a clear width of not less than 68-inches and a clear height of the door opening shall not be less than 80-inches."

(2)   In IBC, Section (F)903.2.2, the words "the entire floor" are deleted and replaced with "a building" and the last paragraph is deleted.

(3)   IBC, Section (F)903.2.4, condition 2, is deleted and replaced with the following: "2. A Group F-1 fire area is located more than three stories above the lowest level of fire department vehicle access."

(4)   IBC, Section (F)903.2.7, condition 2, is deleted and replaced with the following: "2. A Group M fire area is located more than three stories above the lowest level of fire department vehicle access."

(5)   IBC, Sections (F)903.2.8, (F)903.2.8.1, and (F)903.2.8.2, are deleted and replaced with the following: "(F)903.2.8 Group R. An automatic sprinkler system installed in accordance with Section 903.3 shall be provided throughout all buildings with a Group R fire area. Exceptions:

   1.   Detached one- and two-family dwellings and multiple single-family dwellings (townhouses) constructed in accordance with the International Residential Code For One- and Two-Family Dwellings.

   2.   Single story Group R-1 occupancies with fire areas not more than 2,000 square feet that contain no installed plumbing or heating, where no cooking occurs, and constructed of Type I-A, I-B, II-A, or II-B construction.

   3.   Group R-4 fire areas not more than 4,500 gross square feet and not containing more than 16 residents, provided the building is equipped throughout with an approved fire alarm system that is interconnected and receives its primary power from the building wiring and a commercial power system."

(6)   IBC, Section (F)903.2.9, condition 2, is deleted and replaced with the following: "2. A Group S-1 fire area is located more than three stories above the lowest level of fire department vehicle access."

(7)   IBC, Section (F)904.11, is deleted and replaced with the following: "(F)904.11 Commercial cooking systems. The automatic fire-extinguishing system for commercial cooking systems shall be of a type recognized for protection of commercial cooking equipment and exhaust systems. Pre-engineered automatic extinguishing systems shall be tested in accordance with UL 300 and listed and labeled for the intended application. The system shall be installed in accordance with this code, its listing and the manufacturer's installation instructions. Exception: Factory-built commercial cooking recirculating systems that are tested in accordance with UL 710B and listed, labeled, and installed in accordance with Section 304.1 of the International Mechanical Code."

(8)   IBC, Sections (F)904.11.3, (F)904.11.3.1, (F)904.11.4, and (F)904.11.4.1, are deleted.

(9)   IBC, Section (F)907.2.3 Group E:

   (a)   The first sentence is deleted and rewritten as follows: "A manual fire alarm system that initiates the occupant notification system in accordance with Section (F)907.5 and installed in accordance with Section (F)907.6 shall be installed in Group E occupancies."

   (b)   In Exception number 3, starting on line five, the words "emergency voice/alarm communication system" are deleted and replaced with "occupant notification system".

(10)   In IBC, Section (F)908.7, the first sentence is deleted and replaced as follows: "Groups R-1, R-2, R-3, R-4, I-1, and I-4 occupancies"; the exceptions are deleted and the following sentence is added after the first sentence: "A minimum of one carbon monoxide alarm shall be installed on each habitable level."

(11)   In IBC, Section (F)908.7, the following new subsections are added: "(F)908.7.1 Interconnection. Where more than one carbon monoxide alarm is required to be installed within Group R or I-1 occupancies, the carbon monoxide alarms shall be interconnected in such a manner that the activation of one alarm will activate all of the alarms. Physical interconnection of carbon monoxide alarms shall not be required where listed wireless alarms are installed and all alarms sound upon activation of one alarm. The alarm shall be clearly audible in all bedrooms over background noise levels with all intervening doors closed. (F)908.7.2 Power source. In new construction, required carbon monoxide alarms shall receive their primary power from the building wiring where such wiring is served from a commercial source and shall be equipped with a battery backup. Carbon monoxide alarms with integral strobes that are not equipped with battery backup shall be

connected to an emergency electrical system. Carbon monoxide alarms shall emit a signal when the batteries are low. Wiring shall be permanent and without a disconnecting switch other than as required for overcurrent protection.

Exception: Carbon monoxide alarms are not required to be equipped with battery backup where they are connected to an emergency electrical system."

(12)   IBC, Section (F)908.7.1, is renumbered to 908.7.3.

Amended by Chapter 243, 2014 General Session

15A-3-105 Amendments to Chapters 10 through 12 of IBC.

(1)   In IBC, Section 1008.1.9.6, the words "Group I-1 and" are added in the title and in the first sentence before the words "Group I-2" and a new number 8 is added as follows: "8. The secure area or unit with special egress locks shall be located at the level of exit discharge in Type V construction."

(2)   In IBC, Section 1008.1.9.7, a new number 7 is added as follows: "7. The secure area or unit with delayed egress locks shall be located at the level of exit discharge in Type V construction."

(3)   In IBC, Section 1009.7.2, exception 5 is deleted and replaced with the following: "5. In Group R-3 occupancies, within dwelling units in Group R-2 occupancies, and in Group U occupancies that are accessory to a Group R-3 occupancy, or accessory to individual dwelling units in Group R-2 occupancies, the maximum riser height shall be 8 inches (203 mm) and the minimum tread depth shall be 9 inches (229 mm). The minimum winder tread depth at the walk line shall be 10 inches (254 mm), and the minimum winder tread depth shall be 6 inches (152 mm). A nosing not less than 0.75 inch (19.1 mm) but not more than 1.25 inches (32 mm) shall be provided on stairways with solid risers where the tread depth is less than 10 inches (254 mm)."

(4)   In IBC, Section 1009.15, a new exception 6 is added as follows: "6. In occupancies in Group R-3, as applicable in Section 101.2 and in occupancies in Group U, which are accessory to an occupancy in Group R-3, as applicable in Section 101.2, handrails shall be provided on at least one side of stairways consisting of four or more risers."

(5)   In IBC, Section 1011.5, the words ", including when the building may not be fully occupied." are added at the end of the sentence.

(6)   IBC, Section 1024, is deleted.

(7)   In IBC, Section 1028.12, exception 2 is deleted.

(8)   In IBC, Section 1109.8, the following words "shall be capable of operation without a key and" are inserted in the second sentence between the words "lift" and "shall".

(9)   In IBC, Section 1208.4, subparagraph 1 is deleted and replaced with the following: "1. The unit shall have a living room of not less than 165 square feet (15.3 m2) of floor area. An additional 100 square feet (9.3 m2) of floor area shall be provided for each occupant of such unit in excess of two."

Amended by Chapter 297, 2013 General Session

15A-3-106 Amendments to Chapters 13 and 14 of IBC.

IBC, Chapters 13 and 14 are not amended.

Amended by Chapter 153, 2014 General Session

15A-3-106.5 Amendments to Chapter 15 of IBC.

(1)   IBC, Section 1505.8 is deleted.

(2)   IBC, Section 1509.7.2 is deleted.

(3)   IBC, Section 1509.7.4 is deleted and rewritten as follows:

"Photovoltaic panels and modules that are mounted on top of a roof shall:

1. Regardless of the roof assembly classification, be listed and labeled with at least a class C fire classification;

2. Be listed and labeled in accordance with UL 1703; and

3. Be installed in accordance with the manufacturer's installation instructions."

(4)   Subsections (1) through (3) do not apply if the Legislature adopts, with or without amendment, an edition of the IBC that is more recent than the 2012 edition.

Enacted by Chapter 153, 2014 General Session

15A-3-107 Amendments to Chapter 16 of IBC.

(1)   In IBC, Table 1604.5, Risk Category III, in the sentence that begins "Group I-2," a new footnote c is added as follows: "c. Type II Assisted Living Facilities that are I-2 occupancy classifications in accordance with Section 308 shall be Risk Category II in this table."

(2)   In IBC, Section 1605.2, in the portion of the definition for the value of f_2, the words "and 0.2 for other roof configurations" are deleted and replaced with the following: "$f_2 = 0.20 + .025(A-5)$ for other configurations where roof snow load exceeds 30 psf;

$$f_2 = 0 \text{ for roof snow loads of 30 psf (1.44kN/m}^2) \text{ or less.}$$

Where A = Elevation above sea level at the location of the structure (ft./1,000)."

(3)   In IBC, Sections 1605.3.1 and 1605.3.2, exception 2 in each section is deleted and replaced with the following: "2. Flat roof snow loads of 30 pounds per square foot (1.44 kNm²) or less need not be combined with seismic loads. Where flat roof snow loads exceed 30 pounds per square foot (1.44 kNm²), the snow loads may be reduced in accordance with the following in load combinations including both snow and seismic loads. W_s as calculated below, shall be combined with seismic loads.

$$W_s = (0.20 + 0.025(A-5))P_f \text{ is greater than or equal to 0.20 Pf.}$$

Where:

W_s = Weight of snow to be included in seismic calculations

A =   Elevation above sea level at the location of the structure (ft./1,000)

P_f =   Design roof snow load, psf.

For the purpose of this section, snow load shall be assumed uniform on the roof footprint without including the effects of drift or sliding. The Importance Factor, I, used in calculating P_f may be considered 1.0 for use in the formula for W_s".

(4)   IBC, Section 1608.1, is deleted and replaced with the following: "1608.1 General. Except as modified in Sections 1608.1.1, 1608.1.2, and 1608.1.3, design snow loads shall be determined in accordance with Chapter 7 of ASCE 7, but the design roof load shall not be less than that determined by Section 1607."

(5)   A new IBC, Section 1608.1.1, is added as follows: "1608.1.1 Section 7.4.5 of Chapter 7 of ASCE 7 referenced in Section 1608.1 of the IBC is deleted and replaced with the following: Section 7.4.5 Ice Dams and Icicles Along Eaves. Where ground snow loads exceed 75 psf, eaves shall be capable of sustaining a uniformly distributed load of $2p_f$ on all overhanging portions. No other loads except dead loads shall be present on the roof when this uniformly distributed load is applied. All building exits under down-slope eaves shall be protected from sliding snow and ice."

(6)   In IBC, Section 1608.1.2, a new section is added as follows: "1608.1.2 Utah Snow Loads. The snow loads specified in Table 1608.1.2(b) shall be used for the jurisdictions identified in that table. Otherwise, the ground snow load, Pg, to be used in the determination of design snow loads for buildings and other structures shall be determined by using the following formula: $P_g = (P_o^2 + S^2(A - A_o)^2)^{0.5}$ for A greater than A_o, and $P_g = P_o$ for A less than or equal to A_o.

WHERE:

P_g = Ground snow load at a given elevation (psf);

P_o = Base ground snow load (psf) from Table No. 1608.1.2(a);

S = Change in ground snow load with elevation (psf/100 ft.) From Table No. 1608.1.2(a);

A = Elevation above sea level at the site (ft./1,000);

A_o = Base ground snow elevation from Table 1608.1.2(a) (ft./1,000).

The building official may round the roof snow load to the nearest 5 psf. The ground snow load, P_g, may be adjusted by the building official when a licensed engineer or architect submits data substantiating the adjustments.

Where the minimum roof live load in accordance with Section 1607.11 is greater than the design roof snow load, such roof live load shall be used for design, however, it shall not be reduced to a load lower than the design roof snow load. Drifting need not be considered for roof snow loads less than 20 psf."

(7)   IBC, Table 1608.1.2(a) and Table 1608.1.2(b), are added as follows:

"TABLE NO. 1608.1.2(a)

STATE OF UTAH - REGIONAL SNOW LOAD FACTORS

COUNTY	P_o	S	A_o
Beaver	43	63	6.2
Box Elder	43	63	5.2
Cache	50	63	4.5
Carbon	43	63	5.2
Daggett	43	63	6.5
Davis	43	63	4.5
Duchesne	43	63	6.5
Emery	43	63	6.0
Garfield	43	63	6.0
Grand	36	63	6.5
Iron	43	63	5.8
Juab	43	63	5.2
Kane	36	63	5.7
Millard	43	63	5.3
Morgan	57	63	4.5
Piute	43	63	6.2
Rich	57	63	4.1
Salt Lake	43	63	4.5
San Juan	43	63	6.5

	Sanpete	43	63	5.2
	Sevier	43	63	6.0
	Summit	86	63	5.0
	Tooele	43	63	4.5
	Uintah	43	63	7.0
	Utah	43	63	4.5
	Wasatch	86	63	5.0
	Washington	29	63	6.0
	Wayne	36	63	6.5
	Weber	43	63	4.5

TABLE NO. 1608.1.2(B)

REQUIRED SNOW LOADS FOR SELECTED UTAH CITIES AND TOWNS[1,2]

The following jurisdictions require design snow load values that differ from the Equation in the Utah Snow Load Study.

County	City	Elevation	Ground Snow Load (psf)	Roof Snow Load (psf)[6]
Carbon	Price[3]	5550	43	30
	All other county locations[5]	—	—	—
Davis	Fruit Heights[3]	4500–4850	57	40
Emery	Green River[3]	4070	36	25
Garfield	Panguitch[3]	6600	43	30
Rich	Woodruff[3]	6315	57	40
	Laketown[4]	6000	57	40
	Garden City[5]	—	—	—
	Randolph[4]	6300	57	40
San Juan	Monticello[3]	6820	50	35
Summit	Coalville[3]	5600	86	60
	Kamas[4]	6500	114	80
Tooele	Tooele[3]	5100	43	30
Utah	Orem[3]	4650	43	30
	Pleasant Grove[4]	5000	43	30
	Provo[5]	—	—	—
Wasatch	Heber[5]			
Washington	Leeds[3]	3460	29	20
	Santa Clara[3]	2850	21	15
	St. George[3]	2750	21	15
	All other county locations[5]	—	—	—
Wayne	Loa[3]	7080	43	30

[1]The IBC requires a minimum live load – See 1607.11.2.

[2]This table is informational only in that actual site elevations may vary. Table is only valid if site elevation is within 100 feet of the listed elevation. Otherwise, contact the local Building Official.

[3]Values adopted from Table VII of the Utah Snow Load Study.

[4]Values based on site-specific study. Contact local Building Official for additional information.

[5]Contact local Building Official.

[6]Based on Ce = 1.0, Ct = 1.0 and Is = 1.0"

(8)   A new IBC, Section 1608.1.3, is added as follows: "1608.1.3 Thermal Factor. The value for the thermal factor, C_t, used in calculation of P_f shall be determined from Table 7.3 in ASCE 7. Exception: Except for unheated structures, the value of C_t need not exceed 1.0 when ground snow load, P_g is calculated using Section 1608.1.2 as amended."

(9)   IBC, Section 1608.2, is deleted and replaced with the following: "1608.2 Ground Snow Loads. The ground snow loads to be used in determining the design snow loads for roofs in states other than Utah are given in Figure 1608.2 for the contiguous United States and Table 1608.2 for Alaska. Site-specific case studies shall be made in areas designated CS in figure 1608.2. Ground snow loads for sites at elevations above the limits indicated in Figure 1608.2 and for all sites within the CS areas shall be approved. Ground snow load determination for such sites shall be based on an extreme value statistical analysis of data available in the vicinity of the site using a value with a 2-percent annual probability of being exceeded (50-year mean recurrence interval). Snow loads are zero for Hawaii, except in mountainous regions as approved by the building official."

(10)   A new IBC, Section 1613.1.1, is added as follows: "1613.1.1 ASCE 12.7.2 and 12.14.8.1 of Chapter 12 of ASCE 7 referenced in Section 1613.1, Definition of W, Item 4 is deleted and replaced with the following:

4.   Where the flat roof snow load, P_f, exceeds 30 psf, the snow load included in seismic design shall be calculated, in accordance with the following formula: $W_s = (0.20 + 0.025(A - 5))P_f$ is greater than or equal to $0.20\ P_f$.

WHERE:

W_s = Weight of snow to be included in seismic calculations

A = Elevation above sea level at the location of the structure (ft./1,000)

P_f = Design roof snow load, psf.

For the purposes of this section, snow load shall be assumed uniform on the roof footprint without including the effects of drift or sliding. The Importance Factor, I, used in calculating P_f may be considered 1.0 for use in the formula for W_s."

(11)   A new IBC, Section 1613.5, is added as follows: " 1613.5 ASCE 7, Section 13.5.6.2.2 paragraph (e) is modified to read as follows: (e) Penetrations shall have a sleeve or adapter through the ceiling tile to allow for free movement of at least 1 inch (25 mm) in all horizontal directions.

Exceptions:

1.   Where rigid braces are used to limit lateral deflections.

2.   At fire sprinkler heads in frangible surfaces per NFPA 13."

Amended by Chapter 297, 2013 General Session

15A-3-108 Amendments to Chapters 17 through 19 of IBC.

(1)   A new IBC, Section 1807.1.6.4, is added as follows: "1807.1.6.4 Empirical concrete foundation design. Group R, Division 3 Occupancies three stories or less in height, and Group U Occupancies, which are constructed in accordance with Section 2308, or with other methods employing repetitive wood-frame construction or repetitive cold-formed steel structural member construction, shall be permitted to have concrete foundations constructed in accordance with Table 1807.1.6.4."

(2)   A new IBC, Table 1807.1.6.4 is added as follows:

"TABLE 1807.1.6.4

EMPIRICAL FOUNDATION WALLS (1,7,8)

Max. Height	Top Edge Support	Min. Thickness	Vertical Steel (2)	Horizontal Steel (3)	Steel at Openings (4)	Max. Lintel Length	Min. Lintel Length
2'(610 mm)	None	6"	(5)	2- #4 Bars	2- #4 Bars above 1- #4 Bar each side 1- #4 Bar below	2'(610 mm)	2" for each foot of opening width; min. 6"
3'(914 mm)	None	6"	#4@32"	3- #4 Bars	2- #4 Bars above 1- #4 Bar each side 1- #4 Bar below	2'(610 mm)	2" for each foot of opening width; min. 6"
4'(1,219 mm)	None	6"	#4@32"	4- #4 Bars	2- #4 Bars above 1- #4 Bar each side 1- #4 Bar below	3'(914 mm)	2" for each foot of opening width; min. 6"
6'(1,829 mm)	Floor or roof Diaphragm (6)	8"	#4@24"	5- #4 Bars	2- #4 Bars above 1- #4 Bar each side 1- #4 Bar below	6'(1,829 mm)	2" for each foot of opening width; min. 6"
8'(2,438 mm)	Floor or roof Diaphragm (6)	8"	#4@24"	6- #4 Bars	2- #4 Bars above 1- #4 Bar each side 1- #4 Bar below	6'(1,829 mm)	2" for each foot of opening width; min. 6"
9'(2,743 mm)	Floor or roof Diaphragm (6)	8"	#4@16"	7- #4 Bars	2- #4 Bars above 1- #4 Bar each side 1- #4 Bar below	6'(1,829 mm)	2" for each foot of opening width; min. 6"

Over 9'(2,743 mm), Engineering required for each column

Footnotes:

(1) Based on 3,000 psi (20.6 Mpa) concrete and 60,000 psi (414 Mpa) reinforcing steel.

(2) To be placed in the center of the wall, and extended from the footing to within three inches (76 mm) of the top of the wall; dowels of #4 bars to match vertical steel placement shall be provided in the footing, extending 24 inches (610 mm) into the foundation wall.

(3) One bar shall be located in the top four inches (102 mm), one bar in the bottom four inches (102 mm) and the other bars equally spaced between. Such bar placement satisfies the requirements of Section 1805.9. Corner reinforcing shall be provided so as to lap 24 inches (610 mm).

(4) Bars shall be placed within two inches (51 mm) of the openings and extend 24 inches (610 mm) beyond the edge of the opening; vertical bars may terminate three inches (76 mm) from the top of the concrete.

(5) Dowels of #4 bar at 32 inches on center shall be provided in the footing, extending 18 inches (457 mm) into the foundation wall.

(6) Diaphragm shall conform to the requirements of Section 2308.

(7) Footing shall be a minimum of nine inches thick by 20 inches wide.

(8) Soil backfill shall be soil classification types GW, GP, SW, or SP, per Table 1610.1. Soil shall not be submerged or saturated in groundwater."

(3)   In IBC, Section 1904.2, a new exception 1 is added as follows and the current exception is modified to be number 2.

Exceptions:

"1. In ACI Table 4.3.1, for Exposure Class F1, change Maximum w/cm from 0.45 to 0.5 and Minimum f'c from 4,500 psi to 3,000 psi."

(4)   A new IBC, Section 1905.1.11, is added as follows: "1905.1.11 ACI 318, Table 4.2.1." Modify ACI 318, Table 4.2.1 to read as follows: In the portion of the table designated as "Conditions", the Exposure categories and classes are deleted and replaced with the following:

"F0: Concrete elements not exposed to freezing and thawing cycles to include footing and foundation elements that are completely buried in soil.

F1: Concrete elements exposed to freezing and thawing cycles and are not likely to be saturated or exposed to deicing chemicals.

F2: Concrete elements exposed to freezing and thawing cycles and are likely to be saturated, but not exposed to deicing chemicals.

F3: Concrete elements exposed to freezing and thawing cycles and are likely to be saturated and exposed to deicing chemicals."

Amended by Chapter 297, 2013 General Session

15A-3-109 Amendments to Chapters 20 through 22 of IBC.

IBC, Chapters 20 through 22 are not amended.

Enacted by Chapter 14, 2011 General Session

15A-3-110 Amendments to Chapters 23 through 25 of IBC.

(1)   A new IBC, Section 2306.1.5, is added as follows: "2306.1.5 Load duration factors. The allowable stress increase of 1.15 for snow load, shown in Table 2.3.2, Frequently Used Load Duration Factors, Cd, of the National Design Specifications, shall not be utilized at elevations above 5,000 feet (1,524 M)."

(2)   In IBC, Section 2308.6, a new exception is added as follows: "Exception: Where foundation plates or sills are bolted or anchored to the foundation with not less than 1/2 inch (12.7 mm) diameter steel bolts or approved anchors, embedded at least 7 inches (178 mm) into concrete or masonry and spaced not more than 32 inches (816 mm) apart, there shall be a minimum of two bolts or anchor straps per piece located not less than 4 inches (102 mm) from each end of each piece. A properly sized nut and washer shall be tightened on each bolt to the plate."

(3)   IBC, Section 2506.2.1, is deleted and replaced with the following: "2506.2.1 Other materials. Metal suspension systems for acoustical and lay-in panel ceilings shall conform with ASTM C635 listed in Chapter 35 and Section 13.5.6 of ASCE 7, as amended in Section 1613.8, for installation in high seismic areas."

Amended by Chapter 297, 2013 General Session

15A-3-111 Amendments to Chapters 26 through 28 of IBC

IBC, Chapters 26 through 28 are not amended.

Enacted by Chapter 14, 2011 General Session

15A-3-112 Amendments to Chapters 29 through 31 of IBC.

    (1)   In IBC [P] Table 2902.1 the following changes are made:

        (a)   The title for [P] Table 2902.1 is deleted and replaced with the following: "[P] Table 2902.1, Minimum Number of Required Plumbing Facilities a, h".

        (b)   In the row for "E" occupancy in the field for "OTHER" a new footnote i is added.

        (c)   In the row for "I-4" occupancy in the field for "OTHER" a new footnote i is added.

        (d)   A new footnote h is added as follows: "FOOTNOTE: h. When provided, in public toilet facilities there shall be an equal number of diaper changing facilities in male toilet rooms and female toilet rooms."

        (e)   A new footnote i is added to the table as follows: "FOOTNOTE i: Non-residential child care facilities shall comply with additional sink requirements of Utah Administrative Code R430-100-4."

    (2)   In IBC, Section 3006.5, a new exception is added as follows: "Exception: Hydraulic elevators and roped hydraulic elevators with a rise of 50 feet or less."

Amended by Chapter 297, 2013 General Session

15A-3-113 Amendments to Chapters 32 through 35 of IBC.

    (1)   A new section IBC, Section 3401.7, is added as follows: " 3401.7 Parapet bracing, wall anchors, and other appendages. Until June 30, 2014, a building constructed before 1975 shall have parapet bracing, wall anchors, and appendages such as cornices, spires, towers, tanks, signs, statuary, etc. evaluated by a licensed engineer when the building is undergoing structural alterations, which may include structural sheathing replacement of 10% or greater, or other structural repairs. Reroofing or water membrane replacement may not be considered a structural alteration or repair for purposes of this section. Beginning July 1, 2014, a building constructed before 1975 shall have parapet bracing, wall anchors, and appendages such as cornices, spires, towers, tanks, signs, statuary, etc. evaluated by a licensed engineer when the building is undergoing a total reroofing. Parapet bracing, wall anchors, and appendages required by this section shall be evaluated in accordance with 75% of the seismic forces as specified in Section 1613. When allowed by the local building official, alternate methods of equivalent strength as referenced in an approved code under Utah Code, Subsection 15A-1-204(6)(a), will be considered when accompanied by engineer-sealed drawings, details, and calculations. When found to be deficient because of design or deteriorated condition, the engineer's recommendations to anchor, brace, reinforce, or remove the deficient feature shall be implemented.

        Exceptions:

        1.   Group R-3 and U occupancies.

        2.   Unreinforced masonry parapets need not be braced according to the above stated provisions provided that the maximum height of an unreinforced masonry parapet above the level of the diaphragm tension anchors or above the parapet braces shall not exceed one and one-half times the thickness of the parapet wall. The parapet height may be a maximum of two and one-half times its thickness in other than Seismic Design Categories D, E, or F."

    (2)   IBC, Section 3408.4, is deleted and replaced with the following: "3408.4 Seismic. When a change in occupancy results in a structure being reclassified to a higher Risk Category (as defined in Table 1604.5), or when such change of occupancy results in a design occupant load increase of 100% or more, the structure shall conform to the seismic requirements for a new structure.

Exceptions:

1. Specific seismic detailing requirements of this code or ASCE 7 for a new structure shall not be required to be met where it can be shown that the level of performance and seismic safety is equivalent to that of a new structure. A demonstration of equivalence analysis shall consider the regularity, overstrength, redundancy, and ductility of the structure. Alternatively, the building official may allow the structure to be upgraded in accordance with referenced sections as found in an approved code under Utah Code, Subsection 15A-1-204(6)(a).

2. When a change of use results in a structure being reclassified from Risk Category I or II to Risk Category III and the structure is located in a seismic map area where SDS is less than 0.33, compliance with the seismic requirements of this code and ASCE 7 are not required.

3. Where design occupant load increase is less than 25 occupants and the Risk Category does not change."

(3) In IBC, Chapter 35, the referenced standard ICCA117.1-09, Section 606.2, Exception 1 is modified to include the following sentence at the end of the exception: "The minimum clear floor space shall be centered on the sink assembly."

(4) The following referenced standard is added under UL in IBC, Chapter 35:

"Number	Title	Referenced in code section number
2034-2008	Standard of Single- and Multiple-stationCarbon Monoxide Alarms	907.9"

Amended by Chapter 297, 2013 General Session

Part 2 - Statewide Amendments to International Residential Code

15A-3-201 General provision.

(1) The amendments in this part are adopted as amendments to the IRC to be applicable statewide.

(2) The statewide amendments to the following which may be applied to detached one- and two-family dwellings and multiple single-family dwellings shall be applicable to the corresponding provisions of the IRC:

(a) IBC under Part 1, Statewide Amendments to International Building Code;

(b) IPC under Part 3, Statewide Amendments to International Plumbing Code;

(c) IMC under Part 4, Statewide Amendments to International Mechanical Code;

(d) IFGC under Part 5, Statewide Amendments to International Fuel Gas Code;

(e) NEC under Part 6, Statewide Amendments to National Electrical Code; and

(f) IECC under Part 7, Statewide Amendments to International Energy Conservation Code.

Amended by Chapter 189, 2014 General Session

15A-3-202 Amendments to Chapters 1 through 5 of IRC.

(1) In IRC, Section R102, a new Section R102.7.2 is added as follows: "R102.7.2 Physical change for bedroom window egress. A structure whose egress window in an existing bedroom is smaller than required by this code, and that complied with the construction code in effect at the time that the

bedroom was finished, is not required to undergo a physical change to conform to this code if the change would compromise the structural integrity of the structure or could not be completed in accordance with other applicable requirements of this code, including setback and window well requirements."

(2)   In IRC, Section 109:

    (a)   A new IRC, Section 109.1.5, is added as follows: "R109.1.5 Weather-resistant exterior wall envelope inspections. An inspection shall be made of the weather-resistant exterior wall envelope as required by Section R703.1 and flashings as required by Section R703.8 to prevent water from entering the weather-resistive barrier."

    (b)   The remaining sections are renumbered as follows: R109.1.6 Other inspections; R109.1.6.1 Fire- and smoke-resistance-rated construction inspection; R109.1.6.2 Reinforced masonry, insulating concrete form (ICF) and conventionally formed concrete wall inspection; and R109.1.7 Final inspection.

(3)   IRC, Section R114.1, is deleted and replaced with the following: "R114.1 Notice to owner. Upon notice from the building official that work on any building or structure is being prosecuted contrary to the provisions of this code or other pertinent laws or ordinances or in an unsafe and dangerous manner, such work shall be immediately stopped. The stop work order shall be in writing and shall be given to the owner of the property involved, or to the owner's agent or to the person doing the work; and shall state the conditions under which work will be permitted to resume."

(4)   In IRC, Section R202, the following definition is added: "CERTIFIED BACKFLOW PREVENTER ASSEMBLY TESTER: A person who has shown competence to test Backflow prevention assemblies to the satisfaction of the authority having jurisdiction under Utah Code, Subsection 19-4-104(4)."

(5)   In IRC, Section R202, the definition for "CONDITIONED SPACE" is modified by deleting the words at the end of the sentence "being heated or cooled by any equipment or appliance" and replacing them with the following: "enclosed within the building thermal envelope that is directly heated or cooled, or indirectly heated or cooled by any of the following means:

    1.   Openings directly into an adjacent conditioned space.

    2.   An un-insulated floor, ceiling or wall adjacent to a conditioned space.

    3.   Un-insulated duct, piping or other heat or cooling source within the space."

(6)   In IRC, Section R202, the definition of "Cross Connection" is deleted and replaced with the following: "CROSS CONNECTION. Any physical connection or potential connection or arrangement between two otherwise separate piping systems, one of which contains potable water and the other either water of unknown or questionable safety or steam, gas, or chemical, whereby there exists the possibility for flow from one system to the other, with the direction of flow depending on the pressure differential between the two systems (see "Backflow, Water Distribution")."

(7)   In IRC, Section 202, in the definition for gray water a comma is inserted after the word "washers"; the word "and" is deleted; and the following is added to the end: "and clear water wastes which have a pH of 6.0 to 9.0; are non-flammable; non-combustible; without objectionable odors; non-highly pigmented; and will not interfere with the operation of the sewer treatment facility."

(8)   In IRC, Section R202, the definition of "Potable Water" is deleted and replaced with the following: "POTABLE WATER. Water free from impurities present in amounts sufficient to cause disease or harmful physiological effects and conforming to the Utah Code, Title 19, Chapters 4, Safe Drinking Water Act, and 5, Water Quality Act, and the regulations of the public health authority having jurisdiction."

(9)   IRC, Figure R301.2(5), is deleted and replaced with Table R301.2(5a) and Table R301.2(5b) as follows:

"TABLE NO. R301.2(5a)

STATE OF UTAH - REGIONAL SNOW LOAD FACTORS

COUNTY	P_0	S	A_0
Beaver	43	63	6.2
Box Elder	43	63	5.2
Cache	50	63	4.5
Carbon	43	63	5.2
Daggett	43	63	6.5
Davis	43	63	4.5
Duchesne	43	63	6.5
Emery	43	63	6.0
Garfield	43	63	6.0
Grand	36	63	6.5
Iron	43	63	5.8
Juab	43	63	5.2
Kane	36	63	5.7
Millard	43	63	5.3
Morgan	57	63	4.5
Piute	43	63	6.2
Rich	57	63	4.1
Salt Lake	43	63	4.5
San Juan	43	63	6.5
Sanpete	43	63	5.2
Sevier	43	63	6.0
Summit	86	63	5.0
Tooele	43	63	4.5
Uintah	43	63	7.0
Utah	43	63	4.5
Wasatch	86	63	5.0
Washington	29	63	6.0
Wayne	36	63	6.5
Weber	43	63	4.5

TABLE NO. R301.2(5b)

REQUIRED SNOW LOADS FOR SELECTED UTAH CITIES AND TOWNS[1,2]

The following jurisdictions require design snow load values that differ from the Equation in the Utah Snow Load Study.				
County	City	Elevation	Ground Snow Load (psf)	Roof Snow Load (psf)[6]
Carbon	Price[3]	5550	43	30
	All other county locations[5]	–	–	–
Davis	Fruit Heights[3]	4500 – 4850	57	40
Emery	Green River[3]	4070	36	25
Garfield	Panguitch[3]	6600	43	30
Rich	Woodruff[3]	6315	57	40
	Laketown[4]	6000	57	40
	Garden City[5]	–	–	–
	Randolph[4]	6300	57	40
San Juan	Monticello[3]	6820	50	35
Summit	Coalville[3]	5600	86	60
	Kamas[4]	6500	114	80
Tooele	Tooele[3]	5100	43	30
Utah	Orem[3]	4650	43	30
	Pleasant Grove[4]	5000	43	30
	Provo[5]	–	–	–
Wasatch	Heber[5]	–	–	–
Washington	Leeds[3]	3460	29	20
	Santa Clara[3]	2850	21	15
	St. George[3]	2750	21	15
	All other county locations[5]	–	–	–
Wayne	Loa[3]	7080	43	30

[1]The IRC requires a minimum live load - See R301.6.
[2]This table is informational only in that actual site elevations may vary. Table is only valid if site elevation is within 100 feet of the listed elevation. Otherwise, contact the local Building Official.
[3]Values adopted from Table VII of the Utah Snow Load Study.
[4]Values based on site-specific study. Contact local Building Official for additional information.
[5]Contact local Building Official.
[6]Based on Ce = 1.0, Ct = 1.0 and Is = 1.0"

(10)   IRC, Section R301.6, is deleted and replaced with the following: "R301.6 Utah Snow Loads. The snow loads specified in Table R301.2(5b) shall be used for the jurisdictions identified in that table. Otherwise, the ground snow load, P_g, to be used in the determination of design snow loads for buildings and other structures shall be determined by using the following formula: $P_g = (P_o^2 + S^2(A - A_o)^2)^{0.5}$ for A greater than A_o, and $P_g = P_o$ for A less than or equal to A_o.

WHERE:

P_g = Ground snow load at a given elevation (psf);

P_o = Base ground snow load (psf) from Table No. R301.2(5a);

S = Change in ground snow load with elevation (psf/100 ft.) From Table No. R301.2(5a);

A = Elevation above sea level at the site (ft./1,000);

A_o = Base ground snow elevation from Table R301.2(5a) (ft./1,000).

The building official may round the roof snow load to the nearest 5 psf. The ground snow load, Pg, may be adjusted by the building official when a licensed engineer or architect submits data substantiating the adjustments.

Where the minimum roof live load in accordance with Table R301.6 is greater than the design roof snow load, such roof live load shall be used for design, however, it shall not be reduced to a load lower than the design roof snow load. Drifting need not be considered for roof snow loads less than 20 psf."

(11)   In IRC, Section R302.2, the words "Exception: A" are deleted and replaced with the following:

"Exceptions:

1.   A common 2-hour fire-resistance-rated wall is permitted for townhouses if such walls do not contain plumbing or mechanical equipment, ducts or vents in the cavity of the common wall. Electrical installation shall be installed in accordance with Chapters 34 through 43. Penetrations of electrical outlet boxes shall be in accordance with Section R302.4.

2.   In buildings equipped with an automatic residential fire sprinkler system, a".

(12)   In IRC, Section R302.2.4, a new exception 6 is added as follows: "6. Townhouses separated by a common 2-hour fire-resistance-rated wall as provided in Section R302.2."

(13)   In IRC, Section R302.5.1, the words "self-closing device" are deleted and replaced with "self-latching hardware".

(14)   In IRC, Section R303.4, the number "5" is changed to "3" in the first sentence.

(15)   IRC, Sections R311.7.4 through R311.7.4.3, are deleted and replaced with the following: "R311.7.4 Stair treads and risers. R311.7.4.1 Riser height. The maximum riser height shall be 8 inches (203 mm). The riser shall be measured vertically between leading edges of the adjacent treads. The greatest riser height within any flight of stairs shall not exceed the smallest by more than 3/8 inch (9.5 mm).

R311.7.4.2 Tread depth. The minimum tread depth shall be 9 inches (228 mm). The tread depth shall be measured horizontally between the vertical planes of the foremost projection of adjacent treads and at a right angle to the tread's leading edge. The greatest tread depth within any flight of stairs shall not exceed the smallest by more than 3/8 inch (9.5 mm). Winder treads shall have a minimum tread depth of 10 inches (254 mm) measured as above at a point 12 inches (305 mm) from the side where the treads are narrower. Winder treads shall have a minimum tread depth of 6 inches (152 mm) at any point. Within any flight of stairs, the greatest winder tread depth at the 12-inch (305 mm) walk line shall not exceed the smallest by more than 3/8 inch (9.5 mm).

R311.7.4.3 Profile. The radius of curvature at the leading edge of the tread shall be no greater than 9/16 inch (14.3 mm). A nosing not less than 3/4 inch (19 mm) but not more than 1 1/4 inches (32 mm) shall be provided on stairways with solid risers. The greatest nosing projection shall not exceed the smallest nosing projection by more than 3/8 inch (9.5 mm) between two stories, including the nosing at the level of floors and landings. Beveling of nosing shall not exceed 1/2 inch (12.7 mm). Risers shall be vertical or sloped from the underside of the leading edge of the tread above at an angle not more than 30 degrees (0.51 rad) from the vertical. Open risers are permitted, provided that the opening between treads does not permit the passage of a 4-inch diameter (102 mm) sphere.

Exceptions.

1.   A nosing is not required where the tread depth is a minimum of 10 inches (254 mm).

2.   The opening between adjacent treads is not limited on stairs with a total rise of 30 inches (762 mm) or less."

(16)   In IRC, Section R312.1.2, the words "adjacent fixed seating" are deleted.

(17)   IRC, Section R312.2, is deleted.

(18)   IRC, Sections R313.1 through R313.2.1, are deleted and replaced with the following: "R313.1 Design and installation. When installed, automatic residential fire sprinkler systems for townhouses or one- and two-family dwellings shall be designed and installed in accordance with Section P2904."

(19)   A new IRC, Section R315.5, is added as follows: "R315.5 Power source. Carbon monoxide alarms shall receive their primary power from the building wiring when such wiring is served from a commercial source, and when primary power is interrupted, shall receive power from a battery. Wiring shall be permanent and without a disconnecting switch other than those required for over-current protection.

Exceptions:

1.   Carbon monoxide alarms shall be permitted to be battery operated when installed in buildings without commercial power.

2.   Hard wiring of carbon monoxide alarms in existing areas shall not be required where the alterations or repairs do not result in the removal of interior wall or ceiling finishes exposing the structure, unless there is an attic, crawl space or basement available which could provide access for hard wiring, without the removal of interior finishes."

(20)   A new IRC, Section R315.6, is added as follows: "R315.6 Interconnection. Where more than one carbon monoxide alarm is required to be installed within an individual dwelling unit in accordance with Section R315.1, the alarm devices shall be interconnected in such a manner that the actuation of one alarm will activate all of the alarms in the individual unit. Physical interconnection of smoke alarms shall not be required where listed wireless alarms are installed and all alarms sound upon activation of one alarm. Exception: Interconnection of carbon monoxide alarms in existing areas shall not be required where alterations or repairs do not result in removal of interior wall or ceiling finishes exposing the structure, unless there is an attic, crawl space or basement available which could provide access for interconnection without the removal of interior finishes."

(21)   In IRC, Section R403.1.6, a new Exception 4 is added as follows: "4. When anchor bolt spacing does not exceed 32 inches (813 mm) apart, anchor bolts may be placed with a minimum of two bolts per plate section located not less than 4 inches (102 mm) from each end of each plate section at interior bearing walls, interior braced wall lines, and at all exterior walls."

(22)   In IRC, Section R403.1.6.1, a new exception is added at the end of Item 2 and Item 3 as follows: "Exception: When anchor bolt spacing does not exceed 32 inches (816 mm) apart, anchor bolts may be placed with a minimum of two bolts per plate section located not less than 4 inches (102 mm) from each end of each plate section at interior bearing walls, interior braced wall lines, and at all exterior walls."

(23)   In IRC, Section R404.1, a new exception is added as follows: "Exception: As an alternative to complying with Sections R404.1 through R404.1.5.3, concrete and masonry foundation walls may be designed in accordance with IBC Sections 1807.1.5 and 1807.1.6 as amended in Section 1807.1.6.4 and Table 1807.1.6.4 under these rules."

(24)   IRC, Section R501.3, is deleted.

Amended by Chapter 205, 2015 General Session

15A-3-203 Amendments to Chapters 6 through 15 of IRC.

(1)   In IRC, Section N1101.8 (R103.2), all words after the words "herein governed." are deleted and replaced with the following: "Construction documents include all documentation required to be submitted in order to issue a building permit."

(2)   In IRC, Section N1101.14 (R303.3), all wording after the first sentence is deleted.

(3)   In IRC, Table N1102.1.1 (R402.1.1) and Table N1102.1.3 (R402.1.3), the rows for "climate zone 3", "climate zone 5 and Marine 4", and "climate zone 6" are deleted and replaced and a new footnote j is added as follows:

"TABLE N1102.1.1 (R402.1.1)

INSULATION AND FENESTRATION REQUIREMENTS BY COMPONENT[a]

Climate Zone	Fenestration U-Factor[b,e]	Skylight B U-Factor	Glazed Fenestration SHGC	Ceiling R-Value	Wood Frame Wall R-Value	Mass Wall R-Value[i,j]	Floor R-Value	Basement[c] Wall R-Value	Slab[d] R-Valu & Depth	Crawl Space[c] R-Value
3	0.65	0.65	0.40	30	15	5	19	0	0	5/13
5 and Marine 4	0.35	0.60	NR	38	19 or 13 + 5h	13	30 g	10/13	10, 2 ft	10/13
6	0.35	0.60	NR	49	19 or 13 + 5h	15	30 g	10/13	10, 4 ft	10/13

[j]Log walls complying with ICC400 and with a minimum average wall thickness of 5" or greater shall be permitted in Zones 5-8 when overall window glazing is .31 U-factor or lower, minimum heating equipment efficiency is 90 AFUE (gas) or 84 AFUE (oil), and all other component requirements are met."

TABLE N1102.1.3 (R402.1.3)

EQUIVALENT U-FACTORS[a]

Climate Zone	Fenestration U-Factor	Skylight U-Factor	Ceiling U-Factor	Frame Wall U-Factor	Mass Wall U-Factor	Floor U-Factor	Basement Wall U-Factor	Crawl Space Wall U-Factor
3	0.65	0.65	0.035	0.082	0.141	0.047	0.360	0.136
5 and Marine 4	0.35	0.60	0.030	0.060	0.082	0.033	0.059	0.065
6	0.35	0.60	0.026	0.060	0.060	0.033	0.059	0.065

(4)   In IRC, Section N1102.2.1 (R402.2.1), the last sentence is deleted.

(5)   In IRC, Section N1102.2.2 (R402.2.2), the last sentence is deleted.

(6)   In IRC, Section N1102.3.3 (R402.3.3), the last sentence is deleted.

(7)   In IRC, Section N1102.3.4 (R402.3.4), the last sentence is deleted.

(8)   In IRC, Section N1102.4.1 (R402.4.1), in the first sentence, the word "and" is deleted and replaced with the word "or".

(9)   In IRC, Section N1102.4.1.1 (R402.4.1.1), the last sentence is deleted and replaced with the following: "Where allowed by the building official, the builder may certify compliance to components criteria for items which may not be inspected during regularly scheduled inspections."

(10)   In IRC, Section N1102.4.1.2 (R402.4.1.2), the following changes are made:

       (a)   In the first sentence, the words "in Zones 1 and 2, and 3 air changes per hour in Zone 3 through 8" are deleted.

(b)   In the third sentence, the words "Where required by the building official," and the word "third" are deleted.

(c)   The following sentence is inserted after the third sentence: "The following parties shall be approved to conduct testing: Parties certified by BPI or RESNET, or licensed contractors who have completed training provided by Blower Door Test equipment manufacturers or other comparable training."

(11)   In IRC, Section N1102.4.4 (R402.4.4), the last sentence is deleted.

(12)   In IRC, Section N1103.2.2 (R403.2.2), the requirements for total leakage testing are deleted and replaced with the following:

"1.   Postconstruction test: Total leakage shall be less than or equal to 10 cfm (283 L/min) per 100 square feet (9.29 m2) of conditioned floor space when tested at a pressure differential of 0.1 inches w.g. (25 Pa) across the entire system, including the manufacturer's air handler enclosure. All register boots shall be taped or otherwise sealed during the test.

2.   Rough-in test: Total leakage shall be less than or equal to 10 cfm (283 L/min) per 100 square feet (9.29 m2) of conditioned floor area when tested at a pressure differential of at least 0.1 inches w.g. (25 Pa) across the system, including the manufacturer's air handler enclosure. All registers shall be taped or otherwise sealed during the test. If the air handler is not installed at the time of the test, total leakage shall be less than or equal to 7.5 cfm (212 L/min) per 100 square feet (9.29 m2) of conditioned floor area."

(13)   In IRC, Section N1103.2.2 (R403.2.2), the exception for total leakage testing is deleted and replaced with the following: "Exception: The total leakage test is not required for systems with all air handlers and at least 50% of all ducts (measured by length) located entirely within the building thermal envelope."

(14)   In IRC, Section N1103.2.3 (R403.2.3), the words "or plenums" are deleted.

(15)   In IRC, Section N1103.4.2 (R403.4.2), the sentences for "3.", "9.", and the last sentence are deleted.

(16)   In IRC, Section N1103.5 (R403.5), the first sentence is deleted.

(17)   IRC, Section N1104.1 (R404.1) and the exception are deleted, and N1104.1.1 (R404.1.1) becomes N1104.1 (R404.1).

(18)   In IRC, Table N1105.5.2(1) (R405.5.2(1)), the following changes are made under the column STANDARD REFERENCE DESIGN:

(a)   In the row "Air exchange rate", the words "in Zones 1 and 2, and 3 air changes per hour in Zones 3 through 8" are deleted.

(b)   In the row "Heating systems[f, g]", the standard reference design is deleted and replaced with the following:

"Fuel Type: same as proposed design

Efficiencies:

Electric: air source heat pump with prevailing federal minimum efficiencies

Nonelectric furnaces: natural gas furnace with prevailing federal minimum efficiencies

Nonelectric boilers: natural gas boiler with prevailing federal minimum efficiencies

Capacity: sized in accordance with Section N1103.6"

(c)   In the row "Cooling systems[f, h]" the words "As proposed" are deleted and replaced with the following:

"Fuel Type: Electric

Efficiency: in accordance with prevailing federal minimum standards"

(d)   In the row "Service water heating[f, g, h, i]", the words "As proposed" are deleted and replaced with the following:

"Fuel Type: same as proposed design

Efficiency: in accordance with prevailing federal minimum standards

Tank Temperature: 120o F"

(e)   In the row "Thermal distribution systems" the word "none" is deleted and replaced with the following: "Thermal distribution system efficiency (DSE) of .080 shall be applied to both the heating and cooling system efficiencies."

(19)   In Table N1105.5.2(2) (R405.5.2(2)), the number "0.80" is inserted under "Forced air systems" for "Distribution system components located in unconditioned space".

(20)   In IRC, Section M1307.2, the words "In Seismic Design Categories D1 and D2" are deleted.

(21)   The REScheck Software adopted by the United States Department of Energy and modified to meet the requirements of this section shall be used to verify compliance with this section. The software shall address the Total UA alternative approach and account for Equipment Efficiency Trade-offs when applicable per the standard reference design as amended.

(22)   IRC, Section M1411.6, is deleted.

Amended by Chapter 279, 2013 General Session

15A-3-204 Amendments to Chapters 16 through 25 of IRC.

(1)   In IRC, Table M1601.1.1(2), in the section "Round ducts and enclosed rectangular ducts", the word "enclosed" is deleted; the words "14 inches or less" are deleted and replaced with "over 8 inches but less than 15 inches"; the wording "8 inches or less" under duct size, "0.013" under minimum thickness (in.), "30" under equivalent gage no., and "0.0159" under aluminum minimum thickness (in.), are added; and the section "Exposed rectangular ducts" is deleted.

(2)   In IRC, Section M1901.3, the word "only" is inserted between the words "labeled" and "for".

(3)   A new IRC, Section G2401.2, is added as follows: "G2401.2 Meter Protection. Fuel gas services shall be in an approved location and/or provided with structures designed to protect the fuel gas meter and surrounding piping from physical damage, including falling, moving, or migrating ice and snow. If an added structure is used, it must provide access for service and comply with the IBC or the IRC."

Amended by Chapter 297, 2013 General Session

15A-3-205 Amendments to Chapters 26 through 35 of IRC.

(1)   A new IRC, Section P2602.3, is added as follows: "P2602.3 Individual water supply. Where a potable public water supply is not available, individual sources of potable water supply shall be utilized, provided that the source has been developed in accordance with Utah Code, Sections 73-3-1 and 73-3-25, as administered by the Department of Natural Resources, Division of Water Rights. In addition, the quality of the water shall be approved by the local health department having jurisdiction."

(2)   A new IRC, Section P2602.4, is added as follows: "P2602.4 Sewer required. Every building in which plumbing fixtures are installed and all premises having drainage piping shall be connected to a public sewer where the sewer is accessible and is within 300 feet of the property line in accordance with Utah Code, Section 10-8-38; or an approved private sewage disposal system in accordance with Utah Administrative Code, Chapter 4, Rule R317, as administered by the Department of Environmental Quality, Division of Water Quality."

(3)   In IRC, Section P2801.7, all words in the first sentence up to the word "water" are deleted.

(4)   A new IRC, Section P2902.1.1, is added as follows: "P2902.1.1 Backflow assembly testing. The premise owner or his designee shall have backflow prevention assemblies operation tested at the time of installation, repair, and relocation and at least on an annual basis thereafter, or more frequently as required by the authority having jurisdiction. Testing shall be performed by a Certified Backflow Preventer Assembly Tester. The assemblies that are subject to this paragraph are the Spill Resistant Vacuum Breaker, the Pressure Vacuum Breaker Assembly, the Double Check Backflow Prevention Assembly, the Double Check Detector Assembly Backflow Preventer, the Reduced Pressure Principle Backflow Preventer, and Reduced Pressure Detector Assembly."

(5)   IRC, Table P2902.3, is deleted and replaced with the following:

"DEVICE	DEGREE OF HAZARD[a]	APPLICATION[b]	APPLICABLE STANDARDS
BACKFLOW PREVENTION ASSEMBLIES:			
Double check backflow prevention assembly and double check fire protection backflow prevention assembly	Low hazard	Backpressure or backsiphonage Sizes 3/8" - 16"	ASSE 1015, AWWA C510, CSA B64.5, CSA B64.5.1
Double check detector fire protection backflow prevention assemblies	Low hazard	Backpressure or backsiphonage Sizes 3/8" - 16"	ASSE 1048
Pressure vacuum breaker assembly	High or low hazard	Backsiphonage only Sizes 1/2" - 2"	ASSE 1020, CSA B64.1.2
Reduced pressure principle backflow prevention assembly and reduced pressure principle fire protection backflow assembly	High or low hazard	Backpressure or backsiphonage Sizes 3/8" - 16"	ASSE 1013, AWWA C511, CSA B64.4, CSA B64.4.1
Reduced pressure detector fire protection backflow prevention assemblies	High or low hazard	Backpressure or backsiphonage (Fire Sprinkler Systems)	ASSE 1047
Spill-resistant vacuum breaker assembly	High or low hazard	Backsiphonage only Sizes 1/2" - 2"	ASSE 1056
BACKFLOW PREVENTER PLUMBING DEVICES:			
Antisiphon-type fill valves for gravity water closet flush tanks	High hazard	Backsiphonage only	ASSE 1002, CSA B125.3

Backflow preventer for carbonated beverage machines	Low hazard	Backpressure or backsiphonage Sizes 1/4" - 3/8"	ASSE 1022
Backflow preventer with intermediate atmospheric vents	Low hazard	Backpressure or backsiphonage Sizes 1/4" - 3/8"	ASSE 1012, CSA B64.3
Dual check valve type backflow preventers	Low hazard	Backpressure or backsiphonage Sizes 1/4" - 1"	ASSE 1024, CSA B64.6
Hose connection backflow preventer	High or low hazard	Backsiphonage only Sizes 1/2" - 1"	ASSE 1052, CSA B64.2, B64.2.1
Hose connection vacuum breaker	High or low hazard	Backsiphonage only Sizes 1/2", 3/4", 1"	ASSE 1011, CAN/CSA B64.1.1
Atmospheric type vacuum breaker	High or low hazard	Backsiphonage only Sizes 1/2" - 4"	ASSE 1001, CSA B64.1.1
Vacuum breaker wall hydrants, frost resistant, automatic draining type	High or low hazard	Backsiphonage only Sizes 3/4", 1"	ASSE 1019, CSA B64.2.2
OTHER MEANS or METHODS:			
Air gap	High or low hazard	Backsiphonage only	ASME A112.1.2
Air gap fittings for use with plumbing fixtures, appliances and appurtenances	High or low hazard	Backpressure or backsiphonage	ASME A112.1.3

For SI: 1 inch = 25.4 mm

[a] Low Hazard - See Pollution (Section 202), High Hazard - See Contamination (Section 202)

[b] See Backpressure (Section 202), See Backpressure, low head (Section 202), See Backsiphonage (Section 202)

Installation Guidelines: The above specialty devices shall be installed in accordance with their listing and the manufacturer's instructions and the specific provisions of this chapter."

(6)   In IRC, Section P3009.1, all words after the word "urinals" are deleted and the following sentence is added at the end: "Gray water recycling systems for subsurface landscape irrigation shall conform with UAC R317-401 Gray Water Systems."

(7)   A new IRC, Section P3009.1.1, is added as follows: "P3009.1.1 Recording. The existence of a gray water recycling system shall be recorded on the deed of ownership for that property. The certificate of occupancy shall not be issued until the documentation of the recording required under this section is completed by the owner."

(8)   In IRC, Section P3009.2, the words "and systems for subsurface landscape irrigation shall comply with Section P3009.14" are deleted.

(9)   IRC, Section P3009.6, is deleted and replaced with the following: "P3009.6 Potable water connections. The potable water supply to any building utilizing a gray water recycling system shall be protected against backflow by a reduced pressure backflow prevention assembly installed in accordance with Section P2902."

(10)   In IRC, Section P3009.7, the following is added at the end of the sentence: "and other clear water wastes which have a pH of 6.0 to 9.0; are non-flammable, non-combustible; without objectionable odor; non-highly pigmented; and will not interfere with the operation of the sewer treatment facility."

(11)   In IRC, Section P3009.13.3, in the second sentence, the following is added between the words "backflow" and "in": "by a reduced pressure backflow prevention assembly or an air gap installed".

(12)   IRC, Section P3009.14, is deleted and replaced with the following: "Section P3009.14 LANDSCAPE IRRIGATION SYSTEMS. Gray water recycling systems utilized for subsurface irrigation for single family residences shall comply with the requirements of UAC R317-401, Gray Water Systems. Gray water recycling systems utilized for subsurface irrigation for other occupancies shall comply with UAC R317-3, Design Requirements for Wastewater Collection, Treatment and Disposal and UAC R317-4, Onsite Waterwaste Systems."

(13)   In IRC, Section P3103.6, the following sentence is added at the end of the paragraph: "Vents extending through the wall shall terminate not less than 12 inches from the wall with an elbow pointing downward."

(14)   In IRC, Section P3104.4, the following sentence is added at the end of the paragraph: "Horizontal dry vents below the flood level rim shall be permitted for floor drain and floor sink installations when installed below grade in accordance with Chapter 30, and Sections P3104.2 and P3104.3. A wall cleanout shall be provided in the vertical vent."

Amended by Chapter 297, 2013 General Session

15A-3-206 Amendments to Chapters 36 and 44 of IRC.

(1)   In IRC, Section E3902.12, the following words are deleted: "family rooms, dining rooms, living rooms, parlors, libraries, dens, sunrooms, recreation rooms, closets, hallways, and similar rooms or areas. Exception: This section does not apply for a simple move or an extension of a branch circuit or an outlet which does not significantly increase the existing electrical load. This exception does not include changes involving remodeling or additions to a residence."

(2)   IRC, Chapter 44, is amended by adding the following reference standard:

"Standard reference number	Title	Referenced in code section number
USC-FCCCHR 10th Edition Manual of Cross Connection Control	Foundation for Cross-Connection Control and Hydraulic Research University of Southern California Kaprielian Hall 300 Los Angeles CA 90089-2531	Table P2902.3"

Part 3 - Statewide Amendments to International Plumbing Code

15A-3-301 General provision.

The amendments in this part are adopted as amendments to the IPC to be applicable statewide.

Enacted by Chapter 14, 2011 General Session

15A-3-302 Amendments to Chapters 1 and 2 of IPC.

(1)   A new IPC, Section 101.2, is added as follows: "For clarification, the International Private Sewage Disposal Code is not part of the plumbing code even though it is in the same printed volume."

(2)   In IPC, Section 202, the definition for "Backflow Backpressure, Low Head" is deleted.

(3)   In IPC, Section 202, the following definition is added: "Certified Backflow Preventer Assembly Tester. A person who has shown competence to test Backflow prevention assemblies to the satisfaction of the authority having jurisdiction under Utah Code, Subsection 19-4-104(4)."

(4)   In IPC, Section 202, the following definition is added: "Contamination (High Hazard). An impairment of the quality of the potable water that creates an actual hazard to the public health through poisoning or through the spread of disease by sewage, industrial fluids or waste."

(5)   In IPC, Section 202, the definition for "Cross Connection" is deleted and replaced with the following: "Cross Connection. Any physical connection or potential connection or arrangement between two otherwise separate piping systems, one of which contains potable water and the other either water of unknown or questionable safety or steam, gas, or chemical, whereby there exists the possibility for flow from one system to the other, with the direction of flow depending on the pressure differential between the two systems (see "Backflow")."

(6)   In IPC, Section 202, the following definition is added: "Deep Seal Trap. A manufactured or field fabricated trap with a liquid seal of 4" or larger."

(7)   In IPC, Section 202, in the definition for gray water a comma is inserted after the word "washers"; the word "and" is deleted; and the following is added to the end: "and clear water wastes which have a pH of 6.0 to 9.0; are non-flammable; non-combustible; without objectionable odors; non-highly pigmented; and will not interfere with the operation of the sewer treatment facility."

(8)   In IPC, Section 202, the following definition is added: "High Hazard. See Contamination."

(9)   In IPC, Section 202, the following definition is added: "Low Hazard. See Pollution."

(10)   In IPC, Section 202, the following definition is added: "Pollution (Low Hazard). An impairment of the quality of the potable water to a degree that does not create a hazard to the public health but that does adversely and unreasonably affect the aesthetic qualities of such potable water for domestic use."

(11)   In IPC, Section 202, the definition for "Potable Water" is deleted and replaced with the following: "Potable Water. Water free from impurities present in amounts sufficient to cause disease or harmful physiological effects and conforming to the Utah Code, Title 19, Chapter 4, Safe Drinking Water Act, and Chapter 5, Water Quality Act, and the regulations of the public health authority having jurisdiction."

Amended by Chapter 297, 2013 General Session

15A-3-303 Amendments to Chapter 3 of IPC.

(1)   In IPC, Section 303.4, the following exception is added: "Exception: Third-party certification for backflow prevention assemblies will consist of any combination of two certifications, laboratory or field. Acceptable third party laboratory certifying agencies are ASSE, IAPMO, and USC-FCCCHR. USC-FCCCHR currently provides the only field testing of backflow protection assemblies. Also see www.drinkingwater.utah.gov and Division of Drinking Water Rule, Utah Administrative Code, R309-305-6."

(2)   IPC, Section 304.3, Meter Boxes, is deleted.

(3)   IPC, Section 311.1, is deleted.

(4)   In IPC, Section 312.3, the following is added at the end of the paragraph:

"Where water is not available at the construction site or where freezing conditions limit the use of water on the construction site, plastic drainage and vent pipe may be permitted to be tested with air. The following procedures shall be followed:

1.   Contractor shall recognize that plastic is extremely brittle at lower temperatures and can explode, causing serious injury or death.

2. Contractor assumes all liability for injury or death to persons or damage to property or for claims for labor and/or material arising from any alleged failure of the system during testing with air or compressed gasses.

3. Proper personal protective equipment, including safety eyewear and protective headgear, should be worn by all individuals in any area where an air or gas test is being conducted.

4. Contractor shall take all precautions necessary to limit the pressure within the plastic piping.

5. No water supply system shall be pressurized in excess of 6 psi as measured by accurate gauges graduated to no more than three times the test pressure.

6. The pressure gauge shall be monitored during the test period, which should not exceed 15 minutes.

7. At the conclusion of the test, the system shall be depressurized gradually, all trapped air or gases should be vented, and test balls and plugs should be removed with caution."

(5)   In IPC, Section 312.5, the following is added at the end of the paragraph:

"Where water is not available at the construction site or where freezing conditions limit the use of water on the construction site, plastic water pipes may be permitted to be tested with air. The following procedures shall be followed:

1. Contractor shall recognize that plastic is extremely brittle at lower temperatures and can explode, causing serious injury or death.

2. Contractor assumes all liability for injury or death to persons or damage to property or for claims for labor and/or material arising from any alleged failure of the system during testing with air or compressed gasses.

3. Proper personal protective equipment, including safety eyewear and protective headgear, should be worn by all individuals in any area where an air or gas test is being conducted.

4. Contractor shall take all precautions necessary to limit the pressure within the plastic piping.

5. Water supply systems shall be pressure tested to a minimum of 50 psi but not more than 80 psi as measured by accurate gauges graduated to no more than three times the test pressure.

6. The pressure gauge shall be monitored during the test period, which should not exceed 15 minutes.

7. At the conclusion of the test, the system shall be depressurized gradually, all trapped air or gases should be vented, and test balls and plugs should be removed with caution."

(6)   A new IPC, Section 312.10.3, is added as follows: "312.10.3 Tester Qualifications. Testing shall be performed by a Utah Certified Backflow Preventer Assembly Tester in accordance with Utah Administrative Code, R309-305."

Amended by Chapter 297, 2013 General Session

15A-3-304 Amendments to Chapter 4 of IPC.

(1)   In IPC, Table 403.1, the following changes are made:

(a)   The title for Table 403.1 is deleted and replaced with the following: "Table 403.1, Minimum Number of Required Plumbing Facilitiesa, h";

(b)   In the row for "E" occupancy in the field for "OTHER" a new footnote i is added.

(c)   In the row for "I-4" occupancy in the field for "OTHER" a new footnote i is added.

(d)   A new footnote h is added as follows: "FOOTNOTE: h. When provided, in public toilet facilities there shall be an equal number of diaper changing facilities in male toilet rooms and female toilet rooms."

(e)   A new footnote i is added to the table as follows: "FOOTNOTE i: Non-residential child care facilities shall comply with additional sink requirements of Utah Administrative Code R430-100-4."

(2)   A new IPC, Section 406.3, is added as follows: " 406.3 Automatic clothes washer safe pans. Safe pans, when installed under automatic clothes washers, shall be installed in accordance with Section 504.7."

(3)   A new IPC, Section 412.5, is added as follows: "412.5 Public toilet rooms. All public toilet rooms shall be equipped with at least one floor drain."

Amended by Chapter 297, 2013 General Session

15A-3-305 Amendments to Chapter 5 of IPC.

(1)   IPC, Section 502.4, is deleted and replaced with the following: "502.4 Seismic supports. Appliances designed to be fixed in position shall be fastened or anchored in an approved manner. Water heaters shall be anchored or strapped to resist horizontal displacement caused by earthquake motion. Strapping shall be at points within the upper one-third and lower one-third of the appliance's vertical dimensions. At the lower point, the strapping shall maintain a minimum distance of 4 inches (102 mm) above the controls."

(2)   In IPC, Section 504.7.2, the following is added at the end of the section: "When permitted by the code official, the pan drain may be directly connected to a soil stack, waste stack, or branch drain. The pan drain shall be individually trapped and vented as required in Section 907.1. The pan drain shall not be directly or indirectly connected to any vent. The trap shall be provided with a trap primer conforming to ASSE 1018 or ASSE 1044, a barrier type floor drain trap seal protection device meeting ASSE 1072, or a deep seal p-trap."

(3)   A new IPC, Section 504.7.3, is added as follows: "504.7.3 Pan Designation. A water heater pan shall be considered an emergency receptor designated to receive the discharge of water from the water heater only and shall not receive the discharge from any other fixtures, devises, or equipment."

Amended by Chapter 297, 2013 General Session

15A-3-306 Amendments to Chapter 6 of IPC.

(1)   IPC, Section 602.3, is deleted and replaced with the following: "602.3 Individual water supply. Where a potable public water supply is not available, individual sources of potable water supply shall be utilized provided that the source has been developed in accordance with Utah Code, Sections 73-3-1, 73-3-3, and 73-3-25, as administered by the Department of Natural Resources, Division of Water Rights. In addition, the quality of the water shall be approved by the local health department having jurisdiction. The source shall supply sufficient quantity of water to comply with the requirements of this chapter."

(2)   IPC, Sections 602.3.1, 602.3.2, 602.3.3, 602.3.4, 602.3.5, and 602.3.5.1, are deleted.

(3)   A new IPC, Section 604.4.1, is added as follows: "604.4.1 Manually operated metering faucets. Self closing or manually operated metering faucets shall provide a flow of water for at least 15 seconds without the need to reactivate the faucet."

(4)   IPC, Section 606.5, is deleted and replaced with the following: "606.5 Water pressure booster systems. Water pressure booster systems shall be provided as required by Section 606.5.1 through 606.5.11."

(5)   A new IPC, Section 606.5.11, is added as follows: "606.5.11 Prohibited installation. In no case shall a booster pump be allowed that will lower the pressure in the public main to less than the minimum water pressure specified in Utah Administrative Code R309-105-9."

(6)   In IPC, Section 608.1, the words "and pollution" are added after the word "contamination."

(7)   IPC, Table 608.1, is deleted and replaced with the following:

DEVICE	DEGREE OF HAZARD[a]	APPLICATION[b]	APPLICABLE STANDARDS
BACKFLOW PREVENTION ASSEMBLIES:			
Double check backflow prevention assembly and double check fire protection backflow prevention assembly	Low hazard	Backpressure or backsiphonage Sizes 3/8" - 16"	ASSE 1015, AWWA C510, CSA B64.5, CSA B64.5.1
Double check detector fire protection backflow prevention assemblies	Low hazard	Backpressure or backsiphonage Sizes 3/8" - 16"	ASSE 1048
Pressure vacuum breaker assembly	High or low hazard	Backsiphonage only Sizes 1/2" - 2"	ASSE 1020, CSA B64.1.2
Reduced pressure principle backflow prevention assembly and reduced pressure principle fire protection backflow assembly	High or low hazard	Backpressure or backsiphonage Sizes 3/8" - 16"	ASSE 1013, AWWA C511, CSA B64.4, CSA B64.4.1
Reduced pressure detector fire protection backflow prevention assemblies	High or low hazard	Backpressure or backsiphonage (Fire Sprinkler Systems)	ASSE 1047
Spill-resistant vacuum breaker assembly	High or low hazard	Backsiphonage only Sizes 1/2" - 2"	ASSE 1056
BACKFLOW PREVENTER PLUMBING DEVICES:			
Antisiphon-type fill valves for gravity water closet flush tanks	High hazard	Backsiphonage only	ASSE 1002, CSA B125.3
Backflow preventer for carbonated beverage machines	Low hazard	Backpressure or backsiphonage Sizes 1/4" - 3/8"	ASSE 1022
Backflow preventer with intermediate atmospheric vents	Low hazard	Backpressure or backsiphonage Sizes 1/4" - 3/8"	ASSE 1012, CSA B64.3
Dual check valve type backflow preventers	Low hazard	Backpressure or backsiphonage Sizes 1/4" - 1"	ASSE 1024, CSA B64.6

Hose connection backflow preventer	High or low hazard	Backsiphonage only Sizes 1/2" - 1"	ASSE 1052, CSA B64.2, B64.2.1
Hose connection vacuum breaker	High or low hazard	Backsiphonage only Sizes 1/2", 3/4", 1"	ASSE 1011, CAN/ CSA B64.1.1
Atmospheric type vacuum breaker	High or low hazard	Backsiphonage only Sizes 1/2" - 4"	ASSE 1001, CSA B64.1.1
Vacuum breaker wall hydrants, frost resistant, automatic draining type	High or low hazard	Backsiphonage only Sizes 3/4", 1"	ASSE 1019, CSA B64.2.2
OTHER MEANS or METHODS:			
Air gap	High or low hazard	Backsiphonage only	ASME A112.1.2
Air gap fittings for use with plumbing fixtures, appliances and appurtenances	High or low hazard	Backpressure or backsiphonage	ASME A112.1.3

For SI: 1 inch = 25.4 mm

[a] Low Hazard - See Pollution (Section 202), High Hazard - See Contamination (Section 202)

[b] See Backpressure (Section 202), See Backpressure, low head (Section 202), See Backsiphonage (Section 202)

Installation Guidelines: The above specialty devices shall be installed in accordance with their listing and the manufacturer's instructions and the specific provisions of this chapter."

(8) In IPC, Section 608.3, the word "and" after the word "contamination" is deleted and replaced with a comma and the words "and pollution" are added after the word "contamination" in the first sentence.

(9) In IPC, Section 608.5, the words "with the potential to create a condition of either contamination or pollution or" are added after the word "substances".

(10) In IPC, Section 608.6, the following sentence is added at the end of the paragraph: "Any connection between potable water piping and sewer-connected waste shall be protected by an air gap in accordance with Section 608.13.1."

(11) IPC, Section 608.7, is deleted and replaced with the following: "608.7 Stop and Waste Valves installed below grade. Combination stop-and-waste valves shall be permitted to be installed underground or below grade. Freeze proof yard hydrants that drain the riser into the ground are considered to be stop-and-waste valves and shall be permitted."

(12) In IPC, Section 608.11, the following sentence is added at the end of the paragraph: "The coating and installation shall conform to NSF Standard 61 and application of the coating shall comply with the manufacturer's instructions."

(13) IPC, Section 608.13.3, is deleted and replaced with the following: "608.13.3 Backflow preventer with intermediate atmospheric vent. Backflow preventers with intermediate atmospheric vents shall conform to ASSE 1012 or CSA CAN/CSA-B64.3. These devices shall be permitted to be installed on residential boilers only, without chemical treatment, where subject to continuous pressure conditions. The relief opening shall discharge by air gap and shall be prevented from being submerged."

(14) IPC, Section 608.13.4, is deleted.

(15)   IPC, Section 608.13.9, is deleted and replaced with the following: "608.13.9 Chemical dispenser backflow devices. Backflow devices for chemical dispensers shall comply with Section 608.16.7."

(16)   IPC, Section 608.15.3, is deleted and replaced with the following: "608.15.3 Protection by a backflow preventer with intermediate atmospheric vent. Connections to residential boilers only, without chemical treatment, shall be protected by a backflow preventer with an intermediate atmospheric vent."

(17)   IPC, Section 608.15.4, is deleted and replaced with the following: "608.15.4 Protection by a vacuum breaker. Openings and outlets shall be protected by atmospheric-type or pressure-type vacuum breakers. Vacuum breakers shall not be installed under exhaust hoods or similar locations that will contain toxic fumes or vapors. Fill valves shall be set in accordance with Section 425.3.1. Atmospheric Vacuum Breakers - The critical level of the atmospheric vacuum breaker shall be set a minimum of 6 inches (152 mm) above the flood level rim of the fixture or device. Pipe-applied vacuum breakers shall be installed not less than 6 inches (152 mm) above the flood level rim of the fixture, receptor, or device served. No valves shall be installed downstream of the atmospheric vacuum breaker. Pressure Vacuum Breaker - The critical level of the pressure vacuum breaker shall be set a minimum of 12 inches (304 mm) above the flood level of the fixture or device."

(18)   In IPC, Section 608.15.4.2, the following is added after the first sentence: "Add-on-backflow prevention devices shall be non-removable. In climates where freezing temperatures occur, a listed self-draining frost proof hose bibb with an integral backflow preventer shall be used."

(19)   IPC, Section 608.16.2, is deleted and replaced as follows: "608.16.2 Connections to boilers. The potable supply to a boiler shall be protected by an air gap or a reduced pressure principle backflow preventer, complying with ASSE 1013, CSA B64.4 or AWWA C511. Exception: The potable supply to a residential boiler without chemical treatment may be equipped with a backflow preventer with an intermediate atmospheric vent complying with ASSE 1012 or CSA CAN/CSA-B64.3."

(20)   IPC, Section 608.16.3, is deleted and replaced with the following: "608.16.3 Heat exchangers. Heat exchangers shall be separated from potable water by double-wall construction. An air gap open to the atmosphere shall be provided between the two walls.

Exceptions:

1. Single wall heat exchangers shall be permitted when all of the following conditions are met:

    a. It utilizes a heat transfer medium of potable water or contains only substances which are recognized as safe by the United States Food and Drug Administration (FDA);

    b. The pressure of the heat transfer medium is maintained less than the normal minimum operating pressure of the potable water system; and

    c. The equipment is permanently labeled to indicate only additives recognized as safe by the FDA shall be used.

2. Steam systems that comply with paragraph 1 above.

3. Approved listed electrical drinking water coolers."

(21)   In IPC, Section 608.16.4.1, a new exception is added as follows: "Exception: All class 1 and 2 systems containing chemical additives consisting of strictly glycerine (C.P. or U.S.P. 96.5 percent grade) or propylene glycol shall be protected against backflow with a double check valve assembly. Such systems shall include written certification of the chemical additives at the time of original installation and service or maintenance."

(22)   IPC, Section 608.16.7, is deleted and replaced with the following: "608.16.7 Chemical dispensers. Where chemical dispensers connect to the water distribution system, the water supply system shall be protected against backflow in accordance with Section 608.13.1, Section 608.13.2, Section 608.13.5,

Section 608.13.6 or Section 608.13.8. Chemical dispensers shall connect to a separate dedicated water supply separate from any sink faucet."

(23)   IPC, Section 608.16.8, is deleted and replaced with the following: "608.16.8 Portable cleaning equipment. Where the portable cleaning equipment connects to the water distribution system, the water supply system shall be protected against backflow in accordance with Section 608.13.1, Section 608.13.2 or Section 608.13.8."

(24)   A new IPC, Section 608.16.11, is added as follows: "608.16.11 Automatic and coin operated car washes. The water supply to an automatic or coin operated car wash shall be protected in accordance with Section 608.13.1 or Section 608.13.2."

(25)   IPC, Section 608.17, is deleted and replaced with the following: "608.17 Protection of individual water supplies. See Section 602.3 for requirements."

Amended by Chapter 189, 2014 General Session

15A-3-307 Amendments to Chapter 7 of IPC.

(1)   IPC, Section 701.2, is deleted and replaced with the following: "701.2 Sewer required. Every building in which plumbing fixtures are installed and all premises having drainage piping shall be connected to a public sewer where the sewer is accessible and is within 300 feet of the property line in accordance with Utah Code, Section 10-8-38; or an approved private sewage disposal system in accordance with Utah Administrative Code, Rule R317-4, as administered by the Department of Environmental Quality, Division of Water Quality."

(2)   In IPC, Section 712.3.3.1, the following words are added before the word "or": "stainless steel, cast iron, galvanized steel".

Amended by Chapter 297, 2013 General Session

15A-3-308 Amendments to Chapter 8 of IPC.

IPC, Chapter 8, is not amended.

Enacted by Chapter 14, 2011 General Session

15A-3-309 Amendments to Chapter 9 of IPC.

(1)   In IPC, Section 903.1, when the number of inches is to be specified, "12 inches (304.8mm)" is inserted.

(2)   In IPC, Section 903.6, the following sentence is added at the end of the paragraph: "Vents extending through the wall shall terminate not less than 12 inches from the wall with an elbow pointing downward."

(3)   In IPC, Section 905.4, the following sentence is added at the end of the paragraph: "Horizontal dry vents below the flood level rim shall be permitted for floor drain, floor sink, and bath tub installations when installed in accordance with Sections 702.2, 905.2 and 905.3 and provided with a wall clean out."

Amended by Chapter 297, 2013 General Session

15A-3-310 Amendments to Chapter 10 of IPC.

In IPC, Section 1002.4, the following is added at the end of the paragraph: "Approved Means of Maintaining Trap Seals. Approved means of maintaining trap seals include the following, but are not limited to the methods cited:

1.   A listed trap seal primer conforming to ASSE 1018 and ASSE 1044.

2.   A hose bibb or bibbs within the same room.

3.   Drainage from an untrapped lavatory discharging to the tailpiece of those fixture traps which require priming. All fixtures shall be in the same room and on the same floor level as the trap primer.

4.   Barrier type floor drain trap seal protection device meeting ASSE Standard 1072.

5.   Deep seal p-trap".

Amended by Chapter 297, 2013 General Session

15A-3-311 Amendments to Chapter 11 of IPC.

(1)   IPC, Section 1104.2, is deleted and replaced with the following: "1104.2 Combining storm and sanitary drainage prohibited. The combining of sanitary and storm drainage systems is prohibited."

(2)   IPC, Section 1109, is deleted.

Amended by Chapter 297, 2013 General Session

15A-3-312 Amendments to Chapter 12 of IPC.

IPC, Chapter 12, is not amended.

Enacted by Chapter 14, 2011 General Session

15A-3-313 Amendments to Chapter 13 of IPC.

(1)   In IPC, Section 1301.1, all words after the word "urinals" are deleted and the following sentence is added at the end: "Gray water recycling systems for subsurface landscape irrigation shall conform with UAC R317-401 Gray Water Systems."

(2)   A new IPC, Section 1301.1.1, is added as follows: "1301.1.1 Recording. The existence of a gray water recycling system shall be recorded on the deed of ownership for that property. The certificate of occupancy shall not be issued until the documentation of the recording required under this section is completed by the owner."

(3)   In IPC, Section 1301.2, the words "and systems for subsurface landscape irrigation shall comply with Section 1303" are deleted.

(4)   IPC, Section 1301.6, is deleted and replaced with the following: "1301.6 Potable water connections. The potable water supply to any building utilizing a gray water recycling system shall be protected against backflow by a reduced pressure backflow prevention assembly installed in accordance with Section 608."

(5)   In IPC, Section 1301.7, the following is added at the end of the sentence: "and other clear water wastes which have a pH of 6.0 to 9.0; are non-flammable, non-combustible; without objectionable odor; non-highly pigmented; and will not interfere with the operation of the sewer treatment facility."

(6)   In IPC, Section 1302.3, in the second sentence, the following is added between the words "backflow" and "in": "by a reduced pressure backflow prevention assembly or an air gap installed".

(7)   IPC, Section 1303, is deleted and replaced with the following: "Section 1303 SUBSURFACE LANDSCAPE IRRIGATION SYSTEMS. Gray water recycling systems utilized for subsurface irrigation for single family residences shall comply with the requirements of UAC R317-401, Gray Water Systems. Gray water recycling systems utilized for subsurface irrigation for other occupancies shall comply with UAC R317-3, Design Requirements for Wastewater Collection, Treatment and Disposal and UAC R317-4, Onsite Waterwaste Systems."

Amended by Chapter 297, 2013 General Session

15A-3-314 Amendments to Chapter 14 of IPC.

(1)   In IPC, Chapter 14, the following referenced standard is added under ASSE:

"Standard reference number	Title	Referenced in code section number
1072-2007	Performance Requirements for Barrier Type Floor Drain Trap Seal Protection Devices	1004.2"

(2)   In IPC, Chapter 14, the following referenced standard is added:

"Standard reference number	Title	Referenced in code section number
USC-FCCCHR 10th Edition Manual of Cross Connection Control	Foundation for Cross-Connection Control and Hydraulic Research University of Southern California Kaprielian Hall 300 Los Angeles CA 90089-2531	Table 608.1"

Amended by Chapter 297, 2013 General Session

Part 4 - Statewide Amendments to International Mechanical Code

15A-3-401 General provisions.

The following are adopted as amendments to the IMC to be applicable statewide:

(1)   In IMC, Section 202, the definition for "CONDITIONED SPACE" is deleted and replaced with the following: "CONDITIONED SPACE. An area, room, or space enclosed within the building thermal envelope that is directly heated or cooled, or indirectly heated or cooled by any of the following means:

    1.   Openings directly into an adjacent conditioned space.

    2.   An un-insulated floor, ceiling or wall adjacent to a conditioned space.

    3.   Un-insulated duct, piping or other heat or cooling source within the space."

(2)   In IMC, Section 403.2.1, Item 3, is deleted and replaced with the following: "Except as provided in Table 403.3, Note h, where mechanical exhaust is required by Note b in Table 403.3, recirculation of air from such spaces is prohibited. All air supplied to such spaces shall be exhausted, including any air in excess of that required by Table 403.3."

(3)   In IMC, Table 403.3, Note b, is deleted and replaced with the following: "Except as provided in Note h, mechanical exhaust required and the recirculation of air from such spaces is prohibited (see Section 403.2.1, Item 3)."

(4)   In IMC, Table 403.3, Note h is deleted and replaced with the following:

    "1.   For a nail salon where a nail technician files or shapes an acrylic nail, as defined by rule by the Division of Occupational and Professional Licensing, in accordance with Title 63G, Chapter 3, Utah Administrative Rulemaking Act, each nail station where a nail technician files or shapes an acrylic nail shall be provided with:

        a.   a source capture system capable of filtering and recirculating air to inside space not less than 50 cfm per station; or

        b.   a source capture system capable of exhausting not less than 50 cfm per station."

2.   Except as provided in paragraph 3, the requirements described in paragraph 1 apply beginning on July 1, 2020.

3.   The requirements described in paragraph 1 apply beginning on July 1, 2014 if the nail salon is under or begins new construction or remodeling on or after July 1, 2014.

(5)   In IMC, Section 403, a new Section 403.8 is added as follows: "Retrospective effect. Removal, alteration, or abandonment shall not be required, and continued use and maintenance shall be allowed, for a ventilation system within an existing installation that complies with the requirements of this Section 403 regardless of whether the ventilation system satisfied the minimum ventilation rate requirements of prior law."

(6)   In IMC, Table 603.4, in the section "Round ducts and enclosed rectangular ducts", the word "enclosed" is deleted; the words "14 inches or less" are deleted and replaced with "over 8 inches but less than 15 inches"; the wording "8 inches or less" under duct size, "0.013" under minimum thickness (in.), "30" under equivalent gage no., and "0.0159" under aluminum minimum thickness (in.), are added; and the section "Exposed rectangular ducts" is deleted.

(7)   In IMC, Section 1004.2, the first sentence is deleted and replaced with the following: "Boilers and pressure vessels in Utah are regulated by the Utah Labor Commission, Division of Boiler, Elevator and Coal Mine Safety, except those located in private residences or in apartment houses of less than five family units. Boilers shall be installed in accordance with their listing and labeling, with minimum clearances as prescribed by the manufacturer's installation instructions."

(8)   In IMC, Section 1004.3.1, the word "unlisted" is inserted before the word "boilers".

(9)   IMC, Section 1101.10, is deleted.

Amended by Chapter 100, 2014 General Session

Part 5 - Statewide Amendments to International Fuel Gas Code

15A-3-501 General provisions.

The following are adopted as an amendment to the IFGC to be applicable statewide:

(1)   In IFGC, Section 404.9, a new Section 404.9.1, is added as follows: "404.9.1 Meter protection. Fuel gas services shall be in an approved location and/or provided with structures designed to protect the fuel gas meter and surrounding piping from physical damage, including falling, moving, or migrating ice and snow. If an added structure is used, it must still provide access for service and comply with the IBC or the IRC."

(2)   IFGC, Section 409.5.3, is deleted.

(3)   In IFGC, Section 631.2, the following sentence is inserted before the first sentence: "Boilers and pressure vessels in Utah are regulated by the Utah Labor Commission, Division of Boiler, Elevator and Coal Mine Safety, except those located in private residences or in apartment houses of less than five family units."

Amended by Chapter 297, 2013 General Session

Part 6 - Statewide Amendments to National Electrical Code

15A-3-601 General provision.

The following are adopted as amendments to the NEC to be applicable statewide:

(1)   The IRC provisions are adopted as the residential electrical standards applicable to installations applicable under the IRC. All other installations shall comply with the adopted NEC.

(2)   In NEC, Section 310.15(B)(7), the second sentence is deleted and replaced with the following: "For application of this section, the main power feeder shall be the feeder(s) between the main disconnect and the panelboard(s)."

Amended by Chapter 297, 2013 General Session

Part 7 - Statewide Amendments to International Energy Conservation Code

15A-3-701 General provisions.

The following is adopted as an amendment to the IECC to be applicable statewide:

(1)   In IECC, Section C202, the definition for "CONDITIONED SPACE" is deleted and replaced with the following: "CONDITIONED SPACE. An area, room or space enclosed within the building thermal envelope that is directly heated or cooled, or indirectly heated or cooled by any of the following means:

    1.   Openings directly into an adjacent conditioned space.

    2.   An un-insulated floor, ceiling or wall adjacent to a conditioned space.

    3.   Un-insulated duct, piping or other heat or cooling source within the space."

(2)   In IECC, Section C404.4, a new exception is added as follows: "Exception: Heat traps, other than the arrangement of piping and fittings, shall be prohibited unless a means of controlling thermal expansion can be ensured as required in the IPC Section 607.3."

(3)   In IECC, Section R103.2, all words after the words "herein governed." are deleted and replaced with the following: "Construction documents include all documentation required to be submitted in order to issue a building permit."

(4)   In IECC, Section R202, the definition for "CONDITIONED SPACE" is deleted and replaced with the following: "CONDITIONED SPACE. An area, room or space enclosed within the building thermal envelope that is directly heated or cooled, or indirectly heated or cooled by any of the following means:

    1.   Openings directly into an adjacent conditioned space.

    2.   An un-insulated floor, ceiling or wall adjacent to a conditioned space.

    3.   Un-insulated duct, piping or other heat or cooling source within the space."

(5)   In IECC, Section R303.3, all wording after the first sentence is deleted.

(6)   In IECC, Table R402.1.1 and Table R402.1.3, the rows for "climate zone 3", "climate zone 5 and Marine 4, and climate zone 6" are deleted and replaced and a new footnote j is added as follows:

"TABLE R402.1.1

INSULATION AND FENESTRATION REQUIREMENTS BY COMPONENT[a]

Climate Zone	Fenestration U-Factor[b,e]	Skylight B U-Factor	Glazed Fenestration SHGC	Ceiling R-Value	Wood Frame Wall R-Value	Mass Wall R-Value [i,j]	Floor R-Value	Basement[c] Wall R-Value	Slab[d] R-Valu & Depth	Crawl Space[c] R-Value
3	0.65	0.65	0.40	30	15	5	19	0	0	5/13
5 and Marine 4	0.35	0.60	NR	38	19 or 13 + 5h	13	30 g	10/13	10, 2 ft	10/13
6	0.35	0.60	NR	49	19 or 13 + 5h	15	30 g	10/13	10, 4 ft	10/13

[j]Log walls complying with ICC400 and with a minimum average wall thickness of 5" or greater shall be permitted in Zones 5-8 when overall window glazing is .31 U-factor or lower, minimum heating equipment efficiency is 90 AFUE (gas) or 84 AFUE (oil), and all other component requirements are met."

TABLE R402.1.3

EQUIVALENT U-FACTORS[a]

Climate Zone	Fenestration U-Factor	Skylight U-Factor	Ceiling U-Factor	Frame Wall U-Factor	Mass Wall U-Factor	Floor U-Factor	Basement Wall U-Factor	Crawl Space Wall U-Factor
3	0.65	0.65	0.035	0.082	0.141	0.047	0.360	0.136
5 and Marine 4	0.35	0.60	0.030	0.060	0.082	0.033	0.059	0.065
6	0.35	0.60	0.026	0.060	0.060	0.033	0.059	0.065

(7)   In IECC, Section R402.2.1, the last sentence is deleted.

(8)   In IECC, Section R402.2.2, the last sentence is deleted.

(9)   In IECC, Section R402.3.3, the last sentence is deleted.

(10)   In IECC, Section R402.3.4, the last sentence is deleted.

(11)   In IECC, Section R402.4.1, in the first sentence, the word "and" is deleted and replaced with the word "or".

(12)   In IECC, Section R402.4.1.1, the last sentence is deleted and replaced with the following: "Where allowed by the building official, the builder may certify compliance to components criteria for items which may not be inspected during regularly scheduled inspections."

(13)   In IECC, Section R402.4.1.2, the following changes are made:

(a)   In the first sentence, the words "in Zones 1 and 2, and 3 air changes per hour in Zone 3 through 8" are deleted.

(b)   In the third sentence, the words "Where required by the building official," and the word "third" are deleted.

(c)   The following sentence is inserted after the third sentence: "The following parties shall be approved to conduct testing: Parties certified by BPI or RESNET, or licensed contractors who have completed training provided by Blower Door Test equipment manufacturers or other comparable training."

(14)   In IECC, Section R402.4.4, the last sentence is deleted.

(15)   In IECC, Section R403.2.2, the requirements for duct tightness testing are deleted and replaced with the following:

"1.   Postconstruction test: Total leakage shall be less than or equal to 10 cfm (283 L/min) per 100 square feet (9.29 m2) of conditioned floor space when tested at a pressure differential of 0.1 inches w.g. (25 Pa) across the entire system, including the manufacturer's air handler enclosure. All register boots shall be taped or otherwise sealed during the test.

2.   Rough-in test: Total leakage shall be less than or equal to 10 cfm (283 L/min) per 100 square feet (9.29 m2) of conditioned floor area when tested at a pressure differential of at least 0.1 inches w.g. (25 Pa) across the system, including the manufacturer's air handler enclosure. All registers shall be taped or otherwise sealed during the test. If the air handler is not installed at the time of the test, total leakage shall be less than or equal to 7.5 cfm (212 L/min) per 100 square feet (9.29 m2) of conditioned floor area."

(16)   In IECC, Section R403.2.2, the exception for total leakage testing is deleted and replaced with the following: "Exception: The total leakage test is not required for systems with all air handlers and at least 50% of all ducts (measured by length) located entirely within the building thermal envelope."

(17)   In IECC, Section R403.2.3, the words "or plenums" are deleted.

(18)   In IECC, Section R403.4.2, the sentences for "3." and "9." and the last sentence are deleted.

(19)   In IECC, Section R403.5, the first sentence is deleted.

(20)   IECC, Section R404.1 and the exception are deleted, and R404.1.1 becomes R404.1.

(21)   In IECC, Table R405.5.2(1), the following changes are made under the column STANDARD REFERENCE DESIGN:

(a)   In the row "Air exchange rate", the words "in Zones 1 and 2, and 3 air changes per hour in Zones 3 through 8" are deleted.

(b)   In the row "Heating systems[f, g]", the standard reference design is deleted and replaced with the following:

"Fuel Type: same as proposed design

Efficiencies:

Electric: air source heat pump with prevailing federal minimum efficiencies

Nonelectric furnaces: natural gas furnace with prevailing federal minimum efficiencies

Nonelectric boilers: natural gas boiler with prevailing federal minimum efficiencies

Capacity: sized in accordance with Section N1103.6"

(c)   In the row "Cooling systems[f, h]" the words "As proposed" are deleted and replaced with the following:

"Fuel Type: Electric

Efficiency: in accordance with prevailing federal minimum standards"

(d)   In the row "Service water heatingf, g, h, i", the words "As proposed" are deleted and replaced with the following:

"Fuel Type: same as proposed design

Efficiency: in accordance with prevailing federal minimum standards Tank Temperature: 120° F"

(e)   In the row "Thermal distribution systems" the word "none" is deleted and replaced with the following: "Thermal distribution system efficiency (DSE) of .080 shall be applied to both the heating and cooling system efficiencies."

(22)   In IECC, Table R405.5.2(2), the number "0.80" is inserted under "Forced air systems" for "Distribution system components located in unconditioned space".

(23)   The RESCheck Software adopted by the United States Department of Energy and modified to meet the requirements of this section shall be used to verify compliance with this section. The software shall address the Total UA alternative approach and account for Equipment Efficiency Trade-offs when applicable per the standard reference design as amended.

Amended by Chapter 279, 2013 General Session

Part 8 - Installation and Safety Requirements for Mobile Homes Built Before June 15, 1976

15A-3-801 General provision.

Mobile homes built before June 15, 1976 that are subject to relocation, building alteration, remodeling, or rehabilitation shall comply with the following:

(1)   Related to exits and egress windows:

(a)   Egress windows. The home has at least one egress window in each bedroom, or a window that meets the minimum specifications of the U.S. Department of Housing and Urban Development's (HUD) Manufactured Homes Construction and Safety Standards (MHCSS) program as set forth in 24 C.F.R. Parts 3280 and 3282, MHCSS 3280.106 and 3280.404 for manufactured homes. These standards require the window to be at least 22 inches in the horizontal or vertical position in its least dimension and at least five square feet in area. The bottom of the window opening shall be no more than 36 inches above the floor, and the locks and latches and any window screen or storm window devices that need to be operated to permit exiting shall not be located more than 54 inches above the finished floor.

(b)   Exits. The home is required to have two exterior exit doors, located remotely from each other, as required in MHCSS 3280.105. This standard requires that single-section homes have the doors no less than 12 feet, center-to-center, from each other, and multisection home doors no less than 20 feet center-to-center from each other when measured in a straight line, regardless of the length of the path of travel between the doors. One of the required exit doors must be accessible from the doorway of each bedroom and no more than 35 feet away from any bedroom doorway. An exterior swing door shall have a 28-inch-wide by 74-inch-high clear opening and sliding glass doors shall have a 28-inch-wide by 72-inch-high clear opening. Each exterior door other than screen/storm doors shall have a key-operated lock that has a passage latch; locks shall not require the use of a key or special tool for operation from the inside of the home.

(2)   Related to flame spread:

   (a)   Walls, ceilings, and doors. Walls and ceilings adjacent to or enclosing a furnace or water heater shall have an interior finish with a flame-spread rating not exceeding 25. Sealants and other trim materials two inches or less in width used to finish adjacent surfaces within these spaces are exempt from this provision, provided all joints are supported by framing members or materials with a flame spread rating of 25 or less. Combustible doors providing interior or exterior access to furnace and water heater spaces shall be covered with materials of limited combustibility (i.e., 5/16-inch gypsum board, etc.), with the surface allowed to be interrupted for louvers ventilating the space. However, the louvers shall not be of materials of greater combustibility than the door itself (i.e., plastic louvers on a wooden door). Reference MHCSS 3280.203.

   (b)   Exposed interior finishes. Exposed interior finishes adjacent to the cooking range (surfaces include vertical surfaces between the range top and overhead cabinets, the ceiling, or both) shall have a flame-spread rating not exceeding 50, as required by MHCSS 3280.203. Backsplashes not exceeding six inches in height are exempted. Ranges shall have a vertical clearance above the cooking top of not less than 24 inches to the bottom of combustible cabinets, as required by MHCSS 3280.204(e).

(3)   Related to smoke detectors:

   (a)   Location. A smoke detector shall be installed on any ceiling or wall in the hallway or space communicating with each bedroom area between the living area and the first bedroom door, unless a door separates the living area from that bedroom area, in which case the detector shall be installed on the living-area side, as close to the door as practicable, as required by MHCSS 3280.208. Homes with bedroom areas separated by anyone or combination of common-use areas such as a kitchen, dining room, living room, or family room (but not a bathroom or utility room) shall be required to have one detector for each bedroom area. When located in the hallways, the detector shall be between the return air intake and the living areas.

   (b)   Switches and electrical connections. Smoke detectors shall have no switches in the circuit to the detector between the over-current protection device protecting the branch circuit and the detector. The detector shall be attached to an electrical outlet box and connected by a permanent wiring method to a general electrical circuit. The detector shall not be placed on the same branch circuit or any circuit protected by a ground-fault circuit interrupter.

(4)   Related to solid-fuel-burning stoves/fireplaces:

   (a)   Solid-fuel-burning fireplaces and fireplace stoves. Solid-fuel-burning, factory-built fireplaces, and fireplace stoves may be used in manufactured homes, provided that they are listed for use in manufactured homes and installed according to their listing/manufacturer's instructions and the minimum requirements of MHCSS 3280.709(g).

   (b)   Equipment. A solid-fuel-burning fireplace or fireplace stove shall be equipped with an integral door or shutters designed to close the fire chamber opening and shall include complete means for venting through the roof, a combustion air inlet, a hearth extension, and means to securely attach the unit to the manufactured home structure.

      (i)   Chimney. A listed, factory-built chimney designed to be attached directly to the fireplace/fireplace stove and equipped with, in accordance with the listing, a termination device and spark arrester, shall be required. The chimney shall extend at least three feet above the part of the roof through which it passes and at least two feet above the highest elevation of any part of the manufactured home that is within 10 feet of the chimney.

      (ii)   Air-intake assembly and combustion-air inlet. An air-intake assembly shall be installed in accordance with the terms of listings and the manufacturer's instruction. A combustion-air inlet shall conduct the air directly into the fire chamber and shall be designed to prevent material from the hearth from dropping on the area beneath the manufactured home.

      (iii)   Hearth. The hearth extension shall be of noncombustible material that is a minimum of 3/8-inch thick and shall extend a minimum of 16 inches in front and eight inches beyond each side of the fireplace/fireplace stove opening. The hearth shall also extend over the entire surface beneath a fireplace stove and beneath an elevated and overhanging fireplace.

(5)   Related to electrical wiring systems:

  (a)   Testing. All electrical systems shall be tested for continuity in accordance with MHCSS 3280.810, to ensure that metallic parts are properly bonded; tested for operation, to demonstrate that all equipment is connected and in working order; and given a polarity check, to determine that connections are proper.

  (b)   5.2 Protection. The electrical system shall be properly protected for the required amperage load. If the unit wiring employs aluminum conductors, all receptacles and switches rated at 20 amperes or less that are directly connected to the aluminum conductors shall be marked CO/ALA. Exterior receptacles, other than heat tape receptacles, shall be of the ground-fault circuit interrupter (GFI) type. Conductors of dissimilar metals (copper/aluminum or copper-clad aluminum) must be connected in accordance with NEC, Section 110-14.

(6)   Related to replacement furnaces and water heaters:

  (a)   Listing. Replacement furnaces or water heaters shall be listed for use in a manufactured home. Vents, roof jacks, and chimneys necessary for the installation shall be listed for use with the furnace or water heater.

  (b)   Securement and accessibility. The furnace and water heater shall be secured in place to avoid displacement. Every furnace and water heater shall be accessible for servicing, for replacement, or both as required by MHCSS 3280.709(a).

  (c)   Installation. Furnaces and water heaters shall be installed to provide complete separation of the combustion system from the interior atmosphere of the manufactured home, as required by MHCSS.

      (i)   Separation. The required separation may be achieved by the installation of a direct-vent system (sealed combustion system) furnace or water heater or the installation of a furnace and water heater venting and combustion systems from the interior atmosphere of the home. There shall be no doors, grills, removable access panels, or other openings into the enclosure from the inside of the manufactured home. All openings for ducts, piping, wiring, etc., shall be sealed.

      (ii)   Water heater. The floor area in the area of the water heater shall be free from damage from moisture to ensure that the floor will support the weight of the water heater.

Amended by Chapter 297, 2013 General Session

Chapter 4 - Local Amendments Incorporated as Part of State Construction Code

Part 1 - Local Amendments to International Building Code

15A-4-101 General provision.

The amendments in this part are adopted as amendments to the IBC to be applicable to the specified jurisdiction.

Enacted by Chapter 14, 2011 General Session

15A-4-102 Amendments to IBC applicable to Brian Head Town.

The following amendment is adopted as an amendment to the IBC for Brian Head Town, Subsection 15A-3-104(6) that amends IBC, Section (F)903.2.8, is deleted and replaced with the following: "(F)903.2.8 Group R. An automatic sprinkler system installed in accordance with Section (F)903.3 shall be provided throughout all buildings with a Group R fire area.

Exception:

1. Detached one and two family dwellings and multiple single-family dwellings (townhouses) constructed in accordance with the International Residential Code for one and two-family dwellings. Except that an automatic fire sprinkler system shall be installed in all one- and two-family dwellings and townhouses over 3,000 square feet in size of defined living space (garage is excluded from defined living space) in accordance with Section (F)903.3.1 of the International Building Code. In areas not served by Brian Head Town culinary water services, NFPA Standard 1142 for water supplies for rural fire fighting shall apply. Any one- and two-family dwellings and townhouses that are difficult to locate or access, as determined by the authority having jurisdiction, shall be required to follow the guidelines as set forth in the NFPA Standard 1142 regardless of the size of the building.

2. Group R-4 fire areas not more than 4,500 gross square feet and not containing more than 16 residents, provided the building is equipped throughout with an approved fire alarm system that is interconnected and receives its primary power from the building wiring and a commercial power system."

Enacted by Chapter 14, 2011 General Session

15A-4-103 Amendments to IBC applicable to City of Farmington.

The following amendments are adopted as amendments to the IBC for the City of Farmington:

(1) A new IBC, Section (F) 903.2.13, is added as follows: "(F) 903.2.13 Group R, Division 3 Occupancies. An automatic sprinkler system shall be installed throughout every dwelling in accordance with NFPA 13D, when any of the following conditions are present:

1. The structure is over two stories high, as defined by the building code;

2. The nearest point of structure is more than 150 feet from the public way;

3. The total floor area of all stories is over 5,000 square feet (excluding from the calculation the area of the basement and/or garage); or

4. The structure is located on a street constructed after March 1, 2000, that has a gradient over 12% and, during fire department response, access to the structure will be gained by using such street. (If the access is intended to be from a direction where the steep gradient is not used, as determined by the Chief, this criteria shall not apply). Such sprinkler system shall be installed in basements, but need not be installed in garages, under eves or in enclosed attic spaces, unless required by the Chief."

(2)   A new IBC, Section 907.9, is added as follows: "907.9 Alarm Circuit Supervision. Alarm circuits in alarm systems provided for commercial uses (defined as other than one- and two-family dwellings and townhouses) shall have Class "A" type of supervision. Specifically, Type "B" or End-of-line resistor and horn supervised systems are not allowed."

(3)   In NFPA Section 13-07, new sections are added as follows: "6.8.6 FDC Security Locks Required. All Fire Department connections installed for fire sprinkler and standpipe systems shall have approved security locks.

6.10 Fire Pump Disconnect Signs. When installing a fire pump, red plastic laminate signs shall be installed in the electrical service panel, if the pump is wired separately from the main disconnect. These signs shall state: "Fire Pump Disconnect ONLY" and "Main Breaker DOES NOT Shut Off Fire Pump".

22.1.6 Plan Preparation Identification. All plans for fire sprinkler systems, except for manufacturer's cut sheets of equipment shall include the full name of the person who prepared the drawings. When the drawings are prepared by a registered professional engineer, the engineer's signature shall also be included.

22.2.2.3 Verification of Water Supply:

22.2.2.3.1 Fire Flow Tests. Fire flow tests for verification of water supply shall be conducted and witnessed for all applications other than residential unless directed otherwise by the Chief. For residential water supply, verification shall be determined by administrative procedure.

22.2.2.3.2 Accurate and Verifiable Criteria. The design calculations and criteria shall include an accurate and verifiable water supply.

24.2.3.7 Testing and Inspection of Systems. Testing and inspection of sprinkler systems shall include, but are not limited to:

Commercial:

FLUSH-Witness Underground Supply Flush;

ROUGH Inspection-Installation of Riser, System Piping, Head Locations and all Components, Hydrostatic Pressure Test;

FINAL Inspection-Head Installation and Escutcheons, Inspectors Test Location and Flow, Main Drain Flow, FDC Location and Escutcheon, Alarm Function, Spare Parts, Labeling of Components and Signage, System Completeness, Water Supply Pressure Verification, Evaluation of Any Unusual Parameter."

Enacted by Chapter 14, 2011 General Session

15A-4-104 Amendments to IBC applicable to City of North Salt Lake.

The following amendment is adopted as an amendment to the IBC for the City of North Salt Lake, a new IBC, Section (F)903.2.13, is added as follows: "(F)903.2.13 Group R, Division 3 Occupancies. An automatic sprinkler system shall be installed throughout every dwelling in accordance with NFPA 13D, when the following condition is present:

1.   The structure is over 6,200 square feet.

Such sprinkler system shall be installed in basements, but need not be installed in garages, under eves, or in enclosed attic spaces, unless required by the fire chief."

Enacted by Chapter 14, 2011 General Session

15A-4-105 Amendments to IBC applicable to Park City Corporation or Park City Fire District.

(1)   The following amendment is adopted as an amendment to the IBC for the Park City Corporation, in IBC, Section 3409.2, exception 3, is modified to read as follows: "3. Designated as historic under a state or local historic preservation program."

(2)   The following amendments are adopted as amendments to the IBC for the Park City Corporation and Park City Fire District:

(a)   IBC, Section (F)903.2, is deleted and replaced with the following: "(F)903.2 Where required. Approved automatic sprinkler systems in new buildings and structures shall be provided in the location described in this section.

All new construction having more than 6,000 square feet on any one floor, except R-3 occupancy.

All new construction having more than two (2) stories, except R-3 occupancy.

All new construction having three (3) or more dwelling units, including units rented or leased, and including condominiums or other separate ownership.

All new construction in the Historic Commercial Business zone district, regardless of occupancy.

All new construction and buildings in the General Commercial zone district where there are side yard setbacks or where one or more side yard setbacks is less than two and one half (2.5) feet per story of height.

All existing building within the Historic District Commercial Business zone."

(b)   In IBC, Table 1505.1, new footnotes d and e are added as follows: "d. Wood roof covering assemblies are prohibited in R-3 occupancies in areas with a combined rating of more than 11 using Tables 1505.1.1 and 1505.1.2 with a score of 9 for weather factors.

Wood roof covering assemblies shall have a Class A rating in occupancies other than R-3 in areas with a combined rating of more than 11 using Tables 1505.1.1 and 1505.1.2 with a score of 9 for weather factors. The owner of the building shall enter into a written and recorded agreement that the Class A rating of the roof covering assembly will not be altered through any type of maintenance process.

TABLE 1505.1.1

WILDFIRE HAZARD SEVERITY SCALE

Rating	Slope	Vegetation
1	less than or equal to 10%	Pinion-juniper
2	10.1 - 20%	Grass-sagebrush
3	greater than 20%	Mountain brush or softwoods

TABLE 1505.1.2

PROHIBITION/ALLOWANCE OF WOOD ROOFING

Rating	R-3 Occupancy	All Other Occupancies
Less than or equal to 11	Wood roof covering assemblies per Table 1505.1 are allowed	Wood roof covering assemblies per Table 1505.1 are allowed
Greater than or equal to 12	Wood roof covering is prohibited	Wood roof covering assemblies with a Class A rating are allowed"

(c)   IBC, Appendix C, is adopted.

Enacted by Chapter 14, 2011 General Session

15A-4-106 Amendments to IBC applicable to Salt Lake City.

The following amendment is adopted as an amendment to the IBC for Salt Lake City, in IBC, Section 1008.1.9.7, a new exception is added as follows: "Exception: In International Airport areas designated as Group "A" Occupancies where national security interests are present, the use of panic hardware with delayed egress is allowed when all provisions of Section 1008.1.9.7 are met and under item #4 1 second is changed to 2 seconds."

Enacted by Chapter 14, 2011 General Session

15A-4-107 Amendments to IBC applicable to Sandy City.

The following amendments are adopted as amendments to the IBC for Sandy City:

    (1)   A new IBC, Section (F)903.2.13, is added as follows: "(F)903.2.13 An automatic sprinkler system shall be installed in accordance with NFPA 13 throughout buildings containing all occupancies where fire flow exceeds 2,000 gallons per minute, based on Table B105.1 of the 2009 International Fire Code. Exempt locations as indicated in Section 903.3.1.1.1 are allowed. Exception: Automatic fire sprinklers are not required in buildings used solely for worship, Group R Division 3, Group U occupancies and buildings complying with the International Residential Code unless otherwise required by the International Fire Code.

    (2)   A new IBC, Appendix L, is added and adopted as follows: "Appendix L BUILDINGS AND STRUCTURES CONSTRUCTED IN AREAS DESIGNATED AS WILDLAND-URBAN INTERFACE AREAS AL 101.1 General. Buildings and structures constructed in areas designated as Wildland-Urban Interface Areas by Sandy City shall be constructed using ignition resistant construction as determined by the Fire Marshal. Section 502 of the 2006 International Wildland-Urban Interface Code (IWUIC), as promulgated by the International Code Council, shall be used to determine Fire Hazard Severity. The provisions listed in Chapter 5 of the 2006 International Wildland-Urban Interface Code, as modified herein, shall be used to determine the requirements for Ignition Resistant Construction.

        (i)   In Section 504 of the IWUIC Class I IGNITION-RESISTANT CONSTRUCTION a new Section 504.1.1 is added as follows: "504.1.1 General. Subsections 504.5, 504.6, and 504.7 shall only be required on the exposure side of the structure, as determined by the Fire Marshal, where defensible space is less than 50 feet as defined in Section 603 of the 2006 International Wildland-Urban Interface Code.

        (ii)   In Section 505 of the IWUIC Class 2 IGNITION-RESISTANT CONSTRUCTION Subsections 505.5 and 505.7 are deleted."

Enacted by Chapter 14, 2011 General Session

Part 2 - Local Amendments to International Residential Code

15A-4-201 General provision.

    (1)   The amendments in this part are adopted as amendments to the IRC to be applicable to specified jurisdiction.

    (2)   A local amendment to the following which may be applied to detached one and two family dwellings and multiple single family dwellings shall be applicable to the corresponding provisions of the IRC for the local jurisdiction to which the local amendment has been made:

        (a)   IBC under Part 1, Local Amendments to International Building Code;

        (b)   IPC under Part 3, Local Amendments to International Plumbing Code;

(c)   IMC under Part 4, Local Amendments to International Mechanical Code;

(d)   IFGC under Part 5, Local Amendments to International Fuel Gas Code;

(e)   NEC under Part 6, Local Amendments to National Electrical Code; and

(f)   IECC under Part 7, Local Amendments to International Energy Conservation Code.

Amended by Chapter 189, 2014 General Session

15A-4-202 Amendments to IRC applicable to Brian Head Town.

The following amendment is adopted as an amendment to the IRC for Brian Head Town, a new IRC, Section R324, is added as follows: "Section R324 Automatic Sprinkler Systems. An automatic fire sprinkler system shall be installed in all one- and two-family dwellings and townhouses over 3,000 square feet in size of defined living space (garage is excluded from defined living space) in accordance with Section (F)903.3.1 of the International Building Code. In areas not served by Brian Head Town culinary water services, NFPA Standard 1142 for water supplies for rural fire fighting shall apply. Any one- and two-family dwellings and townhouses that are difficult to locate or access, as determined by the authority having jurisdiction, shall be required to follow the guidelines as set forth in the NFPA Standard 1142 regardless of the size of the building."

Enacted by Chapter 14, 2011 General Session

15A-4-203 Amendments to IRC applicable to City of Farmington.

The following amendments are adopted as amendments to the IRC for the City of Farmington:

(1)   In IRC, R324 Automatic Sprinkler Systems, new IRC, Sections R324.1 and R324.2 are added as follows: "R324.1 When required. An automatic sprinkler system shall be installed throughout every dwelling in accordance with NFPA 13D, when any of the following conditions are present:

   1.   the structure is over two stories high, as defined by the building code;

   2.   the nearest point of structure is more than 150 feet from the public way;

   3.   the total floor area of all stories is over 5,000 square feet (excluding from the calculation the area of the basement and/or garage); or

   4.   the structure is located on a street constructed after March 1, 2000 that has a gradient over 12% and, during fire department response, access to the structure will be gained by using such street. (If the access is intended to be from a direction where the steep gradient is not used, as determined by the Chief, this criteria shall not apply).

   R324.2 Installation requirements and standards. Such sprinkler system shall be installed in basements, but need not be installed in garages, under eves or in enclosed attic spaces, unless required by the Chief. Such system shall be installed in accordance with NFPA 13D."

(2)   In IRC, Chapter 44, the following NFPA referenced standards are added as follows:

"TABLE

	Add	
	13D-07	Installation of Sprinkler Systems in One- and Two-family Dwellings and Manufactured Homes, as amended by these rules
	13R-07	Installation of Sprinkler Systems in Residential Occupancies Up to and Including Four Stories in Height"

(3)   In NFPA, Section 13D-07, new sections are added as follows: "1.15 Reference to NFPA 13D. All references to NFPA 13D in the codes, ordinances, rules, or regulations governing NFPA 13D systems shall be read to refer to "modified NFPA 13D" to reference the NFPA 13D as amended by additional regulations adopted by Farmington City.

4.9 Testing and Inspection of Systems. Testing and inspection of sprinkler systems shall include, but are not limited to:

Residential:

ROUGH Inspection-Verify Water Supply Piping Size and Materials, Installation of Riser, System Piping, Head Locations and all Components, Hydrostatic Pressure Test.

FINAL Inspection-Inspectors Test Flow, System Completeness, Spare Parts, Labeling of Components and Signage, Alarm Function, Water Supply Pressure Verification.

5.2.2.3 Exposed Piping of Metal. Exposed Sprinkler Piping material in rooms of dwellings shall be of Metal.

EXCEPTIONS:

a.   CPVC Piping is allowed in unfinished mechanical and storage rooms only when specifically listed for the application as installed.

b.   CPVC Piping is allowed in finished, occupied rooms used for sports courts or similar uses only when the ceiling/floor framing above is constructed entirely of non-combustible materials, such as a concrete garage floor on metal decking.

5.2.2.4 Water Supply Piping Material. Water Supply Piping from where the water line enters the dwelling adjacent to and inside the foundation to the fire sprinkler contractor point-of-connection shall be metal, suitable for potable plumbing systems. See Section 7.1.4 for valve prohibition in such piping. Piping down stream from the point-of-connection used in the fire sprinkler system, including the riser, shall conform to NFPA 13D standards.

5.4 Fire Pump Disconnect Signs. When installing a Fire Pump, Red Plastic Laminate Signs shall be installed in the electrical service panel, if the pump is wired separately from the main disconnect. These signs shall state: "Fire Pump Disconnect ONLY" and "Main Breaker DOES NOT Shut Off Fire Pump".

7.1.4 Valve Prohibition. NFPA 13D, Section 7.1 is hereby modified such that NO VALVE is permitted from the City Water Meter to the Fire Sprinkler Riser Control.

7.6.1 Mandatory Exterior Alarm. Every dwelling that has a fire sprinkler system shall have an exterior alarm, installed in an approved location. The alarm shall be of the combination horn/strobe or electric bell/strobe type, approved for outdoor use.

8.1.05 Plan Preparation Identification. All plans for fire sprinkler systems, except for manufacturer's cut sheets of equipment, shall include the full name of the person who prepared the drawings. When the drawings are prepared by a registered professional engineer, the engineer's signature shall also be included.

8.7 Verification of Water Supply:

8.7.1 Fire Flow Tests: Fire Flow Tests for verification of Water Supply shall be conducted and witnesses for all applications other than residential, unless directed otherwise by the Chief. For residential Water Supply, verification shall be determined by administrative procedure.

8.7.2 Accurate and Verifiable Criteria. The design calculations and criteria shall include an accurate and verifiable Water Supply.

Enacted by Chapter 14, 2011 General Session

15A-4-204 Amendments to IRC applicable to Morgan City Corporation or Morgan County.

    (1)   The following amendment is adopted as an amendment to the IRC for the Morgan City Corporation, in IRC, Section R105.2, Work Exempt From Permit, a new list item number 11 is added as follows: "11. Structures intended to house farm animals, or for the storage of feed associated with said farm animals when all the following criteria are met:

        a.   The parcel of property involved is zoned for the keeping of farm animals or has grandfathered animal rights.

        b.   The structure is setback not less than 50 feet from the rear or side of dwellings, and not less than 10 feet from property lines and other structures.

        c.   The structure does not exceed 1,000 square feet of floor area, and is limited to 20 feet in height. Height is measured from the average grade to the highest point of the structure.

        d.   Before construction, a site plan is submitted to, and approved by the building official. Electrical, plumbing, and mechanical permits shall be required when that work is included in the structure."

    (2)   The following amendment is adopted as an amendment to the IRC for Morgan County, in IRC, Section R105.2, a new list item number 11 is added as follows: "11. Structures intended to house farm animals, or for the storage of feed associated with said farm animals when all the following criteria are met:

        a.   The parcel of property involved is zoned for the keeping of farm animals or has grandfathered animal rights.

        b.   The structure is set back not less than required by the Morgan County Zoning Ordinance for such structures, but not less than 10 feet from property lines and other structures.

        c.   The structure does not exceed 1,000 square feet of floor area, and is limited to 20 feet in height. Height is measured from the average grade to the highest point of the structure.

        d.   Before construction, a Land Use Permit must be applied for, and approved, by the Morgan County Planning and Zoning Department. Electrical, plumbing, and mechanical permits shall be required when that work is included in the structure."

Enacted by Chapter 14, 2011 General Session

15A-4-205 Amendments to IRC applicable to City of North Salt Lake.

The following amendment is adopted as an amendment to the IRC for the City of North Salt Lake, a new IRC, Section R324, is added as follows: "Section R324 Automatic Sprinkler System Requirements. R324.1 When Required. An automatic sprinkler system shall be installed throughout every dwelling when the following condition is present:

1.   The structure is over 6,200 square feet.

R324.2 Installation requirements and standards. Such sprinkler system shall be installed in basements, but need not be installed in garages, under eves, or in enclosed attic spaces, unless required by the fire chief. Such system shall be installed in accordance with NFPA 13D."

Enacted by Chapter 14, 2011 General Session

15A-4-206 Amendments to IRC applicable to Park City Corporation or Park City Fire District.

    (1)   The following amendment is adopted as an amendment to the IRC for the Park City Corporation, Appendix P, of the 2006 IRC is adopted.

(2)   The following amendments are adopted as amendments to the IRC for Park City Corporation and Park City Fire District:

    (a)   IRC, Section R905.7, is deleted and replaced with the following: "R905.7 Wood shingles. The installation of wood shingles shall comply with the provisions of this section. Wood roof covering is prohibited in areas with a combined rating of more than 11 using the following tables with a score of 9 for weather factors.

TABLE

WILDFIRE HAZARD SEVERITY SCALE

Rating	Slope	Vegetation
1	less than or equal to 10%	Pinion-juniper
2	10.1 - 20%	Grass-sagebrush
3	greater than 20%	Mountain brush or softwoods

PROHIBITION/EXEMPTION TABLE

Rating	Wood Roof Prohibition
less than or equal to 11	wood roofs are allowed
greater than or equal to 12	wood roofs are prohibited"

    (b)   IRC, Section R905.8, is deleted and replaced with the following: "R905.8 Wood Shakes. The installation of wood shakes shall comply with the provisions of this section. Wood roof covering is prohibited in areas with a combined rating of more than 11 using the following tables with a score of 9 for weather factors.

TABLE

WILDFIRE HAZARD SEVERITY SCALE

Rating	Slope	Vegetation
1	less than or equal to 10%	Pinion-juniper
2	10.1 - 20%	Grass-sagebrush
3	greater than 20%	Mountain brush or softwoods

PROHIBITION/EXEMPTION TABLE

Rating	Wood Roof Prohibition
less than or equal to 11	wood roofs are allowed
greater than or equal to 12	wood roofs are prohibited"

    (c)   Appendix K is adopted.

Enacted by Chapter 14, 2011 General Session

15A-4-207 Amendments to IRC applicable to Sandy City.

The following amendment is adopted as an amendment to the IRC for Sandy City, a new IRC, Section R324, is added as follows: "Section R324 IGNITION RESISTANT CONSTRUCTION

R324.1 General. Buildings and structures constructed in areas designated as Wildland-Urban Interface Areas by Sandy City shall be constructed using ignition resistant construction as determined by the Fire Marshal. Section 502 of the 2006 International Wildland-Urban Interface Code (IWUIC), as promulgated by the International Code Council, shall be used to determine Fire Hazard Severity. The provisions listed in Chapter 5 of the 2006 IWUIC, as modified herein, shall be used to determine the requirements for Ignition Resistant Construction.

      (i)   In Section 504 of the IWUIC Class I IGNITION-RESISTANT CONSTRUCTION a new Section 504.1.1 is added as follows:

504.1.1 General. Subsections 504.5, 504.6, and 504.7 shall only be required on the exposure side of the structure, as determined by the Fire Marshal, where defensible space is less than 50 feet as defined in Section 603 of the 2006 IWUIC.

      (ii)   In Section 505 of the IWUIC Class 2 IGNITION-RESISTANT CONSTRUCTION Subsections 505.5 and 505.7 are deleted."

Enacted by Chapter 14, 2011 General Session

Part 3 - Local Amendments to International Plumbing Code

15A-4-301 General provision.

The amendments in this part are adopted as amendments to the IPC to be applicable to specified jurisdiction.

Enacted by Chapter 14, 2011 General Session

15A-4-303 Amendments to IPC applicable to South Jordan.

The following amendments are adopted as amendments to the IPC for South Jordan:

      (1)   IPC, Section 312.10.2, is deleted and replaced with the following: "312.10.2 Testing. Reduced pressure principle backflow preventer assemblies, double check-valve assemblies, pressure vacuum breaker assemblies, reduced pressure detector fire protection backflow prevention assemblies, double check detector fire protection backflow prevention assemblies, hose connection backflow preventers, and spill-proof vacuum breakers shall be tested at the time of installation, immediately after repairs or relocation and at least annually. The testing procedure shall be performed in accordance with one of the following standards: ASSE 5013, ASSE 5015, ASSE 5020, ASSE 5047, ASSE 5048, ASSE 5052, ASSE 5056, CSA-B64.10, or CSA-B64.10.1. Assemblies, other than the reduced pressure principle assembly, protecting lawn irrigation systems that fail the annual test shall be replaced with a reduced pressure principle assembly."

      (2)   IPC, Section 608.16.5, is deleted and replaced with the following: "608.16.5 Connections to lawn irrigation systems. The potable water supply to lawn irrigation systems shall be protected against backflow by a reduced pressure principle backflow preventer."

Enacted by Chapter 14, 2011 General Session

Part 4 - Local Amendments to International Mechanical Code

15A-4-401 General provision.

No local amendments to the IMC are adopted.

Enacted by Chapter 14, 2011 General Session

Part 5 - Local Amendments to International Fuel Gas Code

15A-4-501 General provision.

No local amendments to the IFGC are adopted.

Enacted by Chapter 14, 2011 General Session

Part 6 - Local Amendments to National Electrical Code

15A-4-601 General provision.

No local amendments to the NEC are adopted.

Enacted by Chapter 14, 2011 General Session

Part 7 - Local Amendments to International Energy Conservation Code

15A-4-701 General provision.

No local amendments to the IECC are adopted.

Enacted by Chapter 14, 2011 General Session

Chapter 5 - State Fire Code Act

Part 1 - General Provisions

15A-5-101 Title — Adoption of code.

In accordance with Chapter 1, Part 4, State Fire Code Administration Act, the Legislature repeals the State Fire Code in effect on July 1, 2010, and adopts this chapter as the State Fire Code.

Enacted by Chapter 14, 2011 General Session

15A-5-102 Definitions.

As used in this chapter:

(1)   "Appreciable depth" means a depth greater than 1/4 inch.

(2)   "AHJ" means "authority having jurisdiction," which is:

   (a)   the State Fire Marshal;

   (b)   an authorized deputy of the State Fire Marshal; or

   (c)   the local fire enforcement authority.

(3)   "Division" means the State Fire Marshal Division created in Section 53-7-103.

(4)   (a)   "Dwelling Unit" means one or more rooms arranged for the use of one or more individuals living together, as in a single housekeeping unit normally having cooking, living, sanitary, and sleeping facilities.

   (b)   "Dwelling unit" includes a hotel room, dormitory room, apartment, condominium, sleeping room in a nursing home, or similar living unit.

(5)   "Fire jurisdiction" means a contiguous geographic area for which there is a single authority having jurisdiction.

(6)   "IFC" means the edition of the International Fire Code adopted under Section 15A-5-103.

(7)   "NFPA" means the edition of the National Fire Protection Association adopted under Section 15A-5-103.

(8)   "Premixed" means the state of an antifreeze and water solution that results from the solution being prepared by the manufacturer with a quality control procedure that ensures that the antifreeze and water solution does not separate.

(9)   "UL" means Underwriters Laboratories, Inc.

Amended by Chapter 158, 2015 General Session

15A-5-103 Nationally recognized codes incorporated by reference.

The following codes are incorporated by reference into the State Fire Code:

(1)   the International Fire Code, 2012 edition, excluding appendices, as issued by the International Code Council, Inc., except as amended by Part 2, Statewide Amendments and Additions to International Fire Code Incorporated as Part of State Fire Code;

(2)   National Fire Protection Association, NFPA 96, Standard for Ventilation Control and Fire Protection of Commercial Cooking Operations, 2011 edition, except as amended by Part 3, Amendments and Additions to National Fire Protection Association Incorporated as Part of State Fire Code; and

(3)   National Fire Protection Association, NFPA 1403, Standard on Live Fire Training Evolutions, 2012 edition, except as amended by Part 3, Amendments and Additions to National Fire Protection Association Incorporated as Part of State Fire Code.

Amended by Chapter 189, 2014 General Session

Part 2 - Statewide Amendments and Additions to International Fire Code Incorporated as Part of State Fire Code

15A-5-201 General provisions.

The amendments and additions in this part to the IFC are adopted for application statewide.

Enacted by Chapter 14, 2011 General Session

15A-5-202 Amendments and additions to IFC related to administration, permits, definitions and general and emergency planning.

(1)   For IFC, Chapter 1, Scope and Administration:

(a)   IFC, Chapter 1, Section 102.9, is amended by adding the following immediately before the period: "on an emergency basis if:

(a)   the facts known to the fire code official show that an immediate and significant danger to the public health, safety, or welfare exists; and

(b)   the threat requires immediate action by the fire code official.

(2)   In issuing its emergency order, the fire code official shall:

(a)   limit the order to require only the action necessary to prevent or avoid the danger to the public health, safety, or welfare; and

(b)   give immediate notice to the persons who are required to comply with the order, that includes a brief statement of the reasons for the fire code official's order.

(3)   (a)   If the emergency order issued under this section will result in the continued infringement or impairment of any legal right or interest of any party, the party shall have a right to appeal the fire code official's order in accordance with IFC, Chapter 1, Section 108."

        (b)   IFC, Chapter 1, Section 105.6.16, Flammable and combustible liquids, is amended to add the following section: "12. The owner of an underground tank that is out of service for longer than one year shall receive a Temporary Closure Notice from the Department of Environmental Quality and a copy shall be given to the AHJ."

        (c)   In IFC, Chapter 1, Section 108, a new Section 108.4, Notice of right to appeal, is added as follows: "At the time a fire code official makes an order, decision, or determination that relates to the application or interpretation of this chapter, the fire code official shall inform the person affected by the order, decision, or determination of the person's right to appeal under this section. Upon request, the fire code official shall provide a person affected by an order, decision, or determination that relates to the application or interpretation of this chapter a written notice that describes the person's right to appeal under this section."

        (d)   IFC, Chapter 1, Section 109.3, Notice of violation, is amended as follows: On line three, after the words "is in violation of this code," insert in the section the phrase "or other pertinent laws or ordinances".

(2)   For IFC, Chapter 2, Definitions:

    (a)   IFC, Chapter 2, Section 202, General Definitions, the following definition is added for Ambulatory Surgical Center: "AMBULATORY SURGICAL CENTER. A building or portion of a building licensed by the Utah Department of Health where procedures are performed that may render patients incapable of self preservation where care is less than 24 hours."

    (b)   IFC, Chapter 2, Section 202, General Definitions, FOSTER CARE FACILITIES is amended as follows: the word "Foster" is changed to the word "Child."

    (c)   IFC, Chapter 2, Section 202, General Definitions, Occupancy Classification, Educational Group E, Day care facilities, is amended as follows: On line three delete the word "five" and replace it with the word "four". On line four after the word "supervision" add the words "child care centers."

    (d)   IFC, Chapter 2, Section 202, General Definitions, Occupancy Classification, Educational Group E, Five or fewer children is amended as follows: On line one the word "five" is deleted and replaced with the word "four" in both places.

    (e)   IFC, Chapter 2, Section 202, General Definitions, Occupancy Classification, Educational Group E, Five or fewer children in a dwelling unit, the word "five" is deleted and replaced with the word "four" in both places.

    (f)   IFC, Chapter 2, Section 202, General Definitions, Occupancy Classification, Educational Group E, a new section is added as follows: "Child Day Care — Residential Certificate or a Family License. Areas used for child day care purposes with a Residential Certificate R430-50 or a Family License, as defined in Utah Administrative Code, R430-90, Licensed Family Child Care, may be located in a Group R-2 or R-3 occupancy as provided in Residential Group R-3, or shall comply with the International Residential Code in accordance with Section R101.2."

    (g)   IFC, Chapter 2, Section 202, General Definitions, Occupancy Classification, Educational Group E, a new section is added as follows: "Child Care Centers. Areas used for Hourly Child Care Centers, as defined in Utah Administrative Code, R430-60, Child Care Center as defined in Utah Administrative Code, R430-100, or Out of School Time Programs, as defined in Utah Administrative Code, R430-70, may be classified as accessory occupancies."

(h) IFC, Chapter 2, Section 202, General Definitions, Occupancy Classification, Institutional Group I, Group I-1, is amended as follows: On line 8 add "Type I" in front of the words "Assisted living facilities".

(i) IFC, Chapter 2, Section 202, General Definitions, Occupancy Classification, Institutional Group I, Five or fewer persons receiving care is amended as follows: On line four after "International Residential Code" the rest of the section is deleted.

(j) IFC, Chapter 2, Section 202, General Definitions, Occupancy Classification, Institutional Group I, Group I-2, is amended as follows:

    (i) On line three delete the word "five" and insert the word "three".

    (ii) On line six the word "foster" is deleted and replaced with the word "child".

    (iii) On line 10, after the words "Psychiatric hospitals", add the following to the list: "both intermediate nursing care and skilled nursing care facilities, ambulatory surgical centers with five or more operating rooms, and Type II assisted living facilities. Type II assisted living facilities with five or fewer persons shall be classified as a Group R-4. Type II assisted living facilities with at least six and not more than 16 residents shall be classified as a Group I-1 facility".

(k) IFC, Chapter 2, Section 202, General Definitions, Occupancy Classification, Institutional Group I, Group I-4, Day care facilities, Classification as Group E, is amended as follows:

    (i) On line two delete the word "five" and replace it with the word "four".

    (ii) On line three delete the words "2 1/2 years or less of age" and replace with the words "under the age of two".

(l) IFC, Chapter 2, Section 202, General Definitions, Occupancy Classification, Institutional Group Care I, Group I-4, Day care facilities, Five or fewer occupants receiving care in a dwelling unit, is amended as follows: On lines one and two the word "five" is deleted and replaced with the word "four".

(m) IFC, Chapter 2, Section 202, General Definitions, Occupancy Classification, Residential Group R-3, the words "and single family dwellings complying with the IRC" are added after the word "Residential occupancies".

(n) IFC, Chapter 2, Section 202, General Definitions, Occupancy Classification, Residential Group R-3, Care facilities within a dwelling, is amended as follows: On line three after the word "dwelling" insert "other than child care".

(o) IFC, Chapter 2, Section 202, General Definitions, Occupancy Classification, Residential Group R-3, a new section is added as follows: "Child Care. Areas used for child care purposes may be located in a residential dwelling unit when all of the following conditions are met:

    1. Compliance with Utah Administrative Code, R710-8, Day Care Rules, as enacted under the authority of the Utah Fire Prevention Board;

    2. Use is approved by the Utah Department of Health under the authority of the Utah Code, Title 26, Chapter 39, Utah Child Care Licensing Act, and in any of the following categories:

        1.1. Utah Administrative Code, R430-50, Residential Certificate Child Care; or

        1.2. Utah Administrative Code, R430-90, Licensed Family Child Care; and

    3. Compliance with all zoning regulations of the local regulator."

    (p)   IFC, Chapter 2, Section 202, General Definitions, RECORD DRAWINGS, the definition for "RECORD DRAWINGS" is modified by deleting the words "a fire alarm system" and replacing them with "any fire protection system".

Amended by Chapter 158, 2015 General Session

15A-5-202.5 Amendments and additions to Chapters 3 and 4 of IFC.

    (1)   For IFC, Chapter 3, General Requirements:

        (a)   IFC, Chapter 3, Section 304.1.2, Vegetation, is amended as follows: Delete line six and replace it with: "the Utah Administrative Code, R652-122-200, Minimum Standards for Wildland Fire Ordinance".

        (b)   IFC, Chapter 3, Section 308.1.2, Throwing or Placing Sources of Ignition, is deleted and rewritten as follows: "No person shall throw or place, or cause to be thrown or placed, a lighted match, cigar, cigarette, matches, lighters, or other flaming or glowing substance or object on any surface or article where it can cause an unwanted fire."

        (c)   IFC, Chapter 3, Section 310.8, Hazardous and Environmental Conditions, is deleted and rewritten as follows: "When the fire code official determines that hazardous environmental conditions necessitate controlled use of any ignition source, including fireworks, lighters, matches, sky lanterns, and smoking materials, any of the following may occur:

            1.   If the hazardous environmental conditions exist in a municipality, the legislative body of the municipality may prohibit the ignition or use of an ignition source in mountainous, brush-covered, or forest-covered areas or the wildland urban interface area, which means the line, area, or zone where structures or other human development meet or intermingle with undeveloped wildland or land being used for an agricultural purpose.

            2.   Except as provided in paragraph 3, if the hazardous environmental conditions exist in an unincorporated area, the state forester may prohibit the ignition or use of an ignition source in all or part of the areas described in paragraph 1 that are within the unincorporated area, after consulting with the county fire code official who has jurisdiction over that area.

            3.   If the hazardous environmental conditions exist in a metro township created under Title 10, Chapter 2a, Part 4, Incorporation of Metro Townships and Unincorporated Islands in a County of the First Class on and after May 12, 2015, the metro township legislative body may prohibit the ignition or use of an ignition source in all or part of the areas described in paragraph 1 that are within the township."

        (d)   IFC, Chapter 3, Section 311.1.1, Abandoned Premises, is amended as follows: On line 10 delete the words "International Property Maintenance Code and the".

        (e)   IFC, Chapter 3, Section 311.5, Placards, is amended as follows: On line three delete the word "shall" and replace it with the word "may".

        (f)   IFC, Chapter 3, Section 315.2.1, Ceiling Clearance, is amended to add the following: "Exception: Where storage is not directly below the sprinkler heads, storage is allowed to be placed to the ceiling on wall-mounted shelves that are protected by fire sprinkler heads in occupancies meeting classification as light or ordinary hazard."

    (2)   IFC, Chapter 4, Emergency Planning and Preparedness:

        (a)   IFC, Chapter 4, Section 404.2, Where required, Subsection 8, is amended as follows: After the word "buildings" add "to include sororities and fraternity houses".

(b)   IFC, Chapter 4, Section 405.2, Table 405.2, is amended to add the following footnotes:

(i)   "e. Secondary schools in Group E occupancies shall have an emergency evacuation drill for fire conducted at least every two months, to a total of four emergency evacuation drills during the nine-month school year. The first emergency evacuation drill for fire shall be conducted within 10 school days after the beginning of classes. The third emergency evacuation drill for fire, weather permitting, shall be conducted 10 school days after the beginning of the next calendar year. The second and fourth emergency evacuation drills may be substituted by a security or safety drill to include shelter in place, earthquake drill, or lock down for violence. If inclement weather causes a secondary school to miss the 10-day deadline for the third emergency evacuation drill for fire, the secondary school shall perform the third emergency evacuation drill for fire as soon as practicable after the missed deadline."

(ii)   "f. In Group E occupancies, excluding secondary schools, if the AHJ approves, the monthly required emergency evacuation drill can be substituted by a security or safety drill to include shelter in place, earthquake drill, or lock down for violence. The routine emergency evacuation drill for fire must by conducted at least every other evacuation drill."

(iii) "g. A-3 occupancies in academic buildings of institutions of higher learning are required to have one emergency evacuation drill per year, provided the following conditions are met:

(A)   The building has a fire alarm system in accordance with Section 907.2.

(B)   The rooms classified as assembly shall have fire safety floor plans as required in Section 404.3.2(4) posted.

(C)   The building is not classified a high-rise building.

(D)   The building does not contain hazardous materials over the allowable quantities by code."

Amended by Chapter 158, 2015 General Session

Amended by Chapter 352, 2015 General Session

15A-5-203 Amendments and additions to IFC related to fire safety, building, and site requirements.

(1)   For IFC, Chapter 5, Fire Service Features:

(a)   In IFC, Chapter 5, a new Section 501.5, Access grade and fire flow, is added as follows: "An authority having jurisdiction over a structure built in accordance with the requirements of the International Residential Code as adopted in the State Construction Code, may require an automatic fire sprinkler system for the structure only by ordinance and only if any of the following conditions exist:

(i)   the structure:

(A)   is located in an urban-wildland interface area as provided in the Utah Wildland Urban Interface Code adopted as a construction code under the State Construction Code; and

(B)   does not meet the requirements described in Utah Code, Subsection 65A-8-203(3)(a) and Utah Administrative Code, R652-122-200, Minimum Standards for Wildland Fire Ordinance;

(ii)   the structure is in an area where a public water distribution system with fire hydrants does not exist as required in Utah Administrative Code, R309-550-5, Water Main Design;

(iii)   the only fire apparatus access road has a grade greater than 10% for more than 500 continual feet; or

(iv)   (A)   the water supply to the structure does not provide at least 500 gallons fire flow per minute for a minimum of 30 minutes, if the total square foot living space of the structure is equal to or less than 5,000 square feet;

         (B)   the water supply to the structure does not provide at least 750 gallons per minute fire flow for a minimum of 30 minutes, if the total square foot living space exceeds 5,000 square feet, but is equal to or less than 10,000 square feet; or

         (C)   the water supply to the structure does not provide at least 1,000 gallons per minute fire flow for a minimum of 30 minutes, if the total square foot living space exceeds 10,000 square feet."

(b)   In IFC, Chapter 5, Section 506.1, Where Required, is deleted and rewritten as follows: "Where access to or within a structure or an area is restricted because of secured openings or where immediate access is necessary for life-saving or fire-fighting purposes, the fire code official, after consultation with the building owner, may require a key box to be installed in an approved location. The key box shall contain keys to gain necessary access as required by the fire code official. For each fire jurisdiction that has at least one building with a required key box, the fire jurisdiction shall adopt an ordinance, resolution, or other operating rule or policy that creates a process to ensure that each key to each key box is properly accounted for and secure."

(c)   In IFC, Chapter 5, a new Section 507.1.1, Isolated one- and two-family dwellings, is added as follows: "Fire flow may be reduced for an isolated one- and two-family dwelling when the authority having jurisdiction over the dwelling determines that the development of a full fire-flow requirement is impractical."

(d)   In IFC, Chapter 5, a new Section 507.1.2, Pre-existing subdivision lots, is added as follows "Total water supply requirements shall not exceed the fire flows described in Section 501.5(iv) for the largest one- or two-family dwelling, protected by an automatic fire sprinkler system, on a subdivision lot platted before December 31, 1980, unless the municipality or county in which the lot is located provides the required fire flow capacity."

(e)   In IFC, Chapter 5, Section 510.1, Emergency Responder Radio Coverage in New Buildings, is amended by adding: "When required by the fire code official," at the beginning of the first paragraph.

(2)   For IFC, Chapter 6, Building Services and Systems:

(a)   In IFC, Chapter 6, Section 605.11.3.3.1, Access, is deleted and rewritten as follows: "There shall be a minimum three foot wide (914 mm) clear perimeter around the edges of the roof."

(b)   In IFC, Chapter 6, Section 605.11.3.3.2, Pathways, is deleted and rewritten as follows: "The solar installation shall be designed to provide designated pathways. The pathways shall meet the following requirements:

1.   The pathway shall be over areas capable of supporting the live load of fire fighters accessing the roof.

2. The centerline axis pathways shall be provided in both axes of the roof. Centerline axis pathways shall run where the roof structure is capable of supporting the live load of fire fighters accessing the roof.

3. Smoke and heat vents required by Section 910.2.1 or 910.2.2 of this Code, shall be provided with a clear pathway width of not less than three feet (914 mm) to vents.

4. Access to roof area required by Section 504.2 or 1009.16 of this Code, shall be provided with a clear pathway width of not less than three feet (914 mm) around access opening and at least three feet (914 mm) clear pathway to parapet or roof edge."

(c)   In IFC, Chapter 6, Section 605.11.3.2, Residential Systems for One and Two Family Dwellings, is deleted and rewritten as follows: "Access to residential systems for one and two family dwellings shall be provided in accordance with Sections 605.11.3.2.1 through 605.11.3.2.4.

Exception: Reduction in pathways and clear access width shall be permitted where shown that a rational approach has been used and that such reductions are warranted when approved by the Fire Code Official."

(d)   In IFC, Chapter 6, Section 605.11.3.3.3, Smoke Ventilation, is deleted and rewritten as follows: "The solar installation shall be designed to meet the following requirements:

1. Arrays shall be no greater than 150 feet (45.720 mm) by 150 feet (45.720 mm) in distance in either axis in order to create opportunities for fire department smoke ventilation operations.

2. Smoke ventilation options between array sections shall be one of the following:

   2.1. A pathway six feet (1829 mm) or greater in width.

   2.2. A three foot (914 mm) or greater in width pathway and bordering roof skylights or smoke and heat vents when required by Section 910.2.1 or Section 910.2.2 of this Code.

   2.3. Smoke and heat vents designed for remote operation using devices that can be connected to the vent by mechanical, electrical, or any other suitable means, shall be protected as necessary to remain operable for the design period. Controls for remote operation shall be located in a control panel, clearly identified and located in an approved location."

(e)   In IFC, Chapter 6, Section 607.4, Elevator Key Location, is deleted and rewritten as follows: "Firefighter service keys shall be kept in a "Supra-Stor-a-key" elevator key box or similar box with corresponding key system that is adjacent to the elevator for immediate use by the fire department. The key box shall contain one key for each elevator, one key for lobby control, and any other keys necessary for emergency service. The elevator key box shall be accessed using a 6049 numbered key."

(f)   In IFC, Chapter 6, Section 609.1, General, is amended as follows: On line three, after the word "Code", add the words "and NFPA 96".

(3)   For IFC, Chapter 7, Fire-Resistance-Rated Construction, IFC, Chapter 7, Section 703.2, is amended to add the following: "Exception: In Group E Occupancies, where the corridor serves an occupant load greater than 30 and the building does not have an automatic fire sprinkler system installed, the door closers may be of the friction hold-open type on classrooms' doors with a rating of 20 minutes or less only."

Amended by Chapter 158, 2015 General Session

15A-5-204 Amendments and additions to IFC related to fire protection systems.

For IFC, Fire Protection Systems:

(1)   IFC, Chapter 9, Section 901.2, Construction Documents, is amended to add the following at the end of the section: "The code official has the authority to request record drawings ("as builts") to verify any modifications to the previously approved construction documents."

(2)   IFC, Chapter 9, Section 901.4.6, Pump and Riser Room Size, is deleted and replaced with the following: "Pump and Riser Room Size. Fire pump and automatic sprinkler system riser rooms shall be designed with adequate space for all installed equipment necessary for the installation and to provide sufficient working space around the stationary equipment. Clearances around equipment shall be in accordance with manufacturer requirements and not less than the following minimum elements:

901.4.6.1 A minimum clear and unobstructed distance of 12 inches shall be provided from the installed equipment to the elements of permanent construction.

901.4.6.2 A minimum clear and unobstructed distance of 12 inches shall be provided between all other installed equipment and appliances.

901.4.6.3 A clear and unobstructed width of 36 inches shall be provided in front of all installed equipment and appliances, to allow for inspection, service, repair or replacement without removing such elements of permanent construction or disabling the function of a required fire-resistance-rated assembly.

901.4.6.4 Automatic sprinkler system riser rooms shall be provided with a clear and unobstructed passageway to the riser room of not less than 36 inches, and openings into the room shall be clear and unobstructed, with doors swinging in the outward direction from the room and the opening providing a clear width of not less than 34 inches and a clear height of the door opening shall not be less than 80 inches.

901.4.6.5 Fire pump rooms shall be provided with a clear and unobstructed passageway to the fire pump room of not less than 72 inches, and openings into the room shall be clear, unobstructed and large enough to allow for the removal of the largest piece of equipment, with doors swinging in the outward direction from the room and the opening providing a clear width of not less than 68 inches and a clear height of the door opening shall not be less than 80 inches."

(3)   IFC, Chapter 9, Section 903.2.1.2, Group A-2, is amended to add the following subsection: "4. An automatic fire sprinkler system shall be provided throughout Group A-2 occupancies where indoor pyrotechnics are used."

(4)   IFC, Chapter 9, Section 903.2.2, Ambulatory Health Care Facilities, is amended as follows: On line two delete the words "all fire areas floor" and replace with the word "buildings" and delete the last paragraph.

(5)   IFC, Chapter 9, Section 903.2.4, Group F-1, Subsection 2, is deleted and rewritten as follows: "A Group F-1 fire area is located more than three stories above the lowest level of fire department vehicle access."

(6)   IFC, Chapter 9, Section 903.2.7, Group M, Subsection 2, is deleted and rewritten as follows: "A Group M fire area is located more than three stories above the lowest level of fire department vehicle access."

(7)   IFC, Chapter 9, Section 903.2.8 Group R, is amended to add the following: "Exception: Detached one- and two-family dwellings and multiple single-family dwellings (townhouses) constructed in accordance with the International Residential Code for one- and two-family dwellings."

(8)   IFC, Chapter 9, Section 903.2.8, Group R, is amended to add a second exception as follows: "Exception: Group R-4 fire areas not more than 4,500 gross square feet and not containing more than 16 residents, provided the building is equipped throughout with an approved fire alarm system that is interconnected and receives its primary power from the building wiring and a commercial power system."

(9)   IFC, Chapter 9, Section 903.2.8 Group R, is amended to add a third exception as follows: "Exception: Single story group R-1 occupancies with fire areas not more than 2,000 square feet that contain no installed plumbing or heating, where no cooking occurs, and constructed of Type I-A, I-B, II-A, or II-B construction."

(10)   IFC, Chapter 9, Section 903.2.9, Group S-1, Subsection 2, is deleted and rewritten as follows: "A Group S-1 fire area is located more than three stories above the lowest level of fire department vehicle access."

(11)   IFC, Chapter 9, Section 903.3.1.1 is amended by adding the following subsection: "903.3.1.1.2 Antifreeze Limitations. Antifreeze used in a new automatic sprinkler system installed in accordance with NFPA 13 may not exceed a maximum concentration of 38% premixed propylene glycol or 48% premixed glycerin, and the capacity of the system may not exceed 150 gallons."

(12)   IFC, Chapter 9, Section 903.3.1.2 is amended by adding the following subsection: "903.3.1.2.2 Antifreeze Limitations. Antifreeze used in a new automatic sprinkler system installed in accordance with NFPA 13R may not exceed a maximum concentration of 38% premixed propylene glycol or 48% premixed glycerin, and the capacity of the system may not exceed 150 gallons."

(13)   IFC, Chapter 9, Section 903.3.1.3 is amended by adding the following subsection: "903.3.1.3.1 Antifreeze Limitations. Antifreeze used in a new automatic sprinkler system installed in accordance with NFPA 13D may not exceed a maximum concentration of 38% premixed propylene glycol or 48% premixed glycerin, and the capacity of the system may not exceed 150 gallons."

(14)   IFC, Chapter 9, Section 903.3.5, Water supplies, is amended as follows: On line six, after the word "Code", add "and as amended in Utah's State Construction Code".

(15)   IFC, Chapter 9, Section 903.5 is amended to add the following subsection: "903.5.1 Tag and Information. A tag shall be attached to the riser indicating the date the antifreeze solution was tested. The tag shall also indicate the type and concentration of antifreeze solution by volume with which the system is filled, the name of the contractor that tested the antifreeze solution, the contractor's license number, and a warning to test the concentration of the antifreeze solutions at yearly intervals."

(16)   IFC, Chapter 9, Section 904.11, Commercial cooking systems, is deleted and rewritten as follows: "The automatic fire extinguishing system for commercial cooking systems shall be of a type recognized for protection of commercial cooking equipment and exhaust systems. Pre-engineered automatic extinguishing systems shall be tested in accordance with UL300 and listed and labeled for the intended application. The system shall be installed in accordance with this code, its listing and the manufacturer's installation instructions. The exception in Section 904.11 is not deleted and shall remain as currently written in the IFC."

(17)   IFC, Chapter 9, Section 904.11.3, Carbon dioxide systems, and Section 904.11.3.1, Ventilation system, are deleted and rewritten as follows:

(a)   "Existing automatic fire extinguishing systems used for commercial cooking that use dry chemical are prohibited and shall be removed from service."

(b)   "Existing wet chemical fire extinguishing systems used for commercial cooking that are not UL300 listed and labeled are prohibited and shall be either removed or upgraded to a UL300 listed and labeled system."

(18)   IFC, Chapter 9, Section 904.11.4, Special provisions for automatic sprinkler systems, is amended to add the following subsection: "904.11.4.2 Existing automatic fire sprinkler systems protecting commercial cooking equipment, hood, and exhaust systems that generate appreciable depth of cooking oils shall be replaced with a UL300 system that is listed and labeled for the intended application."

(19)   IFC, Chapter 9, Section 904.11.6.2, Extinguishing system service, is amended to add the following: "Exception: Automatic fire extinguishing systems located in occupancies where usage is limited and less than six consecutive months may be serviced annually if the annual service is conducted immediately before the period of usage, and approval is received from the AHJ."

(20)   IFC, Chapter 9, Section 905.3.9 is a new subsection as follows: "Open Parking Garages. Open parking garages shall be equipped with an approved Class I manual standpipe system when fire department access is not provided for firefighting operations to within 150 feet of all portions of the open parking garage as measured from the approved fire department vehicle access. Class I manual standpipe shall be accessible throughout the parking garage such that all portions of the parking structure are protected within 150 feet of a hose connection.

Exception: Open parking garages equipped throughout with an automatic sprinkler system in accordance with Section 903.3.1.1."

(21)   IFC, Chapter 9, Section 905.8, Dry Standpipes, Exception is deleted and rewritten as follows: "Where subject to freezing conditions and approved by the fire code official."

(22)   IFC, Chapter 9, Section 905.11, Existing buildings, and IFC, Chapter 11, Section 1103.6, Standpipes, are deleted.

(23)   In IFC, Chapter 9, Section 906.1, Where Required, the exception under paragraph 1 is deleted and rewritten to read: "Exception: In new and existing Group A, B, and E occupancies equipped with quick response sprinklers, portable fire extinguishers shall be required only in locations specified in items 2 through 6.

(24)   IFC, Chapter 9, Section 907.2.3 Group E:

   (a)   The first sentence is deleted and rewritten as follows: "A manual fire alarm system that initiates the occupant notification system in accordance with Section 907.5 and installed in accordance with Section 907.6 shall be installed in Group E occupancies."

   (b)   Exception number 3, on line five, delete the words, "emergency voice/alarm communication system" and replace with "occupant notification system."

(25)   IFC, Chapter 9, 907.8, Inspection, testing, and maintenance, is amended to add the following sentences at the end of the section: "Increases in nuisance alarms shall require the fire alarm system to be tested for sensitivity. Fire alarm systems that continue after sensitivity testing with unwarranted nuisance alarms shall be replaced as directed by the AHJ."

(26)   IFC, Chapter 9, Section 908.7, Carbon Monoxide Alarms, is deleted and rewritten as follows:

"908.7 Carbon Monoxide Detection.

908.7.1 Groups R-1, R-2, R-3, R-4, I-1, and I-4. Carbon monoxide detection shall be installed on each habitable level of a dwelling unit or a sleeping unit in Groups R-1, R-2, R-3, R-4, I-1, and I-4 occupancies that are equipped with a fuel-burning appliance.

908.7.1.1 If more than one carbon monoxide detector is required, the carbon monoxide detectors shall be interconnected as required in IFC, Chapter 9, Section 907.2.11.3.

908.7.1.2 In new construction, a carbon monoxide detector shall receive its primary power as required under IFC, Chapter 9, Section 907.2.11.4.

908.7.1.3 Upon completion of the installation, a carbon monoxide detector system shall meet the requirements listed in NFPA 720, Installation of Carbon Monoxide Detection and Warning Equipment and UL 2075, Standard for Gas and Vapor Detectors and Sensors.

908.7.2 Group E. A carbon monoxide detection system shall be installed in new buildings that contain Group E occupancies in accordance with IFC, Chapter 9, Sections 908.7.2.1 through 908.7.2.6. A carbon monoxide detection system shall be installed in existing buildings that contain Group E occupancies in accordance with IFC, Chapter 11, Section 1103.9.

908.7.2.1 Where required. In Group E occupancies, a carbon monoxide detection system shall be provided where a fuel-burning appliance, a fuel-burning fireplace, or a fuel-burning forced air furnace is present.

908.7.2.2 Detection equipment. Each carbon monoxide detection system shall be installed in accordance with NFPA 720 and the manufacturer's instructions, and be listed as complying with UL 2075.

908.7.2.3 Locations. Each carbon monoxide detection system shall be installed in the locations specified in NFPA 720.

908.7.2.4 Combination detectors. A combination carbon monoxide/smoke detector is an acceptable alternative to a carbon monoxide detection system if the combination carbon monoxide/smoke detector is listed in accordance with UL 2075 and UL 268.

908.7.2.5 Power source. Each carbon monoxide detection system shall receive primary power from the building wiring if the wiring is served from a commercial source. If primary power is interrupted, each carbon monoxide detection system shall receive power from a battery. Wiring shall be permanent and without a disconnecting switch other than that required for over-current protection.

908.7.2.6 Maintenance. Each carbon monoxide detection system shall be maintained in accordance with NFPA 720. A carbon monoxide detection system that becomes inoperable or begins to produce end-of-life signals shall be replaced."

(27)   IFC Section 908.7.1 is renumbered to 908.7.3.

Amended by Chapter 185, 2015 General Session

15A-5-205 Amendments and additions to IFC related to means of egress and special processes and uses.

(1)   IFC, Chapter 10, Section 1008.1.9.6, Special locking arrangements in Group I-2, is amended as follows:

   (a)   The section title "Special locking arrangements in Group I-2." is rewritten to read "Special locking arrangements in Groups I-1 and I-2."

   (b)   On line three, delete the word "Group", and add the words "Group I-1 and".

   (c)   After existing Item 7 add Item 8 as follows: "8. The secure area or unit with special egress locks shall be located at the level of exit discharge in Type V construction."

(2)   In IFC, Chapter 10, Section 1008.1.9.7, Delayed egress locks, Item 7 is added after the existing Item 6 as follows: "7. The secure area or unit with delayed egress locks shall be located at the level of exit discharge in Type V construction."

(3)   In IFC, Chapter 10, Section [B] 1009.7.2, Stair Treads and Risers, Exception 5 is deleted and replaced with the following: "5. In Group R-3 occupancies, within dwelling units in Group R-2 occupancies, and in Group U occupancies that are accessory to a Group R-3 occupancy, or accessory to individual dwelling units in Group R-2 occupancies, the maximum riser height shall be 8 inches (203 mm) and the minimum tread depth shall be 9 inches (229 mm). The minimum winder tread depth at the walk line shall be 10 inches (254 mm), and the minimum winder tread depth shall be 6 inches (152 mm). A nosing not less than 0.75 inch (19.1 mm) but not more than 1.25 inches (32 mm) shall be provided on stairways with solid risers where the tread depth is less than 10 inches (254 mm)."

(4)   IFC, Chapter 10, Section 1009.12 [B] 1009.15, Handrails, is amended to add the following exception: "6. In occupancies in Group R-3, as applicable in Section 1012 and in occupancies in Group U, which are accessory to an occupancy in Group R-3, as applicable in Section 1012, handrails shall be provided on at least one side of stairways consisting of four or more risers."

(5)   IFC, Chapter 10, Section 1024, Luminous Egress Path Markings, is deleted.

(6)   IFC, Chapter 10, Section 1030.2.1, Security Devices and Egress Locks, is amended to add the following: On line three, after the word "fire", add the words "and building".

Amended by Chapter 199, 2013 General Session

15A-5-205.5 Amendments to Chapter 11 of IFC.

(1)   In IFC, Chapter 11, Section 1103.2 Emergency Responder Radio Coverage in Existing Buildings, is amended as follows: On line two after the title, the following is added: "When required by the fire code official".

(2)   IFC, Chapter 11, Section 1103.5, Sprinkler Systems, is amended to add the following new subsection: "1103.5.3 Group A-2. An automatic fire sprinkler system shall be provided throughout existing Group A-2 occupancies where indoor pyrotechnics are used."

(3)   IFC, Chapter 11, Section 1103.6, Standpipes, is deleted.

(4)   In IFC, Chapter 11, 1103.7, Fire Alarm Systems, is deleted and rewritten as follows: "1103.7, Fire Alarm Systems. The following shall have an approved fire alarm system installed in accordance with Utah Administrative Code Section R710-4:

    1.   a building with an occupant load of 300 or more persons that is owned or operated by the state;

    2.   a building with an occupant load of 300 or more persons that is owned or operated by an institution of higher education; and

    3.   a building with an occupant load of 50 or more persons that is owned or operated by a school district, private school, or charter school.

Exception: the requirements of this section do not apply to a building designated as an Institutional Group I (as defined in IFC 202) occupancy."

(5)   IFC, Chapter 11, 1103.7.1 Group E, 1103.7.2 Group I-1, 1103.7.3 Group I-2, 1103.7.4 Group I-3, 1103.7.5 Group R-1, 1103.7.5.1 Group R-1 Hotel and Motel Manual Fire Alarm System, 1103.7.5.1.1 Group R-1 Hotel and Motel Automatic Smoke Detection System, 1103.7.5.2 Group R-1 Boarding and Rooming Houses Manual Fire Alarm System, 1103.7.5.2.1 Group R-1 Boarding and Rooming Houses Automatic Smoke Detection System, 1103.7.6 Group R-2 and 1103.7.7 Group R-4, are deleted.

(6)   IFC, Chapter 11, Section 1103.9, Carbon Monoxide Alarms, is deleted and rewritten as follows:

"1103.9 Carbon Monoxide Detection.

1103.9.1 Groups R-2, R-3, R-4, I-1, and I-4. Carbon monoxide detection shall be installed on each habitable level of a dwelling unit or a sleeping unit in existing Groups R-2, R-3, R-4, I-1, and I-4 occupancies that are equipped with a fuel-burning appliance.

1103.9.1.1 If more than one carbon monoxide detector is required, they shall be interconnected as required in IFC, Chapter 9, Section 907.2.11.3.

1103.9.1.2 In new construction, a carbon monoxide detector shall receive its primary power as required under IFC, Chapter 9, Section 907.2.11.4.

1103.9.1.3 Upon completion of the installation, the carbon monoxide detector system shall meet the requirements listed in NFPA 720, Installation of Carbon Monoxide Detection and Warning Equipment and UL 2034, Standard for Single and Multiple Carbon Monoxide Alarms.

1103.9.2 Group E. Carbon monoxide detection shall be installed in existing buildings that contain Group E occupancies in accordance with IFC, Chapter 9, Sections 908.7.2.1 through 908.7.2.6."

Amended by Chapter 74, 2014 General Session

15A-5-206 Amendments and additions to IFC related to hazardous materials, explosives, fireworks, and flammable and combustible liquids.

(1)   For IFC, Explosives and Fireworks, IFC, Chapter 56, Section 5601.3, Fireworks, Exception 4 is amended to add the following sentence at the end of the exception: "The use of fireworks for display and retail sales is allowed as set forth in Utah Code, Title 53, Chapter 7, Utah Fire Prevention and Safety Act, Sections 53-7-220 through 53-7-225; Utah Code, Title 11, Chapter 3, County and Municipal Fireworks Act; Utah Administrative Code, R710-2; and the State Fire Code."

(2)   For IFC, Chapter 57, Flammable and Combustible Liquids:

   (a)   IFC, Chapter 57, Section 5701.4, Permits, is amended to add the following at the end of the section: "The owner of an underground tank that is out of service for longer than one year shall receive a Temporary Closure Notice from the Department of Environmental Quality, and a copy shall be given to the AHJ."

   (b)   IFC, Chapter 57, Section 5706.1, General, is amended to add the following special operation: "8. Sites approved by the AHJ".

   (c)   IFC, Chapter 57, Section 5706.2, Storage and dispensing of flammable and combustible liquids on farms and construction sites, is amended to add the following: On line five, after the words "borrow pits", add the words "and sites approved by the AHJ".

(3)   For IFC, Chapter 61, Liquefied Petroleum Gas:

   (a)   IFC, Chapter 61, Section 6101.2, Permits, is amended as follows: On line two, after the word "105.7", add "and the adopted LP Gas rules".

   (b)   IFC, Chapter 61, Section 6103.1, General, is deleted and rewritten as follows: "General. LP Gas equipment shall be installed in accordance with NFPA 54, NFPA 58, the adopted LP Gas rules, and the International Fuel Gas Code, except as otherwise provided in this chapter."

   (c)   Chapter 61, Section 6109.12, Location of storage outside of buildings, is amended as follows: In Table 6109.12, Doorway or opening to a building with two or more means of egress, with regard to quantities 720 or less and 721 — 2,500, the currently stated "5" is deleted and replaced with "10".

   (d)   IFC, Chapter 61, Section 6109.15.1, Automated Cylinder Exchange Stations, is amended as follows: Item # 4 is deleted.

   (e)   IFC, Chapter 61, Section 6110.1, Temporarily out of service, is amended as follows: On line two, after the word "discontinued", add the words "for more than one year or longer as allowed by the AHJ,".

Amended by Chapter 199, 2013 General Session

15A-5-207 Amendments and additions to IFC related to existing buildings and referenced standards.

IFC, Chapter 80, Referenced Standards, is amended as follows:

(1)   Under the heading NFPA - National Fire Protection Association, delete the existing "Standard reference number" with regard to the edition and replace it with the following:

    (a)   "NFPA, Standard 10, Portable Fire Extinguishers, 2010 edition";

    (b)   "NFPA, Standard 11, Low-, Medium- and High-expansion Foam, 2010 edition";

    (c)   "NFPA, Standard 12, Carbon Dioxide Extinguishing Systems, 2008 edition";

    (d)   "NFPA, Standard 12A, Halon 1301 Fire Extinguishing System, 2009 edition";

    (e)   "NFPA, Standard 13, Installation of Sprinkler Systems, 2010 edition";

    (f)   "NFPA, Standard 13D, Installation of Sprinkler Systems in One- and Two-family Dwellings and Manufactured Homes, 2010 edition";

    (g)   "NFPA, Standard 13R, Installation of Sprinkler Systems in Residential Occupancies up to and Including Four Stories in Height, 2010 edition";

    (h)   "NFPA, Standard 14, Installation of Standpipe and Hose Systems, 2010 edition";

    (i)   "NFPA, Standard 17, Dry Chemical Extinguishing Systems, 2009 edition";

    (j)   "NFPA, Standard 17A, Wet Chemical Extinguishing Systems, 2009 edition";

    (k)   "NFPA, Standard 20, Installation of Stationary Pumps for Fire Protection, 2010 edition";

    (l)   "NFPA, Standard 22, Water Tanks for Private Fire Protection, 2008 edition";

    (m)   "NFPA, Standard 24, Installation of Private Fire Service Mains and Their Appurtenances, 2010 edition";

    (n)   "NFPA, Standard 72, National Fire Alarm Code, 2010 edition," all "Referenced in code section numbers" remain the same, except the exclusion of Table 508.1.5;

    (o)   "NFPA, Standard 92B, Smoke Management Systems in Malls, Atria and Large Spaces, 2009 edition";

    (p)   "NFPA, Standard 101, Life Safety Code, 2009 edition";

    (q)   "NFPA, Standard 110, Emergency and Standby Power Systems, 2010 edition";

    (r)   "NFPA 720, Installation of Carbon Monoxide (CO) Detection and Warning Equipment, 2009 edition";

    (s)   "NFPA, Standard 750, Water Mist Fire Protection Systems, 2010 edition"; and

    (t)   "NFPA, Standard 1123, Fireworks Display, 2010 edition."

(2)   Under the heading UL — Underwriters Laboratories, Inc., add the following: "UL2034, Standard for Single and Multiple Station Carbon Monoxide Alarms, 1998."

Amended by Chapter 199, 2013 General Session

15A-5-208 Blasting permits.

(1)   An operational permit is required for the use of any quantity of explosives or explosive materials for the purpose of blasting.

(2)   The State Fire Marshal Division shall issue blasting permits:

    (a)   for those locations where the local fire department that has jurisdiction of the location of the blast does not have a procedure in place for issuing blasting permits; and

(b)   for multiple blasting activities that are part of one project and that involve conducting blasts in the jurisdictions of more than one fire department.

(3)   The State Fire Marshal Division shall adopt rules pursuant to Title 63G, Chapter 3, Utah Administrative Rulemaking Act, as necessary to implement the procedure of issuing blasting permits under this section.

Enacted by Chapter 84, 2012 General Session

Part 3 - Amendments and Additions to National Fire Protection Association Incorporated as Part of State Fire Code

15A-5-301 General provisions.

The amendments and additions in this part to the NFPA are adopted for application statewide.

Enacted by Chapter 14, 2011 General Session

15A-5-302 Amendments and additions to NFPA related to National Fire Alarm Code.

For NFPA 72, National Fire Alarm Code:

(1)   NFPA 72, Chapter 2, Section 2.2, NFPA Publications, is amended to add the following NFPA standard: "NFPA 20, Standard for the Installation of Stationary Pumps for Fire Protection, 2010 edition."

(2)   NFPA 72, Chapter 10, Section 10.4.1, System Designer, Subsection 10.4.1.2(2), is deleted and rewritten as follows: "National Institute of Certification in Engineering Technologies (NICET) fire alarm level II certified personnel."

(3)   NFPA 72, Chapter 10, Section 10.4.2, System Installer, Subsection 10.4.2.2(2), is deleted and rewritten as follows: "National Institute of Certification in Engineering Technologies (NICET) fire alarm level II certified personnel."

(4)   NFPA 72, Chapter 10, Section 10.10, Fire Alarm Signal Deactivation, Subsection 10.10.2, is amended to add the following sentence: "When approved by the AHJ, the audible notification appliances may be deactivated during the investigation mode to prevent unauthorized reentry into the building."

(5)   NFPA 72, Chapter 10, Section 10.15, Protection of Fire Alarm System, is deleted and rewritten as follows: "Automatic smoke detection shall be provided at the location of each fire alarm control unit(s), notification appliance circuit power extenders, and supervising station transmitting equipment to provide notification of fire at the location."

(6)   In NFPA 72, Chapter 10, Section 10.15, a new Exception 1 is added as follows: "When ambient conditions prohibit installation of automatic smoke detection, automatic heat detection shall be permitted."

(7)   In NFPA 72, Chapter 23, Section 23.8.5.9, Signal Initiation — Fire Pump, Subsection 23.8.5.9.3 is added as follows: "Automatic fire pumps shall be supervised in accordance with NFPA 20, Standard for the Installation of Stationary Pumps for Fire Protection, and the AHJ."

(8)   NFPA 72, Chapter 26, Section 26.3.4, Indication of Central Station Service, Subsection 26.3.4.7 is amended as follows: On line two, after the word "notified", insert the words "without delay".

(9)   NFPA 72, Chapter 10, Section 10.4.3 Inspection, Testing, and Maintenance Personnel, Subsection 10.4.3.1, is deleted and rewritten as follows: "Service personnel shall be qualified and experienced in the inspection, testing, and maintenance of fire alarm systems. Qualified personnel shall meet the certification requirements stated in Utah Administrative Code, R710-11-3, Fire Alarm System Inspecting and Testing."

Amended by Chapter 199, 2013 General Session

15A-5-303 Amendments and additions to NFPA related to manufacture, transportation, storage, and retail sales of fireworks.

(1)   For purposes of this section and subject to Subsection (2), the Utah Fire Prevention Board shall adopt standards by rule for the retail sales of consumer fireworks, and in doing so, shall consider the applicable provisions of NFPA 1124, Chapter 7, Retail Sales of Consumer Fireworks.

(2)   NFPA 1124 Manufacture, Transportation, Storage, and Retail Sales of Fireworks and Pyrotechnic Articles:

(a)   In NFPA 1124, Chapter 7, Section 7.2, Special Limits for Retail Sales of Consumer Fireworks, Subsection 7.2.8 is added as follows: "Display of Class C common state approved explosives inside of buildings protected throughout with an automatic fire sprinkler system shall not exceed 25% of the area of the retail sales floor or exceed 600 square feet, whichever is less."

(b)   In NFPA 1124, Chapter 7, Section 7.2, Special Limits for Retail Sales of Consumer Fireworks, Subsection 7.2.9 is added as follows: "Rack storage of Class C common state approved explosives inside of buildings is prohibited."

(c)   NFPA 1124, Chapter 7, Section 7.3.1, Exempt Amounts, Subsection 7.3.1.1, is deleted and rewritten as follows: "Display of Class C common state approved explosives inside of buildings not protected with an automatic fire sprinkler system shall not exceed 125 pounds of pyrotechnic composition."

(d)   NFPA 1124, Chapter 7, Section 7.3.15.2, Height of Sales Displays, Subsection 7.3.15.2.2, is amended as follows: On line three delete "12 ft. (3.66m)" and replace it with "6 ft.".

Enacted by Chapter 14, 2011 General Session

Part 4 - Local Ordinances

15A-5-401 Grandfathering of local ordinances related to automatic sprinkler systems.

An ordinance adopted by a legislative body of a political subdivision that is in effect on June 30, 2010, and that imposes a requirement related to an automatic sprinkler system for a structure built in accordance with the requirements of the International Residential Code as adopted in the State Construction Code may remain in effect on or after July 1, 2010, notwithstanding that the ordinance is not authorized under Subsection 15A-5-203(1).

Amended by Chapter 199, 2013 General Session

National Association of State Contractors Licensing Agencies
NASCLA Membership Information

Membership Benefits

Associate Member

⇨ Online Access to NASCLA "Members Only" website
⇨ Invitation to the Annual Conference
⇨ Annual Complimentary Copy of the NASCLA Contractor State Licensing Information Directory
⇨ Copy of the NASCLA Membership Directory
⇨ Copy of NASCLA's Quarterly Newsletter
⇨ Networking Opportunities with others associated with the construction industry

State Member

⇨ Online Access to NASCLA "Members Only" website
⇨ Invitation to the Annual Conference and Mid Year Meeting
⇨ Annual Complimentary Copy of the NASCLA Contractor State Licensing Information Directory
⇨ Copy of the NASCLA Membership Directory
⇨ Copy of NASCLA's Quarterly Newsletter
⇨ Networking Opportunities with others associated with the construction industry

International Member

⇨ Online Access to NASCLA "Members Only" website
⇨ Invitation to the Annual Conference
⇨ Annual Complimentary Copy of the NASCLA Contractor State Licensing Information Directory
⇨ Copy of the NASCLA Membership Directory
⇨ Copy of NASCLA's Quarterly Newsletter
⇨ Networking Opportunities with others associated with the construction industry

Business Member

⇨ Online Access to NASCLA "Members Only" website
⇨ Invitation to the Annual Conference
⇨ Annual Complimentary Copy of the NASCLA Contractor State Licensing Information Directory
⇨ Copy of the NASCLA Membership Directory
⇨ Copy of NASCLA's Quarterly Newsletter
⇨ Networking Opportunities with others associated with the construction industry
⇨ Sponsorship and Vendor Opportunities at the Annual Conference

NASCLA'S MISSION

"Our national association is dedicated to the assistance of contractor licensing and enforcement agencies, trade associations, and members of the construction industry to best promote mutual interests and improve the quality standards and understanding of regulation in order to enhance protection of the general public.

The organization serves as a clearinghouse of information and resources for its membership, while providing valuable educational and licensure publications to the contracting community."

**NATIONAL ASSOCIATION OF STATE
CONTRACTORS LICENSING AGENCIES**

**23309 N. 17th Drive
Building 1, Unit 110
Phoenix, Arizona 85027**

Phone: (623) 587-9354

Fax: (623) 587-9625

www.nascla.org

APPLICANT INFORMATION

To become a member, please return this form with a check made payable to NASCLA at the address listed above or you may visit our website at www.nascla.org to register online for membership.

If you have any questions, please call NASCLA at (866) 948-3363.

MEMBERSHIP CLASSIFICATIONS

Please read the classifications below and check the box that best describes your membership classification.

❑ **Associate Member:** Limited to contractor trade associations, contracting firms, construction material suppliers and regional (county, city or municipal) contractor licensing agencies.

$125.00 Annual Membership Fee.

❑ **State Member:** Limited to states that have enacted laws to regulate the business of contracting.

$475.00 Annual Membership Fee.

❑ **International Member:** Limited to regulatory agencies from other nations, countries or states other than the 50 United States of America and its territories.

$475.00 Annual Membership Fee.

❑ **Business Member:** Limited to firms whose business is related to the construction industry? These members shall not use the name of the association and its logo or in any manner refer to NASCLA in advertising, selling or soliciting.

$750.00 Annual Membership Fee.

❑ **Affiliate Member:** Limited to former employees and board members of state contractor licensing agencies who are not actively engaged in the contracting business.

$50.00 Annual Membership Fee.

Name: _____

Title: _____

Company: _____

City, State, Zip Code: _____

Phone: _____

Email: _____ Website: _____